T0212748

Lecture Notes in Computer Science 9326

Commenced Publication in 1973
Founding and Former Series Editors:
Gerhard Goos, Juris Hartmanis, and Jan van Leeuwen

More information about this series at http://www.springer.com/series/7410

Günther Pernul · Peter Y A Ryan
Edgar Weippl (Eds.)

Computer Security – ESORICS 2015

20th European Symposium on Research in Computer Security
Vienna, Austria, September 21–25, 2015
Proceedings, Part I

 Springer

Editors
Günther Pernul
University of Regensburg
Regensburg
Germany

Peter Y A Ryan
University of Luxembourg
Luxembourg
Luxembourg

Edgar Weippl
SBA Research
Wien
Austria

ISSN 0302-9743   ISSN 1611-3349   (electronic)
Lecture Notes in Computer Science
ISBN 978-3-319-24173-9   ISBN 978-3-319-24174-6   (eBook)
DOI 10.1007/978-3-319-24174-6

Library of Congress Control Number: 2015948157

LNCS Sublibrary: SL4 – Security and Cryptology

Springer Cham Heidelberg New York Dordrecht London

Springer International Publishing AG Switzerland is part of Springer Science+Business Media
(www.springer.com)

Foreword

It is our great pleasure to welcome you to the 20th European Symposium on Research in Computer Security (ESORICS 2015).

This year's symposium continues its tradition of establishing a European forum for bringing together researchers in the area of computer security, by promoting the exchange of ideas with system developers and by encouraging links with researchers in related areas.

The call for papers attracted 293 submissions – a record in the ESORICS series – from 41 countries. The papers went through a careful review process and were evaluated on the basis of their significance, novelty, technical quality, as well as on their practical impact and/or their level of advancement of the field's foundations. Each paper received at least three independent reviews, followed by extensive discussion. We finally selected 59 papers for the final program, resulting in an acceptance rate of 20 %.

The program was completed with keynote speeches by Sushil Jajodia, George Mason University Fairfax, USA and Richard Clayton, University of Cambridge, UK.

Putting together ESORICS 2015 was a team effort. We first thank the authors for providing the content of the program. We are grateful to the Program Committee, who worked very hard in reviewing papers (more than 880 reviews were written) and providing feedback for authors. There is a long list of people who volunteered their time and energy to put together and organize the conference, and who deserve special thanks: the ESORICS Steering Committee, and its chair Pierangela Samarati in particular, for their support; Giovanni Livraga, for taking care of publicity; Javier Lopez, as workshop chair, and all workshop co-chairs, who organized workshops co-located with ESORICS; and Yvonne Poul for the local organization and the social events.

Finally, we would like to thank our sponsors, HUAWEI, for the financial support and SBA Research, for hosting and organizing ESORICS 2015.

A different country hosts the conference every year. ESORICS 2015 took place in Vienna, Austria at the Vienna University of Technology. We are very happy to have hosted the 20th edition of the symposium in Vienna and we tried to put together a special social program for you, giving you the opportunity to share ideas with other researchers and practitioners from institutions around the world and see all the beautiful sights of Vienna.

We hope that you found this program interesting and thought-provoking and that you enjoyed ESORICS 2015 and Vienna.

July 2015

Günther Pernul
Peter Y A Ryan
Edgar Weippl

Organization

General Chair

Günther Pernul   Universität Regensburg, Germany

Program Chairs

Peter Y A Ryan   University of Luxembourg, Luxembourg
Edgar Weippl   SBA Research & Vienna University of Technology, Austria

Workshops Chair

Javier Lopez   University of Malaga, Spain

Program Committee

Alessandro Armando	Università di Genova, Italy
Vijay Atluri	Rutgers University, USA
Michael Backes	Saarland University, Germany
Feng Bao	Security and Privacy Lab, Huawei, China
David A. Basin	ETH Zurich, Switzerland
Giampaolo Bella	Università di Catania, Italy
Carlo Blundo	Università degli Studi di Salerno, Italy
Stefan Brunthaler	SBA Research, Austria
Ran Canetti	Tel Aviv University, Israel
Liqun Chen	HP Labs, UK
Michael Clarkson	Cornell University, USA
Jason Crampton	University of London, UK
Cas Cremers	University of Oxford, UK
Frédéric Cuppens	Télécom Bretagne, France
Nora Cuppens-Boulahia	Télécom Bretagne, France
Sabrina De Capitani di Vimercati	Università degli Studi di Milano, Italy
Wenliang Du	Syracuse University, USA
Hannes Federrath	University of Hamburg, Germany
Simon Foley	University College Cork, Ireland
Sara Foresti	Università degli Studi di Milano, Italy
Felix Freiling	Friedrich-Alexander-Universität Erlangen-Nürnberg, Germany
Michael Goldsmith	University of Oxford, UK

Dieter Gollmann   TU Hamburg-Harburg, Germany
Dimitris Gritzalis   AUEB, Greece
Joshua Guttman   MTIRE Corp and Worcester Polytechnic, USA
Feng Hao   Newcastle University, UK
Amir Herzberg   Bar-Ilan University, Israel
Xinyi Huang   Fujian Normal University, China
Michael Huth   Imperial College, UK
Sotiris Ioannidis   FORTH, Crete
Sushil Jajodia   George Mason University, USA
Markus Jakobsson   Qualcomm, USA
Sokratis K. Katsikas   University of Piraeus, Greece
Stefan Katzenbeisser   TU Darmstadt, Germany
Florian Kerschbaum   SAP, Germany
Steve Kremer   INRIA Nancy and LORIA, France
Adam J. Lee   University of Pittsburgh, USA
Wenke Lee   Georgia Institute of Technology, USA
Yingjiu Li   Singapore Management University, Singapore
Peng Liu   Pennsylvania State University, USA
Javier Lopez   University of Malaga, Spain
Wenjing Lou   Virginia Polytechnic Institute and State University,
                           USA
Haibing Lu   Santa Clara University, USA
Antonio Maña   Univeristy of Malaga, Spain
Roy Maxion   Carnegie Mellon University, USA
Catherine Meadows   Naval Research Laboratory, USA
Carroll Morgan   University of New South Wales, Australia
John C. Mitchell   Stanford University, USA
Martin Mulazzani   SBA Research, Austria
David Naccache   ENS, France
Rolf Oppliger   eSecurity Technologies, Switzerland
Stefano Paraboschi   Università degli Studi di Bergamo, Italy
Olivier Pereira   UCL Crypto Group, Belgium
Günther Pernul   University of Regensburg, Germany
Bart Preneel   Katholieke Universiteit Leuven, Belgium
Jean-Jacques Quisquater   UCL, Belgium
Kui Ren   University at Buffalo, State University of New York,
                           USA
Mark Ryan   University of Birmingham, UK
Ahmad-Reza Sadeghi   TU Darmstadt, Germany
Pierangela Samarati   Università degli Studi di Milano, Italy
Nitesh Saxena   University of Alabama at Birmingham, USA
Andreas Schaad   SAP, Germany
Steve Schneider   University of Surrey, UK
Jörg Schwenk   Ruhr University Bochum, Germany
Basit Shafiq   Lahore University of Management Sciences, Pakistan
Dimitris E. Simos   SBA Research, Austria

Contents – Part I

Crypto Applications and Attacks

Risk Analysis

Contents – Part II

Authentication

Policies

Applied Security

Networks and Web Security

Towards Security of Internet Naming Infrastructure

Haya Shulman[1,2][✉] and Michael Waidner[1,2]

[1] Fraunhofer Institute for Secure Information Technology (SIT),
Technische Universität Darmstadt, Darmstadt, Germany
[2] Fachbereich Informatik, Technische Universität Darmstadt, Darmstadt, Germany
{haya.shulman,michael.waidner}@sit.fraunhofer.de

Abstract. We study the operational characteristics of the server-side of the Internet's naming infrastructure. Our findings discover common architectures whereby name servers are 'hidden' behind server-side caching DNS resolvers. We explore the extent and the scope of the name servers that use server-side caching resolvers, and find such configurations in at least 38 % of the domains in a forward DNS tree, and higher percents of the domains in a reverse DNS tree. We characterise the operators of the server-side caching resolvers and provide motivations, explaining their prevalence.

Our experimental evaluation indicates that the caching infrastructures are typically run by third parties, and that the services, provided by the third parties, often do not deploy best practices, resulting in misconfigurations, vulnerabilities and degraded performance of the DNS servers in popular domains.

1 Introduction

Domain Name System (DNS), [RFC1034, RFC1035], is the Internet's naming infrastructure; see background in Appendix, Sect. A. DNS plays a central role in the network operation, and its correctness and efficiency are critical to the stability and availability of the Internet. Initially designed to translate domain names to IP addresses, DNS infrastructure has evolved into a complex ecosystem and it is increasingly utilised to facilitate a wide range of applications. Due to the important function that DNS fulfills in the Internet, understanding and characterising it, is critical for security, efficiency and functionality of systems and networks. In this work we utilise Internet scale measurements to study the server-side of the DNS infrastructure. Within our study we find *common configurations* of DNS name servers, that utilise **server-side caching DNS resolvers to handle requests from the client-side resolvers**. In these configurations the DNS name servers are *hidden* behind recursive caching resolvers. In particular, the IP address of the server-side resolver is registered as the authoritative name server in the zone file of the target domain. As a result, client-side resolvers query that IP address (of the server-side resolver) and never communicate with the name

© Springer International Publishing Switzerland 2015
G. Pernul et al. (Eds.): ESORICS 2015, Part I, LNCS 9326, pp. 3–22, 2015.
DOI: 10.1007/978-3-319-24174-6_1

server directly (its IP address is not exposed to the client-side resolvers). In this work we identify and study the name servers supporting such configurations.

Caching constitutes an important building block in the design of scalable network architectures, and offers advantages such as an improved availability, security and reduced latency for responses to clients. Caching proxies are common on the client-side of the DNS infrastructure, where the DNS resolvers are connected to (often a chain of) caching forwarders. Such configurations are, however, much less known, and not studied, on the server-side. In our work, we find and study DNS configurations that use server-side caching resolvers, which handle the DNS requests, and relay them to the name servers. Our finding indicates that the server-side DNS architecture in the Internet is not limited to the traditional model, where the client-side resolution platform (i.e., a client-side resolver possibly connected via a chain of proxies) communicates with the name server directly (see Fig. 11 in Appendix, Sect. A). Our study also shows an increasing shift towards outsourcing DNS services' operation to expert third parties. Outsourcing services is an increasingly common practice in the Internet, [4]; it saves operational and management costs by using expertise and skilled personnel of the third party service provider, e.g., like the services provided by the cloud platforms. We characterise the operators of such caching server-side resolvers, and evaluate the security of domains using server-side caching resolvers. We discover severe vulnerabilities exposing to attacks both the misconfigured networks and other Internet victims. Our findings indicate that the hosts maintained by the third parties are often misconfigured recursive DNS resolvers, that do not support best practices and known security recommendations, e.g., [RFC5452, RFC4697]. Our study shows that many of the networks with the vulnerabilities and misconfigurations are *benign, popular* and often *security aware* – this is in contrast to anecdotal belief that misconfigurations are an artifact of security oblivious networks, [32]. We also explore the challenges that outsourcing DNS operations introduces for adoption of cryptographic defences for DNS.

Our study encompases domains in forward and reverse DNS trees. In a forward DNS tree we study 50K-top Alexa domains and Top-Level Domains (TLDs). In a reverse DNS we study the domains that correspond to IPv4 address blocks, i.e., all the network blocks in classes A, B and C – `x.in-addr.arpa.`, `y.x.in-addr.arpa.` and `z.y.x.in-addr.arpa.` respectively. Forward DNS typically hosts widely used services, such as web and email. Reverse DNS lookups are commonly utilised by security mechanisms, network operators and security researchers. For instance, domains in a reverse DNS tree are used to prevent spam and phishing attacks, to provide topological or geographic information of routers, or to prevent BGP prefix hijacking attacks.

We summarise our findings in Table 1. The first column (to the left), lists the DNS trees that we studied. The second column (to the left) contains the number of registered domains that we tested. This is mainly relevant in the reverse DNS tree, where a large fraction of the domains (that correspond to IPv4 address space) are not registered. The third column (to the left) contains the number of name servers in each domain space. The subsequent two columns report the name

Table 1. Summary of the results reported in this work.

DNS tree	Domains servers	Name	Fixed src port	Predictable src port	Failure w/DNSSEC	Server side cache	Open cache
Forward DNS Alexa	50K	32.5K	4 %	12.7 %	23 %	38 %	6 %
Forward DNS TLDs	568	3.2K	0.8 %	1.6 %	2 %	12 %	3.73 %
rDNS x.in-addr.arpa.	229	1.5K	7 %	14 %	2 %	14 %	8 %
rDNS y.x.in-addr.arpa.	28K	97K	10 %	19 %	32 %	41 %	19 %
rDNS z.y.x.in-addr.arpa.	2,767K	9,687K	14 %	19.5 %	34.5 %	38 %	21 %

servers with open server side resolvers that use fixed or predictable ports. Then
we report on the number of servers that fail with DNSSEC enabled packets. The
two rightmost columns contain the number of servers with server-side resolvers
and with server-side resolvers supporting open recursive resolution respectively.

Organisation

This paper is structured as follows. We review related work and put our results in
context in Sect. 2. In Sect. 3 we present a study of the server-side DNS infrastructure, and describe our methodology for detection of server-side DNS resolvers.
In Sect. 4 we evaluate security of domains that use server-side resolvers, and
conclude this work in Sect. 5. We provide an overview of DNS and DNSSEC in
Appendix, Sect. A.

2   Related Work

In the following section we put our work in context with the related research. In
particular, our work relates to prior studies of the: (1) DNS infrastructure, (2)
misconfigured networks, and (3) DNS security.

2.1   Understanding the DNS Infrastructure

Studying the DNS infrastructure is important for design of Internet systems and
future applications, and for construction and adoption of security mechanisms,
including defences for DNS, e.g., against Denial of Service (DoS), [BCP38], or
cache poisoning attacks, [RFC5452], and for defences that utilise DNS for authentication of services, such as IP prefixes authentication for routing security with
ROVER, [6], or anti-spam mechanisms with SPF, [8].

A number of research works studied the client-side DNS infrastructure and
vulnerabilities, e.g., [13,17,24,31]. On the server-side of the DNS infrastructure,
[20,26] found multiple transitive trust dependencies within the DNS zones. Other
work on the name server-side typically focuses on examining the DNS packets,
exchanged between resolvers and name servers, such as for detection of malicious
domains [1,5] or to detect incorrect uses of DNS, e.g., [3].

In this work we study the server-side *architecture* of the DNS infrastructure. In contrast to client-side resolvers, which the clients can identify by, e.g., inspecting the `hosts` file, the server-side resolvers are *transparent* to the clients, to the client-side resolvers and to network operators. This prevents the clients from being able to identify security vulnerabilities, or sources of failures, or tracking by third party DNS operators.

We also find that often, in contrast to best practices, [RFC5358, BCP140], the server-side third party resolvers support open recursive resolution, i.e., willing to lookup names in *any* domain and not only in the domain which they are 'authoritative' for.

We explore domains' configurations that use server-side resolvers, and illustrate the scope and the extent of this phenomenon in our work. We characterise the operators of the server-side DNS resolvers, and find that these are typically third party service providers.

2.2   Misconfigured Networks

Misconfigured networks pose a significant threat to the stability and availability of the Internet clients and services. Indeed, there is an established correlation between mismanagement and networks reponsible for malicious activities, [32]. Exploiting vulnerabilities in misconfigured networks is a stepping stone towards more sophisticated attacks and they are often abused by the attackers as *proxies* to attack victim networks and clients. Open recursive resolvers, willing to perform a recursive resolution for any Internet client, is a main source of the misconfigurations. Networks, operating open recursive resolvers, pose a particular threat, not only to the clients using their services, but also to the stability of the Internet, as they are frequently exploited in reflection amplification Denial of Service (DoS) attacks on victim networks and services, [22]. Unfortunately, despite the significant operational and research efforts to detect and characterise networks running open resolvers, [24,32], and to provide recommendations to mitigate the threat that they pose, the number of misconfigured networks is still overwhelming. One of the factors for this situation may be a common belief that since the misconfigured networks do not pose internal threat to their operators and clients, there is little incentive to fix the vulnerabilities, [32].

We identify one of the factors responsible for misconfigurations of networks: **outsourcing services to *security oblivious* third parties**. Although outsourcing network and services management to third parties can be effective and convenient, our results indicate that the security of these services should be carefully checked. We show experimentally that the vulnerable services are typically not hosted on the 'misconfigured' networks themselves, but on the networks which the third parties operate. Our findings also indicate that to optimise profit, third parties host multiple services of different customers *on the same hosts*. As a result, a vulnerability in one service, e.g., a web server, can be exploited to attack other services, e.g., DNS or email servers.

We hope that our work will raise awareness to the importance of validating security of the services provided by the third parties. Our message is that the services provided by the third parties should not be blindly relied upon. Clients using third party services should validate the infrastructure of the third party service providers. We design tools that enable clients to infer information about the server side of the DNS infrastructure.

2.3 DNS Security

There is a long history of attacks against the DNS, most notably, DNS cache poisoning, [9,11,12,15,27,28]. In the course of a DNS cache poisoning attack, the attacker hijacks a victim domain by providing spoofed DNS records in DNS responses, thus redirecting clients to incorrect hosts, e.g., for credentials theft or malware distribution. As DNS plays an essential role in networks operation, cache poisoning can inflict economic losses and privacy damages and has a detrimental impact on the functionality and availability of the Internet clients and services. In particular, open recursive resolvers, that do not support source port randomisation and other recommendations, [RFC5452, RFC4697], are a lucrative target for cache poisoning attacks.

We find that often **the server-side resolvers do not support source port randomisation and use fixed or predictable ports for their requests to the name servers** (see columns 4 and 5 in Table 1). Resolvers with predictable ports are even more prevalent in domains in the reverse DNS tree, which is surprising since the reverse DNS is commonly utilised by the security mechanisms, hence it is expected to be better protected.

To mitigate the detrimental damages of cache poisoning attacks, IETF designed and standardised a cryptographic defence for DNS: DNSSEC [RFC4033-RFC4035]. A secure DNS would be resilient to cache poisoning attacks and would facilitate a wide range of applications and systems, such as secure routing (with ROVER [6]), secure email (with PGP keys distribution [29]).

Although proposed in 1997, DNSSEC is still not widely deployed; [18] found that less than 3 % of the DNS resolvers validate DNSSEC records. Important domains, such as the root and top-level domains (TLDs) are signed. However, the fraction of signed zones in lower domains, such as the second level domains (SLDs), is less than 1 %.

While there has been a considerable effort to identify the challenges to DNSSEC deployment, the focus was generally on the issues that large DNSSEC responses incur with the legacy firewalls and middleboxes on the resolver side, e.g., [14,30]. Zones signing was thought to be just a matter of motivation, and a folklore belief was that incentivised operators could sign their domains 'today'.

Our study shows that the server-side resolvers impose obstacles on adoption of DNSSEC, and signing the zones would disrupt the DNS functionality to those domains. The reason is that the server-side resolvers often cannot operate with DNSSEC specific records or flags, [RFC4034-RFC4035], such as the DO bit in EDNS record, [RFC6891], and fail with an exception or a timeout; see the third column from the right, titled 'failure w/DNSSEC', in Table 1.

In a recent work, [25], we studied security of encryption proposals for DNS, and showed that the intermediate proxies foil the security guarantees expected of the encryption schemes.

3 Studying DNS Name Servers

In this section we explore the architecture of the server-side DNS infrastructure. In particular, we answer the following questions: in Sect. 3.1 we consider the *what* - we identify common architectures of DNS name servers that use server-side caching DNS resolvers; in Sect. 3.2 we address the *why* - we study the advantages of such configurations; finally, in Sect. 3.3 we explore the *who* - we characterise the operators of server-side resolvers.

In Sect. 3.4, we introduce our methodology for detecting DNS name servers' architectures that use server-side DNS resolvers, and report on the extent and the scope of this phenomenon among popular domains in forward and in reverse DNS trees; our results and findings are summarised in Table 1.

3.1 Recursive Authoritative Name Servers

Our central finding is a common use of caches, that are configured to relay all the communication between the client-side resolvers and the name servers; see Fig. 1. In particular, we find that a large fraction of the domains in forward and reverse DNS trees are configured in the following way: an authoritative name server is *hidden* behind a server-side resolver. The IP address of the server-side resolver is reported as the name server in the zone file of the target domain (and in its parent). The server-side resolver receives DNS requests from the client-side resolvers and forwards them to the name server hosting the zone file for the target domain. Upon responses from the name server, the server-side resolver caches the DNS records and subsequently returns them to the requesting client-side resolver. Similarly to the standard DNS resolvers functionality, if the requested record is in the cache, the server-side resolver does not forward the query to the name server, but responds from the cache. The setting is illustrated in Fig. 1. We call the servers configured according to this setting the *recursive authoritative name server* (RANS). We report on the fraction of RANSes, among domains in forward and reverse DNS trees, in Table 1. The server-side resolver infrastructure may consist of a number of hosts, whereby a chain of resolver relay the request from one to another, until the request reaches the name server; see Fig. 2. We found that 42 % of the RANSes use more than one host in the server-side resolver infrastructure; we present the measurement methodology that we used in Sect. 3.4.

3.2 Why Use Server-Side Caches?

In this section we attempt to address the following question: **what are the reasons for such configurations?** We list the motivations for configuring caches 'before' the name servers, and compare to similar practices in other systems.

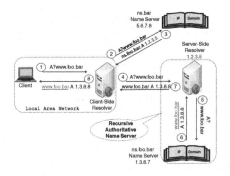

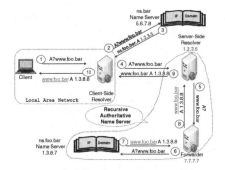

Fig. 1. Resolution for www.foo.bar hosted on a RANS.

Fig. 2. Resolution to a RANS with a chain of server-side resolvers.

Improved Performance and Availability. To speed up access to their servers website operators utilise content delivery networks (CDNs), such as Akamai, these CDNs cache content in their global network and make it available to end users through geographically dispersed *edge servers* that are close to the users. Using CDNs for web content is a known practice. Our study shows that this practice is also common among the naming infrastructure. In particular, utilising distributed resolving hosts to retrieve, cache and supply DNS records to client can reduce latency for clients' requests – the IP address of the resolver can be ANYCAST-ed and the clients will perform lookups against the resolvers that are close to them.

Furthermore, if the name server is connected via a low bandwidth channel to the Internet or if its hardware is not suitable for handling multiple requests, a resolver with high bandwidth connectivity to the Internet or resolver's instance, distributed via ANYCAST, can solve this problem.

Enhanced Security. If the domain operator does not have the required expertise to enhance security of its name server, it can outsource this function to third party DNS operator. It is much more difficult to attack a hidden name server, since its IP address is not known. It is also much easier for the domain operator to prevent attacks, by configuring a firewall rule that allows requests to the name server only from one specific IP address – the resolver of the third party serving the (hidden) name server.

3.3   Who Operates and Uses RANS?

In this section we characterise operators of the server-side resolvers in RANSes, and the domains that use such configurations. To answer the former question we check the owner of the IP address of the server-side resolver, to answer the latter we check the owner of the domain of the name server.

Operators of RANSes. Running `whois` over the IP addresses of the server-side resolvers in RANSes, indicates that at least 57 % of the IP addresses belong to networks of commercial CDNs, [21], (such as Akamai, AT&T, NTT communication, LimeLight, Level 3 Verisign and Google). To identify CDNs, we used the `traceroute` traces, and for each name server's IP address we checked whether `traceroute` from different locations yields different network adapters at the last host before the name server.

Typically, the caching service provided by the caching resolvers in a RANS configuration is purchased for a fee, however we also observed 'anecdotal' configurations, perhaps *free riders*, whereby domains' operators configure the open resolvers run by public open resolvers, e.g., such as Google Public DNS, as the IP addresses of the name servers of their domains.

Customers of RANSes. We use a domain query tool DIG to collect the set of NS records for RANS domains. Then, to characterise the domains with the RANS configuration, we perform the following tests over the NS names that we collected: (1) we check the age of each RANS domain, (2) we check the Alexa rank of the domains and (3) we check the type of domains.

These tests enable us to establish the 'reputation' of the networks which use the RANS configurations.

The age of the RANS domains can be used to establish domains' reputation. In particular, malware domains are typically characterised with a short lived duration (the attackers frequently change domain names to avoid detection) while a long lived domain can be used as an indicatation of legitimate operators. More than 50 % of the RANSes were registered on average a decade ago.

Many of the domains belong to financial institutions, university networks or Internet operators. These results show that many of the RANSes domains, are located in legitimate networks and run by legitimate (and not malicious) network operators.

DOMAIN AGE. Benign domains are usually characterised by a relatively long age. Domains used for malicious purposes instead are typically active only for short periods of time. The average age of benign domains is much higher than the average age of malicious domains. we have estimated that the average age of malicious hostnames is less than 5 weeks.

We utilise `whois` to find the average age of the RANS domains. The average age for domains in Alexa is 517 weeks, for a TLD the differences are very diverse: approximately 18 % are more than 20 years old, 11 % are between 3 and 5 years old, and 71 are less than 2 years old. In a reverse DNS tree, the average domain age is 972 weeks.

ALEXA RANK. We examined the Alexa rank of domains running RANSes, and find that more than 60 % of the RANSes are ranked below 25,000 in Alexa; the results are plotted in Fig. 5.

DOMAIN TYPE. We use a `whois` application over the RANS domains in forward and reverse DNS trees. We process the description field (*descr*) and organisation name (*org-name*) and check the values against a list of universities and network operators that we compiled. Those not appearing on the list, but with keywords such as *university, network, school*, were tested manually. We found that 38 % of the RANSes domains belong to educational sector, most notably universities, approximately 12 % belong to network operators, e.g., Sprint. Approximately

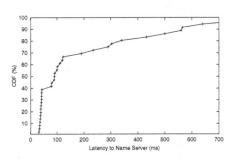

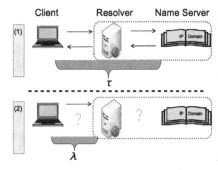

Fig. 3. Latency of the cached responses of the server-side resolver vs. responses from a (hidden) name server.

Fig. 4. Latency probing for the cached (λ seconds) vs. uncached record, i.e., including (τ seconds) latency to the name server.

18 % belong to domains in a financial sector. The rest could not be determined due to unknown or missing description or organisation name in information reported by the whois service.

3.4 Methodology for Detecting RANSes

We use the following techniques to identify domains with RANS architectures: (1) timing side channels, (2) Time-to-Live (TTL) and (3) open recursive resolution.

Timing Side-Channels. We design a timing side channel, which utilises the caching of the server-side resolvers, and allows to identify RANSes. The timing side channel is based on the difference in the latency of the responses relayed by the server-side resolvers to the (hidden) name servers, vs. the latency of the responses returned from the cache of the server-side resolvers. The timing channel is due to the caching of the resolvers. Our evaluation of a target domain foo.bar proceeds as follows: (1) we query a name server of foo.bar for a non-existing (random) subdomain $str.foo.bar, and measure the latency of the response; (2) we repeat the first step with the same query $str.foo.bar and measure the latency. If the name server uses a server-side resolver to handle the DNS queries for clients, then the latency of both responses will differ. In particular, since the record $str.foo.bar in the first query is not in the cache, it is relayed by the server-side resolver to the name server, a subsequent request for the same record is served from the cache. Hence the latency of the first request is higher than the latency of the second request – in this case we mark the name server infrastructure as a RANS. We illustrate the measurement technique in Fig. 4.

To account for a potential noise, such as occasional network load or load balancing mechanisms (where the query is sent to a different name server each time), we repeat the experiment for each name server 20 times, using a different random subdomain $str at each invocation.

The results of the RANSes measurements are plotted in Fig. 3. We set a threshold at 70 ms (and above), which is the typical delay in the Internet.

The values below 70 ms but above 30 ms, were marked as 'suspicious'. To confirm the 'suspicious' RANSes we used an additional TTL-based side channel (described below). As can be seen, the typical latency is above 100 ms. This significant difference in the latency is due to the fact that typically server-side resolvers and the (hidden) name servers are located in different Autonomous Systems (ASes).

Time-to-Live (TTL). Our measurement shows that server-side resolvers support a standard DNS caching mechanisms. Namely, upon receiving a response from the (hidden) name server, the records are sent to the requesting client-side resolver and are cached. The cache reduces the TTL value of the records, until it expires, and the records are evicted form the cache. We utilise the caching to identify server-side resolvers. The idea is to send a request for the same record twice (to the same name server) and check the TTL value of the record in both responses. If the TTL in the second response is lower than the TTL in the first response, then it is a RANS.

Our finding provides one possible explanation to the phenomenon of the inconsistency of TTL values in records within Alexa domains, as reported by [24]. In particular, [24] found that TTL of responses is distorted before reaching the requesting client, and that only 19 % of domains have consistent TTL values. We postulate that the bias could have resulted due to the requests to domains which use RANSes, see Fig. 1, and thus responses were served from the cache of the resolver.

The TTL side channel provides a more accurate metric, than the timing side channel, and enables to detect RANSes, where the latency between the server-side resolver and the (hidden) name server is not significant, e.g., below 30 ms. Although the TTL side channel is more reliable it nevertheless depends on the configuration of the proxy caching resolver. In particular, if the caching resolver does not accurately maintain the TTL of the cached records, the TTL channel cannot be relied upon. In contrast, the timing side channel, albeit less accurate, provides for a more reliable metric. For detection of server-side caching resolvers we recommend to utilise both side channels.

Open Recursion. We found that some of the RANSes are configured as *open resolvers*, i.e., the recursive resolution that they are willing to perform is not limited to a specific domain (for which they are registered as authoritative) but they will look up records in *any* domain.

We call these ORAN Ses. Open recursive resolution is known to expose to attacks and is considered a bad practice.

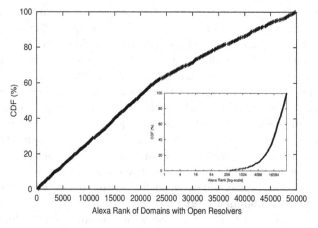

Fig. 5. Alexa rank of ORANSes; the inner graph presents results plotted in log-scale.

Blocking recursive resolution should also be enforced on the server side, and not only on the client side of the DNS infrastructure. On the server-side the goal is to restrict queries only for resources within the domain for which the target name server is authoritative, while serving queries from *any* clients. In contrast, on the client-side, the goal is to allow resolution for resources within *any* domain, but only for a limited set of clients, e.g., those that are located on the same network as the recursive resolver. To identify ORANSes, we set up a domain and sent requests for records within our domain, to the name servers, authoritative for the tested domains within forward and reverse DNS trees. Those servers that forwarded the requests to our name server were marked as ORANSes.

We identified 6 % of open RANSes in 50K-top Alexa domains, 3 % of open RANSes in TLDs, and we found a much larger fraction of the domains in a reverse DNS tree; the results are summarised in Table 1.

We discovered almost $3K$ ORANSes among top 50K Alexa domains and 21 ORANSes among TLDs. This translates to approximately 40 ORANSes in every 1K Alexa domains. We examined the Alexa rank of domains running ORANSes, and report our findings in Fig. 5.

To identify resolvers' chains, i.e., those that use forwarders, we concatenated the destination IP address (to which we sent the DNS request) as a subdomain of our domain; i.e., we sent DNS requests for A record of a resource in `dest-ip.our-domain.tld` domain, where `dest-ip` is the IP address of the server to which we sent the requests. This enabled us to associate the requests that we sent, with the requests that were subsequently received at our name server. Upon receipt of the request on our name server we validated if the request arrived at our name server from the same IP address, as the one to which it was sent. If not, we marked the ORANS as consisting of resolvers' chain. We found that 42 % of the RANSes are using a *chain* of recursive resolvers, consisting of at least two intermediate resolvers; see Fig. 2.

We found that 58 % of the ORANSes use the same source IP in the requests which they forward to the name servers, as the IP addresses on which they receive requests from the clients; namely, support the configuration illustrated in Fig. 1. In particular, 42 % of the DNS requests for A record of a resource in `our-domain.tld` domain, which we sent to the ORANSes, were received at our name server from different IP addresses.

We find that in 84 % of the requests, the IP address to which we sent the request, was located in a different AS than the IP address from which we received the request on our name server.

Misconfigurations. Almost 10 % of the RANSes in 25K-top Alexa domains return responses from a different IP address than the one to which the request was sent by the client-side resolver. In this case, the response (sent from an incorrect IP address of the name server) is ignored by the client side resolver, and after a timeout the query is resent to another name server.

4 Evaluating (in)Security of RANSes

In this section we evaluate the support of best practices and popular defences against cache poisoning by the server-side resolvers in the RANSes and ORANSes configurations.

4.1 Services Coresidence

We find that the server-side resolvers in RANSes frequently serve more than a single service. In particular, we tested for a 'coresidence' between web and DNS servers, in two phases: (1) we use nmap to check for open ports 80 or 443 on server-side resolvers in RANSes; then, in step (2) we use telnet to connect to the web server on port 80, and s_client of openssl to connect web servers that support communication over SSL/TLS, [RFC6101, RFC2246]. We find that more than 60 % of server-side resolvers host web and DNS services on the same machine. Hosting multiple services on the same machine is a known risky practice, in particular, a vulnerability in one service can enable attackers to take control over the host and subvert the security of the other services, e.g., vulnerability in PHP web servers enables attackers to obtain a shell on the victim host, [2].

4.2 Source Port Randomisation

Source port randomisation (SPR) is a main defence against DNS cache poisoning attacks. Resolvers supporting SPR send DNS requests from unpredictable (hopefully randomly selected) source ports. We tested support of SPR among server-side resolvers in ORANSes and RANSes. We first describe the sampling techniques that we used, and then analyse the values of the sampled ports.

Sampling SPR in ORANSes. We triggered, via each ORANS, four consecutive DNS requests to subdomains in our domain www.our-domain.tld, and capture the requests with a tcpdump on a name server hosting a zone file for our domain.

Sampling SPR in RANSes. The measurement of recursive resolvers in RANSes is tricky since we cannot trigger requests to a name server that we control – resolvers in RANSes are limited to resolving requests within a domain which they serve. The approach that we employ is based on a timing side channel due to packet loss inflicted by the attacker via socket overloading between hardware interrupts. The kernels in operating systems (OSes), e.g., Unix variants and Microsoft platforms, use hardware interrupts for event notification purposes in communication with input/output hardware components. Network interface cards (NICs) generate interrupts to notify the kernel of arrival of new packets. Hardware interrupts can impose significant CPU overhead. This is due to the fact that hardware interrupt is associated with context switching of saving and restoring processor state, see details in [16]. After the notification of a new packet arrival the kernel processes the packet, and then invokes TCP/IP protocol processing. However, *arrival of a new packet distrupts protocol processing* since hardware interrupts have higher priority over other tasks. Thus under a high traffic load, the socket may fill up if the interrupt level is high, and when the socket queue is full the arriving packets will be dropped. Techniques to avoid socket overloading was studied in the scope of improving web servers efficiency, e.g., [19,23]. We use the socket overloading technique to elicit side channels for remote detection of port used by the resolver in a RANS. For our measurements, we employ 10 PlanetLab hosts to send the UDP packets' bursts. First we measure latency for requests to the resolver for records that are not in its cache (i.e., we concatenate a random subdomain to requests). Then, to sample if the resolver is using some port p, we send a burst of packets to a port p, causing socket overloading between kernel interrupts; this results in packets' loss. If the resolver used p to send its request to some name server, then the response from the name server to port p is also discarded; after a timeout (typically 1 second) the resolver retransmits the request. We use packet loss from the name server as an indication of hitting the correct port. Notice that a packet loss is caused only when the burst of packets is sent to the same port on which the resolver expects to receive a response. If a burst is sent to a different port, than the one from which the resolver sent its request, no loss will be incurred.

We find that packets of size 500 bytes provide for optimal packets' loss. This is probably due to the fact that they cause maximal number of hardware interrupts and filled the kernel buffers with bytes.

As a result, when the response from the sever arrived between the interrupts, it was discarded since the buffers were full. We first use the socket overloading technique above to sample for known fixed ports, and then for sequential ports. In case of sequential ports, we start with the highest port, probe each port 5 times, and then reduce the port by one, to next port; see Fig. 6.

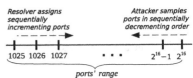

Fig. 6. Meet-in-the-middle port discovery procedure.

Analysing Port Selection. The results are plotted in Figs. 7, 8, and 9. As can be seen almost 10 % of the four consecutive requests contain a fixed port 53, and the similarity across the four requests is very high.

Among TLDs in forward DNS less than 1 % use a fixed port, and among 50K-top Alexa domains 4 % use a fixed port. In a reverse DNS domains that correspond to classes A, B and C – 7 %, 10 %, and 14 % respectively use fixed ports. The most popular (6.58 %) fixed port is 32, 768, then follows a fixed port 53; see distribution of fixed ports in Fig. 7. Most of the requests that did not seem to use predictable ports, contained ports from small ports' ranges, which enables efficient exhaustive search of the ports pool. To calculate the ports' ranges, plotted in Fig. 8, we applied the following function over the ports in our four consecutive requests A, B, C and D: $(ABS(A-B)+ABS(C-D)+ABS(A-D))/3$ As can be seen, only less than 10 % of the requests have ports that differ by $17K$, while more than 90 % differ in less than 256 between them. In contrast, truly random ports would have an average difference of $2^{16}/2$, and would result in a normal distribution. Figure 9 plots the distribution of unpredictable ports in

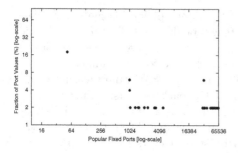

Fig. 7. Distribution of fixed ports in use by RANSes.

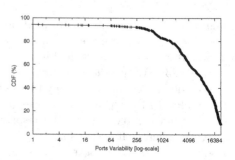

Fig. 8. Ports variability across different DNS requests.

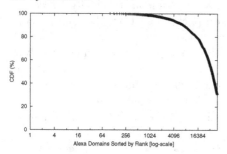

Fig. 9. Distribution of unpredictable ports within 25K-top Alexa domains.

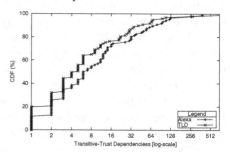

Fig. 10. Transitive-trust dependencies of domains in 50K-top Alexa and TLDs.

use by RANSes in 25K-top Alexa. The curve shows that port unpredictability is correlated with domain popularity – less popular domains use more predictable ports.

4.3 DNSSEC

The root zone and the top-level-domains (TLDs) are signed, but, as our measurements indicate, the adoption of DNSSEC within lower domains is extremely low; see Table 1. An interesting question is, how difficult is it to deploy DNSSEC, and whether there is software support for this. This question is particularly interesting in light of the coresidence of multiple domains, and in light of our discovery of recursive authoritative servers configurations. Our study provides a novel angle to the deployment of DNSSEC, allowing to look into the ability of name servers to support DNSSEC. In particular, previous work either measured the fraction of *signed* zones, [10, 14, 30], or the fraction of *validating resolvers*, [7, 18], however, the ability and the readiness of the name servers to adopt DNSSEC or serve signed zones did not receive sufficient attention. We initiate this investigation in our work.

We sought to measure two quantities: (1) What fraction of open recursive authoritative name servers are 'DNSSEC compatible', i.e., can operate with responses containing DNSSEC records. (2) What fraction of open recursive authoritative name servers perform strict validation of DNSSEC responses.

Evaluation Methodology. We set up three domains[1]: (1) without DNSSEC, (2) correctly signed with DNSSEC, (3) incorrectly signed. Domain (1) was not signed, and served plain DNS responses. Domains (2) and (3), were signed with 1024 bit keys RSA/SHA-1 (algorithm 5), [RFC3110,RFC4034]. Domain (3) served expired keys in DNSKEY records and invalid signatures in RRSIG record.

We found that 39.2 % of the open recursive authoritative name servers could not process signed DNSSEC responses, and returned FMTERROR/SRVFAIL, 29.8 % stripped DNSSEC records from responses and returned plain DNS responses (without signatures and keys). Together this resulted in a bit more than 69 % of servers that can not support DNSSEC. We found that only 30.9 % of the open recursive authoritative name servers return DNSSEC enabled responses, in return to requests for records in signed domains.

We further tested support of EDNS0 among the open recursive authoritative name servers. Clearly, the 30.9 % of them that support DNSSEC also support EDNS0. What about the remaning 69 % that do not support DNSSEC. We found that 52 % of them support EDNS0. In total, we observed that 82 % of the open recursive name servers support EDNS0 while 18 % do not.

To test whether open recursive authoritative name servers perform strict validation of DNSSEC responses, we ran test (2) on the 30.9 % of the open recursive authoritative name servers that could serve signed responses. None of the queries failed, namely, the open recursive authoritative name servers do not support strict DNSSEC validation. This result is consistent with measurements reported in [18], which showed that most recursive DNS resolvers, that support DNSSEC, do not perform strict DNSSEC validation.

4.4 Implications of Vulnerable RANSes

Vulnerabilities in RANSes can be exploited for large scale DNS cache poisoning attacks. In particular, in contrast to the tranditional cache poisoning, where only a single resolver, and the clients using it, fall victims – name servers using vulnerable third party caches expose *any* resolver querying that name server to attacks.

Such vulnerabilities in domains in a forward DNS tree expose to surveillance, distribution of malware, credentials theft, and more. Exploits in domains in a reverse DNS tree can be exploited to subvert security mechanisms, such as anti-spam defences, via PTR records, or routing security, such as ROVER. *Dependency on Vulnerable RANSes.* Best practices for ensuring availability and security of a domain in the DNS infrastructure recommend defining a number of name servers for each domain and configuring these name servers under at least two different parent domains. This redundancy provides for stability of the domain and prevents a single point of failure. In particular, if one of the parent domains is

---

[1] For compliance with anonymisation of the submission the domain names are removed.

not accessible, the domain will remain functional via the other parent domains. As a result of this practice, it is common in a DNS infrastructure for a domain name to depend on many other domains and resolving a single domain name often requires traversing multiple other domains. This phenomenon is called *transitive trust dependency*, introduced in [20]. On the flip side, while ensuring availability, this redundancy introduces a risk in case of dependencies on vulnerable domains. In Fig. 10 we plot the CDF of the number of transitive-trust dependencies in 50K-top Alexa and TLDs: 60 % of Alexa domains depend on 12 or more domains, and 60 % of TLDs depend on 6 or more domains. Subverting one of the domains in a transitive trust dependency chain would impact all the dependant domains.

5   Conclusions

In this work we performed a study of the server-side DNS infrastructure. Our results identify two common phenomena: (1) use of server-side caching DNS resolvers and (2) outsourcing security and availability of the domains to third party service providers. We study the implications of such architectures on the security, availability, and operational characteristics of popular domains in forward and reverse DNS trees, as well as on the design and adoption of security mechanisms for DNS. We show that often server-side resolvers do not support best practices and are vulnerable to cache poisoning attacks. In contrast to client side resolvers, where a vulnerability impacts only the clients on the network of the resolver, a vulnerability in a server-side resolver applies to *any* Internet client querying the vulnerable name server, and not limited to a specific network.

Since the server-side resolvers are transparent to the clients (client-side resolvers or network operators) querying them, the clients have no means to identify such architectures. Hence, the clients cannot validate whether they are vulnerable to cache poisoning attacks or identify failures, e.g., due to use of security mechanisms that the server-side resolvers cannot process, such as signaling of DNSSEC. We design a methodology and implement tools for detection of server-side resolvers and evaluation of their security. The results reported in this work, and the tools that we developed, are of interest and of importance for domain operators and clients, and enable automated evaluation of the security provided by third parties.

Acknowledgements. This research was supported by the German Federal Ministry of Education and Research (BMBF) within EC SPRIDE, by the Hessian LOEWE excellence initiative within CASED, and co-funded by the DFG as part of the CRC 1119 CROSSING.

A   Overview: DNS and DNSSEC

Domain Name System (DNS) is composes of a client-server protocol, used by the resolvers to retrieve domain records in zone files maintained by the name servers.

The resolvers communicate to the name servers using a simple request-response protocol (typically over UDP); for instance, (abstracting out details) to translate www.foo.bar resolvers locate the name server `ns.foo.bar`, authoritative for `foo.bar`, and obtain the IP address of the machine hosting the web server of the website www.foo.bar, see Fig. 11. Resolvers store the DNS records, returned in responses, in their caches for the duration indicated in the Time To Live (TTL) field of each record set.

The resource records in DNS correspond to the different services run by the organisations and networks, e.g., hosts, servers, network blocks.

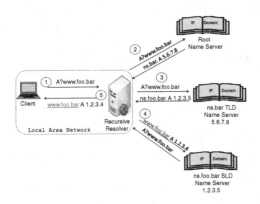

Fig. 11. DNS resolution process for www.foo.bar and the involved DNS servers.

The zones are structured hierarchically, with the root zone at the first level, Top Level Domains (TLDs) at the second level, and millions of Second Level Domains (SLDs) at the third level. The IP addresses of the 13 root servers are provided via the *hints* file, or compiled into DNS resolvers software and when a resolver's cache is empty, every resolution process starts at the root. According to the query in the DNS request, the root name server redirects the resolver, via a `referral` response type, to a corresponding TLD, under which the requested resource is located. There are a number of TLDs types, most notably: *country code TLD* (ccTLD), which domains are (typically) assigned to countries, e.g., `us`, `il`, `de`, and *generic TLD* (gTLD), whose domains are used by organisations, e.g., `com`, `org`, and also US government and military, e.g., `gov`, `mil`. Domains in SLDs can also be used to further delegate subdomains to other entities, or can be directly managed by the organisations, e.g., as in the case of `ibm.com`, `google.com`.

A DNS *domain* is divided into zones, and includes all the nodes of the subtree rooted at the zone. A DNS *zone* constitutes a portion of a domain name space. A zone contains only the nodes that are managed by the name server at the named node. A zone can be divided into subdomains, with its own DNS name servers. At the lowest level of the DNS tree, in the leaves of the tree, the terms 'DNS zone' and a 'DNS domain' become equivalent. For instance, when querying the

root zone for `foo.bar.`, the resolver will be redirected to `bar.` domain, via a
`referral` to the authoritative servers for `bar.` zone. When querying the name
servers of `bar.`, the resolver is issued another `referral` for `foo.bar.` zone.
Notice that `bar.` zone does not include subdomains, e.g., like `foo.bar.`, but
those are delegated from `bar` to their name servers.

When no protection is employed, DNS requests and responses can be
inspected and altered by a MitM attacker. For example, a malicious wireless
client can tap the communication of other clients and can respond to their
DNS requests with maliciously crafted DNS responses, containing a spoofed IP
address, e.g., redirecting the clients to a phishing site. Domain Name System
Security Extensions (DNSSEC) standard [RFC4033, RFC4034, RFC4035] was
designed to address the cache poisoning vulnerability in DNS, by providing *data
integrity* and *origin authenticity* via cryptographic digital signatures over DNS
resource records. The digital signatures enable the recipient, e.g., resolver, that
supports DNSSEC validation, to check that the data in a DNS response is the
same as the data published within the target zone.

DNSSEC defines new resource records (RRs) to store signatures and keys
used to authenticate the DNS responses. For example, a type RRSIG record
contains a signature authenticating an RR-set, i.e., all mappings of a specific type
for a certain domain name. By signing only RR-sets, and not specific responses,
DNSSEC allows signatures to be computed *off-line*, and not upon request; this
is important, both for performance (since signing is computationally intensive)
and security (since the signing key can be stored in a more secure location than
the name server).

To allow clients to authenticate DNS data, each zone generates a signing and
verification key pair, (sk, vk). The signing key sk is used to sign the zone data,
and should be secret and kept offline. Upon queries for records in a domain,
the name server returns the requested RRs, along with the corresponding signatures (in a RRSIG RRs). To prevent replay attacks, each signature has a fixed
expiration date. The clients, i.e., resolvers, should also obtain the zone's public
verification key vk, stored in a DNSKEY RR, which is then used by the clients
to authenticate the origin and integrity of the DNS data.

Resolvers are configured with a set of verification keys for specific zones,
called *trust anchors*; in particular, all resolvers have the verification key (trust
anchor) for the root zone. The resolver obtains other verification keys, which are
not trust anchors, by requesting a DNSKEY resource record from the domain.
To validate these verification keys obtained from DNSKEY, the resolver obtains
a corresponding a DS RR from the parent zone, which contains a hash of the
public key of the child; the resolver accepts the DNSKEY of the child as authentic
if the hashed value in DNSKEY is the same as the value in the DS record at
the parent, and that DS record is properly signed (in a corresponding RRSIG
record). Since the DS record at the parent is signed with the DNSKEY of the
parent, authenticity is guaranteed.

This process constructs a *chain of trust* which allows the resolver to authenticate the public verification key of the target zone. Specifically, the clients

authenticate the public verification key of the zone by constructing a chain of trust starting at the root zone, or another trust anchor, and terminating at the target zone.

References

1. Antonakakis, M., Perdisci, R., Lee, W., Vasiloglou II, N., Dagon, D.: Detecting malware domains at the upper dns hierarchy. In: USENIX Security Symposium, p. 16 (2011)
2. Canali, D., Balzarotti, D., et al.: Behind the scenes of online attacks: an analysis of exploitation behaviors on the web. In: Proceedings of the 20th Annual Network & Distributed System Security Symposium (2013)
3. Chen, Y., Antonakakis, M., Perdisci, R., Nadji, Y., Dagon, D., Lee, W.: DNS noise: measuring the pervasiveness of disposable domains in modern DNS traffic (2014)
4. Feamster, N.: Outsourcing home network security. In: Proceedings of the 2010 ACM SIGCOMM Workshop on Home Networks, pp. 37–42. ACM (2010)
5. Gao, H., Yegneswaran, V., Chen, Y., Porras, P., Ghosh, S., Jiang, J., Duan, H.: An empirical reexamination of global dns behavior. In: Proceedings of the ACM SIGCOMM 2013 Conference on SIGCOMM, pp. 267–278. ACM (2013)
6. Gersch, J., Massey, D.: Rover: Route origin verification using DNS. In: 2013 22nd International Conference on Computer Communications and Networks (ICCCN), pp. 1–9. IEEE (2013)
7. Gudmundsson, O., Crocker, S.D.: Observing DNSSEC Validation in the Wild. In: SATIN, March 2011
8. Herzberg, A.: DNS-based email sender authentication mechanisms: a critical review. Comput. Secur. **28**(8), 731–742 (2009)
9. Herzberg, A., Shulman, H.: Security of patched DNS. In: Foresti, S., Yung, M., Martinelli, F. (eds.) ESORICS 2012. LNCS, vol. 7459, pp. 271–288. Springer, Heidelberg (2012). http://dx.doi.org/10.1007/978-3-642-33167-1_16
10. Herzberg, A., Shulman, H.: DNSSEC: interoperability challenges and transition mechanisms. In: Eighth International Conference on Availability, Reliability and Security (ARES), 2013, Regensburg, Germany, pp. 398–405. IEEE (2013)
11. Herzberg, A., Shulman, H.: Fragmentation Considered Poisonous: or one-domain-to-rule-them-all.org. In: IEEE CNS 2013. The Conference on Communications and Network Security. Washington, IEEE (2013)
12. Herzberg, A., Shulman, H.: Socket overloading for fun and cache poisoning. In: Payne Jr., C.N. (ed.) ACM Annual Computer Security Applications Conference (ACM ACSAC), New Orleans, Louisiana, U.S., December 2013
13. Herzberg, A., Shulman, H.: Vulnerable delegation of DNS resolution. In: Crampton, J., Jajodia, S., Mayes, K. (eds.) ESORICS 2013. LNCS, vol. 8134, pp. 219–236. Springer, Heidelberg (2013). http://dx.doi.org/10.1007/978-3-642-40203-6_13
14. Herzberg, A., Shulman, H.: Retrofitting security into network protocols: the case of DNSSEC. IEEE Internet Compu. **18**(1), 66–71 (2014)
15. Kaminsky, D.: It's the end of the cache as we know it. In: Black Hat Conference, August 2008. http://www.blackhat.com/presentations/bh-jp-08/bh-jp-08-Kaminsky/BlackHat-Japan-08-Kaminsky-DNS08-BlackOps.pdf
16. Kleiman, S.R.: Apparatus and method for interrupt handling in a multi-threaded operating system kernel, US Patent 5,515,538, 7 May 1996

17. Kührer, M., Hupperich, T., Rossow, C., Holz, T.: Exit from hell? reducing the impact of amplification DDoS attacks. In: Proceedings of the 23rd USENIX Security Symposium, San Diego, CA, USA, 20–22 August 2014, pp. 111–125 (2014)
18. Lian, W., Rescorla, E., Shacham, H., Savage, S.: Measuring the practical impact of DNSSEC Deployment. In: Proceedings of USENIX Security (2013)
19. Ramakrishnan, K.: Performance considerations in designing network interfaces. IEEE J. Sel. Areas Commun. 11(2), 203–219 (1993)
20. Ramasubramanian, V., Sirer, E.: Perils of transitive trust in the domain name system. In: Proceedings of the 5th ACM SIGCOMM Conference on Internet Measurement, pp. 35–35. USENIX Association (2005)
21. Rayburn, D.: CDN market getting crowded: Now tracking 28 providers in the industry. Bus. Online Video Blog (2007)
22. Rossow, C.: Amplification hell: Revisiting network protocols for ddos abuse (2014)
23. Salah, K., El-Badawi, K., Haidari, F.: Performance analysis and comparison of interrupt-handling schemes in gigabit networks. Comput. Commun. 30(17), 3425–3441 (2007)
24. Schomp, K., Callahan, T., Rabinovich, M., Allman, M.: On measuring the client-side DNS infrastructure. In: Proceedings of the 2013 Conference on Internet Measurement Conference, pp. 77–90. ACM (2013)
25. Shulman, H.: Pretty bad privacy: pitfalls of DNS encryption. In: Proceedings of the 13th Annual ACM Workshop on Privacy in the Electronic Society, WPES 2014, pp. 191–200 (2014). IETF/IRTF Applied Networking Research Award
26. Shulman, H., Ezra, S.: Poster: On the resilience of DNS infrastructure. In: Proceedings of the 2014 ACM SIGSAC Conference on Computer and Communications Security, pp. 1499–1501. ACM (2014)
27. Shulman, Haya, Waidner, Michael: Fragmentation considered leaking: port inference for DNS poisoning. In: Boureanu, Ioana, Owesarski, Philippe, Vaudenay, Serge (eds.) ACNS 2014. LNCS, vol. 8479, pp. 531–548. Springer, Heidelberg (2014)
28. Stewart, J.: DNS cache poisoning-the next generation (2003)
29. Wouters, P.: Using DANE to Associate OpenPGP public keys with email addresses (2014). http://tools.ietf.org/html/draft-wouters-dane-openpgp-02
30. Yang, H., Osterweil, E., Massey, D., Lu, S., Zhang, L.: Deploying cryptography in internet-scale systems: A case study on dnssec. IEEE Trans. Dependable Secure Comput. 8(5), 656–669 (2011)
31. Yu, Y., Wessels, D., Larson, M., Zhang, L.: Authority server selection of DNS caching resolvers. ACM SIGCOMM Comput. Commun. Rev. 42, 80–86 (2012)
32. Zhang, J., Durumeric, Z., Bailey, M., Liu, M., Karir, M.: On the mismanagement and maliciousness of networks. In: Proceedings of the 21st Annual Network & Distributed System Security Symposium (NDSS 2014), San Diego, California, USA (2014, to appear)

Waiting for CSP – Securing Legacy Web Applications with JSAgents

Mario Heiderich, Marcus Niemietz(✉), and Jörg Schwenk

Horst Görtz Institute for IT-Security, Ruhr-University Bochum, Bochum, Germany
{mario.heiderich,marcus.niemietz,joerg.schwenk}@rub.de

Abstract. Markup Injection (MI) attacks, ranging from classical Cross-Site Scripting (XSS) and DOMXSS to Scriptless Attacks, pose a major threat for web applications, browser extensions, and mobile apps. To mitigate MI attacks, we propose JSAgents, a novel and flexible approach to defeat MI attacks using DOM meta-programming. Specifically, we enforce a security policy on the DOM of the browser at a place in the markup processing chain "just before" the rendering of the markup. This approach has many advantages: Obfuscation has already been removed from the markup when it enters the DOM, mXSS attack vectors are visible, and, last but not least, the (client-side) protection can be individually tailored to fit the needs of web applications.

JSAgents policies look similar to CSP policies, and indeed large parts of CSP can be implemented with JSAgents. However, there are three main differences: (1) Contrary to CSP, the source code of legacy web applications needs not be modified; instead, the policy is adapted to the application. (2) Whereas CSP can only apply one policy to a complete HTML document, JSAgents is able, through a novel cascading enforcement, to apply different policies to each element in the DOM; this property is essential in dealing with JavaScript event handlers and URIs. (3) JSAgents enables novel features like coarse-grained access control: e.g. we may block read/write access to HTML form elements for all scripts, but human users can still insert data (which may be interesting for password and PIN fields).

1   Introduction

Cross-Site Scripting. XSS attacks are one of the major threats to web application security. The goal of an attacker is to execute a (malicious) JavaScript function of his own choice in the context of the target web page. If he succeeds, the Same Origin Policy (SOP) of the browser will grant them full acess to all elements and variables of the target web page (including stored passwords, session cookies, and security tokens), and the script may trigger other potentially harmful actions (drive-by-downloads and alike).

In the literature, three main classes of XSS are described: (1) Reflected XSS, where the attack vector is sent to the target web server in a HTTP request (e.g., a search request), this input is integrated by the server into a dynamically

© Springer International Publishing Switzerland 2015
G. Pernul et al. (Eds.): ESORICS 2015, Part I, LNCS 9326, pp. 23–42, 2015.
DOI: 10.1007/978-3-319-24174-6_2

generated web page, and the attack is executed when this page is rendered. (2) Stored XSS, where the attack vector is stored in a subpage of the target web application (e.g., discussion forum), and the attack is executed each time a victim visits this subpage. (3) DOMXSS [1], where the attack vector is inserted by a (legal) client-side script into the web page. Mutation-based XSS (mXSS) is a recent new variant [2], which has the potential to circumvent several known mitigation techniques, including advanced XSS filters.

HTML5 and Scriptless Attacks. Since the advent of HTML5 (HTML, HTML 5.1 Nightly and HTML.next), new attack techniques are continuously being discovered. Different browser strategies for processing XML, XHTML[1] and HTML content which may all be mixed together can be exploited through SVG images or MathML markup [3]. Even deactivating JavaScript completely, a method repeatedly proposed by security authorities, does not protect against HTML5-based attacks as certain publications [4,5] have shown that *Scriptless Attacks* are possible. Scriptless Attacks additionally complicate the task of server- and client-side filters: It is nearly impossible to decide which HTML5 tags may be dangerous before an attack vector has been published.

Markup Injection Attacks. We will use the term *Markup Injection (MI)* to denote the superclass of attacks formed by Scriptless Attacks and the different kinds of XSS vectors. For a MI attack on a web application to be successful, all three conditions listed below must be fulfilled.

1. *Injectability*. It must be possible to inject potentially malicious markup into a web page.
2. *Executability*. It must be possible for the browser to parse and execute the markup.
3. *Extractability*. It must be possible for the attacker to exfiltrate sensitive information (e.g., session cookies) from the browser and to transfer them to a device where he can retrieve it.

Classical Defense Approaches. As a first line of defense, server- and client-side filters, which have different restrictions, are deployed. Server-side filters must be able to detect JavaScript snippets even if they are obfuscated, a task that becomes harder with every new markup functionality introduced with HTML5. Client-side filters are embedded into the browser (MSIE/ WebKit/ Blink) or can be installed as a plugin (NoScript). In both cases, they have to apply the same policy to all visited web applications, which in many cases proves too weak or too strong.

Novel Defense Approaches. Whereas classical MI countermeasures concentrate on condition (1.) injectability (by detecting and removing markup injections with client- or server-side filters), modern approaches take into account the other two conditions. For example, Content Security Policy (CSP) [6,7] and

---

[1] For example, the different XHTML treatment of self-closing tags.

HTTPonly cookies [8] mitigate extractablility (CSP by allowing HTTP connections only to a small number of white-listed URLs, HTTPonly cookies by making themselves inaccessible from the DOM), and sandboxed Iframes [9] try to prevent executability by restricting script execution.

Content Security Policy. CSP 1.0 is fully supported by all current webbrowser versions. Its main feature is domain whitelisting for `<script>`, `<object>`, `<style>`, `<img>`, `<media>` and `<iframe>` elements, and for fonts and websockets, to mitigate condition 3 (Extractability) for a successful MI attack. For some of these elements (e.g. scripts) this strict whitelisting policy can be relaxed by allowing inline sources through `unsafe-inline`.

CSP 1.1 has a much broader scope: The whitelisting can be applied to a broader set of DOM elements (e.g. through `form-action`), the use of inline scripts can be protected through script nonces, only whitelisted plugins will be activated, client-side XSS filters can be activated, and many more. Thus CSP can be seen as a specification where most research on web application security has been condensed; subsequently CSP is often cited as a comparison for new approaches. However, this comparison is a little weak since CSP 1.1 has to be fully implemented yet. We will nevertheless compare our approach to CSP 1.1 below.

JSAgents Library. Our JSAgents library specifically targets conditions (2.) and (3.) through DOM meta-programming. It is a client-side solution which, in contrast to the client-side XSS filters, can be tailored to a given web application. In addition, it does not have to care about code obfuscation since this has already been removed by the browser. We can restrict execution of any markup, not only JavaScript, thus mitigating XSS and in part Scriptless Attacks (Executability); we can restrict HTTP leakage for elements in the browser's DOM, and we can read-protect certain DOM elements (Extractability). Furthermore, we can write-protect DOM elements; a feature that mitigates complex cross-domain attacks (e.g., through `document.location`). We can enforce different policies for each part of the DOM tree through the use and enforcement of a *cascading* policy language (comparable to CSS).

JSAgents vs. CSP 1.1. With CSP 1.1, stronger security guarantees can be enforced, because CSP is implemented directly in each browser core, it runs with 'browser root privileges'. Through the DOM metaprogramming approach, we can never achieve more than 'page level privileges'. A different CSP 1.1 policy can be applied to each Iframe, but within each Iframe only a one-level, non-cascading security policy is applied. Through Cascading Style Sheets (CSS), web programmers are experienced in cascading style declarations. JSAgents makes use of the CSS syntax to define cascading security policies, where one, two or more iterations over the document's DOM can be made to enforce security rules. This is especially useful for legacy web applications running in a single document context (see below). JSAgents additionally allows to block read and write access to DOM elements and their attributes, a feature that is not part of CSP 1.1 but is currently in discussion for input values on the WHATWG mailing list[2].

Architectural Overview JSAgents. JSAgents uses a static JavaScript library (`jsa.js`) and a customizable configuration file to achieve its application-specific goals: `jsa.js` must be inserted into the web page as the *first* JavaScript function to be executed. Insertion points may include the web application itself, a HTTP proxy, or a browser extension (webapp, proxy, and extension mode). As soon as `jsa.js` is executed, it uses a FrozenDOM approach to stop other active markup from being executed and reads the (cascaded) configuration file. The directives contained in this file are used to set different flags on the elements of the frozen DOM. After all flags are set, the frozen DOM is parsed and all restrictions expressed by the flags are enforced: Elements may be deleted, read- or write-protected, or their actions may be limited to white-listed URLs.

Legacy Web Applications. CSP imposes restrictions on JavaScript event handlers and JavaScript URIs (cf. Section A.2) that makes adoption of CSP nearly impossible for legacy web applications: A complete redesign of each application is necessary to be able to use CSP without the'unsafe-inline' option for scripts. With JSAgents, we can use the fact that policy files can be cascaded to sketch a generic solution for this problem: First we disallow all inline scripts, event handlers, and URIs. Then we can allow those JavaScript embeddings which are essential for a correct functionality of a web page, based on a whitelist extracted from the legacy application. Thus we can achieve the same effect as CSP 1.1 script nonces for inline scripts, but in contrast to CSP 1.1 we can extend this approach to JavaScript URIs and event handlers. We were able to deploy JSAgents successfully for two large classes of legacy applications: (a) Web-mailers and (b) Identity Providers in Single-Sign-On Systems. In both cases, JSAgents could successfully be deployed to enhance security, without affecting functionality. We are confident that, due to the flexibility of our approach, JSAgents can be deployed with nearly all legacy applications. In some cases (1 out of 13 IdPs) we have detected incompatibilities with other large JavaScript libraries, which indicates that we may not be able to achieve 100 % coverage.

Project Evaluation. We evaluated three different aspects of JSAgents: Security, usability, and performance. In Sect. 4, we describe the results of a public challenge to break JSAgents. The goal of our usability evaluation was to show that JSAgents policy files can indeed be adapted to the two classes of web applications mentioned above. During this usability evaluation, we also investigated compatibility with other popular JavaScript libraries: JSAgents is compatible with jQuery, Prototype, and Underscore, but has compatibility issues with RequireJS. Finally, we measured the performance of our solution based on randomly generated HTML code of different sizes. The results can be found in Sect. 5.

---

[2] Write-only Form Elements, http://mikewest.github.io/credentialmanagement/write only/.

Contributions. This paper makes the following contributions:

– *Novelty.* We give a novel, comprehensive, DOM-meta-programming-based approach to defend against MI attacks. We demonstrate the large potential of novel DOM meta-programming features like Object.defineProperty and DOM Mutation Observers.
– *Impact.* We are able to mitigate most attack classes, including mXSS and HTTP request leaks. We describe a flexible and powerful policy language such that JSAgents can be adapted to numerous (legacy) applications scenarios.
– *Usability.* In contrast to CSP, JSAgents can easily be deployed with legacy web applications, since no changes to the source code are necessary.
– *Public Availability.* We present a free open-source project from the JSAgents core that can be used as a universal client-side HTML filter ("DOMPurify" project on GitHub).

2   Related Work

From the large body of research on XSS and beyond, we provide a brief overview of the relevant literature, detailing both scholarly work and research-driven sources pertaining to this subject area.

XSS Mitigation. Server-side mitigation techniques range from a simple character encoding or replacement, to a full rewrite of the HTML code. The advent of DOM XSS was one of the main reasons behind the introduction of XSS filters on the client-side. The IE8 XSS Filter was the first fully integrated solution [10], timely followed by the Chrome XSS Auditor in 2009 [11]. For Firefox, client-side XSS filtering is implemented through the NoScript extension. Unsurprisingly, XSS attacks' mitigation strategies have been covered in numerous publications [12–17]. Noncespaces [18] use randomized XML namespace prefixes as an XSS mitigation technique, which would make detection of the injected content reliable. DSI [19] tries to achieve the same goal based on a process of clasifying HTML content into trusted and untrusted variety on the server side, subsequently changing browser parsing behavior so that the said distinction is taken into account. Blueprint [20] generates a model of the user input on the server-side and transfers it, together with the user-contributed content, to the browser, making its behavior modified by an injection of a JavaScript library for processing the model along with the input.

Mutation-Based (mXSS) and Scriptless Attacks. Weinberger et al. [21] give an example of the innerHTML being used to execute a DOM-based XSS. Comparable XSS attacks based on changes in the HTML markup have been initially described for client-side XSS filters. Vela Nava et al. [22] and Bates et al. [11] have shown that the IE8 XSS Filter could have once been used to "weaponize" harmless strings and turn them into valid XSS attack vectors. This relied on applying a mutation through the regular expressions used by the XSS Filter. Zalewski covers concatenation problems based on NUL strings in *inner-HTML* assignments in the *Browser Security Handbook* [23]. Additionally, he later

dedicates a section to backtick mutation in his volume "The Tangled Web" [24].
Other mutation-based attacks have been reported by Barth et al. [25] and
Heiderich [26]. In the latter, mutation may occur *after* client-side filtering
(WebKit corrected a self-closing script tag before rendering, thus activating the
XSS vector) or *during* XSS filtering (XSS Auditor strips the `code` attribute
value from an applet tag, thus activating a second malicious code source).
Hooimeijer et al. describe the dangers associated with the sanitization of content [27] and claim that they were able to produce a string that would result in a
valid XSS vector *after* sanitization, for every single one of a large number of XSS
vectors. The vulnerabilities described by Kolbitsch et al. may form the basis for
an extremely targeted attack by web malware [28]. Those authors state that the
attack vectors may be prepared for taking into account the mutation behavior
of different browser engines. HTML5 introduces a script-like functionality in its
different tags, making the so called "Scriptless Attacks" (a term coined in [4]) a
real threat. For example, SVG images and their active elements can be used to
steal passwords even if JavaScript is deactivated [5].

3   JSAgents Architecture

3.1   Building Blocks

FrozenDOM. The current version of JSAgents uses a technique called Frozen-
DOM [26, 29–31]. Upon execution of the JSAgents Core Library, the DOM is
stopped from being rendered as a plain-text element (`<plaintext>`) and is being
written right after the `<script>` element that contains JSAgents code. Note that
using plain-text is employed in the sake of supporting legacy browsers; for modern browsers, JSAgents can make use of the Shadow DOM and the `<template>`
element. The interrupted rendering flow allows the library to simultaneously
quickly read the document markup and prevent race conditions introduced by
the injected scripts or markup. In case the application uses a JavaScript templat-
ing engine/MVC framework, JSAgents can directly work on the HTML string
that built before rendering and does not need to rely on `<plaintext>`. Adopting
JSAgents reduces the performance when used on complex websites (see Sect. 5)
but it must be underscored that the user experience on modern browsers (like
Firefox 24+, MSIE9+, and Chrome 30+) is hardly affected at all.

DOM Mutation Observers. By using DOM Mutation Observers (DMO),
JSAgents is able to monitor write-access to selected DOM nodes and trigger
an execution of a callback function in cases where such access has taken place.
This allows us to protect form elements from being overwritten, effectively making a commonly used technique of Web Injects against online banking portals
void. JSAgents can detect scripted form element manipulation because actual
keyboard input into form elements does *not* cause mutation events to be emit-
ted, while, conversely, the scripted access does so. DMO are implemented in all
modern browsers and can be emulated reliably in older versions without DMO
support with the use of `onpropertychange`.

Object.defineProperty(). Almost arbitrary DOM objects can be set into an immutable state by using the ES5 functionality of `Object.defineProperty()`, and thereby be protected from external, potentially malicious, manipulations. By doing so, we can assure a certain level of integrity for the JSAgents library, essentially allowing to introduce tamper safety and detectability of manipulation attempts. Further, it is possible to manage attempts of potentially malicious scripts coveting to gain a write-access to form elements.

Document.querySelectorAll(). By using the `querySelectorAll` API, JSAgents is able to select all elements that match very specific criteria from a given document. Note that the API is similar to the CSS selector API and thereby helps existing front-end developers to precisely select these elements they want to impose the security restrictions and capability control onto. Creating JSAgents policy files is comparable to composing style sheets, as selectors are identical and property-value assignments use common terminology.

3.2   JSAgents Core Library

The Core Library includes the methods that ensure safe deployment and inner workings of JSAgents. The library must be executed as early as possible in the execution flow of the protected website in order to win the basic race condition. When the core library is executed, a sequence of events enumerated and discussed below is started (cf. Fig. 1).[3]

(1) Freezing and Sealing the Original DOM. Markup rendering is stopped by a plain-text element being written into the actual document. Consequently all HTML markup after this element is considered to be simple text and is

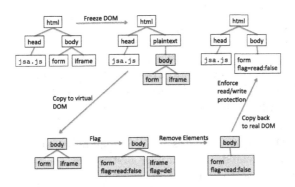

Fig. 1. Processing of a JSAgents protected HTML document.

---

[3] For review purposes, we have copied a password protected ZIP file of the JSAgents code to the following Dropbox URL: https://www.dropbox.com/s/17kjd8hrmjbzy6c/jsa.zip (password: *conference*).

not parsed into DOM objects. This is necessary to win possible attacker-caused race-conditions (for instance based on DOM-clobbering, see below).

```
this.freeze = function () {
    // seal existing document before freezing
    JSA.seal(document);
    // freeze and blind the whole document
    document.write('<plaintext id="' + JSA._random
      +'" style="display:none">');
    document.close();
}
```

Listing 1.1. The code to freeze a document by stopping its execution flow

By calling this.seal(), it is ensured that the áttacker cannot tamper with the existing DOM properties that JS-Agents requires to work (for example DOM traversal, element and attribute manipulation). This technique effectively defeats "DOM clobbering"[4], a way of overwriting the native DOM methods by using HTML injections[5] in any tested browser.

```
this.seal = function (doc) {
  for(var item in doc){
    if(typeof doc[item] ==='function'){
      Object.defineProperty(
      doc, item, {value: doc[item], configurable:false}
      );}}
  return doc;}
```

Listing 1.2. Iterating over all methods to seal them reliably from external access

(2) Content Copying to a "fresh" DOM. We now extract the DOM contents and map them into the safe DOM.

```
// create JSA document to check on
JSA.doc = JSA.create();
//Copy document and assign random ID values
JSA.doc.documentElement.innerHTML ='<html><head>' +
document.getElementById(JSA._random).textContent;
```

Listing 1.3. Creating a virtual DOM and assigning random IDs to each element

(3) Enforcing the given Policies. This is done by iterating over the virtual DOM tree we have created. The enforcer first requests all elements matching the JSAgents policy selectors and, upon receiving one or more elements, passes them to the protected _enforce()_ method. This method is being provided by the JSAgents enforcer module and compares the policy defined capabilities with the actual object's capabilities, eventually taking action in case of any mismatches

---

[4] DOM Clobbering describes malicious declarative DOM manipulation: http://www.thespanner.co.uk/2013/05/16/dom-clobbering/.

[5] For example, the HTML `<img src=x name=getElementById>` would overwrite the method `document.getElementById()` with an image-object.

being identified. The final goal is the removal of either the attributes or the specific attribute values, the prefixing of resource URIs or even the removal of entire elements and there-attached child nodes. However, to make sure the policy directives and their selectors cascade properly (selector precision over selector order), the enforcer initially only flags elements for deletion or manipulation. Only after the final selector's rules have been enforced, the elements are actually removed or modified (see below). By design, the enforcer is being defined and kept as "a module" because adding it to the core library would cause unnecessary overhead – we acknowledge that possible forks and adaptations of JSAgents might prefer building their own enforcers and keep the core library untouched. Using it as a module allows an easy extension and customization; one imaginable scenario would be that a more exotic or legacy browser needs to be supported.

(4) Remove Elements Flagged as del, Domain White-Listing. After all necessary enforcement iterations are completed, the final state of element and attribute flagging is being used as an indicator of whether the element or attribute should be removed or kept in place. Elements are removed if they are flagged as del, or if their source domain does not match any of the whitelisted domains.

```
this.filter = function () {
// remove elements with kill-switch
var elements = JSA.doc.querySelectorAll('*');
for(var index in elements){
if(elements[index].tagName) {
    if(elements[index].getAttribute(JSA._random) ==='del') {
        elements[index].parentNode.removeChild(elements[index
            ])
}}}}
```

Listing 1.4. Deleting marked elements

Note that during the flagging and enforcement no other script in the protected website can be executed[6]. Furthermore, beware that the deletion flags are applied with a token value to make sure that an attacker cannot inject those attributes and force legitimate elements to be deleted. The token changes every time JSAgents runs.

(5) Rendering the Document. Read- or write-access restrictions must be enforced in the "real" DOM. This signifies that the flagged virtual DOM with forbidden elements already removed, is now copied back – as shown in the simplified example: document.body.innerHTML = JSA.doc.body.innerHTML (script content is, if permitted, reactivated separately). During subsequent parsing, restrictions on the parsed elements imposed by the attached flags will be enforced.

---

[6] Only if an external window opened from the same origin injects code, a malicious script may run concurrently to JSAgents. This may happen if only parts of the website are protected with the JSAgents library. Partial library usage is considered a dangerous implementation misbehavior and leads to race conditions that allow policy bypasses.

The core library uses DOM Mutation Observers to get on-time notification on changes happening to the write-protected DOM elements. Only by monitoring access and changes to the existing elements with working observers, a continuous level of write-protection can be guaranteed. All DOM objects flagged with access restrictions are protected – all their property getters are set to return null.

```
var access = document.querySelectorAll('*['+_random+'access
    ]')
for(var elm in access) {
    if(access[elm].tagName) {
        for(var i in access[elm]){
            // null all properties of the protected element
            Object.defineProperty(access[elm], i, {value:
                null});
}}}
```

Listing 1.5. Read access protection for DOM elements

It is possible to allow access for certain trusted DOM methods if required. By default, however, all property access is prohibited. Once write-access to a DOM element with write-access:false is communicated to the JSAgents core function, a wide range of actions becomes available. Depending on the JSAgents policy, the library can block write-access (through restoring the element to its original state), return empty strings upon read-access, and even report attempts of read or write to protected elements.

```
// freeze flagged elements
var freeze = document.querySelectorAll('*['+_random+'freeze
    ]')
for(var elm in freeze) {
    if(freeze[elm].tagName) {
    var observer = new MutationObserver(function(mutations) {
        mutations.forEach(function(mutation) {
        alert('form tamper detected');
        });
    });
    var config = {
        attributes: true,
        childList: true,
        characterData: true
    };
    observer.observe(freeze[elm], config);
    Object.defineProperty(freeze[elm],'value', {set: function
        (){
        return alert('form value tamper detected');
}});}}
```

Listing 1.6. Code to handle write-access control to elements

From this point forward none of the elements and attributes that are violating the JSAgents policies are present. Please note that changing element properties through the keyboard is not registered as a mutation event by the DOM Mutation Observers, as opposed to the write-access by a script. Thus, for example, for write-protected form elements, user input from keyboard is not considered to be write-access, thus laying the foundation for basic access-control functionality.

3.3 JSAgents Modules

The JSAgents library further ships a set of modules that provide functionality not yet available in modern browsers.

(1) A JavaScript implementation of the MD5 hashing algorithm md5.js is being loaded via module; MD5 is being used despite security concerns for performance reasons. The library allows to upgrade to SHA1 and later releases are planned to be shipped with a JavaScript implementation of SHA256. It is important to note that the use cases for hashing algorithms in the JSAgents library do not depend on collision resistance.

(2) An enforcer.js script is used to enforce various JSAgents policies and iterate over the target elements. It also imposes the restrictions or permissions the developer wishes to enforce and grant (as discussed in Sect. 3.2). Furthermore, an extended enforcer allows creation of additional rules – complementary to the already available rules and policies. The enforcer is again not considered a part of the core library because it might be subject to customizations, for instance for a website that uses a specific JavaScript framework.

3.4 JSAgents Policy Files

JSAgents policy files are composed in a JSON format and make use of a very simple and intuitive dictionary of instructions. This allows even novice developers to understand the concept and impact of the policy files rather quickly. Note that the dictionary of available configuration directives might be subject to change as it is now in its prototypic state. The code shown in Listing 1.7 and Listing 1.8 demonstrates the flexibility of JSAgents policy composition. The syntax is designed to closely resemble CSS selectors.

Listing 1.7 makes use of the asterisk-selector which causes the JSAgents engine to indeed choose all available DOM elements on the loaded document and impose the following (very restrictive) directives. As dictated by this policy, no Script, Iframe, Object, Embed, Applet, or SVG elements will be present in the modified DOM. JavaScript and data URIs will be removed from the DOM and so will be the event handlers. All remaining elements will be frozen, for example they cannot be modified by the DOM meta-programming from now on. Read-access to all remaining elements is blocked.

The code shown in Listing 1.8 is a bit more permissive, and demonstrates the "cascading" features of the policy language. Here we can observe an overall of four selectors: the asterisk selector, a selector for head-elements, a selector for form elements and their expected descendants, and, finally, a selector for the

```
{ "*" : {                                    { "*" : {
    "iframe-elements":  false,                   "javascript-uris": false,
    "object-elements":  false,                   "data-uris":       false,
    "embed-elements"  :  false,                  "event-handlers":  false,
    "applet-elements":  false,                   "script-elements": false,
    "svg-elements":     false,                   "style-elements":  false
    "script-elements": false,                },
    "javascript-uris": false,                "head" : {"script-elements":
    "data-uris":        false,                   "same-domain"
    "event-handlers":  false,                }
    "write-access":     false,               "form, input, textarea" : {
    "read-access":      false                   "read-access":   false,
}                                                "write-access": false
                                             },
                                             "#widget" : {
                                                 "script-elements": true
                                             } }
```

Listing 1.7. A high-security policy: All forms of scripting and read/write-access to DOM elements prohibited

Listing 1.8. A low-security policy: Scripting is permitted for scripts living in the page header and a widget container - read-/write-access to form content is prohibited

element(s) applied with the "widget" ID. Depending on the selector, different policies are assigned and will thus be enforced by the JSAgents prototype. None of the elements are permitted to contain script-elements – aside from the head-element which can comprise of script-elements as long as their source points to a same domain resource, and also the element with the "widget" ID. The selected form elements are being protected from arbitrary access. No script can have access to their value properties, all attempts to set their values via JavaScript will be blocked, a read-access will return an empty value. This is interesting for websites which wish to impose better protection for user-generated content in the form elements (account data, passwords, credit card numbers).

The grammar used for the selectors is identical to the CSS grammar and will be parsed by the DOM `document. querySelectorAll()` method for element selection. No deviations from the standard are implemented. Developers can freely use any selector string that is available and supported by the browser. Please note that although the selectors in Listing 1.8 are ordered according to generality, the ordering of selectors is not relevant for the correct functionality as JSAgents will always give preference to stronger selectors. Later versions of the library will also support detailed style directives to avoid HTTP leakage via backgrounds, list bullets, fonts, cursors, and alike. The set of the currently available directives and policies for the JSAgents prototype is described as follows:

(1) **iframe-elements, object-elements, embed-elements.** These policy directives can be set to `true`, `false` or a domain reg-ex. The elements can be permitted, prohibited or only be permitted if the `src` attribute

matches the given domain string. If a directive is set to `false`, all such elements will be removed from the DOM by the JSAgents core library.[7]

(2) **applet-elements.** This policy directive can be set to `true`, `false` or a domain reg-ex. Java applets can be permitted, prohibited, or only be permitted if the code-base or archive attribute matches the given domain string.

(3) **svg-elements.** This policy directive can be set to `true` or `false`. If set to false, no SVG elements can be used inside the selected nodes. This does not exclude the option of using SVG embedded via image elements or CSS. Recent browser versions have proven to be able to safely deal with SVG content – once the SVG data is being loaded as an image rather than a document.

(4) **script-elements.** This policy directive can be set to `true`, `false` or a domain reg-ex. Script elements can be permitted, prohibited, or only be permitted if the src attribute matches the given domain string. Note that the "same-domain" setting does not utilize a regular expression but rather an exact string matching between origin and domain part of the URL that the script element is supposed to load from.

(5) **style-elements.** This policy directive can be set to `true`, `false` or a domain reg-ex. Style (and link) elements can be permitted, prohibited, or only be permitted if the href attribute/ import URIs match the given domain string.

(6) **img-elements.** This policy directive can be used to permit or prohibit images loaded from external URLs. Especially for web-mail software, embedded images and comparable resources allow for advertisers and other parties to track and monitor reception of and reaction to a HTML mail. With prohibition of external sources, an additional layer of privacy will be added. To cope with the needs of modern web-mailers, an additional function `ask()` was added. By using this function, JSAgents leaves the decision of loading or blocking external images to the user, instrumenting a permission-dialog.

(7) **javascript-uris.** This policy directive can be set to `true` or `false`. Once set to `false`, none of the elements hosted by the selected element can be applied with JavaScript URIs. This holds for all attributes supporting URL strings. Note that an element using JavaScript URIs will be completely removed in case that the policy setting prohibits its existence. Several existing tools attempt to rewrite the URL to become a harmless placeholder value, JSAgents nevertheless removes the entire element for security reasons.

(8) **data-uris.** This policy directive can be set to `true` or `false`. Once set to `true`, none of the elements hosted by the selected element can be applied with data URIs. This holds for all attributes supporting URL strings.

---

[7] It should be noted that Java applets can be loaded via object element as well. Future versions of the JSAgents prototype will warn the developer in case a policy prohibits the usage of applets yet allows the arbitrary object usage.

(9) event-handlers. This policy directive can be set to `true` or `false`. If set to `false`, all event handlers will be removed from the selected elements.

(10) write-access. This policy allows setting an element to an immutable state by freezing it and prohibiting access to any of its child properties. This is particularly interesting for form elements as means of keeping external scripts and other active content from varying values, actions and other potentially sensitive data stores. This policy directive can be set to `true` or `false`. Upcoming versions will also allow to define an array of allowed setters, making sure that trusted JavaScript methods are permitted whilst untrusted methods are blocked from modifying form values.

(11) read-access. This policy allows to manage read-access to an element. If set to false, all read-access to its sensitive DOM values will be blocked. Similar to the *freeze*-policy, this directive is particularly interesting for the protection of sensitive data in form elements. The policy directive can be set to `true` or `false`. Upcoming versions will also allow to define an array of allowed setters, ensuring that trusted JavaScript methods are permitted while untrusted methods are blocked from modifying form values.

4   Security Evaluation

Since no formal methods are available to test security against MI attacks (XSS filter bypasses are nearly always found through manual inspection), several semi-formal empirical evaluations have been performed.

Generic Security Features. Unlike other filter tools, JSAgents cannot be bypassed by an attacker utilizing obfuscation, unusual character sets, compressed markup (WBXML) or even mXSS attacks. JSAgents takes the information about the markup that is to be analyzed directly from the browser's DOM. That means that even if a certain version of a given user agent has exploitable flaws that lead to broken markup being parsed into something active and executable, JSAgents can still maintain its protective functionality through analyzing the markup after the browser has processed it.

State-of-the-art Test Vectors. Two major sources of state-of-the-art XSS attack vectors, "RSnake XSS Cheat Sheet" (now maintained by OWASP, 107 unique vectors[8]) and "HTML5 Security Cheatsheet" (139 unique vectors[9]) were used for an initial hardening of JSAgents.

Public Challenge. To test the security features of the JSAgents core, a demo was made available online and announced publicly ("DOMPurify" project hosted on GitHub). Composing an arbitrary HTML string and sanitizing it from XSS and DOM clobbering attacks using our library is made possible through this demo. We received feedback from 31 researchers, with an approximate total of 13,000 attempts to break JSAgents. Only 15 bypasses based on unexpected

---

[8] https://www.owasp.org/index.php/XSS_Filter_Evasion_Cheat_Sheet.
[9] http://html5sec.org.

browser and DOM behaviors as well as DOM clobbering were identified after that test phase and could be mitigated successfully (e.g., DOM-clobbering attacks using a form-node, two input elements applied with the name "attributes" and similar).

Empirical Security Model Based on Browser Capability Tests. The currently employed version of the JSAgents core has been hardened against XSS, DOM Clobbering, Tag Splitting, XML injections, and mXSS attacks by one the authors who is considered as an expert in this field. Further, capability tests for HTML, MathML and SVG elements to harden JSAgents have identified several formerly unknown methods of script execution. This research has resullted in several new attack vectors like using SVG and the `<animate>` element to execute JavaScript from seemingly harmless attributes such as *from*, *to* and *values*, for example leading to XSS Auditor bypasses in WebKit and Blink. Consequently, the JSAgents core was updated and now successfully mitigates these attack vectors.

Preventing Information Leakage. A test-suite was created to enumerate all currently documented ways for browsers to leak information via HTTP requests to third-party servers (images, CSS, videos, HTML manifests, proprietary MSIE features, CSS *image()*). JSAgents was then optimized to spot and later remove those data leaks. This was motivated by a need to allow a web-mailer to present HTML mails without risking data leakage and unwanted tracking. At the same time, it made it possible for the web proxies to provide better anonymity (which they lack based on the fact that proxied HTML is filtered on the server and thereby prone to attacks using obfuscation and exotic HTML features).

5   Performance Evaluation

To measure the execution time of JSAgents we created random HTML files with valid elements and attributes, and arbitrary values. Table 1 shows the performance for files with 10, 100, 608, 1,000, and 10,000 elements. For each test case, Table 1 contains the average time in milliseconds after 25 tests with the web API interface `console.time` (reconstructed for IE10). Next to `console.time`, we worked with the JavaScript profiler of Firebug for Firefox and the native profiler of Chrome to analyze the execution time of our JSAgents functions. Therefore, there are five additional measurements for each test case in FF and GC. We used the policies of Listings 1.7 and 1.8 with the following modifications: (1) For policy 1.7, we used `script-elements: "same-domain"`. (2) For policy 1.8, we omitted the `#widget` definition, since this value was not present in our sample files. Each tested browser was installed on the same virtual machine with an Intel Xeon E5-2470 processor (2,3 GHz), four assigned cores and 4 GB RAM. By reading out the measurements via the profiler, we noticed that the attribute enforcer, source extraction, and innerHTML modification need more execution time than any other parts of JSAgents. By comparing our results, the attribute enforcer is the slowest component if there are at least 37 HTML elements on the website.

Table 1. Performance evaluation in milliseconds.

Elements	IE10	IE11	FF16	FF29	GC36
Policy of Listing 1.8 with					
`script-elements: "same-domain"`					
100	21	23	45	53	25
608	83	114	182	129	77
1,000	132	181	297	208	121
10,000	1,131	1,437	3,064	1,643	1,073
Policy of Listing 1.7 without the `#widget` definition					
100	21	23	49	52	25
608	81	107	179	126	74
1,000	124	173	279	202	117
10,000	1,043	1,403	2,923	1,524	1,031

To make our measurements applicable to real life applications, we computed the average number of HTML elements of the following main pages: Google (145), YouTube (1,302), Facebook (383), Twitter (402), and Yahoo (810). This average number is 608, and for this number (cf. Table 1) JSAgents needs 117 ms to be fully executed for the modified policy of Listing 1.8 with 11 directives inside of one selector, and 114 ms for the modified policy of Listing 1.7 with eight directives inside of three selectors. The modified policy of Listing 1.7 is a little faster than the policy of Listing 1.8; the enforcer is responsible for this behavior because its execution time increases with a higher number of directives.

6   Future Work

JSAgents is a library and framework that can reliably enforce fine-grained policies on the DOM of a website or any other browser-based document. Deploying a security tool on this specific layer has many benefits and enables several novel use cases and docking points for future work and extensions.

Extensibility Through Modularity. Given that the developer can deploy a module right in the time window between the document content being fully loaded and the document being rendered, a large set of additional security and usability enhancements can be implemented. For example accessibility factors of the document can be enriched by JSAgents, since the subtitles can be automatically displayed for videos, markup can be annotated from linked content sources, visibility aspects can be adjusted by applying additional contrast or manipulating font sizes.

Enhancements of the Policy Language. Future revisions will cover policy directives capable of managing permissions to use arbitrary non-HTTP protocol handlers, a flag to enforce "SSL only" resources, and a possibility to pipeline any existing binary resource through a configurable proxy-URL. An implementation of fine-grained DOM property access management will be offered. This is advantageous for developers who wish to use JSAgents with applications that already make use of a plenitude of JavaScript code and DOM interaction.

A   Comparable Approaches

A.1   From XSS Filters to CSP 1.0

Client-side XSS Filters. JSAgents is *not* a classical XSS filter. This is due to the fact that each and every XSS filter must be able to make distinctions between user-supplied and application-supplied markup. Conversely, JSAgents only sees the combination of both (aside from common DOMXSS sources and sinks like `location.href`). However, by employing an approach inherently different from that of any common XSS filters, JSAgents can reliably mitigate several kinds of XSS and markup injection – including DOMXSS and, in part, Scriptless Attacks. If a web application uses third-party input to build some parts of the DOM tree, regardless of whether it is user-supplied, stored, or DOM-based (e.g., `document.URL`, `document.href`, `document.referrer`), it may specify a whitelist of the allowed HTML elements for that very part of the DOM tree. Any other type of element will be deleted by JSAgents. Thus, if JavaScript execution and other potentially malicious HTML5 elements are not allowed in certain parts of the website, these attacks will be blocked. An example of this approach is given in Sect. 5, where a common webmail application assumes that the Iframe containing the body of the rendered email should not contain any active markup.

HTTPonly Cookies. By setting the JSAgents directive `read-access: false` for properties such as `document.cookie`, we effectively turn any cookie into an HTTPonly cookie, so that `document.cookie` can no longer be accessed by scripts. Similar access control can be imposed on form elements to prevent malicious script from stealing its contents or sniffing keystrokes.

Sandboxed Iframes. In their default configuration, sandboxed Iframes have a virtual origin that is different from any other kind of origin. By default, they neither allow script execution nor form submission and they are not permitted to navigate the top level frame (although those restrictions can be lifted gradually). Two of these properties can easily be modeled with JSAgents: We can remove all script and form elements from a selected Iframe. Sandboxed Iframes, however, feature additional properties to gradually release the default security constraints. In its current state JSAgents is not yet able to emulate this functionality.

HTTP Leak Detection/Proxy Injection. Since JSAgents is targeting extractability, it is capable of detecting HTML elements that attempt to load external resources. Depending on the use case, leaking information via direct HTTP requests might compromise privacy promises of a web application. This especially holds for web-mailers and web proxies, where a HTTP request sent to an arbitrary URL or IP would leak user data and timing information, essentially enabling localization and tracking. JSAgents can be instructed to change any of the existing URLs that point to external resources to be prefixed with a proxy URL. This would mean that leakage of sensitive user data is avoided.

A.2   Content Security Policy

Content Security Policy 1.0. Large parts of CSP 1.0 can be implemented and extended with the use of JSAgents. This is achieved by creating a policy that prohibits any form of inline scripting, objects, embeds and applets, while implementing a prefix for external resources (or simply blocking the use of external resources that are coming from a non-whitelisted domain). Therefore, one possible application scenario is to (partly) implement CSP in legacy browsers. However, since JSAgents is not part of the browser core, it is less resistant to higher-privilege attacks (e.g., web injections by local malware). JSAgents can be used as a CSP replacement in browsers that do not support it and as a CSP supplement in browsers with partial or full support.

```
header('X-Content-Security-Policy: script-src'self'; style-
    src 'self'; img-src'self' images.mysite.com);
```
Listing 1.9. Example CSP policy.

The code instances in Listings 1.9 and 1.10 show how an example CSP policy can be emulated using JSAgents, even if the browser itself does not support CSP.

```
{"*" : {
  script-elements: "same-domain",
  style-elements: "same-domain",
  img-elements: "same-domain", "images.mysite.com"
}}
```
Listing 1.10. CSP-emulating JSAgents policy.

CSP 1.1 Script Nonces. Introduced with CSP 1.1, script nonces are a way to permit execution of only those (inline) script elements that have a nonce

Table 2. Comparison between CSP 1.0, 1.1 and JSAgents (Y: available, m: available via module, n: not available).

Feature	CSP 1.0	CSP 1.1	JSAgents
connect-src, font-src, frame-src, img-src, media-src, object-src, script-src, style-src	Y	Y	Y
base-uri, frame-ancestors	n	Y	n
default-src, form-action, plugin-types, referrer, sandbox	n	Y	Y
reflexted-xss, report-uri	n	Y	m
Cascading Properties	n	n	Y
DOM node read-access	n	n	Y
DOM write read-access	n	n	Y
ask() function	n	n	m

attribute with a value identical to a nonce value transmitted in the HTTP header. This makes inline script injection nearly impossible. In cooperation with the web application, JSAgents, inspired by Noncespaces [18], can achieve the same goal: Inline scripts are marked with a fresh nonce value by the web application and the same nonce value is written into a copy of the configuration file. As a result of the jsa.js execution with this unique policy, all inline scripts unmarked with the nonce value from the configuration file will be deleted (Table 2).

References

1. Klein, A.: DOM based cross site scripting or XSS of the third kind (2005). http://www.webappsec.org/projects/articles/071105.shtml
2. Heiderich, M., Schwenk, J., Frosch, T., Magazinius, J., Yang, E.Z.: mxss attacks: attacking well-secured web-applications by using innerhtml mutations. In: CCS (2013)
3. Heiderich, M., Frosch, T., Jensen, M., Holz, T.: Crouching tiger - hidden payload: security risks of scalable vector graphics. In: Proceedings of the 18th ACM conference on Computer and Communications Security, pp. 239–250. ACM (2011)
4. Heiderich, M., Niemietz, M., Schuster, F., Holz; T., Schwenk, J.: Scriptless attacks-stealing the pie without touching the sill. In: ACM Conference on Computer and Communications Security (CCS) (2012)
5. Stone, P.: Pixel perfect timing attacks with html5. http://contextis.co.uk/files/Browser_Timing_Attacks.pdf
6. Sterne, B., Barth, A.: Content security policy 1.0," W3C, Candidate Recommendation, November 2012. http://www.w3.org/TR/2012/CR-CSP-20121115/
7. Barth, A., Veditz, D., West, M.: Content security policy 1.1, w3c editor's draft 12 November 2013. https://dvcs.w3.org/hg/content-security-policy/raw-file/tip/csp-specification.dev.html
8. Barth, A.: HTTP State Management Mechanism, RFC 6265 (Proposed Standard), Internet Engineering Task Force, April 2011. http://www.ietf.org/rfc/rfc6265.txt
9. Hickson, I.: Html living standard - last updated 21 february 2014. http://www.whatwg.org/specs/web-apps/current-work/multipage/the-iframe-element.html
10. Ross, D.: IE8 XSS Filter design philosophy in-depth, April 2008. http://blogs.msdn.com/b/dross/archive/2008/07/03/ie8-xss-filter-design-philosophy-in-depth.aspx
11. Bates, D., Barth, A., Jackson, C.: Regular expressions considered harmful in client-side XSS filters. In: Proceedings of the 19th International Conference on World Wide Web, ser. WWW 2010, pp. 91–100. ACM, New York (2010). http://doi.acm.org/10.1145/1772690.1772701
12. Zuchlinski, G.: The anatomy of cross site scripting. Hitchhiker's World 8, November 2003
13. Bisht, P., Venkatakrishnan, V.N.: XSS-GUARD: precise dynamic prevention of cross-site scripting attacks. In: Zamboni, D. (ed.) DIMVA 2008. LNCS, vol. 5137, pp. 23–43. Springer, Heidelberg (2008)
14. Johns, M.: Code injection vulnerabilities in web applications - exemplified at cross-site scripting. Ph.D. dissertation, University of Passau, Passau, July 2009
15. Gebre, M., Lhee, K., Hong, M.: A robust defense against content-sniffing xss attacks. In: 2010 6th International Conference on Digital Content, Multimedia Technology and its Applications (IDC), pp. 315–320. IEEE (2010)

16. Saxena, P., Molnar, D., Livshits, B.: SCRIPTGARD: automatic context-sensitive sanitization for large-scale legacy web applications. In: Proceedings of the 18th ACM conference on Computer and communications security, pp. 601–614. ACM (2011)

17. Gourdin, B., Soman, C., Bojinov, H., Bursztein, E.: Toward secure embedded web interfaces. In: Proceedings of the Usenix Security Symposium (2011)

18. Gundy, M.V., Chen, H.: Noncespaces: using randomization to defeat cross-site scripting attacks. Comput. Secur. **31**(4), 612–628 (2012)

19. Nadji, Y., Saxena, P., Song, D.: Document structure integrity: a robust basis for cross-site scripting defense. In: NDSS. The Internet Society (2009)

20. Louw, M.T., Venkatakrishnan, V.N.: Blueprint: robust prevention of cross-site scripting attacks for existing browsers. In: Proceedings of the 2009 30th IEEE Symposium on Security and Privacy, ser. SP 2009, pp. 331–34. IEEE Computer Society, Washington, DC (2009). http://dx.doi.org/10.1109/SP.2009.33

21. Weinberger, J., Saxena, P., Akhawe, D., Finifter, M., Shin, R., Song, D.: A systematic analysis of XSS sanitization in web application frameworks. In: Atluri, V., Diaz, C. (eds.) ESORICS 2011. LNCS, vol. 6879, pp. 150–171. Springer, Heidelberg (2011)

22. Nava, E.V., Lindsay, D.: Abusing Internet Explorer 8's XSS Filters. http://p42. us/ie8xss/Abusing_IE8s_XSS_Filters.pdf

23. Zalewski, M.: Browser Security Handbook, July 2010. http://code.google.com/p/browsersec/wiki/Main

24. Zalewski, M.: The Tangled Web: A Guide to Securing Modern Web Applications. No Starch Press, San Francisco (2011)

25. Bug 29278: XSSAuditor bypasses from sla.ckers.org. https://bugs.webkit.org/show_bug.cgi?id=29278

26. Heiderich, M.: Towards Elimination of XSS Attacks with a Trusted and Capability Controlled DOM (2012). http://www-brs.ub.ruhr-uni-bochum.de/netahtml/HSS/Diss/HeiderichMario/diss.pdf

27. Hooimeijer, P., Livshits, B., Molnar, D., Saxena, P., Veanes, M.: Fast and precise sanitizer analysis with bek. In: Proceedings of the 20th USENIX Conference On Security, ser. SEC 2011, p. 1. USENIX Association, Berkeley (2011). http://dl. acm.org/citation.cfm?id=2028067.2028068

28. Kolbitsch, C., Livshits, B., Zorn, B., Seifert, C.: Rozzle: De-Cloaking internet malware. In: Proceedings IEEE Symposium on Security & Privacy (2012)

29. Nava, E.V.: ACS - active content signatures. PST_WEBZINE_0X04, no. 4, December 2006

30. Di Paola, S.: Preventing xss with data binding. http://www.wisec.it/sectou.php?id=46c5843ea4900

31. Heiderich, M., Frosch, T., Holz, T.: IceShield: detection and mitigation of malicious websites with a frozen DOM. In: Sommer, R., Balzarotti, D., Maier, G. (eds.) RAID 2011. LNCS, vol. 6961, pp. 281–300. Springer, Heidelberg (2011)

Analyzing the BrowserID SSO System with Primary Identity Providers Using an Expressive Model of the Web

Daniel Fett, Ralf Küsters[(✉)], and Guido Schmitz

University of Trier, Trier, Germany
{fett,kuesters,schmitzg}@uni-trier.de

Abstract. BrowserID is a complex, real-world Single Sign-On (SSO) System for web applications recently developed by Mozilla. It employs new HTML5 features (such as web messaging and web storage) and cryptographic assertions to provide decentralized login, with the intent to respect users' privacy. It can operate in a primary and a secondary identity provider mode. While in the primary mode BrowserID runs with arbitrary identity providers, in the secondary mode there is one identity provider only, namely Mozilla's default identity provider.

We recently proposed an expressive general model for the web infrastructure and, based on this web model, analyzed the security of the secondary identity provider mode of BrowserID. The analysis revealed several severe vulnerabilities, which have been fixed by Mozilla.

In this paper, we complement our prior work by analyzing the even more complex primary identity provider mode of BrowserID. We do not only study authentication properties as before, but also privacy properties. During our analysis we discovered new and practical attacks that do not apply to the secondary mode: an identity injection attack, which violates a central authentication property of SSO systems, and attacks that break the privacy promise of BrowserID and which do not seem to be fixable without a major redesign of the system. Interestingly, some of our attacks on privacy make use of a browser side channel that, to the best of our knowledge, has not gained a lot of attention so far.

For the authentication bug, we propose a fix and formally prove in a slight extension of our general web model that the fixed system satisfies all the authentication requirements we consider. This constitutes the most complex formal analysis of a web application based on an expressive model of the web infrastructure so far.

As another contribution, we identify and prove important security properties of generic web features in the extended web model to facilitate future analysis efforts of web standards and web applications.

1 Introduction

Single sign-on (SSO) systems have become an important building block for authentication in the web. Over the last years, many different SSO systems have been developed, for example, OpenID, OAuth, and proprietary solutions

© Springer International Publishing Switzerland 2015
G. Pernul et al. (Eds.): ESORICS 2015, Part I, LNCS 9326, pp. 43–65, 2015.
DOI: 10.1007/978-3-319-24174-6_3

such as Facebook Connect. These systems usually allow a user to identify herself to a so-called relying party (RP), which provides some service, using an identity that is managed by an identity provider (IdP), such as Facebook or Google.

Given their role as brokers between IdPs and RPs, the security of SSO systems is particularly crucial: numerous attacks have shown that vulnerabilities in SSO systems compromise the security of many services and users at once (see, e.g., [3, 7, 23–26]).

BrowserID [21] is a relatively new complex SSO system which allows users to utilize any of their existing email addresses as an identity. BrowserID, which is also known by its marketing name *Persona*, has been developed by Mozilla and provides decentralized and federated login, with the intent to respect users' privacy: While in other SSO systems (such as OpenID), by design, IdPs can always see when and where their users log in, Mozilla's intention behind the design of BrowserID was that such tracking should not be possible. Several web applications support BrowserID authentication. For example, popular content management systems, such as Drupal and WordPress allow users to log in using BrowserID. Also Mozilla uses this SSO system on critical web sites, e.g., their bug tracker Bugzilla and their developer network MDN.

The BrowserID implementation is based solely on native web technologies. It uses many new HTML5 web features, such as web messaging and web storage. For example, BrowserID uses the postMessage mechanism for cross-origin inter-frame communication (i.e., communication within a browser between different windows) and the web storage concept of modern browsers to store user data on the client side.

There are two modes for BrowserID: For the best user experience, email providers (IdPs) can actively support BrowserID; they are then called *primary IdPs*. For all other email providers that do not support BrowserID, the user can register her email address at a default IdP, namely Mozilla's `login.persona.org`, the so-called *secondary IdP*.

In [13], we proposed a general and expressive Dolev-Yao style model for the web infrastructure. This web model is designed independently of a specific web application and closely mimics published (de-facto) standards and specifications for the web, for instance, the HTTP/1.1 and HTML5 standards and associated (proposed) standards (mainly RFCs). It is the most comprehensive web model to date. Among others, HTTP(S) requests and responses, including several headers, such as cookie, location, strict transport security (STS), and origin headers, are modeled. The model of web browsers captures the concepts of windows, documents, and iframes, including the complex navigation rules, as well as new technologies, such as web storage and cross-document messaging (postMessages). JavaScript is modeled in an abstract way by so-called scripting processes which can be sent around and, among others, can create iframes and initiate XMLHTTPRequests (XHRs). Browsers may be corrupted dynamically by the adversary.

Based on this general web model, we analyzed the security of the secondary IdP mode of BrowserID [13]. The analysis revealed several severe vulnerabilities, which have since been fixed by Mozilla.

Contributions of this Paper. The main contributions of this paper are that we (i) analyze authentication and privacy properties for the primary mode of BrowserID, where in both cases the analysis revealed new attacks, (ii) identify generic web security properties to ease future analysis efforts, and (iii) slightly extend our web model.

As mentioned before, in [13], we studied the simpler secondary mode of BrowserID only. The primary model studied here is much more complex than the secondary mode (see also the remarks in Sect. 4.2). It involves more components (such as an arbitrary set of IdPs, more iframes), a much more complex communication structure, and requires weaker trust assumptions (for example, some IdPs, and hence, the JavaScript they deliver, might be malicious). Also, in our previous work, we have not considered privacy properties, but authentication properties only.

More specifically, the contributions of this paper can be summarized as follows.

Extension of the Web Model. We slightly extend our web model proposed in [13]. We complement the modeling of the web storage concept of modern browsers by adding sessionStorage [27], which is (besides the already modeled localStorage) heavily used by BrowserID in its primary mode. We also extend the model to include a set of user identities (e.g., user names or email addresses) in addition to user secrets.

Authentication Attack and Security Proof for BrowserID. The authentication properties we analyze are central to any SSO system and correspond to those considered in our previous work: (i) the attacker should not be able to log in at an RP as an honest user and (ii) the attacker should not be able to authenticate an honest user/browser to an RP with an ID not owned by the user (identity injection). While trying to prove these authentication properties for the primary mode of BrowserID, we discovered a new attack which violates property (ii). Depending on the service provided by the RP, this could allow the attacker to track the honest user or to obtain user secrets. We confirmed the attack on the actual implementation and reported it to Mozilla, who acknowledged the attack. We note that this attack does not apply to the secondary mode.

We propose a fix and provide a detailed formal proof based on the (extended) web model which shows that the fixed system satisfies the mentioned authentication properties. This constitutes the most complex formal analysis of a web application based on an expressive model of the web infrastructure, in fact, as mentioned, the most comprehensive one to date. We note that other web models are too limited to be applied to BrowserID (see also Sect. 7).

Privacy Attacks on BrowserID. As pointed out before, BrowserID was designed by Mozilla with the explicit intention to respect users' privacy. Unlike in other SSO systems, when using BrowserID, IdPs should not learn to which RP a user logs in. When trying to formally prove this property, we discovered attacks that show that BrowserID cannot live up to this claim. Our attacks allow malicious

IdPs to check whether or not a user is logged in at a specific RP with little effort. Interestingly, one variant of these attacks exploits a browser side channel which, to our knowledge, has not received much attention in the literature so far. Just as for authentication, we have confirmed the attacks on the actual implementation and reported them to Mozilla [10], who acknowledged the attacks. We have been awarded a bug bounty from the Mozilla Security Bug Bounty Program. Unfortunately, the attacks exploit a design flaw of BrowserID that does not seem to be easily fixable without a major redesign.

Generic Web Security Properties. Our security analysis of BrowserID and the case study in [13] show that certain security properties of the web model need to be established in most security proofs for web standards and web applications. As another contribution, we therefore identify and summarize central security properties of generic web features in our extension of our model and formalize them in a general way such that they can be used in and facilitate future analysis efforts of web standards and web applications.

Structure of this Paper. In Sect. 2, we outline the basic communication model and the web model, including our extensions. We deduce general properties of this model, which are independent of specific web applications, in Sect. 3. For our security analysis, we first, in Sect. 4, provide a description of the BrowserID system, focusing on the primary mode. We then, in Sect. 5, present our attack and the formal analysis of the authentication properties of the (fixed) BrowserID system in primary mode. In Sect. 6, we present our attacks on privacy of BrowserID. Related work is discussed in Sect. 7. We conclude in Sect. 8. In the appendix, we present more details on our web model and some privacy attack variants. Full details of our models and proofs can be found in our technical report [14].

2   The Web Model

In this section, we present a brief overview of our model of the web infrastructure as proposed in [13], along with our extensions (sessionStorage and user identities) mentioned in the introduction. Full details are provided in [14]. We first present the generic Dolev-Yao style communication model which the model is based on.

2.1   Communication Model

The main entities in the communication model are *atomic processes*, which will be used to model web browsers, web servers, DNS servers as well as web and network attackers. Each atomic process has a list of addresses (representing IP addresses) it listens to. A set of atomic processes forms what is called a *system*. The different atomic processes in such a system can communicate via events, which consist of a message as well as a receiver and a sender address. In every step of a run, one event is chosen non-deterministically from the current "pool" of events and is delivered to an atomic process that listens to the receiver address of that event; if different atomic processes can listen to the same address, the atomic process to which the event is delivered is chosen non-deterministically among the possible processes. The (chosen) atomic process can then process the event and output new events, which are added to the pool of events, and so on. More specifically, messages, processes, etc. are defined as follows.

Terms, Messages and Events. As usual in Dolev-Yao models (see, e.g., [1]), messages are expressed as formal terms over a signature. The signature Σ for the terms and messages considered in our web model contains, among others, constants (such as (IP) addresses, ASCII strings, and nonces), sequence and projection symbols, and further function symbols, including those for (a)symmetric encryption/decryption and digital signatures. The equational theory associated with the signature Σ is defined as usual in Dolev-Yao models. Message are defined to be ground terms (terms without variables) and events are of the form $(a{:}f{:}m)$ where a and f are receiver/sender (IP) addresses, and m is a message.

To provide an example of a message, in our web model an HTTP request is represented as a ground term containing a nonce, a method (e.g., GET or POST), a domain name, a path, URL parameters, request headers (such as Cookie), and a message body. Now, for example, an HTTP GET request for the URL http://ex.com/show?p=1 is modeled as the term $r :=$ $\langle \mathsf{HTTPReq}, n_1, \mathsf{GET}, \mathsf{ex.com}, \mathsf{/show}, \langle\langle \mathsf{p}, 1\rangle\rangle, \langle\rangle, \langle\rangle\rangle$, where headers and body are empty. An HTTPS request for r is of the form $\mathsf{enc_a}(\langle r, k'\rangle, \mathsf{pub}(k_{\mathsf{ex.com}}))$, where k' is a fresh symmetric key (a nonce) generated by the sender of the request (typically a browser); the responder is supposed to use this key to encrypt the response.

Atomic Processes, Systems and Runs. Atomic Dolev-Yao processes, systems, and runs of systems are defined as follows.

An *atomic Dolev-Yao (DY) process* is a tuple $p = (I^p, Z^p, R^p, s_0^p)$ where I^p is a set of addresses (the set of addresses the process listens to), Z^p is a set of states (formally, terms), $s_0^p \in Z^p$ is an initial state, and R^p is a relation that takes an event and a state as input and (non-deterministically) returns a new state and a set of events. This relation models a computation step of the process, which upon receiving an event in a given state non-deterministically moves to a new state and outputs a set of messages (events). It is required that the events and states in the output can be computed (more formally, derived in the usual Dolev-Yao style) from the current input event and state.

The so-called *attacker process* is an atomic DY process which records all messages it receives and outputs all messages it can possibly derive from its recorded messages. Hence, an attacker process is the maximally powerful DY process. It carries out all attacks any DY process could possibly perform and is parametrized by the set of sender addresses it may use. Attackers may corrupt other DY processes (e.g., a browser).

A *system* is a (possibly infinite) set of atomic processes. Its state (i.e., the states of all atomic processes in the system) together with a multi-set of waiting events is called a *configuration*.

A *run* of a system for an initial set E_0 of events is a sequence of configurations, where each configuration (except for the first one, which consists of E_0 and the initial states of the atomic processes) is obtained by delivering one of the waiting events of the preceding configuration to an atomic process p (which listens to the receiver address of the event), and which in turn performs a computation step according to its relation R^p.

Scripting Processes. We also define scripting processes, which model client-side scripting technologies, such as JavaScript.

A *scripting process* (or simply, a *script*) is defined similarly to a DY process. It is called by the browser in which it runs. The browser provides it with a (fresh, infinite) set of nonces and state information s. The script then outputs a term s', which represents the new internal state and some command which is interpreted by the browser (see Appendix A). Again, it is required that a script's output is derivable from its input.

Similarly to an attacker process, the so-called *attacker script* R^{att} may output everything that is derivable from the input.

2.2   Web System

A web system formalizes the web infrastructure and web applications. Formally, a *web system* is a tuple $(W, S, \text{script}, E_0)$ with the following components:

The first component, W, denotes a system (a set of DY processes) and contains honest processes, web attacker, and network attacker processes. While a web attacker can listen to and send messages from its own addresses only, a network attacker may listen to and spoof all addresses. Hence, it is the maximally powerful attacker. Attackers may corrupt other parties. In the analysis of a concrete web system, we typically have one network attacker only and no web attackers (as they are subsumed by the network attacker), or one or more web attackers but then no network attacker. Honest processes can either be web browsers, web servers, or DNS servers. The modeling of web servers heavily depends on the specific application (for BrowserID see the modeling in Sect. 5.1). In our security analysis of authentication properties, DNS servers will be subsumed by the attacker, and hence, do not need to be modeled explicitly in this work. The web browser model, which is independent of a specific web application, is presented below.

The second component, S, is a finite set of scripts, including the attacker script R^{att}. In a concrete model, such as our BrowserID model (see Sect. 5.1), the set $S \setminus \{R^{att}\}$ describes the set of honest scripts used in the application under consideration while malicious scripts are modeled by the "worst-case" malicious script, R^{att}.

The third component, script, is an injective mapping from a script in S to its string representation $\text{script}(s)$ (a constant in Σ). Finally, E_0 is a multi-set of events, containing an infinite number of events of the form $(a{:}a{:}\texttt{TRIGGER})$ for every process a in the web system. A *run* of the web system is a run of $\mathcal{W}$ initiated by E_0.

2.3 Web Browsers

We now sketch the model of the web browser, with more details provided in Appendix A. A web browser is modeled as a DY process $(I^p, Z^p, R^p, s_0^p, N^p)$.

An honest browser is thought to be used by one honest user, who is modeled as part of the browser. User actions are modeled as non-deterministic actions of the web browser. For example, the browser itself non-deterministically follows the links in a web page. User data (i.e., passwords and identities) is stored in the initial state of the browser and is given to a web page when needed, similar to the AutoFill feature in browsers.

Besides the user identities and passwords, the state of a web browser (modeled as a term) contains a tree of open windows and documents, lists of cookies, localStorage and sessionStorage data, a DNS server address, and other data (see Appendix A). We note that identities and sessionStorage were not considered in [13].

In the browser state, the *windows* subterm is the most complex one. It contains a window subterm for any open window (which may be many at a time), and inside each window, a list of documents opened in that window (which, again, may contain windows, modeling iframes). A document contains a script loaded from a web server and represents one loaded HTML page.

Scripts may, for example, navigate or create windows, send XHRs and postMessages, submit forms, set/change cookies, localStorage, and sessionStorage data, and create iframes. When activated, the browser provides a script with all data it has access to, such as certain cookies as well as localStorage and sessionStorage.

Browsers can become corrupted, i.e., be taken over by web and network attackers. We model two types of corruption: *close-corruption*, modeling that a browser is closed by the user, and hence, certain data is removed (e.g., session cookies and opened windows), before it is taken over by the attacker, and *full corruption*, where no data is not removed in advance. Once corrupted, the browser behaves like an attacker process.

3 General Security Properties

We have identified central application independent security properties of web features in the web model and formalized them in a general way such that they can be used in and facilitate future analysis efforts of web standards and web applications. In this section, we provide a brief overview of these properties, with precise formulations and proofs presented in [14].

The first set of properties concerns encrypted connections (HTTPS): We show that HTTP requests that were encrypted by an honest browser for an honest receiver cannot be read or altered by the attacker (or any other party). This, in particular, implies correct behavior on the browser's side, i.e., that browsers that are not fully corrupted never leak a symmetric key used for an HTTPS connection to any other party. We also show that honest browsers set the host header in their requests properly, i.e., the header reflects an actual domain name of the receiver, and that only the designated receiver can successfully respond to HTTPS requests.

The second set of properties concerns origins and origin headers. Using the properties stated above, we show that browsers cannot be fooled about the origin of an (HTTPS) document in their state: If the origin of a document in the browser's state is a secure origin (HTTPS), then the document was actually sent by that origin. Moreover, for requests which contain an origin header with a secure origin we prove that such requests were actually initiated by a script that was sent by that origin to the browser. In other words, in this case, the origin header works as expected.

4   The BrowserID System

BrowserID [22] is a decentralized single sign-on (SSO) system developed by Mozilla for user authentication on web sites. It is a complex full-fledged web application deployed in practice, with currently ~47k LOC (excluding some libraries). It allows web sites to delegate user authentication to email providers, identifying users by their email addresses. BrowserID makes use of a broad variety of browser features, such as XHRs, postMessage, local- and sessionStorage, cookies, various headers, etc.

We first, in Sect. 4.1, provide a high-level overview of the BrowserID system. A more detailed description of the BrowserID implementation is then given in Sect. 4.2. The description of the BrowserID system presented in the following as well as our BrowserID model (see Sect. 5.1) is extracted mainly from the BrowserID source code [20] and the (very high-level) official BrowserID documentation [22].

4.1   Overview

The BrowserID system knows three distinct parties: the user, who wants to authenticate herself using a browser, the relying party (RP) to which the user wants to authenticate (log in) with one of her email addresses (say, user@idp.com), and the identity/email address provider, the IdP. If the IdP (idp.com) supports BrowserID directly, it is called a *primary IdP*. Otherwise, a Mozilla-provided service, the so-called *secondary IdP*, takes the role of the IdP. As mentioned before, here we concentrate on the primary IdP mode as the secondary IdP mode was described in detail in [13]. However, we briefly discuss the differences between the two modes at the end of Sect. 4.2.

A primary IdP provides information about its setup in a so-called *support document*, which it provides at a fixed URL derivable from the email domain, e.g., https://idp.com/.well-known/browserid.

A user who wants to log in at an RP with an email address for some IdP has to present two signed documents to the RP: A *user certificate* (UC) and an *identity assertion* (IA). The UC contains the user's email address and the user's public key. It is signed by the IdP. The IA contains the origin of the RP and is signed with the user's private key. Both documents have a limited validity period. A pair consisting of a UC and a matching IA is called a *certificate assertion pair* (CAP) or a *backed identity assertion*. Intuitively, the UC in the CAP tells the RP that (the IdP certified that) the owner of

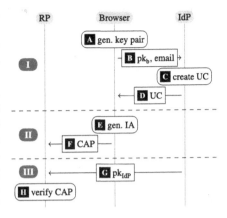

Fig. 1. BrowserID login: basic overview

the email address is (or at least claims to be) the owner of the public key. By the IA contained in the CAP the RP is ensured that the owner of the given public key (i.e., the one who knows the corresponding private key) wants to log in. Altogether, given a valid CAP, RP would consider the user (identified by the email address in the CAP) to be logged in.

The BrowserID authentication process (with a primary IdP) consists of three phases (see Fig. 1): Ⓘ UC provisioning, Ⓘ CAP creation, and Ⓘ CAP verification.

In Phase Ⓘ, (the browser of) the user creates a public/private key pair Ⓐ. She then sends her public key as well as the email address she wants to use to log in at some RP to the respective IdP Ⓑ. The IdP now creates the UC Ⓒ, which is then sent to the user Ⓓ. The above requires the user to be logged in at IdP.

With the user having received the UC, Phase Ⓘ can start. The user wants to authenticate to an RP, so she creates the IA Ⓔ. The UC and the IA are concatenated to a CAP, which is then sent to the RP Ⓕ.

In Phase Ⓘ, the RP checks the authenticity of the CAP. For this purpose, the RP fetches the public key of the IdP Ⓖ, which is contained in the support document. Afterwards, the RP checks the signatures of the UC and the IA Ⓗ. If this check is successful, the RP can, as mentioned before, consider the user to be logged in with the given email address and send her some token (e.g., a cookie with a session ID), which we refer to as an *RP service token*.

4.2 Implementation Details

We now provide a more detailed description of the BrowserID implementation. Since the system is very complex, with many HTTPS requests, XHRs, and postMessages sent between different entities (servers as well as windows and iframes within the browser), we here describe mainly the phases of the login

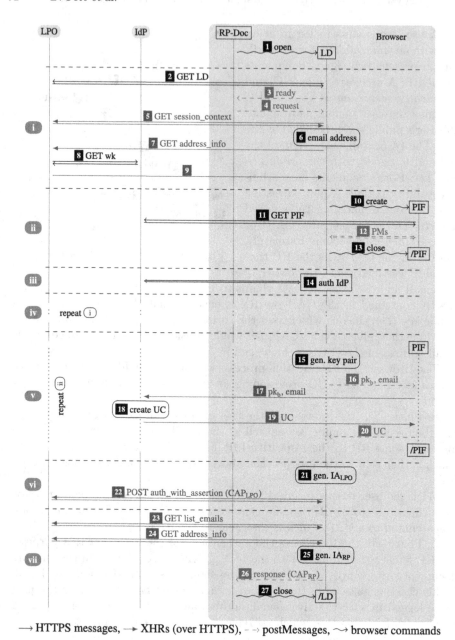

→ HTTPS messages, ⇢ XHRs (over HTTPS), - -> postMessages, ⤳ browser commands

Fig. 2. Simplified BrowserID implementation overview. CIF omitted for brevity.

process without explaining every single message exchange done in the implementation. A more detailed step-by-step description can be found in [14]. Note that BrowserID's specification of IdPs fixes the interface to BrowserID only, but otherwise does not further detail the specification of IdPs. Therefore, in what follows, we consider a typical IdP, namely the example implementation provided by Mozilla [20].

In addition to the parties mentioned so far, the actual BrowserID implementation uses another party, Mozilla's `login.persona.org` (LPO). Among others, LPO provides HTML and JavaScript files that, for security and privacy reasons, cannot be delivered by either IdP or RP. An overview of the implementation is given in Fig. 2. For brevity of presentation, several messages and components, such as the CIF (see below), are omitted in the figure (but not in our analysis).

Windows and iframes in the Browser. By *RP-Doc* we denote the window containing the document loaded from some RP, at which the user wants to log in with an email address hosted by some IdP. RP-Doc typically includes JavaScript from LPO and contains a button "Login with BrowserID". The LPO JavaScript running in RP-Doc opens an auxiliary window called the *login dialog* (LD). Its content is provided by LPO and it handles the interaction with the user. During the login process, a temporary invisible iframe called the *provisioning iframe* (PIF) can be created in the LD. The PIF is loaded from IdP. It is used by LD to communicate (cross-origin) with the IdP via postMessages: As the BrowserID implementation mainly runs under the origin of LPO, it cannot directly communicate with the IdP, thus it uses the PIF as a proxy. Temporarily, the LD may navigate itself to a web page at IdP to allow for direct user interaction with the IdP. We then call this window the *authentication dialog* (AD).

Login Process. To describe the login process, for the sake of presentation we assume for now that the user uses a "fresh" browser, i.e., the user has not been logged in before. As mentioned, the process starts by the user visiting a web site of some RP. After the user has clicked on the login button in RP-Doc, the LD is opened and the interactive login flow is started. We can divide this login flow into seven phases: In Phase ⓘ, the LD is initialized and the user is prompted to provide her email address. Also, LD fetches the support document (see Sect. 4.1) of the IdP via LPO. In Phase ⓘⓘ, LD creates the PIF from the *provisioning URL* provided in the support document. As (by our assumption) the user is not logged in yet, the PIF notifies LD that the user is not authenticated to the IdP. In Phase ⓘⓘⓘ, LD navigates itself away to the *authentication URL* which is also provided in the support document and links to the IdP. Usually, this document will show a login form in which the user enters her password to authenticate to the IdP. After the user has been authenticated to IdP (which typically implies that the IdP sets a session cookie in the browser), the window is navigated back to LPO.

Now, the login flow continues in Phase ⓘⓥ, which basically repeats Phase ⓘ. However, the user is not prompted for her email address (it has previously been saved in the localStorage under the origin of LPO along with a nonce, where the nonce is stored in the sessionStorage). In Phase ⓥ, which essentially repeats Phase ⓘⓘ, the PIF detects that the user is now authenticated to the IdP and the provisioning phase is started (① in Fig. 1): The user's keys are created by LD and stored in the localStorage under the origin of LPO. The PIF forwards the certification request to the IdP, which then creates the UC and sends it back to the PIF. The PIF in turn forwards it to the LD, which stores it in the localStorage under the origin of LPO.

In Phases Ⓥ and Ⓥⅱ, mainly the IA is generated by LD for the origin of RP-Doc and sent (together with the UC) to RP-Doc (Ⅱ in Fig. 1). In the local-Storage, LD stores that the user's email address is logged in at RP. Moreover, to log the user in at LPO, LD generates an IA for the origin of LPO and sends the UC and IA to LPO.

Automatic CAP Creation. In addition to the interactive login presented above, BrowserID also contains an automatic, non-interactive way for RPs to obtain a freshly generated CAP: During initialization within RP-Doc, an invisible iframe called the *communication iframe* (CIF) is created inside RP-Doc. The CIF's JavaScript is loaded from LPO and behaves similar to LD, but without user interaction. The CIF automatically issues a fresh CAP and sends it to RP-Doc under specific conditions: among others, the email address must be marked as logged in at RP in the localStorage. If necessary, a new key pair is created and a corresponding new UC is requested at the IdP. For this purpose, a PIF is created inside the CIF.

Differences to the Secondary IdP Mode. In the secondary IdP mode there are three parties involved only: RP, Browser, and LPO, where LPO also takes the role of an IdP; LPO is the only IdP that is present, rather than an arbitrary set of (external) IdPs. Consequently, in the secondary IdP mode the PIF and the AD do not exist. Moreover, in the primary mode, the behavior of the CIF and the LD is more complex than in the secondary mode. For example, in the primary mode, just like the LD, the CIF might contain a PIF (iframe in iframe) and interact with it via postMessages. Altogether, the secondary IdP case requires much less communication between parties/components and trust assumptions are simpler: in the secondary IdP mode LPO (which is the only IdP in this mode) has to be trusted, in the primary IdP mode some external IdPs might be malicious (and hence, also the scripts they deliver for the PIF and the AD). In [14], Appendix I, we illustrate the differences between the two modes.

5   Analysis of BrowserID: Authentication Properties

In this section, we present the analysis of the BrowserID system with primary IdPs and with respect to authentication properties. As already mentioned, in [13], we analyzed the simpler case with a secondary IdP. Due to the many differences between the secondary and primary mode as described above, the model for the primary case had to be written from scratch in most parts, and hence, the proof is new and much more complex.

We first, in Sect. 5.1, describe our model of BrowserID with primary IdPs, with two central authentication properties one would expect any SSO system to satisfy formalized in Sect. 5.2. As mentioned in the introduction, during the analysis of BrowserID it turned out that one of the security properties is not satisfied and that in fact there is an attack on BrowserID. We confirmed that this attack, which was acknowledged by Mozilla, works on the actual implementation of BrowserID. In Sect. 5.3, the attack is presented along with a fix. In Sect. 5.4, we prove that the fixed BrowserID system with primary IdPs satisfies both authentication properties.

5.1   Modeling of BrowserID with Primary IdPs

We model the BrowserID system with primary IdPs as a web system (in the sense of Sect. 2). Note that, while in Sect. 4 we give only a brief overview of the BrowserID system, our modeling and analysis considers the complete system with primary IdPs, where we have extracted the model from the BrowserID source code [20].

We call a web system $\mathcal{BID} = (\mathcal{W}, \mathcal{S}, \text{script}, E_0)$ a *BrowserID web system* if it is of the form precisely described in [14] and briefly outlined here.

The system $\mathcal{W}$ consists of the (network) attacker process attacker, a finite set B of (initially honest) web browsers, the web server for LPO, a finite set RP of web servers for the relying parties, and a finite set IDP of web servers for the identity providers. (DNS servers are assumed to be dishonest, and hence, are subsumed by attacker.) IdPs and RPs are initially honest and can become corrupted (similar to browsers, by a special message); LPO is assumed to be honest. The definition of the processes in $\mathcal{W}$ follows the description in Sect. 4.2. For RP, we explicitly follow the security considerations in [22] (Cross-site Request Forgery protection, e.g., by checking origin headers and HTTPS only with STS enabled). When RP receives a valid CAP, RP responds with a fresh *RP service token for ID i* where i is the ID (email address) for which the CAP was issued. Intuitively, a client having such a token can use the service of the RP.

The set $\mathcal{S}$ of $\mathcal{BID}$ contains six scripts, with their string representations defined by script: the honest scripts running in RP-Doc, CIF, LD, AD, and PIF, respectively, and the malicious script R^{att}. The scripts for CIF and LD (issued by LPO) are defined in a straightforward way following the implementation outlined in Sect. 4. The scripts for RP-Doc, AD, and PIF follow the example implementation provided by Mozilla [20].

5.2   Authentication Properties of the BrowserID System

While the documentation of BrowserID does not contain explicit security goals, here we state two fundamental authentication properties every SSO system should satisfy. These properties are adapted from [13].

Informally, these properties can be stated as follows: **(A)** *The attacker should not be able to use a service of RP as an honest user.* In other words, the attacker should not get hold of (be able to derive from his current knowledge) an RP service token for an ID of an honest user (browser), even if the browser was closed and then later used by a malicious user (i.e., after a CLOSECORRUPT). **(B)** *The attacker should not be able to authenticate an honest browser to an RP with an ID that is not owned by the browser (identity injection).* We refer the reader to [14] for the formal definitions.

We call a BrowserID web system $\mathcal{BID}$ secure *(w.r.t. authentication)* if the above conditions are satisfied in all runs of the system.

5.3   Identity Injection Attack on BrowserID with Primary IdPs

While trying to prove the above mentioned authentication properties of BrowserID with primary IdPs in our model, we discovered a serious attack, which is sketched below and does not apply to the case with secondary IdPs. We confirmed the attack on the actual implementation and reported it to Mozilla [9], who acknowledged it.

During the provisioning phase Ⓥ (see Fig. 2), the IdP issues a UC for the user's identity and public key provided in [16]. This UC is sent to the LD by the PIF in [20].

If the IdP is malicious, it can issue a UC with different data. In particular, it could replace the email address by a different one, but keep the original public key. This (malicious) UC is then later included in the CAP by LD. The CAP will still be valid, because the public key is unchanged. Now, as the RP determines the user's identity by the UC contained in the CAP, RP issues a service token for the spoofed email address. As a result, the honest user will use RP's service (and typically will be logged in to RP) under an ID that belongs to the attacker, which, for example, could allow the attacker to track actions of the honest user or obtain user secrets. This violates Condition **(B)**.

To fix this problem, upon receipt of the UC in [20], LD should check whether it contains the correct email address and public key, i.e., the one requested by LD in [16]. The same is true for the CIF, which behaves similarly to the LD. Our formal model of BrowserID presented in [14] contains these fixes.

5.4   Security of the Fixed System

For the fixed BrowserID system with primary IdPs, we have proven the following theorem, which says that a fixed BrowserID web system (i.e., the system where the above described fix is applied) satisfies the security properties **(A)** and **(B)**.

Theorem 1. *Let $\mathcal{BID}$ be a fixed BrowserID web system. Then, $\mathcal{BID}$ is secure (w.r.t. authentication).*

We prove Conditions **(A)** and **(B)** separately. For both conditions, we assume that they are not satisfied and lead this to a contradiction. In our proofs, we make use of the general security properties of the web model presented in Sect. 3, which helped a lot in making the proof for the primary IdP model more modular and concise. The complete proof with all details is provided in [14].

6   Privacy of BrowserID

In this section, we study the privacy guarantees of the BrowserID system with primary IdPs. Regarding privacy, Mozilla states that "...the BrowserID protocol never leaks tracking information back to the Identity Provider." [5] and "Unlike other sign-in systems, BrowserID does not leak information back to any server [...] about which sites a user visits." [19].[1] While this is not a formal definition of the level of privacy that BrowserID is supposed to provide, these and other statements[2] make it certainly clear that, unlike for other SSO systems, IdPs should not be able to learn to which RPs their users log in.

In the process of formalizing this intuition in our model of BrowserID and trying to prove this property, we found severe attacks against the privacy of BrowserID which made clear that BrowserID does not provide even a rather weak privacy property in the presence of a malicious IdP. Intuitively, the property says that a malicious IdP (which acts as a web attacker) should not be able to tell whether a user logs in at an honest RP r or some other honest RP r'. In other words, a run in which the user logs in at r at some point should be indistinguishable (from the point of view of the IdP) from the run in which the user logs in at r' instead. Indistinguishability means that the two sequences of messages received by the web attacker in the two runs are statically equivalent in the usual sense of Dolev-Yao models (see [1]), i.e., a Dolev-Yao attacker cannot distinguish between the two sequences. Details of the privacy definition are not important here since our attacks clearly show that privacy is broken for any reasonable definition of privacy. Unfortunately, our attacks are not caused by a simple implementation error, but rather a fundamental design flaw in the BrowserID protocol. Fixes for this flaw are conceivable, but not without major changes to the design of BrowserID as discussed in Sect. 6.2. Such a redesign of BrowserID and a proof of privacy of the redesigned system are therefore out of the scope of this paper, which focuses on the existing and deployed version of BrowserID.

6.1   Privacy Attacks on BrowserID

For our attacks to work, it suffices that the IdP is a web attacker. They work even if all DNS servers, RPs, and LPO are honest, and all parties use encrypted connections. In what follows, we present two variants of the attacks on privacy with three additional interesting variants presented in Appendix B.

PostMessage-Based Attack. The adversary is a malicious IdP that is interested to learn whether a user is logged in at RP r. Figure 3 illustrates the main steps:

---

[1] Clearly, in the current state of BrowserID a malicious LPO server could gather information about users' log in history. However, an integration of the code currently delivered by LPO into the browser, as envisioned, would avoid this issue. Currently, Mozilla's LPO needs to be trusted.

[2] see, for example, https://developer.mozilla.org/en-US/Persona/Why_Persona and http://identity.mozilla.com/post/7669886219.

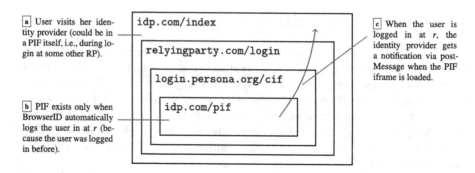

Fig. 3. The three main steps of the privacy attack. Using a specially crafted PIF document, a malicious IdP can notify itself via postMessage when the user is logged in at some RP r.

Step [a]. First, the victim visits her IdP. In BrowserID, email providers serve as IdPs, and therefore it is not unlikely that a user visits this web site (e.g., for checking email). As the IdP usually has some cookie set at the user's browser, it learns the identity of the victim. The IdP now creates a hidden iframe containing the login page of r.

Step [b]. The login page of r (now loaded as an iframe within IdP's web site) includes and runs the BrowserID script. As defined in the BrowserID protocol, the script creates the communication iframe (see "Automatic CAP Creation" in Sect. 4.2), which in turn checks whether the email address is marked as logged in at r in the localStorage of the user's browser. Only then it will try to create a new CAP, for which it needs a PIF (the same as in Phase ⓘⓘ in Fig. 2).

Step [c]. The PIF is loaded from the IdP. (From this action alone, the IdP does not learn where the user wants to log in.) However, instead of the original (honest) PIF document, the IdP can send a modified one that sends a postMessage to the parent of the parent of the parent of its own window, which in this setting is the IdP document that was opened by the user in Step [a]. When the IdP receives this message in the document from Step [a], it knows that the PIF was loaded, and therefore, that the user is currently logged in at r.

Note that the IdP can repeatedly apply the above as long as the user stays on the IdP's web site. During this period, the IdP can see whether or not the user is logged in at the targeted RP. Clearly, the IdP can simultaneously run the attack for different RPs. In particular, the IdP can distinguish whether a user is logged in at RP r or r', which violates the privacy property sketched above. In our formal model, the malicious IdP would run the attacker script R^{att} in `idp.com/index` and in `idp.com/pif` (see Fig. 3) in order to carry out the attack.

Variant 1: Waiting for UC requests. The IdP first acts as in Step [a]. Now, it could passively wait for incoming requests for the PIF document or UC requests on its server, which tell the IdP that a provisioning flow (probably initiated by Step [a]) was started. This variant cannot be executed in parallel and is less reliable in practice, though.

We verified (all variants of) the attacks in our model as well as in a real-world BrowserID setup. Implementing proofs-of-concept required only a few lines of (trivial) JavaScript. In most attack variants, we directly or indirectly use the structure of the windows inside the web browser as a side channel. To our knowledge, this is the first description of this side channel for breaking privacy in browsers. The attacks have been reported to and confirmed by Mozilla [10].

6.2 Fixing the Privacy of BrowserID

Fixing the privacy of BrowserID seems to require a substantial redesign of the system. Regarding the presented attacks, BrowserID's main weakness is the window structure. The most obvious mitigation, modifying the CIF such that it always creates the PIF (even if the user has not logged in before), does not work: To open the PIF, the CIF looks up (in the localStorage) the user's identity at the current RP to derive the address of the PIF. If the user has not logged in before, this information is not available.

Another approach would be to use cross-origin XHRs to replace the features of the PIF. This solution would require a major revision in the inner workings of BrowserID and would not protect against Variant 1.

7 Related Work

The formal treatment of the security of the web infrastructure and web applications based on this infrastructure is a young discipline. Of the few works in this area even less are based on a general model that incorporates essential mechanisms of the web.

Early works in formal web security analysis (see, e.g., [3,11,16,17,25]) are based on very limited models developed specifically for the application under scrutiny. The first work to consider a general model of the web, written in the finite-state model checker Alloy, is the work by Akhawe et al. [2]. Inspired by this work, Bansal et al. [6,7] built a more expressive model, called WebSpi, in ProVerif [8], a tool for symbolic cryptographic protocol analysis. These models have successfully been applied to web standards and applications. Recently, Kumar [18] presented a high-level Alloy model and applied it to SAML single sign-on. However, compared to our model in [13] and its extensions considered here, on the one hand, all above mentioned models are formulated in the specification languages of specific analysis tools, and hence, are tailored towards automation (while we perform manual analysis). On the other hand, the models considered in these works are much less expressive and precise. For example, these models do not incorporate a precise handling of windows, documents, or iframes; cross-document messaging (postMessages) or session storage are not included at all. In fact, several general web features and technologies that have been crucial for the analysis of BrowserID are not supported by these models, and hence, these models cannot be applied to BrowserID. Moreover, the complexity of BrowserID exceeds that of the systems analyzed in these other works in terms of the use of web technologies and the complexity of the protocols. For example, BrowserID in primary mode is a protocol consisting of 48 different (network and inter-frame) messages compared to typically about 10–15 in the protocols analyzed in other models.

The BrowserID system in the primary mode has been analyzed before using the AuthScan tool developed by Bai et al. [4]. Their work focusses on the automated extraction of a model from a protocol implementation. This tool-based analysis did not reveal the identity injection attack, though; privacy properties have not been studied there. Dietz and Wallach demonstrated a technique to secure BrowserID when specific flaws in TLS are considered [12].

8   Conclusion

In this paper, we slightly extended our existing web model, resulting in the most comprehensive model of the web so far. It contains many security-relevant features and is designed to closely mimic standards and specifications for the web. As such, it constitutes a solid basis for the analysis of a broad range of web standards and applications.

Based on this model, we presented a detailed analysis of the BrowserID SSO system in the primary IdP mode. During the security proof of the fundamental authentication requirements (A) and (B), we found a flaw in BrowserID that does not apply to its secondary mode and leads to an identity injection attack, and hence, violates property (B). We confirmed the attack on the actual BrowserID implementation and reported it to Mozilla, who acknowledged it. We proposed a fix and formally proved that the fixed system fulfills both (A) and (B). Among the so far very few efforts on formally analyzing web applications and standards in expressive web models, our analysis constitutes the most complex formal analysis of a web application to date. It illustrates that (manual) security analysis of complex real-world web applications in a detailed web model, while laborious, is feasible and yields meaningful and practically relevant results.

During an attempt to formally analyze the privacy promise of the BrowserID system, we again found practical attacks. These attacks have been reported to and confirmed by Mozilla and, unfortunately, show that BrowserID would have to undergo a substantial redesign in order to fulfill its privacy promise. Interestingly, for our attacks we use a side channel that exploits information about the structure of windows in a browser. To the best of our knowledge, such side channel attacks have not gained much attention so far in the literature.

Finally, we have identified and proven important security properties of general application independent web features in order to facilitate future analysis efforts of web standards and web applications in the web model.

A   Browser Model

Here, we provide a compact overview of our browser model, with full details presented in [14]. A web browser p is modeled as a DY process $(I^p, Z^p, R^p, s_0^p, N^p)$ where I^p is a finite set of (IP) addresses p may listen to and N^p is an infinite set of nonces p may use. The set of states Z^p, the initial state s_0^p, and the relation R^p are sketched next.

A.1   Browser State: Z^p and s_0^p

The set Z^p of states of a browser consists of terms of the form

$$\langle windows, ids, secrets, cookies, localStorage, sessionStorage, keyMapping,$$
$$sts, DNSaddress, nonces, pendingDNS, pendingRequests, isCorrupted \rangle.$$

Windows and Documents. The most important part of the state are windows and documents, both stored in the subterm *windows*. A browser may have several windows open at any time (resembling the tabs and windows in a real browser), each containing a list of documents (the history of visited web pages) of which one is "active", namely the one currently presented to the user in that window. A window may be navigated forward and backward (modeling navigation buttons), deactivating one document and activating its successor or predecessor. Intuitively, a document represents a loaded HTML page. More formally, a document contains (the string representation of) a script, which is meant to model both the static HTML code (e.g., links and forms) as well as JavaScript code. When called by the browser, a script outputs a command which is then interpreted by the browser, such as following a link or issuing an XHR (see below). Documents may also contain iframes, which are represented as windows (*subwindows*) nested inside of document terms. This creates a tree of windows and documents.

Secrets and IDs. This subterm holds the secrets and the identities of the user of the web browser. Secrets (such as passwords) are modeled as nonces and they are indexed by origins (where an origin is a domain name plus the information whether the connection to this domain is via HTTP or HTTPS). Secrets are only released to documents (scripts) with the corresponding origin, similarly to the AutoFill mechanism in browsers. Identities are arbitrary terms that model public information of the user's identity, such as email addresses. Identities are released to any origin. As mentioned in the introduction, identities were not considered in [13].

Cookies, localStorage, and sessionStorage. These subterms contain the cookies (indexed by domains), localStorage data (indexed by origins), and sessionStorage data (indexed by origins and top-level window references) stored in the browser. As mentioned in the introduction, sessionStorage was not modeled in [13].

PROCESSING INPUT MESSAGE *m*

m = FULLCORRUPT: *is Corrupted*:= FULLCORRUPT

m = CLOSECORRUPT: *is Corrupted*:= CLOSECORRUPT

m = TRIGGER: non-deterministically choose *action* from {1,2}

    action = 1: Call script of some active document. Outputs new state and *command*.

        command = HREF: → *Initiate request*

        command = IFRAME: Create subwindow, → *Initiate request*

        command = FORM: → *Initiate request*

        command = SETSCRIPT: Change script in given document.

        command = SETSCRIPTSTATE: Change state of script in given document.

        command = XMLHTTPREQUEST: → *Initiate request*

        command = BACK or FORWARD: Navigate given window.

        command = CLOSE: Close given window.

        command = POSTMESSAGE: Send post Message to specified document.

    action = 2: → *Initiate request to some URL in new window*

m = DNS response: send corresponding HTTP request

m = HTTP(S) response: (decrypt,) find reference.

    reference to window: create document in window

    reference to document: add response body to document's script input

Fig. 4. The basic structure of the web browser relation R^p with an extract of the most important processing steps, in the case that the browser is not already corrupted.

KeyMapping. This term is the equivalent to a certificate authority (CA) certificate store in the browser. Since, for simplicity, the model currently does not formalize CAs, this term simply encodes a mapping assigning domains to their respective public keys.

STS. Domains that are listed in this term are contacted by the web browser over HTTPS only. Connection attempts over HTTP are transparently rewritten to HTTPS. Servers can employ the Strict-Transport-Security header to add their domain to this list.

DNSaddress. This term defines the address of the DNS server used by the browser.

Nonces, pendingDNS, and pendingRequests. These terms are used for bookkeeping purposes, recording the nonces that have been used by the browser so far, the HTTP(S) requests that await successful DNS resolution, and HTTP(S) requests that await a response, respectively.

IsCorrupted. This term indicates whether the browser is corrupted ($\neq \perp$) or not ($= \perp$). A corrupted browser behaves like a web attacker.

Initial State s_0^p. In the browser's initial state, *keyMapping, DNSAddress, secrets,* and *ids* are defined as needed, *isCorrupted* is set to $\bot$, and all other subterms are $\langle\rangle$.

A.2   Web Browser Relation R^p

This relation, outlined in Fig. 4, specifies how the web browser processes incoming messages. The browser may receive special messages that cause it to become corrupted (first two lines in Fig. 4), in which case it acts like the attacker process. As explained in Sect. 2.3, there are two types of corruption: close-corruption and full corruption.

If the browser receives a special trigger message TRIGGER, it non-deterministically chooses one of two actions: (i) Select one of the current documents, trigger its JavaScript, and evaluate the output of the script. Scripts can change the state of the browser (e.g., by setting cookies) and can trigger specific actions (e.g., following a link or creating an iframe), which are modeled as *commands* issued by the script (see the list in Fig. 4). (ii) Follow some URL, with the intuition that it was entered by the user.

As mentioned, some of the above actions can cause the browser to generate new HTTP(S) requests. In this case, the browser first asks the configured DNS server for the IP address belonging to the domain name in the HTTP(S) request. As soon as the DNS response arrives, the browser sends the HTTP(S) request to the respective IP address.

If the HTTP(S) response arrives, its headers are evaluated and the body of the request becomes the script of a newly created document that is then inserted at an appropriate place in the window/document tree. However, if the HTTP(S) response is a response to an XHR (triggered by a script in a document), the body of the response is given to the script of that document for processing when it is called next.

B   Additional Privacy Attack Variants

We here present three additional variants of the privacy attack introduced in Sect. 6.1.

Variant 2: PIF as Attack Source. Step [a] can also be launched from within a PIF itself (i.e., the PIF also takes the role of idp.com/index above). This way, while the user logs in at some r_1, the IdP could check whether the user is logged in at r_2, for any r_2.

Variant 3: Scanning the Window Structure (I). Instead of using a postMessage to alert the IdP's outer document about the existence of the inner PIF document, the outer document could as well repeatedly scan the window tree of the iframe containing r's web site: While the IdP sees almost no information about r's document in the iframe (as it is not same origin), it can see the list of subwindows (i.e., the CIF, and possibly other iframes). For these frames, again, it would see the subwindows, especially the PIF, which it could identify uniquely by checking whether it is same origin with the IdPs outer window.

Variant 4: Scanning the Window Structure (II). In Variant 2, using a same-origin check, the malicious IdP can uniquely identify the PIF in the window structure. This same-origin check could be skipped and it could only be checked whether a PIF is generated, based on the window structure alone. While this is less reliable, this attack could be launched by *any* third party web attacker (not only the IdP to which the user's email address belongs) to check whether the victim is logged in at r or not.

References

1. Abadi, M., Fournet, C.: Mobile values, new names, and secure communication. In: POPL 2001, pp. 104–115. ACM Press (2001)
2. Akhawe, D., Barth, A., Lam, P.E., Mitchell, J., Song, D.: Towards a formal foundation of web security. In: CSF 2010, pp. 290–304. IEEE Computer Society (2010)
3. Armando, A., Carbone, R., Compagna, L., Cuéllar, J., Tobarra, M.L.: Formal analysis of SAML 2.0 Web browser single sign-on: breaking the SAML-based single sign-on for Google Apps. In: FMSE 2008, pp. 1–10. ACM (2008)
4. Bai, G., Lei, J., Meng, G., Venkatraman, S.S., Saxena, P., Sun, J., Liu, Y., Dong, J.S.: AUTHSCAN: automatic extraction of web authentication protocols from implementations. In: NDSS 2013. The Internet Society (2013)
5. Bamberg, W., et al.: Persona FAQ. Mozilla Developer Network Wiki. https://developer.mozilla.org/en-US/Persona/FAQ. Accessed 29 September 2013
6. Bansal, C., Bhargavan, K., Delignat-Lavaud, A., Maffeis, S.: Keys to the cloud: formal analysis and concrete attacks on encrypted web storage. In: Basin, D., Mitchell, J.C. (eds.) POST 2013. LNCS, vol. 7796, pp. 126–146. Springer, Heidelberg (2013)
7. Bansal, C., Bhargavan, K., Maffeis, S.: Discovering concrete attacks on website authorization by formal analysis. In: CSF 2012, pp. 247–262. IEEE Computer Society (2012)
8. Blanchet, B.: An efficient cryptographic protocol verifier based on prolog rules. In: CSFW-14, pp. 82–96. IEEE Computer Society (2001)
9. Bugzilla@Mozilla. Bug 1064254 - Identity Injection Attack on Persona by Malicious IdP, September 2014. https://bugzilla.mozilla.org/show_bug.cgi?id=1064254 (access restricted)
10. Bugzilla@Mozilla. Bug 1120255 - Privacy leak in Persona, January 2015. https://bugzilla.mozilla.org/show_bug.cgi?id=1120255 (access restricted)
11. Chari, S., Jutla, C.S., Roy, A.: Universally Composable Security Analysis of OAuth v2.0. IACR Cryptology ePrint Archive, 2011:526 (2011)
12. Dietz, M., Wallach, D.S.: Hardening persona - improving federated web login. In: NDSS 2014. The Internet Society (2014)
13. Fett, D., Küsters, R., Schmitz, G.: An expressive model for the web infrastructure: definition and application to the BrowserID SSO System. In: S&P 2014, pp. 673–688. IEEE Computer Society (2014)
14. Fett, D., Küsters, R., Schmitz, G.: Analyzing the BrowserID SSO system with primary identity providers using an expressive model of the web. Technical report (2014). http://arxiv.org/abs/1411.7210

15. HTML5, W3C Recommendation, 28 October 2014
16. Jackson, D.: Alloy: a new technology for software modelling. In: Katoen, J.-P., Stevens, P. (eds.) TACAS 2002. LNCS, vol. 2280, p. 20. Springer, Heidelberg (2002)
17. Kerschbaum, F.: Simple cross-site attack prevention. In: SecureComm 2007, pp. 464–472. IEEE Computer Society (2007)
18. Kumar, A.: A lightweight formal approach for analyzing security of web protocols. In: Stavrou, A., Bos, H., Portokalidis, G. (eds.) RAID 2014. LNCS, vol. 8688, pp. 192–211. Springer, Heidelberg (2014)
19. Mills, C.: Introducing BrowserID: a better way to sign in. Identity at Mozilla, 14 July 2011. http://identity.mozilla.com/post/7616727542/
20. Mozilla Identity Team: BrowserID Source Code. BrowserID Repository. https://github.com/mozilla/browserid
21. Mozilla Identity Team: Persona. https://login.persona.org
22. Mozilla Identity Team: Persona. Mozilla developer network. https://developer.mozilla.org/en/docs/persona. Accessed 15 October 2014
23. Somorovsky, J., Mayer, A., Schwenk, J., Kampmann, M., Jensen, M.: On breaking SAML: be whoever you want to be. In: USENIX Security 2012, pp. 397–412. USENIX Association (2012)
24. Sun, S.-T., Beznosov, K.: The devil is in the (implementation) details: an empirical analysis of OAuth SSO systems. In: CCS 2012, pp. 378–390. ACM (2012)
25. Sun, S.-T., Hawkey, K., Beznosov, K.: Systematically breaking and fixing OpenID security: formal analysis, semi-automated empirical evaluation, and practical countermeasures. Comput. Secur. **31**(4), 465–483 (2012)
26. Wang, R., Chen, S., Wang, X.: Signing me onto your accounts through Facebook and Google: a traffic-guided security study of commercially deployed single-sign-on web services. In: S&P 2012, pp. 365–379. IEEE Computer Society (2012)
27. Web Storage - W3C Recommendation, 30 July 2013. http://www.w3.org/TR/webstorage/

System Security

A Practical Approach for Adaptive Data Structure Layout Randomization

Ping Chen[1,2,3], Jun Xu[1(✉)], Zhiqiang Lin[4], Dongyan Xu[3], Bing Mao[2], and Peng Liu[1]

[1] College of Information Sciences and Technology,
The Pennsylvania State University, State College, USA
{pzc10,jxx13,pliu}@ist.psu.edu
[2] State Key Laboratory for Novel Software Technology, Department of Computer
Science and Technology, Nanjing University, Nanjing, China
maobing@nju.edu.cn
[3] Department of Computer Science, Purdue University, West Lafayette, USA
dxu@cs.purdue.edu
[4] Department of Computer Science, University of Texas at Dallas, Richardson, USA
zhiqiang.lin@utdallas.edu

Abstract. Attackers often corrupt data structures to compromise software systems. As a countermeasure, data structure layout randomization has been proposed. Unfortunately, existing techniques require manual designation of randomize-able data structures without guaranteeing the correctness and keep the layout unchanged at runtime. We present a system, called SALADS, that automatically translates a program to a DSSR (Data Structure Self-Randomizing) program. At runtime, a DSSR program dynamically randomizes the layout of each security-sensitive data structure by itself autonomously. DSSR programs regularly re-randomize a data structure when it has been accessed several times after last randomization. More importantly, DSSR programs automatically determine the randomizability of instances and randomize each instance independently. We have implemented SALADS based on gcc-4.5.0 and generated DSSR user-level applications, OS kernels, and hypervisors. Our experiments show that the DSSR programs can defeat a wide range of attacks with reasonable performance overhead.

1 Introduction

In programs developed in `C` or `C++` language, encapsulated data objects, such as `struct` and `class`, are widely used to group a list of logically related variables. Not surprisingly, these encapsulated data structures, the focus of this paper, are often the target or aid of a wide variety of attacks. For instance, attackers often leverage knowledge about data structures defined in a victim program to construct successful exploits against it. This is the case for both application programs and system programs (e.g., operating system kernels and virtual machine monitors). More specifically, a data structure contains a set of fields. Knowledge about a data structure's layout, namely how the fields neighbour each

© Springer International Publishing Switzerland 2015
G. Pernul et al. (Eds.): ESORICS 2015, Part I, LNCS 9326, pp. 69–89, 2015.
DOI: 10.1007/978-3-319-24174-6_4

other inside the data structure, can be very useful to the attacker. For example, knowing the layout of accounting/book-keeping data structures, on-line gaming fraud [10] can be performed by modifying the values of relevant fields; Knowing the layouts of in-stack or in-heap data structures will help construct memory corruption exploits [25]; Guided by the layout of the process control block (PCB), a kernel rootkit is able to hide a process by locating and manipulating certain psssine attacksthat locate a data structure and manipulate specific fields after knowing its layout as *data structure manipulation* attacks.

Randomizing either the location or the layout of the target data structure will significantly raise the bar for data structure manipulation attacks. There have been two lines of research towards achieving such randomizing goals: (1) Address Space Layout Randomization (ASLR) randomly arranges the base addresses of segments (e.g., stack), which has been widely researched and deployed. Recently, fine-grained ASLR techniques have been proposed to achieve randomization at different levels, including page level [5], function level [22], basic block level [28], and instruction level [19,38]. (2) Data Structure Layout Randomization (DSLR) [24,34] reorders the fields or inserts dummy fields in encapsulated data objects (e.g., struct). With DSLR deployed, the layouts of data structures are randomized to break the mono-culture of programs.

However, ASLR or fine-grained ASLR techniques have two limitations: (1) ASLR is vulnerable to memory content leakage [9,11,21,30,31,33,35,42]. By leveraging memory content leakage, an attacker can infer the base addresses of memory regions (e.g., segments or pages) under ASLR. Knowing the offset of the target data structure in the containing region, the attacker can figure out its base address [33]. (2) ASLR can be easily circumvented by rootkits, such as those leveraging Direct Kernel Object Manipulation (DKOM) [7,21,29]. In many cases, a rootkit knows the base address of the target data structure even if ASLR is deployed. For example, kernel global data structures can be located by referring to kernel symbols (i.e., /proc/kallsyms). In other cases, a rootkit has no such knowledge, but it has the privilege to read arbitrary memory and thus can infer such a base address.

In this paper, we present a novel technique, adaptive DSLR, to defend against data structure manipulation attacks. More specifically, we design a compiler-based system, called SALADS[1], to implement our technique. SALADS transforms a program into a Data Structure Self-Randomizing (DSSR) program. A DSSR program periodically re-randomizes a data structure after the data structure has been accessed for a certain number of times since last re-randomization. The re-randomization is independently and asynchronously performed on each instance even if they have the same data structure definition. To avoid errors (e.g., pointer reference corruption), SALADS automatically determines the randomizability of data structure instances without programmer's input and de-randomizes a data structure that might have been unsafely randomized.

SALADS can address the two limitations of ASLR: suppose the base address of the target data structure is exposed when memory content leakage happens or

---

[1] SALADS stands for <u>S</u>elf <u>A</u>daptation of <u>LA</u>yout of <u>D</u>ata <u>S</u>tructures.

when a rootkit is launched. The layout of the data structure is randomized when SALADS is deployed. Therefore, the attacker in general cannot accurately locate specific fields. Even if the attacker could infer the current layout of the target data structure, the attacker could be stopped by the adaptation (i.e., dynamic self-re-randomization). In one attack, the layout inferring part and the data structure manipulation part are typically completed in chronological order. After the layout inferring but before the data structure manipulation, DSSR programs may have already re-randomized the target data structure. Consequently, the attacker would mistakenly manipulate irrelevant fields.

We refer the existing DSLR technique [24, 34] as static DSLR. Compared with static DSLR, our adaptive DSLR offers several unique features: (1) Instead of randomizing data structures layout at compile-time/load-time, DSSR programs generated by SALADS re-randomize data structures at runtime. Without this feature, static DSLR shares the two limitations with ASLR. When memory content leakage happens or when a rootkit is launched, the randomized layout of the target data structure can be reverse engineered (e.g., [6]). Examples of how to reverse engineer the layout are presented in Sect. 2. Once the layout of the target data structure is inferred, the attacker could correctly manipulate specific fields. (2) A DSSR program randomizes each data structure instance independently and asynchronously, regardless of their types. Without this feature, static DSLR can be circumvented in situations where the target data structure is not initialized. For example, rootkits can speculate the layout of the target data structure instance by referring another initialized instance of the same type. In a kernel with static DSLR, the layout inferred in such a way enables the rootkits to successfully manipulate the expected fields. (3) In case an instance is involved in a statement that might cause inconsistency or crash, the DSSR program will restore the instance to its original layout. The restoring process is denoted as de-randomization.

The main contributions of our work are as follows:

- This is the first effort toward runtime adaptive DSLR that is able to address the limitations of ASLR in thwarting data structure manipulation attacks.
- We have implemented a protocol system called SALADS, and we show DSSR programs generated by SALADS can automatically determine the randomizability of data structures without programmers' assistance. Meanwhile, SALADS achieves both cross instance diversity (different randomized layouts for different instances of the same type) and cross time diversity.
- Our experimental results show that on average the performance overhead introduced by SALADS is (1) 6.3 % for application programs (randomly selecting 20 % of data structures to protect in SPECInt2000, httpd-2.0.6, openssh-2.1.1p4, and openssl-0.9.6d); (2) 16.7 % for OS kernels (by selecting 23 security-sensitive data structures to protect in Linux kernel); (3) 4.5 % for hypervisor (by selecting 20 security-sensitive data structures to protect in Xen hypervisor).

2   Overview

2.1   Threat Model

In this paper we focus on data structure manipulation attacks. We subdivide such an attack into three steps: (Step-I) attacker gets the memory location of a data structure instance; (Step-II) attacker figures out its layout; (Step-III) attacker reads/writes certain fields of the instance.

Data Structure Manipulation with Memory Content Leakage in Applications. We take the privilege escalation attack against openssh-2.1.1 (CVE-2001-0144) [13] as an illustrating example. The goal of the attack is to modify the field pw_uid in the instance pw (of type struct passwd) to escalate the remote shell with root privilege. The three steps in this attack are as follows. First, the attacker gets to know the base address of pw; Second, the attacker figures out the layout of pw; Third, the attacker writes the maliciously-crafted value to pw->pw_uid by exploiting an integer truncation bug.

In Fig. 1, we present how to conduct the above privilege escalation attack under ASLR and static DSLR (the base address and the layout of pw are both randomized). At Step-I, an attacker can resort to memory content leakage (e.g., memory disclosure [33], uninitialized memory tracking [11], side channel [9, 30, 42]) (❶). Assuming the attacker has obtained the disclosed memory page that contains pw, he/she can search the signature of struct passwd[2] in the page.

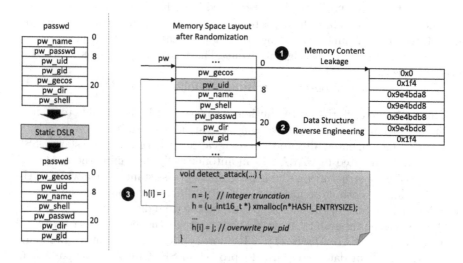

Fig. 1. Privilege escalation in openssh under ASLR and static DSLR

---

[2] Inside struct passwd, pw_uid and pw_gid are identify numbers with small values ($\leq$ 0xffff); pw_passwd, pw_name, pw_shell, and pw_dir are four pointers and their values form an arithmetic progression with common difference of 16; pw_gecos is 0.

If the search succeeds, the attacker can locate the base address of pw. At Step-II, the attacker can reverse engineer the contents of pw to recover locations of specific fields (e.g., pw_uid and pw_gid have unique values (see Footnote 2)) (❷). Since ASLR and static DSLR do not randomize pw at runtime, the attacker can correctly modify pw_uid and pw_gid (❸) to escalate the privilege.

Data Structure Manipulation by Rootkits under ASLR and static DSLR. Many rootkits achieve their goals via manipulating data structures, such as the one presented in [20]. However, ASLR and static DSLR make such manipulation more difficult (by randomizing the base address and the layout of the target data structure). In Sect. 1, we have explained how a rootkit can bypass ASLR and static DSLR. For instance, taskigt is a rootkit that stealthily promotes privileges of a process when the process opens a specific proc file. The rootkit attempts to modify a local data structure instance proc_ent of type proc_dir_entry. Most fields in proc_ent are not initialized, including the target field read_proc (a function pointer). The rootkit can infer read_proc in a global variable proc_root of type proc_dir_entry by reverse engineering (most fields in proc_root are initialized). In this way, the rootkit can locate read_proc in proc_ent (read_proc in proc_ent and proc_root have the same offset). Then the rootkit manipulates read_proc, to make it point to a malicious function.

2.2 System Overview

Key Idea. By breaking any of the three steps in the threat model, we would be able to defeat a data structure manipulation attack. However, since it is hard to eliminate memory content leakage and rootkits, attackers can succeed at Step-I and Step-II even if modern defenses are deployed. Our idea is to disrupt Step-III. Specifically, we adaptively randomize layout of each data structure instance independently at runtime. The key is that the target instance might be re-randomized between Step-II and Step-III. Therefore, the attacker may not accurately access the targeted fields.

Compilation Steps. We design SALADS to realize the above idea. SALADS is built on top of the GNU GCC compiler. Figure 2 shows the compilation steps of SALADS, with the white boxes indicating the original GCC compilation phases. As shown in the figure, SALADS adds two key components to

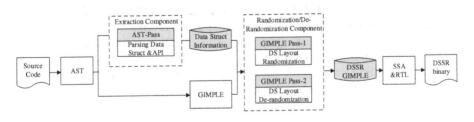

Fig. 2. System overview

GCC: the extraction component and the randomization/de-randomization component. We briefly explain the compilation steps as follows. (1) SALADS parses the source code into an Abstract Syntax Tree (AST). (2) The extraction component (i.e., AST-Pass) traverses the AST to collect required information for the randomization/de-randomization component. (3) SALADS transforms the AST into the GIMPLE representation. (4) The randomization component (i.e., GIMPLE Pass-1) replaces each statement that accesses data structures with DSSR statements. These DSSR statements randomize/re-randomize the layout of the accessed data structures at runtime. (5) The de-randomization component (i.e., GIMPLE Pass-2) inserts de-randomizing statements before each dangerous statement to de-randomize involved data structures. We will explain which statements are dangerous later. (6) SALADS compiles the GIMPLE representation into a DSSR binary in remaining phases (e.g., SSA, RTL). The DSSR binary can self-rerandomize/de-randomize data structure instances at runtime.

3   Design and Implementation of SALADS

3.1   Extraction Component

As shown in Fig. 2, the extraction component is designed to gather definitions of data structures and usages of external and shared APIs. The gathered information is later used by the randomization/de-randomization component.

Extracting Data Structures. For each definition of data structure encountered during AST traversal, the extraction component records the name of the data structure as well as the name, the size and the offset of each field. To calculate the offset or size of a field in a data structure, two challenges need to be tackled. The first one is the alignment. A compiler often allocates fields in a data structure on aligned boundaries. In our design, the extracting component calculates the offsets of fields based on the compiling options specified by the programmers (e.g., #param pack(n)). If no such options are available, the extracting component relies on the default alignment rules to redress the offsets. The second challenge is how to handle arrays with flexible sizes [1]. If a field is an array with flexible size, its size cannot be determined by the compiler. In such a case, SALADS can only arrange this field to the end of the data structure. Correspondingly, SALADS will mark this field as un-randomizable.

Identifying External and Shared APIs. External APIs refer to functions that are used but not defined in a program. The extracting component records usage of all external APIs. For a program, shared APIs are functions defined in this program but publicly used by other programs. For instance, system calls are shared APIs in the Linux kernel. Identifying shared APIs in a program requires knowledge about which functions defined in this program are publicly used by other programs. Such knowledge is often well documented.

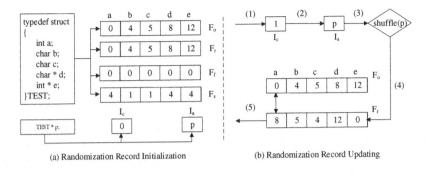

(a) Randomization Record Initialization   (b) Randomization Record Updating

Fig. 3. Initialization and updating of a randomization record

3.2   Randomization Component

The randomization component (i.e., GIMPLE Pass-1) instruments the GIMPLE representation. The instrumented program can self-randomize the layout of data structures at runtime. The instrumentation replaces each statement that contains data structure accesses with a set of DSSR statements, details of which are presented next.

Data Structure Layout Randomization. First, GIMPLE Pass-1 iterates statements in the GIMPLE representation. Second, the pass parses each statement to identify data structure field accesses. For each field access, the pass inserts the DSSR statements before the containing statement. The DSSR statements firstly randomize the layout of the instance. Afterwards, if the access is a read, the DSSR statements maintain the value of the accessed field in a temporary variable. If the access is a write, the DSSR statements use a temporary pointer to point to the after-randomized location of the accessed field. Finally the pass replaces the parsed statement with a new statement. In the new statement, each data structure field access is replaced with the corresponding temporary pointer or the temporary variable.

A statement is parsed as follows. First, the statement is parsed into expressions in a right-to-left order. If an expression is compound (e.g., a+b), it will be decomposed into atomic expressions (e.g., a and b). If an atomic expression is a data structure field access, the parser records the type of the instance, the address of the instance, and the name of the field. In particular, the data structure field access could be nested. For instance, A->B.x involves two nested accesses: A->B and B.x. In such case, the parser firstly parses the outer access and then parses the inner access. In the example of A->B.x, A->B is processed at first and B.x is processed next.

The DSSR statements insertion for data structure field accesses follows the same order as they are parsed. For an access, the inserted DSSR statements include: (1) a gimple statement to invoke the **Initialize_Record** routine. The routine first checks whether this instance is recorded. If not, it initializes a **randomization record**. The randomization record contains following metadata of the instance: I_a (memory address of this instance), I_c (how many times the instance has been accessed since last randomization). A randomization record also maintains the metadata for each field in the instance: F_o (original offset), F_r (after-randomized offset), F_s (size), and F_f (randomization flag). The randomization flag indicates whether a field is randomizable; (2) a GIMPLE statement to invoke the `Update_Record` routine. This routine increases I_c by 1 and then checks whether I_c exceeds a threshold W_m. If so, this routine randomly shuffles the fields in the memory space of the data structure and records the after-randomized offsets into F_r; (3) a GIMPLE statement to call the `Offset_Diff` routine for calculating the offset difference between the randomized layout and the original layout (in term of fields); (4) a GIMPLE statement to assign the after-randomized field (or its location) to a temporary variable (or a pointer).

Example. We present an example in Fig. 4 to illustrate how the randomization component works. Figure 4(a) shows the source code of the program; Fig. 4(b) shows the original GIMPLE representation; Fig. 4(c) shows the GIMPLE representation generated by SALADS. GIMPLE is a three-address representation in static single assignment form [3]. In a GIMPLE representation, temporary variables are defined to store the intermediate values for complex expressions. For example, in Fig. 4(c), to allocate memory for the instance pointed by p, D.2052 is temporarily defined to store the return value of `malloc` (line 15) and afterwards assigned to p (line 16). In particular, we explain how GIMPLE Pass-1 instruments the statement `p->a=1`. Suppose the definition of data structure TEST is identified. First, a GIMPLE statement to invoke Initialize_Record is inserted (line 18 Fig. 4(c)). Initialize_Record initializes I_a as p and I_c as 0. Also Initialize_Record initializes F_s, F_o, and F_f for each field in p. F_s and F_o are determined by the definition of TEST (line 1–7 Fig. 4(a)); F_r is set as the same with F_o; F_f is set as 0 (i.e., randomizable). Second, a GIMPLE statement is inserted to call Update_Record (line 19 Fig. 4(c)). Update_Record updates I_c to be 1 and I_a to be p and uses a routine `Shuffle(p)` to shuffle the layout, which are presented as step-1 to step-3 in Fig. 3. The results are shown in Fig. 3 after step-4. Third, a GIMPLE statement is inserted to call Offset_Diff (line 20 Fig. 4(c)). Offset_Diff

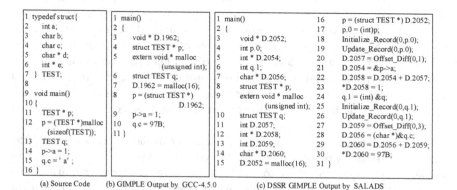

(a) Source Code   (b) GIMPLE Output by GCC-4.5.0   (c) DSSR GIMPLE Output by SALADS

Fig. 4. An example showing how DSSR program generated by SALADS works

calculates difference between the after-randomization offset and original offset (presented as step-5 in Fig. 3). For instance, the offset difference for a in p is 8. Fourth, a GIMPLE statement is inserted to assign the location of the randomized field to a pointer D.2058 (line 22 Fig. 4(c)). Finally, the original statement p->a=1 (line 9 Fig. 4(b)) is replaced with a new statement *D.2058=1 (line 23 Fig. 4(c)).

3.3   De-randomization Component

Data structure randomization may introduce runtime errors. For example, a randomized data structure passed to an un-instrumented library function will be accessed based on the original layout. It will cause program errors because the function may access the irrelevant field in the randomized data structure.

The de-randomization component (i.e., GIMPLE Pass-2) is designed to avoid such errors. First, the pass scans the GIMPLE representation of a program to identify *dangerous statements*. A dangerous statement involves operations on randomized data structures and such operations might cause consequent inconsistency or crash. Second, the pass inserts a statement to invoke the de-randomization routine before a dangerous statement. This routine will restore the data structures involved in the dangerous statement into their original layouts. The dangerous statements appear in two scenarios as follows.

Pointer Involved Dangerous Statements. There are two types of pointer-involved dangerous statements: (1) statements that cast a randomized data structure instance (or a randomized data structure pointer) X to another pointer Y, but X and Y are of different types. Such a statement is dangerous because the subsequent point-to-member operators over Y still access fields according to the original layout; (2) statements that use a pointer to reference a field in a data structure. Suppose there is a statement int *p=&z.a. When z is re-randomized after the assignment, the DSSR program cannot inform p. Consequently, p will point to an irrelevant field instead of a.

For the first type, the inserted de-randomization routine restores X to its original layout and mark it as un-randomizable. For the second type, the de-randomization routine restores the fields (e.g., a) referenced by pointers (e.g., p) to their original locations. Also, the routine marks such fields as un-randomizable.

External and Shared APIs Involved Dangerous Statements. Statements invoking external & shared APIs are dangerous if they pass data structure instances as arguments. For example, when a program calls bind in GNU LIBC with an instance of data structure sockaddr, the sockaddr instance might be randomized. However, bind still uses the sockaddr instance based on its original data structure layout. This will obviously lead to an execution error.

For such an API invoking statement, the inserted de-randomization routine will restore the data structure instances that are passed as arguments to their original layouts and mark them as un-randomizable.

3.4   Other Practical Issues

When there is a deep copy (e.g., plain assignment and `memcpy`) from data structure instance A to another instance B (A and B are with the same type), B shares the identical randomized layout with A. In our design, we directly copy the randomization record of A to B, except I_a and I_c.

If multiple threads access the same data structure instance, the seed of the instance might turn into an un-synchronized state. For user space programs, we leverage `pthread_mutext_lock` and `pthread_mutex_unlock` to keep the execution correct. For kernel space software, the DSSR programs rely on the spinlock interface `spin_lock` and `spin_unlock` to enforce synchronization.

A program might set a written protection attribute for pages that contain data structure instances. If so, DSSR programs firstly change attributes of these pages to make them writable and then randomize layouts of the instances.

4   Evaluation

We have implemented SALADS atop gcc-4.5.0 with an extra of 11 K lines of C code. All evaluation experiments are conducted on an Intel(R) Core(TM) i5 machine with 4GB memory running Fedora Core Release 8 with Linux kernel version 2.6.23.1. In this section, we present the evaluation of the effectiveness and the performance of SALADS system.

4.1   Effectiveness of DSSR Application Programs

How DSSR Applications are Generated. We generate DSSR applications via using SALADS to compile open source programs, including SPECInt2000, `httpd-2.0.6`, `openssh-2.1.1p4`, and `openssl-0.9.6d`. In principle, we should select security-sensitive data structures to randomize. However, we have limited knowledge about such data structures. To be general, we randomly select 20 % of data structures to randomize in each program. In particular, determined security-related data structures are manually added to the randomization set.

How Attacks are Launched. We launch two real world attacks. In the first attack, we exploit the buffer overflow over the array `key_arg` in a data structure instance `session` (of type `ssl_session_st`) in openssl [14]. During the exploitation, the attack firstly overwrites the `key_arg` array and injects the shell codes. Then, the attack uses the pointer field `ciphers` in `session` to calculate the address of the shell codes. By substracting 368 from the pointer `session->ciphers`, the attacker can get the starting address of the shell code. Finally, the attacker redirects the program counter to the shell code. In the second attack, we exploit the integer truncation bug in [13], details of which have been presented before.

We also mimic a memory content leakage attack in the experiment: we insert a routine in each of the tested programs. The routine does two things. First, the routine dumps the page that contains the target data structure instance,

Table 1. Defense results of DSSR applications

Programs	CVE #	Bugs	Data structure	ASLR and DSLR	SALADS
openssl-0.9.6d	CVE-2002-0656	KEY ARG bugs [14]	ssl_session_st	×	✓
openssh-2.1.1	CVE-2001-0144	CRC-32 bug [13]	passwd	×	✓

immediately after the program receives inputs (e.g. socket packets). Second, the routine analyzes the dumped page to locate the base address of the target instance, based on the signature of the data structure. Signature of passwd in openssh has been explained previously. For ssl_session_st, the signature consists of 23 special fields (4 character arrays with 4 corresponding integer lengths, 6 pointer values, and 9 integer values). In addition, the routine can identify fields with unique features: pw_uid in pw is a small integer $\leq$ 0xFFFF; key_arg in session is an 8-byte array which would very likely be separated from other fields by small values ($\leq$ 0x18).

Effectiveness of DSSR. We compile the selected programs with static DSLR and SALADS, respectively. During our experiment, we also enable ASLR in the execution environments. We launch the two attacks to both static DSLR and SALADS compiled applications. Defense results are shown in Table 1. The results demonstrate that when memory content leakage happens, both ASLR and static DSLR cannot defend data structure manipulation attacks. However, SALADS is robust enough to prevent such attacks.

Looking into the Details. Here we discuss the details of how SALADS defeats the two attacks. In the attack against openssh, the memory content leakage enables the attacker to infer the base address of pw and offset of pw_uid at the moment when the leakage happens. The attacker then manipulates the field pw_uid based on the inferred offset. However, a malicious request will trigger at least 5 accesses to pw before it overflows the target instance. Thus the target instance is re-randomized before being manipulated. The story is similar for the attack against openssl: a malicious request will trigger at least 17 accesses to session before it overwrites key_arg.

4.2   Effectiveness of DSSR Kernel and DSSR Hypervisor

How DSSR Linux Kernel and Hypervisor are Generated. Linux kernel-2.6.23.1 contains 11430 data structure definitions. Randomizing all data structures would cause unacceptable overhead. In addition, we observe that many data structures are security in-sensitive and thus, should not be randomized. So we manually select 23 security-sensitive data structures (often used by the rootkits) from Linux kernel-2.6.23.1.

Xen-3.2.0 with Linux kernel-2.6.18.8 contains 11983 data structure definitions. We select 20 data structures from Xen-3.2.0 to randomize, which are widely used in security-sensitive source code files (e.g., mm.c). With the selected data structures, we compile the Linux kernel-2.6.23.1 and Xen-3.2.0 with SALADS.

Table 2. Defense results of deploying DSSR kernel against rootkits

Rootkit name	Data structure	Description	prevented?
hideprocess-2.6	task_struct	hide one process with given PID	√
kbdy-2.6	proc_dir_entry	privilege escalation to the user when open proc file	√
adore-ng-0.56	task_struct, proc_dir_entry, module	hide one process when open proc file	√
taskigt	task_struct,proc_dir_entry	privilege escalation to process when open proc file	√
enyelkm-1.3	proc_dir_entry, module	hide module by modifying the proc read system call	√
int3hook	module	hide process when hijacking int 3	√
synapsys	task_struct,module	give the root privilege to certain proess	√
cleaner-2.6	module	hide the next module of the rootkit	√
linuxfu-2.6	task_struct	hide the process given its name	√
modhide	module	hide the module given its name	√
override	task_struct	hide one process using injected code	√
rmroots	task_struct, module	destroy static data structures to hide	√

How Attacks are Launched. We launch 12 widely used rootkits, as shown in Table 2, in the DSSR Linux kernel. These rootkits manipulate three data structures: `task_struct`, `proc_dir_entry`, and `module`. We also launch a Blue Pill attack against Xen-3.2.0, which reads and then manipulates the `vcpu` data structure with ring0 privilege. All the launched rootkits can circumvent OS level ASLR. The rootkits circumvent static DSLR in a similar way as explained before: speculate the layout of the target instance by referring another known instance of the same type (e.g., `proc_root` is a global variable of type `proc_dir_entry`).

Effectiveness of DSSR. We compile Linux kernel-2.6.23.1 and Xen-3.2.0 with static DSLR and SALADS, respectively. First, we execute the selected rootkits in the static DSLR kernel. These rootkits are enabled to infer the layout the target instance. The effects caused by these rootkits are presented in column 3 of Table 2 (titled as "Description"). Second, we execute the selected

Table 3. Randomization Rate of Data structure in Linux kernel-2.6.23.1 (Size: the memory size of the data structure (bytes); # Operations: the total DSSR statements inserted to handle operations on the data structure; F_t: the total number of fields in the data structure; F_r: the number of fields that can be randomized; I_t: the number of instances that are used; I_r: the number of randomized instances).

Num	Name	Size	# Operations	F_t	F_r	$\gamma = \dfrac{F_r}{F_t}$ (%)	I_t	I_r	$\delta = \dfrac{I_r}{I_t}$(%)
1	sk_buff	180	24770	44	42	95.5	1285	1086	84.5
2	net_device	1280	19918	100	91	91.0	76	72	96.1
3	list_head	8	15595	2	2	100	197391	160347	81.2
4	task_struct	1552	14171	130	97	74.6	386	386	100
5	inode	336	13779	44	25	56.8	5318	4772	89.7
6	device	328	12425	29	18	62.1	393	343	87.3
7	super_block	384	8970	38	25	65.8	23	21	91.3
8	pci_dev	996	7662	43	41	95.3	37	29	78.4
9	socket	40	5111	8	8	100	450	398	88.4
10	Scsi_Host	700	5050	59	56	94.9	40	34	85.0
11	dentry	132	4473	18	11	61.1	5408	5120	94.6
12	urb	104	4452	25	18	72.0	17	17	100
13	scsi_cmnd	304	4401	29	26	89.7	72	66	91.7
14	buffer_head	56	4226	12	9	75.0	8052	5155	64.0
15	file	132	4206	17	10	58.8	3436	2056	59.8
16	net_device_stats	92	4105	23	21	91.3	9	7	77.7
17	sock	364	3846	56	46	82.1	764	587	76.8

rootkits in DSSR kernel and enable them to infer the randomized layout as well. The experiments show two types of results: (1) the rootkit attack is prevented and the kernel continues to work without problems (hideprocess, synapsys, linuxfu-2.6 and override); (2) the rootkit attack causes a kernel panic (the rootkit writes to a pointer which does not point to the location expected by the rootkit). Third, we launch the Blue Pill attack against static DSLR Xen-3.2.0 and DSSR Xen-3.2.0 and enable it to infer the randomized layout. Experiments show that static DSLR Xen is attacked but DSSR Xen is protected.

Looking into the Details. Compared with user space programs, the kernel and the hypervisor contains many more data structure pointers. However, the SALADS system conducts de-randomization for many pointer involved operations. One potential issue is that many instances are de-randomized. For Linux kernel, we calculate the fields randomization rate (the percentage of randomizable fields in all fields) and instance randomization rate (the percentage of randomizable instances in all instances) during booting. In Table 3, we present the results for 17 data structures that are correlated to more operations than others. Field randomization rate for these data structures is 82.2 % and instance randomization rate for these data structures is 80.9 % on average.

4.3 Performance Overhead

Influence of Threshold W_m on Performance Overhead. In SALADS, we set up a threshold W_m to control the times of accesses between two successive randomization. In the first experiment, we use SPECInt2000 benchmark[3] to test how W_m specifically affects the performance overhead introduced by SALADS. All data structures in these programs are randomized. W_m is set to vary from 1 to 10 and for each value, we measure the average performance overhead. The normalized results are shown in Fig. 5. It can be observed that the performance overhead decreases as W_m increases. When W_m grows from 4 to 5, the performance overhead reduces sharply and after that, the performance overhead does not drop obviously. So we set W_m to be 5 by default. All the following experiments are done with $W_m = 5$.

To evaluate the performance overhead introduced by SALADS, we test a variety of programs, including SPECInt2000, `httpd-2.0.6`, `openssh-2.1.1p4` and `openssl-0.9.6d`, Linux kernel 2.6.23.1 and Xen-3.2.0.

To evaluate user space applications, for testing SPECInt2000, we leverage the official benchmark; for testing `httpd`, we use apache benchmark; for testing `opensshl`, we use `openssl speed` [2]; for testing `openssh`, we upload 1.5 GB test-files using `scp` [2] within 1000 times. The evaluation results are shown in Fig. 6. The performance overhead introduced by SALADS ranges from 0.2 % to 23.5 % on average. SALADS introduces higher performance overhead in `gzip`, `gap` and `twolf`. We find that the three programs leverage plenty of data

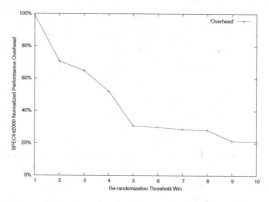

Fig. 5. Influence of W_m on performance

structures to encapsulate data objects (e.g. compressed data, interpret dictionary word, and simulate objects) and frequently operate on these data structures. Consequently, DSSR statements are continuously executed in the three programs, which would cause high performance overhead.

For DSSR Linux kernel and DSSR Xen-3.2.0, we use the Lmbench [26] to evaluate the performance overhead. Specifically, we measure the overhead with the bandwidth and the latency benchmarks. By only randomizing the selected data structures, DSSR Linux kernel introduces 6.7 % to 28.8 % (16.7 % on average) runtime overhead, and DSSR Xen-3.2.0 introduces 0.1 % to 14.8 % (4.5 % on average) runtime overhead. Details are presented in Table 4 in Appendix.

---

[3] We excluded three programs gcc, vortex, and eon in SPECInt2000 since these programs cannot be compiled with gcc-4.5.0.

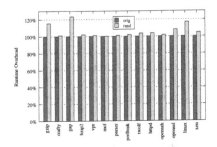

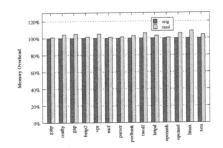

Fig. 6. Runtime overhead

Fig. 7. Memory overhead

4.4 Memory Overhead

We measure the physical memories used by a set of DSSR programs and the corresponding original programs, at randomly selected time points during 1000 runs. As shown in Fig. 7, the memory overhead introduced by SALADS to DSSR programs ranged from 0.7 % (`openssh-2.1.1p4`) to 6.1 % (`twolf`) on average. To measure memory overhead in DSSR kernels, we use the `dmesg` to get the memory usage of the Linux kernel after it is loaded. Both of the original Linux kernel and the DSSR Linux kernel are booted for three times to get the average memory usage. As shown in Fig. 7, the DSSR Linux kernel introduces 8.6 % memory overhead on average. We use the same method for Linux kernel to measure the memory overhead introduced by DSSR Xen-3.2.0. As shown in Fig. 7, DSSR Xen-3.2.0 introduces memory overhead by 4.2 % on average.

5 Discussion

5.1 Analysis of Effectiveness

Our threat model describes a simplified version of data structure manipulation attacks, which only involves one data structure and one specific field. In practice, a data structure manipulation attack often involves multiple data structures and multiple fields. For instance, the rootkit `taskigt` needs to read/manipulate uid, gid, euid, egid in `task_struct` and `read_proc` in `proc_dir_entry`, for a successful attack.

Here we discuss the difficulty introduced by SALADS to a data structure manipulation attack (suppose the original ASLR [32] is deployed). For generality, we assume (1) the attack needs to explore n data structure instances and the ith instance contains l_i fields; (2) the attack needs to read/write m_i fields in the ith instance; (3) the attack attempts to bypass the diversification defenses by brute force; (4) accesses to these instances are completed via one request. Attacks with multiple requests are separated into different attacks.

First, if the attack is against an application and no memory content leakage happens, the attack needs to crack both ASLR and SALADS. To bypass ASLR to refer the base addresses of the n data structures, the attack needs to make at most $2^{19} \times 3$ probes in total, because (1) the data structures may exist in randomized segment of heap, stack, or data; (2) a correct guess of one data structure in a single segment will reveal all other data structures in the same segment. Suppose ASLR has been bypassed and the base addresses of all the instances have been identified. To bypass SALADS to manipulate the correct fields, the attack needs to conduct $\prod_{i=1}^{n} \binom{l_i}{m_i}$ probes. Such a conclusion is based on following facts: (1) all target fields in one single instance are to be accessed in one request, so the attack needs to guess all m_i target fields in the i_{th} instance in one probe; (2) all the n instances are to be accessed in one request, which should be probed in one attempt. Summarily, SALADS complements ASLR to complicate data structure manipulation attacks. For instance, when $n = 2$, $l_1 = 19$, $l_2 = 130$, $m_1 = 1$, and $m_2 = 4$, the expected number of probes to crack SALADS is more than 2^{27} (the values are based on the taskigt rootkit).

Second, if the attack is against an application with memory content leakage or conducted by a rootkit, ASLR (and the static DSLR) is not effective. However, SALADS still works, which has been explained previously. Similarly, the attack needs to make $\prod_{i=1}^{n} \binom{l_i}{m_i}$ probes to bypass SALADS.

5.2 Limitations

In this section, we discuss the limitations of SALADS. First, our design does not explicitly protect the randomization records. Suppose an attacker can read arbitrary memories, including the randomization records. With the records, the attacker can recover the randomized layout. This is a common problem for compiler based defenses, such as Stackguard [12], and G-Free [27]. However, different from existing works, the leaked seeds might be invalid when the attack uses it. The time costs by memory content leakage varies from seconds [33] to weeks, when fine-grained ASLR protection is deployed. Within such a time window, a DSSR program might update the record for multiple times. To protect the randomization records, one possible solution is to adopt the key protection method proposed by Harrison [18]. This technique suggests introducing access control to prevent external code from accessing the key.

Second, an attacker may leverage code-reuse techniques to bypass SALADS. For example, the attacker could reuse the routines (e.g., Update_Record) to get the memory layout of a data structure. Fortunately, code reuse can be effectively handled by existing techniques, such as fine-grained ASLR for instruction areas [16,19,22,28,38] and control flow integrity (CFI) enforcement [4,15,37,40,41].

Third, it is hard to handle the balance between security and efficiency. To obtain the strongest protection, we should randomize all data structures, which, however, would introduce high performance overhead. In our current implementation, we randomize a subset of all data structures, including security-sensitive data structures. Common security-sensitive data structures include those contains authentication information or function pointers. To handle this limitation, we provide users with a white list which contains data structures to be randomized. The users can add security-sensitive data structures into this list. In the near future, we plan to improve our current implementation to randomize more data structures and reduce the overhead.

6 Related Work

Over the past decade, a large number of techniques have been proposed to achieve address space randomization (ASR). These techniques introduce diversification to programs at different granularity [23], including segment level [8,36], page level [5], function level [22], basic block level [28], instruction level [19,38], and memory objects level [17,24,34,39].

In particular, Giuffrida et al. [17] proposed a fine-grained OS-level live randomization technique, including data structure randomization. However, it has several limitations. First, their technique needs to heavily modify the microkernel-based OS; our technique can be directly applied to the targets with light-weight instrumentation. Second, their technique requires to separate a kernel into isolated components, which violates the design principles of modern kernels. Third, it cannot achieve live randomization in the microkernel; whereas our technique can be generically applied to applications, OS kernel and hypervisor code.

Static DSLR [24,34] was proposed to prevent data structure manipulation attacks by modifying the definition of a data structure to reorder the fields. However, static DSLR has several limitations. First, the layout randomized by static DSLR is determined at compile time. Second, static DSLR requires manual efforts to determine which data structure can be randomized. Xin et al. [39] extended static DSLR and proposed using a constraint set to select randomizable data structures. But their techniques cannot handle nested data structures and they ignore all data structures associated with pointer operations.

7 Conclusion

In this paper, we present SALADS, an instrumented compiler that automatically translates a program to a DSSR program. At runtime, a DSSR program adaptively randomizes the layout of each security-sensitive data structure independently. The randomizability of a data structure instance is automatically determined by the DSSR program. Experiments demonstrate both high effectiveness and reasonable performance when applying SALADS to defense against data structure manipulation attacks. As a technique to introduce artificial diversification, SALADS is robust to protect programs in spite of memory leakage and practically applicable to protect OS kernels and hypervisors against rootkits.

Acknowledgement. This work was supported in part by ARO W911NF-13-1-0421 (MURI), NSF CCF-1320605, and NSF CNS-1422594, Chinese National Natural Science Foundation (NSFC 61073027, NSFC 61272078).

A   Details of Lmbench Results

Table 4. Lmbench results

Latency	Linux kernel-2.6.23.1			Linux kernel-2.6.18.8-xen0		
	orig (ms)	r (ms)	O (%)	orig (ms)	r (ms)	O(%)
Simple syscall	0.1559	0.1791	14.9	0.2920	0.2949	1.0
Simple read	0.2239	0.2864	27.9	0.4021	0. 4082	1.5
Simple write	0.1972	0.2539	28.8	0.3658	0.3699	1.1
Simple open/close	1.8732	2.3089	23.2	2.7081	2.7323	0.9
Process fork+exit	60.2857	70.3026	16.6	342.8125	386.5949	12.8
Select on 10 fds	0.4458	0.5069	13.7	0.6874	0.6884	0.1
Select on 100 fds	1.3019	1.5419	18.4	1.7559	1.7688	0.7
Protection fault	0.2289	0.2497	9.1	0.5997	0.6009	0.2
Pipe	5.4670	5.8371	6.7	14.2375	16.3477	14.8
AU_UNIX sock stream	5.9704	7.0496	18.1	13.1883	14.6609	11.2
Bandwidth	orig (MB/s)	r (MB/s)	O (%)	orig (MB/s)	r (MB/s)	O (%)
File I/O	44.71	38.18	17.1	19.30	18.21	6.0
Mmap I/O	7423.26	6671.53	11.2	3023.09	2896.42	4.4
Mem rd	8359.75	7523.35	11.1	3378.98	3245.22	4.1

Table 4 lists the detailed results of testing DSSR Linux kernel (2nd–4th columns) and DSSR Xen-3.2.0 (5th–7th columns) with Lmbench. In particularly, we evaluate the performance overhead introduced by SALADS with two metrics: system latency and bandwidth. For DSSR Linux kernel, file operations (e.g., open/close) have higher performance overhead. Based on our observations, this is possibly because the file-related data structures (e.g., inode) contains many nested definitions which require more DSSR statements to complete the randomization. For DSSR Xen, the randomization mainly affects the local communications (e.g., Pipe) and process-related operations (e.g., process fork). This is probably because more DSSR statements at these points will be executed to access the privileged system components (e.g., MMU, I/O peripherals) and cause traps into the VMM.

References

1. Arrays of length of zero. http://gcc.gnu.org/onlinedocs/gcc/Zero-length.html
2. Openssh   benchmark.   http://blog.famzah.net/2010/06/11/openssh-ciphers-performance-benchmark/
3. Gimple (2015). https://gcc.gnu.org/onlinedocs/gccint/GIMPLE.html

4. Abadi, M., Budiu, M., Erlingsson, U., Ligatti, J.: Control-flow integrity. In: ACM Conference on Computer and Communications Security (CCS 2005) (2005)
5. Backes, M., Nürnberger, S.: Oxymoron: making fine-grained memory randomization practical by allowing code sharing. In: USENIX Security Symposium (Security 2014) (2014)
6. Baliga, A., Ganapathy, V., Iftode, L.: Automatic inference and enforcement of kernel data structure invariants. In: Annual Computer Security Applications Conference (ACSAC 2008) (2008)
7. Berre, S.L.: Bypassing windows 7 kernel aslr (2011). http://dl.packetstormsecurity.net/papers/bypass/NES-BypassWin7KernelAslr.pdf
8. Bhatkar, E., Duvarney, D.C., Sekar, R.: Address obfuscation: an efficient approach to combat a broad range of memory error exploits. In: USENIX Security Symposium (Security 2003) (2003)
9. Bittau, A., Belay, A., Mashtizadeh, A., Mazieres, D., Boneh, D.: Hacking blind. In: IEEE Symposium on Security and Privacy (Oakland 2014) (2014)
10. Bursztein, E., Hamburg, M., Lagarenne, J., Boneh, D.: Openconflict: preventing real time map hacks in online games. In: IEEE Security and Privacy (Oakland 2011) (2011)
11. Chen, H., Mao, Y., Wang, X., Zhou, D., Zeldovich, N., Kaashoek, M.F.: Linux kernel vulnerabilities: state-of-the-art defenses and open problems. In: Asia-Pacific Workshop on Systems (APSys 2011) (2011)
12. Crispin, C., Calton, P., Dave, M., Heather, H., Jonathan, W., Peat, B., Steve, B., Aaron, G., Perry, W., Qian, Z.: Stackguard: automatic adaptive detection and prevention of buffer-overflow attacks. In: USENIX Security Symposium (Security 1998) (1998)
13. CVE-2001-0144. Ssh crc-32 compensation attack detector (2001). http://www.securityfocus.com/bid/2347/discuss
14. CVE-2002-0656. Apache openssl heap overflow exploit (2002). http://www.phreedom.org/research/exploits/apache-openssl/
15. Davi, L., Dmitrienko, A., Egele, M., Fischer, T., Holz, T., Hund, R., Nrnberger, S., Sadeghi, A.-R.: Mocfi: a framework to mitigate control-flow attacks on smartphones. In: Annual Network and Distributed System Security Symposium (NDSS 2012) (2012)
16. Davi, L., Liebchen, C., Sadeghi, A.-R., Snow, K.Z., Monrose, F.: Isomeron: code randomization resilient to (just-in-time) return-oriented programming. In: Annual Network and Distributed System Security Symposium (NDSS 2015) (2015)
17. Giuffrida, C., Kuijsten, A., Tanenbaum, A.S.: Enhanced operating system security through efficient and fine-grained address space randomization. In: USENIX Conference on Security Symposium (Security 2012) (2012)
18. Harrison, K., Xu, S.: Protecting cryptographic keys from memory disclosure attacks. In: Annual IEEE/IFIP International Conference on Dependable Systems and Networks (DSN 2007) (2007)
19. Hiser, J., Nguyen-Tuong, A., Co, M., Hall, M., Davidson, J.: Ilr: Where'd my gadgets go? In: IEEE Symposium on Security and Privacy (Oakland 2012) (2012)
20. Hund, R., Holz, T., Freiling, F.C.: Return-oriented rootkits: bypassing kernel code integrity protection mechanisms. In: USENIX Security Symposium (Security 2009) (2009)
21. Hund, R., Willems, C., Holz, T.: Practical timing side channel attacks against kernel space aslr. In: IEEE Symposium on Security and Privacy (Oakland 2013) (2013)

22. Kil, C., Jim, J., Bookholt, C., Xu, J., Ning, P.: Address space layout permutation (aslp): towards fine-grained randomization of commodity software. In: Annual Computer Security Applications Conference (ACSAC 2006) (2006)
23. Larsen, P., Homescu, A., Brunthaler, S., Franz, M.: Sok: automated software diversity. In: IEEE Symposium on Security and Privacy (Oakland 2014) (2014)
24. Lin, Z., Riley, R.D., Xu, D.: Polymorphing software by randomizing data structure layout. In: Flegel, U., Bruschi, D. (eds.) DIMVA 2009. LNCS, vol. 5587, pp. 107–126. Springer, Heidelberg (2009)
25. Lin, Z., Zhang, X., Xu, D.: Automatic reverse engineering of data structures from binary execution. In: Annual Network and Distributed System Security Symposium (NDSS 2010), San Diego, CA, February 2010
26. McVoy, L., Staelin, C.: lmbench: portable tools for performance analysis. In: USENIX Security Symposium (Security 1996) (1996)
27. Onarlioglu, K., Bilge, L., Lanzi, A., Balzarotti, D., Kirda, E.: G-free: defeating return-oriented programming through gadget-less binaries. In: Annual Computer Security Applications Conference (ACSAC 2010) (2010)
28. Pappas, V., Polychronakis, M., Keromytis, A.: Smashing the gadgets: hindering return-oriented programming using in-place code randomization. In: IEEE Symposium on Security and Privacy (Oakland 2012) (2012)
29. Parvez: Bypassing microsoft windows aslr with a little help by ms-help (2012). http://www.greyhathacker.net/?p=585
30. Seibert, J., Okhravi, H., Söderström, E.: Information leaks without memory disclosures: remote side channel attacks on diversified code. In: ACM Conference on Computer and Communications Security (CCS 2014) (2014)
31. Serna, F.J.: Cve-2012-0769, the case of the perfect info leak (2012). http://zhodiac.hispahack.com/my-stuff/security/Flash_ASLR_bypass.pdf
32. Shacham, H., Page, M., Pfaff, B., Goh, E.-J., Modadugu, N., Boneh, D.: On the effectiveness of address-space randomization. In: ACM Conference on Computer and Communications Security (CCS 2004) (2004)
33. Snow, K.Z., Monrose, F., Davi, L., Dmitrienko, A., Liebchen, C., Sadeghi, A.-R.: Just-in-time code reuse: on the effectiveness of fine-grained address space layout randomization. In: IEEE Symposium on Security and Privacy (Oakland 2013) (2013)
34. Stanley, D.M., Xu, D., Spafford, E.H.: Improved kernel security through memory layout randomization. In: 2013 IEEE 32nd International Performance Computing and Communications Conference (IPCCC), pp. 1–10. IEEE (2013)
35. Strackx, R., Younan, Y., Philippaerts, P., Piessens, F., Lachmund, S., Walter, T.: Breaking the memory secrecy assumption. In: European Workshop on System Security (EUROSEC 2009) (2009)
36. P. Team: Pax address space layout randomization (aslr) (2003). http://pax.grsecurity.net/docs/aslr.txt
37. Wang, Z., Jiang, X.: Hypersafe: a lightweight approach to provide lifetime hypervisor control-flow integrity. In: IEEE Symposium on Security and Privacy (Oakland 2010) (2010)
38. Wartell, R., Mohan, V., Hamlen, K., Lin, Z.: Binary stirring: self-randomizing instruction addresses of legacy x86 binary code. In: ACM Conference on Computer and Communications Security (CCS 2012) (2012)
39. Xin, Z., Chen, H., Han, H., Mao, B., Xie, L.: Misleading malware similarities analysis by automatic data structure obfuscation. In: Burmester, M., Tsudik, G., Magliveras, S., Ilić, I. (eds.) ISC 2010. LNCS, vol. 6531, pp. 181–195. Springer, Heidelberg (2011)

40. Zhang, C., Wei, T., Chen, Z., Duan, L., McCamant, S., Szekeres, L., Song, D., Zou, W.: Practical control flow integrity and randomization for binary executables. In: IEEE Symposium on Security and Privacy (Oakland 2013) (2013)
41. Zhang, M., Sekar, R.: Control flow integrity for cots binaries. In: USENIX Security Symposium (Security 2013) (2013)
42. Zhang, Y., Juels, A., Reiter, M.K., Ristenpart, T.: Cross-vm side channels and their use to extract private keys. In: ACM Conference on Computer and Communications Security (CCS 2012) (2012)

Trustworthy Prevention of Code Injection in Linux on Embedded Devices

Hind Chfouka[1], Hamed Nemati[2(✉)], Roberto Guanciale[2], Mads Dam[2],
and Patrik Ekdahl[3]

[1] University of Pisa, Pisa, Italy
chfouka@di.unipi.it
[2] KTH Royal Institute of Technology, Stockholm, Sweden
{hnnemati,robertog,mfd}@kth.se
[3] Ericsson AB, Lund, Sweden
patrik.ekdahl@ericsson.com

Abstract. We present MProsper, a trustworthy system to prevent code injection in Linux on embedded devices. MProsper is a formally verified run-time monitor, which forces an untrusted Linux to obey the executable space protection policy; a memory area can be either executable or writable, but cannot be both. The executable space protection allows the MProsper's monitor to intercept every change to the executable code performed by a user application or by the Linux kernel. On top of this infrastructure, we use standard code signing to prevent code injection. MProsper is deployed on top of the Prosper hypervisor and is implemented as an isolated guest. Thus MProsper inherits the security property verified for the hypervisor: (i) Its code and data cannot be tampered by the untrusted Linux guest and (ii) all changes to the memory layout is intercepted, thus enabling MProsper to completely mediate every operation that can violate the desired security property. The verification of the monitor has been performed using the HOL4 theorem prover and by extending the existing formal model of the hypervisor with the formal specification of the high level model of the monitor.

1 Introduction

Even if security is a critical issue of IT systems, commodity OSs are not designed with security in mind. Short time to market, support of legacy features, and adoption of binary blobs are only few of the reasons that inhibit the development of secure commodity OSs. Moreover, given the size and complexity of modern OSs, the vision of comprehensive and formal verification of them is as distant as ever. At the same time the necessity of adopting commodity OSs can not be avoided; modern IT systems require complex network stacks, application frameworks etc.

The development of verified low-level execution platforms for system partitioning (hypervisors [11,14], separation kernels [5,15], or microkernels [9]) has enabled an efficient strategy to develop systems with provable security properties without having to verifying the entire software. The idea is to partition the

© Springer International Publishing Switzerland 2015
G. Pernul et al. (Eds.): ESORICS 2015, Part I, LNCS 9326, pp. 90–107, 2015.
DOI: 10.1007/978-3-319-24174-6_5

system into small and trustworthy components with limited functionality running alongside large commodity software components that provide little or no assurance. For such large commodity software it is not realistic to restrict the adversary model. For this reason, the goal is to show, preferably using formal verification, that the architecture satisfies the desired security properties, even if the commodity software is completely compromised.

An interesting usage of this methodology is when the trustworthy components are used as an aid for the application OS to restrict its own attack surface, by proving the impossibility of certain malicious behaviors. In this paper, we show that this approach can be used to implement an embedded device that hosts a Linux system provably free of binary code injection. Our goal is to formally prove that the target system prevents all forms of binary code injection even if the adversary has full control of the hosted Linux and no analysis of Linux itself is performed. This is necessary to make the verification feasible, since Linux consists of million of lines of code and even a high level model of its architecture is subject to frequent changes.

Technically, we use Virtual Machine Introspection (VMI). VMI is a virtualized architecture, where an untrusted guest is monitored by an external observer. VMI has been proposed as a solution to the shortcomings of network-based and host-based intrusion detection systems. Differently from network-based threat detection, VMI monitors the internal state of the guest. Thus, the VMI does not depend on information obtained from monitoring network packets which may not be accurate or sufficient. Moreover, differently from host-based threat detection, VMIs place the monitoring component outside of the guest, thus making the monitoring itself tamper proof. A further benefit of VMI monitors is that they can rely on trusted information received directly from the underlying hardware, which is, as we show, out of the attackers reach.

Our system, MProsper, is implemented as a run-time monitor. The monitor forces an untrusted Linux system to obey the executable space protection policy (usually represented as $W \oplus X$); a memory area can be either executable or writable, but cannot be both. The protection of executable space allows MProsper to intercept all changes to the executable code performed by a user application or by the Linux kernel itself. On top of this infrastructure, we use standard code signing to prevent code injection.

Two distinguishing features of MProsper are its execution on top of a formally verified hypervisor (thus guaranteeing integrity) and the verification of its high level model (thus demonstrating that the security objective is attained). To the best of our knowledge this is the first time the absence of binary code injection has been verified for a commodity OS. The verification of the monitor has been performed using the HOL4 theorem prover and by extending the existing formal model of the hypervisor [14] with the formal specification of the monitor's run-time checks.

The paper is organized as follows: Sect. 2 introduces the target CPU architecture (ARMv7A), the architecture of the existing hypervisor and its interactions with the hosted Linux kernel, the threat model and the existing formal models;

Sect. 3 describes the MProsper architecture and design, it also elaborates on the
additional software required to host Linux; Sect. 4 describes the formal model
of the monitor and formally states the top level goal: absence of code injection;
Sect. 5 presents the verification strategy, by summarizing the proofs that have
been implemented in HOL4; Sect. 6 demonstrates the overhead of MProsper
through standard microbenchmarks, it also presents measures of the code and
proof bases; Finally, Sects. 7 and 8 present the related work and the concluding
remarks.

2   Background

2.1   The Prosper Hypervisor

The Prosper hypervisor supports the execution of an untrusted Linux guest [14]
along with several trusted components. The hosted Linux is paravirtualized; both
applications and kernel are executed unprivileged (in user mode) while privileged
operations are delegated to the hypervisor, which is invoked via hypercalls. The
physical memory region allocated to each component is statically defined. The
hypervisor guarantees spatial isolation of the hosted components; a component
can not directly affect (or be affected by) the content of the memory regions allocated to other components. Thus, the interactions among the hosted components
are possible only via controlled communication channels, which are supervised
by the hypervisor.

The Prosper hypervisor and the MProsper monitor target the ARMv7-A
architecture, which is the most widely adopted instruction set architecture in
mobile computing. In ARMv7-A, the virtual memory is configured via page
tables that reside in physical memory. The architecture provides two levels of
page tables, in the following called L1s and L2s. These tables represent the
configuration of the Memory Management Unit (MMU) and define the access
permissions to the virtual memory. As is common among modern architectures,
the entries of ARMv7 page tables support the NX (No eXecute) attribute: an
instruction can be executed only if it is fetched from a virtual memory area
whose NX bit is not set. Therefore, the system executable code is a subset of the
content of the physical blocks that have at least an executable virtual mapping.

To isolate the components, the hypervisor takes control of the MMU and
configures the pagetables so that no illicit access is possible. This MMU configuration can not be static; the hosted Linux must be able to reconfigure the layout
of its own memory (and the memory of the user programs). For this reason the
hypervisor virtualizes the memory subsystem. This virtualization consists of a
set of APIs that enable Linux to request the creation/deletion/modification of
a page table and to switch the one currently used by the MMU.

Similarly to Xen [3], the virtualization of the memory subsystem is accomplished by direct paging. Direct paging allows the guest to allocate the page
tables inside its own memory and to directly manipulate them while the tables

Table 1. DMMU API

request r	DMMU behavior
$switch(bl)$	makes block bl the active page table
$free_{L1}(bl)$ and $free_{L2}(bl)$	frees block bl, by setting its type to D
$unmap_{L1}(bl, idx)$, $unmap_{L2}(bl, idx)$	unmaps entry idx of the page table stored in block bl
$link_{L1}(bl, idx, bl')$	maps entry idx of block bl to point the L2 stored in bl'
$map_{L2}(bl, idx, bl', ex, wt, rd)$ and $map_{L1}(bl, idx, bl', ex, wt, rd)$	map entry idx of block bl to point to block bl' and granting rights ex, wt, rd to user mode
$create_{L2}(bl)$ and $create_{L1}(bl)$	makes block bl a potential L2/L1, by setting its type to $L2/L1$

are not in active use by the MMU. Once the page tables are activated, the hypervisor must guarantee that further updates are possible only via the virtualization API.

The physical memory is fragmented into blocks of 4 KB. Thus, a 32-bit architecture has 2^{20} physical blocks. We assign a type to each physical block, that can be: *data*: the block can be written by the guest, *L1*: contains part of an L1 page table and should not be writable by the guest, *L2*: contains four L2 page tables and should not be writable by the guest. We call the *L1* and *L2* blocks "potential" page tables, since the hypervisor allows to select only these memory areas to be used as page tables by the MMU.

Table 1 summarizes the APIs that manipulate the page tables. The set of these functions is called DMMU. Each function validates the page type, guaranteeing that page tables are write-protected. A naive run-time check of the page-type policy is not efficient, since it requires to re-validate the L1 page table whenever the *switch* hypercall is invoked. To efficiently enforce that only blocks typed D can be written by the guest the hypervisor maintains a reference counter, which tracks for each block the sum of descriptors providing access in user mode to the block. The intuition is that a hypercall can change the type of a physical block (e.g. allocate or free a page table) only if the corresponding reference counter is zero.

A high level view of the hypervisor architecture is depicted in Fig. 1. The hypervisor is the only component that is executed in privileged mode. It logically consists of three layers: (i) an interface layer (e.g. the exception handlers) that is independent from the hosted software, (ii) a Linux specific layer and (iii) a critical core (i.e. the DMMU), which is the only component that manipulates the sensible resources (i.e. the page tables). Figure 1 demonstrates the behavior of the system when a user process in the Linux guest spawns a new process.

This design has two main benefits: (i) the critical part of the hypervisor is small and does not depend on the hosted software and (ii) the Linux-specific layer

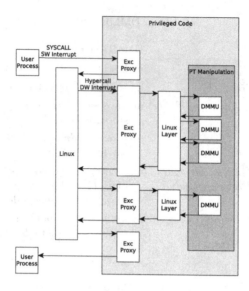

Fig. 1. Hypervisor architecture

enriches the expressiveness of the hypercalls, thus reducing the number of context switches between the hypervisor and the Linux kernel. From a verification point of view, to guarantee security of the complete system it is not necessary to verify functional correctness of the Linux layer; it suffices to verify that this layer never changes directly the sensitive resources and that its execution does not depend on the sensitive data. These tasks can be accomplished using sandboxing techniques [17] or tools for information flow analysis [2].

2.2 The Attack Model

The Linux guest is not trusted, thus we take into account an attacker that has complete control of the partition that hosts Linux. The attacker can force user programs and the Linux kernel to follow arbitrary flows and to use arbitrary data. The attacker can invoke the hypervisor, including the DMMU API, through software interrupts and exceptions. Other transitions into privileged memory are prevented by the hypervisor. The goal of the attacker is "code injection", for example using a buffer overflow to inject malicious executable code. This attack is normally performed by a malicious software that is able to write code into a data storage area of another process, and then cause this code to be executed.

In this paper we exemplify our monitor infrastructure using code signing. Signing the system code is a widely used approach to confirm the software author and guarantee (computationally speaking) that the code has not been altered or corrupted, by use of a cryptographic hash. Many existing code signing systems rely on a public key infrastructure (PKI) to provide both code authenticity and integrity. Here we use code signing to define integrity of the system code: integrity of an executable physical block stands for the block having a valid signature. Similarly, the integrity of the system code depends on the integrity of all executable physical blocks. The valid signatures are assumed to be known by the runtime monitor. We refer to this information as the "golden image" (GI) and it is held by the monitor.

In order to make injected code detectable, we also assume that the attacker is computationally bound; it can not modify the injected code to make its signature compliant with the golden image. We stress that our goal is not to demonstrate the security properties of a specific signature scheme. In fact the monitor can be equipped with an arbitrary signature mechanism and the signature mechanism itself is just one of the possible approaches that can be used to check integrity of the system code. For this reason we do not elaborate further on the computational power of the attacker.

2.3   Formal Model of the Hypervisor

Our formal model is built on top of the existing HOL4 model for ARMv7 [6]. This has been extended with a detailed formalization of the ARMv7 MMU, so that every memory access uses virtual addresses and respects the constraints imposed by the page tables.

An ARMv7 state is a record $\sigma = \langle regs, coregs, mem \rangle \in \Sigma$, where $regs$, $coregs$ and mem, respectively, represent the registers, coprocessors and memory. In the state σ, the function $mode(\sigma)$ determines the current privilege execution mode, which can be either $PL0$ (user mode, used by Linux and the monitor) or $PL1$ (privileged mode, used by the hypervisor).

The system behavior is modeled by a state transition relation $\xrightarrow{l \in \{PL0, PL1\}} \subseteq$ $\Sigma \times \Sigma$, representing the complete execution of a single ARM instruction. Non-privileged transitions ($\sigma \xrightarrow{PL0} \sigma'$) start and end in $PL0$ states. All the other transitions ($\sigma \xrightarrow{PL1} \sigma'$) involve at least one state in privileged level. A transition from $PL0$ to $PL1$ is done by raising an exception, that can be caused by software interrupts, illegitimate memory accesses, and hardware interrupts.

The transition relation queries the MMU to translate the virtual addresses and to check the access permissions. The MMU is represented by the function $mmu(\sigma, PL, va, accreq) \rightarrow pa \cup \{\bot\}$: it takes the state σ, a privilege level PL, a virtual address $va \in 2^{32}$ and the requested access right $accreq \in \{rd, wt, ex\}$, for $readable$, $writable$, and $executable$ in non-privileged respectively, and returns either the corresponding physical address $pa \in 2^{32}$ (if the access is granted) or a fault ($\bot$).

In [14] we show that a system hosting the hypervisor resembles the following abstract model. A system state is modeled by a tuple $\langle \sigma, h \rangle$, consisting of an ARMv7 state σ and an abstract hypervisor state h, of the form $\langle \tau, \rho_{ex}, \rho_{wt} \rangle$. Let $bl \in 2^{20}$ be the index of a physical block and $t \in \{D, L1, L2\}$, $\tau \vdash bl : t$ tracks the type of the block and $\rho_{ex}(bl), \rho_{wt}(bl) \in 2^{30}$ track the reference counters: the number of page tables entries (i.e. entries of physical blocks typed either $L1$ or $L2$) that map to the physical block bl and are executable or writable respectively.

The transition relation for this model is $\langle \sigma, h \rangle \xrightarrow{\alpha} \langle \sigma', h' \rangle$, where $\alpha \in \{0, 1\}$, and is defined by the following inference rules:

- if $\sigma \xrightarrow{PL0} \sigma'$ then $\langle \sigma, h \rangle \xrightarrow{0} \langle \sigma', h \rangle$; instructions executed in non-privileged mode that do not raise exceptions behave equivalently to the standard ARMv7 semantics and do not affect the abstract hypervisor state.
- if $\sigma \xrightarrow{PL1} \sigma'$ then $\langle \sigma, h \rangle \xrightarrow{1} H_r(\langle \sigma', h \rangle)$, where $r = req(\sigma')$; whenever an exception is raised, the hypervisor is invoked through a hypercall, and the reached state is resulting from the execution of the handler H_r.

Here, req is a function that models the hypercall calling conventions; the target hypercall is identified by the first register of σ, and the other registers provide the hypercall's arguments. The handlers H_r formally model the behavior of the memory virtualization APIs of the hypervisor (see Table 1).

Intuitively, guaranteeing spatial isolation means confining the guest to manage a part of the physical memory available for the guest uses. In our setting, this part is determined statically and identified by the predicate $G_m(bl)$, which holds if the physical block bl is part of the physical memory assigned to the guest partition. Clearly, no security property can be guaranteed if the system starts from a non-consistent state; for example the guest can not be allowed to change the MMU behavior by directly writing the page tables. For this reason we introduce a system invariant $I_H(\langle \sigma, h \rangle)$ that is used to constrain the set of consistent initial states. Then the hypervisor guarantees that the invariant is preserved by every transition:

Proposition 1. *Let* $I_H(\langle \sigma, h \rangle)$. *If* $\langle \sigma, h \rangle \xrightarrow{i} \langle \sigma', h' \rangle$ *then* $I_H(\langle \sigma', h' \rangle)$.

We use the function $content : \Sigma \times 2^{20} \to 2^{4096*8}$ that returns the content of a physical block in a system state as a value of 4 KB. Proposition 2 summarizes some of the security properties verified in [14]: the untrusted guest can not directly change (1) the memory allocated to the other components, (2) physical blocks that contain potential page tables, (3) physical blocks whose writable reference counter is zero and (4) the behavior of the MMU.

Proposition 2. *Let* $I_H(\langle \sigma, (\tau, \rho_{wt}, \rho_{ex}) \rangle)$. *If* $\langle \sigma, (\tau, \rho_{wt}, \rho_{ex}) \rangle \xrightarrow{0} \langle \sigma', h' \rangle$ *then:*

2.1 For every bl *such that* $\neg G_m(bl)$ *then* $content(bl, \sigma) = content(bl, \sigma')$
2.2 For every bl *such that* $\tau(bl) \neq D$ *then* $content(bl, \sigma) = content(bl, \sigma')$
2.3 For every bl *if* $content(bl, \sigma) = content(bl, \sigma')$ *then* $\rho_{wt}(bl) > 0$
2.4 For every va, PL, acc *we have* $mmu(\sigma, va, PL, acc) = mmu(\sigma', va, PL, acc)$.

3   Design

We configured the hypervisor to support the interaction protocol of Fig. 2; the monitor mediates accesses to the DMMU layer. Since the hypervisor supervises the changes of the page tables the monitor is able to intercept all modifications

1. For each DMMU hypercall invoked by a guest, the hypervisor forwards the hypercall's request to the monitor.
2. The monitor validates the request based on its validation mechanism.
3. The monitor reports to the hypervisor the result of the hypercall validation.

Fig. 2. The interaction protocol between the Prosper hypervisor and the monitor

to the memory layout. This makes the monitor able to know if a physical block is writable: This is the case if there exists at least one virtual mapping pointing to the block with a guest writable access permission. Similarly it is possible to know if a physical block is executable. Note that the identification of the executable code (also called "working set") does not rely on any information provided by the untrusted guest. Instead, the monitor only depends on HW information, which can not be tampered by an attacker.

The first policy enforced by the monitor is code signature: Whenever Linux requests to change a page table (i.e. causing to change the domain of the working set) the monitor (i) identifies the physical blocks that can be made executable by the request, (ii) computes the block signature and (iii) compares the result with the content of the golden image. This policy is sufficient to prevent code injection that are caused by changes of the memory layout setting, due to the hypervisor forwarding to the monitor all requests to change the page tables.

However, this policy is not sufficient to guarantee integrity of the working set. In fact, operations that modify the content of a physical block that is executable can violate the integrity of the executable code. These operations cannot be intercepted by the monitor, since they are not supposed to raise any hypercall. In fact, a simple write operation in a block typed D does not require the hypervisor intermediation since no modification of the memory layout is introduced. To prevent code injections performed by writing malicious code in an executable area of the memory, the monitor enforces the executable space protection policy $W \oplus X$, preventing physical blocks from being simultaneously writable and executable. As for the hypervisor, a naive run-time check of the executable space protection is not efficient. Instead, we reuse the hypervisor reference counters: we accept a hypercall that makes a block executable (writable) only if the writable (executable) reference counter of the block is zero.

An additional complication comes from the Linux architecture. An unmodified Linux kernel will not survive the policies enforced by the monitor, thus its execution will inevitably fail. For example, when a user process is running there are at least two virtual memory regions that are mapped to the same physical memory where the process executable resides: (i) the user "text segment" and (ii) the "kernel space" (which is an injective map to the whole physical memory). When the process is created, Linux requests to set the text segment as executable and non writable. However, Linux does not revoke its right to write inside this memory area using its kernel space. This setting is not accepted by the monitor, since it violates $X \oplus W$, thus making it impossible to execute a user process.

Instead of adapting a specific Linux kernel we decided to implement a small emulation layer that has two functionalities:

- It proxies all requests from the Linux layer to the monitor. If the emulator receives a request that can be rejected by the monitor (e.g. a request setting as writable a memory region that is currently executable) then the emulator (i) downgrades the access rights of the request (e.g. setting them as non writable) and (ii) stores the information about the suspended right in a private table.
- It proxies all data and prefetch aborts. The monitor looks up in the private table to identify if the abort is due to an access right that has been previously downgraded by the emulator. In this case the monitor attempts (i) to downgrade the existing mapping that conflicts with the suspended access right and (ii) to re-enable the suspended access right.

Note that a malfunction of the emulation layer does not affect the security of the monitor. Namely, we do not care if the emulation layer is functionally correct, but only that it does not access sensible resources directly.

Figure 3 depicts the architecture of MProsper. Both the runtime monitor and the emulator are deployed as two guests of the Prosper hypervisor. The Linux layer prepares a list of requests in a buffer shared with the emulation guest. After the Linux layer returns, the hypervisor activates the emulation guest, which manipulates the requests (or adds new ones) as discussed before. Then the hypervisor iteratively asks the monitor to validate one of the pending requests and upon success it commits the request by invoking the corresponding DMMU function.

Using a dedicated guest on top of the hypervisor permits to decouple the enforcement of the security policies from the other hypervisor functionalities,

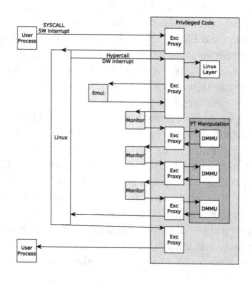

Fig. 3. MProsper's architecture

thus keeping the trusted computing base minimal. Moreover, having the security policy wrapped inside a guest supports both the tamper-resistance and the trustworthiness of the monitor. In fact, the monitor can take advantage from the isolation properties provided by the hypervisor. This avoids malicious interferences coming from the other guests (for example from a process of an OS running on a different partition of the same machine). Finally, decoupling the run-time security policy from the other functionalities of the hypervisor makes the formal specification and verification of the monitor more affordable.

4 Formal Model of MProsper

The formal model of the system (i.e. consisting of the hypervisor, the monitor and the untrusted Linux) is built on top of the models presented in Sect. 2.3. Here we leave unspecified the algorithm used to sign and check signatures, so that our results can be used for different intrusion detection mechanisms. The golden image GI is a finite set of signatures $\{s_1, \ldots, s_n\}$, where the signatures are selected from a domain S. We assume the existence of a function $sig : 2^{4096*8} \rightarrow S$ that computes the signature of the content of a block.

The system behavior is modeled by the following rules:

$$\frac{\langle\sigma,h\rangle \xrightarrow{0} \langle\sigma',h'\rangle}{\langle\sigma,h,GI\rangle \xrightarrow{0} \langle\sigma',h',GI\rangle} \quad \frac{\langle\sigma,h\rangle \xrightarrow{1} \langle\sigma',h'\rangle \ \ validate(req(\langle\sigma,h\rangle),\langle\sigma,h,GI\rangle)}{\langle\sigma,h,GI\rangle \xrightarrow{1} \langle\sigma',h',GI\rangle}$$

$$\frac{\langle\sigma,h\rangle \xrightarrow{1} \langle\sigma',h'\rangle \ \ \neg validate(req(\langle\sigma,h\rangle),\langle\sigma,h,GI\rangle)}{\langle\sigma,h,GI\rangle \xrightarrow{1} \epsilon(\langle\sigma,h,GI\rangle)}$$

User mode transitions (e.g. Linux activities) require neither hypervisor nor monitor intermediation. Proposition 2.1 justifies the fact that, by construction, the transitions executed by the untrusted component can not affect the monitor state; (i) the golden image is constant and (ii) the monitor code can be statically identified and abstractly modeled. Executions in privileged mode require monitor intermediation. If the monitor validates the request, then the standard behavior of the hypervisor is executed. Otherwise the hypervisor performs a special operation to reject the request, by reaching the state that is returned by a function ϵ. Hereafter, the function ϵ is assumed to be the identity. Alternatively, ϵ can transform the state so that the requestor is informed about the rejected operation, by updating the user registers according to the desired calling convention.

The function $validate(req(\langle\sigma, h\rangle), \langle\sigma, h, GI\rangle)$ represents the validation mechanism of the monitor, which checks at run-time possible violations of the security policies. In Table 2 we briefly summarize the policies for the different access requests. Here, PT is a function that yields the list of mappings granted by a page table, where each mapping is a tuple (vb, pb, wt, ex) containing the virtual block mapped (vb), the pointed physical block (pb) and the unprivileged rights to execute (ex) and write (wt). The rules in Table 2 are deliberately more abstract that the ones modeled in HOL4 and are used to intuitively present the behavior of the monitor. For example, the function PT is part of the hardware model and

Table 2. Security policies for the available access requests

request r	$validate(r, \langle \sigma, (\tau, \rho_{wt}, \rho_{ex}), GI \rangle)$ holds iff
$switch(bl)$	always
$free_{L1}(bl)$ and $free_{L2}(bl)$	always
$unmap_{L1}(bl, idx)$, $unmap_{L2}(bl, idx)$ and $link_{L1}(bl, idx, bl')$	$\rho_{ex}(bl) = 0$
$map_{L2}(bl, idx, bl', ex, wt, rd)$ and $map_{L1}(bl, idx, bl', ex, wt, rd)$	$sound_{W \oplus X}(wt, ex, \rho_{wt}, \rho_{ex}, bl') \wedge$ $sound_S(ex, bl', \sigma, GI) \wedge \rho_{ex}(bl) = 0$
$create_{L2}(bl)$ and $create_{L1}(bl)$	$\forall (vb, pb, wt, ex) \in PT(content(bl, \sigma))$ $sound_{W \oplus X}(wt, ex, \rho_{wt}, \rho_{ex}, pb) \wedge$ $sound_S(ex, pb, \sigma, GI)$
	$\forall (vb', pb', wt', ex') \in PT(content(bl, \sigma)).$ $no\text{-}conflict(vb, pb, wt, ex)(vb', pb', wt', ex')$

where

$sound_{W \oplus X}(wt, ex, \rho_{wt}, \rho_{ex}, bl) = (ex \Rightarrow \neg wt \wedge \rho_{wt}(bl) = 0) \wedge (wt \Rightarrow \neg ex \wedge \rho_{ex}(bl) = 0)$

$sound_S(ex, bl, \sigma, GI) = (ex \Rightarrow integrity(GI, bl, content(bl, \sigma)))$

$no\text{-}conflict(vb, pb, wt, ex)(vb', pb', wt', ex') = \left(\begin{array}{l} (vb \neq vb' \wedge pb = pb') \Rightarrow \\ (ex \Rightarrow \neg wt' \wedge wt \Rightarrow \neg ex') \end{array} \right)$

is not explicitly used by the monitor code, that is instead more similar to an iterative program. This makes our verification more difficult, but it also makes the monitor model as near as possible to the actual implementation, enabling further verification efforts that can establish correctness of the implementation.

Note that the monitor always checks that a mapping is not writable and executable simultaneously. Furthermore, if a mapping grants a writable access then the executable reference counter of the pointed physical block must be zero, guaranteeing that this mapping does not conflict (according with the executable space protection policy) with any other allocated page table. Similarly, if a mapping grants an executable access, then the writable reference counter of the pointed block must be zero.

To formalize the top goal of our verification we introduce some auxiliary notations. The working set identifies the physical blocks that host executable binaries and their corresponding content.

Definition 1. *Let σ be a machine state. The working set of σ is defined as*

$$WS(\sigma) = \{ \langle bl, content(bl, \sigma) \rangle \mid \exists pa, va.mmu(\sigma, PL0, va, ex) = pa \wedge pa \in bl \}$$

By using a code signing approach, we say that the integrity of a physical block is satisfied if the signature of the block's content belongs to the golden image.

Definition 2. *Let $cnt \in 2^{4096*8}$ be the 4 KB content of a physical block bl and GI be the golden image. Then $integrity(GI, bl, cnt)$ if, and only if, $sig(bl, cnt) \in GI$.*

Notice that our security property can be refined to fit different anti-intrusion mechanisms. For example, $integrity(GI, bl, cnt)$ can be instantiated with the execution of an anti-virus scanner.

The system state is free of malicious code injection if the signature check is satisfied for the whole executable code. That is:

Definition 3. *Let σ be a machine state, bl be a physical block and GI be the golden image. Then $integrity(GI, \sigma)$ if, only if, for all $\langle bl, cnt \rangle \in WS(\sigma)$, $integrity(GI, bl, cnt)$.*

Finally, we present our top level proof goal: No code injection can succeed.

Proposition 3. *If $\langle \sigma, h, GI \rangle$ is a state reachable from the initial state of the system $\langle \sigma_0, h_0, GI \rangle$ then $integrity(GI, \sigma)$.*

5   Verification Strategy

Our verification strategy consists of introducing a state invariant $I(s)$ that is preserved by any possible transition and demonstrating that the invariant guarantees the desired security properties.

Definition 4. $I(\sigma, (\tau, \rho_{wt}, \rho_{ex}), GI)$ *holds if*

$$I_H(\sigma, (\tau, \rho_{wt}, \rho_{ex})) \wedge$$
$$\forall bl \ . \ (\neg(\tau(bl) = D)) \Rightarrow \forall(vb, pb, wt, ex) \in PT(content(bl, \sigma)).$$
$$sound_{W \oplus X}(wt, ex, \rho_{wt}, \rho_{ex}, pb) \wedge sound_S(ex, pb, \sigma, GI)$$

Clearly, the soundness of the monitor depends on the soundness of the hypervisor, thus I requires that the hypervisor's invariant I_H holds. Notice that the invariant constrains not only the page tables currently in use, but it constrains all potential page tables, which are all the blocks that have type different from D. This allows to speed up the context switch, since the guest simply re-activates a page table that has been previously validated. Technically, the invariant guarantees protection of the memory that can be potentially executable and the correctness of the corresponding signatures.

We verified independently that the invariant is preserved by unprivileged transitions (Theorem 1) and by privileged transitions (Theorem 2). Moreover, Lemma 1 demonstrates that the monitor invariant guarantees that there is no malicious content in the executable memory.

Lemma 1. *If $I(\langle \sigma, (\tau, \rho_{wt}, \rho_{ex}), GI \rangle)$ then $integrity(GI, \sigma)$.*

Proof. The proof is straightforward, following from $sound_S$ of every block that can be executable according with an arbitrary potential page table.   □

Theorem 1 demonstrates that the invariant is preserved by instructions executed by the untrusted Linux. This depends on Lemma 2, which shows that the invariant forbids user transitions to change the content of the memory that is executable.

Lemma 2. *Let* $\langle \sigma, (\tau, \rho_{wt}, \rho_{ex}), GI \rangle \xrightarrow{0} \langle \sigma', h', GI' \rangle$ *and* $I(\langle \sigma, h, GI \rangle)$ *then*

$$\forall bl \ . \ (\neg(\tau(bl) = D)) \Rightarrow \left(\begin{array}{l} PT(content(bl, \sigma')) = PT(content(bl, \sigma)) \wedge \\ \forall (vb, pb, wt, ex) \in PT(content(bl, \sigma')) \ . \\ (ex \Rightarrow content(pb, \sigma) = content(pb, \sigma')) \end{array} \right)$$

Theorem 1. *If* $\langle \sigma, h, GI \rangle \xrightarrow{0} \langle \sigma', h', GI' \rangle$ *and* $I(\langle \sigma, h, GI \rangle)$ *then* $I(\langle \sigma', h', GI' \rangle)$.

Proof. From the inference rules we know that $h' = h$, $GI' = GI$ and that the system without the monitor behaves as $\langle \sigma, h \rangle \xrightarrow{0} \langle \sigma', h \rangle$. Thus, Proposition 1 can be used to guarantee that the hypervisor invariant is preserved ($I_H(\sigma', h')$).

If the second part of the invariant is violated then there must exist a mapping in one (hereafter bl) of the allocated page tables that is compliant with the executable space protection policy in σ and violates the policy in σ'. Namely, $content(bl, \sigma')$ must be different from $content(bl, \sigma)$. This contradicts Proposition 2.2, since the type of the changed block is not data ($\tau(bl) \neq D$).

Finally we must demonstrate that every potentially executable block contains a sound binary. Lemma 2 guarantees that the blocks that are potentially executable are the same in σ and σ' and that the content of these blocks is unchanged. Thus is sufficient to use the invariant $I(\sigma, h, GI)$, to demonstrate that the signatures of all executable blocks are correct. $\square$

To demonstrate the functional correctness of the monitor (Theorem 2 i.e. that the invariant is preserved by privileged transitions) we introduce two auxiliary lemmas: Lemma 3 shows that the monitor correctly checks the signature of pages that are made executable. Lemma 4 expresses that executable space protection is preserved for all hypervisor data changes, as long as a block whose reference counter (e.g. writable; ρ'_{wt}) becomes non zero has the other reference counter (e.g. executable; ρ_{ex}) zero.

Lemma 3. *If* $\langle \sigma, h, GI \rangle \xrightarrow{1} \langle \sigma', (\tau', \rho'_{wt}, \rho'_{ex}), GI' \rangle$ *and* $I(\langle \sigma, h, GI \rangle)$ *then for all* bl, $\tau'(bl) \neq D \Rightarrow \forall (vb', pb', wt, ex) \in PT(content(bl, \sigma')).sound_S(ex, pb', \sigma', GI)$.

Lemma 4. *Assume (i)* $I(\langle \sigma, (\tau, \rho_{wt}, \rho_{ex}), GI \rangle)$, *(ii)* $\forall bl.(\rho_{ex}(bl) = 0 \wedge \rho'_{ex}(bl) > 0) \Rightarrow (\rho_{wt}(bl) = 0)$, *and (iii)* $\forall bl.(\rho_{wt}(bl) = 0 \wedge \rho'_{wt}(bl) > 0) \Rightarrow (\rho_{ex}(bl) = 0)$. *For all blocks* bl, *if* $sound_{W \oplus X}(wt, ex, \rho_{wt}, \rho_{ex}, bl)$ *then* $sound_{W \oplus X}(wt, ex, \rho'_{wt}, \rho'_{ex}, bl)$.

Theorem 2. *If* $\langle \sigma, h, GI \rangle \xrightarrow{1} \langle \sigma', h', GI' \rangle$ *and* $I(\langle \sigma, h, GI \rangle)$ *then* $I(\langle \sigma', h', GI' \rangle)$.

Proof. When the request is not validated ($\neg validate$) than the proof is trivial, since ϵ is the identity function.

If the request is validated by the monitor and committed by the hypervisor, then the inference rules guarantee that $GI' = GI$ and that the system without the monitor behaves as $\langle \sigma, h \rangle \xrightarrow{0} \langle \sigma', h \rangle$. Thus, Proposition 1 can be used to guarantee that the hypervisor invariant is preserved ($I_H(\sigma', h')$). Moreover, Lemma 3 demonstrates that the $sound_S$ part of the invariant holds.

The proof of the second part (the executable space protection) of the invariant is the most challenging task of this formal verification. This basically establishes the functional correctness of the monitor and that its run-time policies are strong enough to preserve the invariant (i.e. they enforce protection of the potentially executable space). Practically speaking, the proof consists of several cases: one for each possible request. The structure of the proof for each case is similar. For example, for $r = map_{L2}(bl, idx, bl', ex, wt, rd)$, we (i) prove that the hypervisor (modeled by the function H_r) only changes entry idx of the page table stored in block bl (that is, all other blocks that are not typed D are unchanged), (ii) we show that only the counters of physical block bl' are changed, and (iii) we establish the hypothesis of Lemma 4. This enables us to infer $sound_{W \oplus X}$ for the unchanged blocks and to reduce the proof to only check the correctness of the entry idx of the page table in the block bl.   □

Finally, Theorem 3 composes our results, demonstrating that no code injection can succeed.

Theorem 3. *Let $\langle \sigma, h, GI \rangle$ be a state reachable from the initial state of the system $\langle \sigma_0, h_0, GI_0 \rangle$ and $I(\langle \sigma_0, h_0, GI_0 \rangle)$, then integrity$(GI, \sigma)$ holds.*

Proof. Theorems 1 and 2 directly show that the invariant is preserved for an arbitrary trace. Then, Lemma 1 demonstrates that every reachable state is free of malicious code injection.   □

6   Evaluation

The verification has been performed using the HOL4 interactive theorem prover. The specification of the high level model of the monitor adds 710 lines of HOL4 to the existing model of the hypervisor. This specification is intentionally low level and does not depend on any high level theory of HOL4. This increased the difficulty of the proof (e.g., it musts handle finite arithmetic overflows), that consists of 4400 lines of HOL4. However, the low level of abstraction allowed us to directly transfer the model to a practical implementation and to identify several bugs of the original design. For example, the original policy for $link_{L1}(bl, idx, bl')$ did not contain the condition $\rho_{ex}(bl) = 0$, allowing to violate the integrity of the working set if a block is used to store an L1 page table and is itself executable.

The monitor code consists of 720 lines of C and the emulator consists of additional 950 lines of code. Finally, 100 lines have been added to the hypervisor to support the needed interactions among the hosted components.

We used LMBench to measure the overhead introduced on user processes hosted by Linux. We focused on the benchmarks "fork", "exec" and "shell", since they require the creation of new processes and thus represent the monitors worst case scenario. As macro-benchmark, we measured in-memory compression of two data streams. The benchmarks have been executed using Qemu to emulate a Beagleboard-Mx. Since we are not interested in evaluating a specific signature

Table 3. Qemu benchmarks

Benchmark	fork	exec	shell	tar -czvf 1.2 KB	tar -czvf 2.8 MB
No monitor	$10240\,\mu s$	$10174\,\mu s$	$42889\,\mu s$	0.05 s	20.95 s
P Emu	$11792\,\mu s$	$11944\,\mu s$	$48473\,\mu s$	0.09 s	21.05 s
P Emu + P Mon	$13965\,\mu s$	$13837\,\mu s$	$54303\,\mu s$	0.10 s	21.02 s
P Emu + U Mon	$17512\,\mu s$	$17154\,\mu s$	$67273\,\mu s$	0.11 s	20.98 s

scheme, we computed the signature of each physical block as the xor of the contained words, allowing us to focus on the overhead introduced by the monitor's infrastructure. Table 3 reports the benchmarks for different prototypes of the monitor, thus enabling to compare the overhead introduced by different design choices. "No monitor" is the base configuration, where neither the monitor or the emulation layer are enabled. In "P Emu" the emulation layer is enabled and deployed as component of the hypervisor. This benchmark is used to measure the overhead introduced by this layer, which can be potentially removed at the cost of modifying the Linux kernel. In "P Emu + P Mon" both the monitor and the emulation layer are deployed as privileged software inside the hypervisor. Finally, in "P Emu + U Mon" the monitor is executed as unprivileged guest.

7 Related Work

Since a comprehensive verification of commodity SW is not possible, it is necessary to architect systems so that the trusted computing base for the desired properties is small enough to be verified, and that the untrusted code cannot affect the security properties. Specialized HW (e.g. TrustZone and TPM) has been proposed to support this approach and has been used to implement secure storage and attestation. The availability of platforms like hypervisors and microkernels extended the adoption of this approach to use cases that go beyond the ones that can be handled using static HW based solutions.

For example, in [8] the authors use the seL4 microkernel to implement a secure access controller (SAC) with the purpose of connecting one front-end terminal to either of two back-end networks one at a time. The authors delegate the complex (and non security critical) functionalities (e.g. IP/TCP routing, WEB front-end) to untrusted Linuxes, which are isolated by the microkernel from a small and trusted router manager. The authors describe how the system's information flow properties can be verified disregarding the behavior of the untrusted Linuxes.

Here, we used the trustworthy components to help the insecure Linux to restrict its own attack surface; i.e. to prevent binary code injection. Practically, our proposal uses Virtual Machine Introspection (VMI), which has been first introduced by Garfinkel et al. [1] and Chen et al. [4]. Similarly to MProsper, other proposals (including Livewire [1], VMWatcher [7] and Patagonix [13]) use VMI, code signing and executable space protection to prevent binary code injection in commodity OSs. However, all existing proposals rely on untrusted hypervisors and their designs have not been subject of formal verification.

Among others non trustworthy VMIs, hytux [10], SecVisor [18] and NICKLE [16] focus on protecting integrity of the sole guest kernel. SecVisor establishes a trusted channel with the user, which must manually confirm all changes to the kernel. NICKLE uses a *shadow memory* to keep copy of authenticated modules and guarantees that any instruction fetch by the kernel is routed to this memory.

OpenBSD 3.3 has been one of the first OS enforcing executable space protection ($W \oplus X$). Similarly, Linux (with the PaX and Exec Shield patches), NetBSD and Microsoft's OSs (using Data Execution Prevention (DEP)) enforce the same policy. However, we argue that due to the size of the modern kernels, trustworthy executable space protection can not be achieved without the external support of a trusted computing base. In fact, an attacker targeting the kernel can circumvent the protection mechanism, for example using *return-oriented programming* [20]. The importance of enforcing executable space protection from a privileged point of view (i.e. by VMI) is also exemplified by [12]. Here, the authors used model checking techniques to identify several misbehaviors of the Linux kernel that violate the desired property.

8 Concluding Remarks

We presented a trustworthy code injection prevention system for Linux on embedded devices. The monitor's trustworthiness is based on two main principles (i) the trustworthy hypervisor guarantees the monitor's tamper resistance and that all memory operations that modify the memory layout are mediated, (ii) the formal verification of design demonstrates that the top security goal is guaranteed by the run-time checks executed by the monitor. These are distinguishing features of MProsper, since it is the first time that absence of binary code injection has been verified for a commodity OS.

Even if the MProsper's formal model is not yet at the level of the actual binary code executed on the machine, this verification effort is important to validate the monitor design; in fact we were able to spot security issues that were not dependent on the specific implementation of the monitor. The high level model of the monitor is actually a state transition model of the implemented code, operating on the actual ARMv7 machine state. Thus the verified properties can be transferred to the actual implementation by using standard refinement techniques (e.g. [19]).

Our ongoing work include the development of a end-to-end secure infrastructure, where an administrator can remotely update the software of an embedded device. Moreover, we are experimenting with other run-time binary analysis techniques that go beyond code signature checking: for example an anti-virus scanner can be integrated with the monitor, enabling to intercept and stop self-decrypting malwares.

Acknowledgments. Work supported by framework grant "IT 2010" from the Swedish Foundation for Strategic Research, and a project grant from Ericsson AB through the KTH ACCESS Linnaeus Excellence Centre.

References

1. Azmandian, F., Moffie, M., Alshawabkeh, M., Dy, J., Aslam, J., Kaeli, D.: Virtual machine monitor-based lightweight intrusion detection. SIGOPS Oper. Syst. Rev. **45**(2), 38–53 (2011)
2. Balliu, M., Dam, M., Guanciale, R.: Automating information flow analysis of low level code. In: Proceedings of the 2014 ACM SIGSAC Conference on Computer and Communications Security, pp. 1080–1091. ACM (2014)
3. Barham, P., Dragovic, B., Fraser, K., Hand, S., Harris, T., Ho, A., Neugebauer, R., Pratt, I., Warfield, A.: Xen and the art of virtualization. ACM SIGOPS Oper. Syst. Rev. **37**(5), 164–177 (2003)
4. Chen, P.M., Noble, B.D.: When virtual is better than real. In: Proceedings of the Eighth Workshop on Hot Topics in Operating Systems, HOTOS 2001, Washington, DC, USA, pp. 133–2001. IEEE Computer Society (2001)
5. Dam, M., Guanciale, R., Khakpour, N., Nemati, H., Schwarz, O.: Formal verification of information flow security for a simple ARM-based separation kernel. In: Proceedings of the 2013 ACM SIGSAC Conference on Computer and Communications Security, pp. 223–234. ACM (2013)
6. Fox, A., Myreen, M.O.: A trustworthy monadic formalization of the ARMv7 instruction set architecture. In: Kaufmann, M., Paulson, L.C. (eds.) ITP 2010. LNCS, vol. 6172, pp. 243–258. Springer, Heidelberg (2010)
7. Jiang, X., Wang, X., Xu, D.: Stealthy malware detection through vmm-based "out-of-the-box" semantic view reconstruction. In: Proceedings of the 14th ACM Conference on Computer and Communications Security, CCS 2007, New York, NY, USA, pp. 128–138. ACM (2007)
8. Klein, G.: From a verified kernel towards verified systems. In: Ueda, K. (ed.) APLAS 2010. LNCS, vol. 6461, pp. 21–33. Springer, Heidelberg (2010)
9. Klein, G., Elphinstone, K., Heiser, G., Andronick, J., Cock, D., Derrin, P., Elkaduwe, D., Engelhardt, K., Kolanski, R., Norrish, M., Sewell, T., Tuch, H., Winwood, S.: seL4: formal verification of an OS kernel. In: Proceedings of SOSP 2009, pp. 207–220. ACM (2009)
10. Lacombe, E., Nicomette, V., Deswarte, Y.: Enforcing kernel constraints by hardware-assisted virtualization. J. Comput. Virol. **7**(1), 1–21 (2011)
11. Leinenbach, D., Santen, T.: Verifying the Microsoft Hyper-V hypervisor with VCC. In: Cavalcanti, A., Dams, D.R. (eds.) FM 2009. LNCS, vol. 5850, pp. 806–809. Springer, Heidelberg (2009)
12. Liakh, S., Grace, M., Jiang, X.: Analyzing and improving Linux kernel memory protection: a model checking approach. In: Proceedings of the 26th Annual Computer Security Applications Conference, pp. 271–280. ACM (2010)
13. Litty, L., Lagar-Cavilla, H.A., Lie, D.: Hypervisor support for identifying covertly executing binaries. In: USENIX Security Symposium, pp. 243–258 (2008)
14. Nemati, H., Guanciale, R., Dam, M.: Trustworthy virtualization of the ARMv7 memory subsystem. In: Italiano, G.F., Margaria-Steffen, T., Pokorný, J., Quisquater, J.-J., Wattenhofer, R. (eds.) SOFSEM 2015-Testing. LNCS, vol. 8939, pp. 578–589. Springer, Heidelberg (2015)

15. Richards, R.: Modeling and security analysis of a commercial real-time operating system kernel. In: Hardin, D.S. (ed.) Design and Verification of Microprocessor Systems for High-Assurance Applications, pp. 301–322. Springer, Heidelberg (2010)

16. Riley, R., Jiang, X., Xu, D.: Guest-transparent prevention of kernel rootkits with VMM-based memory shadowing. In: Lippmann, R., Kirda, E., Trachtenberg, A. (eds.) RAID 2008. LNCS, vol. 5230, pp. 1–20. Springer, Heidelberg (2008)

17. Sehr, D., Muth, R., Biffle, C., Khimenko, V., Pasko, E., Schimpf, K., Yee, B., Chen, B.: Adapting software fault isolation to contemporary CPU architectures. In: USENIX Security Symposium, pp. 1–12 (2010)

18. Seshadri, A., Luk, M., Qu, N., Perrig, A.: SecVisor: a tiny hypervisor to provide lifetime kernel code integrity for commodity OSes. In: Proceedings of Twenty-first ACM SIGOPS Symposium on Operating Systems Principles, SOSP 2007, New York, NY, USA, pp. 335–350. ACM (2007)

19. Sewell, T.A.L., Myreen, M.O., Klein, G.: Translation validation for a verified OS kernel. ACM SIGPLAN Not. 48(6), 471–482 (2013)

20. Shacham, H.: The geometry of innocent flesh on the bone: return-into-libc without function calls (on the x86). In: Proceedings of the 14th ACM Conference on Computer and Communications Security, CCS 2007, New York, NY, USA, pp. 552–561. ACM (2007)

Practical Memory Deduplication Attacks in Sandboxed Javascript

Daniel Gruss[(⊠)], David Bidner, and Stefan Mangard

Graz University of Technology, Graz, Austria
daniel.gruss@iaik.tugraz.at

Abstract. Page deduplication is a mechanism to reduce the memory footprint of a system. Identical physical pages are identified across borders of virtual machines and programs and merged by the operating system or the hypervisor. However, this enables side-channel information leakage through cache or memory access time. Therefore, it is considered harmful in public clouds today, but it is still considered safe to use in a private environment, i.e., private clouds, personal computers, and smartphones.

We present the first memory-disclosure attack in sandboxed Javascript which exploits page deduplication. Unlike previous attacks, our attack does not require the victim to execute an adversary's program, but simply to open a website which contains the adversary's Javascript code. We are not only able to determine which applications are running, but also specific user activities, for instance, whether the user has specific websites currently opened. The attack works on servers, personal computers and smartphones, and across the borders of virtual machines.

Keywords: Memory deduplication · Side-channel attack · Javascript-based attack · Website fingerprinting

1 Introduction

Software-based timing attacks are side-channel attacks which exploit differences in the execution time to derive secret values used during the computation. These timing differences arise from the attacked software itself, different memory types or optimizations implemented in modern computers. For instance, cache attacks exploit the timing difference between a cache access and a memory access caused by a cache miss. An attacker process can measure whether a victim process has evicted one of the attacker's cache lines [13] or whether a victim program has reloaded a cache line the attacker previously evicted from the cache [5,20].

A similar timing difference can be observed between a regular memory access and a pagefault. Upon a pagefault, the operating system loads the data to the given location in virtual memory and returns control to the process. Apart from the difference in the memory access time, pagefault handling is transparent to the user process. This timing difference can be exploited to build a covert channel [17].

© Springer International Publishing Switzerland 2015
G. Pernul et al. (Eds.): ESORICS 2015, Part I, LNCS 9326, pp. 108–122, 2015.
DOI: 10.1007/978-3-319-24174-6_6

Suzaki et al. [16] presented page-deduplication attacks, which enable an attacker on the same physical machine, to determine whether specific programs are running, even across the borders of virtual machines. This is possible, because identical physical pages are merged by the operating system or the hypervisor. After a page is merged write accesses to this page cause a pagefault which is then resolved by the operating system. The timing difference the pagefault causes can be observed by the attacker program. Thus, the attacker learns that somewhere on the same physical machine another instance of this page exists.

JavaScript-based timing attacks have first been described by Felten et al. [3]. They were able to identify recently visited websites if website elements are fetched from the local browser cache instead of the network. A similar attack has been presented by Bortz et al. [2]. More recently Stone [15] presented attacks which exploit timing differences caused by the modification of HTML5 elements. Using their approach, an attacker is able to determine whether specific websites have been visited, and even read pixels from other websites.

In this paper, we present the first page-deduplication attack mounted in sandboxed Javascript. This allows a remote attacker to collect private information, such as whether a program or website is currently opened by a user. In contrast to existing Javascript-based timing attacks, we do not exploit any weaknesses in Javascript or the browser, but timing differences caused by optimizations in the operating system or hypervisor.

Javascript is a scripting language implemented in modern browsers to create interactive elements on websites. It is strictly sandboxed, so it is not possible to access files or system services. The language has no representation of pointers or the virtual address space layout, and less accurate timing information than native code. Oren et al. [12] already demonstrated in a Javascript-based cache attack that timer accuracy is high enough to distinguish cache hits from cache misses. Our attack is possible with less accurate timers, on a microsecond or millisecond basis.

To demonstrate the power of our attack, we show that we can accurately determine whether the user has opened specific websites. Our attack can be applied in a generic way to any system which employs page deduplication, independently of the CPU architecture and in particular independently of the CPU cache structure. This is a significant share of modern personal computers and smartphones.

With our attack, an adversary is not only able to perform the attack remotely through a website, on an arbitrary number of victims, but an adversary is also able to attack a variety of different devices in the same way. Thus, page-deduplication attacks no longer target one specific system, but instead target large numbers of internet users simultaneously. For instance, a website can detect which other websites a user has opened and thereby add more valuable information to user profiles. Furthermore, the attack causes negligible CPU and memory utilization and is thus, hard to detect if placed in a large Javascript framework.

We show that page deduplication must be considered a security threat on any system and not only on public cloud servers. Therefore, we conclude that the only effective countermeasure is to disable page deduplication.

Outline. The remaining paper is organized as follows. In Sect. 2, we provide background information on shared memory and page deduplication, as well as existing attacks. We describe the implementation of our attack in Sect. 3. In Sect. 4.1, we present the performance of our attack in a private cloud and in Sect. 4.2, we present results of our attack on personal computers and smartphones. We discuss countermeasures against page-deduplication attacks in Sect. 5. Finally, we conclude in Sect. 6.

2 Background

2.1 Shared Memory

Operating systems and hypervisors use shared memory to reduce physical memory utilization. Libraries which are used by several programs are loaded into physical memory only once, and are then shared among the processes using it. Thus, multiple programs access the same physical pages mapped within their own virtual address space.

The operating system makes use of shared memory in more cases. When forking a process, the memory is first shared between the parent process and the child process. As soon as one of the processes writes into the shared memory area, a copy-on-write page fault occurs and the operating system creates a copy of the according memory region. Note that write accesses into non-shared memory areas do not incur page faults and thus are significantly faster.

Shared memory is not only used when forking a process, but when starting instances of an already running program, or if a user program explicitly requests shared memory using system calls like `mmap` or `dlopen`. Mapping a file using one of these methods results in a memory region shared with all other proceses mapping the same file.

The form of shared memory we target in this paper is content-based page deduplication. The hypervisor or operating system scans the physical memory for pages with identical content. If identical pages are found, they are remapped to one of the pages, while the other pages are marked as free. Thus, memory is shared between completely unrelated and possibly sandboxed processes, and even between processes running in different virtual machines. If a process modifies its shared data, a copy-on-write page fault occurs and the hypervisor or operating system creates a copy of the memory region. Although searching for identical pages costs CPU time, page deduplication can increase the system performance, by reducing the number of block device accesses, as more data can be held in memory. Therefore, it is especially relevant in small systems like smartphones, besides the primary application in cloud systems.

2.2 Page-Deduplication Attacks

Page-deduplication attacks are a specific type of side-channel attacks, which exploit timing differences in write accesses on deduplicated pages. The first attack on page deduplication was presented by Suzaki et al. [16]. They were able to determine whether specific applications are running in a co-located virtual machine in the cloud. Furthermore, they described the possibility of building covert communication channels between virtual machines by exploiting page deduplication.

In the basic attack scheme, an attacker is able to run a spy program on the victim's system. However, the spy program may be sandboxed or even run in a virtual machine. The spy program fills a page with data it suspects to find in the memory of the victim machine. The hypervisor or operating system constantly deduplicates identical physical pages. When the spy program tries to write to the page again, it can measure the elapsed time and infer whether a copy-on-write page fault occurs or not. Thus, the attacker can determine whether some other process on the same physical machine has an identical page in memory. Such attacks can be performed on both, binary code and static data as well as dynamically generated data.

Owens et al. [14] demonstrated that it is possible to efficiently fingerprint operating systems in co-located virtual machines by exploiting page deduplication. Since then, covert channels based on page deduplication [18,19] have been constructed and evaluated.

At the same time, researchers were able to build more efficient cache attacks if attacker and victim process share memory [5]. Page deduplication introduces a way to share memory with a victim process in a co-located virtual machine in the cloud. The possibility of performing a cache attack on a victim process across virtual machine borders has first been described by Yarom et al. [20]. Since then, several page-deduplication-based cache attacks have been demonstrated [8,9].

3   Description of Our Javascript-Based Attack

Our attack follows the same methodology as the page-deduplication attack presented by Suzaki et al. [16], which was implemented in native code. As our attack is implemented in Javascript, we face several new challenges, such as setting the content of a whole page in physical memory or detecting whether and when page deduplication has occurred.

As described in Sect. 2.2, the first step of a page-deduplication attack is to fill a page with data we expect to find on the system under attack. In native code, this done by filling a page-aligned region in an array with the according data. We found that Javascript engines in common browsers (Firefox and Chrome) perform a call to their own internal `malloc` implementation when creating a large array in Javascript. As a means of optimization, these `malloc` implementations align large memory allocations to page borders. Therefore, creating and filling a large array in Javascript works as in native code, in terms of our attack.

The second step is to wait until the operating system or hypervisor deduplicates our array. In our attacker model, the adversary performs the attack through a website on every visitor. Therefore, we cannot make assumptions about how long it takes until page deduplication has been performed. Instead, we repeatedly write the same value to the same position on the target page and measure the time the write access took. We observed no influence of these repeated writes on whether the page is considered for deduplication. Thus, we can perform the deduplication check in a regular frequency.

The third step is the measurement of the write-access time, to infer whether a page has been deduplicated. This is done by measuring the time a write access on our own page takes. Based on the access time, we decide whether a copy-on-write page fault occurred. In native x86 code, we use the `rdtsc` assembly instruction for this purpose. In Javascript, we can use the function `performance.now()`. The accuracy of this function varies from sub-microsecond to millisecond range. If checking for deduplication of a single page in memory, our attack requires accurate microsecond measurements. However, usually more pages are attacked and thus less accurate timers are sufficient. For instance, when checking for deduplication of a 600 KB image, even an accurate millisecond-based timer can be used to implement our attack. Thus, `performance.now()` is sufficient to distinguish copy-on-write page faults from regular write accesses. Furthermore, `performance.now()` is available independently of the underlying hardware. Therefore, we can attack systems with a variety of different processors using the same Javascript code, such as personal computers or smartphones.

The only remaining question to perform our attack is how to know the data we want to fill the page with. Neither static code and data nor dynamically generated data is necessarily page-aligned. However, if the attacker knows the content of 8192 bytes contiguous in virtual memory, we can fill 4096 pages with data from these 8192 bytes, with every possible offset from the page alignment. Although this allows us to attack systems and programs with random offsets for the targeted data, we found that this is hardly necessary for most cases. For instance, we observed that images and CSS style sheets in websites are page-aligned in memory. This greatly facilitates our attack, as we can trivially extract the page content from a file and include it in our Javascript code.

The resulting attack applies to a wide range of scenarios, from mobile phone usage, over personal computers, to multi-tenant cloud systems. A user on a targeted system accesses a website, which contains the adversary's Javascript code. The Javascript code is then executed. After a few minutes, the Javascript code transmits the results back to the adversary. Our attack not only extracts sensitive information, like the browsing behavior of a user, but it is also extremely powerful due to its scalability. Once the Javascript code is deployed on a website, it automatically attacks anyone who accesses the website. We will demonstrate the attack in different scenarios in the following section.

4   Practical Attacks and Evaluation

In this section, we demonstrate our attack on a KVM-based private cloud server, on Windows 8 personal computers and finally on Android smartphones. In all scenarios, we use the same Javascript source code.

4.1   Cross-VM Attack on Private Clouds

Existing page-deduplication attacks have been demonstrated on public IaaS (Infrastructure-as-a-Service) cloud systems [16,18,19]. In this attack scenario, an adversary tries to be co-located on the same physical server with a targeted virtual machine. Once the adversary is co-located, the adversary extracts sensitive information from other virtual machines, e.g., whether vulnerable versions of specific server applications are running, or whether specific files are currently open.

Although public cloud providers reacted and now disable page deduplication in public IaaS clouds [7], we found that page deduplication is not yet considered a security problem on private cloud systems and servers. Popular Linux server distributions enable page deduplication, either by default, or automatically when reaching a certain memory usage level. For instance, we observed this behavior on Proxmox VE, Redhat Server and Ubuntu Server if configured as a KVM host.

Therefore, we demonstrate our attack in a private IaaS cloud. This is a realistic scenario, for instance in companies where users work on thin clients, connected to a virtual machine in the private IaaS cloud. In this scenario, a victim working in one virtual machine opens a website containing the malicious Javascript code, which is then continuously run in the background in a browser tab. Compared to existing attacks, our attack is possible even if the system does not allow users to start arbitrary programs, or if the user is well-educated to avoid executing programs from an untrusted origin. Furthermore, we want to emphasize that our attack is doubly sandboxed in this scenario, by running in the Javascript sandbox in the virtual machine separated from the targeted program in another virtual machine. That is, the adversary is able to extract sensitive information from the victim's virtual machine and other virtual machines on the same server.

The malicious Javascript code has to stay in memory until page deduplication has been performed. Depending on the system configuration, this can be between 30 sec and several hours. During our tests with 4 GB of physical memory and the default system configuration, we found that our memory is deduplicated after 3 min.

In order to evaluate the accuracy of our attack in Javascript code, we first perform the same attack in native x86 code. Figures 1 and 2 show write-access times on an array containing a 14 MB image file as measured by our native-code spy program within the same virtual machine, with low and high system load. This is equivalent to loading 3584 small images (2–4 KB) and measuring the deduplication of each of them. These write-access times quantify the accuracy of our page deduplication detection. When the image is loaded, we found no measurements to be lower than the expected copy-on-write access time. When having the image not loaded in the browser, we found less than 0.1 % of the measurements to be significantly above the expected regular write-access time. These 0.1 % can lead to false positive copy-on-write detection. However, as there is a timing difference of at least a factor of 10^3, we found an even smaller number of peaks to be above the lowest copy-on-write access times. We subsequently tested our attack using native code in the cross-VM setting and achieved the

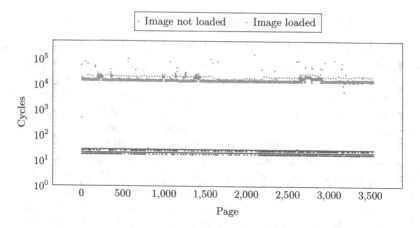

Fig. 1. Timings measured in native code on an otherwise idle Linux KVM virtual machine. The graph shows write-access times on an array containing an image file.

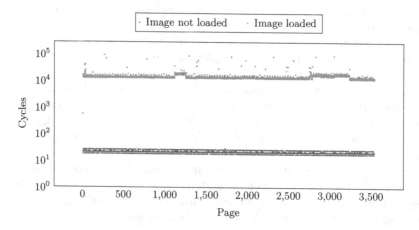

Fig. 2. Timings measured in native code on a Linux KVM virtual machine under high CPU load. The graph shows write-access times on an array containing an image file.

same accuracy. Therefore, we can accurately determine whether an image has been deduplicated and thus, has been loaded by a user.

Subsequently, we measured the performance of our Javascript-based attack. In Figs. 3 and 4, the write-access times on an array containing the same 14 MB image file are shown, but this time measured by our Javascript spy program. Even in with full system load and the browser under attack running in a different virtual machine, page deduplication was detected correctly in all of our measurements. However, in contrast to the native-code implementation of our spy program, we found up to 0.3 % of the pages to be falsely detected as deduplicated when having low system load and 1.1 % on average when having a high system load.

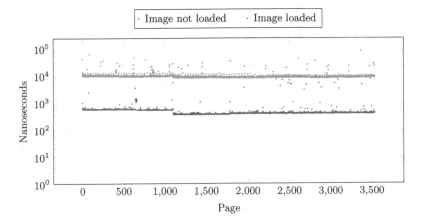

Fig. 3. Timings measured in Javascript on an otherwise idle Linux KVM virtual machine. The graph shows write-access times on an array containing an image file.

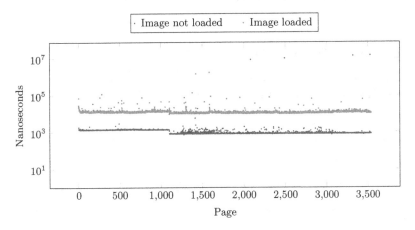

Fig. 4. Timings measured in Javascript on a Linux KVM virtual machine under high CPU load. The graph shows write-access times on an array containing an image file.

We performed this attack on recent versions of the most commonly used browsers, Chrome 40 and Firefox 31. As both browsers load the image file to a page-aligned location in memory, the attack works in exactly the same way and gives the same results for both browsers. Furthermore, we performed the same attack on a browser in a different virtual machine. Even in this setting, we did not find more false positives, and all deduplicated pages were detected successfully.

In order to demonstrate our attack on a real-world scenario, we determine the websites currently opened by a user. In this scenario, the adversary creates arrays containing image data of the websites to detect on the targeted machine. For demonstration purposes, we examined the 10 most-visited websites [1] and chose an image or style sheet file from each website, to determine whether it is currently open in a web browser on the same machine. Furthermore, we generate several pages filled with zeros and several pages filled with random data, to measure reference timings for deduplicated and non-deduplicated pages. When the operating system or hypervisor has tried to deduplicate our pages, the zero-filled pages will have high write-access times, as they are deduplicated. The random-filled pages still have low write-access times, as each random-filled page is unique in the system and therefore not deduplicated. Some websites only contain very small or very few images. In these cases we combine several images to perform the attack more reliably. In all cases we had at least 24 KB of data to measure deduplication.

Figure 5 shows the write-access times to arrays containing image data from these websites, as well as the zero-filled pages and random-filled pages. We can clearly see which websites are currently opened in the browser, because of the higher write-access times, due to the copy-on-write page-fault handling. Based on such measurements, an adversary is able to spy on users' browsing behavior through malicious Javascript code, even across browsers and virtual machine borders.

4.2   Attack on Personal Computers and Smartphones

Our attack is even more precise if performed on a personal computer or smartphone, as the device under attack is only used by a single user at a time. There-

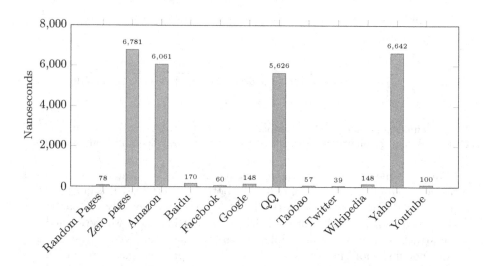

Fig. 5. Write-access times measured in Javascript inside a Linux KVM virtual machine, for images from frequented websites as well as random-filled an zero-filled pages. We measured high access times only for the currently opened websites: Amazon, QQ, Taobao, Wikipedia and Yahoo.

fore, we can create accurate profiles of single users. As in the cross-VM attack, the victim merely needs to access a website containing the malicious Javascript code.

This scenario is not only very simple and realistic, but moreover, it has a huge impact, as it can be applied to popular operating systems like Windows 8 on personal computers, or Android on smartphones. Windows 8 and 8.1 have a market share of around 15 % [11] on personal computers and have page deduplication enabled by default [10]. Android has a market share of 81.5 % [6] on smartphones, but it is device-specific whether page deduplication is enabled by default or not. However, Google recommends [4] that manufacturers enable page deduplication by default on memory-constrained devices, and many manufacturers follow this recommendation. Therefore, we assume that the number of smartphones having page deduplication enabled, and thus vulnerable to this attack, is significant.

In our attack, the malicious Javascript code runs continuously in the background in a browser tab. We found that on our Windows 8.1 test machine, page deduplication has been performed after 15 min on average. On our Android 4.4.4 test device, page deduplication has been performed after 45 min on average. As in the cloud scenario, we can then detect running applications and which specific version of an application is running, or even detect which specific websites are opened by a user. To evaluate the side channel, we again measure the deduplication detection rate for an image loaded in a browser. As we encountered problems with browsers on smartphones loading the 14 MB image file, we now use a 2 MB image file. This is equivalent to performing the same test with 512 small images (2–4 KB).

Figure 6 shows our Javascript-based measurements for the image file, using Firefox 36 on Windows. We can detect page deduplication almost as reliably as in the private-cloud scenario, with less than 2 % false positives. We are able to perform the attack without changes in Internet Explorer 11 and Firefox 36 on Windows, as both return micro- or nanosecond accurate timings via the `window.performance.now()` function. However, Chrome 41 on Windows only allows measuring time in milliseconds. Thus, we cannot measure the timing difference for each single page. Instead, we have to measure the time over a large number of pages at once. When measuring time over 150 write accesses at once, we are able to distinguish whether these 150 pages were deduplicated or not, with only millisecond timer accuracy.

When targeting website usage as a real-world scenario, the adversary creates arrays containing image data of the websites to detect on the targeted machine. As in the private-cloud scenario, we examined the 10 most-visited websites [1]. Figure 7 shows the write-access times to arrays containing image data from these websites, as well as the zero-filled pages and random-filled pages. Again, we clearly see which websites are opened, based on the higher write-access time.

When attacking Android smartphones, we found that although it takes up to one hour until deduplication is performed, the accuracy is not much worse than in the other scenarios we tested. We measured up to 0.8 % of false positives when having the image file not loaded in a browser and up to 0.5 % false negatives when having the image file loaded in a browser. This is slightly less accurate than

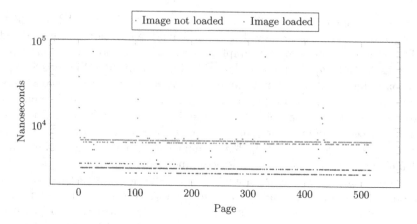

Fig. 6. Timings measured in Javascript on Windows 8.1. The graph shows write-access times on an array containing an image file.

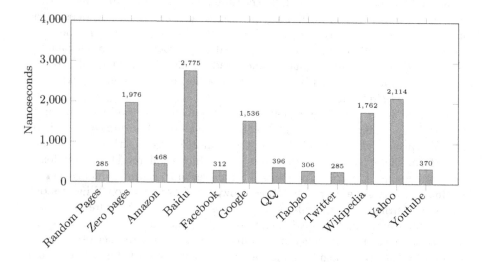

Fig. 7. Write-access times measured in Javascript on Windows 8.1, for images from frequented websites as well as random an zero-filled pages. We measured high access times only for the currently opened websites: Baidu, Google, Wikipedia and Yahoo.

in the other scenarios. Figure 8 shows the timing difference with and without the image loaded by a browser. Again, we examined the 10 most-visited websites [1]. Figure 9 shows the write-access times to arrays containing image data from these websites, as well as the zero-filled pages and random-filled pages. As in all other scenarios, we also see on Android which websites are opened, based on the higher write-access time.

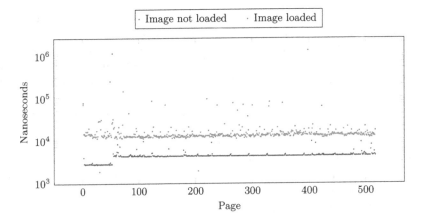

Fig. 8. Timings measured in Javascript on Android 4.4.4. The graph shows write-access times on an array containing an image file.

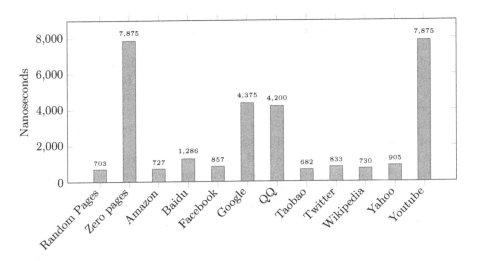

Fig. 9. Write-access times measured in Javascript on Android 4.4.4, for images from frequented websites as well as random an zero-filled pages. We measured high access times only for the currently opened websites: Google, QQ and Youtube.

5   Countermeasures

Our attack shows that even in sandboxed Javascript code, an adversary is able to extract significant sensitive information from real-world applications if the underlying system employs page deduplication. Our specific attack can be prevented on application level, i.e., in the browser executing the adversary's code, or in the applications under attack. However, countermeasures on this level incur limitation of functionality. Disabling page deduplication is the only generic effective countermeasure against page-deduplication attacks.

It is possible prevent or at least weaken our specific attack in Javascript runtime environments by changing the way data is stored in memory, reducing the accuracy of timers, or disabling Javascript execution for untrusted code completely.

Our attack benefits from the fact that we are able to allocate page-sized physically contiguous memory areas. Thus, we are able to define the value of each byte on a physical page. Javascript engines could prevent this by adding small offsets to array indices, so that a few bytes per page cannot be controlled by the attacker. Consequently, the attacker-controlled memory will not be deduplicated. This would cause a small performance impact while impeding page-deduplication attacks in Javascript.

Another optimization we exploit is page alignment of large data, like images, as performed by modern web browsers. However, adding a random offset to the page alignment would not prevent our attack. The adversary can create 4096 copies of a targeted page, and thereby perform the same attack with only a small overhead. Furthermore, such a countermeasure would require manual modification of existing software, and would incur a performance penalty at the same time.

Oren et al. [12] suggested reducing the accuracy of Javascript timers as a countermeasure against Javascript-based cache attacks. However, a reduced timer accuracy would not prevent our attack. It is easily possible to measure the timing over a large number of pages and thereby invoke several copy-on-write page faults, resulting in timing differences in a millisecond range, which can be detected even with coarse-grained timers.

Our attack could also be prevented by disabling the execution of untrusted Javascript, i.e., disables Javascript on websites completely. However, this imposes a significant drawback on functionality of modern browsers and websites. In any case, the attack is still possible if implemented in a browser plugin or smartphone application, where Javascript-level countermeasures do not apply.

However, we think that any form of content-based page deduplication implies a security problem. As writable pages can be generated in any script language, sandboxed or not, and furthermore, we only require coarse-grained timer accuracy, we consider it insecure to perform page deduplication on writable pages. Considering only read-only pages has already been suggested by Suzaki et al. [16] as a countermeasure. Apparently, this countermeasure has not been implemented on the systems we attacked. We assume that one of the reasons is that the hypervisor or operating system is not able to distinguish between read-only pages and writable pages within virtual machines, one of the core applications of page deduplication.

However, not considering writeable pages would prevent page-deduplication attacks in Javascript or other script languages which do not support read-only data. Still, even in case that only read-only pages are merged, an attack could still be possible through browser plugins or smartphone applications on code and static data of targeted binaries, as they are able to load read-only pages or even execute native code. Thus, disabling page deduplication completely is the only way to effectively prevent page-deduplication attacks as presented in this paper.

6   Conclusion

In this paper, we presented the first page-deduplication attack in sandboxed Javascript. In particular, the attack can be launched from any website. We show how the attack can be used to determine whether specific images or websites are currently opened by a user. We demonstrated the attack on private clouds, personal computers and smartphones. In all scenarios, it is even possible to mount the attack across the borders of virtual machines. Thus, we conclude that page deduplication must always be considered vulnerable to attacks as presented in this paper. Systems which have page deduplication enabled cannot be considered secure anymore.

The fact that page-deduplication attacks can be launched through websites marks a paradigm shift, from a targeted attack on a specific system towards large-scale practical attacks launched on a huge number of devices simultaneously. Therefore, we strongly recommend to disable page deduplication.

Acknowledgments.

 The research leading to these results has received funding from the European Union's Horizon 2020 research and innovation programme under grant agreement No 644052 (HECTOR).

Furthermore, this work has been supported by the Austrian Research Promotion Agency (FFG) and the Styrian Business Promotion Agency (SFG) under grant number 836628 (SeCoS).

References

1. Alexa Internet Inc: The top 500 sites on the web, March 2015. http://www.alexa.com/topsites
2. Bortz, A., Boneh, D.: Exposing private information by timing web applications. In: Williamson, C.L., Zurko, M.E., Patel-Schneider, P.F., Shenoy, P.J. (eds.) Proceedings of the 16th International Conference on World Wide Web, WWW 2007, Banff, Alberta, Canada, May 8–12, 2007. pp. 621–628. ACM (2007). http://doi.acm.org/10.1145/1242572.1242656
3. Felten, E.W., Schneider, M.A.: Timing attacks on web privacy. In: Gritzalis, D., Jajodia, S., Samarati, P. (eds.) CCS 2000, Proceedings of the 7th ACM Conference on Computer and Communications Security, Athens, Greece, November 1–4, 2000, pp. 25–32. ACM (2000). http://doi.acm.org/10.1145/352600.352606
4. Google Inc.: Android 4.4 platform optimizations. https://source.android.com/devices/tech/low-ram.html (Feb 2015)
5. Gullasch, D., Bangerter, E., Krenn, S.: Cache Games - Bringing Access-Based Cache Attacks on AES to Practice. In: IEEE Symposium on Security and Privacy - S&P, pp. 490–505. IEEE Computer Society (2011). http://dx.doi.org/10.1109/SP.2011.22

6. International Data Corporation: Android and iOS Squeeze the Competition, February 2015. http://www.idc.com/getdoc.jsp?containerId=prUS25450615

7. Irazoqui, G., Eisenbarth, T., Sunar, B.: Jackpot - Stealing Information From Large Caches via Huge Pages. IACR Cryptology, p. 970, ePrint Archive 2014 (2014). http://eprint.iacr.org/2014/970

8. Irazoqui, G., Inci, M.S., Eisenbarth, T., Sunar, B.: Fine grain Cross-VM Attacks on Xen and VMware are possible! IACR Cryptology, p. 248, ePrint Archive 2014 (2014). http://eprint.iacr.org/2014/248

9. Irazoqui, G., Inci, M.S., Eisenbarth, T., Sunar, B.: Wait a minute! a fast, cross-VM attack on AES. In: Stavrou, A., Bos, H., Portokalidis, G. (eds.) RAID 2014. LNCS, vol. 8688, pp. 299–319. Springer, Heidelberg (2014)

10. Karagounis, B., Sinofsky, S.: Reducing runtime memory in Windows 8, October 2011. http://blogs.msdn.com/b/b8/archive/2011/10/07/reducing-runtime-memory-in-windows-8.aspx

11. Net Applications.com: Desktop Operating System Market Share, February 2015. http://www.netmarketshare.com/operating-system-market-share.aspx

12. Oren, Y., Kemerlis, V.P., Sethumadhavan, S., Keromytis, A.D.: The Spy in the Sandbox - Practical Cache Attacks in Javascript. ArXiv e-prints, February 2015

13. Osvik, D.A., Shamir, A., Tromer, E.: Cache attacks and countermeasures: the case of AES. In: Pointcheval, D. (ed.) CT-RSA 2006. LNCS, vol. 3860, pp. 1–20. Springer, Heidelberg (2006)

14. Owens, R., Wang, W.: Non-Interactive OS Fingerprinting Through Memory De-Duplication Technique in Virtual Machines. In: International Performance Computing and Communications Conference - IPCCC, pp. 1–8. IEEE (2011). http://dx.doi.org/10.1109/PCCC.2011.6108094

15. Stone, P.: Pixel Perfect Timing Attacks with HTML5. Technical report, Context Information Security, June 2013. http://www.contextis.com/files/Browser_Timing_Attacks.pdf

16. Suzaki, K., Iijima, K., Yagi, T., Artho, C.: Memory Deduplication as a Threat to the Guest OS. In: European Workshop on System Security - EUROSEC, pp. 1–6. ACM (2011). http://doi.acm.org/10.1145/1972551.1972552

17. Warner, A., Li, Q., Keefe, T.F., Pal, S.: The impact of multilevel security on database buffer management. In: Martella, G., Kurth, H., Montolivo, E., Bertino, Elisa (eds.) ESORICS 1996. LNCS, vol. 1146. Springer, Heidelberg (1996). http://dx.doi.org/10.1007/978-3-319-11379-1_15

18. Xiao, J., Xu, Z., Huang, H., Wang, H.: A covert channel construction in a virtualized environment. In: Yu, T., Danezis, G., Gligor, V.D. (eds.) the ACM Conference on Computer and Communications Security, CCS 2012, Raleigh, NC, USA, October 16–18, 2012, pp. 1040–1042. ACM (2012). http://doi.acm.org/10.1145/2382196.2382318

19. Xiao, J., Xu, Z., Huang, H., Wang, H.: Security implications of memory deduplication in a virtualized environment. In: 2013 43rd Annual IEEE/IFIP International Conference on Dependable Systems and Networks (DSN), Budapest, Hungary, June 24–27, 2013, pp. 1–12. IEEE (2013). http://doi.ieeecomputersociety.org/10.1109/DSN.2013.6575349

20. Yarom, Y., Falkner, K.: FLUSH+RELOAD: A High Resolution, Low Noise, L3 Cache Side-Channel Attack. In: USENIX Security Symposium, pp. 719–732. USENIX Association (2014). https://www.usenix.org/conference/usenixsecurity14/technical-sessions/presentation/yarom

Cryptography

Computational Soundness
for Interactive Primitives

Michael Backes, Esfandiar Mohammadi, and Tim Ruffing$^{(\boxtimes)}$

CISPA, Saarland University, Saarbrücken, Germany
{backes,mohammadi}@cs.uni-saarland.de, tim.ruffing@mmci.uni-saarland.de

Abstract. We present a generic computational soundness result for interactive cryptographic primitives. Our abstraction of interactive primitives leverages the Universal Composability (UC) framework, and thereby offers strong composability properties for our computational soundness result: given a computationally sound Dolev-Yao model for non-interactive primitives, and given UC-secure interactive primitives, we obtain computational soundness for the combined model that encompasses both the non-interactive and the interactive primitives. Our generic result is formulated in the CoSP framework for computational soundness proofs and supports any equivalence property expressible in CoSP such as strong secrecy and anonymity.

In a case study, we extend an existing computational soundness result by UC-secure blind signatures. We obtain computational soundness for blind signatures in uniform bi-processes in the applied π-calculus. This enables us to verify the untraceability of Chaum's payment protocol in ProVerif in a computationally sound manner.

1 Introduction

Manual security analyses of cryptographic protocols are complex and error-prone. As a result, various automated verification techniques have been developed based on so-called Dolev-Yao models, which abstract cryptographic operations as symbolic terms obeying simple cancellation rules [12,26,35,36,38,40]. Numerous verification tools such as ProVerif [12] and APTE [26] are capable of reasoning about equivalence properties, e.g., strong secrecy and anonymity.

A wide range of these Dolev-Yao models is computationally sound, i.e., the security of a symbolically abstracted protocol entails the security of a suitable cryptographic realization [3,7,14,20,27,29,31,50,52]. However, virtually all of these computational soundness results are inherently restricted to non-interactive primitives such as encryption and signatures.

In contrast, *interactive cryptographic primitives* such as interactive zero-knowledge proofs [43], forward-secure key exchange [37], and blind signatures [25], have gained tremendous attention in the scientific community and widespread deployment in real systems.

The security of interactive primitives is often defined and established in the Universal Composability (UC) framework [17] or similar frameworks [8,44,48],

© Springer International Publishing Switzerland 2015
G. Pernul et al. (Eds.): ESORICS 2015, Part I, LNCS 9326, pp. 125–145, 2015.
DOI: 10.1007/978-3-319-24174-6_7

which allow to prove strong security guarantees in a *composable* manner [23, 24, 41]. In such frameworks, a primitive is secure if its execution is indistinguishable from a setting in which all parties have a private connection to an imaginary trusted machine, called *ideal functionality*, which performs the desired task locally and in a trustworthy manner.

For interactive primitives, ideal functionalities are a suitable abstraction, but for non-interactive primitives, DY-style abstractions have two significant advantages compared to a corresponding abstraction as an ideal functionality (e.g., for encryption schemes or digital signatures): first, as Dolev-Yao models do not incorporate shared memory, the verification of concurrent processes that use Dolev-Yao models is far more efficient, and second, the attacker is purely defined by symbolic rules and is thus much better suited for automatically deriving desired properties such as invariants. There is a rich literature on computationally sound DY-style abstractions. For example, Backes et al. introduced CoSP, a general framework for computational soundness proofs [3], which decouples the treatment of the Dolev-Yao model from the treatment of the language, e.g., the applied π-calculus or RCF. Proving x cryptographic Dolev-Yao models sound for y languages only requires $x + y$ proofs (instead of $x \cdot y$).

Previous work on computational soundness of verification tools for ideal functionalities [47] does not apply to protocols that combine interactive and non-interactive primitives with such computationally sound DY-style abstractions. In this work, we address this gap.

Contribution. We present a generic computational soundness (CS) result for UC-secure interactive primitives. Given a computationally sound Dolev-Yao model for non-interactive primitives and given UC-secure interactive primitives, we show the combined CS for the non-interactive *and* the interactive primitives. This allows us to handle protocols that combine interactive primitives with non-interactive primitives, e.g., protocols that encrypt blind signatures, or protocols that use interactive zero-knowledge proofs about ciphertexts. Our generic method is compatible with any CS result for non-interactive primitives that is cast in the CoSP framework for equivalence properties [6].

In a case study, we apply our method to a recent CS result [6]. We obtain the combined CS for (non-interactive) ordinary signatures and (interactive) blind signatures. The underlying CS result for non-interactive primitives supports uniform bi-protocols, i.e., protocol pairs that always take the same branches and differ only in the messages that they operate on. Consequently, our case study supports uniform bi-processes in the applied π-calculus. Finally, we conduct a computationally sound verification of the untraceability of Chaum's payment protocol [25] in ProVerif.

Remark on Supported Equivalence Properties. The aforementioned CS result [6] is so far the only result established in the CoSP framework for equivalence properties, and is limited to uniform bi-processes. As a result, it is unclear whether a larger class of equivalence properties can be expressed within the existing CoSP framework at all. Thus it is unclear whether our generic result could possibly apply to a larger class of equivalence properties, even though we believe that our core ideas do not fundamentally rely on the specifics of the CoSP framework. The underlying problem is caused by the current embeddings of languages (such as the applied π-calculus) into CoSP. These embeddings do not provide a satisfying solution for concurrency, because they give the attacker full control over the scheduling of even internal scheduling decisions such as the scheduling of concurrent processes. Yet, CS results established with our generic method cover any equivalence properties covered by the underlying CS result for non-interactive primitives. Our work shares this limitation with other state-of-the-art CS results for equivalence properties [27–29].

Overview. To facilitate understanding, we give a brief overview of the proof strategy taken in the paper. Typical CS results for non-interactive primitives ($NIPs$) state that the security of a protocol in a symbolic Dolev-Yao setting DY implies the security of the protocol in a computational setting, where real cryptographic algorithms are used instead of DY-style constructors and destructors (Fig. 1a).

Our proof strategy contains *two* computational settings: one setting with a computational ideal functionality $\mathcal{F}$ and one setting with its UC-secure cryptographic realization IP. For the sake of illustration, we start by explaining our approach with only a single interactive primitive (Fig. 1b).

(i) We transform the computational ideal functionality $\mathcal{F}$ to the symbolic setting by incorporating it into a Dolev-Yao model DY.
(ii) We show CS for the Dolev-Yao model with respect to the ideal functionality $\mathcal{F}$, which lives in the computational setting.
(iii) Under the assumption that IP is a UC-secure cryptographic realization of $\mathcal{F}$, we show CS for the Dolev-Yao model DY with respect to the cryptographic realization IP of the interactive primitive.

Next, we consider the setting of the paper (Fig. 1c). It consists of cryptographic realizations $IP_1, \ldots, IP_n$ of several interactive primitives and additionally of a set of cryptographic realizations $NIPs$ of several non-interactive primitives.

(i) We transform the computational ideal functionalities $\mathcal{F}_1, \ldots, \mathcal{F}_n$ to the symbolic setting by incorporating them into Dolev-Yao models $DY_1, \ldots, DY_n$ (Sect. 5).
(ii) We then consider a unified model $(DY_1, \ldots, DY_n, DY_{NIP_s})$ that consists of the Dolev-Yao models for the interactive primitives as well as a single Dolev-Yao model DY_{NIP_s} that incorporates a set of non-interactive primitives. Under the assumption that DY_{NIP_s} is computationally sound with respect to the cryptographic realizations NIP_s, we show CS for the unified Dolev-Yao model with respect to the algorithms $(\mathcal{F}_1, \ldots, \mathcal{F}_n, NIP_s)$, i.e., with respect to the ideal functionalities plus the cryptographic realizations for the non-interactive primitives (Sect. 6).
(iii) Under the assumption that $IP_1, \ldots, IP_n$ are UC-secure realizations of $\mathcal{F}_1, \ldots, \mathcal{F}_n$, we show CS for the unified Dolev-Yao model with respect to the cryptographic realizations $(IP_1, \ldots, IP_n, NIP_s)$ (Sect. 8).

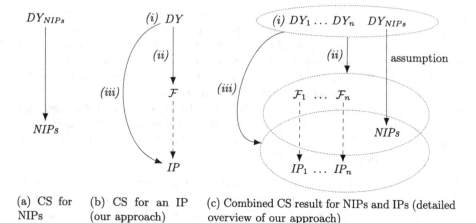

(a) CS for NIPs   (b) CS for an IP (our approach)   (c) Combined CS result for NIPs and IPs (detailed overview of our approach)

Fig. 1. An overview over different types of CS results for non-interactive primitives (NIPs) and interactive primitives (IPs). Solid arrows represent computational soundness. Dashed arrows represent UC-security.

2   Related Work

There is a successful line of research for computational soundness of trace properties [10,27,36,39] such as authentication and for static equivalence properties (i.e., against passive attackers) [2,11,45].

For equivalence properties against active attackers, however, there are only few previous results. The simulatable DY-style library of Backes et al. [4,7] was the first result to show computational soundness against active attackers and for equivalence properties on payloads. For this DY-style library it is not known how to formalize more properties than the secrecy of payloads.

Cortier and Comon-Lundh [27] show computational soundness for observational equivalence for symmetric encryption in the applied π-calculus. The scope of their work is incomparable to our work: their result is restricted to processes that do not contain private channels and abort if a conditional fails, whereas our result is restricted to uniform bi-processes.

An alternative approach to secure abstractions has recently been proposed by Bana and Comon-Lundh [9,10]. Instead of prescribing what an attacker can do and showing that no deviating computational behavior is possible, they pursue the approach to define what is impossible for an attacker (e.g., break the encryption) as first-order logic formulas over symbolic representations. Then, they specify the protocol in question and the existence of a potential attack in the same symbolic model. In their framework, inconsistency of a set of axioms implies security of the protocol. An inherent problem with this style of abstraction is the verification: it is not amenable to general-purpose DY-style verification tools, e.g., ProVerif [12] or Tarmarin [49].

With regard to the composability of computational soundness, Böhl et al. [14] show how a computational soundness result that has been obtained via deduction soundness [32] can be extended to hash functions, MACs, signatures, and symmetric and asymmetric encryption. While they add a set of non-interactive primitives to a given computational soundness result, we add a set of interactive primitives to a given computational soundness result.

There is other work that leverages the strength of the UC framework. Backes et al. [5] prove a computational soundness result for SMPC that is parametric in the same way as our result. However, their result considers only trace properties and is specific to SMPC. Canetti and Herzog [20], extended by Canetti and Gajek [19], show computational soundness for UC-secure key exchange protocols and signatures. There are two major differences to our work. First, their result is specific to the used primitives, while our result can be used for a large class of UC-secure interactive primitives. Second, even though their result holds for equivalence properties, the authors—in contrast to our work—do not show that their result can be combined with computationally sound Dolev-Yao models for non-interactive primitives.

Dahl and Damgård [33] show the computational soundness of a certain class of two-party protocols with respect to UC security, i.e., symbolic security implies computational UC security. While they use the UC framework to obtain strong, composable computational security for protocols that use certain non-interactive primitives, we use the UC framework to obtain ordinary, non-composable computational security for protocols that use UC-secure interactive primitives.

Küsters et al. [46] and Küsters et al. [47] leverage non-interference techniques for ideal functionalities in Java programs. While their method is capable of covering a large class of protocols and interactive primitives, it does not encompass DY-style abstractions of non-interactive primitives such as encryption. Thus, they have to represent all non-interactive primitives as ideal functionalities. Since the abstraction that uses ideal functionalities inherently contains shared memory between protocol parties, automated verification techniques are forced to deal with numerous interleaving runs and the verification costs significantly increase with the number of ideal functionalities. We show that UC-secure ideal functionalities of interactive primitives can be combined with computationally sound DY-style abstractions of non-interactive primitives, thereby minimizing the amount of ideal functionalities.

Fournet et al. [42] show computational soundness for the refinement type system F7 (and later F*) by relying on ideal functionalities as abstraction. The required type annotations serve as local invariants and make the verification feasible, even with shared memory and many interleaving runs. First steps have been undertaken towards automated type inference [53] for the type annotations; however, the automation is incomplete and still requires a significant amount of human interaction. As the type system is for the computational setting (against a computational attacker), automated type derivation is inherently harder than in a symbolic setting (against a symbolic attacker).

Delaune et al. [34] and Böhl and Unruh [15] transfer simulation-based security completely into the symbolic setting, including symbolic composition theorems. However, these results do not guarantee computational soundness.

3   Review of the CoSP Framework for Equivalence

We review the CoSP framework for equivalence properties [6], in which we cast our computational soundness result.

Symbolic Model. In CoSP, symbolic abstractions of protocols and of the attacker are formulated in a symbolic model $\mathbf{M} = (\mathbf{C}, \mathbf{N}, \mathbf{T}, \mathbf{D})$: a set of free functions $\mathbf{C}$, an infinite set $\mathbf{N}$ of nonces, a set $\mathbf{T}$ of terms (formed by constructors and nonces), and a set $\mathbf{D}$ of destructors, i.e., partial functions from terms to terms.

Protocols. Protocols are represented as infinite trees with the following nodes: *computation nodes* are used for drawing fresh nonces and applying constructors and destructors; *input nodes* and *output nodes* are used for sending and receiving terms; *control nodes* are used for allowing the attacker to schedule the protocol. A computation node is annotated with its arguments and has two outgoing edges: a yes-edge, used for the application of constructors, for drawing a nonce, and for the successful application of a constructor or destructor, and a no-edge, used for the failed application of a constructor or destructor. Nodes have explicit *references* to other nodes whose terms they use.

Symbolic Operations. We model the capabilities of the symbolic attacker as operations that the attacker can perform on protocol messages. A *symbolic operation* is a finite tree, whose nodes are labeled with constructors, destructors, nonces from the symbolic model $\mathbf{M}$, or pointers to messages that the protocol has sent to the attacker. There is a natural evaluation function $eval_O$ that evaluates a symbolic operation O in a bottom-up fashion on a list of terms, resulting in a term or the error symbol $\bot$.

Symbolic Execution. A *symbolic execution* is a path through a protocol tree. Formally, a symbolic execution of a protocol Π is a (finite) list of triples (V_i, ν_i, f_i) as follows. Initially, we have $V_1 = \varepsilon$, ν_1 is the root of Π, and f_1 is an empty partial function mapping node identifiers to terms. For every two consecutive tuples (V, ν, f) and (V', ν', f') in the list, let $\tilde{\nu}$ be the nodes referenced by ν and define $\underline{\tilde{t}}$ through $\tilde{t}_j := f(\tilde{\nu}_j)$. Figure 2 depicts a case distinction over ν for defining valid successors V', ν', and f'. Each V_i is called *symbolic view.*

Given a view V, V_{Out} is the list of terms t contained in $(\mathtt{out}, t) \in V$. $V_{Out\text{-}Meta}$ is the list of terms l contained in $(\mathtt{control}, (l, l')) \in V$. V_{In} (the *attacker strategy*) is the list of terms that contains only entries of V of the form $(\mathtt{in}, (*, O))$ or $(\mathtt{control}, (*, l'))$, and the first term has been masked with the symbol $*$.

```
switch ν with
    case computation node with constructor, destructor or nonce F
        if m := F(t̃) ≠ ⊥ then
            V' := V; ν' := the yes-successor of ν; f' := f(ν := m)
        else
            V' := V; ν' := the no-successor of ν; f' := f
    case input node
        if there is a term t ∈ T and a symbolic operation O on M with eval_O(V_Out) = t then
            ν' := the successor of ν; V' := V :: (in, (t, O)); f' := f(ν := t)
    case output node
        ν' := the successor of ν; V' := V :: (out, t̃₁); f' := f
    case control node with out-metadata l
        ν' := the successor of ν with some in-metadata l'
        f' := f; V' := V :: (control, (l, l'))
```

Fig. 2. Symbolic execution

Symbolic Knowledge and Equivalent Views. The *symbolic knowledge* of the attacker comprises the results of all the symbolic operations that the attacker can perform on messages output by the protocol. Given a view V, the *symbolic knowledge* K_V is a function from symbolic operations on $\mathbf{M}$ of arity $|V_{Out}|$ to $\{\top, \bot\}$, where $\top$ unifies all results of $eval_O(V_{Out})$ that are not $\bot$.

Two views are *equivalent* if they *(i)* have the same structure (i.e., the same order of out, in, and control entries), *(ii)* have the same out-metadata (i.e., $V_{Out\text{-}Meta} = V'_{Out\text{-}Meta}$), and *(iii)* lead to the same knowledge (i.e., $K_V = K_{V'}$).

Symbolic Indistinguishability. Finally, we define two protocols to be *symbolically indistinguishable* if the two protocols lead to equivalent views when faced with the same attacker strategy.

Computational Implementation. On the computational side, the constructors and destructors in a symbolic model are realized with cryptographic algorithms, which we call *computational implementations*. A computational implementation is a family $\mathbf{A} = (A_x)_{x \in \mathbf{C} \cup \mathbf{D} \cup \mathbf{N_P}}$ of deterministic polynomial-time algorithms $\mathbf{A}_F$ for each constructor or destructor $F \in \mathbf{C} \cup \mathbf{D}$ well as a probabilistic polynomial-time (ppt) algorithm A_N for drawing protocol nonces $N \in \mathbf{N}$.

Computational Execution. The *computational execution* of a protocol is the interaction between a ppt machine called the *computational challenger* and a ppt attacker $\mathcal{A}$. The transcript of the execution contains the computational counterparts of a symbolic execution. The computational challenger traverses the protocol tree and interacts with the attacker: at a computation node the corresponding algorithm is run and depending on whether the algorithm succeeds or outputs $\bot$, either the yes-branch or the no-branch is taken; at an output node, the message is sent to the attacker; at an input node a message is received by the attacker; and at a control node the attacker is asked which edge to take.

Computational Indistinguishability. The CoSP framework for indistinguishability properties [6] uses *termination-insensitive computational indistinguishability* [54] (tic-indistinguishability) to capture that two protocols are computationally indistinguishable. In comparison to the standard notion of indistinguishability, tic-indistinguishability does not require the interactive machines to be polynomial-time; instead, it only considers decisions that were made for polynomially-bounded prefixes of the interaction.

Given two machines A, B and a polynomial p, we write $\Pr[\langle A|B \rangle \Downarrow_{p(k)} x]$ for the probability that the interaction between A and B terminates within $p(k)$ steps and B outputs x.

Two machines A and B are *tic-indistinguishable* [54] *for a machine* $\mathcal{A}$ ($A \approx_{tic}^{\mathcal{A}} B$) if for all p, there is a negligible function μ such that for all $z, a, b \in \{0,1\}^*$ with $a \neq b$, $\Pr[\langle A(k)|\mathcal{A}(k,z)\rangle \Downarrow_{p(k)} a] + \Pr[\langle B(k)|\mathcal{A}(k,z)\rangle \Downarrow_{p(k)} b] \leq 1 + \mu(k)$. Here, z represents an auxiliary string. We call A and B *tic-indistinguishable* ($A \approx_{tic} B$) if $A \approx_{tic}^{\mathcal{A}} B$ for all ppt machines $\mathcal{A}$.

We define a pair of protocols to be *computationally indistinguishable* if the corresponding challengers are tic-indistinguishable. With the previously introduced notions, we define *computational soundness*, which states that symbolic indistinguishability implies computational indistinguishability.

Definition 1 (Computational Soundness). *Let a symbolic model* **M** *and a class* P *of efficient protocols be given. A computational implementation* **A** *of* **M** *is* computationally sound *for* **M** *if every pair of protocols in* P *is computationally indistinguishable whenever it is symbolically indistinguishable.*

4   Review of the UC Framework

We briefly review the UC framework [17], as we use it to establish our computational soundness result. The UC framework is designed to enable a modular analysis of security protocols. In this framework, the security of a protocol ϕ is defined by comparing the protocol with a setting in which all parties have a private connection to a trusted machine $\mathcal{F}$, called *ideal functionality*, which performs the desired protocol task locally. The ideal functionality $\mathcal{F}$ serves as an abstraction of this task. A protocol ϕ *UC-realizes* an ideal functionality $\mathcal{F}$ if for all ppt machines $\mathcal{A}$ (the *attacker*) there is a ppt machine $\mathcal{S}$ (the *simulator*) such that no ppt machine $\mathcal{Z}$ (the *environment*) can distinguish an interaction with ϕ and $\mathcal{A}$ from an interaction with $\mathcal{F}$ and $\mathcal{S}$. The environment is connected to the protocol and the attacker in the real setting or to the functionality and the simulator in the ideal setting.

Each machine M has two different input tapes. First, it has a *subroutine input tape*, which is used when another machine M', e.g., the environment $\mathcal{Z}$, calls them as a local subroutine. Second, each machine has a *network tape*, which is connected to the attacker $\mathcal{A}$ or the simulator $\mathcal{S}$.

The order in which computations are performed in UC is as follows. The execution starts with the environment $\mathcal{Z}$. Its execution pauses whenever it writes a message to an input tape of another machine M'. At this point, M' is activated and runs until M', in turn, writes a message to a tape of another machine M''.

5   Ideal Functionalities in the Symbolic Model

We abstract interactive primitives in the symbolic model as ideal functionalities. As a simple example, consider two parties A and B running an interactive key exchange. For example in the applied π-calculus, this is modeled as three parallel processes $A \mid P \mid B$, where P is the symbolic key exchange abstraction that generates a fresh key and sends it to both parties on private channels.

Formalizing Ideal Functionalities. An ideal functionality $\mathcal{F}$ in CoSP is symbolically abstracted as a CoSP protocol with only computation nodes; it will serve as a subroutine in another protocol. Technically, $\mathcal{F}$ excepts five parameters *state, sid, sender, input,* and *rand* as input. Since destructors and algorithms in CoSP are stateless as opposed to machines in UC, we model the state explicitly by the first parameter. A message sent to $\mathcal{F}$ is modeled by the parameters *sender* and *input*, where *sender* represents an identifier of the sending party and *input* the contents. If the message comes from the attacker, *sender* is *null()*. The *sid* parameter gives $\mathcal{F}$ access to its session id. The last parameter *rand* is a fresh randomness for $\mathcal{F}$.

For the output, $\mathcal{F}$ contains *result nodes*. They indicate the end of an invocation of $\mathcal{F}$, and the messages computed by the reached result nodes encode $\mathcal{F}$'s output.

Ideal Functionalities in the Symbolic Model. An ideal functionality yields a potentially complex destructor $D_{\mathcal{F}}$ with the same behavior as the symbolic operation. To combine ideal functionalities for interactive primitives with Dolev-Yao models for non-interactive primitives, we formulate the aforementioned process P, which models the ideal task, essentially as an application of the destructor $D_{\mathcal{F}}$.

An application of the destructor corresponds to a message sent to the UC machine implementing the ideal functionality. This allows a CoSP protocol to use the ideal functionality like a subroutine (as in the UC framework).

Definition 2 (Ideal Destructor). *Let* $\mathbf{F}$ *be an ideal model (a set of ideal functionalities) based on the symbolic model* $\mathbf{M} = (\mathbf{C}, \mathbf{N}, \mathbf{T}, \mathbf{D})$, *and let* $\mathcal{F} \in \mathbf{F}$.
The ideal destructor of $\mathcal{F}$ *is a destructor* $D_{\mathcal{F}} : \mathbf{T}^5 \to \mathbf{T}$ *with* $(t_{state}, t_{sid}, t_{sender}, t_{input}, t_{rand}) \mapsto t_{res}$. *Here* t_{res} *is the term produced by the reached result node in the symbolic execution of* $\mathcal{F}$ *with parameters* $t_{state}, t_{sid}, t_{sender}, t_{input}, t_{rand}$.

Extended Symbolic Model. Given destructors $D_{\mathcal{F}}$ for $\mathcal{F} \in \mathbf{F}$ and a symbolic model $\mathbf{M} = (\mathbf{C}, \mathbf{N}, \mathbf{T}, \mathbf{D})$ (for non-interaction primitives), the *extended symbolic model* is $\mathbf{M_F} := (\mathbf{C}, \mathbf{N}, \mathbf{T}, \mathbf{D_F})$ where $\mathbf{D_F} := \mathbf{D} \cup \{D_{\mathcal{F}}/5 \mid \mathcal{F} \in \mathbf{F}\}$.

6   Ideal Functionalities in the Computational Model

As a first step to prove computational soundness, we explain how to leverage existing computational soundness results for non-interactive primitives. The formulation of $\mathcal{F}$ as a destructor $D_{\mathcal{F}}$ enables us to consider an ideal computational execution, in which $D_{\mathcal{F}}$ is implemented by a computational variant (called *the canonical algorithm*) $A_{\mathcal{F}}$ of $\mathcal{F}$.

Definition 3 (Canonical Algorithm). *Let an extended symbolic model $\mathbf{M_F}$ based on $\mathbf{M}$ and a computational implementation $\mathbf{A}$ of $\mathbf{M}$ be given. The canonical algorithm of $\mathcal{F}$ is the algorithm $A_{\mathcal{F}} : \mathbb{N} \times (\{0,1\}^*)^5 \rightarrow \{0,1\}^*$ with $(b_{state}, b_{sid}, b_{sender}, b_{input}, b_{rand}) \mapsto b_{res}$. It runs the an unbounded variant of the computational execution of $\mathcal{F}$ and stops if the first reached result node is reached. (An attacker is not involved, because $\mathcal{F}$ contains only computation nodes.) The output b_{res} is the bitstring computed by the that node. The first argument of $A_{\mathcal{F}}$ represents the security parameter and the other arguments determine the inputs.*

Ideal Implementations. Recall that we extend a symbolic model $\mathbf{M}$ by ideal destructors $D_{\mathcal{F}}$, resulting in a new symbolic model $\mathbf{M_F}$. Analogously, we extend a computational implementation $\mathbf{A}$ for $\mathbf{M}$ by the canonical algorithms $A_{\mathcal{F}}$, given that each $A_{\mathcal{F}}$ is computable in polynomial-time. Writing $A_{\mathcal{F}}$ instead of $A_{D_{\mathcal{F}}}$, the resulting *ideal implementation* $\mathbf{A_F} := (A_x)_{x \in \mathbf{C} \cup \mathbf{D_F} \cup \mathbf{N}}$ implements $\mathbf{M_F}$.

Computational Soundness for the Ideal Functionalities. Assume we have a computational soundness result for the implementations of non-interactive primitives (e.g., A_{enc} and A_{dec}). That is, the Dolev-Yao model without the special destructor $D_{\mathcal{F}}$ (only consisting of *enc* and *dec*) is computational sound. Then we can show that also the Dolev-Yao model *with* the destructor $D_{\mathcal{F}}$ is computationally sound given that $D_{\mathcal{F}}$ is implemented by $A_{\mathcal{F}}$.

The following lemma states the computational soundness of the ideal functionalities, which are ideal implementations in the computational model. To establish the lemma, we need some natural *protocol conditions* (Appendix A). They ensure *(i)* that inputs and outputs of the ideal functionalities are actually plugged to input and output nodes, *(ii)* that sessions and state are handled correctly and *(iii)*, that fresh randomness is provided for each call of the ideal functionality (the *rand* argument). Within a concrete symbolic calculus, syntactic criteria that imply the protocol conditions can be introduced.

Lemma 1 (Soundness of Ideal Implementations). *Let $\mathbf{M_F}$ be an extended symbolic model based on $\mathbf{M}$, and let $\mathbf{A}$ be a computationally sound implementation of $\mathbf{M}$ for protocols Π in a class of protocols P that fulfills the protocol conditions (Appendix A). Suppose that $\mathbf{M_F}$ has the ideal implementation $\mathbf{A_F}$. Suppose that for every $\Pi \in \mathrm{P}$, we have that the full protocol $\hat{\Pi}$ is in P.*

Then the ideal implementation $\mathbf{A_F}$ is computationally sound for $\mathbf{M_F}$ and P.

For the proof of the lemma (see the full version [30]), we construct a *full* protocol $\hat{\Pi}$ from Π by inlining the calls to ideal implementations: Each computation node ν with destructor $D_{\mathcal{F}}$ is replaced by the tree of the ideal functionality $\mathcal{F}$. The parameters of $\mathcal{F}$ are connected to the nodes referenced by ν and the subtree rooted at the yes-successor of ν is appended to every result node of $\mathcal{F}$. The proof basically uses the fact that the full protocol $\hat{\Pi}$ does not use any of the ideal destructors $D_{\mathcal{F}}$. Thus the computational soundness of $\mathbf{M}$ applies.

7 Real Protocols in CoSP

In the ideal computational execution, the interactive primitives are not implemented by their actual cryptographic realizations: while $A_{\mathcal{F}}$ is computational, it is merely an algorithmic representation of the ideal functionality $\mathcal{F}$. To close the gap to a real interactive protocol, we assume that there is a an interactive protocol ϕ that is a UC-secure realization of $\mathcal{F}$.

Formally, we define a *real algorithm* A_ϕ, which has the same interface as an algorithm $A_{\mathcal{F}}$, i.e., it takes bitstrings $b_{state_1}, b_{sid}, b_{sender}, b_{input}, b_{rand}$ as input and produces a triple $(b'_{state_1}, b_{receiver}, b_{output})$ of bitstrings as output.

The arguments directly correspond to the arguments of canonical algorithms of ideal functionalities, and the same intuition should be applied in general. In contrast to an ideal functionality however, there is no "joint state" between the participants of a real protocol. To enforce this statically, the state argument $state_1$ only represents the state of one single protocol party P.

Since the algorithms can output a state, each UC protocol can be reformulated as a real algorithm in our model. If we have a cryptographic realization for every $\mathcal{F}$ in an ideal model $\mathbf{F}$, we can extend a computational implementation $\mathbf{A}$ to a *real implementation* $\mathbf{A}_\Phi$. $\mathbf{A_F}$ and $\mathbf{A}_\Phi$ allow us to compare an ideal implementation of the interactive primitives with a real one, as in the UC framework.

To simplify notation, we write A_θ to denote an interactive algorithm that is either the canonical algorithm for an ideal functionality $\theta = \mathcal{F}$ or the algorithm for a real protocol $\theta = \phi$.

To make use of the UC framework, we first bring interactive algorithms to the UC setting by constructing machines in the UC sense from them. We write $\mu(\theta)$ for the machine that runs A_θ internally. It basically provides an interface to a computational CoSP execution that activates $\mu(\theta)$ whenever A_θ should be executed. In case that $\theta = \phi$ is a real algorithm, we require that $\mu(\theta)$ separates the state of distinct protocol parties. This models a real protocol execution as the parties can only communicate via the attacker.

8 Computational Soundness for Interactive Primitives

As a final step, we prove computational soundness for the interactive primitives. We leverage the composability of UC security: If the real protocol ϕ is a UC-secure realization of the ideal functionality $\mathcal{F}$, then instances of $\mathcal{F}$ used in a larger protocol can be replaced securely by instances of ϕ.

Using the UC framework, we would like to show an analogous result in our model: if the machine $\mu(\phi)$ is a UC-secure realization of $\mu(\mathcal{F})$, then instances of the canonical algorithm $A_{\mathcal{F}}$ used in a larger protocol can be replaced securely by instances of the real algorithm A_ϕ. Consequently, if $A_{\mathcal{F}}$ is a computational sound implementation of the destructor $D_{\mathcal{F}}$, then A_ϕ is a computational sound implementation of the destructor $D_{\mathcal{F}}$.

We require that the ideal functionality $\mathcal{F}$ and the real protocol ϕ adhere to few technical conditions. We explain why these conditions are necessary, what they exactly are, and why they do not constitute fundamental restrictions.

Problems. Our goal is to consider a UC environment $\mathcal{Z}$ that runs a computational CoSP execution but does not handle computation nodes with the destructor $D_{\mathcal{F}}$. Instead, this task should be delegated to a UC machine. For a interactive algorithm A_θ however, the standard machine $\mu(\theta)$ does not suffice for this purpose:

One problem stems from the fact that in the CoSP execution run by $\mathcal{Z}$, communication with the attacker happens only when an input or an output node is reached in the CoSP protocol. However, the machine $\mu(\theta)$ could just not adhere to this restriction and exchange messages with the attacker machine even if the CoSP execution run by $\mathcal{Z}$ does not currently process an input or an output node.

The second problem concerns only the ideal setting, and consists of a lack of information of the environment $\mathcal{Z}$. The CoSP view output by the environment must contain the communication between $\mathcal{F}$ and the simulator $\mathcal{S}$, but this communication is not visible for $\mathcal{Z}$ in UC. In fact, $\mu(\mathcal{F})$ and $\mathcal{S}$ can exchange arbitrary messages without even noticed by $\mathcal{Z}$.

To understand why this second problem does not arise in the real setting, consider w.l.o.g. the dummy attacker $\mathcal{A}_d$ that will only relay communication between the environment $\mathcal{Z}$ and the machine $\mu(\phi)$.[1] Thus $\mathcal{Z}$ is informed about all communication between $\mu(\phi)$ and $\mathcal{A}_d$.

Technical Remedy. In the proof of our main theorem, we build a wrapper machine $\tilde{\mu}(\theta)$ around every machine $\mu(\theta)$. It reports to the environment $\mathcal{Z}$ that communication took place between $\mu(\theta)$ and the attacker, but not what communication. To ensure that the wrapper machine can be used instead, we assume that the ideal functionality $\mathcal{F}$ and the real protocol ϕ are *good*, i.e. we require them to adhere to one technical condition each. We describe the conditions here only informal. Exact definitions can be found in the full version [30].

Condition on the Ideal Functionality. The condition on the ideal functionality basically states that the simulator can force $\mu(\mathcal{F})$ to produce output to the environment. This helps in a situation where the real attacker sends a message to $\mu(\phi)$, which sends in turn a message m to the environment. In the ideal setting, the simulator must force $\mu(\mathcal{F})$ to send a message indistinguishable from m to the environment immediately, without replying to the simulator first, because such a reply would be reported to the environment by the wrapper machine $\tilde{\mu}(\mathcal{F})$.

Condition on the Real Protocol. The condition on the real protocol ensures that a message from the environment to $\mu(\phi)$ leads to a output message to the attacker immediately. Here the excluded situation is that the real protocol machine $\mu(\phi)$ answers a request from the environment immediately, whereas the ideal machine

---

[1] Canetti shows [17] that it suffices to prove security against a dummy attacker $\mathcal{A}_d$, which acts as proxy for the environment $\mathcal{Z}$.

$\mu(\mathcal{F})$ would have to talk to the simulator first, which is not possible without being reported to the environment by the wrapper machine $\tilde{\mu}(\mathcal{F})$.

Discussion. We stress that both the conditions for the ideal functionality and the conditions for the real protocol are rather technical requirements instead of severe restrictions. The conditions are fulfilled by virtually all natural interactive primitives such as blind signatures [41], zero-knowledge proofs [16], oblivious transfer [17], and secure function evaluation [17]. In some cases, a technical reformulation of the ideal functionality or the real protocol is necessary. For instance, a real protocol that provides access to its results via an request interface would violate our condition; however it can be formulated such that it reports the results to the environment without being asked.

Furthermore, the condition for the ideal functionality seems to exclude adaptive corruption models. The reason is that these models typically require the ideal functionality to report parts of its internal state corresponding to a corrupted party to the simulator, after the simulator decides to corrupt that party. Still, by modeling corruption in a slightly different but still natural manner, a reformulation is possible. We refer to the full version [30] for a detailed discussion.

The main cause for the two technical conditions is a discrepancy between the UC framework and the CoSP framework. We use the latter in order to leverage existing results [6]. As a result, we inherit the restrictions that stem from the way previous embeddings resolved non-deterministic choices, e.g., concurrent computations: the distinguisher has full control over all scheduling decisions of concurrent computations and is fully aware of the execution state with respect to control flow. As a consequence the distinguisher can observe that communication between the simulator and the ideal functionality takes place. This is in contrast to the UC framework, where the distinguisher (the environment) cannot observe this communication.

Main Result. The main theorem, which is proven in the full version [30], states that we can extend a computational soundness result for equivalence properties to a computational soundness result for interactive primitives that are soundly abstracted by ideal functionalities.

Theorem 1. *Let $\mathbf{M_F}$ be an extended symbolic model based on $\mathbf{M}$, and let $\mathbf{A}_{\Phi}$ be a computational implementation of $\mathbf{M_F}$ based on $\mathbf{A}$. Let P be a class of CoSP protocols such that every protocol in P fulfills the protocol conditions for interactive primitives (Appendix A). Suppose that every $\mathcal{F} \in \mathbf{F}$ is a good ideal functionality and every $\phi \in \Phi$ is a good real protocol (see the full version [30]). Suppose that for every ideal functionality $\mathcal{F} \in \mathbf{F}$ and the corresponding real protocol $\phi \in \Phi$, we have that $\mu(\phi)$ UC-realizes $\mu(\mathcal{F})$.*

If $\mathbf{A}$ is a computationally sound implementation of $\mathbf{M}$ for P with respect to equivalence properties, then $\mathbf{A}_{\Phi}$ is a computationally sound implementation of $\mathbf{M_F}$ for P with respect to equivalence properties.

Limitations. While our result can be used with a wide range of natural two-party and multi-party primitives in the UC framework, it comes with several limitations.

First, since UC security is a very strong notion, some interactive primitives cannot be achieved in the UC framework, or they can only achieved under additional assumptions, or they require less efficient protocols than under ordinary security definitions. For instance, zero-knowledge proofs and oblivious-transfer are impossible without additional assumptions [17,22]. However, these primitives are possible if a common reference string (CRS) and authenticated message transfer (e.g., using a public-key infrastructure) is assumed [17,18]. Another example is UC-secure key exchange, which is, depending on the formulation, strictly stronger than standard key exchange [21], and thus requires less efficient protocols. We refer to Canetti [17, 2005 revision] for a comprehensive overview over different primitives in the UC framework.

Second, our result cannot be used to abstract *non-interactive* primitives using the UC framework. (While such abstractions are not desirable for automated verification (see Sect. 2), they might be desirable to achieve composability.) The culprit is the condition for the real protocol. Recall that it imposes that the protocol does not immediately reply to the environment, i.e., to the caller. While this is a natural assumption for interactive primitives,[2] it is very unnatural for non-interactive primitives. Indeed, all meaningful "protocols" that realize ideal functionalities for public-key encryption and signatures proposed by Canetti [17] violate the condition that we impose upon real protocols, because they perform the cryptographic operation locally without network communication involving the attacker. However, we are not aware of any natural *interactive* protocol, which cannot be reformulated to adhere to the technical conditions outlined above.

9   Case Study: Untraceable Payments

Untraceable payments, proposed by Chaum [25], allow a payer to perform a payment to a payee, say a shop, via a bank. In Chaum's protocol, a payer basically buys a coupon, i.e., a signed random bitstring, such that the bank does not know the coupon. Then, the user can pay with this coupon at a shop, and the shop will check the validity of the coupon with the bank. As the main cryptographic tool for untraceable payments Chaum suggests *blind signatures*, which guarantee that the bank neither learns the message nor the signature while signing the message.

We verify the untraceability of the payments with the verification tool ProVerif [12] using a UC-secure abstraction of blind signatures by Fischlin [41]. Our computational soundness theorems entail that the result of ProVerif's verification carries over to the computational realization of untraceable payments.

---

[2] It is the very nature of interactive protocols that a message is sent on the network, i.e., the protocol activates the attacker, before it reports results to the caller.

Ideal Blind Signatures and Their Realization. Our ideal functionality $\mathcal{F}$ for blind signatures models a scenario with one bank BANK and n users USER$_i$. It consists of a setup phase and offers a signing oracle to the users. In the setup phase, the bank generates signature keys or receives them from the attacker. Then, the functionality distributes the verification keys to the bank BANK and all users.

Upon a signing request (Sign, sid, m, vk') from USER$_i$, the functionality for an honest USER$_i$ waits for the attacker to deliver the message, signs the message m using the stored signing key sk, and sends the result to USER$_i$. For a malicious USER$_i$, the ideal functionality $\mathcal{F}$ informs $\mathcal{A}$ about the message. Then it informs the bank that a signature is being requested.

Fischlin [41] showed the existence of a protocol that UC-realizes an ideal functionality for blind signatures under standard cryptographic assumptions. Our functionality differs in details from the one in [41]. Using Fischlin's construction ϕ, we can prove realization if we require that the signature scheme, used by the ideal functionality is unforgeable. The proof is essentially only a modification of the proof in [41], and can be found in the full version [30].

Computational Soundness of Signatures and Blind Signatures. We rely on a symbolic model $\mathbf{M}_{sig}$ for digital signatures. (It contains also public-key encryption, which we do not use). The model is computationally sound in CoSP for uniform bi-protocols with respect to a computational implementation $\mathbf{A}_{sig}$ [6]. The aforementioned ideal functionality $\mathcal{F}$ for blind signatures and its UC-secure realization ϕ yields a CoSP destructor $D_{\mathcal{F}}$ and a real implementation A_ϕ, respectively. Symbolically, we extend $\mathbf{M}_{sig}$ by $D_{\mathcal{F}}$, resulting in $\mathbf{M}_{sig,bsig}$. Computationally, we extend $\mathbf{A}_{sig}$ by A_ϕ, resulting in $\mathbf{A}_{sig,bsig}$. Finally, Theorem 1 and the computational soundness for signatures in uniform bi-processes in the applied π-calculus [6, Theorem 3] yield the computational soundness of our case study.

Theorem 2. *Let Q be an applied-π bi-process on the symbolic model $\mathbf{M}_{sig,bsig}$ that is randomness-safe [6] and fulfills the protocol conditions (Appendix A). If Q is uniform, then the computational bi-protocol corresponding to Q, which uses the computational implementation $\mathbf{A}_{sig,bsig}$, is computationally indistinguishable.*

Uniform Bi-protocols. We leverage a computational soundness result [6], which is restricted to uniform bi-protocols. Bi-protocols are pairs of protocols that always take the same branches and differ only in the messages that they operate on.

Uniform bi-protocols cannot express equivalence between protocols with processes of different structure. For example, consider a protocol Π_1 with a client process that sends some request to a server twice. If the requests are unlinkable to each other, then formally, the client process is equivalent to a protocol Π_2 with the parallel composition of two client processes that send one request each. However, Π_1 and Π_2 have different structure, i.e., they differ in more than the terms they operate on. Thus a uniform bi-protocol cannot model this unlinkability.

A uniform bi-process [13] in the applied π-calculus is the counterpart of a uniform bi-protocol in CoSP. A bi-process is a pair of processes that only differ in the terms they operate on. Formally, they contain expressions of the form *choice*[*a, b*], where *a* is used in the left process and *b* is used in the right one. A bi-process Q can only reduce if both its processes can reduce in the same way. We consider the variant of the applied π-calculus used for the original CoSP embedding [3]. The operational semantics is defined in terms of *structural equivalence* ($\equiv$) and *internal reduction* ($\rightarrow$); for a precise definition of the applied π-calculus, we refer to [12]. Formally, a bi-process Q in the applied π-calculus is *uniform* if left(Q) $\rightarrow R_{\text{left}}$ implies that $Q \rightarrow R$ for some bi-process R with left(R) $\equiv R_{\text{left}}$, and symmetrically for right(Q) $\rightarrow R_{\text{right}}$ with right(R) $\equiv R_{\text{right}}$.

Verifying Untraceability in ProVerif. ProVerif [12] is an automated verification tool that can prove the uniformity of bi-processes in the applied π-calculus [1]. We use a wrapper process (Fig. 3) in the applied π-calculus that enforces the protocol conditions from Appendix A.

This wrapper maintains the session identifier in a way that is compatible with UC, maintains the state of the ideal functionality, and offers an interface that is compatible with our computational soundness result for interactive primitives.

Model in ProVerif. We used ProVerif to model a small untraceable payment system with two payers and one payee, say a shop owner. We modeled the scenario in which the bank is compromised and two honest payers purchase coupons. Then, one of the payers uses the coupon, and the shop owner leaks the coupon to the bank by cashing it. We modeled the scenario as a process for the ideal functionality of blind signatures and one bi-process that models both the payers and the shop owner. Since we consider untraceability, the bank is not modeled explicitly, it is the attacker.

To help ProVerif terminate, we replaced the process that executes the very complex destructor $D_{\mathcal{F}}$ by an equivalent process consisting of a series of *let* and *if* commands. As there is no communication in the equivalent process, the modified protocol differs only in the fact that it offers more scheduling possibilities: the attacker can schedule other processes in the middle of the computation, which is not possible in the unmodified process with the atomic destructor $D_{\mathcal{F}}$. Thus any attack possible on the unmodified process is also possible on the modified one.

Our code [51] has about 200 lines of code. ProVerif proves uniformity within under a second on a machine with an Intel i7 CPU (2 GHz) and 4 GB RAM.

Even though the symbolic model $\mathbf{M}_{sig}$ includes a length function, we did not include the corresponding length destructor in the case study, because ProVerif does otherwise not terminate. Nevertheless, our verification is computationally sound, because the length functions in the underlying result [6] are only necessary to handle public-key encryption, which is not part of $\mathbf{M}_{sig}$ in our case study.

Formally, we present the following lemma, which can be useful beyond our case study when applying the result of [6]. The lemma states that we can ignore a destructor d in the symbolic analysis of a bi-protocol, if *(i)* d is not used in the bi-protocol and *(ii)* d can be simulated using other destructors and constructors.

Lemma 2. *Let* $\mathbf{M} = (C, \mathbf{N}, \mathbf{T}, \mathbf{D})$ *be a symbolic model. Consider the model* $\mathbf{M}' = (C, \mathbf{N}, \mathbf{T}, \mathbf{D}')$ *with* $\mathbf{D}' = \mathbf{D} \setminus \{d\}$. *Let* Π *be a bi-protocol on* $\mathbf{M}'$.

Assume there is a function simD with the following property: given any symbolic operation O_d in $\mathbf{M}$, and any view V, but only the symbolic knowledge $K_V^{\mathbf{M}'}$ of $\mathbf{M}'$, simD outputs a symbolic operation O_{simD} on $\mathbf{M}'$ that simulates d, i.e., $O_{simD}(\underline{t}) = d(O_d(\underline{t}))$ for all sequences of terms $\underline{t} \in \mathbf{T}^*$.

Then Π is indistinguishable in the symbolic model $\mathbf{M}$ if it is indistinguishable in the symbolic model $\mathbf{M}'$.

In the full version [30], we prove the lemma and give a function *SimLength* that simulates the destructor *"length"* used in [6].

Plugging everything together, the successful ProVerif verification, Theorem 2, and Lemma 2 prove for our case study bi-process that any realization adhering to the implementation conditions of $\mathbf{A}_{sig,bsig}$ [6] is computationally indistinguishable.

```
let functionalityWrapper_F =
  (* initialize *)
  in(initInputC_F, any_value);
  new attSessC; new protSessInC; new commonSessC;
  out(attC, attSessC);
  out(initOutputC_F, protSessInC);
  new stateC; new resC; new sid;
  (
    (* initialize state *)
    out(stateC, null())
  )
  |
  !(
    (
      (* receive from attacker *)
      in(attSessC, attInput);
      out(commonSessC, (attInput, attSessC))
    ) | (
      (* receive from protocol party *)
      in(protSessInC, (protInput, protParty));
      out(commonSessC, (protInput, protParty))
    ) | (
      (* handle both types of input *)
      in(commonSessC, (input, sender));
      in(stateC, state);
      new rand;
      (* execute ideal functionality *)
      let (state', (receiver, output)) =
        D_F(state, sid, input, sender, rand) in
      out(resC, (state',(receiver, output)))
    ) | (
      (* process outputs *)
      in(resC, (state', (receiver, output)));
      out(receiver, output);
      out(stateC, state')
    )
  )
).
```

Fig. 3. The wrapper for the ideal functionality

Acknowledgments. We thank the reviewers for their helpful and valuable comments. This work was supported by the German Ministry for Education and Research (BMBF) through funding for the Center for IT-Security, Privacy and Accountability (CISPA) and the German Universities Excellence Initiative.

A   Protocol Conditions

Given a CoSP protocol Π, consider the directed graph $ref(\Pi)$ which has the property that a node ν_s is successor of a node ν_p if and only if ν_p references ν_s in its annotations. It is a tree because nodes may only reference nodes which are on the path to the root in the protocol tree. For a node ν of Π, the *reference tree of ν* is the subtree of $ref(\Pi)$ which is rooted at ν and reachable from there. We say that a node ν *is determined* by a node ν' if on the path (through $ref(\Pi)$) from ν to ν' exclusive, every node has exactly one successor. The corresponding path is called *reference path to ν'*.

We require that the following criteria are met for for all ideal functionalities $\mathcal{F}$ and all computation nodes ν with a destructor $D_{\mathcal{F}}$.

1. We say that two interactive nodes *belong to the same session* if and only if one of them is contained in the reference tree of the *state* argument node of the other. Two interactive nodes with destructor $D_{\mathcal{F}} \in \mathbf{F}$ are required to be part of the same session if and only if they have the same *sid* argument node.
2. Let ν' be the bottom-most predecessor of ν that belongs to the same session, if any. Let be the output computed by ν' in a computational execution of the protocol. On the path from ν' to ν, there are the following nodes:
   - Three computation nodes ν_{state}, $\nu_{receiver}$ and ν_{output} which produce the bitstrings *state*, *receiver* and *output*, respectively. They are determined by ν'. Their reference paths to ν' contain only computation nodes and ν is in the yes-subtree of all these computation nodes.
   - If and only if in a computational execution of the protocol, the bitstring produced by $\nu_{receiver}$ is $A_{null}()$, an output node referencing ν_{output}.
3. The *state* argument of ν is ν_{state} or a computation node with constructor $null()$.
4. ν_{state} is not referenced by other nodes than ν.
5. The *sender* argument is a computation node with constructor *null* if and only if the *input* argument is an input node.
6. The *rand* argument of ν is a computation node ν_{rand} with nonce $N \in \mathbf{N}$. On a path trough ν_{rand}, there is no other computation node with nonce N. ν_{rand} is not referenced by other nodes than ν.

References

1. Abadi, M., Fournet, C.: Mobile values, new names, and secure communication. In: POPL 2001, pp. 104–115. ACM (2001)
2. Abadi, M., Baudet, M., Warinschi, B.: Guessing attacks and the computational soundness of static equivalence. In: Aceto, L., Ingólfsdóttir, A. (eds.) FOSSACS 2006. LNCS, vol. 3921, pp. 398–412. Springer, Heidelberg (2006)

3. Backes, M., Hofheinz, D., Unruh, D.: CoSP: a general framework for computational soundness proofs. In: CCS 2009, pp. 66–78. ACM (2009)
4. Backes, M., Laud, P.: Computationally sound secrecy proofs by mechanized flow analysis. In: CCS, pp. 370–379. ACM (2006)
5. Backes, M., Maffei, M., Mohammadi, E.: Computationally sound abstraction and verification of secure multi-party computations. In: FSTTCS 2010, pp. 352–363. Schloss Dagstuhl (2010)
6. Backes, M., Mohammadi, E., Ruffing, T.: Computational soundness results for ProVerif. In: Abadi, M., Kremer, S. (eds.) POST 2014. LNCS, vol. 8414, pp. 42–62. Springer, Heidelberg (2014)
7. Backes, M., Pfitzmann, B., Waidner, M.: A composable cryptographic library with nested operations (extended abstract). In: CCS 2003, pp. 220–230. ACM (2003)
8. Backes, M., Pfitzmann, B., Waidner, M.: The reactive simulatability (RSIM) framework for asynchronous systems. Inf. Comput. **205**(12), 1685–1720 (2007)
9. Bana, G., Comon-Lundh, H.: A computationally complete symbolic attacker for equivalence properties. In: CCS 2014, pp. 609–620 (2014)
10. Bana, G., Comon-Lundh, H.: Towards unconditional soundness: computationally complete symbolic attacker. In: Degano, P., Guttman, J.D. (eds.) POST 2012. LNCS, vol. 7215, pp. 189–208. Springer, Heidelberg (2012)
11. Baudet, M., Cortier, V., Kremer, S.: Computationally sound implementations of equational theories against passive adversaries. In: Caires, L., Italiano, G.F., Monteiro, L., Palamidessi, C., Yung, M. (eds.) ICALP 2005. LNCS, vol. 3580, pp. 652–663. Springer, Heidelberg (2005)
12. Blanchet, B., Abadi, M., Fournet, C.: Automated verification of selected equivalences for security protocols. In: LICS, pp. 331–340 (2005)
13. Blanchet, B., Fournet, C.: Automated verification of selected equivalences for security protocols. In: LICS 2005, pp. 331–340. IEEE (2005)
14. Böhl, F., Cortier, V., Warinschi, B.: Deduction soundness: prove one, get five for free. In: CCS 2013, pp. 1261–1272. ACM (2013)
15. Böhl, F., Unruh, D.: Symbolic universal composability. In: CSF 2013. IEEE (2013)
16. Camenisch, J., Krenn, S., Shoup, V.: A framework for practical universally composable zero-knowledge protocols. In: Lee, D.H., Wang, X. (eds.) ASIACRYPT 2011. LNCS, vol. 7073, pp. 449–467. Springer, Heidelberg (2011)
17. Canetti, R.: Universally Composable Security: A New Paradigm for Cryptographic Protocols. Full and revised version of FOCS 2001 paper. IACR ePrint Archive: 2000/067/20130717:020004 (2013)
18. Canetti, R., Fischlin, M.: Universally composable commitments. In: Kilian, J. (ed.) CRYPTO 2001. LNCS, vol. 2139, pp. 19–23. Springer, Heidelberg (2001)
19. Canetti, R., Gajek, S.: Universally Composable Symbolic Analysis of Diffie-Hellman based Key Exchange. IACR ePrint Archive: 2010/303 (2010)
20. Canetti, R., Herzog, J.: Universally composable symbolic security analysis. J. Cryptol. **24**(1), 83–147 (2011)
21. Canetti, R., Krawczyk, H.: Security analysis of IKE's signature-based key-exchange protocol. In: Yung, M. (ed.) CRYPTO 2002. LNCS, vol. 2442, pp. 143–161. Springer, Heidelberg (2002)
22. Canetti, R., Kushilevitz, E., Lindell, Y.: On the limitations of universally composable two-party computation without set-up assumptions. J. Cryptol. **19**(2), 68–86 (2003)
23. Canetti, R., Lindell, Y., Ostrovsky, R., Sahai, A.: Universally composable two-party and multi-party secure computation. In: STOC 2002, pp. 494–503. ACM (2002)

24. Chandran, N., Goyal, V., Sahai, A.: New constructions for UC secure computation using tamper-proof hardware. In: Smart, N. (ed.) EUROCRYPT 2008. LNCS, vol. 4965, pp. 545–562. Springer, Heidelberg (2008)

25. Chaum, D.: Blind Signatures for Untraceable Payments. In: CRYPTO 1982, pp. 199–203. Plenum Press (1982)

26. Cheval, V.: APTE: an algorithm for proving trace equivalence. In: Ábrahám, E., Havelund, K. (eds.) TACAS 2014. LNCS, vol. 8413, pp. 587–592. Springer, Heidelberg (2014)

27. Comon-Lundh, H., Cortier, V.: Computational Soundness of Observational Equivalence. In: CCS 2008, pp. 109–118. ACM (2008)

28. Comon-Lundh, H., Cortier, V., Scerri, G.: Security proof with dishonest keys. In: Degano, P., Guttman, J.D. (eds.) POST 2012. LNCS, vol. 7215, pp. 149–168. Springer, Heidelberg (2012)

29. Comon-Lundh, H., Hagiya, M., Kawamoto, Y., Sakurada, H.: Computational soundness of indistinguishability properties without computable parsing. In: Ryan, M.D., Smyth, B., Wang, G. (eds.) ISPEC 2012. LNCS, vol. 7232, pp. 63–79. Springer, Heidelberg (2012)

30. Computational Soundness for Interactive Primitives (full version of this paper). https://www.infsec.cs.uni-saarland.de/~mohammadi/interactive.html

31. Cortier, V., Kremer, S., Küsters, R., Warinschi, B.: Computationally sound symbolic secrecy in the presence of hash functions. In: Arun-Kumar, S., Garg, N. (eds.) FSTTCS 2006. LNCS, vol. 4337, pp. 176–187. Springer, Heidelberg (2006)

32. Cortier, V., Warinschi, B.: A Composable Computational Soundness Notion. In: CCS 2011, pp. 63–74. ACM (2011)

33. Dahl, M., Damgård, I.: Universally composable symbolic analysis for two-party protocols based on homomorphic encryption. In: Nguyen, P.Q., Oswald, E. (eds.) EUROCRYPT 2014. LNCS, vol. 8441, pp. 695–712. Springer, Heidelberg (2014)

34. Delaune, S., Kremer, S., Pereira, O.: Simulation based security in the applied Pi calculus. In: FSTTCS 2009, pp. 169–180. Schloss Dagstuhl (2009)

35. Delaune, S., Kremer, S., Ryan, M.: Verifying privacy-type properties of electronic voting protocols. J. Comput. Secur. 17(4), 435–487 (2009)

36. Delaune, S., Kremer, S., Ryan, M.D., Steel, G.: Formal analysis of protocols based on TPM state registers. In: CSF, pp. 66–80. IEEE (2011)

37. Diffie, W., Van Oorschot, P.C., Wiener, M.J.: Authentication and authenticated key exchanges. Des. Codes Crypt. 2(2), 107–125 (1992)

38. Dolev, D., Yao, A.C.: On the security of public key protocols. IEEE Trans. Inf. Theory 29(2), 198–208 (1983)

39. Dougherty, D.J., Guttman, J.D.: An algebra for symbolic Diffie-Hellman protocol analysis. In: Palamidessi, C., Ryan, M.D. (eds.) TGC 2012. LNCS, vol. 8191, pp. 164–181. Springer, Heidelberg (2013)

40. Even, S., Goldreich, O.: On the security of multi-party ping-pong protocols. In: FOCS 1983, pp. 34–39. IEEE (1983)

41. Fischlin, M.: Round-optimal composable blind signatures in the common reference string model. In: Dwork, C. (ed.) CRYPTO 2006. LNCS, vol. 4117, pp. 60–77. Springer, Heidelberg (2006)

42. Fournet, C., Kohlweiss, M., Strub, P.-Y.: Modular code-based cryptographic verification. In: CCS 2011, pp. 341–350. ACM (2011)

43. Goldwasser, S., Micali, S., Rackoff, C.: The knowledge complexity of interactive proof systems. SIAM J. Comp. 18(1), 186–207 (1989)

44. Hofheinz, D., Shoup, V.: GNUC: a new universal composability framework. J. Cryptol. **28**(3), 423–508 (2013)
45. Kremer, S., Mazaré, L.: Adaptive soundness of static equivalence. In: Biskup, S., López, J. (eds.) ESORICS 2007. LNCS, vol. 4734, pp. 610–625. Springer, Heidelberg (2007)
46. Küsters, R., Scapin, E., Truderung, T., Graf, J.: Extending and applying a framework for the cryptographic verification of java programs. In: Abadi, M., Kremer, S. (eds.) POST 2014. LNCS, vol. 8414, pp. 220–239. Springer, Heidelberg (2014)
47. Küsters, R., Truderung, T., Graf, J.: A framework for the cryptographic verification of java-like programs. In: CSF 2012, pp. 198–212. IEEE (2012)
48. Küsters, R., Tuengerthal, M.: The IITM Model: a Simple and Expressive Model for Universal Composability. IACR ePrint Archive: 2013/025 (2013)
49. Meier, S., Schmidt, B., Cremers, C., Basin, D.: The TAMARIN prover for the symbolic analysis of security protocols. In: Sharygina, N., Veith, H. (eds.) CAV 2013. LNCS, vol. 8044, pp. 696–701. Springer, Heidelberg (2013)
50. Micciancio, D., Warinschi, B.: Soundness of formal encryption in the presence of active adversaries. In: Naor, M. (ed.) TCC 2004. LNCS, vol. 2951, pp. 133–151. Springer, Heidelberg (2004)
51. ProVerif code of the case study. https://www.infsec.cs.uni-saarland.de/~mohammadi/paper/case_study_untraceable_payments.zip
52. Sprenger, C., Backes, M., Basin, D., Pfitzmann, B., Waidner, M.: Cryptographically sound theorem proving. In: CSFW 2006, pp. 153–166. IEEE (2006)
53. Swamy, N., Weinberger, J., Schlesinger, C., Chen, J., Livshits, B.: Verifying high-erorder programs with the Dijkstra Monad. In: PLDI 2013, pp. 387–398. ACM (2013)
54. Unruh, D.: Termination-insensitive computational indistinguishability (and applications to computational soundness). In: CSF 2011, pp. 251–265. IEEE (2011)

Verifiably Encrypted Signatures: Security Revisited and a New Construction

Christian Hanser[1], Max Rabkin[2,3]([✉]), and Dominique Schröder[2]

[1] IAIK, Graz University of Technology, Graz, Austria
christian.hanser@iaik.tugraz.at
[2] CISPA, Saarland University, Saarbrücken, Germany
mrabkin@mpi-inf.mpg.de
[3] International Max Planck Research School for Computer Science,
Saarbrücken, Germany
dschroede@mmci.uni-saarland.de

Abstract. In structure-preserving signatures on equivalence classes (SPS-EQ-$\mathcal{R}$), introduced at ASIACRYPT 2014, each message M in $(\mathbb{G}^*)^\ell$ is associated to its projective equivalence class, and a signature commits to the equivalence class: anybody can transfer the signature to a new, scaled, representative.

In this work, we give the first black-box construction of a public-key encryption scheme from any SPS-EQ-$\mathcal{R}$ satisfying a simple new property which we call perfect composition. The construction does notinvolve any non-black-box technique and the implication is that such SPS-EQ-$\mathcal{R}$ cannot be constructed from one-way functions in a black-box way. The main idea of our scheme is to build a verifiable encrypted signature (VES) first and then apply the general transformation suggested by Calderon et al. (CT-RSA 2014).

The original definition of VES requires that the underlying signature scheme be correct and secure in addition to other security properties. The latter have been extended in subsequent literature, but the former requirements have sometimes been neglected, leaving a hole in the security notion. We show that Calderon et al.'s notion of resolution independence fills this gap.

Keywords: Structure preserving signatures · Verifiably encrypted signatures · Resolution independence · Public-key encryption

1 Introduction

Structure-preserving signatures on equivalence classes (SPS-EQ-$\mathcal{R}$s) have been introduced at ASIACRYPT 2014, and a corrected instantiation was given in a joint

C. Hanser—Part of this work was done while visiting CISPA (Saarbrücken, Germany); supported by COST Action IC1306. Further supported by EU FP7 through project MATTHEW (GA No. 610436) and EU Horizon 2020 through project PRISMACLOUD (GA No. 644962).

© Springer International Publishing Switzerland 2015
G. Pernul et al. (Eds.): ESORICS 2015, Part I, LNCS 9326, pp. 146–164, 2015.
DOI: 10.1007/978-3-319-24174-6_8

work with Fuchsbauer [9]. In an SPS-EQ-$\mathcal{R}$, each message M is a vector of group elements from a group of prime order p, and a signature commits the signer only to its projective equivalence class $[M]_{\mathcal{R}} = \{\lambda M : \lambda \in \mathbb{Z}_p^*\}$: anybody can transfer the signature to a new representative, scaling the message by an arbitrary factor and obtaining a new signature for the scaled message. SPS-EQ-$\mathcal{R}$s have many applications such as anonymous credentials [6] and have appealing properties, such as being compatible with Groth-Sahai zero-knowledge proofs [15]. In this work, we show how to construct verifiably encrypted signatures and public-key encryption from an SPS-EQ-$\mathcal{R}$.

Verifiably Encrypted Signatures. Bob wants to buy a theater ticket with an electronic check. That is, he wants to exchange one document, signed by himself, for another document, signed by the theater. If he sends the check before receiving the ticket, he worries that the theater will cash his check without issuing the ticket. On the other hand, the theater is not willing to issue the ticket without receiving a check.

A verifiably encrypted signature scheme (VES), introduced by Boneh et al. [3], can be used to resolve this impasse. A VES has two forms of signatures: plain and encrypted. Both forms of signature can be verified, and if the signer refuses to reveal the plain signature at the end of negotiations, the other party can appeal to a trusted third party (called the arbiter), who can recreate a plain signature given the corresponding encrypted signature.

Thus, in our example, the theater can provisionally send Bob a ticket with an encrypted signature, and once they receive Bob's signed check they can reveal the corresponding plain signature, and thus validate the provisional ticket. If they fail to do so, Bob can take the encrypted signature to the arbiter. The arbiter's investigation will reveal that Bob has indeed upheld his side of the deal, and so recreate the corresponding plain signature, giving Bob the ticket he has paid for. This protocol has the advantage that the arbiter need not participate unless there is a dispute.

VES from SPS-EQ-$\mathcal{R}$. We introduce a simple new property for SPS-EQ-$\mathcal{R}$ schemes, called *perfect composition*, which is satisfied by an existing construction in the generic group model, and show how to construct VESes from such schemes. In particular, this is the first VES construction from any kind of structure-preserving signature scheme, underlining the versatility of SPS-EQ-$\mathcal{R}$s. In our construction, each message is associated to a projective equivalence class. To create a plain signature, the signer signs one representative; to create an encrypted signature, she signs another. The scaling factor between these two representatives depends on the arbiter's key, allowing the arbiter to recover the plain signature from the encrypted one using the SPS-EQ-$\mathcal{R}$'s *change representative* algorithm.

Public-Key Encryption from SPS-EQ-$\mathcal{R}$. If the SPS-EQ-$\mathcal{R}$ allows perfect composition, then our VES construction satisfies resolution duplication, a property introduced very recently by Calderon et al. [5], which requires that a signature extracted by the arbiter is identical to that which would have been created by the signer. Not only does this prevent discrimination between arbiter-issued and signer-issued signatures, but VESes satisfying this property imply public-key encryption. This is particularly interesting because it is not possible to construct PKE from ordinary signatures (or equivalently, from one-way functions) in a black-box way. Looking at this from the other side, it means that such an SPS-EQ-$\mathcal{R}$ cannot be constructed (black-box) from one-way functions.

1.1 Our Contribution

Our main contribution is twofold:

Verifiably Encrypted Signatures. We propose the first black-box construction of verifiably encrypted signature scheme from any structure-preserving signature scheme on equivalence classes satisfying a simple property. This construction does *not* combine an encryption scheme with an SPS-EQ-$\mathcal{R}$. Furthermore, all our security proofs hold in the standard model, under the Diffie-Hellman Inversion assumption.

We also revisit the security definitions of VES. The original definition of VES [3] requires that the underlying (ordinary) signature scheme be correct and secure in addition to other security properties. The latter properties have been extended in subsequent literature [18,27] but the requirements on the underlying scheme are sometimes neglected. We show that with this omission, resolution independence is absolutely essential not only to the unforgeability, but even to the correctness, of the underlying signature scheme. From the alternative viewpoint, we show that security including resolution independence is sufficient for the correctness and security of the underlying signature scheme.

Public-Key Encryption. We propose the first black-box construction of a CPA-secure public-key encryption scheme from any structure-preserving signature scheme on equivalence classes allowing perfect composition. The construction follows the idea of Calderon et. al [5]; it is black-box and does not involve known non-black-box techniques such as zero-knowledge. Given the well-known impossibility results, this shows that SPS-EQ-$\mathcal{R}$s allowing perfect composition cannot be constructed from one-way functions in a black-box way.

1.2 Related Work

Verifiably encrypted signatures and a first instantiation in the random oracle model were proposed by Boneh et al. [3]. After their invention, several instantiations were suggested in the RO model [26,29] and in the standard model [8,22,27]. The security model is treated in [3,5,18,27].

Impagliazzo and Rudich [20] show in their seminal work that cryptographic primitives can be classified as lying in one of two "worlds". The "Minicrypt" world contains those primitives that are equivalent to the weakest known assumption, the existence of one-way functions (OWFs), such as digital signatures [14, 17,19,21,24]. The second world, "Cryptomania", includes primitives that require stronger assumptions such as public-key encryption (PKE), key-agreement (KA), oblivious transfer (OT) [4,11,12,25,28] and now SPS-EQ-$\mathcal{R}$.

1.3 Outline

In Sect. 2 we state the preliminaries. In Sect. 3 we discuss the relationship between resolution independence and the correctness and unforgeability of the underlying signature scheme of a VES. Then, in Sect. 4, we show how to generically build a VES from an SPS-EQ-$\mathcal{R}$ scheme. In Sect. 5, we then discuss the implication of PKE by certain SPS-EQ-$\mathcal{R}$. Finally, we conclude this paper in Sect. 6.

2 Preliminaries

A function $\epsilon : \mathbb{N} \to \mathbb{R}^+$ is called *negligible* if for all $c > 0$ there is a k_0 such that $\epsilon(k) < 1/k^c$ for all $k > k_0$. In the remainder of this paper, we use ϵ to denote such a negligible function. By $a \xleftarrow{\$} A$, we denote that a is chosen uniformly at random from the set A. We use the notation $A(a_1, \ldots, a_n; r)$ if we make the randomness r used by a probabilistic algorithm $A(a_1, \ldots, a_n)$ explicit.

Definition 1 (Bilinear Map). *Let $\mathbb{G}_1$, $\mathbb{G}_2$ and $\mathbb{G}_T$ be cyclic groups of prime order p, where we denote $\mathbb{G}_1$ and $\mathbb{G}_2$ additively and $\mathbb{G}_T$ multiplicatively. We write $\mathbb{G}_i^*$ for $\mathbb{G}_i \setminus \{0_{\mathbb{G}_i}\}$ where $i \in \{1, 2\}$. Let P and $\hat{P}$ be generators of $\mathbb{G}_1$ and $\mathbb{G}_2$, respectively. We call $e \colon \mathbb{G}_1 \times \mathbb{G}_2 \to \mathbb{G}_T$ a bilinear map or pairing if it is efficiently computable and the following holds:*

Bilinearity: $e(aP, b\hat{P}) = e(P, \hat{P})^{ab} \quad \forall\, a, b \in \mathbb{Z}_p$.
Non-degeneracy: $e(P, \hat{P}) \neq 1_{\mathbb{G}_T}$, *i.e.,* $e(P, \hat{P})$ *generates* $\mathbb{G}_T$.

If $\mathbb{G}_1 = \mathbb{G}_2$, then e is *symmetric* (Type-1) and *asymmetric* (Type-2 or 3) otherwise. For Type-2 pairings there is an efficiently computable isomorphism $\Psi \colon \mathbb{G}_2 \to \mathbb{G}_1$; for Type-3 pairings no such isomorphism is known. Type-3 pairings are currently the optimal choice in terms of efficiency and security trade-off [7].

Definition 2 (Bilinear Group Generator). *A polynomial-time algorithm BGGen is a bilinear-group generator if it takes as input a security parameter 1^κ and outputs $\mathsf{BG} = (p, \mathbb{G}_1, \mathbb{G}_2, \mathbb{G}_T, e, P, \hat{P})$ where the common group order p of the groups $\mathbb{G}_1, \mathbb{G}_2$ and $\mathbb{G}_T$ is a prime of bit-length κ, e is a pairing, and P and $\hat{P}$ are generators of $\mathbb{G}_1$ and $\mathbb{G}_2$, respectively.*

In this work we assume BGGen to be deterministic.[1]

Definition 3 (Diffie-Hellman Inversion Assumption (DHI) [23]). *Let $\mathbb{G}$ be a group of prime order p with $\log_2 p = \kappa$ and let $a \xleftarrow{\$} \mathbb{Z}_p^*$. Then, for every PPT adversary $\mathcal{A}$ there is a negligible function $\epsilon(\cdot)$ such that $\Pr\left[\frac{1}{a}P \leftarrow \mathcal{A}(P, aP)\right] \leq \epsilon(\kappa)$.*

---

[1] This is e.g. the case for BN-curves [2], the most common choice for Type-3 pairings.

2.1 Digital Signatures

Definition 4 (Digital Signature Scheme). *A* digital signature scheme *consists of the following polynomial time algorithms:*

$\mathsf{KeyGen}(1^\kappa)$**:** *A probabilistic algorithm that takes input a security parameter* $\kappa \in \mathbb{N}$ *and outputs a key pair* $(\mathsf{sk}, \mathsf{pk})$ *for message space* $\mathcal{M}$.

$\mathsf{Sign}(m, \mathsf{sk})$**:** *A probabilistic algorithm that takes input a message* $m \in \mathcal{M}$, *a secret key* sk *and outputs a signature* σ.

$\mathsf{Verify}(m, \sigma, \mathsf{pk})$**:** *A deterministic algorithm that takes input a message* $m \in \mathcal{M}$, *a signature* σ, *a public key* pk *and outputs* 1 *if* σ *is a valid signature for* M *under* pk *and* 0 *otherwise.*

A digital signature scheme is *secure* if it is *correct* and existentially unforgeable under adaptively chosen-message attacks. We define the properties below:

Definition 5 (Correctness). *A digital signature scheme* $(\mathsf{KeyGen}, \mathsf{Sign}, \mathsf{Verify})$ *is called* correct *if*

$$\forall \kappa > 0 \; \forall (\mathsf{sk}, \mathsf{pk}) \xleftarrow{\$} \mathsf{KeyGen}(1^\kappa) \; \forall m \in \mathcal{M} : \quad \mathsf{Verify}(m, \mathsf{Sign}(m, \mathsf{sk}), \mathsf{pk}) = 1$$

Definition 6 (EUF-CMA). *A digital signature scheme* $(\mathsf{KeyGen}, \mathsf{Sign}, \mathsf{Verify})$ *is called* existentially unforgeable under adaptively chosen-message attacks *if for all PPT algorithms* $\mathcal{A}$ *having access to a signing oracle* $\mathcal{O}(\cdot, \mathsf{sk})$, *there is a negligible function* $\epsilon(\cdot)$ *such that:*

$$\Pr\left[\begin{matrix} (\mathsf{sk}, \mathsf{pk}) \xleftarrow{\$} \mathsf{KeyGen}(1^\kappa), \\ (m^*, \sigma^*) \xleftarrow{\$} \mathcal{A}^{\mathcal{O}(\cdot, \mathsf{sk})}(\mathsf{pk}) \end{matrix} : \begin{matrix} m^* \notin Q \; \wedge \\ \mathsf{Verify}(m^*, \sigma^*, \mathsf{pk}) = 1 \end{matrix} \right] \le \epsilon(\kappa),$$

where Q *is the set of queries which* $\mathcal{A}$ *has issued to the signing oracle* $\mathcal{O}$.

2.2 Structure-Preserving Signatures on Equivalence Classes

In a structure-preserving signature scheme [1], public keys, messages and signatures consist only of group elements of a bilinear group. The verification algorithm verifies a signature solely through group membership tests and by evaluating pairing-product equations.

An SPS-EQ-$\mathcal{R}$ scheme is a structure-preserving signature scheme that is defined either on the message space $(\mathbb{G}_1^*)^\ell$ or $(\mathbb{G}_2^*)^\ell$, where $\ell > 1$ and $|\mathbb{G}_1| = |\mathbb{G}_2| = p$ is prime. Since $\mathbb{Z}_p^\ell$ is a vector space, it is possible to define—in analogy to the projective space—a projective equivalence relation $\sim_\mathcal{R}$ that partitions $\mathbb{Z}_p^\ell$ into projective equivalence classes. This equivalence relation then further propagates onto $(\mathbb{G}_i^*)^\ell$ for $i \in \{1, 2\}$.

Now, an SPS-EQ-$\mathcal{R}$ scheme signs such equivalence classes by signing arbitrary representatives of such classes. When given a message-signature pair, anyone can derive a valid message-signature pair for every other representative of this class. This is done by multiplying each message vector component by the same scalar and by consistently updating the corresponding signature. Clearly, this requires unforgeability to be defined with respect to equivalence classes. This means that after querying signatures for messages M_i, no adversary should be able to output a forgery for a message M^* belonging to a class different from the classes $[M_i]_{\mathcal{R}}$.

We restate the syntax and the security properties of structure-preserving signatures on equivalence classes from [9,10,16]:

Definition 7 (Structure-Preserving Signature Scheme on Equivalence Classes (SPS-EQ-$\mathcal{R}$)). *An SPS-EQ-$\mathcal{R}$ scheme* SPSEQ *on* $(\mathbb{G}_i^*)^\ell$ *consists of the following polynomial-time algorithms:*

BGGen$_{\mathcal{R}}(1^\kappa)$: *A deterministic bilinear-group generation algorithm, which on input a security parameter κ outputs a bilinear group* BG.

KeyGen$_{\mathcal{R}}$(BG, ℓ): *A probabilistic algorithm, which on input a bilinear group* BG *and a vector length $\ell > 1$ outputs a key pair* (sk, pk).

Sign$_{\mathcal{R}}(M, sk)$: *A probabilistic algorithm, which on input a representative $M \in (\mathbb{G}_i^*)^\ell$ of an equivalence class $[M]_{\mathcal{R}}$ and a secret key* sk *outputs a signature σ for the representative M of equivalence class $[M]_{\mathcal{R}}$.*

ChgRep$_{\mathcal{R}}(M, \sigma, \lambda, pk)$: *A probabilistic algorithm, which on input a representative $M \in (\mathbb{G}_i^*)^\ell$ of an equivalence class $[M]_{\mathcal{R}}$, a signature σ for M, a scalar λ and a public key* pk *returns an updated message-signature pair (M', σ'), where $M' = \lambda M$ is the new representative and σ' its updated signature.*

Verify$_{\mathcal{R}}(M, \sigma, pk)$: *A deterministic algorithm, which given a representative $M \in (\mathbb{G}_i^*)^\ell$, a signature σ and a public key* pk *outputs 1 if σ is valid for M under* pk *and 0 otherwise.*

VKey$_{\mathcal{R}}($sk, pk$)$: *A deterministic algorithm, which given a secret key* sk *and a public key* pk *checks both keys for consistency and returns 1 on success and 0 otherwise.*

Definition 8 (Correctness). *An SPS-EQ-$\mathcal{R}$ scheme* SPSEQ *on* $(\mathbb{G}_i^*)^\ell$ *is called correct if for all security parameters $\kappa \in \mathbb{N}$, for all $\ell > 1$, all bilinear groups* BG $\leftarrow$ BGGen$_{\mathcal{R}}(1^\kappa)$, *all key pairs* (sk, pk) $\xleftarrow{\$}$ KeyGen$_{\mathcal{R}}$(BG, ℓ), *all messages $M \in (\mathbb{G}_i^*)^\ell$ and all $\lambda \in \mathbb{Z}_p^*$ we have:*

$$\mathsf{VKey}_{\mathcal{R}}(\mathsf{sk}, \mathsf{pk}) = 1 \quad and$$

$$\Pr\left[\mathsf{Verify}_{\mathcal{R}}(M, \mathsf{Sign}_{\mathcal{R}}(M, \mathsf{sk}), \mathsf{pk}) = 1\right] = 1 \quad and$$

$$\Pr\left[\mathsf{Verify}_{\mathcal{R}}(\mathsf{ChgRep}_{\mathcal{R}}(M, \mathsf{Sign}_{\mathcal{R}}(M, \mathsf{sk}), \lambda, \mathsf{pk}), \mathsf{pk}) = 1\right] = 1.$$

Definition 9 (EUF-CMA). *An SPS-EQ-$\mathcal{R}$ scheme* SPSEQ *on* $(\mathbb{G}_i^*)^\ell$ *is called existentially unforgeable under adaptively chosen-message attacks if, for all PPT algorithms $\mathcal{A}$ having access to a signing oracle $\mathcal{O}($sk, $M)$, there is a negligible function $\epsilon(\cdot)$ such that:*

$$\Pr\left[\begin{array}{l} \mathsf{BG} \leftarrow \mathsf{BGGen}_{\mathcal{R}}(1^\kappa), \\ (\mathsf{sk}, \mathsf{pk}) \xleftarrow{\$} \mathsf{KeyGen}_{\mathcal{R}}(\mathsf{BG}, \ell), \\ (M^*, \sigma^*) \xleftarrow{\$} \mathcal{A}^{\mathcal{O}(\mathsf{sk}, \cdot)}(\mathsf{pk}) \end{array} : \begin{array}{l} [M^*]_{\mathcal{R}} \neq [M]_{\mathcal{R}} \; \forall M \in Q \; \wedge \\ \mathsf{Verify}_{\mathcal{R}}(M^*, \sigma^*, \mathsf{pk}) = 1 \end{array} \right] \leq \epsilon(\kappa),$$

where Q is the set of queries that $\mathcal{A}$ has issued to the signing oracle $\mathcal{O}$.

We now introduce the following new property:

Definition 10. *An SPS-EQ-$\mathcal{R}$ scheme* SPSEQ *allows perfect composition if for all random tapes r and tuples* $(\mathsf{sk}, \mathsf{pk}, M, \sigma, \lambda)$:

$$\mathsf{VKey}_{\mathcal{R}}(\mathsf{sk}, \mathsf{pk}) = 1 \qquad \sigma \leftarrow \mathsf{Sign}_{\mathcal{R}}(M, \mathsf{sk}; r) \qquad M \in (\mathbb{G}_i^*)^{\ell} \qquad \lambda \in \mathbb{Z}_p^*$$

it holds that $(\lambda M, \mathsf{Sign}_{\mathcal{R}}(\lambda M, \mathsf{sk}; r)) = \mathsf{ChgRep}_{\mathcal{R}}(M, \sigma, \lambda, \mathsf{pk}; 1)$.

Intuitively, this requires that $\mathsf{ChgRep}_{\mathcal{R}}$ executed with random coins fixed to 1 updates only the parts of a signature that are affected by updating the representative from M to λM, not changing the randomness of $\mathsf{Sign}_{\mathcal{R}}$.

In [10], a standard model SPS-EQ-$\mathcal{R}$ construction is presented. Unfortunately, it does not satisfy the above definition, but the scheme in [9], which is secure in the generic group model, does.

2.3 Verifiably Encrypted Signatures

Below, we give the abstract model of verifiably encrypted signatures, adapted from [3].

Definition 11 (Verifiably Encrypted Signature Scheme (VES)). *A verifiably encrypted signature scheme* VES *consists of the following polynomial time algorithms:*

$\mathsf{AKeyGen}(1^{\kappa})$: *Given a security parameter κ, this probabilistic algorithm outputs a key pair* $(\mathsf{ask}, \mathsf{apk})$, *where* ask *is the private key and* apk *the corresponding public key of the arbiter.*

$\mathsf{KeyGen}(1^{\kappa})$: *Given a security parameter κ, this probabilistic algorithm outputs a private signing key* sk *and a public verification key* pk *for message space $\mathcal{M}$.*

$\mathsf{Sign}(m, \mathsf{sk})$: *Given a message $m \in \mathcal{M}$ and a signing key* sk, *this probabilistic algorithm outputs a signature σ under* sk *on m.*

$\mathsf{Verify}(m, \sigma, \mathsf{pk})$: *Given a message $m \in \mathcal{M}$ and a public key* pk, *this deterministic algorithm outputs 1 iff σ is a valid signature on m under* pk *and 0 otherwise.*

$\mathsf{VESign}(m, \mathsf{sk}, \mathsf{apk})$: *Given a message $m \in \mathcal{M}$, a signing key* sk *and an arbiter public key* apk, *this probabilistic algorithm outputs an encrypted signature ω under* sk *on message m.*

$\mathsf{VEVerify}(m, \omega, \mathsf{pk}, \mathsf{apk})$: *Given a message $m \in \mathcal{M}$, an encrypted signature ω, a public key* pk *and an arbiter public key* apk, *this deterministic algorithm outputs 1 if ω is a valid encrypted signature on m under* pk *and 0 otherwise.*

$\mathsf{Resolve}(m, \omega, \mathsf{ask}, \mathsf{pk})$: *Given a message $m \in \mathcal{M}$, an encrypted signature ω, an arbiter secret key* ask *and a public key* pk, *this (probabilistic) algorithm outputs a valid signature σ on m under* pk.

We call a VES *secure* if it is *complete, unforgeable, opaque, extractable, abuse free* and *resolution independent*. We define these properties below.

Completeness says that any honestly computed VES always verifies and that moreover the arbiter can always extract a valid signature.

Definition 12 (Completeness). *A VES* VES *is* complete *if for all* $\kappa > 0$*, all* $(\mathsf{ask}, \mathsf{apk}) \xleftarrow{\$} \mathsf{AKeyGen}(1^\kappa)$*, all* $(\mathsf{sk}, \mathsf{pk}) \xleftarrow{\$} \mathsf{KeyGen}(1^\kappa)$*, and all messages* $m \in \mathcal{M}$*, for* $\omega \xleftarrow{\$} \mathsf{VESign}(m, \mathsf{sk}, \mathsf{apk})$ *it holds that*

$$\Pr\left[\mathsf{VEVerify}(m, \omega, \mathsf{pk}, \mathsf{apk}) = 1\right] = 1 \quad and$$
$$\Pr\left[\mathsf{Verify}(m, \mathsf{Resolve}(m, \omega, \mathsf{ask}, \mathsf{pk}), \mathsf{pk}) = 1\right] = 1.$$

Unforgeability says that it should be infeasible to produce a valid encrypted signature for an unknown secret key.

Definition 13 (Unforgeability). *A VES* VES *is* unforgeable *if for all PPT algorithms* $\mathcal{A}$ *having access to oracles* $\mathcal{O} \leftarrow \{\mathsf{VESign}(\cdot, \mathsf{sk}, \mathsf{apk}), \mathsf{Resolve}(\cdot, \cdot, \mathsf{ask}, \mathsf{pk}), \mathsf{Sign}(\cdot, \mathsf{sk})\}$*, there is a negligible function* $\epsilon(\cdot)$ *such that:*

$$\Pr\left[\begin{array}{l} (\mathsf{ask}, \mathsf{apk}) \xleftarrow{\$} \mathsf{AKeyGen}(1^\kappa), \\ (\mathsf{sk}, \mathsf{pk}) \xleftarrow{\$} \mathsf{KeyGen}(1^\kappa), \\ (m^*, \omega^*) \xleftarrow{\$} \mathcal{A}^{\mathcal{O}}(\mathsf{pk}, \mathsf{apk}) \end{array} : \begin{array}{l} m^* \notin Q \ \wedge \\ \mathsf{VEVerify}(m^*, \omega^*, \mathsf{pk}, \mathsf{apk}) = 1 \end{array}\right] \le \epsilon(\kappa),$$

where Q *is the set of messages which were queried to the oracles.*

Opacity basically requires that only the arbiter should be able to pull out the underlying signature.

Definition 14 (Opacity). *A VES* VES *is* opaque *if for all PPT algorithms* $\mathcal{A}$ *having access to oracles* $\mathcal{O} \leftarrow \{\mathsf{VESign}(\cdot, \mathsf{sk}, \mathsf{apk}), \mathsf{Resolve}(\cdot, \cdot, \mathsf{ask}, \mathsf{pk})\}$*, there is a negligible function* $\epsilon(\cdot)$ *such that:*

$$\Pr\left[\begin{array}{l} (\mathsf{ask}, \mathsf{apk}) \xleftarrow{\$} \mathsf{AKeyGen}(1^\kappa), \\ (\mathsf{sk}, \mathsf{pk}) \xleftarrow{\$} \mathsf{KeyGen}(1^\kappa), \\ (m^*, \sigma^*) \xleftarrow{\$} \mathcal{A}^{\mathcal{O}}(\mathsf{pk}, \mathsf{apk}) \end{array} : \begin{array}{l} m^* \notin Q \ \wedge \\ \mathsf{Verify}(m^*, \sigma^*, \mathsf{pk}) = 1 \end{array}\right] \le \epsilon(\kappa),$$

where Q *is the set of messages queried to the* Resolve *oracle.*

In addition to the above property, we have to guarantee that it is indeed possible for the arbiter to extract the underlying signature, which is covered by the following property.

Definition 15 (Extractability). *A VES* VES *is* extractable *if for all PPT algorithms* $\mathcal{A}$ *having access to oracles* $\mathcal{O} \leftarrow \{\mathsf{Resolve}(\cdot, \cdot, \mathsf{ask}, \cdot)\}$*, there is a negligible function* $\epsilon(\cdot)$ *such that:*

$$\Pr\left[\begin{array}{l} (\mathsf{ask}, \mathsf{apk}) \xleftarrow{\$} \mathsf{AKeyGen}(1^\kappa), \\ (\mathsf{pk}^*, m^*, \omega^*) \xleftarrow{\$} \mathcal{A}^{\mathcal{O}}(\mathsf{apk}) \end{array} : \begin{array}{l} \sigma \xleftarrow{\$} \mathsf{Resolve}(m^*, \omega^*, \mathsf{ask}, \mathsf{pk}^*) \ \wedge \\ \mathsf{VEVerify}(m^*, \omega^*, \mathsf{pk}^*, \mathsf{apk}) = 1 \ \wedge \\ \mathsf{Verify}(m^*, \sigma, \mathsf{pk}^*) = 0 \end{array}\right] \le \epsilon(\kappa).$$

Abuse freeness guarantees that even if an adversary is colluding with the arbiter, it is unable to forge a valid encrypted signature.

Definition 16 (Abuse Freeness). *A VES* VES *is abuse free if for all PPT algorithms $\mathcal{A}$ having access to oracles $\mathcal{O} \leftarrow \{\text{VESign}(\cdot, \text{sk}, \text{apk})\}$, there is a negligible function $\epsilon(\cdot)$ such that:*

$$\Pr\left[\begin{array}{l} (\text{ask}, \text{apk}) \xleftarrow{\$} \text{AKeyGen}(1^\kappa), \\ (\text{sk}, \text{pk}) \xleftarrow{\$} \text{KeyGen}(1^\kappa), \\ (m^*, \omega^*) \xleftarrow{\$} \mathcal{A}^\mathcal{O}(\text{pk}, \text{ask}, \text{apk}) \end{array} : \begin{array}{l} m^* \notin Q \ \wedge \\ \text{VEVerify}(m^*, \omega^*, \text{pk}, \text{apk}) = 1 \end{array} \right] \leq \epsilon(\kappa),$$

where Q is the set of messages queried to the VESign *oracle.*

Extractability and abuse freeness were introduced by Rückert and Schröder in [27].

Additionally, Calderon et al. [5] have identified another property that is called resolution independence. This property is crucial for a VES to be secure, as we will discuss in Sect. 3.

Definition 17 (Resolution Independence). *A VES* VES *is resolution independent if for all $\kappa > 0$, all $(\text{ask}, \text{apk}) \xleftarrow{\$} \text{AKeyGen}(1^\kappa)$, $(\text{sk}, \text{pk}) \xleftarrow{\$} \text{KeyGen}(1^\kappa)$, and all messages m, the outputs of* Sign(m, sk) *and* Resolve$(m, \text{VESign}(m, \text{sk}, \text{apk}),$ ask, pk$)$ *are distributed identically.*

In [5], the authors showed that VES constructions imply public key encryption if they additionally satisfy a property called *resolution duplication*. Loosely speaking, a VES is resolution duplicate if the signatures returned by the signer and the arbiter are identical.

Definition 18 (Resolution Duplication). *A VES* VES *is resolution duplicate if it is resolution independent and fulfills the following properties:*

Deterministic Resolution: *The algorithm* Resolve *is deterministic.*
Extraction: *There exists an additional PPT algorithm* Extract$(\cdot, \cdot, \cdot)$, *such that for all $\kappa > 0$, all $(\text{ask}, \text{apk}) \xleftarrow{\$} \text{AKeyGen}(1^\kappa)$, $(\text{sk}, \text{pk}) \xleftarrow{\$} \text{KeyGen}(1^\kappa)$, $m \in \mathcal{M}$, and random tapes $r \in \{0,1\}^*$, it is the case that*

$$\text{Extract}(m, \text{sk}, r) = \text{Resolve}(m, \text{VESign}(m, \text{sk}, \text{apk}; r), \text{ask}, \text{pk}).$$

Up to now numerous standard-model VES constructions have been proposed, but not all constructions so far are resolution-duplicate; in particular not the ones with a randomized Resolve algorithm [5].

3   The Importance of Resolution Independence

In Boneh et al.'s original definition of a VES [3], the underlying signature scheme is required to be secure, in addition to the security properties of the encrypted signatures: completeness, unforgeability and opacity. Rückert and Schröder [27] added the properties of extractability and abuse freeness, and Calderon et al. [5] added the properties of resolution independence, but both omit (or are at least unclear about) the requirement that the underlying signature scheme be secure. Indeed, the latter paper says that they "additionally provide the adversary with access to the Sign oracle, as otherwise the underlying signature scheme could be completely broken and the VES would still be considered unforgeable." In fact, it can be completely broken anyway.

We will show that, with this omission, resolution independence is absolutely essential to not only the unforgeability, but even the correctness, of the underlying scheme. Resolution independence supplies the necessary glue to connect the security properties of the encrypted scheme to the underlying scheme. Contrapositively, we show that security including resolution independence is sufficient for the correctness and security of the underlying signature scheme, so that does not need to be proven separately. To be clear, we formally define what is meant by the underlying signature scheme.

Definition 19. *Let* VES *be a VES. Then we call* Sig $=$ (SKeyGen, Sign, Verify) *the underlying signature scheme of* VES, *where* SKeyGen(1^κ) *outputs* (sk, pk) $\xleftarrow{\$}$ KeyGen(1^κ).

3.1   Counterexample

We now show that completeness, unforgeability, opacity, extractability and abuse freeness together do not imply the correctness or security of the underlying scheme.

Let VES $=$ (AKeyGen, KeyGen, Sign, Verify, VESign, VEVerify, Resolve) be a VES with messages of length n, and let VES$'$ $=$ (AKeyGen, KeyGen, Sign$'$, Verify, VESign, VEVerify, Resolve) where Sign$'(m, \text{sk})$ computes and outputs Sign(0^n, sk).

Theorem 1. *If* VES *is complete, unforgeable, opaque, extractable and abuse free, then so is* VES$'$.

Proof. The adversary in the unforgeability game must output a valid encrypted signature, but the set of valid encrypted signatures in VES and VES$'$ are the same, and we have only weakened the oracles (by making Sign provide signatures only on 0^n), so unforgeability is preserved. The other properties do not mention the Sign algorithm at all, so they are unaffected. $\square$

This scheme is intuitively both incorrect (as the signatures produced by Sign$'$ cannot be verified) and insecure (as it gives away a forgery as soon as it is called on a message other than 0^n. Nevertheless, VES$'$ is secure as defined in [27], since their definition does not include the security of the underlying signature scheme. It is also much more catastrophically insecure than the separating example in [5, Sect. 3], which motivated the definition of resolution independence.

Theorem 2. *The underlying signature scheme* Sig *of* VES$'$ *is neither correct nor secure.*

3.2 Filling the Gap

Lemma 1. *If* VES *is a complete and resolution independent VES, then its underlying signature scheme* Sig *is correct.*

Proof. By completeness, for all $\kappa > 0$, $(\mathsf{ask}, \mathsf{apk}) \xleftarrow{\$} \mathsf{AKeyGen}(1^\kappa), (\mathsf{sk}, \mathsf{pk}) \xleftarrow{\$} \mathsf{KeyGen}(1^\kappa)$ and all messages $m \in \mathcal{M}$, for $\omega \xleftarrow{\$} \mathsf{VESign}(m, \mathsf{sk}, \mathsf{apk})$, with probability 1,

$$\mathsf{Verify}(m, \mathsf{Resolve}(m, \omega, \mathsf{ask}, \mathsf{pk}), \mathsf{pk}) = 1.$$

By resolution independence, $\mathsf{Resolve}(m, \omega, \mathsf{ask}, \mathsf{pk})$ is identically distributed to $\mathsf{Sign}(m, \mathsf{sk})$, so with probability 1,

$$\mathsf{Verify}(m, \mathsf{Sign}(m, \mathsf{sk}), \mathsf{pk}) = 1. \qquad \square$$

Lemma 2. *If* VES *is an opaque and resolution independent VES, then its underlying signature scheme* Sig *is EUF-CMA-secure.*

Proof. Let VES be a resolution independent VES, and let Sig be the underlying signature scheme. We assume that there is an efficient adversary $\mathcal{A}$ breaking the EUF-CMA security of Sig with non-negligible probability, and construct an adversary $\mathcal{B}$ that uses $\mathcal{A}$ to break the opacity of VES.

$\mathcal{B}$ takes as input an arbiter's public key apk and a signer's public key pk (with unknown corresponding private keys ask and sk), and passes pk as input to $\mathcal{A}$. Whenever $\mathcal{A}$ tries to query the Sign oracle on message m, $\mathcal{B}$ forwards m to its VESign oracle, obtaining $\omega = \mathsf{VESign}(m, \mathsf{sk}, \mathsf{apk})$; $\mathcal{B}$ then queries (m, ω) to its Resolve oracle, obtaining $\sigma = \mathsf{Resolve}(m, \mathsf{VESign}(m, \mathsf{sk}, \mathsf{apk}), \mathsf{ask}, \mathsf{pk})$, which it returns to $\mathcal{A}$. When $\mathcal{A}$ outputs (m^*, σ^*), $\mathcal{B}$ outputs the same.

By resolution independence, $\mathsf{Sign}(m, \mathsf{sk})$ and $\mathsf{Resolve}(m, \mathsf{VESign}(m, \mathsf{sk}, \mathsf{apk}), \mathsf{ask}, \mathsf{pk})$ are identically distributed, so we perfectly simulate $\mathcal{A}$'s Sign oracle.

If $\mathcal{A}$ never queried m^* to Sign, then $\mathcal{B}$ never queried m^* to Resolve, and so $\mathcal{B}$ has the same non-negligible success probability as $\mathcal{A}$. $\qquad \square$

Theorem 3. *If a VES is complete, opaque and resolution independent, then its underlying signature scheme* Sig *is correct and secure.*

Proof. By Lemmas 1 and 2. $\qquad \square$

4 Verifiably Encrypted Signatures from SPS-EQ-$\mathcal{R}$

In Scheme 1, we show how a VES can be built using any SPS-EQ-$\mathcal{R}$ construction that allows perfect composition as a black box. In particular, the VES construction only requires the SPS-EQ-$\mathcal{R}$ construction to be correct, EUF-CMA secure and to fulfill perfect composition (Definition 10).

Note 1. Observe that, independently of the instantiation of Scheme 1 with a concrete SPS-EQ-$\mathcal{R}$, the efficiency of the Verify resp. VEVerify can be improved by precomputing parts of the pairing product equations that solely depend on P and pk resp. A and pk, and including the resulting $\mathbb{G}_T$ elements into (the updated) user public key pk.

AKeyGen(1^κ): Given a security parameter κ, compute BG $\leftarrow$ BGGen$_\mathcal{R}(1^\kappa)$, pick $a \overset{\$}{\leftarrow} \mathbb{Z}_p^*$, compute $A \leftarrow aP$ and output (ask, apk) $\leftarrow$ $(a, (\text{BG}, A))$.

KeyGen(1^κ): Given a security parameter κ, compute BG $\leftarrow$ BGGen$_\mathcal{R}(1^\kappa)$ and output (sk, pk) $\overset{\$}{\leftarrow}$ KeyGen$_\mathcal{R}(\text{BG}, \ell = 3)$.

Sign(m, sk; (r_1, r_2)): Given a message $m \in \mathbb{Z}_p^*$, secret key sk and a random tape $(r_1, r_2) \in \{0,1\}^*$, pick $s \overset{\$}{\leftarrow} \mathbb{Z}_p^*$ using r_1 and compute $\sigma' \leftarrow$ Sign$_\mathcal{R}((msP, sP, P), \text{sk}; r_2)$ using the remaining coins r_2. Finally, output $\sigma \leftarrow (\sigma', sP)$.

Verify(m, σ, pk): Given a message $m \in \mathbb{Z}_p^*$, a signature $\sigma = (\sigma', S)$ and a public key pk, output whatever Verify$_\mathcal{R}((mS, S, P), \sigma', \text{pk})$ outputs.

VESign(m, sk, apk; (r_1, r_2)): Given a message $m \in \mathbb{Z}_p^*$, secret key sk, the arbiter public key apk $= A$ and a random tape $(r_1, r_2) \in \{0,1\}^*$, pick $s \overset{\$}{\leftarrow} \mathbb{Z}_p^*$ using r_1 and compute $\omega' \leftarrow$ Sign$_\mathcal{R}((msA, sA, A), \text{sk}; r_2)$ using the remaining coins r_2. Finally, output $\omega \leftarrow (\omega', sA)$.

VEVerify(m, ω, pk, apk): Given a message $m \in \mathbb{Z}_p^*$, an encrypted signature $\omega = (\omega', W)$, a public key pk and an arbiter public key apk $= A$, output whatever Verify$_\mathcal{R}((mW, W, A), \omega', \text{pk})$ outputs.

Resolve(m, ω, ask, pk): Given a message $m \in \mathbb{Z}_p^*$, an encrypted signature $\omega = (\omega', sA)$, a public key pk and an arbiter secret key ask $\leftarrow a$, check whether VEVerify(m, ω, pk, apk) $\overset{?}{=} 1$ and return $\perp$ if this is not the case. Otherwise, compute $((msP, sP, P), \sigma') \leftarrow$ ChgRep$_\mathcal{R}((msA, sA, A), \omega, \frac{1}{a}, \text{pk}; 1)$ and output $\sigma \leftarrow (\sigma', sP)$.

Scheme 1. A VES Construction from SPS-EQ-$\mathcal{R}$.

In the following, we are going to analyze the security of Scheme 1 and prove completeness, unforgeability, opacity and abuse freeness as well as resolution duplication.

Theorem 4. *The VES in Scheme 1 is complete.*

Proof. The completeness proof of Scheme 1 is straight-forward and therefore omitted here. $\qquad\square$

Theorem 5. *The VES in Scheme 1 is unforgeable given that the underlying SPS-EQ-$\mathcal{R}$ scheme is unforgeable.*

Proof. We assume that there is an efficient adversary $\mathcal{A}$ winning the unforgeability game with non-negligible probability; then we are able to construct an adversary $\mathcal{B}$ that uses $\mathcal{A}$ to break the EUF-CMA security of the underlying SPS-EQ-$\mathcal{R}$ scheme with non-negligible probability.

$\mathcal{B}$ obtains pk$_\mathcal{R}$ of the SPS-EQ-$\mathcal{R}$ scheme with $\ell = 3$ (and thereby implicitly the bilinear group BG) from the challenger $\mathcal{C}$ of the EUF-CMA security game, and sets pk $\leftarrow$ pk$_\mathcal{R}$. Then $\mathcal{B}$ picks $a \overset{\$}{\leftarrow} \mathbb{Z}_p^*$, computes $A \leftarrow aP$ and sets

$(\mathsf{ask}, \mathsf{apk}) \leftarrow (a, (\mathsf{BG}, A))$. Next, $\mathcal{B}$ sets up a list $L \leftarrow \emptyset$ to keep track of representatives queried to $\mathcal{C}$, runs $\mathcal{A}$ on $(\mathsf{pk}, \mathsf{apk})$ and answers $\mathcal{A}$'s oracle queries to the Resolve oracle as in the real game and simulates queries to all other oracles as follows:

$\mathsf{Sign}(\cdot, \mathsf{sk})$: If $\mathcal{A}$ submits a query for $m \in \mathbb{Z}_p^*$, $\mathcal{B}$ queries $\mathcal{C}$'s signing oracle for the message (msP, sP, P) for $s \xleftarrow{\$} \mathbb{Z}_p^*$, gets in return a corresponding signature σ', sets $L[m] \leftarrow L[m] \cup \{(msA, sA, A)\}$ and gives $\sigma \leftarrow (\sigma', sP)$ to $\mathcal{A}$.

$\mathsf{VESign}(\cdot, \mathsf{sk}, \mathsf{apk})$: If $\mathcal{A}$ submits a query for $m \in \mathbb{Z}_p^*$, $\mathcal{B}$ queries $\mathcal{C}$'s signing oracle for the message (msA, sA, A) for $s \xleftarrow{\$} \mathbb{Z}_p^*$, gets in return a corresponding signature ω', sets $L[m] \leftarrow L[m] \cup \{(msA, sA, A)\}$ and gives $\omega \leftarrow (\omega', sA)$ as encrypted signature to $\mathcal{A}$.

If at some point $\mathcal{A}$ outputs a valid encrypted message-signature pair $(m^*, \omega^* = (\omega'^*, W^*))$, such that it has not previously queried m^* to any of the oracles, then $\mathcal{B}$ will output $((m^*W^*, W^*, A), \omega'^*)$ to $\mathcal{C}$.

Note that the distribution of all values returned to $\mathcal{A}$ during the simulation is identical to the distribution of these values during a real game.

By construction, $((m^*W^*, W^*, A), \omega'^*)$ constitutes a valid SPS-EQ-$\mathcal{R}$ message-signature pair. It remains to show that for $M^* = (m^*W^*, W^*, A)$, the class $[M^*]_{\mathcal{R}}$ is different from all classes represented by elements in L, if m^* is different from all messages queried to the oracles. VEVerify demands that the third vector component of M^* be A, which uniquely determines the representative for each class and allows for comparison. Now, if there is some $M_i = (m_i W_i, W_i, A) \in L$ queried to the VESign or the Sign oracle coinciding with M^* in the second component, then both vectors still differ in the first component for $m^* \neq m_i$. Likewise, if they coincide in the first component for $m^* \neq m_i$, then they cannot have equal second components. Hence, $M^* \neq M_i$ for any M_i in L.   □

Theorem 6. *The VES in Scheme 1 is opaque given that the DHI assumption holds in $\mathbb{G}_1$ and that the underlying SPS-EQ-$\mathcal{R}$ is unforgeable.*

Proof. We assume that there is an efficient adversary $\mathcal{A}$ winning the opacity game with non-negligible probability. Then we are able to construct an adversary $\mathcal{B}$ that uses $\mathcal{A}$ either to break with non-negligible probability the EUF-CMA security of the underlying SPS-EQ-$\mathcal{R}$ scheme (Type-1 adversary) if $\mathcal{A}$ has neither queried the VESign nor the Resolve oracle for m^*; or the DHI assumption (Type-2 adversary) if $\mathcal{A}$ has only queried the VESign but not the Resolve oracle for m^*.

In the following, $\mathcal{B}$ guesses $\mathcal{A}$'s strategy, i.e., the type of forgery $\mathcal{A}$ will conduct. We are now going to describe the setup, the initialization of the environment, the reduction and the abort conditions for each type.

Type-1: $\mathcal{B}$ obtains $\mathsf{pk}_{\mathcal{R}}$ of the SPS-EQ-$\mathcal{R}$ scheme with $\ell = 3$ (and thereby implicitly the bilinear group BG) from the challenger $\mathcal{C}$ of the EUF-CMA security game and sets $\mathsf{pk} \leftarrow \mathsf{pk}_{\mathcal{R}}$. Furthermore, $\mathcal{B}$ picks $a \xleftarrow{\$} \mathbb{Z}_p^*$, computes $A \leftarrow aP$ and sets $(\mathsf{ask}, \mathsf{apk}) \leftarrow (a, (\mathsf{BG}, A))$. Next, $\mathcal{B}$ runs $\mathcal{A}$ on $(\mathsf{pk}, \mathsf{apk})$ and answers $\mathcal{A}$'s oracle queries to the Resolve oracle as in the real game and simulates queries to the other oracle as follows:

VESign($\cdot$, sk, apk): If $\mathcal{A}$ submits a query for $m \in \mathbb{Z}_p^*$, $\mathcal{B}$ queries $\mathcal{C}$'s signing oracle for the message (msA, sA, A) for $s \xleftarrow{\$} \mathbb{Z}_p^*$, then $\mathcal{B}$ gets in return a signature ω' and outputs (ω', sA).

If at some point $\mathcal{A}$ outputs a valid message-signature pair (m^*, σ^*) with $\sigma^* = (\sigma'^*, S^*)$, and neither has queried to the VESign nor to the Resolve oracle for m^*, then $\mathcal{B}$ will output $((m^* S^*, S^*, P), \sigma'^*)$ to $\mathcal{C}$. In case that $\mathcal{A}$ has queried the VESign oracle for m^*, $\mathcal{B}$ will abort.

Note that the distribution of all values returned to $\mathcal{A}$ during the simulation is identical to the distribution of these values during a real game, which makes the simulation perfect.

By construction, $((m^* S^*, S^*, P), \sigma'^*)$ constitutes a valid SPS-EQ-$\mathcal{R}$ message-signature pair. It remains to show that for $M^* = (m^* S^*, S^*, P)$, the class $[M^*]_{\mathcal{R}}$ is different from all classes queried to $\mathcal{C}$, if m^* is different from all messages queried to the VESign oracle. Verify demands that the third vector component of M^* be P, which uniquely determines the representative for each class and allows for comparison. Now, if there is some $M_i = (m_i S_i, S_i, P)$ coinciding with M^* in the second component, then both vectors still differ in the first component for $m^* \neq m_i$. Likewise, if they coincide in the first component for $m^* \neq m_i$, then they cannot have equal second components. Hence, $M^* \neq M_i$ for any M_i queried to $\mathcal{C}$.

Type-2: In the following, let $\mathbf{p}$ be some fixed probability, which we will set later. $\mathcal{B}$ obtains an instance (P, aP) of the DHI problem in group $\mathbb{G}_1 \in \mathsf{BG}$ (and thereby implicitly the bilinear group BG) from the challenger $\mathcal{C}$. $\mathcal{B}$ executes $(\mathsf{sk}, \mathsf{pk}) \xleftarrow{\$} \mathsf{KeyGen}_{\mathcal{R}}(\mathsf{BG})$, runs $\mathcal{A}$ on $(\mathsf{pk}, \mathsf{apk} \leftarrow (\mathsf{BG}, A))$ for $A \leftarrow aP$, sets up a list $L \leftarrow \emptyset$ and simulates queries to the oracles as follows:

VESign($\cdot$, sk, apk): If $\mathcal{A}$ submits a query for $m \in \mathbb{Z}_p^*$, $\mathcal{B}$ picks $s \xleftarrow{\$} \mathbb{Z}_p^*$ and random coins r_2, sets
- $W \leftarrow sA$ with probability $\mathbf{p}$, or
- $W \leftarrow s(P + A)$ with probability $1 - \mathbf{p}$, and

runs $\omega' \leftarrow \mathsf{Sign}_{\mathcal{R}}((mW, W, A), \mathsf{sk}; r_2)$. Then, it sets $\omega \leftarrow (\omega', W)$, stores $L[m] \leftarrow (s, r_2, \omega)$ and returns ω.

Resolve($\cdot$, $\cdot$, ask, pk): If $\mathcal{A}$ submits a query for $m \in \mathbb{Z}_p^*$ and ω, then $\mathcal{B}$ checks whether VEVerify$(m, \omega, \mathsf{pk}, \mathsf{apk}) \stackrel{?}{=} 1$ and returns $\perp$ if this is not the case. Otherwise, it retrieves the entry $(s, r_2, \omega = (\omega', W)) \leftarrow L[m]$. If $W \stackrel{?}{=} s(P + A)$, then $\mathcal{B}$ aborts. Otherwise, $\mathcal{B}$ computes $\sigma' \leftarrow \mathsf{Sign}_{\mathcal{R}}((msP, sP, P), \mathsf{sk}; r_2)$ and returns $\sigma \leftarrow (\sigma', sP)$.

If at some point $\mathcal{A}$ outputs a valid message-signature pair $(m^*, \sigma^* = (\sigma'^*, S^*))$ and has queried the VESign oracle for m^*, but not the Resolve oracle, then $\mathcal{B}$ retrieves $(s^*, r_2^*, \omega^*) \leftarrow L[m^*]$. If $S^* = s^* P$, then $\mathcal{B}$ aborts. Otherwise, we have $S^* = s^*(\frac{1}{a}P + P)$ and $\mathcal{B}$ outputs $\frac{1}{a}P \leftarrow \frac{1}{s^*}S^* - P$ as a solution to the DHI problem.

Note that the distribution of all values returned to $\mathcal{A}$ during the simulation is identical to the distribution of these values during a real game, which makes the simulation perfect.

Let q_R be the number of resolve queries. Then, with probability $\mathbf{p}^{q_R}$, $\mathcal{B}$ does not abort during the simulation. Given that the simulation works out, $\mathcal{A}$ outputs a "useful" forgery with probability $1 - \mathbf{p}$. In total, $\mathcal{B}$ is able to return a solution to the DHI problem with probability $\mathbf{p}^{q_R}(1 - \mathbf{p})$. The function $f(\mathbf{p}) = \mathbf{p}^{q_R}(1 - \mathbf{p})$ reaches its maximum for $\frac{q_R}{q_R+1}$ and after few calculations we obtain $f(\mathbf{p}) = O(\frac{1}{q_R})$. Therefore, if $\mathcal{A}$ is able to break the opacity of the scheme with non-negligible probability $\epsilon(\kappa)$, then $\mathcal{B}$ is able to break the DHI assumption with non-negligible probability $O(\frac{\epsilon(\kappa)}{q_R})$.   □

Theorem 7. *The VES in Scheme 1 is unconditionally extractable.*

Theorem 8. *The VES in Scheme 1 is abuse free given that the underlying SPS-EQ-$\mathcal{R}$ scheme is unforgeable.*

The following theorem states that Scheme 1 is resolution duplication. In particular, it is resolution independent, the importance of which was established in Sect. 3. It will allow also us to derive a PKE scheme (cf. Sect. 5).

Theorem 9. *The VES in Scheme 1 is resolution duplicate given that the underlying SPS-EQ-$\mathcal{R}$ scheme allows perfect composition.*

The proofs of Theorems 7–9 are given in Appendix A.

5   Public-Key Encryption from SPS-EQ-$\mathcal{R}$

In this section, we show how to convert any SPS-EQ-$\mathcal{R}$ satisfying perfect composition (Definition 10) into a public-key encryption scheme. This connection is somewhat surprising, as it is well known that regular signature schemes do not imply public-key encryption (in a black-box way). However, there is no contradiction as SPS-EQ-$\mathcal{R}$ have more structure than a regular signature scheme.

The basic idea is to instantiate the transformation of Calderon et al. [5]. This transformation turns any secure, resolution duplicate VES scheme into a public-key encryption scheme, in a black-box way. We have already shown how to construct a secure VES scheme, and that it is resolution duplicate, in Sect. 4. The basic idea of the transformation is an application of the Goldreich-Levin trick [14] to the setting of VES. That is, we view $\langle \sigma, r \rangle$ as the hard-core predicate for VESign, i.e., given ω and r it should be hard to predict the value of $\langle \sigma, r \rangle$. This intuition is formally shown in the following lemma.

Lemma 3. *Let* VES *be a VES and let* $b(x, r) := \langle x, r \rangle \bmod 2$ *for any x and r such that $|x| = |r|$. Then, if the VES is opaque for all messages $m \in \mathcal{M}$, all* (ask, apk) $\xleftarrow{\$}$ AKeyGen(1^κ) *and* (sk, pk) $\xleftarrow{\$}$ KeyGen(1^κ)*, it is hard to compute* $b(\sigma, r)$ *given m,* apk, pk, $\omega \xleftarrow{\$}$ VESign(m, sk, apk)*, and $r \xleftarrow{\$} \{0, 1\}^{|\sigma|}$, where $\sigma :=$* Resolve(ω, ask, pk)*.*

The proof is given in [5] and follows that of Goldreich [13] closely. It leads to the following construction of a CPA-secure public-key encryption scheme (EKeyGen, Enc, Dec) as follows:

- EKeyGen(1^κ): Output $(\mathsf{apk}, \mathsf{ask}) \xleftarrow{\$} \mathsf{AKeyGen}(1^\kappa)$.
- Enc(m, apk) : Generate signing keys $(\mathsf{sk}, \mathsf{pk}) \xleftarrow{\$} \mathsf{KeyGen}(1^\kappa)$ and pick a random tape r and $r_\sigma \xleftarrow{\$} \{0,1\}^{|\sigma|}$. Now, compute $\omega := \mathsf{VESign}(0, \mathsf{sk}, \mathsf{apk}; r)$, $\sigma \xleftarrow{\$} \mathsf{Extract}(m, \mathsf{sk}, r)$, and set $c_0 := m \oplus \langle \sigma, r_\sigma \rangle$. Output $c = (\mathsf{pk}, \omega, r_\sigma, c_0)$.
- Dec(c, ask) : Parse $c = (\mathsf{pk}, \omega, r_\sigma, c_0)$ and return $\perp$ if $\mathsf{VEVerify}(0, \omega, \mathsf{pk}, \mathsf{apk}) = 0$. Otherwise, compute $\sigma := \mathsf{Resolve}(0, \mathsf{pk}, \omega, \mathsf{ask}, \mathsf{pk})$ and output $m := c_0 \oplus \langle \sigma, r_\sigma \rangle$.

Regarding security, it was shown that the above construction is CPA secure [5]:

Theorem 10. *If the verifiably encrypted signature is resolution duplicate (according to Definition 18) and opaque, then the above scheme is IND-CPA secure.*

6 Conclusion

We have shown that the property of resolution independence is crucial, not only for constructing public-key encryption from verifiably encrypted signatures, but even for the correctness and security of the VES.

We gave for the first time a construction of resolution duplicate (and in particular resolution independent) VES from SPS-EQ-$\mathcal{R}$. Our VES has short keys and signatures. This result demonstrates further applications of SPS, and SPS-EQ-$\mathcal{R}$ in particular. Using our VES, we constructed public-key encryption. Since the construction is generic, it proves that SPS-EQ-$\mathcal{R}$s allowing perfect composition cannot be constructed from one-way functions.

References

1. Abe, M., Fuchsbauer, G., Groth, J., Haralambiev, K., Ohkubo, M.: Structure-preserving signatures and commitments to group elements. In: Rabin, T. (ed.) CRYPTO 2010. LNCS, vol. 6223, pp. 209–236. Springer, Heidelberg (2010)
2. Barreto, P.S.L.M., Naehrig, M.: Pairing-friendly elliptic curves of prime order. In: Preneel, B., Tavares, S. (eds.) SAC 2005. LNCS, vol. 3897, pp. 319–331. Springer, Heidelberg (2006)
3. Boneh, D., Gentry, C., Lynn, B., Shacham, H.: Aggregate and verifiably encrypted signatures from bilinear maps. In: Biham, E. (ed.) EUROCRYPT 2003. LNCS, vol. 2656, pp. 416–432. Springer, Heidelberg (2003)
4. Boneh, D., Papakonstantinou, P.A., Rackoff, C., Vahlis, Y., Waters, B.: On the impossibility of basing identity based encryption on trapdoor permutations. In: 49th FOCS, pp. 283–292. IEEE Computer Society Press, Philadelphia, 25–28 October 2008
5. Calderon, T., Meiklejohn, S., Shacham, H., Waters, B.: Rethinking verifiably encrypted signatures: a gap in functionality and potential solutions. In: Benaloh, J. (ed.) CT-RSA 2014. LNCS, vol. 8366, pp. 349–366. Springer, Heidelberg (2014)
6. Camenisch, J.L., Lysyanskaya, A.: Dynamic accumulators and application to efficient revocation of anonymous credentials. In: Yung, M. (ed.) CRYPTO 2002. LNCS, vol. 2442, p. 61. Springer, Heidelberg (2002)

7. Chatterjee, S., Menezes, A.: On cryptographic protocols employing asymmetric pairings - the role of ψ revisited. Discrete Appl. Math. **159**(13), 1311–1322 (2011). http://www.sciencedirect.com/science/article/pii/S0166218X11001648

8. Fuchsbauer, G.: Commuting signatures and verifiable encryption. In: Paterson, K.G. (ed.) EUROCRYPT 2011. LNCS, vol. 6632, pp. 224–245. Springer, Heidelberg (2011)

9. Fuchsbauer, G., Hanser, C., Slamanig, D.: EUF-CMA-secure structure-preserving signatures on equivalence classes. Cryptology ePrint Archive, Report 2014/944 (2014). http://eprint.iacr.org/2014/944

10. Fuchsbauer, G., Hanser, C., Slamanig, D.: Practical round-optimal blind signatures in the standard model. In: Gennaro, R., Robshaw, M. (eds.) CRYPTO 2015. LNCS, vol. 9216, pp. 233–253. Springer, Heidelberg (2015)

11. Gertner, Y., Kannan, S., Malkin, T., Reingold, O., Viswanathan, M.: The relationship between public key encryption and oblivious transfer. In: 41st FOCS, pp. 325–335. IEEE Computer Society Press, Redondo Beach, 12–14 November 2000

12. Gertner, Y., Malkin, T., Myers, S.: Towards a separation of semantic and CCA security for public key encryption. In: Vadhan, S.P. (ed.) TCC 2007. LNCS, vol. 4392, pp. 434–455. Springer, Heidelberg (2007)

13. Goldreich, O.: Foundations of Cryptography: Basic Tools, vol. 1. Cambridge University Press, Cambridge (2001)

14. Goldreich, O., Levin, L.A.: A hard-core predicate for all one-way functions. In: 21st ACM STOC, pp. 25–32. ACM Press, Seattle, 15–17 May 1989

15. Groth, J., Sahai, A.: Efficient non-interactive proof systems for bilinear groups. In: Smart, N.P. (ed.) EUROCRYPT 2008. LNCS, vol. 4965, pp. 415–432. Springer, Heidelberg (2008)

16. Hanser, C., Slamanig, D.: Structure-preserving signatures on equivalence classes and their application to anonymous credentials. In: Sarkar, P., Iwata, T. (eds.) ASIACRYPT 2014. LNCS, vol. 8873, pp. 491–511. Springer, Heidelberg (2014)

17. Håstad, J., Impagliazzo, R., Levin, L.A., Luby, M.: A pseudorandom generator from any one-way function. SIAM J. Comput. **28**(4), 1364–1396 (1999)

18. Hess, F.: On the security of the verifiably-encrypted signature scheme of boneh, gentry, lynn and shacham. Inf. Process. Lett. **89**(3), 111–114 (2004)

19. Impagliazzo, R., Luby, M.: One-way functions are essential for complexity based cryptography (extended abstract). In: 30th FOCS, pp. 230–235. IEEE Computer Society Press, Research Triangle Park, 30 October - 1 November 1989

20. Impagliazzo, R., Rudich, S.: Limits on the provable consequences of one-way permutations. In: 21st ACM STOC, pp. 44–61. ACM Press, Seattle, 15–17 May 1989

21. Lamport, L.: Constructing digital signatures from a one-way function. Technical report SRI-CSL-98, SRI International Computer Science Laboratory, October 1979

22. Lu, S., Ostrovsky, R., Sahai, A., Shacham, H., Waters, B.: Sequential aggregate signatures and multisignatures without random oracles. In: Vaudenay, S. (ed.) EUROCRYPT 2006. LNCS, vol. 4004, pp. 465–485. Springer, Heidelberg (2006)

23. Pfitzmann, B., Sadeghi, A.-R.: Anonymous fingerprinting with direct non-repudiation. In: Okamoto, T. (ed.) ASIACRYPT 2000. LNCS, vol. 1976, p. 401. Springer, Heidelberg (2000)

24. Rompel, J.: One-way functions are necessary and sufficient for secure signatures. In: 22nd ACM STOC, pp. 387–394. ACM Press, Baltimore, 14–16 May 1990

25. Rosen, A., Segev, G.: Chosen-ciphertext security via correlated products. In: Reingold, O. (ed.) TCC 2009. LNCS, vol. 5444, pp. 419–436. Springer, Heidelberg (2009)

26. Rückert, M.: Verifiably encrypted signatures from RSA without NIZKs. In: Roy, B., Sendrier, N. (eds.) INDOCRYPT 2009. LNCS, vol. 5922, pp. 363–377. Springer, Heidelberg (2009)

27. Rückert, M., Schröder, D.: Security of verifiably encrypted signatures and a construction without random oracles. In: Shacham, H., Waters, B. (eds.) Pairing 2009. LNCS, vol. 5671, pp. 17–34. Springer, Heidelberg (2009)

28. Vahlis, Y.: Two Is a crowd? a black-box separation of one-wayness and security under correlated inputs. In: Micciancio, D. (ed.) TCC 2010. LNCS, vol. 5978, pp. 165–182. Springer, Heidelberg (2010)

29. Zhang, F., Safavi-Naini, R., Susilo, W.: Efficient verifiably encrypted signature and partially blind signature from bilinear pairings. In: Johansson, T., Maitra, S. (eds.) INDOCRYPT 2003. LNCS, vol. 2904, pp. 191–204. Springer, Heidelberg (2003)

A Omitted Proofs

Theorem 7. *The VES in Scheme 1 is unconditionally extractable.*

Proof. This follows directly from the correctness property of any SPS-EQ-$\mathcal{R}$ scheme. To see this, observe that for (m, ω) with $\omega = (\omega', sA)$ it holds that $\mathsf{VEVerify}_{\mathcal{R}}((msA, sA, A), \omega', \mathsf{pk}) = 1$ if and only if $\mathsf{Verify}_{\mathcal{R}}((msP, sP, P), \sigma', \mathsf{pk}) = 1$, where $((msP, sP, P), \sigma') \leftarrow \mathsf{ChgRep}_{\mathcal{R}}((msA, sA, A), \omega', \frac{1}{a}, \mathsf{pk}; 1)$, since

$$[(msA, sA, A)]_{\mathcal{R}} = [(msP, sP, P)]_{\mathcal{R}}. \qquad \Box$$

Theorem 8. *The VES in Scheme 1 is abuse free given that the underlying SPS-EQ-$\mathcal{R}$ scheme is unforgeable.*

Proof. We assume that there is an efficient adversary $\mathcal{A}$ winning the abuse freeness game with non-negligible probability; then we are able to construct an adversary $\mathcal{B}$ that uses $\mathcal{A}$ to break the EUF-CMA security of the underlying SPS-EQ-$\mathcal{R}$ scheme with non-negligible probability.

$\mathcal{B}$ obtains $\mathsf{pk}_{\mathcal{R}}$ of the SPS-EQ-$\mathcal{R}$ scheme with $\ell = 3$ (and thereby implicitly the bilinear group BG) from the challenger $\mathcal{C}$ of the EUF-CMA security game, sets $\mathsf{pk} \leftarrow \mathsf{pk}_{\mathcal{R}}$. Furthermore, $\mathcal{B}$ picks $a \xleftarrow{\$} \mathbb{Z}_p^*$, computes $A \leftarrow aP$ and sets $(\mathsf{ask}, \mathsf{apk}) = (a, (\mathsf{BG}, A))$. Next, $\mathcal{B}$ runs $\mathcal{A}$ on $(\mathsf{pk}, \mathsf{ask}, \mathsf{apk})$ and answers $\mathcal{A}$'s oracle queries as follows:

$\mathsf{VESign}(\cdot, \mathsf{sk}, \mathsf{apk})$: If $\mathcal{A}$ submits a query for $m \in \mathbb{Z}_p^*$, $\mathcal{B}$ queries $\mathcal{C}$'s signing oracle for the message $(m \cdot sA, sA, A)$ for $s \xleftarrow{\$} \mathbb{Z}_p^*$, gets in return a corresponding encrypted signature ω' and gives $\omega \leftarrow (\omega', sA)$ to $\mathcal{A}$.

If at some point $\mathcal{A}$ outputs a valid encrypted message-signature pair $(m^*, \omega^* = (\omega'^*, W^*))$, such that it has not previously queried m^* to any of the oracles, then $\mathcal{B}$ will output $((m^*W^*, W^*, A), \omega'^*)$ to $\mathcal{C}$. In case that $\mathcal{A}$ has queried the VESign oracle for m^*, $\mathcal{B}$ will abort.

Note that the distribution of all values returned to $\mathcal{A}$ during the simulation is identical to the distribution of these values during a real game.

By construction, $((m^*W^*, W^*, A), \omega'^*)$ constitutes a valid SPS-EQ-$\mathcal{R}$ message-signature pair. It remains to show that for $M^* = (m^*W^*, W^*, A)$, the class $[M^*]_{\mathcal{R}}$ is different from all classes queried to $\mathcal{C}$, if m^* is different from all messages queried to the VESign oracle. VEVerify demands that the third vector component of M^* be A, which uniquely determines the representative for each class and allows for comparison. Now, if there is some $M_i = (m_i \cdot W_i, W_i, A)$ coinciding with M^* in the second component, then both vectors still differ in the first component for $m^* \neq m_i$. Likewise, if they coincide in the first component for $m^* \neq m_i$, then they cannot have equal second components. Hence, assuming that $m^* \neq m_i$ and $M^* = M_i$ for some M_i queried to $\mathcal{C}$, immediately gives a contradiction. $\square$

Theorem 9. *The VES in Scheme 1 is resolution duplicate given that the underlying SPS-EQ-$\mathcal{R}$ scheme allows perfect composition.*

Proof. Here, we have to show (1) that the outputs of $\mathsf{Sign}(m, \mathsf{sk})$ and $\mathsf{Resolve}(m, \mathsf{VESign}(m, \mathsf{sk}, \mathsf{apk}), \mathsf{ask}, \mathsf{pk})$ are distributed identically, (2) that $\mathsf{Resolve}$ is deterministic and (3) that there exists a PPT algorithm $\mathsf{Extract}(\cdot, \cdot, \cdot)$, such that for all $(\mathsf{ask}, \mathsf{apk}) \stackrel{\$}{\leftarrow} \mathsf{AKeyGen}(1^\kappa)$, $(\mathsf{sk}, \mathsf{pk}) \stackrel{\$}{\leftarrow} \mathsf{KeyGen}(1^\kappa)$, $m \in \mathcal{M}$, and random tapes $r \in \{0,1\}^*$, it is the case that

$$\mathsf{Extract}(m, \mathsf{sk}, r) = \mathsf{Resolve}(m, \mathsf{VESign}(m, \mathsf{sk}, \mathsf{apk}; r), \mathsf{ask}, \mathsf{pk}).$$

Property (2) is easy to see, since $\mathsf{Resolve}$ controls the internal randomness of $\mathsf{ChgRep}_{\mathcal{R}}$, runs it with randomness 1 and, thereby, executes it deterministically. All other parts of $\mathsf{Resolve}$ are deterministic as well.

The extract algorithm for Property (3) can be specified as $\mathsf{Extract}(m, \mathsf{sk}, r) :=$ $\mathsf{Sign}(m, \mathsf{sk}; r) = \mathsf{Sign}(m, \mathsf{sk}; (r_1, r_2)) = (\mathsf{Sign}_{\mathcal{R}}((msP, sP, P), \mathsf{sk}; r_2), sP)$ where s is drawn uniformly from $\mathbb{Z}_p^*$ using random coins r_1. For the RHS, we have

$\mathsf{Resolve}(m, \mathsf{VESign}(m, \mathsf{sk}, \mathsf{apk}; r_2), \mathsf{ask}, \mathsf{pk}) =$

$\mathsf{Resolve}(m, (\mathsf{Sign}_{\mathcal{R}}((msA, sA, A), \mathsf{sk}; r_2), sA), \mathsf{ask}, \mathsf{pk}) =$

$(\mathsf{ChgRep}_{\mathcal{R}}((msA, sA, A), \mathsf{Sign}_{\mathcal{R}}((msA, sA, A), \mathsf{sk}; r_2), \dfrac{1}{a}, \mathsf{pk}; 1)[2], sP),$

where s and t are as above. If the underlying SPS-EQ-$\mathcal{R}$ scheme allows perfect composition, this gives the same output as the specified $\mathsf{Extract}$ algorithm. With regard to (1) observe that Property (3) and the fact that the $\mathsf{Extract}$ algorithm can be expressed by Sign implies that the distributions of $\mathsf{Sign}(m, \mathsf{sk})$ and $\mathsf{Resolve}(m, \mathsf{VESign}(m, \mathsf{sk}, \mathsf{apk}), \mathsf{ask}, \mathsf{pk})$ are identical. $\square$

Interleaving Cryptanalytic Time-Memory Trade-Offs on Non-uniform Distributions

Gildas Avoine[1,2]([✉]), Xavier Carpent[3], and Cédric Lauradoux[4]

[1] INSA de Rennes, IRISA UMR 6074, F-35043 Rennes, France
gildas.avoine@irisa.fr
[2] Institut Universitaire de France, Paris, France
[3] Université Catholique de Louvain, B-1348 Louvain-la-Neuve, Belgium
[4] INRIA, Rennes, France

Abstract. Cryptanalytic time-memory trade-offs (TMTO) are famous tools available in any security expert toolbox. They have been used to break ciphers such as A5/1, but their efficiency to crack passwords made them even more popular in the security community. While symmetric keys are generated randomly according to a uniform distribution, passwords chosen by users are in practice far from being random, as confirmed by recent leakage of databases. Unfortunately, the technique used to build TMTOs is not appropriate to deal with non-uniform distributions. In this paper, we introduce an efficient construction that consists in partitioning the search set into subsets of close densities, and a strategy to explore the TMTOs associated to the subsets based on an interleaved traversal. This approach results in a significant improvement compared to currently used TMTOs. We experimented our approach on a classical problem, namely cracking 7-character NTLM Hash passwords using an alphabet with 34 special characters. This resulted in speedups ranging from 16 to 76 (depending on the input distribution) over rainbow tables, which are considered as the most efficient variant of time-memory trade-offs.

1 Introduction

Security experts are often facing the problem of guessing secret values such as passwords. Performing an exhaustive search in the set of possible secrets is an ad-hoc approach commonly used. In practice, the search time can usually be reduced (on average) by exploiting side information on the values to be guessed. For example, a password cracker checks the most commonly used passwords and their variants before launching an exhaustive search. This optimization is very effective, as described in [7,15]. More generally, the distribution of the secrets can be exploited to reduce the average cryptanalysis time [14].

An alternative to an exhaustive search is the cryptanalytic time-memory trade-off (TMTO) technique, introduced by Hellman in 1980 [9]. It consists for an adversary in precalculating values that are then used to speed up the attack itself. The precalculation is quite expensive but they are done once, and the cryptanalysis time is significantly reduced if a large memory is used to store

© Springer International Publishing Switzerland 2015
G. Pernul et al. (Eds.): ESORICS 2015, Part I, LNCS 9326, pp. 165–184, 2015.
DOI: 10.1007/978-3-319-24174-6_9

the precalculation. Nowadays, TMTOs are used by most password crackers, for example Ophcrack that is considered to be the most efficient password cracker, which implements a TMTO variant due to Oechslin [16] and known as the *rainbow tables*.

Unfortunately, TMTOs do not behave well with non-uniform distributions of secrets because TMTOs, by construction, uniformly explore the set of considered secrets. Duplicating secrets in the search set for instance artificially creates a non-uniform distribution but this approach does not make sense in practice due to the excessive waste of memory. Providing an efficient solution would be very impactful in practice, though, not only for cracking passwords, but also for solving any problem that can be reduced to a chosen plaintext attack. For example, anonymization techniques based on hashing email addresses or MAC addresses are vulnerable targets for non-uniform TMTOs.

This paper introduces a technique to make cryptanalytic time-memory trade-offs compliant with non-uniform distributions. More precisely, the approach consists in (i) dividing a set into subsets of close densities, and (ii) exploring the related time-memory trade-offs in an interleaved way (instead of sequentially) defined by a density-related metric. The technique significantly improves the cryptanalysis time when considering non-uniform distributions: we applied our technique to crack passwords and demonstrated that we are up to 76 times faster than state-of-the-art techniques [16] when considering real-life password distributions.

After an introduction to TMTOs in Sect. 2, we describe and analyze our technique in Sect. 3 and explain how to interleave the TMTOs in Sect. 4. Section 5 explains the memory allocation, and Sect. 6 provides experimental results.

2   Cryptanalytic Time-Memory Trade-Offs

2.1   Hellman Scheme

Hellman introduced in [9] a method to do an efficient cryptanalysis of a one-way function, the cryptanalytic time-memory trade-off (or TMTO). Given y, the goal is to discover x such that $h(x) = y$, with $h : A \to B$ a one-way function (such as a hash function or a block cipher). As its name suggests, it is a trade-off between two simple solutions, the exhaustive search and the lookup table. The exhaustive search consists in computing h over all possible input values in A, checking every time if the image corresponds to y. It requires no memory or precalculation, but on average $|A|/2$ evaluations of h. The lookup table approach creates offline a huge table mapping all inputs in A with their image through h. During the online phase (when queried with an image), this approach requires no h evaluation and is very quick, but the precalculation cost is $N = |A|$ evaluations of h, and more importantly the N mappings are saved in memory. Hellman's method on the other hand, has an offline cost of $O(N)$, and an online cost of $O(N^2/M^2)$ for M units of memory.

2.2 Oechslin Scheme

There has been quite a few variants to Hellman's method, but arguably the most significant improvement is the *rainbow table*, introduced by Oechslin in [16]. Rainbow tables are faster in practice than Hellman tables [12,16], and are implemented in many popular tools, especially in the password-cracking scene (see e.g. Ophcrack [17], RainbowCrack [20]).

Rainbow tables are heavily inspired from Hellman tables and their behavior is similar. In the offline phase, a series of chains of hashes is built, by alternating $h : A \rightarrow B$, the hash function to be inverted, and $r_i : B \rightarrow A$, a *reduction function*. The goal of the reduction function is to output an arbitrary point in A in an efficient and deterministic way, and with outputs uniformly distributed in A (given inputs uniformly distributed in B). A typical reduction function set is:

$$r_i(y) = (y + i) \bmod |A|.$$

A different reduction function r_i is used at each iteration i (this is the major difference with Hellman tables where the same reduction function is used in a table[1]). Chains start with an arbitrary point in A. They are all of a given length t, and m chains are built this way. Of all the points in the chains, only the starting and ending points are saved. Figure 1 depicts the construction of a rainbow table.

Tables are said to be *perfect* [4,16] or *clean* [2] when they contain no merges. A major advantage of rainbow tables over Hellman tables is that in rainbow tables, collisions only result in merges when they happened in the same column (whereas collisions always lead to merges in Hellman tables). In that case, merging chains result in duplicate ending points. It is therefore very easy to remove these chains and create clean tables. Clean tables have a maximal size (on average, only a given number of different ending points may be obtained by

$$
\begin{array}{|c|c c c c c c|}
\hline
X_{1,1} & \xrightarrow{r_1 \circ h} X_{1,2} & \xrightarrow{r_2 \circ h} \cdots & \xrightarrow{r_{i-1} \circ h} X_{1,i} & \xrightarrow{r_i \circ h} \cdots & \xrightarrow{r_{t-1} \circ h} & X_{1,t} \\
X_{2,1} & \xrightarrow{r_1 \circ h} X_{2,2} & \xrightarrow{r_2 \circ h} \cdots & \xrightarrow{r_{i-1} \circ h} X_{2,i} & \xrightarrow{r_i \circ h} \cdots & \xrightarrow{r_{t-1} \circ h} & X_{2,t} \\
\vdots & \vdots & \ddots & \vdots & \ddots & & \vdots \\
X_{j,1} & \xrightarrow{r_1 \circ h} X_{j,2} & \xrightarrow{r_2 \circ h} \cdots & \xrightarrow{r_{i-1} \circ h} X_{j,i} & \xrightarrow{r_i \circ h} \cdots & \xrightarrow{r_{t-1} \circ h} & X_{j,t} \\
\vdots & \vdots & \ddots & \vdots & \ddots & & \vdots \\
X_{m,1} & \xrightarrow{r_1 \circ h} X_{m,2} & \xrightarrow{r_2 \circ h} \cdots & \xrightarrow{r_{i-1} \circ h} X_{m,i} & \xrightarrow{r_i \circ h} \cdots & \xrightarrow{r_{t-1} \circ h} & X_{m,t} \\
\hline
\end{array}
$$

Fig. 1. Structure of a rainbow table. The framed columns, respectively the starting points and the ending points, are the parts stored in memory.

---

[1] Multiple tables with different reduction functions are used in both Hellman and rainbow tables, although there are much more tables in typical settings for Hellman tables.

computing chains from all possible starting points), and have a bounded probability of success of about 86 %. In order to have a higher probability of success,
several rainbow tables are computed, using a different reduction function set for
each (a typical number is 4).

The online phase works as follows. Given an image y, the goal is to find x
such that $h(x) = y$. The first step is to compute $r_{t-1}(y)$, and check whether
it appears in the ending points list. If an ending point $X_{j,t}$ matches $r_{t-1}(y)$,
a chain is rebuilt from $X_{j,1}$ up to $X_{j,t-1}$, and $h(X_{j,t-1})$ is compared to y. If
they are equal, the search stops here and the preimage is $x = X_{j,t-1}$. If they
differ (this situation is called a *false alarm* and is due to the collisions created
by the reduction functions), the search goes on to the next table, where $r_{t-1}(y)$
is computed for that table. When all tables are searched in the last column, the
next step is to compute $r_{t-1}(h(r_{t-2}(y)))$ and to proceed to the next column. This
procedure goes on until the answer is found, or until all t columns are searched
through, in which case the search fails (as said previously, the number of tables
can be adjusted to make this event extremely rare).

2.3   Related Works

There exists many variants of the original cryptanalytic time-memory trade-off
introduced by Hellman [9], in particular the distinguished points [8,11,21] and
the rainbow tables [16]. The choice on which variant to apply depends on the
parameters (space size, memory, probability of success), and the applicability of
their various optimizations (see [6,12,16] for discussions on their comparison).
Lately however, rainbow tables have been shown [12] to be superior to the other
trade-offs in most practical scenarios, and maximal tables have the best online
performance (despite being slower to precompute). That being said, the interleaving technique discussed in this paper can be easily adapted to other variants
or to non-maximal rainbow tables.

Maximal-Sized Rainbow Tables. This work focuses on clean maximal-sized
rainbow tables. Clean rainbow tables have been analyzed extensively [4,12]. Some
earlier results on maximal-size rainbow tables from [4] that are relevant for the
rest of the analysis are cited below for reference.

Result 1. *The probability of success of a set of ℓ clean rainbow tables of maximal
size is:*

$$P^* \approx 1 - e^{-2\ell}.$$

Result 2. *The average number of h evaluations during a search in column k
(column 0 being the rightmost one) of a set of ℓ clean rainbow tables of maximal
size with chains of size t is:*

$$C_k = k + (t - k + 1)q_{t-k+1},$$

with

$$q_i = 1 - \frac{i(i-1)}{t(t+1)}.$$

Result 3. *The average number of h evaluations during the online phase of a set of ℓ clean rainbow tables of maximal size with m chains of size t on a problem set of size N is:*

$$T = \sum_{k=1}^{t} \left(1 - \left(1 - \frac{m}{N}\right)^{\ell}\right) \left(1 - \frac{m}{N}\right)^{(k-1)\ell} \sum_{i=1}^{k} \ell C_k + \left(1 - \frac{m}{N}\right)^{t\ell} \sum_{k=1}^{t} \ell C_k.$$

Rainbow Table Improvements. Rainbow tables have had a few improvements of their own. Although they are not considered in this article, they are worth mentioning as they are independent and complementary to the interleaving technique.

Checkpoints, introduced by Avoine, Junod and Oechslin in [3] are additional data related to the chain that is stored alongside the starting points and the ending points. Their goal is to alleviate the overhead due to false alarms at the cost of a bit of extra memory.

Efficient storage is important in time-memory trade-offs, as more chains translates directly into faster online time. Techniques to store starting and ending points efficiently are discussed in [2].

Ending point truncation (as described for instance in [12]) is another effort to reduce memory usage. Truncating the ending points reduces storage required for chains, and thus more chains can be stored in the same amount of memory. A drawback is that it introduces additional false alarms and thus increases online cost somewhat, but a modest amount of truncation has been shown to be valuable.

Non-uniform Distribution. Working with non-uniform distribution is the core aspect of our work, and several approaches have been proposed [10,13].

A possible means to favor some passwords over some others is to introduce a bias in the reduction functions [10]. However, the technique suffers from implementation issues and is not profitable in practice, as stated in [10].

Markov chains have been used to search through probable passwords instead of improbable ones [13,15]. This is essentially the adaptation of dictionary attacks on time-memory trade-offs, as it allows to search for some passwords at the expense of not covering some others. Interleaving is different in that it aims at covering a given set, but searching through it in an efficient way, given its probability distribution. As detailed in Sect. 6, we used statistics on common passwords to guide the partitioning of the input set. One could alternatively use the technique described in [13] to determine the partitioning.

3   Interleaving

3.1   Description

The nature of rainbow tables dictates that each point of the input set is recovered using on average the same time. There is no bias in the coverage either: each point is covered a priori with the same probability. In order to work efficiently with a non-uniform input distribution, the technique introduced in this paper consists in (1) dividing the TMTO into several *sub-TMTOs* and (2) balancing the online search between the sub-TMTOs.

The TMTO is divided into several sub-TMTOs such that each subdivision of the input set is close to be uniform. For instance, if one wants to build a TMTO against passwords containing alphanumeric and special characters, two sub-TMTOs can be built on a partition of the input set: alphanumeric passwords on one side, and passwords containing special characters on the other side. As illustrated on Fig. 2, this makes sense because the first set (A_1) is considerably larger although most users choose their passwords in the second set (A_2). We say that the first set has a higher *password density* than the second one. This density disparity is not exploited in regular TMTOs while Sect. 5 demonstrates that a TMTO covering a high-density subset should be devoted a higher memory.

Formally, let the input set A be partitioned into n input subsets[2] $[A]_b$ of size $|[A]_b| = [N]_b$. Each subset has a probability p_b that the answer to the challenge in the online phase lies in $[A]_b$. The part of the trade-off dedicated to $[A]_b$ is named "sub-TMTO b". The memory is divided and a slice $[M]_b = \rho_b M$ is allocated for each sub-TMTO b, where M is the total memory available for the trade-off. Each sub-TMTO b is built on $[A]_b$ using a memory of $[M]_b$, exactly in the same way than a regular TMTO.

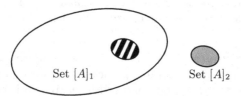

Set $[A]_1$ Set $[A]_2$

Fig. 2. Input set divided into two sets of different densities

In order to search through the sub-TMTOs, one naive approach could be to search through each of them one by one. However, this technique is very slow when the point to recover ends up being in one of the last sub-TMTOs. A more efficient approach consists in balancing the search between the sub-TMTOs: at every step of the online search, the balancer decides which sub-TMTO will be visited, as illustrated in Fig. 3 when 2 sub-TMTOs are considered. The search in a sub-TMTO is performed in the same way than in classical rainbow tables. The order of visits is chosen deterministically in a way that minimizes the average online time, as described in Sect. 4.

---

[2] For notations that already exist for rainbow tables, the convention adopted throughout the article to avoid confusion is to surround them with brackets, as summarized in Table 1.

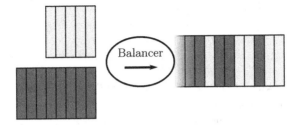

Fig. 3. The TMTO balancer defines the order of visit of the sub-TMTOs.

Table 1. Notations used in this paper.

	Meaning	Notes
n	number of subsets (and sub-TMTOs)	
$[A]_b$	input subset	$\bigcup_{b=1}^{n}[A]_b = A,\ [A]_b \cap [A]_{b'} = \emptyset\ \forall b \neq b'$
$[N]_b$	input subset size	$[N]_b = |[A]_b|,\ \sum_{b=1}^{n}[N]_b = N$
p_b	intrinsic probability of subset $[A]_b$	$p_b = \Pr(x \in [A]_b|h(x)),\ \sum_{b=1}^{n}p_b = 1$
$[M]_b$	memory size for sub-TMTO b	$\sum_{b=1}^{n}[M]_b = M$
ρ_b	memory proportion for sub-TMTO b	$\rho_b M = [M]_b,\ \sum_{b=1}^{n}\rho_b = 1$
$[m]_b$	number of chains of the sub-TMTO b	$[m]_b = \frac{[M]_b}{2\lceil \log_2 N \rceil}$
$[t]_b$	length of chains of the sub-TMTO b	$[t]_b = \frac{2[N]_b}{[m]_b} - 1$
$\hat{t}$	total number of steps of the TMTO	$\hat{t} = \sum_{b=1}^{n}[t]_b$
$[C_i]_b$	cost for column i of sub-TMTO b	see Theorem 2

3.2 Analysis

Notations. In the analysis done in this article, the same number ℓ of tables is used in each sub-TMTO. It is also possible to use a different number of tables per sub-TMTO, but this results in a different probability of success for each of them.

A step is defined as being a search in one column for the ℓ tables of a given sub-TMTO. One could choose to define a step as being a search in a column for a single table of a given sub-TMTO, but doing so results in a negligible difference of performance at the cost of a more complicated analysis and implementation.

The notations used in this paper are presented in Table 1.

Online Phase

Probability of Success. The probability of success is the same in rainbow tables that use interleaving than in the undivided case, provided clean tables of maximal size are used.

Theorem 1. *The probability of success of a set of interleaved clean rainbow tables of maximal size is:*
$$P^* \approx 1 - e^{-2\ell}.$$

Proof. The probability of success is

$$P^* = \sum_{b=1}^{n} p_i P_i^*,$$

with P_i^* the probability of success of the sub-TMTO i. Since each sub-TMTO is a clean rainbow table of maximal size, we have that $P_i^* \approx 1 - e^{-2\ell}$, as computed in Result 1. The results follows from $\sum_{b=1}^{n} p_i = 1$.

Average Time. The average search time for interleaved rainbow tables is given in Theorem 2. An example of the average speedup realized is given in Sect. 6.

Theorem 2. *The average number of hash operations required in the online phase of a set of interleaved clean rainbow tables of maximal size, given a set of n input subset sizes $\{[N]_1, ..., [N]_n\}$, intrinsic probabilities $\{p_1, ..., p_n\}$, numbers of chains $\{[m]_1, ..., [m]_n\}$, and a vector $V = (V_1, ..., V_{\hat{t}})$ representing the order of visits (i.e. V_k is the sub-TMTO chosen at step k) is:*

$$T = \sum_{k=1}^{\hat{t}} p_{V_k} \left[1 - \left(1 - \frac{[m]_{V_k}}{[N]_{V_k}} \right)^{\ell} \right] \left[1 - \frac{[m]_{V_k}}{[N]_{V_k}} \right]^{(S_k-1)\ell} \sum_{i=1}^{k} \ell[C_{S_i}]_{V_i}$$

$$+ \left[\sum_{b=1}^{n} p_b \left(1 - \frac{[m]_b}{[N]_b} \right)^{[t]_b \ell} \right] \sum_{b=1}^{n} \sum_{s=1}^{[t]_b} \ell[C_s]_b, \qquad (1)$$

with $\hat{t} = \sum_{b=1}^{n} [t]_b$ the total maximum number of steps[3], and S_k the number of steps for the sub-TMTO V_k after k steps in total, that is:

$$S_k = \#\{i \le k | V_i = V_k\}.$$

Proof. The formula is a relatively direct adaptation of the average time in the undivided case (Result 3) to the interleaved case. Let y be the given hash in the online phase, and $x \in A$ be the the preimage of y. The average cryptanalysis time for a TMTO is:

$$T = \sum_{k}^{\hat{t}} \Pr(\text{search succeeds at step } k) \times (\text{cost up to step } k)$$

$$+ \Pr(\text{search fails}) \times (\text{cost of a complete search}).$$

V_k is the sub-TMTO chosen to visit at some step k. V_k has been visited $S_k - 1$ times until step k. The probability $\Pr(\text{search succeeds at step } k)$ is therefore:

$$p_{V_k} \left(1 - \left(1 - \frac{[m]_{V_k}}{[N]_{V_k}} \right)^{\ell} \right) \left(1 - \frac{[m]_{V_k}}{[N]_{V_k}} \right)^{(S_k-1)\ell}. \qquad (2)$$

---

[3] $\hat{t}$ is used instead of t in order to avoid confusion with the number of columns of the undivided TMTO, which is a different number.

The first factor in (2) is simply $\Pr(x \in [A]_{V_k})$ *(the search may not succeed otherwise). Then, for the search to succeed at step k (or step S_k within the sub-TMTO V_k), it must have failed up to now. This is the third factor in (2). The expression* $\frac{[m]_{V_k}}{[N]_{V_k}}$ *is the probability that x lies within any column of any table of the sub-TMTO V_k, provided that $x \in [A]_{V_k}$. The expression* $\left(1 - \frac{[m]_{V_k}}{[N]_{V_k}}\right)^{(S_k-1)\ell}$ *is then just the probability that x is not in any of the $(S_k - 1)\ell$ first columns visited, provided that $x \in [A]_{V_k}$. Finally, the second factor in (2) expresses the probability that x lies within one of the ℓ columns visited at this step[4], provided that $x \in [A]_{V_k}$ and that it has not been found up to now.*

The value "cost up to step k" is the sum of the cost of each step up to the current one. For each step $i \leq k$, the sub-TMTO visited is V_i (and it is its S_i-th visit), and the associated cost is $[C_{S_i}]_{V_i}$ (see Result 2).

The probability $\Pr(search\ fails)$ *is:*

$$\sum_{b=1}^{n} p_b \left(1 - \frac{[m]_b}{[N]_b}\right)^{[t]_b \ell}. \tag{3}$$

A failed search means that x is not in any of the $[t]_b$ columns of the sub-TMTO b where b is such that $x \in [A]_b$. Since the subsets $[A]_i$ form a partition of A, the law of total probability gives (3). The factor $\left(1 - \frac{[m]_b}{[N]_b}\right)^{[t]_b \ell}$ *is the probability that x is not in any of the $[t]_b$ columns of the sub-TMTO b, given $x \in [A]_b$.*

Finally, the "cost of a complete search" is the sum of the cost of each step in all sub-TMTOs, that is $\sum_{b=1}^{n} \sum_{s=1}^{[t]_b} \ell [C_s]_b$. This expression could also be written $\sum_{k=1}^{\hat{t}} \ell [C_{S_k}]_{V_k}$, but the former expression is closer to its counterpart in Theorem 3 and also highlights that the cost of failure is independent of the order of visits V.

Note that Theorem 2 for interleaved rainbow tables is a generalization of Result 3 for classical rainbow tables. In particular, if $n = 1$ and $V = (1, 1, ..., 1)$ with $|V| = t$, Theorem 2 gives the same equation as Result 3.

Worst-Case Time. A drawback of the interleaving is that it has in general a worse worst-case time than an undivided TMTO. The worst-case in interleaved rainbow tables corresponds to the second factor of the last term in (1), that is:

$$\sum_{b=1}^{n} \sum_{s=1}^{[t]_b} \ell [C_s]_b. \tag{4}$$

Note that it is independent of the subset probabilities and the order of visits.

---

[4] Note that one would normally stop the search as soon as x is found rather than continuing with all ℓ tables of this step. This results in a more complex formula for the average time, and a negligible difference numerically.

Offline Phase. Precalculation of an interleaved TMTO consists in precalculation of each sub-TMTO independently. Precalculation of a clean rainbow table set of m chains requires to build $m_1 = \alpha m$ chains, where α is a factor depending on how close to tables of maximal size the implementer wants to get (typical numbers for α are 20–50).

The precalculation cost is the same regardless of the order of visit (since this only regards the online phase), and asymptotically independent of the memory allocation for each sub-TMTO. In particular, it is the same as in the undivided case, as shown in Theorem 3.

Theorem 3. *The number of hash operations required in the precalculation phase of a set of interleaved clean rainbow tables, given a set of n input subset sizes $\{[N]_1, ..., [N]_n\}$, numbers of chains $\{[m]_1, ..., [m]_n\}$, and given α, the overhead factor for clean tables, is:*

$$P \approx 2\alpha\ell N.$$

Proof. The precalculation consists in computing, for each sub-TMTO b and for each of its ℓ tables, $[m_1]_b = \alpha[m]_b$ chains of $[t_b]$ points.

$$P = \sum_{b=1}^{n} \ell[m_1]_b[t]_b.$$

By replacing the definition of $[t]_b$ for clean tables, we get

$$P = \sum_{b=1}^{n} \ell[m_1]_b \left(\frac{2[N]_b}{[m]_b} - 1\right) \approx \sum_{b=1}^{n} \ell 2\alpha[N]_b.$$

The approximation $\left(\frac{2[N]_b}{[m]_b} - 1\right) \approx \frac{2[N]_b}{[m]_b}$ is good because, typically, $[t]_b \gg 1$. For unusually small tables, the cost is slightly overestimated. The conclusion follows from $\sum_{b=1}^{n} [N]_b = N$

Storage. In this analysis, a naive storage consisting in storing both the starting and ending points on $\lceil\log_2 N\rceil$ bits is used. This explains why the number of chains $[m]_b$ is given as $\frac{[M]_b}{2\lceil\log_2 N\rceil}$ in Table 1.

Other options could be envisaged, such as storing the starting points on $\lceil\log_2[m_1]_b\rceil$ bits and the ending points on $\lceil\log_2[N]_b\rceil$ bits, or even better, using prefix-suffix decomposition or compressed delta encoding [2]. These storage techniques improve the memory efficiency and therefore implicitly the global efficiency of the trade-off. In fact, they are even more beneficial for interleaved sub-TMTOs than for an undivided TMTO, because sub-TMTOs operate on smaller subsets, and can therefore benefit from a more substantial reduction of the memory.

However, taking these into account makes both the analysis of interleaved sub-TMTOs and their comparison with an undivided TMTO quite a bit more complex. It is nevertheless strongly encouraged to take these storage improvements into consideration for practical implementations, and for figuring out the optimal memory allocation (as discussed in Sect. 5.2) for such practical implementations.

4   Order of Visit

4.1   Discussion

This section discusses the order of visit of the columns of the sub-TMTOs. Before every step during the search, a decision is made regarding in which sub-TMTO to search through during this step. This decision should be made easily and quickly, and the goal is to have an order of visit that minimizes the average search time.

What is suggested is that a metric is computed for each sub-TMTO b. This metric is defined as being the probability to find a solution in $[A]_b$ at the next step, divided by the average amount of work at the next step in sub-TMTO b (Definition 1).

Definition 1. *The metric associated to the k-th step of sub-TMTO b is:*

$$\eta(b, k) = \frac{\Pr(x \ found \ at \ the \ k\text{-}th \ step \ in \ sub\text{-}TMTO \ b)}{\mathbb{E}[work \ for \ the \ k\text{-}th \ step \ in \ sub\text{-}TMTO \ b]},$$

with x, an answer in the online phase.

The sub-TMTO that should be visited is the one with the highest metric. This metric is quantified for the rainbow scheme case in Sect. 4.2.

4.2   Analysis

It has been shown in [4] that the probability for the preimage to be in any column is m/N. This probability is thus independent of the column visited. Moreover, it may be seen from Result 2 that the cost is monotonically increasing towards the left columns in a rainbow table. This means that it is always preferable to visit the rightmost column that is not yet visited first. Therefore, the metric is only computed for each sub-TMTO rather than for each column, since the choice of the column is implicitly the rightmost one[5].

Theorem 4. *The metric associated to the k-th step of sub-TMTO b is:*

$$\eta(b, k) = \frac{p_b \times \left(1 - \left(1 - \frac{[m]_b}{[N]_b}\right)^\ell\right)\left(1 - \frac{[m]_b}{[N]_b}\right)^{(k-1)\ell}}{\ell[C_k]_b}.$$

Proof. The numerator in Definition 1 is the probability addressed in equation (2) in the proof of Theorem 2. The denominator, the expected work required at step k in sub-TMTO b is denoted $[C_k]_b$, and is computed as indicated in Result 2. Since the search is done in ℓ tables, the total work done at this step on average is $\ell[C_k]_b$.

---

[5] Note that in rainbow tables with checkpoints [3], this is not entirely the case (columns where checkpoints are placed often have a slightly cheaper cost than the the the column immediately to their right, for instance). Nevertheless, the search is performed from right to left as well in such tables (see [3]), and experiments show that the gain of reorganizing columns visit for taking this into account is extremely small.

The Lemma 1 provided below helps demonstrating Theorem 5.

Lemma 1. *The metric $\eta(b,k)$ from Theorem 4 is a decreasing function of k.*

Proof. The numerator of $\eta(b,k)$ is decreasing, because both $\left(1 - \left(1 - \frac{[m]_b}{[N]_b}\right)^{\ell}\right)$

and p_b are constant, and because $\left(1 - \frac{[m]_b}{[N]_b}\right)^{(k-1)\ell}$ is decreasing (since $\frac{[m]_b}{[N]_b} > 0$).

The denominator is an increasing function of k since the cost of a step is increasingly expensive towards the left of a rainbow table.

Theorem 5. *The metric given in Theorem 4 is optimal, that is it minimizes T from Theorem 2 given a set of n input subset sizes $\{[N]_1, ..., [N]_n\}$, intrinsic probabilities $\{p_1, ..., p_n\}$ and numbers of chains $\{[m]_1, ..., [m]_n\}$.*

Proof. See Appendix A.

5   Input Set Partition and Memory Allocation

5.1   Input Set Partition

Dividing a set into subsets generates a time overhead for the online phase of the time-memory trade-off. Doing so is worth it if the gain outweighs this overhead. The ratio $\frac{p_b}{[N]_b}$ represents the individual probability of occurrence for each point of the $[A]_b$ subset, and is intuitively a measure of the "density" of $[A]_b$. It makes sense to divide a set when it contains subsets of unbalanced densities. A TMTO covering a high-density subset should be devoted a higher memory and searched through more rapidly than usual, and vice versa. Once the considered set is partitioned into subsets, one may compute the expected online time given using Theorem 2.

5.2   Memory Allocation

Given a partition $\{[N]_1, ..., [N]_n\}$ of the input set and their intrinsic probabilities $\{p_1, ..., p_n\}$, a memory size must be assigned to each subset. Given $[N]_b$, we have $[M]_b = \rho_b M$. The expression T given in Theorem 2 is not simple enough to determine analytically an optimal memory allocation. Instead, the memory allocation can be done solving an optimization problem that consists in minimizing T by changing the variables $\rho_1, ..., \rho_n$.

When the number of subsets n is small, the memory allocation can be found easily with a grid search. That is, T is evaluated at discretized values of the parameters $\rho_1, ..., \rho_n$ (with $\sum_{i=1}^{n} \rho_i = 1$), and the point where T is minimal is kept as the selected memory allocation.

This technique however becomes quite costly when the number of subsets n is too large, or when the desired resolution of the discretization is too thin. Metaheuristic techniques of local search such as Hill Climbing [19] can be used instead to search for the optimal memory allocation more efficiently.

6   Results

In this section, the interleaving technique is illustrated on password cracking.

6.1   Statistics

In order to determine the password distribution, two publicly-available datasets have been considered: "RockYou" and "10 million combos". The RockYou dataset originated from www.rockyou.com, a gaming website that lost 32.6 million unencrypted passwords in 2009. Among those passwords 14.3 million are unique. The *10 million combos* was released by Mark Burnett in 2015. This 10 million passwords dataset contains passwords from various hack sources according to the author from which 5.18 million are unique. These datasets are for example used for wordlist attacks by the well-known password crackers Hashcat [1] and John the Ripper [18].

Tables 2 and 3 present some statistics on these datasets (the results are shown up to length of 7). Each cell of the two tables represents the per mille of passwords that have the length indicated on the left, and that correspond to the character set indicated on the top. More precisely: "Special" relates to passwords with at least a special character[6], "Lower" to passwords containing only lowercase letters, "Upper" to passwords containing only uppercase letters, "Digit" to passwords containing only digits, "Alpha" to passwords containing only letters (at least one lowercase and one uppercase), "Alnum" to passwords containing letters and digits (at least one letter and one digit). Such statistics can then be used to feed the parameters for the interleaving technique.

Table 2. Statistics for the "RockYou" dataset (expressed in per mille).

Length	Special	Lower	Upper	Digit	Alpha	Alnum
0	0.000	0.000	0.000	0.000	0.000	0.000
1	0.000	0.002	0.000	0.002	0.000	0.000
2	0.000	0.024	0.002	0.005	0.000	0.001
3	0.002	0.153	0.010	0.032	0.003	0.006
4	0.007	1.384	0.052	0.634	0.026	0.055
5	0.283	28.930	1.401	6.550	0.511	3.013
6	3.022	122.316	4.528	69.899	2.131	58.435
7	5.709	83.980	3.034	19.684	1.848	78.546

---

[6] Here, a special character is one of {!"#$%&'()*+,-./:;<=>?@[\]^_`{|}~␣. These are the characters denoted as such in the "XP special" table of the Ophcrack software [17].

Table 3. Statistics for the "10 million combos" dataset (expressed in per mille).

Length	Special	Lower	Upper	Digit	Alpha	Alnum
0	0.000	0.000	0.000	0.000	0.000	0.000
1	0.000	0.000	0.000	0.000	0.000	0.000
2	0.000	0.000	0.000	0.000	0.000	0.000
3	0.004	0.292	0.026	0.153	0.034	0.083
4	0.057	17.357	0.490	14.212	0.515	1.890
5	0.145	31.451	0.804	7.427	1.489	8.194
6	0.782	117.591	2.965	70.308	6.604	56.200
7	1.024	74.965	1.742	20.857	3.306	64.425

6.2 RockYou

We decided to set A to the set of passwords of the special character set (96 characters) of length 7 or less, which corresponds to the same set covered in the "XP special" table of the Ophcrack software [17]. Likewise, we set the total memory to 8 GB, which is about the memory used for this table. With these settings, an undivided TMTO has an average cryptanalysis time of $T = 6.27 \times 10^9$ operations (obtained from Result 3).

We chose the following partition: $[A]_1$ is set to the passwords of length 7 (exactly) that contain at least one special character, and $[A]_2$ the rest of the passwords. This gives the following parameters for the RockYou dataset:

$$[N]_1 = 96^7 - 62^7 = 7.16 \times 10^{13} \qquad\qquad p_1 = 0.0143$$
$$[N]_2 = N - [N]_1 = 4.31 \times 10^{12} \qquad\qquad p_2 = 0.9857.$$

The probabilities are taken from Table 2, and are adjusted such that the sum of probabilities up to length 7 is 1.

Figure 4 represents T according to ρ_1: the memory allocation is optimal when $\rho_1 = 0.5957$, with $T = 3.81 \times 10^8$ operations, which represents a speedup of about 16.45 with respect to the undivided case[7].

6.3 10 Million Combos

This second dataset presents comparable statistics to RockYou. Applying the same partitioning, we have:

$$[N]_1 = 96^7 - 62^7 = 7.16 \times 10^{13} \qquad\qquad p_1 = 0.0026$$
$$[N]_2 = N - [N]_1 = 4.31 \times 10^{12} \qquad\qquad p_2 = 0.9974.$$

---

[7] For instance, in terms of time elapsed on a laptop capable of performing 3×10^6 SHA-1 operations per second, and on a memory of 8 GB, this corresponds to 34'50" (for the undivided case) reduced to 2'07" (for the interleaved case) on average.

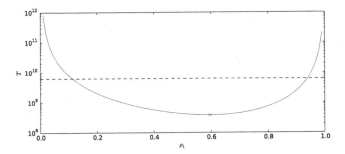

Fig. 4. Memory allocation for the RockYou database: the solid line represents the average number of operations as a function of the proportion ρ_1 of the memory devoted to the first sub-TMTO. The cross mark is the optimal memory allocation, and the dashed line represents the cost of an undivided TMTO, about 16.45 times slower.

This partitioning yields an even better result: $T = 1.42 \times 10^8$ at the optimal memory division $\rho_1 = 0.4695$, which represents a speedup of 44.29. This further improvement with respect to RockYou is due to p_1 being even smaller in the case of the 10 million combos dataset, which results in a stronger disparity in the densities of A_1 and A_2.

In order to improve further the gain, one may partition A into more subsets. This was tried with three subsets: we sorted the cells of Table 3 in increasing order of density, and chose the partitioning that produced the best results (see Appendix B for details on the subsets chosen). These subsets correspond to:

$$[N]_1 = 7.16 \times 10^{13} \qquad p_1 = 0.0026$$
$$[N]_2 = 4.27 \times 10^{12} \qquad p_2 = 0.1962$$
$$[N]_3 = 4.67 \times 10^{10} \qquad p_2 = 0.8012.$$

The average time is of 8.20×10^7, which represents a speedup of 76.48. The optimal memory decomposition was found using Hill Climbing [19]:

$$\rho_1 = 0.5604 \qquad \rho_2 = 0.3931 \qquad \rho_3 = 0.0466.$$

Partitioning into four subsets or more did not yield a better speedup in our experiments.

6.4   Discussion

Interleaving produces a gain over the classical method of 16.45, 44.29 and 76.48, respectively for RockYou with 2 subsets, 10 million combos with 2 subsets, and 10 million combos with 3 subsets. The gain thus strongly depends on the input distribution, and can be arbitrarily big. On the other hand, interleaving may not be profitable at all when the input distribution is close to uniform.

Increasing the number of subsets allows for a finer division of the input set, and is worthwhile when the resulting subsets have important differences of density. It has however an overhead, which means that in practice (at least for the distributions described in Sect. 6.1), the optimal size of the partitioning is relatively small.

Barkan, Biham and Shamir showed [5] that the cost of a search using a time-memory trade-offs is theoretically lower-bounded. With an appropriate input distribution, one could go below that bound using interleaving, which may seem to be in contradiction with the results of [5]. However, these results were provided in a context of uniform input distribution, so the bound is not violated since the assumptions are different.

7   Conclusion

This paper introduces a technique to magnify the efficiency of cryptanalytic time-memory trade-offs when the considered distribution of secrets is non-uniform. It consists – during the precalculation phase – in dividing the input set into smaller subsets of unbalanced densities and applying a time-memory trade-off on every subset. As importantly, the contribution also consists of a method to interleave – during the attack phase – the exploration of the time-memory trade-offs. For that, a metric to select at each step the time-memory trade-off to be explored is introduced, and a proof of optimality is provided.

Questions such as how the efficiency changes when a TMTO built on some distribution is applied to another distribution, or whether it is possible to find optimal memory division analytically remain to be explored.

The efficiency of the technique is practically demonstrated to crack 7-character passwords selected in a 96-character alphabet. Password length and alphabet size have been chosen in compliance with tools currently used by security experts to crack LM Hash passwords. The password distributions used to evaluate the efficiency of the technique come from recently leaked password databases of well-known websites. It has been shown that the time required to crack such passwords is divided by up 76 when the technique introduced in this paper is applied, compared to current methods. The efficiency can be even better when considering distributions with a higher standard deviation. As far as we know, this is the first time an improvement on time-memory trade-off divides by more than two the cracking time since Hellman's seminal work.

Acknowledgments. We thank the anonymous reviewers for their constructive comments.

A   Proof of Theorem 5

For the sake of clarity, the following simplified notations are used in this proof:

$$f(b,k) = p_b \left(1 - \left(1 - \frac{[m]_b}{[N]_b}\right)^\ell\right)\left(1 - \frac{[m]_b}{[N]_b}\right)^{(k-1)\ell},$$

$$g(b,k) = \ell[C_k]_b.$$

Let V be a vector describing an arbitrary order of visit. Let V^* be a vector describing the order of visit dictated by the metric given in Theorem 4. V is thus an arbitrary permutation of V^*. S_k (resp. S_k^*) is defined as in Theorem 2, that is how many times V_k (resp. V_k^*) has been visited up to step k included:

$$S_k = \#\{i \leq k | V_i = V_k\},$$
$$S_k^* = \#\{i \leq k | V_i^* = V_k^*\}.$$

Additionally, let $\sigma(b, k)$ be the position of the k-th apparition of the sub-TMTO b in V (and $\sigma^*(b, k)$ its V^* equivalent). In particular, the following identity binds these notations:

$$\sigma(V_i, S_i) = \sigma^*(V_i^*, S_i^*) = i \quad \forall 1 \leq i \leq \hat{t}.$$

The goal is to minimize (1), that is:

$$
T = \sum_{k=1}^{\hat{t}} p_{V_k} \left[1 - \left(1 - \frac{[m]_{V_k}}{[N]_{V_k}} \right)^{\ell} \right] \left[1 - \frac{[m]_{V_k}}{[N]_{V_k}} \right]^{(S_k-1)\ell} \sum_{i=1}^{k} \ell[C_{S_i}]_{V_i}
$$
$$
+ \left[\sum_{b=1}^{n} p_b \left(1 - \frac{[m]_b}{[N]_b} \right)^{[t]_b \ell} \right]^{[t]_b \ell} \sum_{b=1}^{n} \sum_{s=1}^{[t]_b} \ell[C_s]_b
$$
$$
= \sum_{k=1}^{\hat{t}} f(V_k, S_k) \sum_{i=1}^{k} g(V_i, S_i) + constant.
$$

Note that the second term of this expression is constant, regardless of the choice for V. Therefore, in order to prove the optimality of the metric and thus the optimality of the choice of V^*, it suffices to show that $G \geq G^*$, with:

$$
G = \sum_{k=1}^{\hat{t}} f(V_k, S_k) \sum_{i=1}^{k} g(V_i, S_i), \tag{5}
$$

$$
G^* = \sum_{k=1}^{\hat{t}} f(V_k^*, S_k^*) \sum_{i=1}^{k} g(V_i^*, S_i^*), \tag{6}
$$

and with V any permutation of V^*. Equation 5 can be re-written such that sub-TMTOs are considered in consecutive order rather than considering them in the order of visit (this is a mere re-ordering of the terms in the sum):

$$
G = \sum_{b=1}^{n} \sum_{k=1}^{[t]_b} f(b, k) \sum_{i=1}^{\sigma(b,k)} g(V_i, S_i),
$$

and likewise for the sum in (6). It is now possible to factorize the difference $G - G^*$ as such:

$$
G - G^* = \sum_{b=1}^{n} \sum_{k=1}^{[t]_b} f(b, k) \left[\sum_{i=1}^{\sigma(b,k)} g(V_i, S_i) - \sum_{i=1}^{\sigma^*(b,k)} g(V_i^*, S_i^*) \right]. \tag{7}
$$

Some terms cancel each other out in the two sums of the bracketed factor in (7), i.e. terms that appear in both sums. Let $\Delta_{b,k}^+$ (resp. $\Delta_{b,k}^-$) be the set of positions in V (resp. V^*) that only appear in the left (resp. right) sum. Formally,

$$\Delta_{b,k}^+ = \{j < \sigma(b,k) \mid \sigma^*(V_j, S_j) > \sigma^*(b,k)\},$$
$$\Delta_{b,k}^- = \{j < \sigma^*(b,k) \mid \sigma(V_j^*, S_j^*) > \sigma(b,k)\}.$$

This allows to rewrite the difference (7) as:

$$G - G^* = \sum_{b=1}^{n} \sum_{k=1}^{[t]_b} f(b,k) \left[\sum_{i \in \Delta_{b,k}^+} g(V_i, S_i) - \sum_{i \in \Delta_{b,k}^-} g(V_i^*, S_i^*) \right]. \tag{8}$$

By construction, the following implication holds between Δ^+ and Δ^-:

$$\sigma(b,k) \in \Delta_{b',k'}^+ \iff \sigma^*(b',k') \in \Delta_{b,k}^-. \tag{9}$$

Indeed, we have:

$$\sigma(b,k) \in \Delta_{b',k'}^+$$
$$\iff \sigma(b,k) < \sigma(b',k') \wedge \sigma^*(V_{\sigma(b,k)}, S_{\sigma(b,k)}) > \sigma^*(b',k')$$
$$\iff \sigma(b,k) < \sigma(b',k') \wedge \sigma^*(b,k) > \sigma^*(b',k') \tag{10}$$

The first equivalence is the definition of $\Delta_{b,k}^+$, and the second comes from the fact that $V_{\sigma(b,k)} = b$ and $S_{\sigma(b,k)} = k$, by definition of V and S. Likewise,

$$\sigma^*(b',k') \in \Delta_{b,k}^-$$
$$\iff \sigma^*(b',k') < \sigma^*(b,k) \wedge \sigma(V_{\sigma^*(b',k')}^*, S_{\sigma^*(b',k')}^*) > \sigma(b,k)$$
$$\iff \sigma^*(b',k') < \sigma^*(b,k) \wedge \sigma(b',k') > \sigma(b,k) \tag{11}$$

The implication (9) comes from the equivalence between (10) and (11). As a particular case of (9), we have:

$$j \in \Delta_{b,k}^- \iff \sigma(b,k) \in \Delta_{V_j^*,S_j^*}^+.$$

This means that for each negative term $-f(b,k)g(V_j^*, S_j^*)$ in (8), there is also a positive counterpart $f(V_j^*, S_j^*)g(b,k)$. This allows to rewrite the difference (8) as a simple sum of opposed crossed terms:

$$G - G^* = \sum \left[f(V_j^*, S_j^*)g(b,k) - f(b,k)g(V_j^*, S_j^*) \right]. \tag{12}$$

We have that $\sigma^*(b,k) > j = \sigma^*(V_j^*, S_j^*)$, for all $j \in \Delta_{b,k}^-$, by definition of $\Delta_{b,k}^-$. Moreover, since the metric used to construct V^* is decreasing (see Lemma 1), we have that:

$$\eta(b,k) \geq \eta(b',k'),$$
$$f(b,k)g(b',k') \geq f(b',k')g(b,k),$$

for all b, k, b', k' such that $\sigma^*(b,k) < \sigma^*(b',k')$. Using this fact in (12) shows that each term of the sum is positive, and thus $G \geq G^*$.

B   Subsets of 10 Million Combos

The partition in three subsets that yields the best speedup on the 10 million combos dataset is depicted in Table 4.

Table 4. Subset indices for the partitioning done on 10 million combos.

Length	Special	Lower	Upper	Digit	Alpha	Alnum
0	3	3	3	3	3	3
1	3	3	3	3	3	3
2	3	3	3	3	3	3
3	3	3	3	3	3	3
4	3	3	3	3	3	3
5	2	3	3	3	3	3
6	2	3	3	3	2	3
7	1	3	2	2	2	2

References

1. Atom: The Hashcat password cracker (2014). http://hashcat.net/hashcat/
2. Avoine, G., Carpent, X.: Optimal storage for rainbow tables. In: Lee, H.-S., Han, D.-G. (eds.) ICISC 2013. LNCS, vol. 8565, pp. 144–157. Springer, Heidelberg (2014)
3. Avoine, G., Junod, P., Oechslin, P.: Time-memory trade-offs: false alarm detection using checkpoints. In: Maitra, S., Veni Madhavan, C.E., Venkatesan, R. (eds.) INDOCRYPT 2005. LNCS, vol. 3797, pp. 183–196. Springer, Heidelberg (2005)
4. Avoine, G., Junod, P., Oechslin, P.: Characterization and improvement of time-memory trade-off based on perfect tables. ACM Trans. Inf. Syst. Secur. TISSEC **11**(4), 1–22 (2008)
5. Barkan, E., Biham, E., Shamir, A.: Rigorous Bounds on cryptanalytic time/memory tradeoffs. In: Dwork, C. (ed.) CRYPTO 2006. LNCS, vol. 4117, pp. 1–21. Springer, Heidelberg (2006)
6. Barkan, E.P.: Cryptanalysis of ciphers and protocols. Ph.D. thesis, Technion - Israel Institute of Technology, Haifa, Israel, March 2006
7. Bonneau, J.: The science of guessing: analyzing an anonymized corpus of 70 million passwords. In: IEEE Symposium on Security and Privacy - S&P 2012, San Francisco, CA, USA. IEEE Computer Society, May 2012
8. Denning, D.: Cryptography and Data Security, p. 100. Addison-Wesley, Boston (1982)
9. Hellman, M.: A cryptanalytic time-memory trade off. IEEE Trans. Inf. Theory IT **26**(4), 401–406 (1980)
10. Hoch, Y.Z.: Security analysis of generic iterated hash functions. Ph.D. thesis, Weizmann Institute of Science, Rehovot, Israel, August 2009

11. Hong, J., Jeong, K.C., Kwon, E.Y., Lee, I.-S., Ma, D.: Variants of the distinguished point method for cryptanalytic time memory trade-offs. In: Chen, L., Mu, Y., Susilo, W. (eds.) ISPEC 2008. LNCS, vol. 4991, pp. 131–145. Springer, Heidelberg (2008)

12. Lee, G.W., Hong, J.: A comparison of perfect table cryptanalytic tradeoff algorithms. Cryptology ePrint Archive, report 2012/540 (2012)

13. Lestringant, P., Oechslin, P., Tissières, C.: Limites des tables rainbow et comment les dépasser en utilisant des méthodes probabilistes optimisées (in French). In: Symposium sur la sécurité des technologies de l'information et des communications - SSTIC, Rennes, France, June 2013

14. Massey, J.L.: Guessing and entropy. In: International Symposium on Information Theory - ISIT 1994, Trondheim, Norway, p. 204. IEEE, June 1994

15. Narayanan, A., Shmatikov, V.: Fast dictionary attacks on passwords using time-space tradeoff. In: ACM Conference on Computer and Communications Security - CCS 2005, Alexandria, VA, USA, pp. 364–372. ACM, November 2005

16. Oechslin, P.: Making a faster cryptanalytic time-memory trade-off. In: Boneh, D. (ed.) CRYPTO 2003. LNCS, vol. 2729, pp. 617–630. Springer, Heidelberg (2003)

17. Oechslin, P.: The ophcrack password cracker (2014). http://ophcrack.source forge.net/

18. Peslyak, A.: The John the Ripper password cracker (2014). http://www.openwall. com/john/

19. Russell, S.J., Norvig, P.: Artificial Intelligence: A Modern Approach, vol. 2. Pearson Education, Upper Saddle River (2003)

20. Shuanglei, Z.: The RainbowCrack project (2014). http://project-rainbowcrack. com/

21. Standaert, F.-X., Rouvroy, G., Quisquater, J.-J., Legat, J.-D.: A time-memory tradeoff using distinguished points: new analysis & FPGA results. In: Kaliski, B.S., Koç, C.K., Paar, C. (eds.) CHES 2002. LNCS, vol. 2523, pp. 593–609. Springer, Heidelberg (2002)

Efficient Message Authentication Codes
with Combinatorial Group Testing

Kazuhiko Minematsu$^{(\boxtimes)}$

NEC Corporation, Kawasaki, Japan
k-minematsu@ah.jp.nec.com

Abstract. Message authentication code, MAC for short, is a symmetric-key cryptographic function for authenticity. A standard MAC verification only tells whether the message is valid or invalid, and thus we can not identify which part is corrupted in case of invalid message. In this paper we study a class of MAC functions that enables to identify the part of corruption, which we call group testing MAC (GTM). This can be seen as an application of a classical (non-adaptive) combinatorial group testing to MAC. Although the basic concept of GTM (or its keyless variant) has been proposed in various application areas, such as data forensics and computer virus testing, they rather treat the underlying MAC function as a black box, and exact computation cost for GTM seems to be overlooked. In this paper, we study the computational aspect of GTM, and show that a simple yet non-trivial extension of parallelizable MAC (PMAC) enables $O(m + t)$ computation for m data items and t tests, irrespective of the underlying test matrix we use, under a natural security model. This greatly improves efficiency from naively applying a black-box MAC for each test, which requires $O(mt)$ time. Based on existing group testing methods, we also present experimental results of our proposal and observe that ours runs as fast as taking single MAC tag, with speed-up from the conventional method by factor around 8 to 15 for $m = 10^4$ to 10^5 items.

Keywords: Message authentication code · Combinatorial group testing · Data corruption · Provable security

1 Introduction

Message authentication code (MAC) is a symmetric-key cryptographic function for authenticity. A MAC function, F, takes a secret key K and a message M to produce a tag $T = F(K, M)$. A legitimate user with key K first takes (M, T) and later verifies the validity of a tuple (M', T'), which may be corrupted from (M, T), by computing $T'' = F(K, M')$ and checking if $T'' = T'$ holds or not. While MAC-based integrity check is simple and efficient, if verification fails one can not obtain any further information on what part of message is corrupted. On the other extreme side, by partitioning data into m items, say 4K-byte sectors of

© Springer International Publishing Switzerland 2015
G. Pernul et al. (Eds.): ESORICS 2015, Part I, LNCS 9326, pp. 185–202, 2015.
DOI: 10.1007/978-3-319-24174-6_10

HDD, and taking tags for each item, we can always identify all corrupted items. However this can be impractical due to a huge impact to the storage.

This tread-off between the number of tags and the information on corruption can be improved by taking multiple MAC tags for overlapping parts of data items. If we carefully choose overlapping parts it allows us to identify the corrupted items if they are few. This is an interesting application of combinatorial group testing (CGT) to message authentication, as pointed out by literatures in various applications areas. Here, CGT is a method to identify defectives from a large number of samples using group tests (see Du and Hwang [15] for a good summary). For example, Goodrich et al. [20] proposed a MAC scheme combined with CGT for data forensics applications. Crescenzo et al. [11] proposed a MAC scheme for corruption localization not only restricted to identification. For schemes other than MAC, Crescenzo, Jiang and Safavi-Naini proposed corruption-localizing hash schemes [12] and it was further improved and extended at [8,10] incorporating the theory of CGT. We can find various applications such as computer virus testing [13] and HDD integrity check [17]. Relationship between CGT and signature batch verification was studied by Zaverucha and Stinson [30].

CGT has been extensively studied from the viewpoints of combinatorics and coding theory. In particular, non-adaptive CGT (NCGT) using t tests for m items is specified by a $t \times m$ binary test matrix, and there are numerous results on the efficient matrix constructions with primary focus on the number of tests (rows), both deterministic and randomized, see e.g. Du and Hwang [15] and Ngo and Du [24]. In application of NCGT to MAC, we first choose a test matrix and then take MAC tags following the chosen test matrix. We call such combined MAC scheme group testing MAC (GTM). GTM can in principle use any of known test matrix designs. In this paper, we study the computational cost of GTM. This has not been deeply explored by previous researches as they assume MAC function as a black box. Naturally we need to compute t MAC tags for distinct parts of m items, and standard MAC needs $O(m)$ time for computing a tag for m items (assuming constant item length). Hence the computation cost is $O(w)$ where w is the weight of test matrix, which is at most $O(mt)$. In practice GTM requires many overlapping items between distinct tests to have good ability in corruption identification, thus the computation cost is quite higher than taking single tag for all items as long as MAC function is used as a black box. In this paper, we show that a special form of MAC enables to reduce the computation cost of GTM to $O(m + t)$ for any matrix of t tests and m items. The crux of our proposal is the introduction of a parallelizable MAC defined over a vector space which efficiently handles empty string (bit string of length zero) without computation. This is a simple yet non-trivial extension of a parallelizable blockcipher-based MAC called PMAC [7,26]. Additionally our scheme also enables efficient incremental update of data items in the same manner to PMAC, and even the update of test matrix. To analyze the security of our proposal we consider several formal security notions, and show that our scheme is secure with respect to them, in a concrete provable security framework proposed by Bellare et al. [3]. Our notions are rather straightforward extension of those for deterministic MAC [5,6], and have some similarities with those seen in [12,20].

We also present experimental implementation of our scheme, using existing NCGT matrix constructions and AES blockcipher. We show that our scheme achieves essentially the same speed as the single tag computation, which is the speed of AES itself if each item is sufficiently long. The factor of speed-up compared to the conventional scheme is dependent on the matrix, and in our experiments it is expected to be around 8 to 15 for 10^4 to 10^5 items. The implementation results show that differences from theory and practice are quite small.

2 Preliminaries

Let $\{0,1\}^{\bullet}$ be the set of all binary strings, including the empty string ε. We write the bit length of $X \in \{0,1\}^{\bullet}$ by $|X|$. Here $|\varepsilon| = 0$. We define $\{0,1\}^{*} \stackrel{\text{def}}{=} \{0,1\}^{\bullet} \setminus \varepsilon$. We define a vector space consisting of m non-empty strings as $\{0,1\}^{*m} \stackrel{\text{def}}{=} (\{0,1\}^{*})^{m}$. Similarly let $\{0,1\}^{\bullet m} \stackrel{\text{def}}{=} (\{0,1\}^{\bullet})^{m}$ as a vector space consisting of m possibly empty strings, which we call extended vector space. Here note that (ε, v) and (v, ε) for $v \neq \varepsilon$ are distinct elements of $\{0,1\}^{\bullet 2}$. Let $M = (M[1], \ldots, M[m])$ and $M' = (M'[1], \ldots, M'[m])$ be vectors of m strings in $\{0,1\}^{*m}$. We define $\mathrm{diff}(M, M') = \{i : M[i] \neq M'[i]\}$ and $\Delta(M, M') = (Y[1], \ldots, Y[m])$ where $Y[i] = 1$ if $M[i] \neq M'[i]$ and otherwise $Y[i] = 0$. Let $x \odot 1 = x$ and $x \odot 0 = \varepsilon$ for any $x \in \{0,1\}^{*}$, and for $B = (B[1], \ldots, B[m]) \in \{0,1\}^{m}$, we let $M \odot B = (M[1] \odot B[1], \ldots, M[m] \odot B[m]) \in \{0,1\}^{\bullet m}$. Moreover, let $M \ominus B \in \{0,1\}^{*m}$ be a vector obtained by removing all empty strings from $M \odot B$. For example if $M = (M[1], M[2], M[3], M[4])$ and $B = (1,0,1,0)$ we have $M \odot B = (M[1], \varepsilon, M[3], \varepsilon)$ and $M \ominus B = (M[1], M[3])$.

For $n \times m$ binary matrix $\mathbb{M}$, $\mathbb{M}_i$ denotes the i-the row, $\mathbb{M}_{i,j}$ denotes the entry at i-th row and j-th column. We let $\mathcal{J}(\mathbb{M}_i) \stackrel{\text{def}}{=} \{j : \mathbb{M}_{i,j} = 1\}$. We also let $\mathrm{Hw}(\mathbb{M}) = \sum_i |\mathcal{J}(\mathbb{M}_i)|$ to denote the hamming weight of $\mathbb{M}$.

Keyed Function and Random Function. For keyed function $F : \mathcal{K} \times \mathcal{X} \to \mathcal{Y}$ with key $K \in \mathcal{K}$, we may simply write $F_K : \mathcal{X} \to \mathcal{Y}$ if key space is obvious, or even write as $F : \mathcal{X} \to \mathcal{Y}$ if being keyed with K is obvious. If $E_K : \mathcal{X} \to \mathcal{X}$ is a keyed permutation, or a blockcipher, E_K is a permutation over $\mathcal{X}$ for every $K \in \mathcal{K}$. Its inverse is denoted by E_K^{-1}. A tweakable keyed permutation, also known as tweakable blockcipher (TBC) [23] is a family of keyed permutation (blockcipher) over $\mathcal{X}$ indexed by a public parameter called tweak $V \in \mathcal{V}$. It is written as $\widetilde{E}_K : \mathcal{V} \times \mathcal{X} \to \mathcal{X}$. The encryption of TBC is written as $C = \widetilde{E}_K^V(M)$ for plaintext M, tweak V and ciphertext C, and the decryption is written as $M = \widetilde{E}_K^{-1,V}(C)$. For two keyed functions, $F_K, F'_{K'} : \mathcal{X} \to \mathcal{Y}$, we say they are compatible, i.e. they have the same input and output domains. Here, the key spaces are not necessarily identical. Let $\mathrm{Func}(n, m)$ be the set of all functions $\{0,1\}^n \to \{0,1\}^m$, and let $\mathrm{Perm}(n)$ be the set of all permutations over $\{0,1\}^n$. A uniform random function (URF) having n-bit input and m-bit output is a function family uniformly distributed over $\mathrm{Func}(n, m)$. We write $X \xleftarrow{\$} \mathcal{X}$ to denote the uniform sampling of X over $\mathcal{X}$. Then a URF is expressed as $\mathsf{R} \xleftarrow{\$} \mathrm{Func}(n, m)$. A uniform random permutation (URP) over n-bit space is similarly denoted by $\mathsf{P} \xleftarrow{\$} \mathrm{Perm}(n)$. We also define tweakable URP. Let $\mathcal{V}$ be a set of tweak and $\mathrm{Perm}^{\mathcal{V}}(n)$ be the set of all functions $\mathcal{V} \times \{0,1\}^n \to \{0,1\}^n$ such that, for any $f \in \mathrm{Perm}^{\mathcal{V}}(n)$ and $v \in \mathcal{V}$, $f(v, *)$ is a permutation. A tweakable n-bit URP with tweak $V \in \mathcal{V}$ is denoted by $\widetilde{\mathsf{P}} \xleftarrow{\$} \mathrm{Perm}^{\mathcal{V}}(n)$. In addition, a URF $\mathsf{R} : \mathcal{V} \times \mathcal{X} \to \mathcal{Y}$ is also called a tweakable URF when $V \in \mathcal{V}$ is used as a tweak in the application we discuss, and we also write it as $\widetilde{\mathsf{R}} : \mathcal{V} \times \mathcal{X} \to \mathcal{Y}$.

Pseudorandom Function. For c oracles, $O_1, O_2, \ldots, O_c$, $\mathcal{A}^{O_1, O_2, \ldots, O_c}$ denotes the adversary $\mathcal{A}$ querying these c oracles. Let $F_K, G_{K'} : \mathcal{X} \to \mathcal{Y}$ be two compatible keyed functions, and let $\mathcal{A}$ be an adversary trying to distinguish them using queries with 1-bit final output. Then the (chosen-plaintext attack, CPA) advantage of $\mathcal{A}$ is defined as

$$\mathrm{Adv}^{\mathrm{cpa}}_{F_K, G_{K'}}(\mathcal{A}) \stackrel{\mathrm{def}}{=} \Pr[\mathcal{A}^{F_K} \Rightarrow 1] - \Pr[\mathcal{A}^{G_{K'}} \Rightarrow 1],$$

where $\mathcal{A}^{F_K} \Rightarrow 1$ denotes the event that $\mathcal{A}$'s final output is 1 after queries to F_K. The probability is defined over a uniform sampling of K and internal randomness of $\mathcal{A}$. If F and G are tweakable, a tweak in a query is arbitrarily chosen by the adversary. Using URF R compatible with F_K, we define

$$\mathrm{Adv}^{\mathrm{prf}}_{F_K}(\mathcal{A}) \stackrel{\mathrm{def}}{=} \mathrm{Adv}^{\mathrm{cpa}}_{F_K, \mathsf{R}}(\mathcal{A}).$$

In a similar manner, using URP P compatible with a keyed permutation E_K we define $\mathrm{Adv}^{\mathrm{prp}}_{E_K}(\mathcal{A}) \stackrel{\mathrm{def}}{=} \mathrm{Adv}^{\mathrm{cpa}}_{E_K, \mathsf{P}}(\mathcal{A})$. For tweakable keyed permutation $\widetilde{E}_K$, we also define $\mathrm{Adv}^{\mathrm{tprp}}_{\widetilde{E}_K}(\mathcal{A}) \stackrel{\mathrm{def}}{=} \mathrm{Adv}^{\mathrm{cpa}}_{\widetilde{E}_K, \widetilde{\mathsf{P}}}(\mathcal{A})$, where $\widetilde{\mathsf{P}}$ is a tweakable URP compatible with $\widetilde{E}_K$.

If adversary $\mathcal{A}$ is with time complexity, it means the total computation time and memory of $\mathcal{A}$ required for query generation and final decision, in some fixed model. If there is no description on time complexity of $\mathcal{A}$, it means $\mathcal{A}$ has no computational restriction. Conventionally we say F_K is a pseudorandom function (PRF) if $\mathrm{Adv}^{\mathrm{cpa}}_{F_K}(\mathcal{A})$ is negligible for all practical adversaries (though the formal definition [19] requires F_K to be a function family). Similarly we say F_K is a pseudorandom permutation (PRP) if $\mathrm{Adv}^{\mathrm{prp}}_{F_K}(\mathcal{A})$ is negligible and F_K is invertible. Tweakable PRP (TPRP) is similarly defined with $\mathrm{Adv}^{\mathrm{tprp}}_{\widetilde{E}_K}(\mathcal{A})$. We also introduce the notion of tweakable PRF, which is essentially a PRF containing tweak space as a part of input.

3   MAC for Corruption Identification

3.1   Combinatorial Group Testing

We start with a brief introduction of CGT and its application to MAC. CGT was originally formulated by Dorfman [14] for medical testing of blood supplies during World War II. Formally, let us assume that we have a set of m items,

$\mathbf{M} = \{M[1], \ldots, M[m]\}$, and each item is either normal or defective. The goal is to identify the defective items among $\mathbf{M}$ using group testing, that is, we choose a subset $\mathbf{S} \subset \mathbf{M}$ and query if $\mathbf{S}$ contains at least one defective item. A response to a query is said to be positive if it indicates the existence of at least one defective, and otherwise said to be negative. We usually assume a prior knowledge or assumption about the maximum number of possible defective items, and the central question of CGT is how to form effective tests to identify all defective items. If each query is not depending on responses of other queries, the scheme is called non-adaptive CGT (NCGT), which is specified by a $t \times m$ binary test matrix $\mathbb{Q}$. Here, t denotes the number of tests and $\mathbb{Q}_{i,j} = 1$ denotes that $M[j]$ is included in the i-th test. The construction of test matrix is deeply related to the combinatorics and coding theory and there are numerous studies on the construction of test matrix. See Du and Hwang [15] for a collection of these results. It is known that we need $t = O(d^2 \log m)$ non-adaptive tests to identify all defective items if there are at most d defective items, hence we can greatly reduce the number of tags from naively taking m tags. When $d = 1$ there is a simple Hamming code based matrix achieving $t = \lceil \log m \rceil$. For $d > 1$ deterministic construction achieving $\Theta(d^2 \log m)$ is known [25], however, finding a construction achieving the minimum number of tests (not asymptotically) is generally not easy and remains as a vital research topic.

A conventional approach to GTM is as follows, which is also seen in the previous studies [11,20]. For m data items represented as a vector $M = (M[1], \ldots, M[m]) \in \{0,1\}^{*m}$, we first prepare a conventional MAC function defined over input space of $\{0,1\}^*$ (or $\{0,1\}^\bullet$), say HMAC, and using it with an appropriate input encoding, we build a MAC function for vector space $\mathrm{MAC}_K : \{0,1\}^{*m} \to \{0,1\}^n$. We also prepare a $t \times m$ test matrix $\mathbb{Q}$. Then for each $\mathbb{Q}_i$ we compute

$$T[i] = \mathrm{MAC}_K(M \ominus \mathbb{Q}_i) \tag{1}$$

to obtain the legitimate MAC tag vector, $T = (T[1], \ldots, T[t])$. Later, given potentially corrupted items, $M' = (M'[1], \ldots, M'[m])$, and T, we compute $T' = (T'[1], \ldots, T'[t])$ where $T'[i] = \mathrm{MAC}_K(M' \ominus \mathbb{Q}_i)$, and compare T and T', obtain $Z = \Delta(T, T')$. From the property of $\mathbb{Q}$, if $0 \leq |\mathrm{diff}(M, M')| \leq d$ holds true Z is uniquely mapped to $\Delta(M, M')$, i.e. the indexes of all corrupted items. This procedure is also called decoding in the field of CGT. It is possible to prove that producing T' such that Z does not correctly indicate $\Delta(M, M')$ implies a successful forgery against MAC_K (See Sect. 3.6).

As mentioned there are plenty of efficient construction methods for $\mathbb{Q}$ from the literature, deterministic or random, with various additional properties, and we can basically adopt any of them with any MAC. What we here ask is the computation cost given $\mathbb{Q}$. Defining the unit of computation as an internal operation of MAC to process each item, e.g. the compression function of HMAC-SHA2, the conventional approach described above, taking MAC as a black box, generally requires $O(\mathrm{Hw}(\mathbb{Q})) \leq O(mt)$ computation, which can be significantly larger than $O(m)$, the time for taking one MAC tag for M. Once given $\mathbb{Q}$ and MAC_K it is possible to find some optimizations, however this will be cumbersome as we need ad-hoc optimization for each $\mathbb{Q}$. In the following, we show that a simple parallelizable MAC enables to reduce the computation cost to $O(m+t)$ for any $\mathbb{Q}$ with t rows. Usually m is much greater than t thus our result implies that GTM can run mostly as fast as single MAC computation.

3.2 MAC for Extended Vector Space

Let $\mathcal{V}$ and $\mathcal{V}'$ be sets of integers used as tweak spaces. Let $\overline{F}_K : \mathcal{V} \times \{0,1\}^* \to \{0,1\}^n$ be a keyed function and let $F_K : \mathcal{V} \times \{0,1\}^{\bullet} \to \{0,1\}^n$ be defined as $F_K(i,x) = \overline{F}_K(i,x)$ if $x \neq \varepsilon$ and $F_K(i,x) = 0^n$ otherwise, for any $i \in \mathcal{V}$. Let $G_{K'} : \mathcal{V}' \times \{0,1\}^n \to \{0,1\}^n$ be a tweakable keyed permutation over n bits. We may write $F_K^i(x)$ and $G_{K'}^j(z)$ to denote $F_K(i,x)$ and $G_{K'}(j,z)$.

Let $\mathsf{gtm}[F_K, G_{K'}]$ be a MAC function which takes an extended vector $X \in \{0,1\}^{\bullet m}$ for fixed m and outputs an n-bit tag with tweak $h \in \mathcal{V}'$, defined as

$$\mathsf{gtm}[F_K, G_{K'}](h, X) = G_{K'}^h(F_K^1(X[1]) \oplus \ldots \oplus F_K^m(X[m])). \qquad (2)$$

For example, if $m = 3$ and $a, b \in \{0,1\}^*$, $\mathsf{gtm}[F_K, G_{K'}](h, (a, \varepsilon, b)) = G_{K'}^h(F_K^1(a) \oplus F_K^3(b))$ holds. Assuming $|X[i]| \leq n$ for all $i \leq m$ and the use of n-bit blockcipher E_K for instantiations of F and G, gtm is similar to parallelizable blockcipher-based MAC called PMAC [7,26]. However, we observe important differences that in PMAC the input X is in $\{0,1\}^{\bullet}$ and we apply partitioning to X into n-bit blocks, and the last item $X[m]$ is directly XORed to the state. Moreover, PMAC does not allow $X[i]$ to be empty for any i,[1] thus to process $X \in \{0,1\}^{\bullet m}$ with PMAC we need some encoding of X into $\{0,1\}^{\bullet}$. In Sect. 3.6 we will prove that $\mathsf{gtm}[F_K, G_{K'}]$ is a tweakable PRF: $\mathcal{V}' \times \{0,1\}^{\bullet m} \to \{0,1\}^n$ if $\overline{F}_K$ is a tweakable PRF with tweak space $\mathcal{V} = \{1, \ldots, m\}$, and $G_{K'}$ is an n-bit tweakable PRP with tweak space $\mathcal{V}'$.

We stress that (2) is not secure if input space contains extended vectors of different number of strings (i.e. m can be changed). Indeed, if m could be changed we have the same outputs for $X = (X[1])$ and $X' = (X[1], \varepsilon)$. Such attack can be prevented by taking the number of component strings as a part of G's tweak. We prefer (2) for its simplicity and the fact that gtm for fixed m is enough to provide a secure GTM for any fixed-size, $t \times m$ test matrix.

3.3 Efficient Group Testing MAC

Given a $t \times m$ test matrix $\mathbb{Q}$ and a list of m items denoted by $M \in \{0,1\}^{*m}$, now what we want to compute is

$$T[i] = \mathsf{gtm}[F_K, G_{K'}](i, M \odot \mathbb{Q}_i) \text{ for all } i = 1, \ldots, t. \qquad (3)$$

Since any test that includes $M[j]$ adds $F_K^j(M[j])$ to its internal state, $F_K^j(M[j])$ can be shared for all tests that include $M[j]$. In other words, the computation

---

[1] Unless entire input is an empty string.

of (3) can be done by reading each $M[j]$, computing $F_K^j(M[j])$, and XORing to the state memory block for the i-th test (denoted by $S[i]$) for all i such that $\mathbb{Q}_{i,j} = 1$. Then we compute $T[i] = G_{K'}^i(S[i])$ for all i. This requires m calls of F and t calls of G using t state memory blocks for any $\mathbb{Q}$. Note that such computation can not be done by a black-box application of PMAC with input encoding (from $\{0,1\}^{\bullet m}$ to $\{0,1\}^\bullet$).

We write this procedure as $\mathsf{GTM}[F_K, G_{K'}].\mathrm{Tag}$, which uses gtm as a subroutine but in a decomposed way described above. It is shown in Fig. 1. A simple procedure for the corruption identification, also known as *naive decoder*, is to apply $\mathsf{GTM}[F_K, G_{K'}].\mathrm{Tag}$ for the (possibly corrupted) data items, and removes all data items which is included in a test with negative outcome, i.e. a test that correctly passed. The remaining items are considered to be corrupted. This procedure is defined as $\mathsf{GTM}[F_K, G_{K'}].\mathrm{Ident}$. Moreover, we require that $\mathsf{GTM}[F_K, G_{K'}]$ to work as an ordinal MAC for the whole data items or each subset specified by $\mathbb{Q}_i$. The corresponding verification functions are defined as $\mathsf{GTM}[F_K, G_{K'}].\mathrm{Verify}$ and $\mathsf{GTM}[F_K, G_{K'}].\mathrm{Verify}^{(i)}$ shown in Fig. 1. The corresponding security notions will be described in Sect. 3.4.

In the definition of GTM we assume $M \in \{0,1\}^{*m}$, however extension to $M \in \{0,1\}^{\bullet m}$ is trivially possible by additional input encoding for F.

Properties. We remark that $\mathrm{gtm}[F_K, G_{K'}]$ is parallelizable. It also supports incremental update in the same manner to PMAC. For example, if we have $T[i] =$

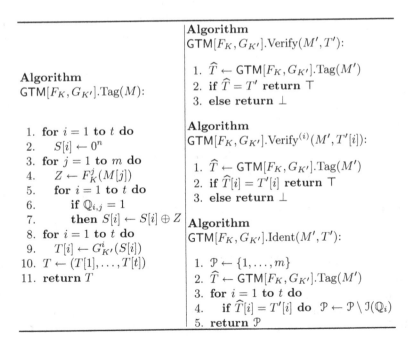

Fig. 1. $\mathsf{GTM}[F_K, G_{K'}]$ with $t \times m$ test matrix $\mathbb{Q}$.

$\text{gtm}[F_K, G_{K'}](i, M \odot \mathbb{Q}_i)$ for some i and j with $\mathbb{Q}_{i,j} = 1$, re-computation of $T[i]$ with incremental update of $M[j]$ to $M'[j] \neq M[j]$ requires two invocations of F and G, i.e., we apply $G_{K'}^{-1,i}$ to $T[i]$ and compute $F_K^j(M[j]) \oplus F_K^j(M'[j])$ to renew the state, and finally apply $G_{K'}^i$ to the state to renew $T[i]$. This incremental update is useful when the data is large and frequently updated by items.

We also remark that even the incremental update of $\mathbb{Q}$ (i.e. a change in the test matrix) is efficiently handled. For instance, if we want to change $\mathbb{Q}_{i,j} = 0$ to $\mathbb{Q}_{i,j} = 1$ then we add $F_K^j(M[j])$ to $G_{K'}^{-1,i}(T[i])$. However, we have not investigated the practical application of this functionality.

3.4   Security Notions

To consider the security of our proposal, we need formal security notions. Generally GTM can be considered as an extension of deterministic MAC, having input in $\{0,1\}^{*m}$ and output in $(\{0,1\}^n)^t$ with a $t \times m$ binary matrix $\mathbb{Q}$ as a public parameter, equipped with corruption identification procedure in addition to tagging and verification procedures. Therefore we make our notions as natural extensions of those for deterministic MACs [5,6]. We intend to define our notions so that they can be satisfied if item subset specified by a test (i.e. $\{M[j] : \mathbb{Q}_{i,j} = 1\}$) is processed by a PRF, independent for each test, and the underlying $\mathbb{Q}$ is appropriate for both MAC and corruption identification. We later show that $\text{GTM}[F_K, G_{K'}]$ is in fact secure with respect to our notions.

Let $\mathbb{Q}$ be a $t \times m$ binary matrix. Let $\text{MAC}_{\mathbf{K}} : \mathcal{M} \to \mathcal{T}$ with $\mathcal{M} = \{0,1\}^{*m}$ and $\mathcal{T} = (\{0,1\}^n)^t$ be a GTM scheme using test matrix $\mathbb{Q}$. We also let $\text{MAC}_{\mathbf{K}}^{(i)} : \mathcal{M} \to \{0,1\}^n$ for $i = 1, \ldots, t$ to denote the corresponding MAC for the i-th test, that is, $\text{MAC}_{\mathbf{K}}(M) = (\text{MAC}_{\mathbf{K}}^{(1)}(M), \ldots, \text{MAC}_{\mathbf{K}}^{(t)}(M))$.

To define the security notions for MAC, we introduce several oracles.

Definition 1. *Let $M, M' \in \mathcal{M} = \{0,1\}^{*m}$ and $T, T', \widehat{T} \in \mathcal{T} = (\{0,1\}^n)^t$. Let $\text{MAC}_{\mathbf{K}}$.Tag be tagging oracle which takes M and returns output as $T = \text{MAC}_{\mathbf{K}}(M)$. Let $\text{MAC}_{\mathbf{K}}$.Verify be the verification oracle which takes $(M', T') \in \mathcal{M} \times \mathcal{T}$ and evaluates $\widehat{T} = \text{MAC}_{\mathbf{K}}(M')$, and returns $\top$ if $T' = \widehat{T}$ (i.e. it is valid) and otherwise $\bot$ (i.e. it is invalid). We define verification-i oracle $\text{MAC}_{\mathbf{K}}$.Verify$^{(i)}$ which takes $(M', T'[i])$ to compute $\widehat{T}[i] = \text{MAC}_{\mathbf{K}}^{(i)}(M')$ and returns $\top$ if $\widehat{T}[i] = T'[i]$, and $\bot$ otherwise. We also define identification oracle $\text{MAC}_{\mathbf{K}}$.Ident which takes (M', T') and computes the index set of possibly corrupted items, simply obtained by evicting $\mathfrak{I}(\mathbb{Q}_i)$ from $\{1, \ldots, m\}$ for all i such that i-th test is failed.*

By setting $\text{MAC}_{\mathbf{K}} = \text{GTM}[F_K, G_{K'}]$, these oracles are formally defined by Fig. 1.

We define the following three security notions. Let $\mathcal{O}_T$, $\mathcal{O}_V$, $\mathcal{O}_V^{(i)}$, and $\mathcal{O}_I$ respectively denote tagging, verification, verification-i, and identification oracles for $\text{MAC}_{\mathbf{K}}$. Here we fix the number of items, m, and $t \times m$ test matrix $\mathbb{Q}$.

1. **Tag vector forgery (TVF).** Let $\mathcal{A}_1$ be the adversary who queries $(\mathcal{O}_T, \mathcal{O}_V)$. Suppose $\mathcal{A}_1$ obtains $(M_1, T_1), \ldots, (M_q, T_q)$ via q (adaptive, chosen-plaintext)

queries to $\mathcal{O}_T$ (where $(M_i, T_i) \in \{0,1\}^{*m} \times (\{0,1\}^n)^t$) and then determines $(M', T') \in \{0,1\}^{*m} \times (\{0,1\}^n)^t$ as a query to $\mathcal{O}_V$. We say $\mathcal{A}_1$ forges if $\mathcal{A}_1$ receives $\top$ from $\mathcal{O}_V$ and $(M', T') \neq (M_i, T_i)$ for all $i = 1, \ldots, q$. The advantage of $\mathcal{A}_1$ is defined as

$$\mathrm{Adv}^{\mathrm{mac}}_{\mathrm{MAC_K}}(\mathcal{A}_1) \stackrel{\mathrm{def}}{=} \Pr[\mathcal{A}_1^{\mathcal{O}_T, \mathcal{O}_V} \text{ forges }]. \tag{4}$$

We say $\mathrm{MAC_K}$ is secure against tag vector forgery if $\mathrm{Adv}^{\mathrm{mac}}_{\mathrm{MAC_K}}(\mathcal{A}_1)$ is negligibly small for all practical adversaries.

2. **Tag string forgery (TSF).** Fix $i \in \{1, \ldots, t\}$. Let $\mathcal{A}_2$ be the adversary who queries $(\mathcal{O}_T, \mathcal{O}_V^{(i)})$. Suppose $\mathcal{A}_2$ first obtains (M_j, T_j) for $j = 1, \ldots, q$ via q queries to $\mathcal{O}_T$, and then determines a query to $\mathcal{O}_V^{(i)}$ as $(M', T'[i])$. We say $\mathcal{A}_2$ forges if $\mathcal{A}_2$ receives $\top$ from $\mathcal{O}_V^{(i)}$ and $(M' \ominus \mathbb{Q}_i, T'[i]) \neq (M_j \ominus \mathbb{Q}_i, T_j[i])$ for all $j = 1, \ldots, q$. The advantage of $\mathcal{A}_2$ is defined as

$$\mathrm{Adv}^{\mathrm{mac}(i)}_{\mathrm{MAC_K}}(\mathcal{A}_2) \stackrel{\mathrm{def}}{=} \Pr[\mathcal{A}_2^{\mathcal{O}_T, \mathcal{O}_V^{(i)}} \text{ forges }], \tag{5}$$

and we say $\mathrm{MAC_K}$ is secure against tag string forgery if $\mathrm{Adv}^{\mathrm{mac}(i)}_{\mathrm{MAC_K}}(\mathcal{A}_2)$ is negligibly small for all practical adversaries, for all $i = 1, \ldots, t$.

3. **Corruption misidentification (CM).** Let $\mathcal{A}_3$ be a d-corruptive adversary who first performs q distinct queries to $\mathcal{O}_T$ and obtains $(M_1, T_1), \ldots, (M_q, T_q)$, and then queries (M', T') to $\mathcal{O}_I$ such that $T' = T_i$ for some i and $1 \leq |\mathrm{diff}(M', M_i)| \leq d$. We say $\mathcal{A}_3$ forges if (1) we have $T_i = T_j$ for some $i \neq j$ or (2) all T_is are unique and $\mathcal{O}_I$ returns $\mathcal{P} \subseteq \{1, \ldots, m\}$ such that $\mathcal{P} \neq \mathrm{diff}(M', M_i)$ (where index i is uniquely determined from T'). We define

$$\mathrm{Adv}^{\mathrm{ident}(d)}_{\mathrm{MAC_K}}(\mathcal{A}_3) \stackrel{\mathrm{def}}{=} \Pr[\mathcal{A}_3^{\mathcal{O}_T, \mathcal{O}_I} \text{ forges}]. \tag{6}$$

For some fixed d, we say $\mathrm{MAC_K}$ is secure against corruption misidentification if $\mathrm{Adv}^{\mathrm{ident}(d)}_{\mathrm{MAC_K}}(\mathcal{A}_3)$ is negligibly small for all practical d-corrupting adversaries.

We will call these notions as TVF, TSF, and CM-security respectively. Note that in CM-security we safely let the adversary win if it finds a tag vector collision while querying $\mathcal{O}_T$. Finally we say $\mathrm{MAC_K}$ is secure if it is secure with respect to all three notions.

Requirements on Test Matrix. To fulfill all of our security notions, test matrix $\mathbb{Q}$ needs to satisfy some conditions. We naturally assume that all rows of $\mathbb{Q}$ are unique. In the standard scenario of NCGT, it is known that $\mathbb{Q}$ should be at least d-separable[2], that is, unions (bitwise logical OR) of up to d columns of $\mathbb{Q}$ are all distinct. Here a union can include no column of $\mathbb{Q}$ which is all-zero vector, and thus $\mathbb{Q}$ cannot have all-zero column. A stronger definition is d-disjunct which means that any union of up to d columns does not contain a column

---

[2] It is also written as $\bar{d}$-separable, and in this case d-separable means that unions of exactly d columns are distinct.

of Q. This notion is useful in practice since if Q is d-disjunct, correct decoding (corruption identification in our case) is always possible by naive decoder mentioned earlier which simply evicts all items used in at least one test that was negative. Moreover, we could always detect the existence of more than d defective items. See e.g. [15,16,24] for more details. Following these observations we set $\mathsf{GTM}[F_K, G_{K'}]$.Ident as naive decoder and require Q to be d-disjunct for CM-security with d-corrupting adversaries. The existence of all-zero column also immediately implies a trivial attack against TVF-security.

TSF-security is independent of Q because Q_i specifies the input space of $\mathsf{MAC}_K^{(i)}$, and if $\mathsf{MAC}_K^{(i)}$ is an independent, secure MAC for each i, TSF-security is trivially satisfied for any Q.

For TVF-security, however, we require that Q contains an all-one row, which shows a separation between TSF and TVF-securities.

Proposition 1. *For any GTM using $t \times m$ test matrix Q, if Q does not contain an all-one row, TVF-security can be broken using at most $t + 1$ queries.*

Proof. Let us assume Q has no all-one row. Let a and b be two distinct non-empty strings. Then, for each $i = 1, \ldots, t$ the adversary queries $M_i = (M_i[1], \ldots, M_i[m])$ to the tagging oracle, where $M_i[j] = a$ if $Q_{i,j} = 1$ and $M_i[j] = b$ if $Q_{i,j} = 0$, and receives $T_i = (T_i[1], \ldots, T_i[t])$. Then the adversary queries (M', T') to the verification oracle, where $M' = (a, \ldots, a)$ and $T'[j] = T_j[j]$. This query is always accepted. $\square$

Consequently we require the following.

Definition 2. *We say $t \times m$ test matrix Q is sound for d-corruptive adversaries, if Q is d-disjunct and contains an all-one row.*

In the following, without loss of generality we assume that if Q is sound for d-corruptive adversaries, Q_1 is the all-one row.

3.5   Remarks

Multiple Verification Queries. For simplicity the notions defined at Sect. 3.4 require that the adversary uses one query to $\mathcal{O}_V$ or $\mathcal{O}_V^{(i)}$ or $\mathcal{O}_I$. They can be extended so that the adversary can use $q_v > 1$ queries to these oracles, and from the result of [4] we could generally prove that if MAC_K is secure with the case $q_v = 1$, it is also secure when $q_v > 1$. A more rigorous analysis will be given in the full version.

The Need of Tag String Security. We remark that TSF-security notion is rather optional as if MAC_K is secure against tag vector forgery, any forgery is detectable by checking a tag for the all-one row. We think however one may want to quickly check authenticity of a part of data items ($M \ominus Q_i$) by computing tag for Q_i. Tag computation for $M \ominus Q_i$ can be significantly faster than computing a tag for the all-one row. If MAC_K is only TVF-secure and not TSF-secure, a forgery against $M \ominus \mathbb{Q}_i$ may not be detected until a user performs a tag verification for the all-one row.

Extending CM-security. Notions of TVF and TSF securities allow the adversary to freely choose tags at the final query, while that of CM-security does not (i.e. adversary can not arbitrarily choose T' in querying $\mathcal{O}_I$, only to choose it from $T_1, \ldots, T_q$). However this is unlikely to hold when MAC tags are stored at the same storage as data items. In addition, a user may be interested in corruption localization, that is, finding a superset of corrupted items (i.e. allowing some false positives in the guess) if exact identification of all corrupted items is difficult. These important extensions are already mentioned and independently studied. For example, corruption localization was studied by [8, 11–13], and identification of corrupted items under tag corruption was described at [20].

We remark that these extensions also have been studied in the field of CGT design. If $M \odot \mathbb{Q}_i$ for some i is not corrupted but $T[i] = \mathrm{gtm}(i, M \odot \mathbb{Q}_i)$ is corrupted to $T'[i]$, the corresponding test is considered as invalid, that is, a false positive occurs at the i-th test. Test matrix that can tolerate false positives, and even false negatives[3], has been studied in the literature, such as Cheraghchi [9], Thierry-Mieg [27] and Ngo et al. [25]. Some of these papers also study the case where final output is only required to be a superset of corrupted items with an allowable margin, which is a form of corruption localization. By using test matrices from these studies, it would be possible to built a GTM scheme having CM-security notion with some extended model allowing a more freedom in choosing a query to $\mathcal{O}_I$ (e.g. (M', T') with $|\mathrm{diff}(M', M_i)| \leq d_1$ and $|\mathrm{diff}(T', T_i)| \leq d_2$ for some d_1, d_2) and corruption identification with some false positives. Formalizing these ideas and providing a concrete security result using existing results on CGT will be an interesting future direction.

3.6   Provable Security of GTM

We first prove that $\mathrm{gtm}[F_K, G_{K'}]$ is a tweakable PRF for input domain $\{0,1\}^{\bullet m}$, tweak space $\mathcal{V} = \{1, \ldots, t\}$. In what follows we fix the $t \times m$ test matrix $\mathbb{Q}$ and assume it is sound for d-corruptive adversaries.

Theorem 1. *Let* $\mathrm{gtm}[\widetilde{\mathsf{R}}, \widetilde{\mathsf{P}}] : \mathcal{V} \times \{0,1\}^{\bullet m} \to \{0,1\}^n$ *be the tweakable keyed function defined as (2), using a tweakable URF,* $\widetilde{\mathsf{R}}$, *compatible with* F_K *and tweakable URP,* $\widetilde{\mathsf{P}}$, *compatible with* $G_{K'}$. *Then we have*

$$\mathrm{Adv}^{\mathrm{prf}}_{\mathrm{gtm}[\widetilde{\mathsf{R}}, \widetilde{\mathsf{P}}]}(\mathcal{A}) \leq \frac{q^2}{2^n} \tag{7}$$

for any adversary $\mathcal{A}$ *using* q *queries.*

---

[3] It corresponds to successful MAC forgeries, which we consider negligibly small chance to occur.

Proof. Let $\mathsf{gtm}[\widetilde{\mathsf{R}}, \widetilde{\mathsf{R}}']$ be the function that substitutes $\widetilde{\mathsf{P}}$ with $\widetilde{\mathsf{R}}'$, an independent tweakable URF compatible with $\widetilde{\mathsf{P}}$. Let $\widetilde{\mathsf{R}}_{\mathrm{gtm}}$ be the tweakable URF compatible with $\mathsf{gtm}[\widetilde{\mathsf{R}}, \widetilde{\mathsf{P}}]$. Then we have

$$\mathbf{Adv}^{\mathrm{prf}}_{\mathsf{gtm}[\widetilde{\mathsf{R}},\widetilde{\mathsf{P}}]}(\mathcal{A}) \leq \mathbf{Adv}^{\mathrm{cpa}}_{\mathsf{gtm}[\widetilde{\mathsf{R}},\widetilde{\mathsf{P}}],\mathsf{gtm}[\widetilde{\mathsf{R}},\widetilde{\mathsf{R}}']}(\mathcal{A}') + \mathbf{Adv}^{\mathrm{cpa}}_{\mathsf{gtm}[\widetilde{\mathsf{R}},\widetilde{\mathsf{R}}'],\widetilde{\mathsf{R}}_{\mathrm{gtm}}}(\mathcal{A}'') \tag{8}$$

for some adversaries $\mathcal{A}'$, $\mathcal{A}''$ using q queries. The first term in the right hand side of (8) is simply bounded by an extended form of PRP/PRF switching lemma (e.g. [6]) and we have $\mathbf{Adv}^{\mathrm{cpa}}_{\mathsf{gtm}[\widetilde{\mathsf{R}},\widetilde{\mathsf{P}}],\mathsf{gtm}[\widetilde{\mathsf{R}},\widetilde{\mathsf{R}}']}(\mathcal{A}') \leq q^2/2^{n+1}$. To analyze the second term, let $(V_i, X_i) \in \{1,\ldots,t\} \times \{0,1\}^{\bullet m}$ with $X_i = (X_i[1],\ldots,X_i[m])$ be the i-th query of $\mathcal{A}''$ accessing $\mathsf{gtm}[\widetilde{\mathsf{R}}, \widetilde{\mathsf{R}}']$. From the assumption we have $(V_i, X_i) \neq (V_j, X_j)$ if $i \neq j$. Let $S_i = \bigoplus_{j=1,\ldots,m, X_i[j] \neq \varepsilon} \widetilde{\mathsf{R}}^j(X_i[j])$, which denotes the i-th input (with tweak V_i) to $\widetilde{\mathsf{R}}'$ for the i-th query made by $\mathcal{A}''$ accessing to $\mathsf{gtm}[\widetilde{\mathsf{R}}, \widetilde{\mathsf{R}}']$. Here $\widetilde{\mathsf{R}}^j$ is not computed for input being ε following (2).

Since $\mathsf{gtm}[\widetilde{\mathsf{R}}, \widetilde{\mathsf{R}}']$ can be seen as a variant of classical Carter-Wegman MAC, the second term is bounded by the collision probability of (V, S) against non-adaptive strategy in the same manner to the analysis of [6,26], and we have

$$\mathbf{Adv}^{\mathrm{cpa}}_{\mathsf{gtm}[\widetilde{\mathsf{R}},\widetilde{\mathsf{R}}'],\widetilde{\mathsf{R}}_{\mathrm{gtm}}}(\mathcal{A}'') \leq \max \Pr_{\mathsf{gtm}[\widetilde{\mathsf{R}},\widetilde{\mathsf{R}}']}[(V_i, S_i) = (V_j, S_j) \text{ for some } i \neq j] \tag{9}$$

$$\leq \max \sum_{i<j, V_i=V_j} \Pr_{\mathsf{gtm}[\widetilde{\mathsf{R}},\widetilde{\mathsf{R}}']}[S_i = S_j], \tag{10}$$

where the maximum is taken for $(V_1, X_1),\ldots,(V_q, X_q)$. Without loss of generality we focus on the event $S_1 = S_2$ and assume $X_1[1] \neq X_2[1]$ and $V_1 = V_2$. If $X_1[1] \neq \varepsilon$ and $X_2[1] \neq \varepsilon$, $S_1 \oplus S_2 = \widetilde{\mathsf{R}}^{(1)}(X_1[1]) \oplus \widetilde{\mathsf{R}}^{(1)}(X_2[1]) \oplus \delta$, where δ is independent of $\widetilde{\mathsf{R}}^{(1)}$ (as it is a sum of some outputs of $\widetilde{\mathsf{R}}^{(2)},\ldots,\widetilde{\mathsf{R}}^{(m)}$ or 0^n). If $X_1[1] = \varepsilon$ and $X_2[1] = x \neq \varepsilon$ (or vice versa), $S_1 \oplus S_2 = \widetilde{\mathsf{R}}^{(1)}(x) \oplus \delta$ holds. For both cases the probability of $S_1 \oplus S_2 = 0^n$ is clearly $1/2^n$. Thus the right hand side of (10) is bounded by $\binom{q}{2}/2^n < q^2/2^{n+1}$. This concludes the proof.   □

Theorem 2. *Let $\widetilde{\mathsf{R}}$ and $\widetilde{\mathsf{P}}$ be the tweakable URF and tweakable URP compatible with F_K and $G_{K'}$ in $\mathsf{GTM}[F_K, G_{K'}]$. Then, we have*

$$\mathbf{Adv}^{\mathrm{mac}}_{\mathsf{GTM}[\widetilde{\mathsf{R}},\widetilde{\mathsf{P}}]}(\mathcal{A}_1) \leq \frac{5t^2 q^2}{2^n}, \tag{11}$$

$$\mathbf{Adv}^{\mathrm{mac}(i)}_{\mathsf{GTM}[\widetilde{\mathsf{R}},\widetilde{\mathsf{P}}]}(\mathcal{A}_2) \leq \frac{5t^2 q^2}{2^n} \text{ for all } i = 1,\ldots,t, \tag{12}$$

$$\mathbf{Adv}^{\mathrm{ident}(d)}_{\mathsf{GTM}[\widetilde{\mathsf{R}},\widetilde{\mathsf{P}}]}(\mathcal{A}_3) \leq \frac{6t^2 q^2}{2^n}, \tag{13}$$

where $\mathcal{A}_j$ for $j = 1, 2, 3$ uses q queries to $\mathcal{O}_T$ and a query to $\mathcal{O}_V$ (for $j = 1$) or $\mathcal{O}_V^{(i)}$ (for $j = 2$) or $\mathcal{O}_I$ (for $j = 3$).

Proof. For (11), let $\widetilde{\mathsf{R}}_{\mathsf{gtm}}$ be the tweakable URF compatible with $\mathsf{gtm}[\widetilde{\mathsf{R}}, \widetilde{\mathsf{P}}]$. Let $\mathsf{R}_i : \{0,1\}^{*c_i} \to \{0,1\}^n$ be the independent URF where $c_i = |\mathfrak{I}(\mathbb{Q}_i)|$, and let $\widetilde{\mathsf{R}}_{\mathsf{GTM}}$ be an ideal primitive for $\mathsf{GTM}[\widetilde{\mathsf{R}}, \widetilde{\mathsf{P}}]$, which takes $M \in \{0,1\}^{*m}$ and outputs $T = (T[1], \ldots, T[t])$ for $T[i] = \mathsf{R}_i(M \ominus \mathbb{Q}_i)$. We observe that a tagging query to $\mathsf{GTM}[\widetilde{\mathsf{R}}, \widetilde{\mathsf{P}}]$ yields queries to $\mathsf{gtm}[\widetilde{\mathsf{R}}, \widetilde{\mathsf{P}}](i, \cdot)$ for each $i = 1, \ldots, t$. Thus we have

$$\mathsf{Adv}^{\mathsf{mac}}_{\mathsf{GTM}[\widetilde{\mathsf{R}},\widetilde{\mathsf{P}}]}(\mathcal{A}_1) \leq \mathsf{Adv}^{\mathsf{cpa}}_{\mathsf{GTM}[\widetilde{\mathsf{R}},\widetilde{\mathsf{P}}],\widetilde{\mathsf{R}}_{\mathsf{GTM}}}(\mathcal{A}'_1) + \mathsf{Adv}^{\mathsf{mac}}_{\widetilde{\mathsf{R}}_{\mathsf{GTM}}}(\mathcal{A}_1) \tag{14}$$

$$\leq \mathsf{Adv}^{\mathsf{prf}}_{\mathsf{gtm}[\widetilde{\mathsf{R}},\widetilde{\mathsf{P}}]}(\mathcal{A}''_1) + \frac{1}{2^n} \tag{15}$$

$$\leq \frac{t^2(q+1)^2}{2^n} + \frac{1}{2^n}, \tag{16}$$

where $\mathcal{A}'_1$ uses $q+1$ queries, and $\mathcal{A}''_1$ uses $t(q+1)$ queries. The second inequality follows from the fact that, to forge $\widetilde{\mathsf{R}}_{\mathsf{GTM}}$, the adversary has to guess $T'[1] = \mathsf{R}_1(M' \ominus \mathbb{Q}_1) = \mathsf{R}_1(M')$ given tags for $M_1, \ldots, M_q$ for certain $M' \neq^\forall M_i$. Thus $T'[1]$ is independent and uniformly random over n bits. The last inequality follows from Theorem 1.

For (12), the bound is similarly derived as

$$\mathsf{Adv}^{\mathsf{mac}(i)}_{\mathsf{GTM}[\widetilde{\mathsf{R}},\widetilde{\mathsf{P}}]}(\mathcal{A}_2) \leq \mathsf{Adv}^{\mathsf{cpa}}_{\mathsf{GTM}[\widetilde{\mathsf{R}},\widetilde{\mathsf{P}}],\widetilde{\mathsf{R}}_{\mathsf{GTM}}}(\mathcal{A}'_2) + \mathsf{Adv}^{\mathsf{mac}(i)}_{\widetilde{\mathsf{R}}_{\mathsf{GTM}}}(\mathcal{A}_2) \tag{17}$$

$$\leq \mathsf{Adv}^{\mathsf{prf}}_{\mathsf{gtm}[\widetilde{\mathsf{R}},\widetilde{\mathsf{P}}]}(\mathcal{A}''_2) + \frac{1}{2^n} \tag{18}$$

$$\leq \frac{(tq+1)^2}{2^n} + \frac{1}{2^n} \tag{19}$$

where $\mathcal{A}''_2$ uses $(tq+1)$ queries to $\mathsf{gtm}[\widetilde{\mathsf{R}}, \widetilde{\mathsf{P}}](i, \cdot)$ or $\widetilde{\mathsf{R}}_{\mathsf{gtm}}(i, \cdot)$. The second inequality follows from that the adversary needs to guess $\mathsf{R}_i(M' \ominus \mathbb{Q}_i)$ for some M' satisfying $M' \ominus \mathbb{Q}_i \neq M_1 \ominus \mathbb{Q}_i, \ldots, M_q \ominus \mathbb{Q}_i$, and the last follows from Theorem 1.

For (13), we observe that the adversary must find a pair of distinct M and M' causing an *exploitable* collision between tag strings, throughout accessing tagging oracle, since otherwise it reduces to the original combinatorial problem setting where tests never fail, and thus the identification oracle never fails due to d-disjunctness of $\mathbb{Q}$. Here, an exploitable collision means that there exists a pair of distinct (M, M') such that for some $i \in \{1, \ldots, t\}$ with $M \ominus \mathbb{Q}_i \neq M' \ominus \mathbb{Q}_i$ we have $T[i] = T'[i]$, for $(T[1], \ldots, T[t]) = \mathsf{GTM}[\widetilde{\mathsf{R}}, \widetilde{\mathsf{P}}](M)$ and $(T'[1], \ldots, T'[t]) = \mathsf{GTM}[\widetilde{\mathsf{R}}, \widetilde{\mathsf{P}}](M')$. Here, note that an exploitable collision at the final identification query directly means a win but an exploitable collision invoked at tagging queries also implies a win. Hence the advantage is bounded by the probability of exploitable collision throughout the game.

We then define a collision-finding game, where adversary $\mathcal{A}$ (adaptively) queries a tagging oracle implementing a GTM, $\mathsf{MAC_K}$. Let $M_i \in \{0,1\}^{*m}$ be the i-th query and $T_i \in (\{0,1\}^n)^t$ be the i-th response. We assume $\mathcal{A}$ never makes duplicate queries, and say $\mathcal{A}$ wins there is an exploitable collision, i.e. $T_i[h] = T_j[h]$ for some $1 \leq i < j \leq q$ and $h \in \{1, \ldots, t\}$, and we denote the probability of win by $\mathsf{Adv}^{\mathsf{coll}}_{\mathsf{MAC_K}}(\mathcal{A})$. Then we have

$$\mathbf{Adv}_{\mathsf{GTM}[\widetilde{\mathsf{R}},\widetilde{\mathsf{P}}]}^{\mathrm{ident}(d)}(\mathcal{A}_3) \leq \mathbf{Adv}_{\mathsf{GTM}[\widetilde{\mathsf{R}},\widetilde{\mathsf{P}}]}^{\mathrm{coll}}(\mathcal{A}_3') \tag{20}$$

$$\leq \mathbf{Adv}_{\mathsf{gtm}[\widetilde{\mathsf{R}},\widetilde{\mathsf{P}}]}^{\mathrm{prf}}(\mathcal{A}_3'') + \mathbf{Adv}_{\mathsf{R}_{\mathsf{GTM}}}^{\mathrm{coll}}(\mathcal{A}_3') \tag{21}$$

$$\leq \frac{t^2(q+1)^2}{2^n} + \frac{t(q+1)^2}{2^{n+1}}, \tag{22}$$

where $\mathcal{A}_3'$ uses $(q+1)$ queries, $\mathcal{A}_3''$ uses $t(q+1)$ queries. The first term of the last inequality follows from Theorem 1, and the second term follows from the fact that $\widetilde{\mathsf{R}}_{\mathsf{GTM}}$'s outputs are completely random and a simple counting of events ($T_i[h] = T_j[h]$ for some $1 \leq i < j \leq q$ and $h \in \{1,\dots,t\}$) having probability $1/2^n$. This concludes the proof. □

Practical Instantiations. The above analysis shows security bounds based on information-theoretic primitives, however we can easily derive the security bounds with practical instantiations having computational security. For concrete instantiations, $\widetilde{\mathsf{R}}$ in $\mathsf{gtm}[\widetilde{\mathsf{R}},\widetilde{\mathsf{P}}]$ can be instantiated by HMAC-SHA2 or CMAC [2] with AES, where tweak is (e.g.) encoded into a fixed-length sequence and prepended to to input. Also $\widetilde{\mathsf{P}}$ can be instantiated by a computationally-secure TBC. It can be instantiated by a blockcipher mode of operation such as XEX [26] or a dedicated constructions, such as Threefish [18] or TBCs by Jean et al. [22] which are used in their proposals for CAESAR competition for authenticated encryption [1]. If we use CMAC with n-bit URP for $\widetilde{\mathsf{R}}$ and XEX with another n-bit URP for $\widetilde{\mathsf{P}}$, and each data item is at most $n\ell$ bits, then combining the provable security bounds of CMAC, shown by Iwata and Kurosawa [21], and XEX and Theorem 2, the resulting security bounds (for TVF, TSF and CM) are shown to be $O(\sigma^2/2^n)$, where $\sigma = q\ell w \leq q\ell mt$ and $w = \mathrm{Hw}(\mathbb{Q})$ with a small constant. When URP is substituted with a real blockcipher, deriving computational counterparts is also standard, see e.g. Bellare et al. [3].

4   Experimental Implementation

We implemented our algorithm with two existing CGT methods. The first is *Shifted Traversal Design* (STD) by Thierry-Mieg [27]. Thierry-Mieg and Bailly also developed a tool to produce CGT test matrix based on STD, Interpool [28]. The second is *Chinese Reminder Sieve* (CRS) proposed by Eppstein et al. [16].

The first method, STD, is based on the repetition and rotation of sub-matrix. A parameter set of STD is written as (n, q, k), where n denotes the number of items, q denotes the number of tests in a layer and k denotes the number of layers. Here k specifies redundancy in the design and each item is included exactly in k tests. We need q to be a prime and $q < n$ and $k \leq q+1$. The number of tests is $q \cdot k$. Each test contains $\lfloor n/q \rfloor$ or $\lfloor n/q \rfloor + 1$ items. Let $\Gamma(q, n)$ be $\min\{\gamma : q^{\gamma+1} \geq n\}$. Then STD can identify t corrupted items if $t \cdot \Gamma(q, n) \leq q$ and $k = t \cdot \Gamma(q, n) + 1$ hold. Moreover with E observation errors (false positives or negatives) it works if $t \cdot \Gamma(q, n) + 2E \leq q$ and $k = t \cdot \Gamma(q, n) + 2E + 1$ hold. See [27] for details.

The second method, CRS, is based on number theory and its test matrix is specified by a sequence of powers of primes, $(t_1, \ldots, t_k) = (p_1^{e_1}, \ldots, p_k^{e_k})$, satisfying $\prod_j t_j \geq n^d$, where n denotes the number of items and d denotes the number of corrupted items that can be identified. Test matrix consists of k sub-matrices and j-th sub-matrix is determined by t_j and has t_j rows (tests). Thus CRS consists of $t = \sum_j t_j$ tests. Reference [16] suggests a backtracking search to find an appropriate sequence $(t_1, \ldots, t_k)$ and shows a Python code doing it.

Details. We chose several parameter settings for both STD and CRS methods, and implemented our algorithm for tag computation. Verification and corruption identification procedures are not implemented at this moment. For STD we chose $(n, q, k) = (940, 13, 13)$ with 169 tests and $(2000, 11, 11)$ with 121 tests, and for CRS we chose $(n, d) = (10^4, 2)$ and $(10^4, 5)$ and $(10^5, 2)$. Number of tests are 89, 378, and 131 respectively. We did not include the all-one row as the effect to performance is quite small.

To implement $\mathsf{GTM}[F_K, G_{K'}]$, we used CMAC for F_K^j, where tweak j is encoded as a 4-byte sequence and prepended to the input, and used XEX for $G_{K'}^i$, both with AES-128. Each tag is 16 bytes. For storing a large binary test matrix, a natural way is to have an array, $A[i][j]$, which denotes the j-th item index to be included in the i-th test, as employed by Interpool. In C language we can store it as a two-dimensional array of pointers. This expression, which we call item-index expression, is however quite inefficient to implement $\mathsf{GTM}[F_K, G_{K'}]$.Tag in Fig. 1, since it incurs a search over A for every item. Instead we made the inverse array, $B[i][j]$, which denotes the j-th test index used in the i-th item, which we call test-index expression. Using this expression the algorithm of Fig. 1 is easily implemented, where lines 4 and 5 are replaced with simple successive reading of array B.

For comparison we also implemented a conventional computation of $\mathsf{gtm}[F_K, G_{K'}]$, which uses $\mathsf{gtm}[F_K, G_{K'}](i, \cdot)$ as a black-box tweakable MAC function for each test index i, using item-index array. This needs $\mathsf{Hw}(\mathbb{Q})$ calls of F and t calls of G.

We used a standard C implementation of AES using four 1K-byte tables, called T-tables, on Intel CPU (Ivybridge Core i7 3770, 3.4 GHz), running 64-bit Windows. Here AES-128 runs at 13.3 cycles/byte.

The implementation results are shown in Table 1 for STD and Table 2 for CRS, where each item has a fixed length, from 16 to 2048 bytes, shown in the first row. The data items are randomly generated. The figures denote the average cycles for input byte (i.e. total cycles divided by the total bytes of all data items). These tables show that the speed of our algorithm is much faster than the conventional one, and it is mostly the same as AES itself if each data item is more than 1K bytes. In theory the speed-up of the proposed scheme from the conventional one is proportional to $\mathsf{Hw}(\mathbb{Q})/(m + t)$ for m items and t tests. The actual speed-up factor is 8 to 15 in our experiments for data items of 2K bytes, and the difference from the ratio $\mathsf{Hw}(\mathbb{Q})/(m + t)$ is quite small.

Table 1. Implementation results for STD, with parameter (n, q, k).

Parameter $(940, 13, 13)$, $\mathrm{Hw}(\mathbb{Q}) = 12,220$, $\mathrm{Hw}(\mathbb{Q})/(m+t) = 11.01$								
$(m, t) = (940, 169)$	16	32	64	128	256	512	1024	2048
Proposed	63.4	64.0	26.8	20.5	17.3	15.7	14.8	14.4
Conventional	430.2	312.2	249.4	219.8	200.4	190.8	186.7	184.0
Parameter $(2000, 11, 11)$, $\mathrm{Hw}(\mathbb{Q}) = 22,220$, $\mathrm{Hw}(\mathbb{Q})/(m+t) = 10.47$								
$(m, t) = (2000, 121)$	16	32	64	128	256	512	1024	2048
Proposed	55.3	33.9	27.3	20.2	16.8	15.1	14.5	14.1
Conventional	361	259.7	206.9	180.7	166.8	159.5	155.9	153.8

Table 2. Implementation results for CRS, with parameter (n, d).

Parameter $(10^4, 5)$, $\mathrm{Hw}(\mathbb{Q}) = 150,000$, $\mathrm{Hw}(\mathbb{Q})/(m+t) = 14.45$								
$(m, t) = (10^4, 378)$	16	32	64	128	256	512	1024	2048
Proposed	60.9	37.6	25.8	20	17.1	15.6	14.8	14.5
Conventional	492.4	353.5	285	251.4	233	226.9	218.2	215.5
Parameter $(10^4, 2)$, $\mathrm{Hw}(\mathbb{Q}) = 80,000$, $\mathrm{Hw}(\mathbb{Q})/(m+t) = 7,92$								
$(m, t) = (10^4, 89)$	16	32	64	128	256	512	1024	2048
Proposed	51	30.8	22.6	18.4	16.4	15.3	14.7	14.5
Conventional	259.5	189.7	156.1	135.5	125.7	121.2	117.7	116.3
Parameter $(10^5, 2)$, $\mathrm{Hw}(\mathbb{Q}) = 1,000,000$, $\mathrm{Hw}(\mathbb{Q})/(m+t) = 9.98$								
$(m, t) = (10^5, 131)$	16	32	64	128	256	512	1024	2048
Proposed	49.7	31.9	23	18.6	16.3	15.1	14.5	14.1
Conventional	319.6	237.5	190.7	171.6	158.1	148.9	144.1	141.5

5   Concluding Remarks

This paper has studied a class of MAC function which is used with combinatorial group testing to identify the part of corruption. While such MAC function generally needs $O(mt)$ computation for m data items and t tests, we propose to use a variant of PMAC to reduce the cost to $O(m + t)$ irrespective of the contents of these tests. From our experiments, we observe that an AES-based implementation of our scheme can in fact run as fast as AES itself for practical size of problems. An important next direction is to investigate practical impact of our proposal to real-life security applications for which a group testing MAC is useful.

Interestingly, the idea shown here can not work fine in the keyless setting, say by replacing F and G by keyless hash functions, since the resulting incremental hash function is quite weak against generalized birthday attack [29], and thus we need to greatly increase the internal state (the output size of F). The problem here seems deeply related to the construction of secure, space-efficient incremental hash function, and needs further study.

Acknowledgments. The author would like to thank Kengo Mori, Jun Furukawa and Toshihiko Okamura for fruitful discussions, and Hiroyasu Kubo for initial-stage implementation, and anonymous reviewers for helpful comments.

References

1. CAESAR : competition for authenticated encryption: security, applicability, and robustness. http://competitions.cr.yp.to/index.html/
2. Recommendation for block cipher modes of operation: the CMAC mode for authentication. NIST special publication 800–38B (2005), national institute of standards and technology
3. Bellare, M., Desai, A., Jokipii, E., Rogaway, P.: A concrete security treatment of symmetric encryption. In: FOCS 1997, pp. 394–403. IEEE Computer Society (1997). http://dx.doi.org/10.1109/SFCS.1997.646128
4. Bellare, M., Goldreich, O., Mityagin, A.: The Power of verification queries in message authentication and authenticated encryption. Cryptology ePrint Archive, Report 2004/309 (2004). http://eprint.iacr.org/
5. Bellare, M., Kilian, J., Rogaway, P.: The security of the cipher block chaining message authentication code. J. Comput. Syst. Sci. **61**(3), 362–399 (2000)
6. Black, J.A., Rogaway, P.: CBC MACs for arbitrary-length messages: the three-key constructions. In: Bellare, M. (ed.) CRYPTO 2000. LNCS, vol. 1880, pp. 197–215. Springer, Heidelberg (2000)
7. Black, J.A., Rogaway, P.: A block-cipher mode of operation for parallelizable message authentication. In: Knudsen, L.R. (ed.) EUROCRYPT 2002. LNCS, vol. 2332, pp. 384–397. Springer, Heidelberg (2002). http://dx.doi.org/10.1007/3-540-46035-7_25
8. De Bonis, A., Di Crescenzo, G.: Combinatorial group testing for corruption localizing hashing. In: Fu, B., Du, D.-Z. (eds.) COCOON 2011. LNCS, vol. 6842, pp. 579–591. Springer, Heidelberg (2011). http://dx.doi.org/10.1007/978-3-642-22685-4_50
9. Cheraghchi, M.: Noise-resilient group testing: limitations and constructions. Discrete Appl. Math. **161**(1–2), 81–95 (2013). http://dx.doi.org/10.1016/j.dam.2012.07.022
10. Di Crescenzo, G., Arce, G.: Data forensics constructions from cryptographic hashing and coding. In: Shi, Y.Q., Kim, H.-J., Perez-Gonzalez, F. (eds.) IWDW 2011. LNCS, vol. 7128, pp. 494–509. Springer, Heidelberg (2012). http://dx.doi.org/10.1007/978-3-642-32205-1_39
11. Di Crescenzo, G.D., Ge, R., Arce, G.R.: Design and analysis of DBMAC, an error localizing message authentication code. In: GLOBECOM 2004, pp. 2224–2228. IEEE (2004). http://dx.doi.org/10.1109/GLOCOM.2004.1378404
12. Di Crescenzo, G., Jiang, S., Safavi-Naini, R.: Corruption-localizing hashing. In: Backes, M., Ning, P. (eds.) ESORICS 2009. LNCS, vol. 5789, pp. 489–504. Springer, Heidelberg (2009). http://dx.doi.org/10.1007/978-3-642-04444-1_30
13. Di Crescenzo, G.D., Vakil, F.: Cryptographic hashing for virus localization. In: Jahanian, F. (ed.) WORM 2006. pp. 41–48. ACM Press (2006). http://doi.acm.org/10.1145/1179542.1179550
14. Dorfman, R.: The detection of defective members of large populations. Ann. Math. Stat. **14**(4), 436–440 (1943)
15. Du, D., Hwang, F.: Combinatorial Group Testing and Its Applications: Series on Applied Mathematics. World Scientific, Singapore (2000). http://books.google.co.jp/books?id=KW5-CyUUOggC

16. Eppstein, D., Goodrich, M.T., Hirschberg, D.S.: Improved combinatorial group testing algorithms for real-world problem sizes. SIAM J. Comput. **36**(5), 1360–1375 (2007). http://dx.doi.org/10.1137/050631847

17. Fang, J., Jiang, L.Z., Yiu, S., Hui, L.C.: Hard disk integrity check by hashing with combinatorial group testing. In: CSA 2009, pp. 1–6 (2009). http://dx.doi.org/10.1109/CSA.2009.5404206

18. Ferguson, N., Lucks, S., Schneier, B., Whiting, D., Bellare, M., Kohno, T., Callas, J., Walker, J.: Skein hash function. SHA-3 Submission (2008). http://www.skein-hash.info/

19. Goldreich, O.: Modern Cryptography, Probabilistic Proofs and Pseudorandomness. Algorithms and Combinatorics. Springer, Heidelberg (1998)

20. Goodrich, M.T., Atallah, M.J., Tamassia, R.: Indexing information for data forensics. In: Ioannidis, J., Keromytis, A.D., Yung, M. (eds.) ACNS 2005. LNCS, vol. 3531, pp. 206–221. Springer, Heidelberg (2005). http://dx.doi.org/10.1007/11496137_15

21. Iwata, T., Kurosawa, K.: OMAC: one-key CBC MAC. In: Johansson, T. (ed.) FSE 2003. LNCS, vol. 2887, pp. 129–153. Springer, Heidelberg (2003)

22. Jean, J., Nikolic, I., Peyrin, T.: Tweaks and keys for block ciphers: the TWEAKEY framework. In: Sarkar, P., Iwata, T. (eds.) ASIACRYPT 2014. LNCS, vol. 8874, pp. 274–288. Springer, Heidelberg (2014). http://dx.doi.org/10.1007/978-3-662-45608-8_15

23. Liskov, M., Rivest, R.L., Wagner, D.: Tweakable block ciphers. In: Yung, M. (ed.) CRYPTO 2002. LNCS, vol. 2442, pp. 31–46. Springer, Heidelberg (2002). http://dx.doi.org/10.1007/3-540-45708-9_3

24. Ngo, H.Q., Du, D.Z.: A Survey on combinatorial group testing algorithms with applications to DNA library screening. DIMACS Series in Discrete Mathematics and Theoretical Computer Science (2000)

25. Ngo, H.Q., Porat, E., Rudra, A.: Efficiently decodable error-correcting list disjunct matrices and applications (Extended Abstract). In: Aceto, L., Henzinger, M., Sgall, J. (eds.) ICALP 2011, Part I. LNCS, vol. 6755, pp. 557–568. Springer, Heidelberg (2011). http://dx.doi.org/10.1007/978-3-642-22006-7_47

26. Rogaway, P.: Efficient instantiations of tweakable blockciphers and refinements to modes OCB and PMAC. In: Lee, P.J. (ed.) ASIACRYPT 2004. LNCS, vol. 3329, pp. 16–31. Springer, Heidelberg (2004). http://dx.doi.org/10.1007/978-3-540-30539-2_2

27. Thierry-Mieg, N.: A new pooling strategy for high-throughput screening: the shifted transversal design. BMC Bioinform. **7**, 28 (2006). http://www.biomedcentral.com/content/pdf/1471-2105-7-28.pdf

28. Thierry-Mieg, N., Bailly, G.: Interpool: interpreting smart-pooling results. Bioinformatics **24**(5), 696–703 (2008)

29. Wagner, D.: A generalized birthday problem. In: Yung, M. (ed.) CRYPTO 2002. LNCS, vol. 2442, pp. 288–304. Springer, Heidelberg (2002). http://dx.doi.org/10.1007/3-540-45708-9_19

30. Zaverucha, G.M., Stinson, D.R.: Group testing and batch verification. In: Kurosawa, K. (ed.) ICITS 2009. LNCS, vol. 5973, pp. 140–157. Springer, Heidelberg (2010). http://dx.doi.org/10.1007/978-3-642-14496-7_12

Symmetric-Key Based Proofs of Retrievability Supporting Public Verification

Chaowen Guan[1]([✉]), Kui Ren[1], Fangguo Zhang[1,2,3], Florian Kerschbaum[4], and Jia Yu[1,5]

[1] Department of Computer Science and Engineering,
University at Buffalo, Buffalo, USA
{chaoweng,kuiren}@buffalo.edu, isszhfg@mail.sysu.edu.cn
[2] School of Information Science and Technology, Sun Yat-sen University,
Guangzhou, China
[3] Guangdong Key Laboratory of Information Security Technology,
Guangzhou, China
[4] SAP, Karlsruhe, Germany
florian.kerschbaum@sap.com
[5] College of Information Engineering, Qingdao University, Qingdao, China

Abstract. Proofs-of-Retrievability enables a client to store his data on a cloud server so that he executes an efficient auditing protocol to check that the server possesses all of his data in the future. During an audit, the server must maintain full knowledge of the client's data to pass, even though only a few blocks of the data need to be accessed. Since the first work by Juels and Kaliski, many PoR schemes have been proposed and some of them can support dynamic updates. However, all the existing works that achieve public verifiability are built upon traditional public-key cryptosystems which imposes a relatively high computational burden on low-power clients (e.g., mobile devices).

In this work we explore *indistinguishability obfuscation* for building a Proof-of-Retrievability scheme that provides public verification while the encryption is based on symmetric key primitives. The resulting scheme offers light-weight storing and proving at the expense of longer verification. This could be useful in apations where outsourcing files is usually done by low-power client and verifications can be done by well equipped machines (e.g., a third party server). We also show that the proposed scheme can support dynamic updates. At last, for better assessing our proposed scheme, we give a performance analysis of our scheme and a comparison with several other existing schemes which demonstrates that our scheme achieves better performance on the data owner side and the server side.

Keywords: Cloud storage · Proofs of retrievability · Indistinguishability obfuscation

1 Introduction

Nowadays, storage outsourcing (e.g., Google Drive, Dropbox, etc.) is becoming increasingly popular as one of the applications of cloud computing. It enables

© Springer International Publishing Switzerland 2015
G. Pernul et al. (Eds.): ESORICS 2015, Part I, LNCS 9326, pp. 203–223, 2015.
DOI: 10.1007/978-3-319-24174-6_11

clients to access the outsourced data flexibly from any location. However, the storage provider (i.e., server) is not necessarily trusted. This situation gives rise to a need that a data owner (i.e., client) can efficiently verify that the server indeed stores the entire data. More precisely, a client can run an efficient *audit* protocol with the untrusted server where the server can pass the audit only if it maintains knowledge of the client's *entire* outsourced data. Formally, this implies two guarantees that the client wants from the server: *Authenticity* and *Retrievability*. Authenticity ensures that the client can verify the correctness of the data fetched from the server. On the other hand, Retrievability provides assurance that the client's data on the server is intact and no data loss has occurred. Apparently, the client should not need to download the entire data from server to verify the data's integrity, since this may be prohibitive in terms of bandwidth and time. Also, it is undesirable for the server to read all of the client's outsourced data during an audit protocol.

One method that achieves the above is called Proofs of Retrievability (PoR) which was initially defined and constructed by Juels and Kaliski [1]. Mainly, PoR schemes can be categorized into two classes: privately verifiable ones and publicly verifiable ones. Note that privately verifiable PoR systems normally only involve symmetric key primitives, which are cheap for the data owner in encrypting and uploading its files. However, in such systems the guarantees of the data's authenticity and retrievability largely depend on the data owners themselves due to the fact that they need to regularly perform verifications (e.g., auditing) in order to react as early as possible in case of a data loss. Nowadays, users create and upload data everywhere using low power devices, such as mobile phones. Obviously, such privately verifiable PoR system would inevitably impose expensive burdens on low power data owners in the long run. On the other hand, in this scenario with low power users, it is reasonable to have a well equipped server (trusted or semi-trusted) perform auditing on behalf of data owner which requires publicly verifiable PoR systems. However, all of the existing PoR schemes that achieve public verifiability are constructed based on traditional public key cryptography which implies more complex and expensive computations compared to simple and symmetric key cryptographic primitives. (This observation can also be spotted in outsourced computing schemes that support public verification [34–36].) That means a PoR scheme using public key cryptographic primitives incurs relatively expensive overheads on low-capability clients. One might want to construct a public verifiable PoR scheme without relying on traditional public key cryptographic primitives. One cryptographic primitive that can help to overcome this constraint is *indistinguishability obfuscation* ($i\mathcal{O}$) which achieves that obfuscations of any two distinct (equal-size) programs that implement the same functionality are computationally indistinguishable from each other. $i\mathcal{O}$ has become so important since the recent breakthrough result of Garg et al. in [2]. Garg et al. proposed the first candidate construction of an efficient indistinguishability obfuscator for general programs which are written as boolean circuits. Subsequently, Sahai and Waters [3] showed the power of $i\mathcal{O}$ as a cryptographic primitive: they used $i\mathcal{O}$ to construct denial encryption, public-key encryption, and much more from pseudorandom functions. Most recently, by exploiting $i\mathcal{O}$, Ramchen et al. [4] built a fully secure signature scheme with fast signing and Boneh et al. [5] proposed a multiparty key exchange protocol, an efficient traitor tracing system and more.

Our work. In this paper, we explore this new primitive, $i\mathcal{O}$, for building PoR. In particular, we modify Shacham and Waters' privately verifiable PoR scheme [6] and apply $i\mathcal{O}$ to construct a publicly verifiable PoR scheme. Our results share a similar property with Ramchen et al.'s signing scheme [4], that is, storing and proving are fast at the expense of longer public verification. Such "imbalance" could be useful in applications where outsourcing files is usually done by low-power client and verifications can be done by well equipped machines (a semi-trusted third party). Our contributions are summarized as follows:

1. We explore building proof-of-retrievability systems from obfuscation. The resulting PoR scheme offers light-weight outsourcing, because it requires only symmetric key operations for the data owner to upload files to the cloud server. Likewise, the server also requires less workload during an auditing compared to existing publicly verifiable PoR schemes.
2. We show that the proposed PoR scheme can support dynamic updates by applying the Merkle hash tree technique. We first build a modified B+ tree over the file blocks and the corresponding block verification messages σ. Then we apply the Merkle hash tree to this tree for ensuring authenticity and freshness.
3. Note that the current $i\mathcal{O}$ construction candidate will incur a large amount of overhead for generating obfuscation, but it is only a one-time cost during the preprocessing stage of our system. Therefore its cost can be amortized over plenty of future operations. Except for this one-time cost, we show that our proposed scheme achieves good performance on the data owner side and the cloud server side by analysis and comparisons with other recent existing PoR schemes.

Indistinguishability obfuscation indeed provides attractive and interesting features, but the current $i\mathcal{O}$ candidate construction offers impractical generation and evaluation. Given the fact that the development of $i\mathcal{O}$ is still in its nascent stages, in Appendix, we discuss several possible future directions in works on obfuscation in addition to those discussed in [2].

1.1 Related Work

Proof of Retrievability and Provable Data Possession. The first PoR scheme was defined and constructed by Juels and Kaliski [1], and the first Provable Data Possession (PDP) was concurrently defined by Ateniese et al. [7]. The main difference between PoR and PDP is the notion of security that they achieve. Concretely, PoR provides stronger security guarantees than PDP does. A successful PoR audit guarantees that the server maintains knowledge of *all* of the client's outsourced data, while a successful PDP audit only ensures that the server is retaining *most* of the data. That means, in a PDP system a server that lost a small amount of data can still pass an audit with significant probability. Some PDP schemes [8] indeed provide full security. However, those schemes requires the server to read the client's entire data during an audit. If the data is large, this becomes totally impractical. A detailed comparison can be found in [9]. Since the introduction of PoR and PDP they have received much research attention. On the one hand, subsequent works [6,10–12] for static data focused on the improvement of communication efficiency and exact security. On the other hand, the works of [13–15] showed how to construct dynamic PDP scheme supporting efficient updates. Although many efficient PoR schemes have been proposed since the work of Juels et al., only a few of them supports efficient dynamic update [16–18].

Observe that in publicly verifiable PoR systems, an external verifier (called auditor) is able to perform an auditing protocol with the cloud server on behalf of the data owner. However, public PoR systems do not provide any security guarantees when the user and/or the external verifier are dishonest. To address this problem Armknecht et al. recently introduced the notion of *outsourced proofs of retrievability* (OPoR) [19]. In particular, OPoR protects against the collusion of any two parties among the malicious auditor, malicious users and the malicious cloud server. Armknecht et al. proposed a concrete OPoR scheme, named Fortress, which is mainly built upon the private PoR scheme in [6]. In order to be secure in the OPoR security model, Fortress also employs a mechanism that enables the user and the auditor to extract common pseudorandom bits using a time-dependent source without any interaction.

Indistinguishability Obfuscation. Program obfuscation aims to make computer programs "unintelligible" while preserving their functionality. The formal study of obfuscation was started by Barak et al. [20] in 2001. In their work, they first suggested a quite intuitive notion called *virtual black-box* obfuscation, for which they also showed impossibility. Motivated by this impossibility, they proposed another important notion of obfuscation called *indistinguishability obfuscation* (*iO*), which asks that obfuscations of any two distinct (equal-size) programs that implement the same functionalities are computationally indistinguishable from each other. A recent breakthrough result by Garg et al. [2] presented the first candidate construction of an efficient indistinguishability obfuscator for general programs that are written as boolean circuits. The proposed construction was build on the multilinear map candidates [21,22].

The works of Garg et al. [2] also showed how to apply indistinguishability obfuscation to the construction of functional encryption schemes for general circuits. In subsequent work, Sahai and Waters [3] formally investigated what can be built from indistinguishability obfuscation and showed the power of indistinguishability obfuscation as a cryptographic primitive. Since then, many new applications of general-purpose obfuscation have been explored [24–28]. Most recently, the works of Boneh et al. [5] and Ramchen et al. [4] re-explore the constructions of some existing cryptographic primitives through the lens of obfuscation, including broadcast encryption, traitor tracing and signing. Those proposed constructions indeed obtain some attractive features, although current obfuscation candidates incur prohibitive overheads. Precisely, Boneh et al.'s broadcast encryption achieves that ciphertext size is independent of the number of users, and their traitor tracing system achieves full collusion resistance with short ciphertexts, secret keys and public keys. On the other hand, Ramchen et al. [4] proposed an *imbalanced* signing algorithm, which is ideally significantly faster than comparable signatures that are not built upon obfuscation. Here "imbalanced" means the signing is fast at the expense of longer verification.

2 Preliminaries

In this section we define proof-of-retrievability, indistinguishability obfuscation, and variants of pseudorandom functions (PRFs) that we will make use of. All the variants of PRFs that we consider will be constructed from one-way functions.

2.1 Proofs of Retrievability

Below, we give the definition of publicly verifiable PoR scheme in a way similar to that in [6]. A proof of retrievability scheme defines four algorithms, KeyGen, Store, Prove and Verify, which are specified as follows:

$(pk, sk) \leftarrow$ **KeyGen**(1^λ). On input the security parameter λ, this randomized algorithm generates a public-private keypair (pk, sk).

$(M^*, t) \leftarrow$ **Store**(sk, M). On input a secret key sk and a file $M \in \{0, 1\}^*$, this algorithm processes M to produce M^*, which will be stored on the server, and a tag t. The tag t contains information associated with the file M^*.

$(0, 1) \leftarrow$ **Audit(Prove, Verify)**. The randomized proving and verifying algorithms together define an Audit-protocol for proving file retrievability. During protocol execution, both algorithms take as input the public key pk and the file tag t output by Store. **Prove** algorithm also takes as input the processed file description M^* that is output by Store, and **Verify** algorithm takes as input public verification key VK. At the end of the protocol, **Verify** outputs 0 or 1, with 1 indicating that the file is being stored on the server. We denote a run of two parties executing such protocol as:

$$\{0, 1\} \leftarrow (\mathbf{Verify}(pk, VK, t) \rightleftharpoons \mathbf{Prove}(pk, t, M^*)).$$

Correctness. For all keypairs (pk, sk) output by KeyGen, for all files $M \in \{0, 1\}^*$, and for all (M^*, t) output by Store(sk, M), the verification algorithm accepts when interacting with the valid prover:

$$(\mathbf{Verify}(pk, VK, t) \rightleftharpoons \mathbf{Prove}(pk, t, M^*)) = 1.$$

2.2 Obfuscation Preliminaries

We recall the definition of indistinguishability obfuscation from [2,3].

Definition 1. *Indistinguishability Obfuscation (iO). A uniform PPT machine iO is called an indistinguishability obfuscator for a circuit class* $\{C_\lambda\}_{\lambda \in \mathbb{N}}$ *if the following conditions are satisfied:*

- *For all security parameters* $\lambda \in \mathbb{N}$, *for all* $C \in C_\lambda$, *for all inputs* x, *we have that* $\Pr[C'(x) = C(x) : C' \leftarrow iO(\lambda, C)] = 1$.
- *For any (not necessarily uniform) PPT distinguisher (Samp, D), there exists a negligible function* $negl(\cdot)$ *such that the following holds: if for all security parameters* $\lambda \in \mathbb{N}$, $\Pr[\forall x, C_0(x) = C_1(x) : (C_0; C_1; \tau) \leftarrow Samp(1^\lambda)] > 1 - negl(\lambda)$, *then we have*

$$|\Pr[D(\tau, iO(\lambda, C_0)) = 1 : (C_0; C_1; \tau) \leftarrow Samp(1^\lambda)] -$$
$$\Pr[D(\tau, iO(\lambda, C_1)) = 1 : (C_0; C_1; \tau) \leftarrow Samp(1^\lambda)]| \leq negl(\lambda).$$

2.3 Puncturable PRFs

A pseudorandom function (PRF) is a function $F : \mathcal{K} \times \mathcal{M} \to \mathcal{Y}$ with $K \xleftarrow{\$} \mathcal{K}$ such that the function $F(K, \cdot)$ is indistinguishable from random. A constrained PRF [29] is a PRF $F(K, \cdot)$ that is able to evaluate at certain portions of the input space and nowhere else. A *puncturable* PRF [3,29] is a type of constrained PRF that enables the evaluation at all bit strings of a certain length, except for any polynomial-size set of inputs. Concretely, it is defined with two PPT algorithms $(\mathsf{Eval}_F, \mathsf{Puncture}_F)$ such that the following two properties hold:

- **Functionality Preserved under Puncturing.** For every PPT algorithm $\mathcal{A}$ with input 1^λ outputs a set $S \subseteq \{0,1\}^n$, for all $x \in \{0,1\}^n \backslash S$, we have

$$\Pr[\mathsf{Eval}_F(K\{S\}, x) = F(K, x) : K \xleftarrow{\$} \mathcal{K}, K\{S\} \leftarrow \mathsf{Puncture}_F(K, S)] = 1$$

- **Pseudorandom at Punctured Points.** For every pair of PPT algorithms $(\mathcal{A}_1, \mathcal{A}_2)$ such that $\mathcal{A}_1(1^\lambda)$ outputs a set $S \subseteq \{0,1\}^n$ and a state σ, consider an experiment where $K \xleftarrow{\$} \mathcal{K}, K\{S\} \leftarrow \mathsf{Puncture}_F(K, S)$. It holds that

$$|\Pr[\mathcal{A}_2(\sigma, K\{S\}, S, F(K, S)) = 1)] -$$
$$\Pr[\mathcal{A}_2(\sigma, K\{S\}, S, U_{m(\lambda) \cdot |S|}) = 1]| \leq negl(\lambda)$$

3 Security Definitions

The security definitions of *Authenticity* and *Retrievability* in [17,18] are essentially equivalent to the security definition of *Soundness* in [6]. Note that the security definitions in [17,18] are for dynamic PoR systems, while the one in [6] considers only static PoR systems. The only difference between a static PoR scheme and a dynamic PoR scheme is that the latter one supports secure dynamic updates, including modification, deletion and insertion. This affects the access to oracles in the security game. Below we present the security definitions for static PoR systems in the same way as [17,18] and then point out how to obtain the security definitions for dynamic PoR systems based on the static one.

3.1 Security Definitions on Static PoR

Authenticity. Authenticity requires that the client can always detect if any message sent by the server deviates from honest behavior. More precisely, consider the following game between a challenger $\mathcal{C}$, a malicious server $\widetilde{\mathcal{S}}$ and an honest server $\mathcal{S}$ for the adaptive version of authenticity:

- The challenger initializes the environment and provides $\widetilde{\mathcal{S}}$ with public parameters.
- The malicious sever $\widetilde{\mathcal{S}}$ specifies a valid protocol sequence $P = (op_1, op_2, \cdots , op_{\text{poly}(\lambda)})$ of polynomial size in the security parameter λ. The specified operations op_t can be either Store or Audit. $\mathcal{C}$ executes the protocol with both $\widetilde{\mathcal{S}}$ and an honest server $\mathcal{S}$.

If at execution of any op_j, the message sent by $\widetilde{\mathcal{S}}$ differs from that of the honest server $\mathcal{S}$ and $\mathcal{C}$ does not output reject, the adversary $\widetilde{\mathcal{S}}$ wins and the game results in 1, else 0.

Definition 2. *A static PoR scheme is said to satisfy adaptive* **Authenticity***, if any polynomial-time adversary $\widetilde{\mathcal{S}}$ wins the above security game with probability no more than* $\text{negl}(\lambda)$.

Retrievability. Retrievability guarantees that whenever a malicious server can pass the audit test with non-negligible probability, the server must know the entire content of $\mathcal{M}$; and moreover, $\mathcal{M}$ can be recovered by repeatedly running the Audit-protocol between the challenger $\mathcal{C}$ and the server $\widetilde{\mathcal{S}}$. More precisely, consider the following security game:

- The challenger initializes the environment and provides $\widetilde{\mathcal{S}}$ with public parameters.
- The malicious server $\widetilde{\mathcal{S}}$ specifies a protocol sequence $P = (op_1, op_2, \cdots , op_{\text{poly}(\lambda)})$ of polynomial size in terms of the security parameter λ. The specified operations op_t can be either Store or Audit. Let $\mathcal{M}$ be the correct content value.
- The challenger $\mathcal{C}$ sequentially executes the respective protocols with $\widetilde{\mathcal{S}}$. At the end of executing P, let $st_{\mathcal{C}}$ and $st_{\widetilde{\mathcal{S}}}$ be the final configurations (states) of the challenger and the malicious server, respectively.
- The challenger now gets black-box rewinding access to the malicious server in its final configuration $st_{\widetilde{\mathcal{S}}}$. Starting from the configurations $(st_{\mathcal{C}}, st_{\widetilde{\mathcal{S}}})$, the challenger runs the Audit-protocol repeatedly for a polynomial number of times with the server $\widetilde{\mathcal{S}}$ and attempts to extract out the content value as $\mathcal{M}'$.

If the malicious server $\widetilde{S}$ passes the Audit-protocol with non-negligible probability and the extracted content value $\mathcal{M}' \neq \mathcal{M}$, then this game outputs 1, else 0.

Definition 3. *A static PoR scheme is said to satisfy* **Retrievability**, *if there exists an efficient extractor $\mathcal{E}$ such that for any polynomial-time $\widetilde{S}$, if $\widetilde{S}$ passes the Audit-protocol with non-negligible probability, and then after executing the Audit-protocol with $\widetilde{S}$ for a polynomial number of times, the extractor $\mathcal{E}$ outputs content value $\mathcal{M}' \neq \mathcal{M}$ only with negligible probability.*

The above says that the extractor $\mathcal{E}$ will be able to extract out the correct content value $\mathcal{M}' = \mathcal{M}$ if the malicious server $\widetilde{S}$ can maintain a non-negligible probability of passing the Audit-protocol. This means the server must retain full knowledge of $\mathcal{M}$.

3.2 Security Definitions on Dynamic PoR

The security definitions for dynamic PoR systems are the same as those for static PoR systems, except that the oracles which the malicious server $\widetilde{S}$ has access to are including Read, Write and Audit. Precisely, the security game for Authenticity is the same as the for static PoR schemes, except that the malicious server $\widetilde{S}$ can get access to Read, Write and Audit oracles. This means that the specified operations op_t by $\widetilde{S}$ in the protocol sequence $P = (op_1, op_2, \cdots, op_{\mathrm{poly}(\lambda)})$ can be either Read, Write or Audit. Similarly, the security game for Retrievability is the same as that for static PoR systems, except that the malicious server $\widetilde{S}$ can get access to Read, Write and Audit oracles. Note that the winning condition for both games remain unchanged.

4   Constructions

In this section we first give the construction of a static publicly verifiable PoR system. Then we discuss how to extend this static PoR scheme to support efficient dynamic updates.

Before presenting our proposed constructions, we analyze a trivial construction of a publicly verifiable PoR scheme using $i\mathcal{O}$. Let n be the number of file blocks, λ_1 be the size of a file block (here assume every file block is equally large), λ_2 be the size of a block tag σ and I be the challenge index set requested by the verifier. Since $i\mathcal{O}$ can hide secret information, which is embedded into the obfuscated program, from the users, one might construct a scheme as: (1) set the tag for a file block m_i as the output of a PRF $F(k, m_i)$ with secret key k; (2) embed key k into the verification program and obfuscate it; (3) this verification program simply checks the tags for the challenged file blocks to see if they are valid outputs of the PRF. Observe that this verification program takes as inputs a challenge index set, the challenged file blocks and the corresponding file tags. Therefore, the circuit for this verification program will be of size $O(poly(|I| \cdot \log n + |I| \cdot \lambda_1 + |I| \cdot \lambda_2))$, where $|I|$ is the size of index set I and $poly(x)$ is a polynomial in terms of x. Clearly, this method also costs much a lot of bandwidth due to the fact that it does not provide an aggregated proof.

While in our construction we modify the privately verifiable PoR scheme in [6]. For consistency with the above analysis, assume that file blocks are not further divided into sectors. Then the verification program takes as input a challenge index set I, an aggregation of the challenged file blocks μ and an aggregated σ'. Consequently the circuit for the verification program will have size $O(poly(|I| \cdot \log n + \lambda_1 + \lambda_2))$, which is much smaller than that in the trivial construction. Clearly, the trivial construction will lead to a significantly larger obfuscation of the verification program.

Similarly, we analyze the circuit's size when a file block is further split into s sectors, as the scheme in [6] did. Let the size of a sector in a file block be λ_3. The circuit size in the trivial construction will remain unchanged, $O(poly(|I| \cdot \log n + |I| \cdot \lambda_1 + |I| \cdot \lambda_2))$. While the circuit in our construction will have size $O(poly(|I| \cdot \log n + s \cdot \lambda_3 + \lambda_3)) \approx O(poly(|I| \cdot \log n + \lambda_1 + \lambda_3))$, which is still much smaller than that in the trivial construction. As we can see, exploiting $i\mathcal{O}$ is not trivial although it is a powerful cryptographic primitive.

4.1 Static Publicly Verifiable PoR Scheme

We modify Shacham and Waters' privately verifiable PoR scheme in [6] and combine it with $i\mathcal{O}$ to give a publicly verifiable PoR scheme. Recall that in the scheme in [6], a file F is processed using erasure code and then divided into n blocks. Also note that each block is split into s sectors. This allows for a tradeoff between storage overhead and communication overhead, as discussed in [6].

Before presenting the construction of the proposed static PoR scheme, we give a brief discussion on how we apply indistinguishability obfuscation to the PoR scheme in [6]. For doing that, we need to utilize a key technique introduced in [3], named *punctured programs*. At a very high-level, the idea of this technique is to modify a program (which is to be obfuscated) by surgically removing a key element of the program, without which the adversary cannot win the security game it must play, but in a way that does not change the functionality of the program. Note that, in Shacham and Waters' PoR scheme, for each file block, σ_i is set as $f_{prf}(i) + \sum_{j=1}^{s} \alpha_j m_{ij}$, where the secret key k_{prf} for PRF f is specific for one certain file M. That means for different files, it uses different PRF key k_{prf}'s. As to make it a *punctured* PRF that we want in the obfuscated program, we eliminate this binding between PRF key k_{prf} and file M, and the same PRF key k_{prf} will be used in storing many different files. Thus, the PRF key k_{prf} will be randomly chosen in client KeyGen step, not in Store step. The security will be maintained after this modification, due to the fact that it still provides σ_i with randomness without adversary getting the PRF key.

The second main change is related to the construction of a file tag t. Note that, in Shacham and Waters' scheme, $t = n \| c \| \mathsf{MAC}_{k_{mac}}(n \| c)$, where $c = \mathsf{Enc}_{k_{enc}}(k_{prf} \| \alpha_1 \| \cdots \| \alpha_s)$. In our proposed scheme, the randomly selected elements $\alpha_1, \cdots, \alpha_s$ will be removed. Instead, we use another PRF key $f_{prf'}$ to generate s pseudorandom numbers, which will reduce the communication cost by $(s \cdot \lceil \log p \rceil)$, where $\log p$ means each element $\alpha_i \in \mathbb{Z}_p$. As a consequence of these two changes, the symmetric key encryption component c is no longer needed and σ_i will be made as $f_{prf}(i) + \sum_{j=1}^{s} f_{prf'}(j) \cdot m_{ij}$.

Let $F_1(k_1, \cdot)$ be a puncturable PRF mapping $\lceil \log N \rceil$-bit inputs to $\lceil \log \mathbb{Z}_p \rceil$. Here N is a bound on the number of blocks in a file. Let $F_2(k_2, \cdot)$ be a puncturable PRF mapping $\lceil \log s \rceil$-bit inputs to $\lceil \log \mathbb{Z}_p \rceil$. Let $\mathsf{SSig}_{ssk}(x)$ be the algorithm generating a signature on x.

KeyGen(). Randomly choose two PRF key $k_1 \in \mathcal{K}_1$, $k_2 \in \mathcal{K}_2$ and a random signing keypair $(svk, ssk) \xleftarrow{R} \mathsf{SK}_g$. Set the secret key $sk = (k_1, k_2, ssk)$. Let the public key be svk along with the verification key VK which is an indistinguishability obfuscation of the program Check defined as below.

Store(sk, M). Given file M and secret key $sk = (k_1, k_2, ssk)$, proceed as follows:
1. apply the erasure code to M to obtain M';
2. split M' into n blocks, and each block into s sectors to get $\{m_{ij}\}$ for $1 \le i \le n, 1 \le j \le s$;
3. set the file tag $t = n \| \mathsf{SSig}_{ssk}(n)$
4. for each i, $1 \le i \le n$, compute $\sigma_i = F_1(k_1, i) + \sum_{j=1}^s F_2(k_2, j) \cdot m_{ij}$;
5. set as the outputs the processed file $M' = \{m_{ij}\}$, $1 \le i \le n, 1 \le j \le s$, the corresponding file tag t and $\{\sigma_i\}, 1 \le i \le n$.

Verify(svk, VK, t). Given the tag t, parse $t = n \| \mathsf{SSig}_{ssk}(n)$ and use svk to verify the signature on t; if the signature is invalid, reject and halt. Otherwise, pick a random l-element subset I from $[1, n]$, and for each $i \in I$, pick a random element $v_i \in \mathbb{Z}_p$. Send set $Q = \{(i, v_i)\}$ to the prover.

Parse the prover's response to obtain $\mu_1, \cdots, \mu_s, \sigma \in \mathbb{Z}_p^{s+1}$. If parsing fails, reject and halt. Otherwise, output $\mathsf{VK}(Q = \{(i, v_i)\}_{i \in I}, \mu_1, \cdots, \mu_s, \sigma)$.

> Check:
> Inputs: $Q = \{(i, v_i)\}_{i \in I}, \mu_1, \cdots, \mu_s, \sigma$
> Constants: PRF keys k_1, k_2
> **if** $\sigma = \sum_{(i, v_i) \in Q} v_i \cdot F_1(k_1, i) + \sum_{j=1}^s F_2(k_2, j) \cdot \mu_j$ **then** output 1
> **else** output $\perp$

Prove(t, M'). Given the processed file M', $\{\sigma_i\}, 1 \le i \le n$ and an l-element set Q sent by the verifier, parse $M' = \{m_{ij}\}, 1 \le i \le n, 1 \le j \le s$ and $Q = \{(i, v_i)\}$. Then compute

$$\mu_j = \sum_{(i, v_i) \in Q} v_i m_{ij} \text{ for } 1 \le j \le s, \quad \text{and} \quad \sigma = \sum_{(i, v_i)} v_i \sigma_i,$$

and send to the prove in response the values $\mu_1, \cdots, \mu_s$ and σ.

4.2 PoR Scheme Supporting Efficient Dynamic Updates

A PoR scheme supporting dynamic updates means that it enables modification, deletion and insertion over the stored files. Note that, in the static PoR scheme, each σ_i associated with $m_{ij_{1 \le j \le s}}$ is also bound to a file block index i. If an update is executed in this static PoR scheme, it requires to change every σ_i corresponding to the involved file blocks, and the cost could probably be expensive. Let's say the client needs to insert a file block F_i into position i. We can see that this insertion manipulation requires to update the indices in σ_j's for all $i \le j \le n$. On average, a single insertion incurs updates on $n/2$ σ_j's.

In order to offer efficient insertion, we need to disentangle σ_i from index i. Concretely, $F_1(k_1, \cdot)$ should be erased in the computing of σ_i, which leads to a modified $\sigma_i' = \sum_{j=1}^{s} F_2(k_2, j) \cdot m_{ij}$. However, this would make the scheme insecure, because a malicious server can always forge, e.g., $\sigma_i'/2 = \sum_{j=1}^{s} F_2(k_2, j) \cdot (m_{ij}/2)$ for file block $\{m_{ij}/2\}_{1 \le j \le s}$ with this σ_i'.

Instead, we build σ_i as $F_1(k_1, r_i) + \sum_{j=1}^{s} F_2(k_2, j) \cdot m_{ij}$, where r_i is a random element from $\mathbb{Z}_p$. Clearly, we can't maintain the order of the stored file blocks without associating σ_i with index i. To provide the guarantee that every up-to-date file block is in the designated position, we use a modified B+ tree data structure with standard Merkle hash tree technique.

Observe that, unlike Shacham and Waters' scheme where the file is split into n blocks after being erasure encoded, the construction here assumes that each file block is encoded 'locally'. (Cash et al.'s work [17] also started with this point.) That is, instead of using an erasure code that takes the entire file as input, we use a code that works on small blocks. More precisely, the client divides the file M into n blocks, i.e., $M = (m_1, m_2, \cdots, m_n)$, and then encodes each file block m_i individually into a corresponding codeword block $c_i = \mathsf{encode}(m_i)$. Next, the client performs the following PoR scheme to create σ_i for each c_i. Auditing works as before: The verifier randomly selects l indices from $[1, n]$ and l random values, and then challenges the server to respond with a proof that is computed with those l random values and corresponding codewords specified by the l indices. Note that, in this construction, each codeword c_i will be further divided into s sectors, $(c_{i1}, c_{i2}, \cdots, c_{is})$ during the creation of σ_i. A more detailed discussion about this and analysis of how to better define block size can be found in the appendices in [6,17].

Let $F_1(k_1, \cdot)$ be a puncturable PRF mapping $\lceil \log N \rceil$-bit inputs to $\lceil \log \mathbb{Z}_p \rceil$. Here N is a bound on the number of blocks in a file. Let $F_2(k_2, \cdot)$ be a puncturable PRF mapping $\lceil \log s \rceil$-bit inputs to $\lceil \log \mathbb{Z}_p \rceil$. Let $\mathsf{Enc}_k / \mathsf{Dec}_k$ be a symmetric key encryption/decryption algorithm, and $\mathsf{SSig}_{ssk}(x)$ be the algorithm generating a signature on x.

KeyGen(). Randomly choose puncturable PRF keys $k_1 \in \mathcal{K}_1$ $k_2 \in \mathcal{K}_2$, a symmetric encryption key $k_{enc} \in \mathcal{K}_{enc}$ and a random signing keypair $(svk, ssk) \xleftarrow{R} \mathsf{SK}_g$. Set the secret key $sk = (k_1, k_2, k_{enc}, ssk)$. Let the public key be svk along with the verification key VK which is an indistinguishability obfuscation of the program CheckU defined as below.

Store(sk, M). Given file M and secret key $sk = (k_1, k_2, k_{enc}, ssk)$, proceed as follows:

1. split M' into n blocks and apply the erasure code to each block m_i to obtain the codeword block m_i', then divide each block m_i' into s sectors to get $\{m_{ij}'\}$ for $1 \le i \le n, 1 \le j \le s$;
2. for each i, $1 \le i \le n$, choose a random element $r_i \in \mathbb{Z}_p$ and compute
   $$\sigma_i = F_1(k_1, r_i) + \sum_{j=1}^{s} F_2(k_2, j) \cdot m_{ij}';$$
3. set $c = \mathsf{Enc}_{k_{enc}}(r_1 \| \cdots \| r_n)$ and the file tag $t = n \| c \| \mathsf{SSig}_{ssk}(n \| c)$;
4. set as the outputs the processed file $M' = \{m_{ij}'\}$, $1 \le i \le n, 1 \le j \le s$, the corresponding file tag t and $\{\sigma_i\}, 1 \le i \le n$.

Verify(svk, VK, t). Given the file tag t, parse $t = n\|c\|\mathsf{SSig}_{ssk}(n\|c)$ and use svk to verify the signature on t; if the signature is invalid, reject and halt. Otherwise, pick a random l-element subset I from $[1, n]$, and for each $i \in I$, pick a random element $v_i \in \mathbb{Z}_p$. Sent set $Q = \{(i, v_i)\}$ to the prover.

Parse the prover's response to obtain $\mu_1, \cdots, \mu_s, \sigma \in \mathbb{Z}_p^{s+1}$. If parsing fails, reject and halt. Otherwise, output $\mathrm{VK}(Q = \{(i, v_i)\}_{i \in I}, \mu_1, \cdots, \mu_s, \sigma, t)$.

CheckU:
Inputs: $Q = \{(i, v_i)\}_{i \in I}, \mu_1, \cdots, \mu_s, \sigma, t$
Constants: PRF keys k_1, k_2, symmetric encryption key k_{enc}
$\quad n\|c\|\mathsf{SSig}_{ssk}(n\|c) \leftarrow t$
$\quad r_1, \cdots, r_n \leftarrow Dec_{k_{enc}}(c)$
$\quad$**if** $\sigma = \sum_{(i,v_i) \in Q} v_i \cdot F_1(k_1, r_i) + \sum_{j=1}^s F_2(k_2, j) \cdot \mu_j$ **then** output 1
$\quad$**else** output $\bot$

Prove(t, M'). Given the processed file M', $\{\sigma_i\}, 1 \le i \le n$ and an l-element set Q sent by the verifier, parse $M' = \{m'_{ij}\}, 1 \le i \le n, 1 \le j \le s$ and $Q = \{(i, v_i)\}$. Then compute

$$\mu_j = \sum_{(i,v_i) \in Q} v_i m'_{ij} \text{ for } 1 \le j \le s, \quad \text{and} \quad \sigma = \sum_{(i,v_i)} v_i \sigma_i,$$

and send to the prove in response the values $\mu_1, \cdots, \mu_s$ and σ.

Modified B+ Merkle tree. In our construction, we organize the data files using a modified B+ tree, and then apply a standard Merkle Hash tree to provides guarantees of freshness and authenticity. In this modified B+ tree, each node has at most three entries. Each entry in leaf node is data file's σ and is linked to its corresponding data file in the additional bottom level. The internal nodes will no longer have index information. Before presenting the tree's construction, we first define some notations. We denote an entry's corresponding computed σ by $label(\cdot)$, the rank of an entry (i.e., the number of file blocks that can be reached from this entry) by $rank(\cdot)$, descendants of an entry by $child(\cdot)$, left/right sibling of an entry by $len(\cdot)/ren(\cdot)$.

- entry w in leaf node: $label(w) = \sigma$, $len(w)$ (if w is the leftmost entry, $len(w) = 0$) and $ren(w)$ ((if w is the rightmost entry, $ren(w) = 0$);
- entry v in internal node and root node: $rank(v)$, $child(v)$ $len(v)$ and $ren(v)$, where $len(v)$ and $ren(v)$ conform to the rules above.

An example is illustrated in Fig. 1a. Following the definitions above, entry v_1 in root node R contains: (1) $rank(v_1) = 3$, because w_1, w_2 and w_3 can be reached from v_1; (2) $child(v_1) = w_1\|w_2\|w_3$; (3) $len(v_1) = 0$; (4) $ren(v_1) = v_2$. Entry w_2 in leaf node W_1 contains: (1) $label(w_2) = \sigma_2$; (2) $len(w_2) = w_1$; (3) $ren(w_2) = w_3$. Note that the arrows connecting the entries in leaf nodes with F's means that each entry is associated with its corresponding file block. Precisely, e.g., entry w_1 is associated with the first data block F_1 and $label(w_1) = \sigma_1$.

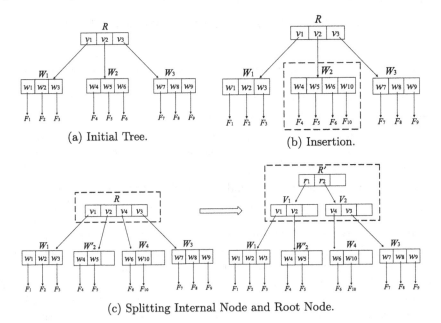

(a) Initial Tree.

(b) Insertion.

(c) Splitting Internal Node and Root Node.

Fig. 1. An example of a modified B+ tree.

To search for a σ and its corresponding file block, we need two additional values of each entry, $low(\cdot)$ and $high(\cdot)$. $low(\cdot)$ gives the lowest-position data block that can be reached from an entry, and $high(\cdot)$ defines the highest-position data block that can be reached from an entry. Observe that these two values need not be stored for every entry in the tree. We can compute them on the fly using the ranks. For the current entry r, assume we know $low(r)$ and $high(r)$. Let $child(r) = v_1\|v_2\|v_3$. Then $low(v_i)$'s and $high(v_i)$'s can be computed with entry's $rank$ value in the following way: (1) $low(v_1) = low(r)$ and $high(v_1) = low(v_1) + rank(v_1) - 1$; (2) $low(v_2) = high(v_1) + 1$ and $high(v_2) = low(v_2) + rank(v_2) - 1$; (3) $low(v_3) = high(v_2) + 1$ and $high(v_3) = high(r)$.

Using the entries' $rank$ values, we can reach the i-th data block (i.e., i-th entry) in the leaf nodes. The search starts with entry v_1 in root node. Clearly, for the start entry of the tree, we have $low(v_1) = 1$. On each entry v during the search, if $i \in [low(v), high(v)]$, we proceed the search along the pointer from v to its children; otherwise, check the next entry on v's right side. We continue until we reach the i-th data block. For instance, say we want to read the 6-th data block in Fig. 1a. We start with entry v_1, and the search proceeds as follows:

1. compute $high(v_1) = low(v_1) + rank(v_1) - 1 = 3$;
2. $i = 6 \notin [low(v_1), high(v_1)]$, then check the next entry, v_2;
3. compute $low(v_2) = high(v_1) + 1 = 4$, $high(v_2) = low(v_2) + rank(v_2) - 1 = 6$;
4. $i \in [low(v_2), high(v_2)]$, then follow the pointer leading to v_2's children;
5. get $child(v_2) = w_4\|w_5\|w_6$;

6. now in leaf node, check each entry from left to right, and find w_6 be the entry connecting to the wanted data block.

Now it is only left to define the Merkle hash tree on this modified B+ tree. Note that in our modified B+ tree, each node have at most 3 entries. Let upper case letter denote node and lower case one denote entry. For each entry, the hashing value is computed as follows:

- **Case 0**: w is an entry in a leaf node, compute $f(w) = h(label(w)) = h(\sigma)$,
- **Case 1**: v is an entry in an internal node and it's descendent is node V', compute $f(v) = h(rank(v)\|f(V'))$.

For each node (internal node or leaf node) consisting of entries v_1, v_2, v_3 from left to right, we define $f(V) = h(f(v_1)\|f(v_2)\|f(v_3))$. For instance, in Fig. 1.a, the hashing value for the root node is $f(R) = h(f(v_1)\|f(v_2)\|f(v_3))$, where $f(v_i) = h(rank(v_i)\|f(W_i))$ and $f(W_i) = h(f(w_{(i-1)*3+1})\|f(w_{(i-1)*3+2})\|f(w_{(i-1)*3+3}))$.

With this Merkle hash tree built over the modified B+ tree, the client keeps track of the root digest. Every time after fetching a data block, the client fetches its corresponding σ as well. Also the client receives the hashing values associated with other entries in the same node along the path from root to the data block. Then the client can verify the authenticity and freshness with the Merkle tree. Say the client needs to verify the authenticity and freshness of block F_3 in Fig. 1a, where he/she possesses the root digest $f(R)$. The path from root to F_3 will be $(R \to W_1)$. For verification, besides σ_3, the client also receives $f(w_1), f(w_2)$ in node W_1 and $f(v_2), f(v_3)$ in node R.

Update. The main manipulations are updating the data block and updating the Merkle tree. Note that the update affects only nodes along the path from a wanted data block to root on the Merkle tree. Therefore, the running time for updating the Merkle tree is $O(logn)$. Also to update the Merkle tree, some hashing values along the path from a data block to root are needed from the server. Clearly, the size of those values will be $O(logn)$. Update operations include Modification, Deletion and Insertion. The update operations over our modified B+ tree mostly conform to the procedures of standard B+ tree. A slight difference lies in the Insertion operation when splitting node, due to the fact that our modified B+ tree doesn't have index information.

First, we discuss Modification and Deletion. To modify a data block, the client simply computes the data block's new corresponding σ and updates the Merkle tree with this σ to obtain a new root digest. Then the client uploads the the new data block and the new σ. After receiving this new σ, the server just needs to update the Merkle tree along the path from the data block to root. To delete a data block, the server simply deletes the unwanted data block by the client and then updates the Merkle tree along the path from this data block to root.

Next, we give the details of Insertion. If the leaf node where the new data block will be inserted is not full, the procedure is the same as Modification. Otherwise, the leaf node needs to be split, and then the entry that leads to this leaf node will also be split into two entries, with one entry leading to each leaf node. Note that unlike operations on standard B+ tree, we don't copy the index of the third entry (i.e., the index of the new generated node) to its parent's node. Instead, we simply create a new entry with a pointer leading to the node and record the corresponding information as defined above. If the root node needs to be divided, the depth of this Merkle tree will increment by 1. An example of updating is shown as Fig. 1b and c. Say the client wants to insert a new file block F_{10} in the 7-th position. First, it locates the position in the way mentioned above. Note that we can locate the 6-th position or the 7-th position. Here we choose to locate the 6-th position and insert a new entry w_{10} behind w_6 in left node W_2 . (If choosing to locate the 7-th position, one should put the new entry before w_7.) Next, the information corresponding to this new file block F_{10} will be written into entry w_{10} with a pointer pointing from w_{10} to F_{10}, as shown in Fig. 1b. Since it exceeds the maximum number of entries that a node can have, this leaf node W_2 needs to be split into two leaf nodes, W_2' and W_4 with two non-empty entries in each node (this conforms to the rules of updating a B+ tree), as shown in Fig. 1c. At the same time, a new entry v_4 is created in the root node R with a pointer leading v_4 to leaf node W_4. Similarly, this root node R is split into two internal nodes, V_1 and V_1. Finally, a new root note R' is built, which has two entries and two pointers leading to V_1 and V_2, respectively. Note that, now the root node has entries r_1 and r_2, where r_1 is the start entry of this tree, meaning $low(r_1) = 1$. We also have $rank(r_1) = rank(V_1) = rank(v_1) + rank(v_2) = 5$ and $rank(r_2) = 5$.

4.3 Security Proofs

Theorem 1. *The proposed static PoR scheme satisfied* **Authenticity** *as specified in Sect. 3.1, assuming the existence of secure indistinguishability obfuscators, existentially unforgeable signature schemes and secure puncturable PRFs.*

Theorem 2. *The proposed static PoR scheme satisfies* **Retrievability** *as specified in Sect. 3.1.*

The detailed proof for Theorem 1 is given in the full version of this paper [23]. The proof for Theorem 2 will be identical to that in [6], because in our scheme, a file is processed using erasure code before being divided into n blocks, the same as that in [6] where the proof was divided into two parts, Sects. 4.2 and 4.3.

5 Analysis and Comparisons

In this section, we give an analysis of our proposed scheme and then compare it with other two recently proposed schemes.

Our scheme requires the data owner to generate an obfuscated program during the preprocessing stage of the system. With the current obfuscator candidate, it indeed costs the data owner a somewhat large amount of overhead, but this is a one-time effort which can be amortized over plenty of operations in the future. Thus, we focus on the analysis on the computation and communication overheads incurred during writing and auditing operations rather than those in

Table 1. Comparison with existing dynamic PoRs.

Scheme	Write cost on server	Write bandwidth	Auditing cost server read	Verifiability	Dynamic
Iris [16]	$O(\beta)$	$O(\beta)$	$O(\beta\lambda\sqrt{n})$	Private	YES
Cash et al. [17]	$O(\beta\lambda(\log n)^2)$	$O(\beta\lambda(\log n)^2)$	$O(\beta\lambda(\log n)^2)$	Private	YES
Shi et al. [18]	$O(\beta\log n) +$ $O(\lambda\log n)$	$O(\beta) +$ $O(\lambda\log n)$	$O(\beta\lambda\log n)$	Public	YES
This paper	$O(\beta) +$ $O(\lambda\log n)$	$O(\beta) +$ $O(\lambda\log n)$	$O(\beta\lambda)$	Public	YES

the preprocessing step. Like the private PoR system in [6] the data owner can efficiently store files on the cloud server, and it takes the cloud server less overhead during an auditing protocol than in a public-key-based scheme. The cost on the client device is mainly incurred by the operations over symmetric key primitives, which are known to be much faster than public key cryptographic primitives. The cost analysis on the server side is shown as Table 1.

In Table 1 showing a comparison with existing dynamic PoR schemes we let β be the block size in number of bits, λ be the security parameter and n be the number of blocks. We compare our scheme with the state-of-the-art scheme [18], since a comparison between Shi et al.'s scheme and Cash et al.'s scheme is given in [18]. Note that Shi et al.'s scheme needs amortized cost $O(\beta\log n)$ for writing on the server side, due to the fact that an erasure-coding needs to be done on the entire data file after $\Theta(n)$ updates, while our scheme uses an erasure code that works on file blocks, instead of taking the entire file as inputs (more details and discussions can be found in Sect. 4). That means, in our system modifying a block does not require a change of the erasure codes of the entire file. Thus, the cost for writing is only proportional to the block size being written. On the other hand, during an auditing protocol, Shi et al.'s scheme incurs overhead $O(\beta\lambda\log n)$ on the server side, due to the features of the server-side storage layout. In their scheme, one single file will be stored as three parts, including raw data part R, erasure-coded copy of the entire file C and hierarchical log structure part H that stores the up-to-date file blocks in erasure-coded format. Thus, during one auditing operation, Shi et al.'s scheme needs to check $O(\lambda)$ random blocks from C and $O(\lambda)$ random blocks from each filled level in H. While, in our scheme, the server performs every writing over the wanted block directly, not storing the update block separately. Thus, our scheme only requires $O(\lambda)$ random blocks of one file to check authenticity during auditing. (Note that this $O(\lambda)$ usually would be $\Omega(\sqrt{n}\beta)$ if no pseudorandom permutation over the locations of the file blocks is performed, because a small number proportional to $O(\lambda)$ might render the system insecure. Please refer to [17] for more details.) Note that it is most likely that the auditing protocol is executed between a well-equipped verification machine and the server, and the operations on server side only involve symmetric key primitives. Therefore, it will not have noticeable effects on the system's overall performance.

Clearly, the improvement in our work mainly results from $i\mathcal{O}$'s power that secret keys can be embedded into the obfuscated verification program without secret keys being learnt by user. However, the current obfuscator candidate [2] provides a construction running in impractical, albeit polynomial, time. (Note that it is reasonable and useful that the obfuscated program is run on well-equipped machines.) Although $i\mathcal{O}$'s generation and evaluation is not fast now [30], studies on implementing practical obfuscation are developing fast [31]. It is plausible that obfuscations with practical performance will be achieved in the not too distant future. Note that the improvement on obfuscation will directly lead to an improvement on our schemes.

6   Conclusions

In this paper, we explore *indistinguishability obfuscation* to construct a publicly verifiable Proofs-of-Retrievability (PoR) scheme that is mainly built upon symmetric key cryptographic primitives. We also show how to modify the proposed scheme to support dynamic updates using a combination of a modified B+ tree and a standard Merkle hash tree. By analysis and comparisons with other existing schemes, we show that our scheme is efficient on the data owner side and the cloud server side. Although it consumes a somewhat large amount of overheads to generate an obfuscation, it is only a one-time effort during the preprocessing stage of the system. Therefore, this cost can be amortized over all of future operations. Also note that the improvement on obfuscation will directly lead to an improvement on our schemes.

Acknowledgments. This work is supported in part by US National Science Foundation under grant CNS-1262277 and the National Natural Science Foundation of China (Nos. 61379154 and U1135001).

A   Discussions and Future Directions Towards $i\mathcal{O}$

As pointed out in [2], the current obfuscation constructions runs in impractical polynomial-time, and it is an important objective to improve the efficiency for $i\mathcal{O}$ usage in real life applications. Also Apon et al.'s showed the inefficiency in $i\mathcal{O}$'s generation and evaluation in [30]. In this section, we give discussions on three possible future directions in Obfuscation, in addition to those in [2].

A.1   Outsourced and Joint Generation of Indistinguishability Obfuscation

Image the scenario in our proposed publicly verifiable PoR system, where users store their data on the same cloud server using the same PoR scheme but with different secret keys. One naive approach with $i\mathcal{O}$ would be requiring each user to generate his/her own individual obfuscated program for public verification. This means that each user needs to afford the prohibitively expensive overhead for $i\mathcal{O}$'s generation on his/her own. Note that for the same PoR scheme, the verification procedures are the same but with different user's secret key. Also note that each user "embeds" his/her own secret keys into the obfuscated verification in a way that anyone else can't learn anything about the embedded secret values. Hence, we can have several users jointly and securely generate one obfuscated verification program, where each user uses his/her own secret key as part of the input to the generation. One promising way could be using Secure multiparty computation. Observe that this generated obfuscated program has almost the same computation as the one with only one user's secret key embedded. The only differences between this jointly generated obfuscation and the individual-user-generated obfuscation are that (1) the jointly generated obfuscation is implanted with more than one user's secret key; (2) the jointly generated obfuscation needs one more step to identify which user's secret key it will use.

On the other hand, outsourced computing is useful in applications where relatively low-power devices need to compute expensive and time-consuming functions. Clearly, as for relatively low-power individual computers, the overhead caused by the current $i\mathcal{O}$ construction candidate is impractical. Thus, it would be promising to find a specific way to efficiently outsource $i\mathcal{O}$'s generation.

A.2   Reusability and Universality of Indistinguishability Obfuscation

Reusability is related to $i\mathcal{O}$'s joint generation to some extent. In the scenario considered above, the jointly generated obfuscated program is embedded with a group of users' private key. This means that the same obfuscated program can be used by verifiers on behalf of different users in this group.

Universality is relevant to an obfuscated program's functionalities. More Concretely, an universal $i\mathcal{O}$ is supposed to support multiple functionalities. A *straightforward* example would be the obfucation-based functional encryption scheme in [2]. Recall that in their construction, the secret key sk_f for a function f is an obfuscated program. For this obfuscated program to become universal, sk_f would need to be associated with more than one function. In this case, e.g., an universal obfuscated program sk_f can be associated with a class of similar functions $f = (f_1, f_2, \cdots, f_k)$. This means that sk_f's holder can obtain $f_1(m), f_2(m), \cdots, f_k(m)$ from an encryption of m.

Recently, Hohenberger et al. [32] has shown that $i\mathcal{O}$ can provide some other cryptographic primitives with universality. They employed $i\mathcal{O}$ to construct universal signature aggregators, which can aggregate across schemes in various algebraic settings (e.g., RSA, BLS). Prior to this universal signature aggregator, the aggregation of signatures can only be built if all the signers use the same signing algorithm and shared parameters. On the contrary, the universal signature aggregator enables the aggregation of the users' signatures without requiring them to execute the same signing behavior, which indicates a compressed authentication overhead.

A.3   Obfuscation for Specific Functions

The current $i\mathcal{O}$ construction candidate provides a way for obfuscating general circuits and runs in impractical polynomial-time. Note that an obfuscation designed for some particular simple function with practical performance, such as computing two vectors' inner product, can also be wanted. (like Wee's work in STOC'05 [33]) This means that we want to obfuscate such simple functions in a practical way that might be specific for those functions. Note that, for example, a practical obfuscated program computing the inner product of two vectors, where one vector is an input to this program and the other one is embedded into the program without user learning its knowledge, could be useful in applications like computational biometrics. Also, it is really likely that such a practical obfuscation for a specified function can be used as a building block to construct an obfuscation supporting more complex functionalities by combining with other existing practical cryptographic primitives.

References

1. Juels, A., Kaliski, Jr., B.S.: PORs: Proofs of retrievability for large files. In: ACM CCS, pp. 584–597 (2007)
2. Garg, S., Gentry, C., Halevi, S., Raykova, M., Sahai, A., Waters, B.: Candidate indistinguishability obfuscation and functional encryption for all circuits. In: FOCS, pp. 40–49 (2013)
3. Sahai, A., Waters, B.: How to use indistinguishability obfuscation: deniable encryption, and more. In: STOC, pp. 475–484 (2014)
4. Ramchen, K., Waters, B.: Fully secure and fast signing from obfuscation. In: ACM CCS, pp. 659–673 (2014)
5. Boneh, D., Zhandry, M.: Multiparty key exchange, efficient traitor tracing, and more from indistinguishability obfuscation. In: Garay, J.A., Gennaro, R. (eds.) CRYPTO 2014, Part I. LNCS, vol. 8616, pp. 480–499. Springer, Heidelberg (2014)
6. Shacham, H., Waters, B.: Compact proofs of retrievability. In: Pieprzyk, J. (ed.) ASIACRYPT 2008. LNCS, vol. 5350, pp. 90–107. Springer, Heidelberg (2008)
7. Giuseppe, A., Randal, B., Reza, C., Herring, J., Kissner, L., Peterson, Z., Song, D.: Provable data possession at untrusted stores. In: ACM CCS, pp. 598–609 (2007)
8. Benabbas, S., Gennaro, R., Vahlis, Y.: Verifiable delegation of computation over large datasets. In: Rogaway, P. (ed.) CRYPTO 2011. LNCS, vol. 6841, pp. 111–131. Springer, Heidelberg (2011)
9. Küpçü, A.: Efficient cryptography for the next generation secure cloud: protocols, proofs, and implementation. Lambert Academic Publishing, Saarbrücken (2010)
10. Ateniese, G., Kamara, S., Katz, J.: Proofs of storage from homomorphic identification protocols. In: Matsui, M. (ed.) ASIACRYPT 2009. LNCS, vol. 5912, pp. 319–333. Springer, Heidelberg (2009)
11. Bowers, K.D., Juels, A., Oprea, A.: Proofs of retrievability: theory and implementation. In: The ACM Workshop on Cloud Computing Security, pp. 43–54 (2009)
12. Dodis, Y., Vadhan, S., Wichs, D.: Proofs of retrievability via hardness amplification. In: Reingold, O. (ed.) TCC 2009. LNCS, vol. 5444, pp. 109–127. Springer, Heidelberg (2009)
13. Ateniese, G., Pietro, R.D., Mancini, L.V., Tsudik, G.: Scalable and efficient provable data possession. In: SecureComm 2008, pp. 9:1–9:10. ACM, New York (2008)

14. Dynamic provable data possession. In: ACM CCS, pp. 213–222 (2009)
15. Wang, Q., Wang, C., Li, J., Ren, K., Lou, W.: Enabling public verifiability and data dynamics for storage security in cloud computing. In: Backes, M., Ning, P. (eds.) ESORICS 2009. LNCS, vol. 5789, pp. 355–370. Springer, Heidelberg (2009)
16. Stefanov, E., van Dijk, M., Juels, A., Oprea, A.: Iris: a scalable cloud file system with efficient integrity checks. In: ACSAC, pp. 229–238 (2012)
17. Cash, D., Küpçü, A., Wichs, D.: Dynamic proofs of retrievability via oblivious RAM. In: Johansson, T., Nguyen, P.Q. (eds.) EUROCRYPT 2013. LNCS, vol. 7881, pp. 279–295. Springer, Heidelberg (2013)
18. Shi, E., Stefanov, E., Papamanthou, C.: Practical dynamic proofs of retrievability. In: ACM CCS, pp. 325–336 (2013)
19. Armknecht, F., Bohli, J.M., Karame, G.O., Liu, Z., Reuter, C.A.: Outsourced proofs of retrievability. In: ACM CCS, pp. 831–843 (2014)
20. Barak, B., Goldreich, O., Impagliazzo, R., Rudich, S., Sahai, A., Vadhan, S.: On the (Im)possibility of obfuscating programs. In: Kilian, J. (ed.) CRYPTO 2001. LNCS, vol. 2139, pp. 1–18. Springer, Heidelberg (2001)
21. Coron, J.-S., Lepoint, T., Tibouchi, M.: Practical multilinear maps over the integers. In: Canetti, R., Garay, J.A. (eds.) CRYPTO 2013, Part I. LNCS, vol. 8042, pp. 476–493. Springer, Heidelberg (2013)
22. Garg, S., Gentry, C., Halevi, S.: Candidate multilinear maps from ideal lattices. In: Johansson, T., Nguyen, P.Q. (eds.) EUROCRYPT 2013. LNCS, vol. 7881, pp. 1–17. Springer, Heidelberg (2013)
23. Guan, C., Ren, K., Zhang, F., Kerschbaum, F., Yu, J.: A symmetric-key based proofs of retrievability supporting public verification. full version. http://ubisec. cse.buffalo.edu/files/PoR_from_iO.pdf
24. Barak, B., Bitansky, N., Canetti, R., Kalai, Y.T., Paneth, O., Sahai, A.: Obfuscation for evasive functions. In: Lindell, Y. (ed.) TCC 2014. LNCS, vol. 8349, pp. 26–51. Springer, Heidelberg (2014)
25. Brakerski, Z., Rothblum, G.N.: Virtual black-box obfuscation for all circuits via generic graded encoding. In: Lindell, Y. (ed.) TCC 2014. LNCS, vol. 8349, pp. 1–25. Springer, Heidelberg (2014)
26. Garg, S., Gentry, C., Halevi, S., Raykova, M.: Two-round secure MPC from indistinguishability obfuscation. In: Lindell, Y. (ed.) TCC 2014. LNCS, vol. 8349, pp. 74–94. Springer, Heidelberg (2014)
27. Goldwasser, S., Gordon, S.D., Goyal, V., Jain, A., Katz, J., Liu, F.-H., Sahai, A., Shi, E., Zhou, H.-S.: Multi-input functional encryption. In: Nguyen, P.Q., Oswald, E. (eds.) EUROCRYPT 2014. LNCS, vol. 8441, pp. 578–602. Springer, Heidelberg (2014)
28. Hohenberger, S., Sahai, A., Waters, B.: Replacing a random oracle: full domain hash from indistinguishability obfuscation. In: Nguyen, P.Q., Oswald, E. (eds.) EUROCRYPT 2014. LNCS, vol. 8441, pp. 201–220. Springer, Heidelberg (2014)
29. Boneh, D., Waters, B.: Constrained pseudorandom functions and their applications. In: Sako, K., Sarkar, P. (eds.) ASIACRYPT 2013, Part II. LNCS, vol. 8270, pp. 280–300. Springer, Heidelberg (2013)
30. Apon, D., Huang, Y., Katz, J., Malozemoff, A.J.: Implementing cryptographic program obfuscation. IACR Cryptol. ePrint Arch. **2014**, 779 (2014)
31. Ananth, P., Gupta, D., Ishai, Y., Sahai, A.: Optimizing obfuscation: avoiding barrington's theorem. In: ACM CCS, pp. 646–658 (2014)
32. Hohenberger, S., Koppula, V., Waters, B.: Universal signature aggregators. IACR Cryptol. ePrint Arch. **2014**, 745 (2014)

33. Wee, H.: On obfuscating point functions. In: STOC, pp. 523–532 (2005)
34. Gennaro, R., Gentry, C., Parno, B.: Non-interactive verifiable computing: outsourcing computation to untrusted workers. In: Rabin, T. (ed.) CRYPTO 2010. LNCS, vol. 6223, pp. 465–482. Springer, Heidelberg (2010)
35. Parno, B., Raykova, M., Vaikuntanathan, V.: How to delegate and verify in public: verifiable computation from attribute-based encryption. In: Cramer, R. (ed.) TCC 2012. LNCS, vol. 7194, pp. 422–439. Springer, Heidelberg (2012)
36. Kerschbaum, F.: Outsourced private set intersection using homomorphic encryption. In: ASIACCS, pp. 85–86 (2012)

DTLS-HIMMO: Achieving DTLS Certificate Security with Symmetric Key Overhead

Oscar Garcia-Morchon$^{(\boxtimes)}$, Ronald Rietman, Sahil Sharma, Ludo Tolhuizen, and Jose Luis Torre-Arce

Philips Group Innovation, Research, Eindhoven, The Netherlands
{oscar.garcia,ronald.rietman,sahil.sharma,ludo.tolhuizen,
jose.luis.torre.arce}@philips.com

Abstract. Billions of devices are being connected to the Internet creating the Internet of Things (IoT). The IoT not only requires strong security, like current Internet applications, but also efficient operation. The recently introduced HIMMO scheme enables lightweight and collusion-resistant identity-based key sharing in a non-interactive way, so that any pair of Internet-connected devices can securely communicate.

This paper firstly reviews the HIMMO scheme and introduces two extensions that e.g. enable implicit credential verification without the need of traditional digital certificates. Then, we show how HIMMO can be efficiently implemented even in resource-constrained devices, enabling combined key agreement and credential verification more efficiently than using ECDH-ECDSA. We further explain how HIMMO helps to secure the Internet and IoT by introducing the DTLS-HIMMO operation mode. DTLS, the datagram version of TLS, is becoming the standard security protocol in the IoT, although it is very frequently discussed that it does not offer the right performance for IoT scenarios. Our design, implementation, and evaluation show that DTLS-HIMMO operation mode achieves the security properties of the DTLS-Certificate security suite while exhibiting the overhead of symmetric-key primitives without requiring changes in the DTLS standard.

Keywords: HIMMO · Lightweight · (D)TLS · Quantum · TTP infrastructure.

1 Introduction

The Internet of Things (IoT) is connecting billions of smart devices deployed in critical applications like healthcare, distributed control systems, smart cities and smart energy. The IoT not only needs strong security solutions, like today's Internet, but also efficient approaches to secure the data exchanges between smart devices, and between smart devices and the Internet.

The Transport Layer Security (TLS) [5] and its Datagram version (DTLS) are two of the most important protocols used to secure the Internet. DTLS is becoming the security standard to secure the IoT since it is required by many Machine to Machine standards such as LWM2M. However, it is very frequently

G. Pernul et al. (Eds.): ESORICS 2015, Part I, LNCS 9326, pp. 224–242, 2015.
DOI: 10.1007/978-3-319-24174-6_12

discussed that DTLS and its cipher suites are too heavy for many IoT use cases. In some cases, resource limitations (e.g., memory or energy) of end devices may prohibit the support of the standard algorithms. In other cases, the large number of devices and lack of user interface make the managing of large amounts of credentials for all those devices extremely complex. In some situations, devices are managed over a cellular connection and each extra byte of consumed bandwidth incurs costs. It is estimated that currently 70 % of the IoT devices have security risks and are often poorly managed [1]. At the same time, the advent of quantum computers will endanger all key agreement primitives used in (D)TLS except pre-shared keys [3]. Thus, there is a need for a solution that is secure, efficient, scalable, simple to use, and if possible, quantum-secure.

The HIMMO scheme [10] is a fully-collusion resistant key pre-distribution scheme that enables lightweight identity-based key sharing between devices in a single message, which is ideal for real-time IoT interactions. This paper builds on the HIMMO scheme and describes a couple of extensions, e.g., enabling implicit credential verification without the need of traditional digital certificates. Next, we show how HIMMO can be efficiently implemented even on resource-constrained devices. We further put HIMMO in the context of the IoT and describe the design, implementation, and evaluation of the (D)TLS-HIMMO operation mode as a lightweight alternative to existing public-key based solutions. This new operation mode for (D)TLS allows us to achieve security properties of a (D)TLS-certificate exchange – key agreement, mutual authentication of client and server, and verification of credentials – with the resource needs of symmetric-key primitives.

The rest of this paper is organized as follows. Section 2 describes the features of IoT scenarios, security needs, and relevant IoT security standards. Section 3 reviews the HIMMO scheme. Section 4 presents an efficient algorithm for key agreement and performance results. Section 5 introduces the (D)TLS-HIMMO operation mode. In Sect. 6, we compare DTLS-HIMMO with existing (D)TLS alternatives. Section 7 concludes this paper and discusses future work.

2   Preliminaries

We consider a network of low-resource devices that should be capable to pairwise communicate with each other. In order to secure this communication, each pair of devices should be able to generate a common key. In the HIMMO scheme and in the extensions we discuss in this paper, one or more Trusted Third Parties (TTPs) provide all devices with secret information, termed keying material, that will be used in generating such common keys. It is assumed that the TTP can provide the keying material in a secure manner.

2.1   Security Standards in the Internet (of Things)

The Internet is protected by two main standard protocols, the Internet Protocol Security (IPSec) and the Transport Layer Security (TLS). IPSec offers security at network layer while TLS protects exchange of information between applications at transport layer. Both IPSec and TLS have an initial phase enabling authentication of peers, agreement on a session key, negotiation on the cipher-suite, etc. Afterwards, the data flow can be secured in the sense of confidentiality, authenticity, integrity and freshness by making use of the agreed session keys.

The TLS protocol runs on top of TCP and is used to secure our HTTP Internet connections when we access the bank online, we do the tax computation, or when we access some healthcare services. The Internet is further evolving to connect many smart objects creating the Internet of Things (IoT) comprising smart meters, healthcare devices, etc. In a typical use case, devices communicate end-to-end with a back-end server, reporting information such as energy consumption, maintenance data, etc. by means of protocols such LWM2M that are protected by Datagram Transport Layer Security (DTLS), the equivalent of TLS running on UDP. Note that DTLS builds on TLS, and therefore both protocols are very similar, the only differences are a few extensions ensuring that protocol can run on UDP. There are more than 200 known cipher-suites for TLS, e.g. see [2]. OpenSSL is one of the most common and used libraries implementing TLS and most of its different cipher-suites. For the Internet of Things, other libraries such as CyaSSL[1] are also popular due to their smaller footprint and simple API supporting more than 70 cipher-suites.

2.2 DTLS-PSK

Pre Shared Key (PSK) mode is a set of ciphersuites applicable to both TLS and DTLS [6]. Although not in common use on the Internet, (D)TLS-PSK is widely employed by IoT devices since it has very low resource needs. The ciphersuite TLS_PSK_WITH_AES_128_CCM_8 [13], for instance, uses PSK as the authentication and key exchange algorithm.

In DTLS-PSK, both clients and servers may have pre-shared keys with different parties, the client indicates which key to use with the PSK-identity in the *ClientKeyExchange* message. The server may help the client in selecting the identity to use with the *PSK-identity-hint* in the *ServerKeyExchange* message. For IoT devices, the PSK identity can be based on the domain name of the server and, thus, the *PSK-identity-hint* need not be sent by the server [17], so the *ServerKeyExchange* is optional. The credentials (the pre-shared keys themselves) are stored as part of hardware modules, such as SIM cards, and sometimes, on the firmware of resource-constrained devices themselves. The session keys for the DTLS record session are derived from the PSK using the TLS Pseudo Random Function (PRF) as defined in [5]. The cookie exchange is used to prevent denial of service attacks on the server. The Constrained Application Protocol (CoAP) [16] mandates the use of TLS_PSK_WITH_AES_128_CCM_8 for the use with shared secrets [17].

---

[1] Cyassl. http://www.yassl.com/yaSSL/Products-cyassl.html.

2.3   Attack Model and Security Goals

With the HIMMO-DTLS extension, we aim at ensuring all security properties of DTLS-PSK [6] including also the capability of credential verification.
This work does not provide other security features such as perfect forward secrecy
or non-repudiation. We assume that the TTP can securely distribute the keying
materials to the devices. However, an attacker can later monitor, eavesdrop, and
modify message exchanges. We further assume that the attacker can compromise
arbitrary devices and extract secret keying material which he can combine to
attack the system.

3   HIMMO and HIMMO Extensions

HIMMO is a Key Pre-Distribution Scheme (KPS), a concept introduced by Matsumoto and Imai in 1987 [12]. An elegant and efficient KPS, based on symmetric
polynomials, has been introduced by Blundo *et al.* [4]. There was no KPS that
is both efficient and not prone to efficient attacks of multiple colluding (or compromised) nodes, see the references in [9], until recently the HIMMO scheme
solved this problem. This section reviews the operation of the HIMMO scheme
that enables any pair of devices in a system to directly agree on a common
symmetric-key based on their identifiers and a secret key generating polynomial
as introduced in [10]. The underlying security principles on which HIMMO relies
have been analyzed in [7,8]. Furthermore, this section describes two protocol
extensions of the HIMMO scheme as described in [9].

We use the following notation: for each integer x and positive integer M,
we denote by $\langle x \rangle_M$ the unique integer $y \in \{0, 1, \ldots, M - 1\}$ such that $x \equiv y$
mod M.

3.1   HIMMO Operation

Like any KPS, HIMMO requires a trusted third party (TTP), and three phases
can be distinguished in its operation [12].

In the **setup phase**, the TTP selects positive integers B, b, m and α, where
$m \geq 2$. The number B is the bit length of the identifiers that will be used in
the system, while b denotes the bit length of the keys that will be generated.
The TTP generates the public modulus N, an odd number of length exactly
$(\alpha+1)B+b$ bits (so $2^{(\alpha+1)B+b-1} < N < 2^{(\alpha+1)B+b}$). It also randomly generates
m distinct secret moduli $q_1, \ldots, q_m$ of the form $q_i = N - 2^b \beta_i$, where $0 \leq \beta_i < 2^B$
and at least one of $\beta_1, \ldots, \beta_m$ is odd. Finally, the TTP generates the secret
root keying material, that consists of the coefficients of m bi-variate symmetric
polynomials of degree at most α in each variable. For $1 \leq i \leq m$, the i-th root
keying polynomial $R^{(i)}(x, y)$ is written as

$$R^{(i)}(x, y) = \sum_{j=0}^{\alpha} \sum_{k=0}^{\alpha} R_{j,k}^{(i)} x^j y^k \text{ with } 0 \leq R_{j,k}^{(i)} = R_{k,j}^{(i)} \leq q_i - 1. \quad (1)$$

In the **keying material extraction phase**, the TTP provides each node ξ in the system, with $0 \leq \xi < 2^B$, the coefficients of the key generating polynomial G_ξ:

$$G_\xi(y) = \sum_{k=0}^{\alpha} G_{\xi,k} y^k \tag{2}$$

where

$$G_{\xi,k} = \langle \sum_{i=1}^{m} \langle \sum_{j=0}^{\alpha} R_{j,k}^{(i)} \xi^j \rangle_{q_i} \rangle_N. \tag{3}$$

In the **key generation phase**, a node ξ wishing to communicate with node η with $0 \leq \eta < 2^B$, computes:

$$K_{\xi,\eta} = \langle \langle G_\xi(\eta) \rangle_N \rangle_{2^b} \tag{4}$$

It can be shown that $K_{\xi,\eta}$ and $K_{\eta,\xi}$ need not be equal. However, as shown in Theorem 1 in [9], for all identifiers ξ and η with $0 \leq \xi, \eta \leq 2^B$,

$$K_{\xi,\eta} \in \{ \langle K_{\eta,\xi} + jN \rangle_{2^b} \mid 0 \leq |j| \leq 2m \}. \tag{5}$$

In order to perform key reconciliation, i.e. to make sure that ξ and η use the same key to protect their future communications, the initiator of the key generation (say node ξ) sends to the other node, simultaneously with an encrypted message, information on $K_{\xi,\eta}$ that enables node η to select $K_{\xi,\eta}$ from the candidate set $C = \{ \langle K_{\eta,\xi} + jN \rangle_{2^b} \mid 0 \leq |j| \leq 2m \}$. No additional communication thus is required for key reconciliation. The key $K_{\xi,\eta}$ will be used for securing future communication between ξ and η. As an example of information used for key reconciliation, node ξ sends to node η the number $r = \langle K_{\xi,\eta} \rangle_{2^s}$, where $s = \lceil \log_2(4m+1) \rceil$. Node η can efficiently obtain the integer j such that $|j| \leq 2m$ and $K_{\xi,\eta} \equiv K_{\eta,\xi} + jN \mod 2^b$ by using that $jN \equiv K_{\xi,\eta} - K_{\eta,\xi} \equiv r - K_{\eta,\xi} \mod 2^s$. As N is odd, the latter equation allows for determination of j. As r reveals the s least significant bits of $K_{\xi,\eta}$, only the $b - s$ most significant bits $K_{\xi,\eta}$, that is, the number $\lfloor 2^{-s} K_{\xi,\eta} \rfloor$, should be used as key.

3.2   Implicit Certification and Verification of Credentials

Implicit certification and verification of credentials is further enabled on top of the basic HIMMO scheme. A node that wants to register with the system provides the TTP with its credentials, e.g., device type, manufacturing date, etc. The TTP, which can also add further information to the node's credentials such as a unique node identifier or the issue date of the keying material and its expiration date, obtains the node's identity as $\xi = H(credentials)$, where H is a public hash function. When a first node with identity ξ wants to securely send a message M to a second node with identity η, the following steps are taken.

- Step 1: Node ξ computes a common key $K_{\xi,\eta}$ with node η, and uses $K_{\xi,\eta}$ to encrypt and authenticate its credentials and M, say $e = E_{K_{\xi,\eta}}(credentials|M)$.

- Step 2: Node ξ sends (ξ, e, r) to node η, where r is data helping node η to find $K_{\xi,\eta}$.
- Step 3: Node η receives (ξ', e', r'). Using r', it computes its common key $K_{\eta,\xi'}$ with ξ' to decrypt e' obtaining the message M and verifying the authenticity of the received message. Furthermore, it checks whether the *credentials'* in e' correspond with ξ', that is, it validates if $\xi' = H(credentials')$.

This method not only allows for direct secure communication of message M, but also for implicit certification and verification of ξ's credentials because the key generating polynomial assigned to a node is linked to its credentials by means of H. If the output size of H is long enough, e.g., 256 bits, the input (i.e., the credentials) contains a unique node identifier, and if H is a secure one-way hash function, then it is infeasible for an attacker to find any other set of credentials leading to the same identity ξ. The fact that credential verification might be prone to birthday attacks motivates the choice for the relation between identifier and key sizes, namely, $B = 2b$. In this way, the scheme provides an equivalent security level for credential verification and key generation. The capability for credential verification enables e.g. the verification of the expiration date of the credentials (and the keying material) of a node, or verification of the access roles of the sender node ξ.

3.3 Enhancing Privacy by Using Multiple TTPs

Using multiple TTPs was introduced by Matsumoto and Imai [12] for KPS and can also be elegantly supported by HIMMO [9]. In this set-up, a number of TTPs provide a node with keying materials linked to the node's identifier during the keying material extraction phase. Upon reception, the device combines the different keying materials by adding the coefficients of the key generating polynomials modulo N. Without increasing the resource requirements at the nodes, this scheme enjoys two interesting properties. First, privacy is enhanced since a single TTP cannot eavesdrop the communication links. In fact, all TTPs should collude to monitor the communication links. Secondly, compromising a sub-set of TTPs does not break the overall system.

4   Implementation and Performance

HIMMO has been designed keeping in mind that we want to achieve very good performance. In this section, we explain how the key generation algorithm in Eq. 4 can be implemented in a very efficient way for the specific choice $N = 2^{B(\alpha+1)+b} - 1$, taking into account that the size of the identifiers (B bits) is small compared to the size of the coefficients of the polynomial G_ξ $((\alpha+1)B+b$ bits). Algorithm 1 shows this optimized key generation algorithm that applies an approximation of the well-known Horner algorithm for evaluating polynomials in which the specific choice of N is taken into account. In the appendix, we motivate some steps of the algorithm and show that

$$\langle\langle\sum_{j=0}^{\alpha} G_{\xi,j}\eta^j\rangle_N\rangle_{2^b} \in \{key, \langle key + 1\rangle_{2^b}\}. \tag{6}$$

Algorithm 1. Optimized key generation

1: **INPUT:** B, b, α, η, $G_{\xi,j}$ with $j \in \{0,\ldots,\alpha\}$
2: **OUTPUT:** key
3: $key \leftarrow \langle G_{\xi,\alpha}\rangle_{2^b}$
4: $temp \leftarrow \lfloor\frac{G_{\xi,\alpha}}{2^b}\rfloor$
5: **for** $j = \alpha - 1$ **to** 0 **do**
6:    $temp \leftarrow temp \times \eta + \lfloor\frac{G_{\xi,j}}{2^{(\alpha-1-j)B+b}}\rfloor$
7:    $key \leftarrow \langle key \times \eta\rangle_{2^b} + \langle G_{\xi,j}\rangle_{2^b}$
8:    $key \leftarrow \langle key + \lfloor\frac{temp}{2^{(j+2)B}}\rfloor\rangle_{2^b}$
9:    $temp \leftarrow \lfloor\frac{(temp)_{2^{(j+2)B}}}{2^B}\rfloor$
10: **end for**
11: **return** key

We note that part of the coefficients $G_{\xi,j}$ with $j \in \{0,\ldots,\alpha\}$ is not used in Algorithm 1. This allows for a further optimization in which only the required parts of the coefficients are stored, namely the b least significant bits and the jB most significant bits of each coefficient $G_{\xi,j}$.

Figure 1 provides a brief summary of the performance of the HIMMO scheme implemented in C and assembler on the 8-bit CPU ATMEGA128L. The first graph shows the key generation time for $\alpha = 26$ as a function of $b = B$. In the next two graphs we see – as a function of α and for $b = B = 128$ – the key generation time and the size of the key generating function.

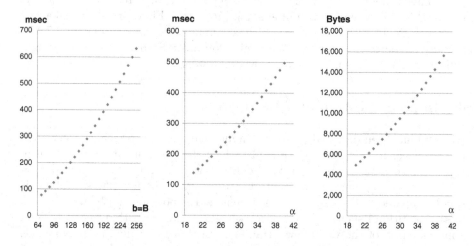

Fig. 1. HIMMO Performance: on the left, performance for $\alpha = 26$ as a function of $b = B$; in the middle and right, performance for $b = B = 128$ as a function of α.

Table 1. HIMMO performance and comparison with ECDH and ECDH + ECDSA.

	CPU time	Key material + code	RAM	Exchanged data	Security properties
ECDH [11]	3.97 s	16018 B	1774 B	480 B	Key agreement
ECDH + ECDSA [11]	11.9 s	35326 B	3284 B	704 B	Key agreement and credential verification
HIMMO	0.290 s	7560 B	1220 B	448 B	Key agreement and credential verification

Table 1 compares the performance HIMMO using security parameters $\alpha = 26$ and $2b = B = 160$ with that of ECDH and/or ECDSA for a security level of 80 bits. We illustrate a simple interaction scenario between two nodes: a first node ξ wants to send in a secure way information to η, and η wants to securely receive the message from ξ and verify its credentials. The first two protocols involve communicating before node ξ can send an encrypted message, whereas HIMMO allows node ξ to directly compute the key with η based on its identifier and send the encrypted message. Also, notice that ECDH only provides key agreement, to get key agreement and verification of credentials, it is needed to use also ECDSA, increasing the resource requirements. For this implementation, we use the ATMEGA128L processor running at 8 MHz since it is a typical resource-constrained device used in the IoT. Other less constrained devices are emerging featured by longer word size (32-bit) and slightly higher clock frequency. In Table 1, CPU refers to the overall computing needs, the memory refers to the amount of information that needs to be stored in flash, RAM is the RAM memory needs, exchanged data refers to the amount of data exchanged between ξ and η, and finally, the security properties illustrate the features of the security protocols.

5   (D)TLS-HIMMO

TLS and DTLS are two of the protocols to protect the Internet today, while DTLS is becoming the standard for the IoT. Existing (D)TLS operational modes have pros and cons. PSK is efficient but does not scale well. Raw-public key scales well but does not offer authentication and is prone to man-in-the-middle attacks. Certificate-based schemes are too expensive in some scenarios, in particular IoT related ones, and most of those schemes would also be broken with quantum computers. This motivates our research in a new (D)TLS cipher suite based on HIMMO that:

- has the low operational cost of DTLS-PSK,
- enables mutual authentication and credential verification as with certificate-based schemes,
- is scalable like public-key cryptography and infrastructure,
- is resilient to attacks using quantum computers.

To this end, we extend the DTLS-PSK mode, which is based on identities, without changing the standard so that it can work with HIMMO. The main difference from the usual PSK profile lies in using identities to generate a pairwise symmetric key and, then, deriving the session keys from the pairwise symmetric key. A TTP provisions keying material to client nodes and the server as shown in Eq. 2 during an initial setup (e.g. manufacture stage). HIMMO can be directly used in (D)TLS-PSK mode by exchanging HIMMO's identifiers in the *ClientKeyExchange* and *ServerKeyExchange* messages. Creation of a new profile to indicate DTLS-HIMMO (e.g. TLS_DTLS-HIMMO_WITH_AES_128_CCM_8) can also be considered, but requires standardization.

5.1   DTLS-HIMMO Configurations

The existing PSK profile, such as the one used in TLS_PSK_WITH_AES_128_CCM_8, involves the exchange of two fields, the *PSK-identity* and *PSK-identity-hint*, in the *ClientKeyExchange* and *ServerKeyExchange* messages respectively. Instead of sending a PSK identifier, we use these fields, which can be up to 128 bytes long [17], to exchange HIMMO information.

Table 2 illustrates these fields of information with exemplary lengths. First, we find an identifier/flag indicating the use of DTLS-HIMMO. Next, we find a DTLS-HIMMO message type. The third and fourth field refer to the number of TTPs and their identifiers, respectively. These are the TTPs associated with generating and distributing the key material of the client and server. These two fields are followed by an identifier field. Next, we optionally find the HIMMO credentials length as well as the credentials themselves. Finally, a field that contains the key reconciliation data is optionally present. The interpretation of the identifier field and the absence of presence of the optional fields is derived from the Message Type field.

This message format is used in the *PSK-identity-hint* and *PSK-identity* fields of the *ServerKeyExchange* and *ClientKeyExchange* messages. With these fields we can enable different ways of using HIMMO with DTLS-PSK. If only the HIMMO identifier is exchanged in the identifier field, then only mutual authentication is achieved between client and server. Alternatively, the client, or server, or both of them might exchange their credentials. The credentials could be any information that today is exchanged in regular digital certificates and, for IoT scenarios, information such as manufacturer, device type, date of manufacturing, etc. In this case, the exchange enables unilateral or mutual implicit credential verification of the parties. We note that in this case, the identifier field does not contain the HIMMO identifier but a unique random value that concatenated

Table 2. Exemplary format of the *PSK-identity-hint* and *PSK-identity* fields enabling DTLS-HIMMO; Length in Bytes; N = Number of TTPs; M = mandatory, O = optional

	HIMMO flag	Message type	Number of TTPs	TTP ID	Identifier	HIMMO credentials length	HIMMO credentials	Reconcilliation data
Length	2	1	1	N	B	1	0 ... (122 − B − N)	N
M/O	M	M	M	M	M	O	O	O

Table 3. Modes of operation of DTLS-HIMMO profile

	Client sends HIMMO's ID	Client sends HIMMO's credentials
Server sends HIMMO's ID	**Messages exchanged**	
	ClientKeyExchange: Client ID and Reconciliation data ServerKeyExchange: Server ID	ClientKeyExchange: Clients credentials and Reconciliation data ServerKeyExchange: Server ID
	Computations	
	Two HIMMO evaluations	Two HIMMO evaluations One hash evaluation
	Properties	
	Mutual authentication	Mutual authentication Verification of client's credentials
Server sends HIMMO's credentials	**Messages exchanged**	
	ClientKeyExchange: Client ID and Reconciliation data ServerKeyExchange: Servers credentials	ClientKeyExchange: Clients credentials and Reconciliation data ServerKeyExchange: Servers credentials
	Computations	
	Two HIMMO evaluations One hash evaluation	Two HIMMO evaluations Two hash evaluations
	Properties	
	Mutual authentication Verification of server's credentials	Mutual authentication Verification of the credentials of client and server

with the information in the *HIMMO credentials length* and *HIMMO credentials* is hashed to obtain the HIMMO identifier. The reason for this construction was explained in Sect. 3.2. Finally, we note that the reconciliation data is only exchanged in the *ClientKeyExchange* message since it is the server the one performing this operation.

These two different options give rise to four (two each for client and server) different combinations whose features are explained in Table 3.

5.2   (D)TLS-HIMMO Handshake

The HIMMO enabled PSK message exchanges comprises multiple steps:

- Step 1: The client sends a *ClientHello* message to the server indicating use of the PSK mode, such as the TLS_PSK_WITH_AES_128_CCM_8.
- Step 2: The usual *HelloVerifyRequest* message, with a cookie, is sent from the server to the client.
- Step 3: The client replies back with *ClientHello* along with the cookie.
- Step 4: The server replies with *ServerHello*, *ServerKeyExchange* and *ServerHelloDone*. The *PSK-identity-hint* of the *ServerKeyExchange* contains the DTLS-HIMMO fields as in the exemplary format shown in Table 2.
- Step 5: The client sends the *ClientKeyExchange* with the *PSK-identity* field containing the DTLS-HIMMO fields as shown in Table 2. It also sends the usual *ChangeCipherSpec* and *Finished* messages to the server.
- Step 6: The Server would send back the usual *ChangeCipherSpec* and *Finished* messages to the client.

The client computes the symmetric pairwise key as follows:

- Step 1: If the server sent its credentials, as indicated in the DTLS-HIMMO fields, compute *ID-Server* = H(*Server Identifier* || *Server HIMMO Credentials Length* || *Server HIMMO-credentials*). In case the server sent the HIMMO identifier then set *ID-Server* = *Server HIMMO-Identifier*.
- Step 2: If the client is also using credentials, compute *ID-Client* = H(*Client Identifier* || *Client HIMMO Credentials Length* || *Client HIMMO-credentials*). Otherwise, set *ID-Client* = *Client HIMMO-Identifier*.
- Step 3: Compute the pairwise key $K_{\text{ID-Client, ID-Server}}$ as shown in Eq. 4.

Similarly, the server, upon receipt of the *ClientKeyExchange* message computes the pairwise key as:

- Step 1: Depending upon whether the client sent its credentials or its HIMMO identifier, compute *ID-Client* as shown in the steps followed by the client before. In the same manner, depending upon whether the server uses credentials or its HIMMO identifier, compute *ID-Server*.
- Step 2: Compute the pairwise key $K_{\text{ID-Server, ID-Client}}$ using the key reconciliation data sent by the client to arrive at the symmetric pairwise key.

Note that the respective key generating polynomials ($G_{\xi,k}$ in Eq. 2) in the devices would be configured with either the HIMMO identifier or the hash of the concatenation of the identifier, the length of the credentials and the credentials for its identity ξ, depending upon which mode of operation is used (see Table 3). Once the client and server have computed the pairwise key, it can be part of the input to the standard (D)TLS pseudo-random function used to derive the session keys for the DTLS session as is done with the PSK profile. The DTLS *Finished* message authenticates the handshake, and thus, authenticates both parties as having the correct keying material. If the communicating peer is using HIMMO credentials for the key exchange, then the successful completion of the *Finished* message implies that the credentials it provided are correct and, thus, authenticates the credentials of the peer.

5.3   Privacy Protection

Protecting the privacy of the communication links is fundamental. HIMMO and its extensions can be used to ensure the privacy of the involved communication parties.

A first aspect is the protection of the exchanged credentials that might contain some private information that should not be exposed to the other party, if not authenticated before, or to a passive eavesdropper. This can be achieved by the following simple extension of the DTLS handshake. The credentials are encrypted with the pairwise key shared with the other party. For instance, in the DTLS-HIMMO exchange, the client protects its credentials by encrypting them with the HIMMO key shared with the server and that is computed after the reception of the *ServerKeyExchange* message. Thus, the *ClientKeyExchange* could contain the Client's HIMMO identifier and encrypted HIMMO credentials. The server uses the HIMMO identifier to obtain the common pairwise key, and decrypts the client's credentials. Neither a fake server nor an attacker eavesdropping the communication is able to learn the client's credentials.

The usage of raw-public keys with out-of-band verification or of digital certificates requires some type of public-key infrastructure that allows validating the authenticity of the involved public-keys or installing the digital certificates in a secure way. A certification authority (CA), or a hierarchy of CAs, plays this role in today's public-key infrastructure (PKI). HIMMO relies on a TTP whose role is similar to that of a CA. Like a CA, the TTP is in charge of validating the identity of a joining node and securely distributing its key generating function. The difference is that a single TTP could be misused and the TTP (or anyone having access to it) could eavesdrop or alter the ongoing data exchanges between any pair of nodes in a passive way. As explained in Sect. 3.3, the usage of multiple TTPs avoids this situation, since each device then registers with several TTPs and combines the received key generating polynomials from each TTP. In this way, the generated keys between any pair of entities of the system depend on the information shared by all the involved TTPs. An active attacker that can compromise a TTP can act as follows: he sets up a new server and tries to make a client authenticate to that server by setting the number of TTPs in the *ServerKeyExchange* message equal to one. One way to protect against this attack is a policy that a client only authenticates if the number of TTPs in the *SeverKeyExchange* message is at least two.

5.4   TTP Infrastructure

The introduction of an infrastructure of TTPs for the DTLS-HIMMO profile would mean the creation of an alternative to today's PKI. As outlined above, each entity in the system would register with a number of TTPs and receive the corresponding key generating polynomials, each linked to the same or related credentials. Each entity would store this information either combined, as explained in Sect. 3.3, or independently. In this case, the TTP identifiers can be exchanged between client and server during a DTLS-HIMMO handshake. In a first step, the server provides in the *ServerKeyExchange* message the TTP identifiers from which it received its key generating polynomials. In a second step, the client answers with the common or chosen TTPs in the *ClientKeyExchange* message.

Such an infrastructure brings new challenges but also advantages. Today, if a CA is compromised, then it is not possible to easily recover since certificates are often not signed by more than one CA. On the other hand, if they are, recovering is feasible, but this rapidly increases the bandwidth and computational requirements since all those certificates need to be exchanged and verified. This is not the case for above TTP Infrastructure since the capture of a single TTP does not break the whole system and using more than a TTP (e.g., t) involves practically the same bandwidth and computational resources as when a single one is used.

5.5 Security Considerations of (D)TLS-HIMMO

In [9], it is shown that a collusion attack in HIMMO amounts to solving a close vector problem in a certain lattice, and that the minimum required number of nodes, and thus the lattice dimension, is $(\alpha + 1)(\alpha + 2)/2$. If α is large enough, $\alpha > 25$, an approximate solution of this close vector problem, using the default LLL [14] implementation of Sage [15], and Babai's nearest plane algorithm, fails to give a good result, while the lattice dimension becomes too large for exact methods, for which the running time and memory requirements grow exponentially in the lattice dimension. While it is quite likely that more elaborate approximate classical algorithms would give better results, thus increasing the minimum required value of α somewhat, currently no quantum algorithm exists that would speed up the approximate lattice methods, nor is it foreseen that the quantum speed-ups in the exact lattice algorithms, which use enumeration techniques, are sufficient to crack HIMMO for these values of α. Therefore, the scheme presented in this paper could be an interesting approach to ensure secure digital communications in the Internet in a post-quantum world.

6 Performance of DTLS-HIMMO and Comparison with Existing (D)TLS Alternatives

We have implemented the DTLS-HIMMO operation mode such that the client and server run on a Intel Core i5-3437U @ 1.90 GHz with Windows 7 Enterprise. The DTLS-HIMMO extension is carried out by using DTLSv1.2 in PSK mode as starting point as explained in Sect. 5. The HIMMO-based DTLS operation modes include: (i) HIMMO enabling mutual authentication, (ii) HIMMO enabling mutual authentication and server verification, and (iii) HIMMO enabling mutual authentication and client and server verification. We compare DTLS-HIMMO with (iv) DTLS in PSK mode, (v) DTLS certificates enabling server verification only and (vi) DTLS certificates with both server and client verification. Both modes are implemented using the ECDHE and ECDSA using the NIST secp256r1 curve for ECC computations. All of the analyzed DTLS operation modes rely on a 128-bit AES in CCM operation mode to secure the DTLS record layer.

Table 4 provides a qualitative comparison of the above DTLS modes of operation against their performance and security properties. Performance-wise we discuss the resource requirements on the client and server and the communication overhead. Security-wise we consider the capability of the handshakes for key agreement, authentication, information verification, and scalability.

Due to the identity-based nature of HIMMO, the verification of the client or server credentials only costs one additional hash computation. For this reason, the communication overhead can be kept at a very low level compared with certificates. For ECDHE + ECDSA, key agreement and verification of information requires several scalar ECC point multiplications, while HIMMO only requires a polynomial evaluation.

Table 4. Qualitative comparison of the HIMMO based PSK profile with other algorithms. All algorithms allow for key agreement

DTLS mode	Client CPU Needs	Server CPU Needs	Handshake size	Authentication	Information verification	Scalability
DTLS-HIMMO	HIMMO key generation	HIMMO key generation Key reconciliation	Low	Mutual	No	$G_\xi(x)$ installation
DTLS-HIMMO(SA) (Server authentication)	1 SHA-256 HIMMO key generation	HIMMO key generation Key reconciliation	Low	Mutual	Server authentication	$G_\xi(x)$ installation
DTLS-HIMMO (Mutual authentication)	1 SHA-256 HIMMO key generation	1 SHA-256 HIMMO key generation Key reconciliation	Low	Mutual	Server and Client	$G_\xi(x)$ installation
PSK	-	-	Low	Mutual	No	Installation of PSKs
ECDHE + ECDSA (Server authentication)	Three ECC point multiplications	One ECC point multiplication	High	Unilateral	Server verification	Root Certificate installation
ECDHE + ECDSA (Mutual authentication)	Three ECC point multiplications	Three ECC point multiplication	Higher	Mutual	Server and client verification	Root Certificate installation

This qualitative comparison is supported by the experimental results in which we have measured (i) the elapsed time, (ii) the amount of data exchanged, and (iii) the ratio between data exchanged and payload in three different scenarios for different DTLS modes of operation:

- the DTLS connection is established and 1 KB of data are exchanged,
- the DTLS connection is established and 10 KB of data are exchanged, and
- the DTLS connection is established and 100 KB of data are exchanged.

Figure 2 depicts the total amount of exchanged data for all the cipher suites. This includes the headers of the underlying protocols (UDP, IP, etc.) as well as the transfer of 1 KB of data. On the left side of Fig. 3 we see the required time to establish a secure connection and send the data for different cipher suites. On the right side of this figure we observe the ratio between the required bandwidth and the exchanged payload. In both figures, from top to bottom: (1) ECDH-ECDSA with mutual authentication, (2) ECDH-ECDSA with server authentication, (3) HIMMO with mutual verification of client's and server's credentials ($t = 5, B = 256, b = 32, \alpha = 17$), (4) HIMMO with mutual authentication ($t = 5, B = 32, b = 32, \alpha = 50$) and (5) PSK. We notice that DTLS-PSK is the fastest followed by DTLS-HIMMO without credential verification capabilities. DTLS-HIMMO with credential verification capabilities becomes slightly more expensive since B needs to be larger than the generated key in this case. We also observe that the value of the security parameter α does not heavily impact the performance of the scheme remaining around a factor 8 faster than the ECC alternative. We note that in this experiment HIMMO is configured to generate a key 128 bit long by combining five ($t = 5$) instances in parallel. For the cases of mutual authentication and mutual credential verification we use HIMMO parameters ($B = 32, b = 32, \alpha = 50$) and ($B = 256, b = 32, \alpha = 17$) respectively. This implies that an attacker has to deal with lattices of dimensions as high as 1377 and 1368, respectively, for the HI problem [8]. It is also worth noting that in all cases the cryptographic operations involved in the transfer of data are negligible

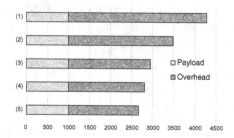

Fig. 2. Exchanged data.

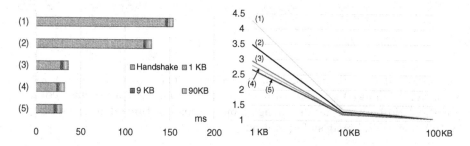

Fig. 3. DTLS connection time (left) and ratio between total exchanged data and payload (right).

compared with the DTLS handshake. Figure 2, right side, shows that the usage of schemes relying on long keys might not be the best solution for use cases in which little payload needs to be exchanged.

These figures together with Fig. 1 show several advantages of HIMMO compared with other alternatives. The first one is that IoT applications that involve the exchange of little data, frequently under 10 KB, can benefit from HIMMO since it offers a better ratio between the amount of transmitted payload and the overall amount of transmitted data. This is due to HIMMO's identity based nature that does not require the exchange of public-keys or long certificates. As a result, the underlying constrained networks are less overloaded, thus enabling IoT applications with less costs to network operators. The second advantage is that same back-end can handle many more clients with the same resources. This prevents potential DoS attacks and decreases again the price to enable those applications. Finally, we remark that Fig. 3 shows the DTLS connection time between two powerful devices. In a real world IoT scenario one of those devices will have much lower capabilities. However, HIMMO can be still implemented in a very efficient way as illustrated in Fig. 1.

7   Conclusions

The HIMMO scheme is the first Key Pre-distribution scheme that is simultaneously efficient and secure (in terms of collusion resistance). Specific choices of the HIMMO parameters enable very efficient implementations that, combined with the implicit credential certification and verification, improve the performance of related public-key schemes by one order of magnitude. HIMMO can be embedded in TLS and DTLS, the security protocols used to secure the Internet, without requiring any changes in the standards, but offering a significantly improved performance security trade-off. In fact, the DTLS-PSK mode can be extended with HIMMO to achieve functionality that today is only possible with public-key cryptography and a public-key infrastructure, but at the speed and memory requirements of a symmetric-key handshake. The DTLS-HIMMO handshake offers mutual authentication of client and server, implicit verification of their credentials costing a single hash computation, client's privacy-protection by sending its credentials in encrypted format, and support of multiple TTPs.

We finally remark that HIMMO is post-quantum secure as known attacks involve solving a close vector problem in a lattice for which currently no quantum algorithm exists that would speed up the approximate lattice methods, nor is it foreseen that the quantum speed-ups in the exact lattice algorithms, which use enumeration techniques, are sufficient to crack HIMMO.

Appendix: Proof of Correctness of Optimized Algorithm

Algorithm 1 is an approximation to Horner's algorithm for polynomial evaluation modulo N, taking into account that N is of the special form $N = 2^{(\alpha+1)B+b}$ and that the argument η is small. In this appendix, we motivate some of the steps in Algorithm 1, and prove (6) which states that the output of the algorithm nearly is the wanted key.

Each intermediate value in Horner's algorithm for computing $\langle \sum_{j=0}^{\alpha} G_{\xi,j} \eta^j \rangle_N$ is obtained as

$$\langle temp_j \rangle_N = \langle temp_{j+1} \times \eta + G_{\xi,j} \rangle_N$$

for $j = \alpha - 1, \ldots, 0$. As $0 \le \eta < 2^B$, we can write $temp_{j+1} \times \eta + G_{\xi,j} = temp_j = temp_j^H \times 2^{(\alpha+1)B+b} + temp_j^L$, where $temp_j^H$ and $temp_j^L$ are b and $(\alpha + 1)B + b$ bits long, respectively. As $N = 2^{(\alpha+1)B+b} - 1$, we thus have that $\langle temp_j \rangle_N = \langle temp_j^H + temp_j^L \rangle_N \approx temp_j^H + temp_j^L$. This is only an approximation because there might be a carry in the addition of $temp_j^H$ and $temp_j^L$, requiring a second reduction. We will show that this second reduction is needed at most once during the calculation, and ignoring it leads to a difference of one (mod 2^b) between the wanted key and the value returned by the algorithm, so that (6) is satisfied. The modular reduction happens when the value of key is updated with the contribution of the MSB stored in $temp$ after being shifted $(j + 2)B$ bits and added to key (Line 8).

We now state and prove the main property of Algorithm 1. Let b, B, α be positive integers and let $N := 2^{(\alpha+1)B+b} - 1$. For $0 \leq i \leq \alpha$, let $0 \leq G_i \leq N-1$, and let $0 \leq \eta \leq 2^B - 1$. We are interested in obtaining the key K, defined as

$$K := \langle \langle \sum_{i=0}^{\alpha} G_i \eta^i \rangle_N \rangle_{2^b}. \tag{7}$$

For $0 \leq i \leq \alpha - 1$, we write

$$G_i = \gamma_i 2^{(\alpha-i-1)B+b} + \delta_i \text{ with } 0 \leq \delta_i \leq 2^{(\alpha-i-1)B+b} - 1. \tag{8}$$

We rewrite Algortihm 1, where we added indices to the variables that will be useful in the analysis the algorithm:

$k_\alpha := \langle G_\alpha \rangle_{2^b}; \tau_\alpha := \lfloor \frac{G_\alpha}{2^b} \rfloor;$
for $j := \alpha - 1$ downto 0 do
begin $\sigma_j := \tau_{j+1} \times \eta + \gamma_j;$
$\qquad k_j := \langle k_{j+1} \times \eta + \langle G_j \rangle_{2^b} + \lfloor \frac{\sigma_j}{2^{(j+2)B}} \rfloor \rangle_{2^b};$
$\qquad \tau_j := \lfloor \frac{\langle \sigma_j \rangle_{2^{(j+2)B}}}{2^B} \rfloor$
end;
key:= k_0

Theorem 1. *If $\alpha < 2^B$, then either $K = key$ or $K = \langle key + 1 \rangle_{2^b}$.*

For proving the above theorem, we define $\Lambda_\alpha, \Lambda_{\alpha-1}, \ldots, \Lambda_0$ as

$$\Lambda_\alpha := G_\alpha \text{ and for } 0 \leq j \leq \alpha - 1, \Lambda_j := \eta \Lambda_{j+1} + G_j - \lfloor \frac{\sigma_j}{2^{(j+2)B}} \rfloor N. \tag{9}$$

By induction on j, it is easy to see that for $0 \leq j \leq \alpha$, $\Lambda_j \equiv \sum_{i=j}^{\alpha} G_i \eta^{i-j}$ mod N. Note that $\sum_{i=j}^{\alpha} G_i \eta^{i-j}$ is the j-th iterate of the evaluation of $\sum_{i=0}^{\alpha} G_i \eta^i$ using Horner's algorithm.

We will show below (Proposition 2) that for each j,

$$0 \leq \Lambda_j - \tau_j 2^{(\alpha-j)B+b} \leq (\alpha - j + 1) 2^{(\alpha-j)B+b}.$$

As a consequence, if $\alpha < 2^B$, then $0 \leq \Lambda_0 - \tau_0 2^{\alpha B+b} < N$. The algorithm implies that $0 \leq \tau_0 \leq 2^B - 1$, and so $0 \leq \tau_0 \leq \Lambda_0 < N + 2^B - 1$. As $\sum_{j=0}^{\alpha} G_j \eta^j \equiv \Lambda_0$ mod N, we conclude that $\langle \sum_{j=0}^{\alpha} G_j \eta^j \rangle_N = \langle \Lambda_0 \rangle_N \in \{\Lambda_0, \Lambda_0 - N\}$, and so

$$K \in \{\langle \Lambda_0 \rangle_{2^b}, \langle \Lambda_0 + 1 \rangle_{2^b}\}. \tag{10}$$

In Proposition 3, we show that $\Lambda_j \equiv k_j$ for $0 \leq j \leq \alpha$. Combining this result with (10) proves the theorem.

For $0 \leq j \leq \alpha$, we define

$$r_j := \Lambda_j - 2^{(\alpha-j)B+b} \tau_j.$$

Proposition 1. *For $0 \le j \le \alpha - 1$, we have that $r_j = 2^{(\alpha-j-1)B+b}\langle\sigma_j\rangle_{2^B} + \eta r_{j+1} + \delta_j + \lfloor\frac{\sigma_j}{2^{(j+2)B}}\rfloor$.*

Proof. Let $0 \le j \le \alpha - 1$. From the definitions of $\Lambda_j, \Lambda_{j+1}, r_j \; r_{j+1}$ and σ_j we readily find that

$$r_j = 2^{(\alpha-1-j)B+b}(\sigma_j - 2^B\tau_j) + \eta r_{j+1} + \eta\delta_j - \lfloor\frac{\sigma_j}{2^{(j+2)B}}\rfloor N.$$

Writing $\sigma_j = \lfloor\frac{\sigma_j}{2^{(j+2)B}}\rfloor 2^{(j+2)B} + \langle\sigma_j\rangle_{2^{(j+2)B}}$, and using that $N = 2^{(\alpha+1)B+b} - 1$, we obtain that

$$r_j = 2^{(\alpha-1-j)B+b}(\langle\sigma_j\rangle_{2^{(j+2)B}} - 2^B\tau_j) + \lfloor\frac{\sigma_j}{2^{(j+2)B}}\rfloor + \eta r_{j+1} + \eta\delta_j.$$

The proposition now follows from observing that

$$\langle\sigma_j\rangle_{2^{(j+2)B}} = 2^B\lfloor\frac{\langle\sigma_j\rangle_{2^{(j+2)B}}}{2^B}\rfloor + \langle\langle\sigma_j\rangle_{2^{(j+2)B}}\rangle_{2^B} = 2^B\tau_j + \langle\sigma_j\rangle_{2^B}.$$

$\square$

Proposition 2. *For $0 \le j \le \alpha$ we have that $r_j \le (\alpha - j + 1)2^{(\alpha-j)B+b} - 1$.*

Proof. By induction on j. As $r_\alpha = \langle G_\alpha\rangle_{2^b} \le 2^b - 1$, the proposition is true for $j = \alpha$.
Now let $0 \le j \le \alpha-1$. The algorithm immediately implies that $\tau_{j+1} \le 2^{(j+2)B}-1$ (make distinctions for $j = \alpha - 1$ and $j < \alpha - 1$ for showing this). Moreover,

$$\gamma_j = \lfloor\frac{G_j}{2^{(\alpha-j-1)B}}\rfloor \le \frac{G_j}{2^{(\alpha-j-1)B+b}} \le \frac{N-1}{2^{(\alpha-j-1)B+b}} \le 2^{(j+2)B} - 1.$$

We conclude that

$$\sigma_j = \tau_{j+1}\eta + \gamma_j < 2^{(j+2)B}(\eta + 1) < 2^{(j+3)B}, \quad \text{and so}$$

$$\lfloor\frac{\sigma_j}{2^{(j+2)B}}\rfloor \le 2^B - 1. \tag{11}$$

According to (8), we have that $\delta_j \le 2^{(\alpha-1-j)B+b}-1$, and clearly $\langle\sigma_j\rangle_{2^B} \le 2^B-1$. Combining these inequalities with (11) and Proposition 2, we infer that

$$r_j \le 2^{(\alpha-j-1)B+b}(2^B - 1) + (2^{(\alpha-1-j)B+b} - 1) \; + \eta r_{j+1} + (2^B - 1)$$

$$= 2^{(\alpha-j)B+b} + \eta r_{j+1} + 2^B - 2 < 2^{(\alpha-j)B+b} + 2^B(r_{j+1} + 1).$$

According to the induction hypothesis, $r_{j+1} \le (\alpha - j)2^{(\alpha-j-1)B+b} - 1$, and so

$$r_j \le (\alpha - j + 1)2^{(\alpha-j)B+b} - 1.$$

$\square$

Proposition 3. *For $0 \le j \le \alpha$, we have that $k_j = \langle\Lambda_j\rangle_{2^b}$.*

Proof. By induction on j. The proposition is true for $j = \alpha$.
Now let $0 \le j \le \alpha - 1$. The definition of Λ_j implies that

$$\Lambda_j = \eta\Lambda_{j+1}+G_j-\lfloor\frac{\sigma_j}{2^{(j+2)B}}\rfloor(2^{(\alpha+1)B+b}-1) \equiv \eta\langle\Lambda_{j+1}\rangle_{2^b}+\langle G_j\rangle_{2^b}+\lfloor\frac{\sigma_j}{2^{(j+2)B}}\rfloor \pmod{2^b}.$$

As $k_{j+1} \equiv \Lambda_{j+1} \pmod{2^b}$, the definition of k_j implies the proposition. $\square$

References

1. HP report: Internet of Things Research Study. www.fortifyprotect.com. Accessed 21 August 2014
2. TLS Ciphersuites. https://www.thesprawl.org/research/tls-and-ssl-cipher-suites
3. NIST workshop on cybersecurity in a post-quantum world (2015). http://www.nist.gov/itl/csd/ct/post-quantum-crypto-workshop-2015.cfm
4. Blundo, C., de Santis, A., Herzberg, A., Kutten, S., Vaccaro, U., Yung, M.: Perfectly secure key distribution for dynamic conferences. Inf. Comput. **146**, 1–23 (1998)
5. Dierks, T., Rescorla, E.: The Transport Layer Security (TLS) Protocol Version 1.2. RFC 5246 (Proposed Standard), August 2008. Updated by RFCs 5746, 5878, 6176
6. Eronen, P., Tschofenig, H.: Pre-Shared Key Ciphersuites for Transport Layer Security (TLS). RFC 4279 (Proposed Standard), December 2005
7. García-Morchón, O., Gómez-Pérez, D., Gutiérrez, J., Rietman, R., Tolhuizen, L.: The MMO problem. In: Proceedings of ISSAC 2014, pp. 186–193. ACM (2014)
8. García-Morchón, O., Rietman, R., Shparlinski, I.E., Tolhuizen, L.: Interpolation and approximation of polynomials in finite fields over a short interval from noisy values. Exp. Math. **23**, 241–260 (2014)
9. García-Morchón, O., Gómez-Pérez, D., Gutiérrez, J., Rietman, R., Schoenmakers, B., Tolhuizen, L.: HIMMO - A Lightweight, Fully Colluison Resistant Key-Predistribution Scheme. Cryptology ePrint Archive, Report 2014/698 (2014). http://eprint.iacr.org/
10. Garcia-Morchón, O., Tolhuizen, L., Gomez, D., Gutierrez, J.: Towards full collusion resistant ID-based establishment of pairwise keys. In: Extended abstracts of the Third Workshop on Mathematical Cryptology (WMC 2012) and the Third International Conference on Symbolic Computation and Cryptography (SCC 2012), pp. 30–36 (2012)
11. Liu, A., Ning, P.: Tinyecc: a configurable library for elliptic curve cryptography in wireless sensor networks. In: Proceedings of the 7th International Conference on Information Processing in Sensor Networks, IPSN 2008, pp. 245–256. IEEE Computer Society, Washington, DC (2008)
12. Matsumoto, T., Imai, H.: On the key predistribution system: a practical solution to the key distribution problem. In: Pomerance, C. (ed.) CRYPTO 1987. LNCS, vol. 293, pp. 185–193. Springer, Heidelberg (1988)
13. McGrew, D., Bailey, D.: AES-CCM Cipher Suites for Transport Layer Security (TLS). RFC 6655 (Proposed Standard), July 2012
14. Nguyen, P.Q., Vallée, B. (eds.): The LLL Algorithm - Survey and Applications. Springer, Heidelberg (2010)
15. Sage. http://www.sagemath.org
16. Shelby, Z., Hartke, K., Bormann, C.: The Constrained Application Protocol (CoAP). RFC 7252 (Proposed Standard), June 2014
17. Tschofenig, H.: A Datagram Transport Layer Security (DTLS) 1.2 Profile for the Internet of Things, August 2014

Short Accountable Ring Signatures
Based on DDH

Jonathan Bootle, Andrea Cerulli, Pyrros Chaidos, Essam Ghadafi$^{(\boxtimes)}$,
Jens Groth, and Christophe Petit

University College London, London, UK
e.ghadafi@ucl.ac.uk

Abstract. Ring signatures and group signatures are prominent crypto-graphic primitives offering a combination of privacy and authentication. They enable individual users to anonymously sign messages on behalf of a group of users. In ring signatures, the group, i.e. the ring, is chosen in an ad hoc manner by the signer. In group signatures, group membership is controlled by a group manager. Group signatures additionally enforce accountability by providing the group manager with a secret tracing key that can be used to identify the otherwise anonymous signer when needed. Accountable ring signatures, introduced by Xu and Yung (CARDIS 2004), bridge the gap between the two notions. They provide maximal flexibility in choosing the ring, and at the same time maintain accountability by supporting a designated opener that can identify sign-ers when needed.

We revisit accountable ring signatures and offer a formal security model for the primitive. Our model offers strong security definitions incorporating protection against maliciously chosen keys and at the same time flexibility both in the choice of the ring and the opener. We give a generic construction using standard tools. We give a highly efficient instantiation of our generic construction in the random oracle model by meticulously combining Camenisch's group signature scheme (CRYPTO 1997) with a generalization of the one-out-of-many proofs of knowledge by Groth and Kohlweiss (EUROCRYPT 2015). Our instantiation yields signatures of logarithmic size (in the size of the ring) while relying solely on the well-studied decisional Diffie-Hellman assumption. In the process, we offer a number of optimizations for the recent Groth and Kohlweiss one-out-of-many proofs, which may be useful for other applications.

Accountable ring signatures imply traditional ring and group signa-tures. We therefore also obtain highly efficient instantiations of those primitives with signatures shorter than all existing ring signatures as well as existing group signatures relying on standard assumptions.

The research leading to these results has received funding from the European Research Council under the European Union's Seventh Framework Programme (FP/2007–2013)/ERC Grant Agreement n. 307937 and EPSRC grant EP/J009520/1.
P. Chaidos was supported by an EPSRC scholarship (EP/G037264/1 – Security Science DTC).

G. Pernul et al. (Eds.): ESORICS 2015, Part I, LNCS 9326, pp. 243–265, 2015.
DOI: 10.1007/978-3-319-24174-6_13

Keywords: Accountable ring signatures · Group signatures · One-out-of-many zero-knowledge proofs

1 Introduction

Significant effort has been devoted to the study of signature schemes with privacy properties that allow a signer to remain anonymous within a set of users. Two prominent examples of anonymous signature schemes are ring signatures [RST01] and group signatures [CvH91]. Ring signatures allow a signer to choose any *ad hoc* set of users, i.e. a ring, and sign anonymously on behalf the ring. Group signatures also allow a signer to sign anonymously on behalf of a group of users but here group membership is controlled by a designated group manager. The advantage of group signatures is accountability; in case of abuse, the group manager can revoke anonymity and identify the signer.

Accountable ring signatures [XY04] bridge the gap between ring signatures and group signatures. They offer the flexibility of freely choosing the ring of users when creating a signature and at the same time enforce accountability by including an opener who can open a signature and reveal who signed it. The combination of flexibility and accountability allows applications where ring signatures or group signatures are less suitable. Consider, for instance, an online forum that wants to offer anonymity to users but also wants to be able to trace people who violate the code of conduct. A forum can achieve this by allowing user posts with accountable ring signatures where the owner is the specified opener. This system is decentralized and flexible since different fora can have their own opener keys and users do not have to register with each individual forum they post to. Another potential application is an auction system where bids are public but unsuccessful bidders want anonymity. Bidders sign bids with the seller as opener and at the end of the auctions the seller can disclose the winner in a verifiable way.

Our Contribution. We introduce a new security model for *accountable* ring signatures. The signer specifies, in addition to a set of users that could have produced the signature, the public key of an opening entity, which will be able to remove anonymity. This opening mechanism offers protection against misbehaving signers while at the same time not relying on a single, centralized group manager. Our security definitions are stringent and when possible incorporate protection against maliciously chosen keys.

We provide a generic construction of accountable ring signatures from standard cryptographic tools. We also give a concrete instantiation, combining ideas from Camenisch's group signature [Cam97] with a generalization of the one-out-of-many proof of knowledge of Groth and Kohlweiss [GK15]. The most efficient ring and group signatures [ACJT00, CL02, CKS09, BBS04, DKNS04, CG05, Ngu05, GK15] in the literature are in the random oracle model [FS87] and so is ours. However, the only other assumption we make is the hardness of the well-established decisional Diffie-Hellman problem.[1]

From a technical viewpoint, we offer two optimisations of Groth-Kohlweiss one-out-of-many proofs. One perspective on their proof system is that they form a binary tree and prove that one of the leaves is selected. We generalise their approach to n-ary trees, allowing us to fine-tune the parameters for better performance. For $N = n^m$, our optimisations reduce the number of group elements in the 1-out-of-N proof from $4m$ to $2m$ with little impact on the number of field elements or computational cost. Also, while their proofs can be used for ElGamal encryption, which is what we need for our scheme, this imposes an overhead in all parts of their protocol. We deploy more efficient Pedersen commitments in some parts of the proof, thus limiting the overhead of ElGamal.

The end result is an accountable ring signature scheme with efficient computation and very small signatures. Namely, for a ring with $N = \text{poly}(\lambda)$ users, we obtain signatures of size approximately $\frac{5}{2}\lambda \log_2 N$ bits, which is smaller than all existing group and ring signatures based on standard assumptions.

Related Work. Accountable ring signatures were informally defined by Xu and Yung [XY04]. Their security model mitigates the trust on the opener by using several openers and a threshold decryption mechanism, whereas we reduce the trust in the opener by allowing users to choose arbitrary openers (and leaving it to the verifier to decide whether they trust the opener). It would be easy to generalize our definitions to accommodate threshold decryption as well. Xu and Yung rely on the tamper-resistance of smart cards to ensure that the signatures contain some footprint of the signer. In our model, we require the signer to provide a proof that his signature is well-formed. Finally, Xu and Yung require the existence of trapdoor permutations whereas we rely on the hardness of the Decision Diffie-Hellman (DDH) problem.

Our security model for accountable ring signatures is also very similar to the identity escrow extension by Dodis et al. [DKNS04], except that we allow for an arbitrary choice of opener and we require openers to prove correctness of their decisions. The construction in [DKNS04] relies on the strong RSA assumption whereas we rely on, in our opinion, the more established DDH assumption.

Traceable ring signatures [FS08] and linkable ring signatures [LWW04] also offer some restricted form of accountability. In traceable ring signatures, any couple of signatures produced by the same user will reveal her identity. In linkable group signatures, it is possible to efficiently decide whether two signatures were produced by the same user but without revealing his identity. Unique ring signatures [FZ13] encompass both traceable and linkable ring signatures.

Formal security models for group signatures were introduced by Bellare et al. [BMW03] in the static case and by Kiayias and Yung [KY05] and Bellare et al. [BSZ05] in the partially dynamic case where users can join the

---

[1] An important advantage of working over a discrete logarithm group is that so do many standard signature schemes, e.g., DSS. We therefore already have many users with suitable public verification keys in a standard cyclic group, e.g., NIST's 256-bit elliptic curve group P. 256.

group at any time. A formal security model for ring signatures was provided by
Bender et al. [BKM09].

The first practical and provably secure group signature was due to Ateniese
et al. [ACJT00]. Their scheme was later improved by Camenisch and Lysyanskaya to allow efficient revocation of group member using dynamic accumulators
[CL02]. Both schemes yield signatures of constant size and are based on the
DDH and the strong RSA assumptions, in the random oracle model. Boneh
et al. [BBS04] also constructed constant size group signatures under the strong
Diffie-Hellman and the Decision Linear assumption in pairing groups. Other
pairing-based schemes include [ACHdM05, NSN04, CG05, BW07, Gro07, CKS09,
LPY12]. Recently, Langlois et al. [LLNW14] gave an efficient lattice-based group
signature scheme supporting revocation, based on the hardness of approximat-
ing the shortest independent vectors problem in lattice of dimension n within a
factor $\tilde{O}(n^{1.5})$. Our scheme achieves roughly the same signature sizes as theirs
under an arguably more standard and better understood assumption.

Constant-size ring signatures can also be based on the strong RSA assumption [DKNS04] and on pairing assumptions [Ngu05]. Very recently, Groth and
Kohlweiss provided a ring signature scheme based on the discrete logarithm
assumption in the random oracle model, which is asymptotically more efficient
than previous ones. Our accountable ring signature scheme extends Groth and
Kohlweiss' scheme to enforce accountability and due to our optimisations, we
get a performance improvement as well.

2   Defining Accountable Ring Signatures

We write $y = A(x; r)$ when the algorithm A on input x and randomness r
outputs y. We write $y \leftarrow A(x)$ for the process of setting $y = A(x; r)$ where
r is sampled at random. We also write $y \leftarrow S$ for sampling y uniformly at
random from a set S. Given two functions $f, g : \mathbb{N} \to [0, 1]$ we write $f(\lambda) \approx g(\lambda)$
if $|f(\lambda) - g(\lambda)| = \lambda^{-\omega(1)}$. We say f is negligible if $f(\lambda) \approx 0$ and that f is
overwhelming if $f(\lambda) \approx 1$. By PPT we mean running in probabilistic polynomial
time in the relevant security parameter λ.

An accountable ring signature scheme over a PPT setup Setup is a tuple of
polynomial-time algorithms (OKGen, UKGen, Sign, Vfy, Open, Judge).

Setup(1^λ): Given the security parameter, produces public parameters pp used
    (sometimes implicitly) by the rest of the scheme. The public parameters
    define key spaces PK, DK, VK, SK with efficient algorithms for sampling and
    deciding membership.

OKGen(pp): Given the public parameters pp, produces a public key $pk \in$ PK and
    secret key $dk \in$ DK for an opener. Without loss of generality, we assume dk
    defines pk deterministically and write $pk = \text{OKGen}(pp, dk)$ when computing
    pk from dk.

UKGen(pp): Given the public parameters pp, produces a verification key $vk \in$
    VK and a secret signing key $sk \in$ SK for a user. We can assume sk deter-
    ministically determines vk and write $vk = \text{UKGen}(pp, sk)$ when computing
    vk from sk.

Sign(pk, m, R, sk): Given an opener's public key, a message, a ring (i.e. a set of verification keys) and a secret key, produces a ring signature σ. The algorithm returns the error symbol $\perp$ if the inputs are malformed, i.e., if $pk \notin$ PK, $R \not\subset$ VK, $sk \notin$ SK or $vk =$ UKGen(pp, sk) $\notin R$.

Vfy(pk, m, R, σ): Given an opener's public key, a message, a ring and a signature, returns 1 if accepting the signature and 0 otherwise. We assume the algorithm always returns 0 if the inputs are malformed, i.e., if $pk \notin$ PK or $R \not\subset$ VK.

Open(m, R, σ, dk): Given a message, a ring, a ring signature and an opener's secret key, returns a verification key vk and a proof ψ that the owner of vk produced the signature. If any of the inputs are invalid, i.e., $dk \notin$ DK or σ is not a valid signature using $pk =$ OKGen(pp, dk), the algorithm returns $\perp$.

Judge($pk, m, R, \sigma, vk, \psi$): Given an opener's public key, a message, a ring, a signature, a verification key and a proof, returns 1 if accepting the proof and 0 otherwise. We assume the algorithm returns 0 if σ is invalid or $vk \notin R$.

An accountable ring signature scheme should be correct, fully unforgeable, anonymous and traceable as defined below.

Definition 1 (Perfect correctness). *An accountable ring signature scheme is perfectly correct if for any PPT adversary* $\mathcal{A}$

$$\Pr\left[\begin{array}{c} pp \leftarrow \text{Setup}(1^\lambda); (vk, sk) \leftarrow \text{UKGen}(pp); \\ (pk, m, R) \leftarrow \mathcal{A}(pp, sk); \sigma \leftarrow \text{Sign}(pk, m, R, sk) \; : \\ \text{If } pk \in \text{PK}, R \subset \text{VK}, vk \in R \text{ then Vfy}(pk, m, R, \sigma) = 1 \end{array}\right] = 1.$$

We remark that correctness of the opening algorithm (w.r.t. an honestly generated opener key) is implied by the other requirements.

Full unforgeability ensures that an adversary, who may control the opener, can neither falsely accuse an honest user of producing a ring signature nor forge ring signatures on behalf of an honest ring. The former should hold even when all other users in the ring are corrupt. This requirement combines the non-frameability of group signatures [BSZ05] and the unforgeability of ring signatures [BKM09] requirements.

Definition 2 (Full Unforgeability). *An accountable ring signature scheme is fully unforgeable if for any PPT adversary* $\mathcal{A}$

$$\Pr\left[\begin{array}{c} pp \leftarrow \text{Setup}(1^\lambda); (pk, vk, m, R, \sigma, \psi) \leftarrow \mathcal{A}^{\text{UKGen,Sign,Reveal}}(pp) : \\ \left(vk \in Q_{\text{UKGen}} \setminus Q_{\text{Reveal}} \;\wedge\; (pk, vk, m, R, \sigma) \notin Q_{\text{Sign}}\right. \\ \wedge \; \text{Judge}(pk, m, R, \sigma, vk, \psi) = 1) \\ \vee \; \left(R \subset Q_{\text{UKGen}} \setminus Q_{\text{Reveal}} \;\wedge\; (pk, \cdot, m, R, \sigma) \notin Q_{\text{Sign}}\right. \\ \wedge \; \text{Vfy}(pk, m, R, \sigma) = 1) \end{array}\right] \approx 0.$$

- UKGen *runs* $(vk, sk) \leftarrow$ UKGen(pp) *and returns* vk. Q_{UKGen} *is the set of verification keys* vk *that have been generated by this oracle.*
- Sign *is an oracle that on query* (pk, vk, m, R) *returns* $\sigma \leftarrow$ Sign(pk, m, R, sk) *if* $vk \in R \cap Q_{\text{UKGen}}$. Q_{Sign} *contains the queries and responses* (pk, vk, m, R, σ).
- Reveal *is an oracle that when queried on* $vk \in Q_{\text{UKGen}}$ *returns the corresponding signing key* sk. Q_{Reveal} *is the list of verification keys* vk *for which the corresponding signing key has been revealed.*

Anonymity ensures that a signature does not reveal the identity of the ring member who produced it without the opener explicitly wanting to open the particular signature. We allow the adversary to choose the secret signing keys of the users which implies anonymity against full key exposure attacks [BKM09] where the users' secret signing keys have been revealed. Our definition also captures unlinkability as used in [XY04]: if an adversary can link signatures by the same signer, it can break anonymity.

Definition 3 (Anonymity). *An accountable ring signature scheme is anonymous if for any PPT adversary* $\mathcal{A}$

$$\Pr \left[\begin{array}{l} pp \leftarrow \text{Setup}(1^\lambda); b \leftarrow \{0, 1\}; (pk, dk) \leftarrow \text{OKGen}(pp): \\ \mathcal{A}^{\text{Chal}_b, \text{Open}}(pp, pk) = b \end{array} \right] \approx \frac{1}{2}.$$

- Chal$_b$ *is an oracle that the adversary can only call once. On query* (m, R, sk_0, sk_1) *it runs* $\sigma_0 \leftarrow$ Sign(pk, m, R, sk_0); $\sigma_1 \leftarrow$ Sign(pk, m, R, sk_1). *If* $\sigma_0 \neq \bot$ *and* $\sigma_1 \neq \bot$ *it returns* σ_b, *otherwise it returns* $\bot$.
- Open *is an oracle that on a query* (m, R, σ) *returns* Open(m, R, σ, dk). *If* σ *was obtained by calling* Chal$_b$ *on* (m, R), *the oracle returns* $\bot$.

Traceability ensures that the specified opener can always identify the ring member who produced a signature and that she is able to produce a valid proof for her decision.

Definition 4 (Traceability). *An accountable ring signature scheme is traceable if for any PPT adversary* $\mathcal{A}$

$$\Pr \left[\begin{array}{l} pp \leftarrow \text{Setup}(1^\lambda); (dk, m, R, \sigma) \leftarrow \mathcal{A}(pp); \\ pk \leftarrow \text{OKGen}(pp, dk); (vk, \psi) \leftarrow \text{Open}(m, R, \sigma, dk): \\ \text{Vfy}(pk, m, R, \sigma) = 1 \ \wedge \ \text{Judge}(pk, m, R, \sigma, vk, \psi) = 0 \end{array} \right] \approx 0.$$

Tracing soundness ensures that a signature cannot trace to two different users; only one person can be identified as the signer even when all users as well as the opener are fully corrupt. Similarly to the setting of group signatures [SSE+12], this requirement is vital for some applications, e.g., where users might be rewarded for signatures they produced, or to avoid shifting blame when signatures are used as evidence of abuse.

Definition 5 (Tracing Soundness). *An accountable ring signature scheme satisfies tracing soundness if for any PPT adversary* $\mathcal{A}$

$$\Pr \left[\begin{array}{l} pp \leftarrow \text{Setup}(1^\lambda); (m, \sigma, R, pk, vk_1, vk_2, \psi_1, \psi_2) \leftarrow \mathcal{A}(pp): \\ \forall i \in \{1, 2\}, \ \text{Judge}(pk, m, R, \sigma, vk_i, \psi_i) = 1 \wedge \ vk_1 \neq vk_2 \end{array} \right] \approx 0.$$

2.1 Ring and Group Signatures from Accountable Ring Signatures

We will now relate accountable ring signatures to ring signatures and group signatures by showing that the latter are implied by accountable ring signatures.

Ring Signatures. Traditional ring signatures [RST01] do not have an opener and their security requires anonymity of the signer and unforgeability [RST01, BKM09]. By simply regarding the opener's public key as part of the signature and ignoring the opening and judge algorithms, we obtain a traditional ring signature scheme from an accountable ring signature. Correctness and anonymity follow from those of the accountable ring signature, whereas unforgeability is implied by full unforgeability and traceability.

Group Signatures. Bellare et al. [BMW03] defined group signatures for static groups, where the population of the group is fixed once and for all at the setup time, and where the group manager additionally acts as the designated opener. Besides, correctness, their model requires full anonymity and full traceability. The latter requires that an adversary in possession of the group master secret key who can corrupt members of the group, cannot produce a new signature that does not trace to a user in set of corrupt users. An accountable ring signature satisfying our security definitions gives rise to a group signature scheme as follows: We fix the group manager as the designated opener and set the corresponding decryption key as the group master secret key $gmsk$ used as the tracing key. In the setup, the group members generate their personal key pairs and we publish the ring containing the public keys of the members as part of the group signature public key. Group signatures are then just accountable ring signatures w.r.t. this ring. Full anonymity follows from the anonymity of the accountable ring signature scheme, whereas full traceability follows from full unforgeability and traceability.

The group public key in our scheme is quite large since it grows linearly in the number of members. However, this is a cost that can be amortized over many signatures. An advantage of the group signature scheme on the other hand is that it can easily be made dynamic. The group manager can enrol or remove users by adding or deleting their verification keys from the group public key [DKNS04]. In the dynamic group signature scheme, the group public key is changing and group signatures must be verified against the group as it was at the time of signing, but for scenarios where the group is not changing too often or where great flexibility is desired this is a price worth paying.

3 Preliminaries

We define here the tools and assumptions we use.

Cyclic Groups and Assumptions. A group generator $\mathcal{G}$ is a PPT algorithm that on input 1^λ (for a security paremeter λ) returns a description $gk = (\mathbb{G}, q, g)$ of a group $\mathbb{G}$ of prime order q and a generator g. We assume the group has associated polynomial time algorithms for computing group operations and deciding membership.

The Discrete Logarithm (DL) assumption holds relative to $\mathcal{G}$ if for all PPT adversaries $\mathcal{A}$

$$\Pr\left[gk = (\mathbb{G}, q, g) \leftarrow \mathcal{G}(1^\lambda); x \leftarrow \mathbb{Z}_q; h := g^x : \mathcal{A}(gk, h) = x\right] \approx 0.$$

The Decisional Diffie-Hellman (DDH) assumption holds relative to $\mathcal{G}$ if for all PPT adversaries $\mathcal{A}$

$$\Pr\left[\begin{array}{l} gk = (\mathbb{G}, q, g) \leftarrow \mathcal{G}(1^\lambda); x, y, z \leftarrow \mathbb{Z}_q; b \leftarrow \{0, 1\}; \\ h := g^x; u := g^y; v := g^{(1-b)xy+bz} : \mathcal{A}(gk, h, u, v) = b \end{array}\right] \approx \frac{1}{2}.$$

The DDH assumption relative to $\mathcal{G}$ implies the DL assumption relative to $\mathcal{G}$. The DDH assumption is believed to hold when $\mathbb{G}$ is an appropriately chosen subgroup of elliptic curve groups or multiplicative groups of large characteristic finite fields.

One-way Function. A function $f : X \rightarrow Y$ (over setup gk, which defines the function f, the domain X and range Y) is *one-way* if f is polynomial-time computable and is hard to invert, i.e. for all PPT adversaries $\mathcal{A}$

$$\Pr\left[gk \leftarrow \mathcal{G}(1^\lambda); x \leftarrow \mathrm{X}; y := f(x) : \mathcal{A}(gk, y) = x\right] \approx 0.$$

We will instantiate f via group exponentiation, i.e. $x \mapsto g^x$ with domain $\mathbb{Z}_q$ and range $\mathbb{G}$. The one-wayness of f is then implied by the DL assumption.

Non-Interactive Zero-Knowledge (NIZK) Proofs. A NIZK proof system (over a setup gk) for an NP-relation $\mathcal{R}$ defining the language $\mathcal{L}_\mathcal{R} := \{s \mid \exists w : (s, w) \in \mathcal{R}\}$, where s is a statement and w is a witness, is a tuple of polynomial-time algorithms (CRSGen, Prove, PVfy). CRSGen(gk) generates a common reference string crs; Prove(crs, s, w) returns a proof π that $(s, w) \in \mathcal{R}$; PVfy(crs, s, π) verifies that π is a valid proof for $s \in \mathcal{L}_\mathcal{R}$ outputting a bit accordingly.

Perfect completeness of the proof system requires that for any crs generated by CRSGen and any pair $(s, w) \in \mathcal{R}$ we have $\Pr[\mathrm{PVfy}(crs, s, \mathrm{Prove}(crs, s, w))] = 1$. Additionally, we require *soundness* and *zero-knowledge*, which are as follows:

– Soundness: For all PPT adversaries $\mathcal{A}$, we have

$$\Pr\left[\begin{array}{l} gk \leftarrow \mathcal{G}(1^\lambda); crs \leftarrow \mathrm{CRSGen}(gk); (s, \pi) \leftarrow \mathcal{A}(gk, crs) : \\ \mathrm{PVfy}(crs, s, \pi) = 1 \ \wedge \ s \notin \mathcal{L}_\mathcal{R} \end{array}\right] \approx 0.$$

– Zero-Knowledge: There exist PPT algorithms (SimCRSGen, SimProve), where SimCRSGen(gk) outputs a simulated reference string crs and possibly a simulation trapdoor τ, and SimProve(crs, s, τ) produces a simulated proof (without knowing a witness). We require that

$$\Pr\left[gk \leftarrow \mathcal{G}(1^\lambda); crs \leftarrow \mathrm{CRSGen}(gk) : \mathcal{A}^{\mathrm{Prove}}(gk, crs) = 1\right]$$

$$\approx \Pr\left[gk \leftarrow \mathcal{G}(1^\lambda); (crs, \tau) \leftarrow \mathrm{SimCRSGen}(gk) : \mathcal{A}^{\mathrm{Sim}}(gk, crs) = 1\right],$$

where on query $(s, w) \in \mathcal{R}$, Sim returns $\pi \leftarrow \mathrm{SimProve}(crs, s, \tau)$.

Sigma-Protocols. We will in our instantiation use NIZK proofs in the random oracle model obtained by applying the Fiat-Shamir transformation [FS87] to interactive Σ-protocols, which are 3-move protocols that allow a prover to convince a verifier that a certain statement is true.

A Σ-protocol for a relation $\mathcal{R}$ w.r.t. a setup gk is a tuple $(\mathcal{G}_{crs}, \mathcal{P}, \mathcal{V})$. $\mathcal{G}_{crs}(gk)$ generates a common reference string crs; $\mathcal{P}(crs, s, w)$ generates an initial message a; $\mathcal{P}(x)$ computes a response z to a random challenge x. $\mathcal{V}(crs, s, a, x, z)$ verifies the proof and outputs 1 for acceptance or 0 for rejection.

Besides completeness, we require Σ-protocols to have *Special Honest Verifier Zero-Knowledge (SHVZK)* and *n-Special Soundness* [GK15]:

- SHVZK: Given any statement $s \in \mathcal{L}_{\mathcal{R}}$ and any verifier challenge x, it is possible to simulate a transcript of the protocol.
- n-Special Soundness: For any statement s, from n accepting transcripts $\{(a, x_i, z_i)\}_{i=1}^n$ for $s \in \mathcal{L}_{\mathcal{R}}$ where the challenges x_i are distinct, we can extract w s.t. $(s, w) \in \mathcal{R}$.

Signature of Knowledge. A *Signature of Knowledge* (SoK) for an NP-relation $\mathcal{R}$ w.r.t. a setup gk is a tuple (SoKSetup, SoKSign, SoKVerify). SoKSetup(gk) outputs public parameters pp; SoKSign(pp, s, w, m) outputs a signature σ_{SoK} on m if $(s, w) \in \mathcal{R}$; SoKVerify(pp, $s, m, \sigma_{\mathsf{SoK}}$) outputs 1 if σ_{SoK} is a valid signature on m or 0 otherwise. The (game-based) security definition for signatures of knowledge (*SimExt*) [CL06], besides correctness, requires *Simulatability* and *Extractability*. We consider a *stronger* generalisation of the latter called f-extractability [BCKL08]:

- Simulatability: There are PPT algorithms (SoKSimSetup, SoKSimSign), where SoKSimSetup(gk) outputs public parameters pp and some trapdoor τ, whereas SoKSimSign(pp, τ, s, m) outputs a signature σ_{SoK}, such that

$$\Pr\left[gk \leftarrow \mathcal{G}(1^\lambda); (\mathsf{pp}, \tau) \leftarrow \mathrm{SoKSimSetup}(gk) : \mathcal{A}^{\mathrm{SoKSim}}(gk, \mathsf{pp}) = 1\right]$$

$$\approx \Pr\left[gk \leftarrow \mathcal{G}(1^\lambda); \mathsf{pp} \leftarrow \mathrm{SoKSetup}(gk) : \mathcal{A}^{\mathrm{SoKSign}}(gk, \mathsf{pp}) = 1\right],$$

for all PPT adversaries $\mathcal{A}$, where SoKSim(s, w, m) returns SoKSimSign(pp, τ, s, m) if $(s, w) \in \mathcal{R}$ and $\bot$ otherwise.
- f-Extractability: For all PPT adversaries $\mathcal{A}$, there exists a polynomial time algorithm SoKExtract such that:

$$\Pr\left[\begin{array}{l} gk \leftarrow \mathcal{G}(1^\lambda); (\mathsf{pp}, \tau) \leftarrow \mathrm{SoKSimSetup}(gk); \\ (s, m, \sigma_{\mathsf{SoK}}) \leftarrow \mathcal{A}^{\mathrm{SoKSim}}(gk, \mathsf{pp}); \\ y \leftarrow \mathrm{SoKExtract}(\mathsf{pp}, \tau, s, m, \sigma_{\mathsf{SoK}}) : \\ (s, m, \sigma_{\mathsf{SoK}}) \in Q_{\mathrm{SoKSim}} \vee \mathrm{SoKVerify}(\mathsf{pp}, s, m, \sigma_{\mathsf{SoK}}) = 0 \\ \vee \left(\exists w \text{ s.t. } (s, w) \in \mathcal{R} \wedge y = f(w)\right) \end{array}\right] \approx 1.$$

In the above, Q_{SoKSim} is a list of queries to the SoKSimSign oracle. Note that our extractability definition is stronger than that of [CL06], as we allow the adversary to ask for signatures w.r.t. statements for which it does know the witness. In the definition, if f is the identity function, we get the standard notion of extractability.

Signatures of knowledge in the random oracle model can be efficiently realized by applying the Fiat-Shamir transformation to Σ-protocols. Applying the transformation to Σ-protocols having quasi-unique responses (i.e. given an accepting transcript, it is infeasible to find a different accepting response w.r.t. the same initial message and challenge) provides weak simulation-extractability [FKMV12], where the extractor needs to rewind the prover. To get straight-line f-extractability, i.e. without rewinding [Fis05], we additionally encrypt a function f of the witness with a public key in the reference string and prove that the encrypted value is consistent with the witness. This way we get both full weak extractability and straightline f-extractability simultaneously.

Commitment Scheme. A non-interactive commitment scheme (over a setup gk) consists of two polynomial-time algorithms $(\mathrm{CGen}, \mathrm{Com}_{ck})$, where $\mathrm{CGen}(gk)$ outputs a commitment key ck, and Com_{ck} is a randomized algorithm that on input a message m and a randomness r outputs a commitment c. To open a commitment, one reveals m and r allowing anyone to verify that c is indeed a commitment to m. We require that the scheme is *hiding* and *binding*. Hiding requires that for all PPT stateful adversaries $\mathcal{A}$

$$\mathrm{Pr}\left[\begin{array}{l} gk \leftarrow \mathcal{G}(1^\lambda); ck \leftarrow \mathrm{CGen}(gk); (m_0, m_1) \leftarrow \mathcal{A}(gk, ck); \\ b \leftarrow \{0,1\}; c \leftarrow \mathrm{Com}_{ck}(m_b) : \mathcal{A}(c) = b \end{array}\right] \approx \frac{1}{2}.$$

Binding requires that for all polynomial-time stateful adversaries $\mathcal{A}$

$$\mathrm{Pr}\left[\begin{array}{l} gk \leftarrow \mathcal{G}(1^\lambda); ck \leftarrow \mathrm{CGen}(gk); (m_0, r_0, m_1, r_1) \leftarrow \mathcal{A}(gk, ck): \\ m_0 \neq m_1 \ \wedge \ \mathrm{Com}_{ck}(m_0, r_0) = \mathrm{Com}_{ck}(m_1, r_1) \end{array}\right] \approx 0.$$

Pedersen commitments [Ped91] are of the form $c = g^r h^m$ where $r \leftarrow \mathbb{Z}_q^*$, $h \leftarrow \mathbb{G}$ and $m \in \mathbb{Z}_q$. They are perfectly hiding and computationally binding assuming the DL assumption holds. We exploit the fact that the Pedersen commitment scheme is homomorphic, i.e., for all correctly generated gk, ck and all $m, m', r, r' \in \mathbb{Z}_q$

$$\mathrm{Com}_{ck}(m; r) \cdot \mathrm{Com}_{ck}(m'; r') = \mathrm{Com}_{ck}(m + m'; r + r').$$

We will use a variant of the Pedersen commitment scheme to commit to multiple messages at once as shown in Fig. 1.

$\mathrm{CGen}(gk)$	$\mathrm{Com}_{ck}(m_1, \ldots, m_n)$
$h_1, \ldots, h_n \leftarrow \mathbb{G}$.	If $(m_1, \ldots, m_n) \notin \mathbb{Z}_q^n$ return $\bot$.
Return $ck := (h_1, \ldots, h_n)$.	$r \leftarrow \mathbb{Z}_q$; Return $c := g^r \prod_{i=1}^n h_i^{m_i}$.

Fig. 1. Pedersen commitment to multiple elements.

IND-CPA Public-Key Encryption. A public-key encryption scheme (over setup gk) consists of three algorithms (PKEGen, Enc, Dec). PKEGen(gk) is a probabilistic algorithm that generates a public key and decryption key pair (pk, dk). Without loss of generality, we assume pk can be efficiently computed given dk and write $pk = \mathrm{PKEGen}(gk, dk)$ for this computation which returns $\bot$ if dk is not valid. Enc(pk, m) is a probabilistic algorithm which returns a ciphertext c if all its inputs are valid and $\bot$ otherwise. Dec(dk, c) is a deterministic algorithm that decrypts the ciphertext and returns either the message m or the failure symbol $\bot$. We assume that gk, which is an implicit input to Enc and Dec, defines the public key, decryption key, message, randomness and ciphertext spaces PK, DK, M, Rnd and C.

We also require that the scheme is *indistinguishable under chosen plaintext attacks (IND-CPA)*, i.e., for all PPT stateful adversaries $\mathcal{A}$

$$\Pr\left[\begin{array}{l} gk \leftarrow \mathcal{G}(1^\lambda); (pk, dk) \leftarrow \mathrm{PKEGen}(gk) \\ (m_0, m_1) \leftarrow \mathcal{A}(gk, pk); b \leftarrow \{0,1\}; c \leftarrow \mathrm{Enc}(pk, m_b) \end{array} : \mathcal{A}(c) = b \right] \approx \frac{1}{2},$$

where we require $\mathcal{A}$ outputs $m_0, m_1 \in \mathrm{M}$.

We will in our instantiation use ElGamal encryption described in Fig. 2, which is IND-CPA secure if the DDH assumption holds relative to $\mathcal{G}$ where $gk = (\mathbb{G}, q, g) \leftarrow \mathcal{G}(1^\lambda)$. We also note that ElGamal ciphertexts are homomorphic, similarly to Pedersen commitments. We have PK $:= \mathbb{G}^*$, DK $:= \mathbb{Z}_q^*$, M $:= \mathbb{G}$, Rnd $:= \mathbb{Z}_q$, and C $:= \mathbb{G}^2$.

PKEGen(gk)	Enc(pk, m)	Dec($dk, c = (u, v)$)
$dk \leftarrow \mathbb{Z}_q^*; pk := g^{dk}$.	If $pk \notin \mathbb{G}^*$ or $m \notin \mathbb{G}$ return $\bot$.	If $dk \notin \mathbb{Z}_q^*$ or $c \notin \mathbb{G}^2$ return $\bot$.
Return (pk, dk).	$r \leftarrow \mathbb{Z}_q$; Return $c := (pk^r, g^r m)$.	Return $m := vu^{-\frac{1}{dk}}$.

Fig. 2. ElGamal encryption.

4   Constructing Accountable Ring Signatures

Our generic construction (shown in Fig. 3) uses a one-way function f, an IND-CPA public-key encryption scheme, a signature of knowledge, and a zero-knowledge proof of membership, all of which share the same setup gk. The setup gk defines domain SK and range VK for f, and key, message, randomness and ciphertext spaces PK, DK, M, Rnd, C for the encryption scheme. The range of f and the message space of the encryption scheme need to be compatible such that VK $\subseteq$ M.

The idea is that an opener will have a key pair for the encryption scheme and the user will have a secret key sk and corresponding verification key $vk = f(sk)$. To sign a message m w.r.t. a ring R, the signer first encrypts her verification key under the opener's public key and provides a signature of knowledge on m proving the ciphertext encrypts a verification key in the ring and that she knows the secret key associated with the encrypted verification key. To open a

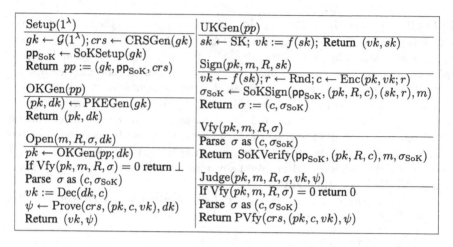

Setup(1^λ)	UKGen(pp)
$gk \leftarrow \mathcal{G}(1^\lambda); crs \leftarrow$ CRSGen(gk) $\mathrm{pp_{SoK}} \leftarrow$ SoKSetup(gk) Return $pp := (gk, \mathrm{pp_{SoK}}, crs)$	$sk \leftarrow$ SK; $vk := f(sk)$; Return (vk, sk)
	Sign(pk, m, R, sk)
OKGen(pp)	$vk \leftarrow f(sk); r \leftarrow$ Rnd; $c \leftarrow$ Enc($pk, vk; r$)
$(pk, dk) \leftarrow$ PKEGen(gk) Return (pk, dk)	$\sigma_{\mathrm{SoK}} \leftarrow$ SoKSign($\mathrm{pp_{SoK}}, (pk, R, c), (sk, r), m$) Return $\sigma := (c, \sigma_{\mathrm{SoK}})$
	Vfy(pk, m, R, σ)
Open(m, R, σ, dk)	Parse σ as $(c, \sigma_{\mathrm{SoK}})$
$pk \leftarrow$ OKGen($pp; dk$) If Vfy(pk, m, R, σ) = 0 return $\perp$ Parse σ as $(c, \sigma_{\mathrm{SoK}})$ $vk := $ Dec(dk, c) $\psi \leftarrow$ Prove($crs, (pk, c, vk), dk$) Return (vk, ψ)	Return SoKVerify($\mathrm{pp_{SoK}}, (pk, R, c), m, \sigma_{\mathrm{SoK}}$)
	Judge($pk, m, R, \sigma, vk, \psi$)
	If Vfy(pk, m, R, σ) = 0 return 0 Parse σ as $(c, \sigma_{\mathrm{SoK}})$ Return PVfy($crs, (pk, c, vk), \psi$)

Fig. 3. A generic construction for accountable ring signatures.

signature, the opener decrypts the ciphertext to obtain the user's verification key and provides an NIZK proof of correct decryption.

The relations $\mathcal{R}_{\mathrm{sig}}$ and $\mathcal{R}_{\mathrm{open}}$ associated with the signature of knowledge and the NIZK system, respectively, are as follows:

$$\mathcal{R}_{\mathrm{sig}} := \left\{ \begin{array}{c} ((pk, R, c), (sk, r)) : \\ R \subset \mathrm{VK} \ \wedge \ vk := f(sk) \in R \ \wedge \ c = \mathrm{Enc}(pk, vk; r) \end{array} \right\}.$$

$$\mathcal{R}_{\mathrm{open}} := \left\{ \begin{array}{c} ((pk, c, vk), dk) : \\ pk = \mathrm{PKEGen}(gk; dk) \in \mathrm{PK} \ \wedge \ vk = \mathrm{Dec}(dk, c) \ \wedge \ vk \in \mathrm{VK} \end{array} \right\}.$$

We prove the following theorem in Appendix A.

Theorem 1. *The accountable ring signature construction in Fig. 3 is perfectly correct, anonymous, fully unforgeable, traceable, and satisfies tracing soundness if the building blocks satisfy the security definitions in Sect. 3.*

Since all the building blocks can be constructed from (doubly enhanced) trapdoor permutations, we get as a corollary that trapdoor permutations imply the existence of accountable ring signatures.

5   Efficient Instantiation

We give here an efficient instantiation of the generic construction from Fig. 3. The instantiation is secure in the random oracle model under the well-established DDH assumption. As specified in Sect. 3, we instantiate f with group exponentiation and the IND-CPA encryption scheme with ElGamal. We will get the Signature of Knowledge and NIZK proof for the relations $\mathcal{R}_{\mathrm{sig}}$ and $\mathcal{R}_{\mathrm{open}}$ by applying the Fiat-Shamir transform to suitable Σ-protocols for these relations. Thanks to the straightline f-Extractability of our instantiation of the signature of knowledge, we can answer the adversary's Open queries in the anonymity game by extracting $vk = f(sk)$ from σ_{SoK} without rewinding.

Details of the Σ-Protocols. For all Σ-protocols, the setup includes the group description gk and the common reference string $crs := (ck, ek)$, where $ck \leftarrow \text{CGen}(gk)$, $(ek, \tau) \leftarrow \text{PKEGen}(gk)$ and $ek = g^\tau$ for $\tau \leftarrow \mathbb{Z}_q^*$, for the Pedersen commitment scheme and the ElGamal encryption scheme, respectively. The proofs of the lemmata can be found in Appendix B.

Committed bits. We first give a Σ-protocol for a commitment B having an opening consisting of sequences of bits, where in each sequence there is exactly one 1. More precisely, we give in Fig. 4 a Σ-protocol $(\mathcal{G}_{crs}, \mathcal{P}_1, \mathcal{V}_1)$ for the relation

$$\mathcal{R}_1 = \left\{ \begin{array}{c} (B, (b_{0,0}, \ldots, b_{m-1,n-1}, r)): \\ (\forall i, j : b_{j,i} \in \{0, 1\}) \wedge (\forall j : \sum_{i=0}^{n-1} b_{j,i} = 1) \wedge B = \text{Com}_{ck}(b_{0,0}, \ldots, b_{m-1,n-1}; r) \end{array} \right\}$$

The main idea is to prove that $b_{j,i}(1 - b_{j,i}) = 0$ for all i, j, and also that $\sum_{i=1}^{n} b_{j,i} = 1$.

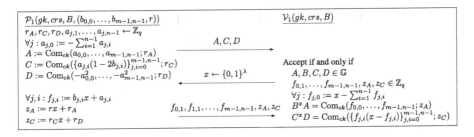

Fig. 4. Σ-protocol for relation $\mathcal{R}_1$.

Lemma 1. *The Σ-protocol in Fig. 4 is perfectly complete, perfect SHVZK, computational 3-special sound and has quasi-unique responses.*

List Containing Encryption of 1. We now describe a Σ-protocol that a list of N ElGamal ciphertexts $(c_0, \ldots, c_{N-1})$ includes an encryption of 1. More precisely, we give a Σ-protocol $(\mathcal{G}_{crs}, \mathcal{P}_2, \mathcal{V}_2)$ (see Fig. 5) for the relation:

$$\mathcal{R}_2 = \left\{ ((\{c_i\}_{i=0}^{N-1}), (\ell, r)) : (\forall i, c_i \in \mathbb{G}^2) \wedge \ell \in \{0, \ldots, N-1\} \wedge c_\ell = \text{Enc}_{ek}(1; r) \right\}$$

This generalizes easily to other homomorphic encryption and commitment schemes.

Since we can pad the list with copies of the last ciphertext (at little extra cost in the protocol), we may assume $N = n^m$. We will later discuss the efficiency implications of different choices of n. The idea behind our Σ-protocol is to prove knowledge of an index ℓ for which the product $\prod_{i=0}^{N-1} c_i^{\delta_{\ell,i}}$ is an encryption of 1, where as usual $\delta_{\ell,i} = 1$ when $i = \ell$ and $\delta_{\ell,i} = 0$ otherwise. We have $\delta_{\ell,i} = \prod_{j=0}^{m-1} \delta_{\ell_j, i_j}$, where $\ell = \sum_{j=0}^{m-1} \ell_j n^j$ and $i = \sum_{j=0}^{m-1} i_j n^j$ are the n-ary representations of ℓ and i respectively.

The prover first commits to m sequences of n bits $(\delta_{\ell_j,0}, \ldots, \delta_{\ell_j,n-1})$. It runs the Σ-protocol in Fig. 4 to prove that the commitment is well-formed. On receiving a challenge x, the prover discloses elements $f_{j,i} = \delta_{\ell_j,i}x + a_{j,i}$ as in Fig. 4. Observe that for every $i \in \{0, \ldots, N-1\}$, the product $\prod_{j=0}^{m-1} f_{j,i_j}$ is the evaluation at x of the polynomial $p_i(x) = \prod_{j=0}^{m-1}(\delta_{\ell_j,i}x + a_{j,i})$. For $0 \leq i \leq N-1$, we have:

$$p_i(x) = \prod_{j=0}^{m-1} \delta_{\ell_j,i_j}x + \sum_{k=0}^{m-1} p_{i,k}x^k = \delta_{\ell,i}x^m + \sum_{k=0}^{m-1} p_{i,k}x^k, \tag{1}$$

for some coefficients $p_{i,k}$ depending on ℓ and $a_{j,i}$. Note that $p_{i,k}$ can be computed by the prover independently of x, and that $p_\ell(x)$ is the only degree m polynomial amongst $p_0(x), \ldots, p_{N-1}(x)$. From these coefficients and some random noise values ρ_k, the prover computes ciphertexts $G_k := \prod_{i=0}^{N-1} c_i^{p_{i,k}} \cdot \mathrm{Enc}_{ek}(1; \rho_k)$ and includes them in the initial message. These ciphertexts are then used to cancel out the low degree terms in (1). Namely, if c_ℓ is an encryption of 1, the following product is an encryption of 1 for any x

$$\prod_{i=0}^{N-1} c_i^{\prod_{j=0}^{m-1} f_{j,i_j}} \cdot \prod_{k=0}^{m-1} G_k^{-x^k} = \left(\prod_{i=0}^{N-1} c_i^{\delta_{\ell,i}}\right)^{x^m}.$$

$\mathcal{P}_2(gk, crs, (c_0, \ldots, c_{N-1}), (\ell, r))$		$\mathcal{V}_2(gk, crs, (c_0, \ldots, c_{N-1}))$
$r_B, \rho_k \leftarrow \mathbb{Z}_q$		
$B := \mathrm{Com}_{ck}(\delta_{\ell_0,0}, \ldots, \delta_{\ell_{m-1},n-1}; r_B)$		
$(A,C,D) \leftarrow \mathcal{P}_1(gk, crs, B, (\{\delta_{\ell_j,i}\}_{j=0}^{m-1,n-1}, r_B))$		
For $k = 0, \ldots, m-1$		
$\quad G_k = \prod_{i=0}^{N-1} c_i^{p_{i,k}} \cdot \mathrm{Enc}_{ek}(1; \rho_k)$	$\xrightarrow{\;A,B,C,D,\{G_k\}_{k=0}^{m-1}\;}$	Accept if and only if
$\quad$ using $p_{i,k}$ from (1)		$A, B, C, D, G_0, \ldots, G_{m-1} \in \mathbb{G}$
	$\xleftarrow{\;x \leftarrow \{0,1\}^\lambda\;}$	$f_{0,1}, \ldots, f_{m-1,n-1}, z_A, z_C, z \in \mathbb{Z}_q$
		$\mathcal{V}_1(gk, crs, B, x, A, B, C, \{f_{j,i}\}_{j=0,i=1}^{m-1,n-1}, z_A, z_C) = 1$
$(f_{0,1}, \ldots, f_{m-1,n-1}, z_A, z_C) \leftarrow \mathcal{P}_1(x)$	$\xrightarrow{\;f_{0,1}, \ldots, f_{m-1,n-1}, z_A, z_C, z\;}$	$\forall j : f_{j,0} := x - \sum_{i=1}^{n-1} f_{j,i}$
$z := rx^m - \sum_{k=0}^{m-1} \rho_k x^k$		$\prod_{i=0}^{N-1} c_i^{\prod_{j=1}^{m} f_{j,i_j}} \cdot \prod_{k=0}^{m-1} G_k^{-x^k} = \mathrm{Enc}_{ek}(1; z)$

Fig. 5. Σ-protocol for a list $c_0, \ldots, c_{N-1}$ containing an encryption of 1

Lemma 2. *Let $m \geq 2$. The Σ-protocol in Fig. 5 is perfectly complete, SHVZK, $(m+1)$-special sound and has quasi-unique responses.*

Correct Signature. We give in Fig. 6 a Σ-protocol for the relation $\mathcal{R}_{\mathrm{sig}} = \{((pk, m, R, c), (sk, r)) : sk \in \mathbb{Z}_q \wedge vk = g^{sk} \in R \subset \mathbb{G}^* \wedge c = \mathrm{Enc}_{pk}(vk; r)\}$

Lemma 3. *The Σ-protocol in Fig. 6 is perfectly complete, SHVZK, $m+1$-special sound and has quasi-unique responses.*

Lemma 4. *Applying the Fiat-Shamir transformation to the protocol in Fig. 6 with SoKSetup as in Sect. 5 produces a signature of knowledge in the random oracle model, that is extractable and straightline f-extractable.*

$\mathcal{P}_{sig}(gk, crs, (pk, m, R, c), (r, sk))$		$\mathcal{V}_{sig}(gk, crs, (pk, m, R, c))$
$s, t, r_a, r_b \leftarrow \mathbb{Z}_q; d \leftarrow \mathrm{Enc}_{ek}(g^{sk}; t)$		
$A \leftarrow \mathrm{Enc}_{pk}(g^s; r_a); B \leftarrow \mathrm{Enc}_{ek}(g^s; r_b)$	d, A, B, a_2	**Accept iff**
$c_0 := d \cdot \mathrm{Enc}_{ek}(vk_0^{-1}; 0), \ldots, c_{N-1} := d \cdot \mathrm{Enc}_{ek}(vk_{N-1}^{-1}; 0)$	$\xrightarrow{\hspace{2cm}}$	$R \subset \mathbb{G}; pk \in \mathbb{G}^*; d, A, B \in \mathbb{G}^2$
$a_2 \leftarrow \mathcal{P}_2(gk, crs, (c_0, \ldots, c_{N-1}), (\ell, t))$	$x \leftarrow \{0,1\}^\lambda$	$z_s, z_a, z_b \in \mathbb{Z}_q$
	$\xleftarrow{\hspace{2cm}}$	
$z_s := sk \cdot x + s ; z_a := rx + r_a ; z_b := tx + r_b$	z_a, z_b, z_s, z_2	$c^x A = \mathrm{Enc}_{pk}(g^{z_s}; z_a)$
$z_2 \leftarrow \mathcal{P}_2(x)$	$\xrightarrow{\hspace{2cm}}$	$d^x B = \mathrm{Enc}_{ek}(g^{z_s}; z_b)$
		$\mathcal{V}_2(gk, crs, (c_0, \ldots, c_{N-1}), a_2, x, z_2) = 1$

Fig. 6. Σ-protocol for $\mathcal{R}_{sig}$.

Proof. For simulatability, SoKSimSetup is identical to SoKSetup and SoKSimSign programs the random oracle to simulate proofs. Simulatability then follows from SHVZK.

For extractability we rely on rewinding, $m + 1$ special soundness and quasi-unique responses, using [FKMV12]. For straightline f-extractability, we use the trapdoor τ to decrypt d in the proof transcript and obtain $vk = f(sk)$. $\square$

Correct Opening. Writing out the details of ElGamal encryption we get

$$\mathcal{R}_{open} = \left\{ \begin{array}{c} ((pk, c, vk), dk) : \\ dk \in \mathbb{Z}_q \wedge pk = g^{dk} \neq 1 \wedge c = (u, v) \in \mathbb{G}^2 \wedge vk \in \mathbb{G} \wedge (v/vk)^{dk} = u \end{array} \right\}$$

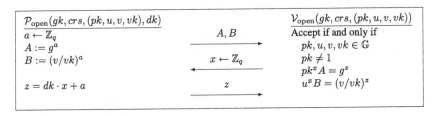

$\mathcal{P}_{open}(gk, crs, (pk, u, v, vk), dk)$		$\mathcal{V}_{open}(gk, crs, (pk, u, v, vk))$
$a \leftarrow \mathbb{Z}_q$	A, B	**Accept if and only if**
$A := g^a$	$\xrightarrow{\hspace{1.5cm}}$	$pk, u, v, vk \in \mathbb{G}$
$B := (v/vk)^a$	$x \leftarrow \mathbb{Z}_q$	$pk \neq 1$
	$\xleftarrow{\hspace{1.5cm}}$	$pk^x A = g^z$
$z = dk \cdot x + a$	z	$u^x B = (v/vk)^z$
	$\xrightarrow{\hspace{1.5cm}}$	

Fig. 7. Σ-protocol for correct decryption.

Lemma 5. *The Σ-protocol in Fig. 7 is perfectly complete, perfect SHVZK, perfect 2-special sound and has unique responses. Also, applying the Fiat-Shamir transformation to it produces a NIZK proof.*

Efficiency of Our Schemes. The efficiency of our schemes is determined by the signature of knowledge of Fig. 6. For a ring of $N = n^m$ users, this requires the prover to send $m + 4$ ElGamal ciphertexts, 4 Pedersen commitments and $m(n - 1) + 6$ elements of $\mathbb{Z}_q$. A full accountable ring signature includes an additional ElGamal encryption, i.e. $2m + 12$ group elements and $m(n-1) + 6$ field elements in total.

A signature can be computed using $mN + 3mn + 2m + 12$ group exponentiations as follows. Computing A, C and D in the bit proof requires $2mn + 3$ exponentiations since exponentiation by $(1 - 2b_{i,j})$ amounts to a multiplication. By construction of c_i in Fig. 6, the first components of all c_i are identical in

Fig. 5, so computing the first components of all G_k costs $2m$ exponentiations. The second components of all G_k requires $mN + m$ exponentiations. We also need 9 exponentiations to compute B in Fig. 5, d, A and B in Fig. 6, and the ElGamal encryption of the public key.

Signatures can be verified using $N + 2mn + 2m + 15$ group exponentiations as follows: $N + 2m + 3$ exponentiations for the last verification equation in Fig. 5, $2mn + 4$ for the equations in Figs. 4 and 8 for the first two verification equations in Fig. 6.

Our schemes can be instantiated over any group $\mathbb{G}$ where the DDH problem is computationally hard. Let us say the security parameter λ determines the bit size of the field elements as $|q| \approx \lambda$ bits and let $N = \text{poly}(\lambda)$. When group elements are much larger than field elements, say more than a factor λ, it is convenient to choose a large n. For instance, setting $n = \lambda + 1$ (in which case $m = O(1)$) the communication complexity amounts to a constant number of group elements and $m\lambda + 6$ field elements. When group and field elements are of roughly the same size, as can be the case for elliptic curve groups, our signatures have total size $m(n + 1) + 18$ elements. Setting $n = 4$ gives communication of roughly $5 \log_4 N + 18 = \frac{5}{2} \log_2 N + 18$ elements.

In Fig. 8, we compare our instantiation with prior work. Since our signatures require a logarithmic number of group elements, they enjoy shorter sizes than all previous signatures based on RSA and/or DDH assumptions, for sufficiently large security parameters. Indeed, a constant number of RSA ring elements typically requires $O(\lambda^3)$ bits whereas the elliptic curve instantiation of our protocol achieves $O(\lambda \log N)$ bit size. As long as λ is large enough and $N \leq 2^{\lambda^2}$, our signatures will be shorter. Our signatures are also a factor 2.8 shorter than Groth and Kohlweiss ring signatures.

Scheme	Signature Size	Assumptions	Type
[ACJT00]	$3\mathbb{Z}_n^* + 4\mathbb{Z}$	Strong RSA	Group
[CL02]	$6\mathbb{Z}_n^* + 8\mathbb{Z}$	Strong RSA	Group
[DKNS04]	$12\mathbb{Z}_n^* + 12\mathbb{Z}$	Strong RSA	Ring/Group
[CG05]	$4\mathbb{Z}_n^* + 4\mathbb{Z}$	Strong RSA + DDH	Group
[GK15]	$(4 \log_2 N)\mathbb{G} + (3 \log_2 N + 1)\mathbb{Z}_q^*$	DDH	Ring
Ours	$(\log_2 N + 12)\mathbb{G} + \frac{1}{2}(3 \log_2 N + 12)\mathbb{Z}_q^*$	DDH	Ring/Group

Fig. 8. Efficiency comparison between our instantiation and most efficient group and ring signatures based on RSA and/or DDH assumptions. $\mathbb{Z}_n^*, \mathbb{Z}, \mathbb{G}, \mathbb{Z}_q^*$ represent the size of RSA ring elements, integers, group elements and field elements, respectively.

A   Proof of Theorem 1

Proof. Perfect correctness follows from that of the building blocks and is easy to verify. Lemmata 6–9 complete the rest of the proof.

Lemma 6. *The accountable ring signature scheme in Fig. 3 is anonymous.*

Proof. We start by replacing the algorithm SoKSetup of the signature of knowledge with SoKSimSetup, and when answering the challenge query, we use SoKSimSign instead of SoKSign. By the SimExt security of the SoK, the adversary has a negligible probability in distinguishing between the two settings. This ensures that the signature of knowledge σ_{SoK} reveals no information about the underlying witness.

Next, we replace the algorithm CRSGen of the NIZK system with SimCRSGen and when answering opening queries, we use SimProve instead of Prove. By the zero-knowledge property of the NIZK system, the adversary has a negligible probability in distinguishing between the two settings.

Now, we modify the Open oracle into Open' such that instead of decrypting the ciphertext, we run SoKExtract to extract the verification key vk from the signature of knowledge σ_{SoK}. By the SimExt security of the signature of knowledge, with overwhelming probability in each query, we get the same vk as the plaintext of c.

As we are no longer using the decryption algorithm, by the IND-CPA security of the encryption scheme, the probability of $\mathcal{A}$ winning the anonymity game is close to $\frac{1}{2}$.

Lemma 7. *The accountable ring signature scheme in Fig. 3 is fully unforgeable.*

Proof. We start by running the Setup algorithm as normal with the exception that here we replace SoKSetup with SoKSimSetup. We forward pp to the adversary. By the simulatability of the signature of knowledge, the adversary has a negligible probability in distinguishing between the two settings. From now on, we use SoKSimSign instead of SoKSign when answering Sign queries. The adversary can win in two ways:

- **Case I:** The adversary forges a valid ring signature on a message m w.r.t. an honest ring R where $(pk, \cdot, m, R, \sigma) \notin Q_{\mathsf{Sign}}$. By the SimExt security of the signature of knowledge, we can extract a valid witness for the statement $(pk, R, c) \in \mathcal{L}_{\mathcal{R}_{\mathrm{sig}}}$ from which we obtain (vk, sk) such that $vk := f(sk) \in R$. We use this to break the one-wayness of the function f which contradicts the security of the function f.
- **Case II:** The adversary outputs a valid ring signature $\sigma := (c, \sigma_{\mathsf{SoK}})$ on a message m w.r.t. a ring R and a proof ψ that the honest user with key vk produced the signature while such user never did so.
  We start by guessing the user the adversary is going to frame. We have a probability $\frac{1}{\eta(\lambda)}$ of guessing correctly, where $\eta(\lambda)$ is a polynomial representing an upper bound on the number of honest users $\mathcal{A}$ uses in the game. By the soundness of the NIZK system, ψ is a proof for a valid statement $(pk, c, vk) \in \mathcal{L}_{\mathcal{R}_{\mathrm{open}}}$. In the game, we abort if $\mathcal{A}$ asks for the secret key of the user we guessed. For all other honest users, we have chosen their key pairs ourselves and thus know their secret keys.

Again, by the SimExt of the signature of knowledge, with overwhelming probability, we can extract a valid witness for the statement $(pk, R, c) \in \mathcal{L}_{\mathcal{R}_{\text{sig}}}$ from σ_{SoK}, from which we obtain (vk, sk) such that $vk := f(sk) \in R$. We use this to break the one-wayness of f which contradicts the security of the function f.

Lemma 8. *The accountable ring signature scheme in Fig. 3 is traceable.*

Proof. By the security of the signature of knowledge, we are able to extract a valid witness from σ_{SoK} part of the valid signature $\sigma = (c, \sigma_{\text{SoK}})$ the adversary outputs. The witness thus satisfies $vk = f(sk)$ where $vk \in R \subset \text{VK}$, $pk \in \text{PK}$ and $c = \text{Enc}(pk, vk; r)$ for some $r \in \text{Rnd}$ and $sk \in \text{SK}$.

Since $pk = \text{PKEGen}(gk; dk)$, we see from $pk \neq \bot$ that $dk \in \text{DK}$. Correctness of the encryption algorithm implies that $\text{Dec}(dk, c) = vk$, which is the first part of the opening algorithm's output. Now the opening algorithm has a statement (pk, c, vk) and a corresponding witness dk. By the completeness of the NIZK proof system, ψ will verify correctly. This means that the Judge algorithm will output 1 which is a contradiction.

Lemma 9. *The construction satisfies tracing soundness if* SoK *is SimExt secure, the NIZK proof system is sound and the encryption scheme is perfectly correct.*

Proof. The SimExt security of the signature of knowledge ensures that from any signature σ_{SoK} (w.r.t. a statment s) output by the adversary, we can extract a valid witness w such that $(s, w) \in \mathcal{R}_{\text{sig}}$ which eliminates the case that the adversary forges a signature for a statement $s^* \notin \mathcal{L}_{\mathcal{R}_{\text{sig}}}$. If this is not the case, we can use such an adversary to construct another adversary against the SimExt security of the signature of knowledge.

The soundness of the NIZK system for the relation $\mathcal{R}_{\text{open}}$ ensures that ciphertext c contained in the ring signature decrypts to vk, which eliminates the case that the adversary can produce a proof ψ for a statement $s^* \notin \mathcal{L}_{\mathcal{R}_{\text{open}}}$. Finally, the perfect correctness of the public-key encryption scheme (which is regarded as a perfectly-binding commitment scheme) ensures that a ciphertext has a unique decryption.

B   Security Proofs of Our Σ-Protocols

B.1   Proof of Lemma 1

Proof. Perfect completeness follows by inspection. The SHVZK simulator, given a challenge x, can simulate the transcript by picking $f_{0,1}, \ldots, f_{m-1,n-1}, z_A, z_C \leftarrow \mathbb{Z}_q$, $C \leftarrow \mathbb{G}$ and computing $f_{j,0} := x - \sum_{i=1}^{n-1} f_{j,i}$, $A := \text{Com}_{ck}(f_{0,0}, \ldots, f_{m-1,n-1}, z_A)B^{-x}$, $D = \text{Com}_{ck}(\{f_{i,j}(x - f_{i,j})\}_{i,j=0}^{m-1,n-1}; z_C)C^{-x}$. In both simulations and real proofs, $f_{0,1}, \ldots, f_{m-1,n-1}, z_A, z_C$ and C are independent, uniformly random and uniquely determine $\{f_{j,0}\}_{j=0}^{m-1}, A, D$, so the simulation is perfect. We also have quasi-unique responses, since two different valid answers

$f_{0,1}, \ldots, f_{m-1,n-1}, z_A, z_C$ and $f'_{0,1}, \ldots, f'_{m-1,n-1}, z'_A, z'_C$ to one challenge would break the binding property of $B^x A$ and $C^x D$.

We prove 3-special soundness in three parts. First, we show that any answers to 3 (actually 2) different challenges provide an opening of B. Second, we show that these answers imply that committed values are bits. Finally, we show that they imply that the sum of the committed values is 1. For the first part, suppose that a prover has answered two different challenges x, x' correctly with answers $(f_{0,1}, \ldots, f_{m-1,n-1}, z_A, z_C)$ and $(f'_{0,1}, \ldots, f'_{m-1,n-1}, z'_A, z'_C)$. Since we have $B^x A = \mathrm{Com}_{ck}(f_{0,0}, \ldots, f_{m-1,n-1}; z_A)$ and $B^{x'} A = \mathrm{Com}_{ck}(f'_{0,0}, \ldots, f'_{m-1,n-1}; z'_A)$, from the first verification equation we have $B^{x-x'} = \mathrm{Com}_{ck}(f_{0,0} - f'_{0,0}, \ldots, f_{m-1,n-1} - f'_{m-1,n-1}; z_A - z'_A)$. Thus $b_{i,j} = \frac{f_{i,j} - f'_{i,j}}{x - x'}$, with $r = \frac{z_A - z'_A}{x - x'}$, gives us an opening of B. The first verification equation also gives an opening $(a_0, \ldots, a_0; r_A)$ of A using $a_{j,i} = f_{j,i} - x b_{j,i}$ and $r_A = z_A - x r$. Note that by the binding properties of the commitment scheme, the prover cannot know a second opening of A or B, and must respond to any challenge with $f_{j,i} = b_{j,i} x + a_{j,i}$. We can get openings of C and D to values $c_{j,i}, d_{j,i}$ from the second equation in a similar way.

By the second verification equation, the values satisfy $c_{j,i} x + d_{j,i} = f_{j,i}(x - f_{j,i}) = b_{j,i}(1 - b_{j,i})x^2 + (1 - 2b_{j,i})a_{j,i} x - a_{j,i}^2$. If this holds for three different x, x' and x'' then the polynomials are identical. So, $b_{j,i}(1 - b_{j,i}) = 0$ and $b_{j,i} \in \{0, 1\}$ for all i, j.

By construction we have $\sum_{i=0}^{n-1} f_{j,i} = \sum_{i=0}^{n-1} b_{j,i} x + \sum_{i=0}^{n-1} a_{j,i} = x$ for all $j = 0, \ldots, m - 1$. This holds for two challenges x and x'. Therefore $\sum_{i=0}^{n-1} b_{j,i} = 1$. $\square$

B.2 Proof of Lemma 2

Proof. First we prove perfect completeness. By the perfect completeness of the Σ-protocol in Fig. 4 we have that $\mathcal{V}_1$ always accepts. Correctness of the last equation follows from the homomorphic property of ElGamal encryption since

$$
\prod_{i=0}^{N-1} c_i^{\prod_{j=0}^{m-1} f_{j,i_j}} \cdot \prod_{k=0}^{m-1} G_k^{-x^k} = \prod_{i=0}^{N-1} c_i^{p_i(x)} \cdot \prod_{k=0}^{m-1} \left(\prod_{i=0}^{N-1} c_i^{p_{i,k}} \cdot \mathrm{Enc}(1; \rho_k) \right)^{-x^k}
$$

$$
= \prod_{i=0}^{N-1} c_i^{p_i(x)} \cdot \prod_{k=0}^{m-1} \left(\prod_{i=0}^{N-1} c_i^{-p_{i,k} x^k} \cdot \mathrm{Enc}(1; -x^k \rho_k) \right)
$$

$$
= \prod_{i=0}^{N-1} c_i^{p_i(x)} \cdot \prod_{i=0}^{N-1} c_i^{-\sum_{k=0}^{m-1} p_{i,k} x^k} \cdot \mathrm{Enc}\left(1; -\sum_{k=0}^{m-1} x^k \rho_k\right)
$$

$$
= \prod_{i=0}^{N-1} c_i^{\delta_{\ell,i} x^m} \cdot \mathrm{Enc}\left(1; -\sum_{k=0}^{m-1} x^k \rho_k\right) = c_\ell^{x^m} \mathrm{Enc}\left(1; -\sum_{k=0}^{m-1} x^k \rho_k\right)
$$

$$
= \mathrm{Enc}(1; r x^m) \cdot \mathrm{Enc}\left(1; -\sum_{k=0}^{m-1} x^k \rho_k\right) = \mathrm{Enc}(1; z).
$$

We now describe a special honest verifier zero-knowledge simulator. It picks $B \leftarrow \mathbb{G}$ and $G_1, \ldots, G_{m-1} \leftarrow \mathbb{G}^2$. It runs the SHVZK simulator for $\mathcal{P}_1$ to simulate $A, C, D, z_A, z_C, f_{0,1}, \ldots, f_{m-1,n-1}$ and computes the $f_{j,0}$'s accordingly. It picks $z \leftarrow \mathbb{Z}_q$ and computes G_0 from the last verification equation.

By the DDH assumption, $G_1, \ldots, G_{m-1}$ in a real proof are indistinguishable from picking random pairs in $\mathbb{G}^2$ as in the simulation. We get independent, uniformly random B and z in both real proofs and simulations. By the perfect SHVZK of the simulator for $\mathcal{P}_1$ we also have the same distribution of $A, B, C, f_{j,i}, z_A, z_C$ as in a real proof. Finally, G_0 is uniquely determined by the last verification equation in both real proofs and in simulations, so the two are indistinguishable. The last verification equation uniquely determines z, thus quasi-unique responses follow from the quasi-unique responses of the underlying Σ-protocol for $\mathcal{R}_1$.

Now we prove the protocol is $(m+1)$-special sound. Suppose an adversary can produce $(m+1)$ different accepting responses $(f_{j,i}^{(0)}, z^{(0)}), \ldots, (f_{j,i}^{(m)}, z^{(m)})$ with respect to $m+1$ different challenges $x^{(0)}, \ldots, x^{(m)}$ and the same initial message. Assume that $m > 1$. We use 3-special soundness of the Σ-protocol for $\mathcal{R}_1$ to extract openings $\delta_{\ell_j,i}, a_{j,i}$ for B and A with $\delta_{\ell_j,i} \in \{0,1\}$ and $\sum_{i=0}^{n-1} \delta_{\ell_j,i} = 1$. The openings define $\ell := \sum_{j=0}^{m-1} \ell_j n^j$, where ℓ_j is the index of the only 1 in the sequence $(\delta_{\ell_j,0}, \ldots, \delta_{\ell_j,n-1})$. Following the proof, all answers satisfy $f_{j,i}^{(e)} = \delta_{\ell_j,i} x^{(e)} + a_{j,i}$ for $0 \le e \le m$, with overwhelming probability due to the binding property of the commitment scheme.

From $\delta_{\ell_j,i}, a_{j,i}$ we can compute the polynomials $p_i(x) = \prod_{j=0}^{m-1}(\delta_{\ell_j,i} x + a_{j,i})$. Note that $p_\ell(x)$ is the only such polynomial with degree m in x. Based on this observation we rewrite the last verification equation as: $c_\ell^{x^m} \cdot \prod_{k=0}^{m-1} \tilde{G}_k^{x^k} = \mathrm{Enc}(1; z)$. Here the $\tilde{G}_k$ values are derived from the initial statement and $\delta_{\ell_j,i}, a_{j,i}$. This equation holds for $x^{(0)}, \ldots, x^{(m)}$. Consider the Vandermonde matrix with the eth row given by $(1, x^{(e)}, \ldots, (x^{(e)})^m)$. The $x^{(e)}$ values are distinct, so the matrix is invertible. We can thus obtain a linear combination $\theta_0, \ldots, \theta_n$ of the rows producing the vector $(0, \ldots, 0, 1)$. We deduce $c_\ell = \prod_{e=0}^{m} \left(c_\ell^{(x^{(e)})^m} \cdot \prod_{k=0}^{m-1} \tilde{G}_k^{(x^{(e)})^k} \right)^{\theta_e} = \mathrm{Enc}\left(1; \sum_{e=0}^{m} \theta_e z^{(e)}\right)$, which provides an opening of c_ℓ to the plaintext 1 with randomness $r = \sum_{e=0}^{m} \theta_e z^{(e)}$. $\square$

B.3   Proof of Lemma 3

Proof. Perfect completeness follows by direct verification and the perfect completeness of $(\mathcal{P}_2, \mathcal{V}_2)$. The SHVZK simulator chooses $z_a, z_b, z_s \leftarrow \mathbb{Z}_q$ and $d \leftarrow \mathbb{G}^2$ at random and computes A, B from the verification equations. It runs the perfect SHVZK simulator for $\mathcal{P}_2$ to get a_2 and z_2. By the DDH assumption, d is indistinguishable from the ciphertexts in the real proof. In Both real proofs and simulations, z_a, z_b, z_t are uniformly random and uniquely determine A, B giving us SHVZK. Since the verification equations uniquely determine z_a, z_b and z_s and $(\mathcal{P}_2, \mathcal{V}_2)$ has quasi-unique responses, so must this protocol.

For $(m+1)$-special soundness, consider accepting answers z_a, z_b, z_s and z_a', z_b', z_s' to distinct challenges x and x'. From the first verification equation we get $c^{x-x'} = \mathrm{Enc}_{pk}(g^{z_s - z_s'}; z_a - z_a')$ giving $sk = \frac{z_s - z_s'}{x - x'}$ and $r = \frac{z_a - z_a'}{x - x'}$. The second verification equation gives $d^{x-x'} = \mathrm{Enc}_{pk}(g^{z_s - z_s'}; z_b - z_b')$ so d also encrypts g^{sk}. Finally, $(m+1)$-special soundness of the Σ-protocol for $\mathcal{R}_2$ then shows that $g^{sk} \in R$. $\square$

B.4   Proof of Lemma 5

Proof. Perfect completeness follows by direct verification. The SHVZK simulator picks $z \leftarrow \mathbb{Z}_q$ and computes A, B from the verification equations. Both in real proofs and simulated proofs z is uniformly random and the verification equations determine the initial message uniquely, so we have perfect simulation. As the first verification equation determines z we have unique responses.

For 2-special soundness, let z and z' be accepting answers to distinct challenges x, x'. The first verification equation gives $pk^{x-x'} = g^{z-z'}$, so $dk = \frac{z-z'}{x-x'}$. The second gives $u^{x-x'} = (v/vk)^{z-z'}$, which shows $u = (v/vk)^{dk}$. Thus, vk was encrypted in (u, v). □

References

ACHdM05. Ateniese, G., Camenisch, J., Hohenberger, S., de Medeiros, B.: Practical group signatures without random oracles. Cryptology ePrint Archive, Report 2005/385 (2005). http://eprint.iacr.org/

ACJT00. Ateniese, G., Camenisch, J.L., Joye, M., Tsudik, G.: A practical and provably secure coalition-resistant group signature scheme. In: Bellare, M. (ed.) CRYPTO 2000. LNCS, vol. 1880, pp. 255–270. Springer, Heidelberg (2000)

BBS04. Boneh, D., Boyen, X., Shacham, H.: Short group signatures. In: Franklin, M. (ed.) CRYPTO 2004. LNCS, vol. 3152, pp. 41–55. Springer, Heidelberg (2004)

BCKL08. Belenkiy, M., Chase, M., Kohlweiss, M., Lysyanskaya, A.: P-signatures and noninteractive anonymous credentials. In: Canetti, R. (ed.) TCC 2008. LNCS, vol. 4948, pp. 356–374. Springer, Heidelberg (2008)

BKM09. Bender, A., Katz, J., Morselli, R.: Ring signatures: stronger definitions, and constructions without random oracles. J. Cryptology **22**(1), 114 (2009)

BMW03. Bellare, M., Micciancio, D., Warinschi, B.: Foundations of group signatures: formal definitions, simplified requirements, and a construction based on general assumptions. In: Biham, E. (ed.) EUROCRYPT 2003. LNCS, vol. 2656. Springer, Heidelberg (2003)

BSZ05. Bellare, M., Shi, H., Zhang, C.: Foundations of group signatures: the case of dynamic groups. In: Menezes, A. (ed.) CT-RSA 2005. LNCS, vol. 3376, pp. 136–153. Springer, Heidelberg (2005)

BW07. Boyen, X., Waters, B.: Full-domain subgroup hiding and constant-size group signatures. In: Okamoto, T., Wang, X. (eds.) PKC 2007. LNCS, vol. 4450, pp. 1–15. Springer, Heidelberg (2007)

Cam97. Camenisch, J.L.: Efficient and generalized group signatures. In: Fumy, W. (ed.) EUROCRYPT 1997. LNCS, vol. 1233, pp. 465–479. Springer, Heidelberg (1997)

CG05. Camenisch, J.L., Groth, J.: Group signatures: better efficiency and new theoretical aspects. In: Blundo, C., Cimato, S. (eds.) SCN 2004. LNCS, vol. 3352, pp. 120–133. Springer, Heidelberg (2005)

CKS09. Camenisch, J., Kohlweiss, M., Soriente, C.: An accumulator based on bilinear maps and efficient revocation for anonymous credentials. In: Jarecki, S., Tsudik, G. (eds.) PKC 2009. LNCS, vol. 5443, pp. 481–500. Springer, Heidelberg (2009)

264   J. Bootle et al.

CL02.   Camenisch, J.L., Lysyanskaya, A.: Dynamic accumulators and application to efficient revocation of anonymous credentials. In: Yung, M. (ed.) CRYPTO 2002. LNCS, vol. 2442, pp. 61–76. Springer, Heidelberg (2002)

CL06.   Chase, M., Lysyanskaya, A.: On signatures of knowledge. In: Dwork, C. (ed.) CRYPTO 2006. LNCS, vol. 4117, pp. 78–96. Springer, Heidelberg (2006)

CvH91. Chaum, D., van Heyst, E.: Group signatures. In: Davies, D.W. (ed.) EUROCRYPT 1991. LNCS, vol. 547, pp. 257–265. Springer, Heidelberg (1991)

DKNS04. Dodis, Y., Kiayias, A., Nicolosi, A., Shoup, V.: Anonymous identification in Ad Hoc groups. In: Cachin, C., Camenisch, J.L. (eds.) EUROCRYPT 2004. LNCS, vol. 3027, pp. 609–626. Springer, Heidelberg (2004)

Fis05. Fischlin, M.: Communication-efficient non-interactive proofs of knowledge with online extractors. In: Shoup, V. (ed.) CRYPTO 2005. LNCS, vol. 3621, pp. 152–168. Springer, Heidelberg (2005)

FKMV12. Faust, S., Kohlweiss, M., Marson, G.A., Venturi, D.: On the non-malleability of the Fiat-Shamir transform. In: Galbraith, S., Nandi, M. (eds.) INDOCRYPT 2012. LNCS, vol. 7668, pp. 60–79. Springer, Heidelberg (2012)

FS87.   Fiat, A., Shamir, A.: How to prove yourself: practical solutions to identification and signature problems. In: Odlyzko, A.M. (ed.) CRYPTO 1986. LNCS, vol. 263, pp. 186–194. Springer, Heidelberg (1987)

FS08.   Fujisaki, E., Suzuki, K.: Traceable ring signature. IEICE Trans. 91–A(1), 83 (2008)

FZ13.   Franklin, M., Zhang, H.: Unique ring signatures: a practical construction. In: Sadeghi, A.-R. (ed.) FC 2013. LNCS, vol. 7859, pp. 162–170. Springer, Heidelberg (2013)

GK15.   Groth, J., Kohlweiss, M.: One-out-of-many proofs: or how to leak a secret and spend a coin. In: Oswald, E., Fischlin, M. (eds.) EUROCRYPT 2015. LNCS, vol. 9057, pp. 253–280. Springer, Heidelberg (2015)

Gro07. Groth, J.: Fully anonymous group signatures without random oracles. In: Kurosawa, K. (ed.) ASIACRYPT 2007. LNCS, vol. 4833, pp. 164–180. Springer, Heidelberg (2007)

KY05.   Kiayias, A., Yung, M.: Group signatures with efficient concurrent join. In: Cramer, R. (ed.) EUROCRYPT 2005. LNCS, vol. 3494, pp. 198–214. Springer, Heidelberg (2005)

LLNW14. Langlois, A., Ling, S., Nguyen, K., Wang, H.: Lattice-based group signature scheme with verifier-local revocation. In: Krawczyk, H. (ed.) PKC 2014. LNCS, vol. 8383, pp. 345–361. Springer, Heidelberg (2014)

LPY12. Libert, B., Peters, T., Yung, M.: Group signatures with almost-for-free revocation. In: Safavi-Naini, R., Canetti, R. (eds.) CRYPTO 2012. LNCS, vol. 7417, pp. 571–589. Springer, Heidelberg (2012)

LWW04. Liu, J.K., Wei, V.K., Wong, D.S.: Linkable spontaneous anonymous group signature for ad hoc groups. In: Wang, H., Pieprzyk, J., Varadharajan, V. (eds.) ACISP 2004. LNCS, vol. 3108, pp. 325–335. Springer, Heidelberg (2004)

Ngu05. Nguyen, L.: Accumulators from bilinear pairings and applications. In: Menezes, A. (ed.) CT-RSA 2005. LNCS, vol. 3376, pp. 275–292. Springer, Heidelberg (2005)

NSN04. Nguyen, L., Safavi-Naini, R.: Efficient and provably secure trapdoor-free group signature schemes from bilinear pairings. In: Lee, P.J. (ed.) ASI-ACRYPT 2004. LNCS, vol. 3329, pp. 372–386. Springer, Heidelberg (2004)

Ped91. Pedersen, T.P.: Non-interactive and information-theoretic secure verifiable secret sharing. In: Feigenbaum, J. (ed.) CRYPTO 1991. LNCS, vol. 576, pp. 129–140. Springer, Heidelberg (1992)

RST01. Rivest, R.L., Shamir, A., Tauman, Y.: How to leak a secret. In: Boyd, C. (ed.) ASIACRYPT 2001. LNCS, vol. 2248, pp. 552–565. Springer, Heidelberg (2001)

SSE+12. Sakai, Y., Schuldt, J.C.N., Emura, K., Hanaoka, G., Ohta, K.: On the security of dynamic group signatures: preventing signature hijacking. In: Fischlin, M., Buchmann, J., Manulis, M. (eds.) PKC 2012. LNCS, vol. 7293, pp. 715–732. Springer, Heidelberg (2012)

XY04. Xu, S., Yung, M.: Accountable ring signatures: a smart card approach. In: Quisquater, J.-J., Paradinas, P., Deswarte, Y., El Kalam, A.A. (eds.) Smart Card Research and Advanced Applications VI. IFIP, vol. 153, pp. 271–286. Springer, Boston (2004)

Updatable Hash Proof System
and Its Applications

Rupeng Yang[1,2], Qiuliang Xu[1](✉), Yongbin Zhou[2](✉), Rui Zhang[2](✉),
Chengyu Hu[1], and Zuoxia Yu[1,2]

[1] School of Computer Science and Technology,
Shandong University, Jinan 250101, China
orbbyrp@gmail.com, xql@sdu.edu.cn
[2] State Key Laboratory of Information Security (SKLOIS), Institute of Information
Engineering (IIE), Chinese Academy of Sciences (CAS), Beijing, China
{zhouyongbin,r-zhang}@iie.ac.cn

Abstract. To tackle with physical attacks to real world cryptosystems, leakage resilient cryptography was developed. In this setting, the adversary is allowed to have access to the internal state of a cryptographic system, thus violates the black-box reduction used in cryptography. Especially when considering continual memory leakage (CML), i.e., there is no predetermined bound on the leakage of the internal information, the task is extremely tough.

In this paper, we solve this problem by introducing a new primitive called updatable hash proof system (UHPS). A UHPS can be viewed as a special Hash proof system (HPS), which served as a fundamental tool in constructing public key encryption (PKE) schemes in both leakage-free and leaky settings. A remarkable property of UHPS is that by simply substituting the HPS component with a UHPS component in a PKE scheme, one obtains a new PKE scheme secure in the CML setting. Moreover, the resulting PKE scheme enjoys the same advantage of the original HPS-based PKE, for instance, still "compatible" with known transforms [8,20,24,32]. We then give instantiations of UHPS from widely-accepted assumptions, including the symmetric external Diffie-Hellman assumption and the d-linear assumption. Interestingly, we notice that when instantiated with concrete assumptions, the resulting chosen-ciphertext secure PKE scheme is by far the most efficient.

1 Introduction

Side-channel attacks are fatal for a real-world cryptosystem. Notably, such attacks can violate the black-box "provable" security of schemes [3,5,17,21,22, 30,34]. For instance, the only known working attack for AES is via side-channel attacks [30]. Moreover, it is also possible to launch such an attack remotely, e.g., the timing attacks could break OpenSSL run on a network server [5].

R. Yang — This work was mainly done when doing the internship at SKLOIS, IIE, CAS.

G. Pernul et al. (Eds.): ESORICS 2015, Part I, LNCS 9326, pp. 266–285, 2015.
DOI: 10.1007/978-3-319-24174-6_14

Even worse, via the cold-boot attack, one can read the secret keys stored in the memory directly [17].

As for a countermeasure, engineers are always required to implement the scheme in an environment approximate to the theoretical assumptions, e.g., using extra protection circuits, adding random circles to CPU occupations, or adding metal shields against electromagnetic radiation. But in a word, there is no guarantee whether they have actually realized the design goal.

Leakage Resilient Cryptography. On the other hand, theorists intended to investigate this problem in a more rigorous way, so the leakage resilient cryptography came up. Micali and Reyzin [27] first introduced the notion of physically observable cryptography, where they assumed "computation and only computation leaks information" about the internal state. Many works follows their approach [12,14,31]. However, their assumption could not capture the cold-boot attack (memory attack) [17], namely, information leakage of the whole internal state can appear any time during the life span of the scheme.

To cope with memory attacks, Akavia et al. [2] proposed the *bounded memory leakage* (BML) model, where adversaries can obtain arbitrary function of the whole secret state, as long as the total leakage is limited to a certain amount of bits. But this model is not strong enough since the adversary may launch many attacks and it is not evident to bound the information leakage to a predetermined value.

One way to capture more realistic attackers is to relax the restriction imposed on the leakage function. Dodis et al. [10] proposed the auxiliary input model where the leakage can be arbitrary large and only with the restriction that the secret key is computationally hard to compute given the leakage information.

Another (and maybe a more realistic) way is to consider continual leakage directly. Brakerski et al. [4] and Dodis et al. [9] proposed the *continual memory leakage* (CML) model. In their models, the entire lifetime of the scheme is partitioned into some periods, and at the end of each period, the internal secret state of the scheme is updated. The adversary is allowed to obtain bounded leakage from the *entire* internal secret state during each time period, just as in the BML setting, but the total leakage over the lifetime of the scheme is *unbounded*.

Continual Memory Leakage Model. One may think that it is easy to construct cryptographic schemes in the CML setting. For example, one can construct continual memory leakage resilient (CML) public key encryption (PKE) schemes by generating multiple independent instances of a normal PKE scheme, encrypting messages under all public keys and decrypting with a fresh secret key at each time period. However, this does not satisfy realistic requirements. One reason is that the size of the public key and ciphertexts depend on the number of time periods throughout the lifetime of the scheme. Besides, secret keys not used at present must be stored in some external leak-free storage and key updating can only be executed privately. To exclude such trivial solution, which will not provide actual guidance in practice, the compactness (i.e. all parameters are independent of number of time periods) and the ability of publicly key updating (i.e. secret keys can be updated with only the public parameters) are required for constructions of cryptographic schemes in the CML setting.

In fact, it is rather involved to construct cryptographic schemes in the CML setting. When considering CML-PKE schemes, only a few constructions are known so far [4,11,23,26]. Most of them are based on concrete number-theoretic assumptions directly. Especially, no *practical* chosen-ciphertext (CCA) secure PKE schme has been presented in this model yet. Therefore, new techniques for constructing CML-PKE schemes are desired.

Hash Proof System. Since first introduced by Cramer and Shoup [8], hash proof system (HPS) gained great success in constructing various cryptographic schemes, such as password-based authenticated key exchange [15], lossy trapdoor functions [19], (leak-free) CCA-secure PKE schemes [8,24] and PKE schemes in the BML setting [18,28,32,33].

Especially, when constructing PKE schemes in the BML setting, the technique of HPS is essential to obtain leakage resilience. The bottom line is that multiple secret keys are mapped to a single public key in an HPS-based PKE scheme, thus the adversary cannot determine which secret key is in use even bounded leakage is given. Meanwhile, honestly generated ciphertexts are computationally indistinguishable from dishonest ciphertexts, whose decryptings are not determined by the public key but the secret key decrypting it. So the BML adversary cannot decrypt ciphertexts of an HPS-based PKE scheme (actually, they cannot obtain any information from these ciphertexts).

Considering that attacks launched in each time period in the CML setting can just be viewed as bounded memory attacks, one may naturally think that by augmenting HPS with the publicly key updating ability, it can be applied to construct CML-PKE schemes straightforwardly. But this simple idea seems *not* working: the publicly key updating ability seems incompatible with HPS.

To see this, recall that an HPS is based on a collection of hash functions indexed by a set of secret keys. When evaluating the hash function on an element in the domain, different secret keys may lead to the same result, and we say such secret keys are "equivalent on this element". All secret keys are mapped to some public keys and those mapped to the same public key will be equivalent on every element in a specific subset of its domain. Also, the subset membership problem (SMP), which demands a PPT algorithm to distinguish a uniform element in this subset from a uniform element in its complement, is hard in HPS, and that leads to the ciphertexts indistinguishability in an HPS-based PKE scheme.

When updating secret keys of HPS in the CML setting, one should generate a new secret key mapped to the same public key. Thus the new key and the old key will be equivalent on every element in the specific subset. But they will not be equivalent on every element in the domain. So an adversary can break the underlying SMP of HPS via the "GUC attack", namely, generating a secret key, updating it, and checking whether they are equivalent on the challenge element.

Therefore, the following two questions arise naturally: Whether HPS is still effective for building PKEs in the CML setting? If yes, how?

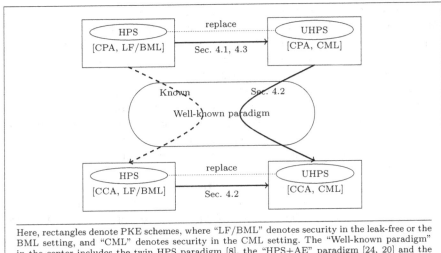

Here, rectangles denote PKE schemes, where "LF/BML" denotes security in the leak-free or the BML setting, and "CML" denotes security in the CML setting. The "Well-known paradigm" in the center includes the twin HPS paradigm [8], the "HPS+AE" paradigm [24, 20] and the "HPS+OT-LF" paradigm [32].

Fig. 1. Constructing CML-PKE schemes from UHPS and its relation with HPS-based PKE schemes.

1.1 Our Results

In this paper, we investigate these two questions and pose affirmative answers to them. More precisely, we show that in general, an HPS based PKE scheme is in fact secure against continuous memory attacks, as long as the underlying HPS fulfill some additional requirements.

First, we require that secret keys are updated in some pattern, namely, updated keys and old keys are equivalent on elements in a superset of the specific subset. Next, as a substitute of the SMP, we require that elements chosen uniformly from the specific subset and from that superset are computationally indistinguishable. We remark that the GUC attack is not applicable to this indistinguishability. But updating secret keys with certain patterns will cause new problems since the adversary is able to obtain leakage about secret keys continually and thus may learn this pattern (we will discuss how this threatens security of PKE schemes in the proof sketch of Theorem 5). Therefore, we require that all updated keys appear independent and uniform to the adversary, although they are updated with certain patterns.

We call an HPS with these properties "updatable hash proof system" (UHPS), and show how to instantiate it with some widely-accepted assumptions, e.g. the symmetric external Diffie-Hellman (SXDH) assumption and the d-linear assumption in bilinear groups. Interestingly, our instantiations are just extensions of the DDH-based HPS in [8] and one can realize them via modifying existing implementations of DDH-based HPS.

The functionalities of UHPS are summarized in Fig. 1. In particular, by simply substituting the HPS component in an HPS-based PKE with a UHPS component, one obtains a CML-PKE scheme. Interestingly, we show that well-known transforms that upgrade weak (e.g. CPA-secure) PKE schemes into strong (i.e. CCA-secure) PKE schemes are still effective for the resulting CML-PKE schemes. The reason why UHPS is effective in constructing CML-PKE is that honest ciphertexts and dishonest ciphertexts are still indistinguishable when secret keys are updated in some pattern. Also, the key indistinguishability in UHPS can guarantee that real secret keys as well as the pattern are hidden from CML adversaries. So they cannot obtain any information from these ciphertexts just as in the BML setting.

We remark that when instantiated with concrete assumptions, our CCA-secure CML-PKE schemes are much more efficient compared to known results. To show this, we give a brief overview of known constructions of CCA-secure CML-PKE schemes in Sect. 1.2, and give a concrete efficiency comparison between these schemes and our schemes in Sect. 5.2. Besides, we observe that several frameworks for constructing hybrid encryption schemes, including the framework of "constrained CCA (CCCA) secure KEM + authenticated encryption (AE) scheme" [20] and the tag KEM/DEM framework [1], are also robust in the CML setting. Also, it is worth noting that PKE schemes in Wichs's PhD thesis [36] can be viewed as instantiations of our CPA-secure PKE schemes. In fact, our work provides a modular way to reconsider their schemes and makes the construction of CML-PKE schemes more concise and conceptual simpler.

1.2 Related Work

Now we give a brief overview of approaches applicable to construct CCA-secure CML-PKE schemes. In principle, the Naor-Yung paradigm [29,35] is robust against continuous memory attacks. That is to say, in the CML setting, one can transform any CPA-secure PKE scheme to be CCA-secure. Alternatively, the CHK transformation [6] can also provide CCA-secure CML-PKE schemes given suitable building blocks, e.g., identity based encryption schemes with continual master key leakage resilience [26]. Recently, a contemporaneous work [23] also shows that one can construct CCA-secure CML-PKE schemes from a variant of lossy trapdoor function. We remark that due to lack of suitable underlying building blocks, the latter two approaches are only applicable to a weaker CML setting where no leakage is allowed during key update.

2   Preliminaries

In this section, we review some useful notations and notions.

Notations. Let S be a finite set, we use $\|S\|$ and $U(S)$ to denote the size of S and the uniform distribution over S respectively. Also, we write $x \xleftarrow{\$} S$ to indicate that x is sampled uniformly from S. For a bit string $s \in \{0,1\}^*$, we use $\|s\|$ to denote the length of s. We use $[n]$ to denote the set $\{1, 2, \ldots, n\}$ for any positive integer n. We write $negl(\cdot)$ to denote a negligible function. Let $\mathcal{X} = \{X_n\}_{n \in \mathbb{N}}$ and $\mathcal{Y} = \{Y_n\}_{n \in \mathbb{N}}$ be two ensembles of random variables. We use $\mathcal{X} \overset{s}{\approx} \mathcal{Y}$ to denote that $\mathcal{X}$ and $\mathcal{Y}$ are statistically indistinguishable and use $\mathcal{X} \overset{c}{\approx} \mathcal{Y}$ to denote that $\mathcal{X}$ and $\mathcal{Y}$ are computationally indistinguishable.

Linear Algebra. Let q be a prime, we introduce some notations of linear algebra over $\mathbb{Z}_q$. We use bold uppercase letters $(\boldsymbol{X})$ to denote matrices and lowercase letters with arrow $(\vec{x})$ to denote vectors. All vectors used in this paper are column vectors. Let $\vec{v}_1, \ldots, \vec{v}_m$ be m vectors in $\mathbb{Z}_q^n$, then we denote by $span(\vec{v}_1, \ldots, \vec{v}_m)$ the linear space spanned by these vectors. Assuming $\mathcal{V}$ is a subspace of $\mathbb{Z}_q^n$ with dimension $d < n$, we denote by $\mathcal{V}^{\perp}$ the orthogonal space of $\mathcal{V}$. We use $Rk_d(\mathbb{Z}_q^{n \times k})$ to denote the set of $n \times k$-matrices with rank d.

Entropy and Extractors. The min-entropy of a discrete random variable X, which measures the worst case predictability of X, is defined as $H_{\infty}(X) = - \log(\max_x \Pr[X = x])$. It is often useful to work with the average case of min-entropy that was first defined in [13] as $\widetilde{H}_{\infty}(X \mid Y) = - \log(\mathbb{E}_{y \leftarrow Y}[\max_x \Pr[X = x \mid Y = y]])$. To obtain nearly perfect randomness from sources with high (average case) min-entropy, one can use the (average case) randomness extractor.

Definition 1 ([13]). *A function $Ext : \mathcal{X} \times \{0,1\}^t \to \mathcal{Y}$ is an (average case) (k, ϵ)-strong extractor if for all pairs of random variables (X, I) such that X is distributed over $\mathcal{X}$ and $H_{\infty}(X \mid I) \geq k$ $(\widetilde{H}_{\infty}(X \mid I) \geq k)$, it holds that $\Delta((Ext(X, R), R, I), (Y, R, I)) \leq \epsilon$ where R is uniform over $\{0,1\}^t$ and Y is uniform over $\mathcal{Y}$.*

Such (average case) randomness extractors can be constructed directly from any universal hash family [7] as long as $k \geq \log(\|\mathcal{Y}\|) + 2 \log(1/\epsilon)$, and the later primitive can be further constructed directly from natural algebraic operations (e.g. linear combination in $\mathbb{Z}_q$ for a prime q).

3   Updatable Hash Proof System

In this section, we define the notion of UHPS, which is a variant of HPS. Since we intend to use UHPS to construct PKE schemes in the CML setting, publicly key updating ability is demanded and we need properties to support this in UHPS. But as stated in Sect. 1, HPS with publicly key updating ability will suffer from the GUC attack, which breaks the intractability of underlying SMP. Thus we need a substitute of SMP immune to this attack. This is formalized as the subset indistinguishability in UHPS. However, to apply the subset indistinguishability, all secret keys have to be updated in some pattern, which may bring new problems as the adversary may learn this pattern via requesting continual leakage. Therefore, we define some key indistinguishabilities in UHPS here to solve these potential problems. Although several additional properties are defined in UHPS, we observe that they have already been fulfilled by existing instantiations of HPS to some degree and will not take too much extra overhead.

Similar to a normal HPS, a UHPS is based on a collection of hash functions $\mathcal{H} = \{\mathcal{H}_{sk} : \mathcal{C} \to \mathcal{K}\}_{sk \in \mathcal{SK}}$. Also there exists an efficiently computable projection φ from $\mathcal{SK}$ to $\mathcal{PK}$, and a specific set $\mathcal{V} \subset \mathcal{C}$ such that for any $sk_1, sk_2 \in \mathcal{SK}$, $\varphi(sk_1) = \varphi(sk_2)$ if and only if $\forall x \in \mathcal{V}, \mathcal{H}_{sk_1}(x) = \mathcal{H}_{sk_2}(x)$. Further, for every $x \in \mathcal{V}$, there exists a witness $w \in \mathcal{W}$ proving this. Besides, for any $x \notin \mathcal{V}$, $H_\infty(\mathcal{H}_{sk}(x)|\varphi(sk))$ is usually required to be large enough when $sk \xleftarrow{\$} \mathcal{SK}$, and this is formalized as the universality in UHPS.

Here, we provide the publicly key updating ability via algebraic operations and require that UHPS is key homomorphic, i.e. $\mathcal{SK}$ and $\mathcal{K}$ are finite groups with an efficiently computable operation "$+$" and $\forall sk_1, sk_2 \in \mathcal{SK}, \forall x \in \mathcal{C}$, we have $\mathcal{H}_{sk_1+sk_2}(x) = \mathcal{H}_{sk_1}(x) + \mathcal{H}_{sk_2}(x)$. Now, we can update a secret key sk by adding it with a specific secret key sk^* s.t. $\forall x \in \mathcal{V}, \mathcal{H}_{sk^*}(x) = 0$. Since $\forall x \in \mathcal{V}, \mathcal{H}_{sk+sk^*}(x) = \mathcal{H}_{sk}(x) + \mathcal{H}_{sk^*}(x) = \mathcal{H}_{sk}(x)$, we have $\varphi(sk+sk^*) = \varphi(sk)$, which indicates that the new key and the old key are mapped to the same public key.

For secret keys will be updated continually, fresh updating key is required each time. So we require $span(sk^*)$, which is a specific set such that $\forall sk^{*\prime} \in span(sk^*), \mathcal{H}_{sk^*}(x) = 0 \to \mathcal{H}_{sk^{*\prime}}(x) = 0$, to be efficiently samplable given an initial updating key sk^*. To generate the initial updating key, we also demand that $\forall L \subseteq \mathcal{C}, ker(L) = \{sk \mid \forall x \in L, \mathcal{H}_{sk}(x) = 0\}$ is efficiently samplable given a trapdoor $T \in \mathcal{T}$ for L. Besides, due to the requirement for security proofs of PKE schemes, we require that given trapdoors $T_1, T_2 \in \mathcal{T}$ for subsets $L_1, L_2 \subseteq \mathcal{C}$ respectively, it is efficient to generate a trapdoor $T_3 \in \mathcal{T}$ for $L_1 \cup L_2$.

We stress that although we have provided mechanisms to update secret keys in UHPS, we will not fix an updating policy, and one can choose various approaches to performing key update in different scenarios.

Now we present the formal definition.

Definition 2. *Let λ be a polynomial of the security parameter n, and indicates the bits of challenge information that can be obtained by the distinguisher for "partial key indistinguishability". A λ-UHPS $\mathfrak{H}$ consists of five algorithms:*

- *__Instance Generation.__ $\mathfrak{H}.Param(1^n)$: The instance generation algorithm takes as input the security parameter 1^n, and outputs an instance $\mathbf{H} = (\mathcal{C}, \mathcal{V}, \mathcal{H}, \mathcal{K}, \mathcal{SK}, \mathcal{PK}, \mathcal{T}, \mathcal{W}, \varphi)$ of UHPS with a trapdoor $T^* \in \mathcal{T}$ for $\mathcal{V}$. Here, all sets in $\mathbf{H}$ are finite non-empty sets.*
- *__Subset Sampling.__ $\mathfrak{H}.VSamp(\mathbf{H})$: The subset sampling algorithm outputs $x \xleftarrow{\$} \mathcal{V}$ with a witness $w \in \mathcal{W}$ for $x \in \mathcal{V}$.*
- *__Complement Sampling.__ $\mathfrak{H}.ISamp(\mathbf{H})$: The complement sampling algorithm outputs $x \xleftarrow{\$} \mathcal{C}\backslash\mathcal{V}$ with a trapdoor $T \in \mathcal{T}$ for $\{x\}$. We remark that we can tolerant a negligible statistical error here, namely, we only require that the sampled elements are statistically indistinguishable from $U(\mathcal{C}\backslash\mathcal{V})$.*
- *__Public Evaluation.__ $\mathfrak{H}.Pub(\mathbf{H}, pk, x, w)$: Given $pk \in \mathcal{PK}$ and $x \in \mathcal{V}$ with its witness $w \in \mathcal{W}$, the public evaluation algorithm outputs $k \in \mathcal{K}$.*
- *__Private Evaluation.__ $\mathfrak{H}.Priv(\mathbf{H}, sk, x)$: Given $sk \in \mathcal{SK}$ and $x \in \mathcal{C}$, the private evaluation algorithm outputs $k = \mathcal{H}_{sk}(x)$.*

Moreover, we require that $\mathfrak{H}$ has four basic properties, indicating its correctness and hardness requirements:

1. **Correctness.** For any instance $\boldsymbol{H}$, any (sk, pk) s.t. $pk = \varphi(sk)$, and any $x \in \mathcal{V}$ with its witness w, we have $\mathfrak{H}.Pub(\boldsymbol{H}, pk, x, w) = \mathfrak{H}.Priv(\boldsymbol{H}, sk, x)$.

2. **Subset Indistinguishability.** As a substitute of SMP, this indicates the indistinguishability between elements in $\mathcal{V}$ and not in $\mathcal{V}$, namely, for arbitrary positive integer l, let $(\boldsymbol{H}, T^*) \leftarrow \mathfrak{H}.Param(1^n)$, $x \xleftarrow{\$} \mathcal{V}$, $sk_1, \ldots, sk_l \xleftarrow{\$} ker(\mathcal{V})$, $x' \xleftarrow{\$} \mathcal{C}\backslash\mathcal{V}$, and $sk'_1, \ldots, sk'_l \xleftarrow{\$} ker(\mathcal{V} \cup \{x'\})$, then we have $(\boldsymbol{H}, x, sk_1, \ldots, sk_l) \overset{c}{\approx} (\boldsymbol{H}, x', sk'_1, \ldots, sk'_l)$.

3. **Full Key Indistinguishability.** For any PPT adversary $\mathcal{A} = (\mathcal{A}_1, \mathcal{A}_2)$, it is hard to distinguish whether two secret keys are "linearly dependent", i.e. for some function δ negligible in n, we have

$$\Pr[(\boldsymbol{H}, T^*) \leftarrow \mathfrak{H}.Param(1^n); T \leftarrow \mathcal{A}_1(\boldsymbol{H}, T^*); b \xleftarrow{\$} \{0,1\};$$
$$sk, sk_1 \xleftarrow{\$} ker(L); sk_0 \xleftarrow{\$} span(sk) : \mathcal{A}_2(sk, sk_b) = b] - \frac{1}{2} = \delta$$

where L is a subset of $\mathcal{C}$ for which T is a trapdoor.

4. **Partial Key Indistinguishability.** When only partial information is revealed, it is hard to determine whether an updating key is legal. More precisely, for arbitrary function f with range $\{0,1\}^\lambda$, let $(\boldsymbol{H}, T^*) \leftarrow \mathfrak{H}.Param(1^n)$, $x \xleftarrow{\$} \mathcal{C}\backslash\mathcal{V}$, $sk_1, sk_2 \xleftarrow{\$} ker(\mathcal{V} \cup \{x\})$, $sk'_2 \xleftarrow{\$} ker(\mathcal{V})$, then we have $(\boldsymbol{H}, sk_1, f(\boldsymbol{H}, sk_1, sk_2), x) \overset{s}{\approx} (\boldsymbol{H}, sk_1, f(\boldsymbol{H}, sk_1, sk'_2), x)$. Note that the function f must be independent of x.

In order to indicate how secret keys mapped to the same public key behave in evaluating hash functions on elements not in $\mathcal{V}$, we define the "universality" of UHPS similarly to that of normal HPS with only minimal variance due to the need of keeping some algebra properties of UHPS.

Definition 3 (*Universal UHPS*). *Let τ be a function on n. Then a UHPS is τ-universal if for each instance $\boldsymbol{H}$, for any $pk \in \mathcal{PK}$ and any $x \in \mathcal{C}\backslash\mathcal{V}$, we have $H_\infty(\mathcal{H}_{SK}(x) \mid \varphi(SK) = pk) \geq \tau$ where SK is a random variable with distribution $U(\mathcal{SK})$.*

Definition 4 (*Universal$_2$ UHPS*). *Let τ be a function on n. Then a UHPS is τ-universal$_2$ if for each instance $\boldsymbol{H}$, we can augment it with an efficiently computable functions η from $\mathcal{C} \times \mathcal{K}$ to $\mathcal{Y}$, and for any $pk \in \mathcal{PK}$, any $x, x^* \in \mathcal{C}\backslash\mathcal{V}$ s.t. $x \neq x^*$, any $y \in \mathcal{Y}$, we have $H_\infty(\eta(x, \mathcal{H}_{SK}(x)) \mid \varphi(SK) = pk, \eta(x^*, \mathcal{H}_{SK}(x^*)) = y) \geq \tau$, where SK is a random variable with distribution $U(\mathcal{SK})$.*

Interestingly, universal$_2$ UHPS can be constructed directly from universal ones by applying the approach in [8] and we give more details about the construction in the full version.

4   Building CML-PKE from UHPS

In this section, we demonstrate the usefulness of UHPS: By substituting a HPS component in the PKE schemes with a UHPS components, some well-established paradigms remain effective in building CML-PKE schemes. As a by-product, the new schemes from UHPS can inherit many interesting features from the corresponding HPS-based schemes. For example, all CCA-secure PKE schemes constructed in this paper can be transformed into tag-KEM/DEM [1], therefore, can be extended to threshold PKE schemes in the CML setting; besides, the scheme from UHPS plus AE can be formalized in the "CCCA KEM + AE" framework. In general, UHPS is applicable to almost all known HPS-based PKE schemes.

Key update is a must for CML-PKE schemes. This is because otherwise the adversary can learn the entire secret state by repeatedly requesting more and more leakage, and no security can be guaranteed then. An adversary considered in this case is further allowed to learn any bounded leakage information (namely, up to λ_M bits) in each time period. In some cases, we will consider update phases separately, so we also give another bound λ_U on the size of leakage during key updating. We remark that no information can be leaked after the challenge phase, since otherwise the adversary can embed the challenge ciphertext into the leakage query and obtain information about the message. We give the formal definition of PKE schemes in the CML setting as well as its security definition with various security level (namely, the CPA-security and the adaptive CCA-security[1]) in the full version.

Two scenarios are mainly considered in the CML setting, namely, the one not allowing leakage during key update (i.e. $\lambda_U = 0$) and the one allowing leakage during key update (i.e. $\lambda_U = \lambda_M > 0$). The primary difference between constructions of PKE schemes in these two cases is that constructions in the latter case have a more involved key update algorithm. Here, we focus on constructions in the former case and only consider constructions in the latter case in Sect. 4.3. Due to the limit of space, all security proofs and some constructions are omitted and will be given in the full version.

4.1   A CPA-Secure Scheme

We start with a CPA-secure CML-PKE scheme from UHPS, which will help us understand how UHPS functions in constructing CML-PKE schemes. The resulting PKE scheme Π_1, which is a variant of the HPS-based CPA-secure PKE scheme [8], consists of four algorithms:

– **Parameters.** Denote n as the security parameter. Let $\mathfrak{H}$ be a τ-universal λ-UHPS and $(\boldsymbol{H}, T^*) \leftarrow \mathfrak{H}.Param(1^n)$ be an instance of $\mathfrak{H}$. Let $Ext : \mathcal{K} \times \{0,1\}^d \rightarrow \{0,1\}^\iota$ be an average case (τ, δ)-strong extractor where δ is negligible

---

[1] We only consider adaptive CCA secuirty in this paper, so we will just write CCA instead of adaptive CCA for short.

in n and $\tau - \iota \geq 2\log(1/\delta)$. Sample $sk^* \xleftarrow{\$} ker(\mathcal{V})$ with T^*. The public parameter of Π_1 is $Params = (\boldsymbol{H}, sk^*, Ext)$.

- **Key Generation.** The key generation algorithm of Π_1 samples $\overline{sk} \xleftarrow{\$} \mathcal{SK}$ and evaluates $pk = \varphi(\overline{sk})$. Then it sets $PK = pk$ and $SK = \overline{sk} + sk^{*\prime}$ where $sk^{*\prime} \xleftarrow{\$} span(sk^*)$.

- **Encryption.** Given a public key $PK = pk$, to encrypt a message $M \in \{0,1\}^\iota$, the encryption algorithm samples $rand \xleftarrow{\$} \{0,1\}^d$ and runs $\mathfrak{H}.VSamp(\boldsymbol{H})$ to sample $C \xleftarrow{\$} \mathcal{V}$ with a witness w. Then it evaluates $K = \mathfrak{H}.Pub(\boldsymbol{H}, pk, C, w)$, and $\Psi = Ext(K, rand) \oplus M$, Finally, it outputs $CT = (C, \Psi, rand)$ as ciphertext.

- **Decryption.** Given a secret key $SK = sk$, to decrypt a ciphertext $CT = (C, \Psi, rand)$, the decryption algorithm computes $K' = \mathfrak{H}.Priv(\boldsymbol{H}, sk, C)$ and outputs $M' = \Psi \oplus Ext(K', rand)$.

- **Key Update.** Given a secret key $SK = sk$, the update algorithm samples $sk^{*\prime} \xleftarrow{\$} span(sk^*)$ and outputs a new key $SK' = sk + sk^{*\prime}$.

Correctness. Let $SK_i = sk^{(i)}$ be the secret key obtained by applying the update algorithm i times to the initial secret key generated by $KeyGen$ and $PK = pk$ be the public key. It is obvious that the correctness holds if for any honestly generated ciphertext $CT = (C, \Psi, rand)$, and for arbitrary natural number i, we have $\mathfrak{H}.Priv(\boldsymbol{H}, sk^{(i)}, C) = \mathfrak{H}.Pub(\boldsymbol{H}, pk, C, w)$ where w is the witness for $C \in \mathcal{V}$. This follows directly from the correctness of UHPS because $\varphi(sk^{(i)}) = \varphi(\overline{sk} + sk^{*\prime}) = pk$, where $sk^{*\prime} \in span(sk^*)$.

Security. Security of Π_1 is guaranteed by Theorem 5 stated as follows.

Theorem 5. *Π_1 is secure against chosen-plaintext attacks in the CML setting with period leakage amount $\lambda_M = \lambda$ and $\lambda_U = 0$.*

Proof Sketch. Similarly to security proofs of PKE schemes constructed from a normal HPS, we prove Theorem 5 by first altering the way in which the challenge ciphertext is generated, i.e., a challenge ciphertext $CT^* = (C^*, \Psi^*, rand^*)$ s.t. $C^* \notin \mathcal{V}$ is generated instead. This is indistinguishable from an honestly generated ciphertext due to the subset indistinguishability of UHPS. However, we cannot subsequently apply the universal property of UHPS to complete the proof directly. This is because all secret keys throughout lifetime of the scheme will still decrypt CT^* correctly, and the adversary who can obtain leakage about these secret keys continually may learn enough knowledge to break the scheme. Therefore, we should argue that such leakage information will not provide the adversary with practical assistance. It is sufficient to establish the indistinguishability between the real secret keys (i.e. secret keys generated and updated honestly) and the ideal secret keys (i.e. secret keys chosen uniformly over keys mapped to the public key). We do this in two steps. First we apply the full key indistinguishability of UHPS to argue that real secret keys and "semi-ideal" secret keys are indistinguishable. Here we use "semi-ideal" to denote secret keys generated honestly and updated with fresh updating keys chosen uniformly from

$ker(\mathcal{V} \cup \{C^*\})$. However, semi-ideal secret keys can still decrypt CT^* correctly. Fortunately, indistinguishability between semi-ideal secret keys and ideal secret keys can be derived from partial key indistinguishability of UHPS since the adversary can only obtain bounded leakage in each time period.

4.2 CCA-Secure Schemes

Then we move on to CCA-secure CML-PKE schemes, which is the main contribution of UHPS. Generally, the bottom line to construct CCA-secure PKE schemes is to prevent the adversary from querying unintended ciphertexts whose decryption will damage the security of the scheme. This is usually performed by applying a suitable authentication.

Three main paradigms are proposed to construct CCA-secure PKE schemes from HPS. In [8], the construction applies a universal$_2$ HPS to provide the authentication and applies a universal HPS to mask the message. Another approach is to employ a single universal$_2$ HPS together with an AE scheme to provide both the authentication and the privacy [24]. Besides, in [32], a new paradigm avoiding the usage of universal$_2$ HPS is given and it applies a universal HPS to mask the message and a one time lossy filter (OT-LF) to provide the authentication. We observe that UHPS is applicable to all these three paradigms. More precisely, by substituting HPS with corresponding UHPS, we can obtain CCA-secure PKE scheme in the CML setting.

We remark that our universal$_2$ UHPS is far less efficient compared to our universal UHPS and it has a much larger secret key, thus the scheme from universal UHPS plus OT-LF can achieve both the best efficiency and the best leakage rate (which will be defined in Sect. 5.2) among all three schemes. So we only present its construction here, and give the other two constructions in Appendix A.

Roughly speaking, an OT-LF is a family of functions indexed by a public key F_{pk} as well as a tag t. Each function will be injective unless the tag comes from some specific set. Moreover, it is hard to generate or even recognize such non-injective tags without a trapdoor F_{td} associated with F_{pk}. We refer the reader to [32] for more details about OT-LF. The presented PKE scheme Π_2 consists of four algorithms:

- **Parameters.** Denote n as the security parameter. Let $\mathfrak{H}$ be a τ-universal λ-UHPS and $(\boldsymbol{H}, T^*) \leftarrow \mathfrak{H}.Param(1^n)$ be an instance of $\mathfrak{H}$. Let $LF = (LF.Gen, LF.Eval, LF.LTag, LF.DITag)$ be a $(\mathcal{K}, \ell_{LF})$-OT-LF with the tag space $\mathcal{C} \times \{0,1\}^l \times \{0,1\}^d \times \mathcal{T}_c$. Let $Ext : \mathcal{K} \times \{0,1\}^d \to \{0,1\}^\iota$ be an average case $(\tau - \ell_{LF}, \delta)$-strong extractor where δ is negligible in n and $\tau - \ell_{LF} - \iota \geq 2\log(1/\delta)$. Sample $sk^* \xleftarrow{\$} ker(\mathcal{V})$ with T^*. The public parameter of Π_2 is $Params = (\boldsymbol{H}, sk^*, Ext, LF)$.

- **Key Generation.** The key generation algorithm of Π_2 samples $\overline{sk} \xleftarrow{\$} \mathcal{SK}$, evaluates $pk = \varphi(\overline{sk})$, and runs $LF.Gen(1^n)$ to obtain F_{pk}. Then it sets $PK = (pk, F_{pk})$ and $SK = \overline{sk} + sk^{*\prime}$ where $sk^{*\prime} \xleftarrow{\$} span(sk^*)$.

- **Encryption.** Given a public key $PK = (pk, F_{pk})$, to encrypt a message $M \in \{0,1\}^\iota$, the encryption algorithm samples $rand \xleftarrow{\$} \{0,1\}^d$, $t_c \xleftarrow{\$} \mathcal{T}_c$, and runs $\mathfrak{H}.VSamp(\boldsymbol{H})$ to sample $C \xleftarrow{\$} \mathcal{V}$ with a witness w. Then it evaluates $K = \mathfrak{H}.Pub(\boldsymbol{H}, pk, C, w)$, $\Psi = Ext(K, rand) \oplus M$, and $\Upsilon = LF_{F_{pk},t}(K)$ where $t = (t_a, t_c)$ and $t_a = (C, \Psi, rand)$. Finally, it outputs $CT = (C, \Psi, rand, \Upsilon, t_c)$ as ciphertext.

- **Decryption.** Given a secret key $SK = sk$, to decrypt a ciphertext $CT = (C, \Psi, rand, \Upsilon, t_c)$, the decryption algorithm computes $K' = \mathfrak{H}.Priv(\boldsymbol{H}, sk, C)$ and checks whether $\Upsilon = LF_{F_{pk},t}(K')$ where $t = ((C, \Psi, rand), t_c)$. If $\Upsilon = LF_{F_{pk},t}(K')$, the decryption algorithm outputs $M' = \Psi \oplus Ext(K', rand)$. Otherwise, it rejects with $\bot$.

- **Key Update.** Given a secret key $SK = sk$ the update algorithm samples $sk^{*\prime} \xleftarrow{\$} span(sk^*)$ and outputs a new key $SK' = sk + sk^{*\prime}$.

Correctness of Π_2 follows directly from correctness of Π_1 and security of Π_2 is guaranteed by Theorem 6 stated as follows.

Theorem 6. Π_2 *is secure against a posteriori chosen-ciphertext attacks in the CML setting with period leakage amount* $\lambda_M = \min(\lambda, \tau - (\iota + \ell_{LF} + \omega(\log n)))$ *and* $\lambda_U = 0$.

Proof Sketch. Proof of Theorem 6 is similar to that of Theorem 5, however, the simulator has to deal with decryption oracle queries here. Fortunately, all decryption oracle queries can be answered by the simulator directly until the "partial key indistinguishability" of UHPS is employed in the proof. As this is a statistical indistinguishability, the simulator can answer decryption oracle queries unless the decryption of the submitted ciphertext is not determined by the public key. This occurs only when a ciphertext $CT = (C, \Psi, rand, \Upsilon, t_c)$ with $C \notin \mathcal{V}$ is queried. But such queries cannot pass the verification in the decryption algorithm with a non-negligible probability. To see this, recall that $\tilde{H}_\infty(\mathcal{H}_{sk}(C))$ is large when $C \notin \mathcal{V}$ since the underlying UHPS is universal and leakage in each time period is bounded, where sk is the current secret key. Also, it is hard for the adversary to sample a non-injective function of OT-LF. Therefore, the adversary can generate the correct Υ with only a negligible probability. We remark that for privacy, lossy function of OT-LF need to be used when generating the challenge ciphertext and that is why we should use an OT-LF rather than a family of injective one-way functions.

4.3 PKE Schemes with Leakage During Key Update

We stress that, our claim that UHPS is effective in constructing CML-PKE schemes is in fact valid in the setting where leakage during key update is allowable. Compared to PKE schemes in Sects. 4.1 and 4.2, which are only proved secure in the CML setting without leakage during key update, schemes secure in this section have nothing more than a better key updating policy. This is based on the ideas of [11,25]. More precisely, the secret key of the PKE scheme consists of multiple secret keys of UHPS, and can be updated by computing linear combinations of secret keys of UHPS consist in it.

As more involved algebra operations are introduced here, three additional properties of UHPS are required. First, we require that for each instance $\mathcal{H}$ and any secret key $sk \in \mathcal{SK}$, we have $span(sk) = \{r \circ sk \mid r \in \mathbb{Z}\}$ where $r \circ sk$ is denoted as the key obtained by adding sk r times. Assume the order of $\mathcal{K}$ is q, then for any secret key sk, we can sample $sk' \xleftarrow{\$} span(sk)$ by just sampling $r \xleftarrow{\$} \mathbb{Z}_q$ and computing $sk' = r \circ sk$. Next, we require that q is prime. The last requirement is that $ker(\mathcal{V})$ is m-decomposable, namely, $ker(\mathcal{V})$ can be represented by m uniform and independent keys in $ker(\mathcal{V})$. More precisely, for any $l \geq m$, let $sk_i \xleftarrow{\$} ker(\mathcal{V})$ for $i \in [l]$, then with all but negligible probability, we have "sampling $sk' \xleftarrow{\$} ker(\mathcal{V})$" is equivalent to "first sampling $sk'_1 \xleftarrow{\$} span(sk_1), \ldots, sk'_l \xleftarrow{\$} span(sk_l)$ then computing $sk' = sk'_1 + \ldots + sk'_l$", where the probability is taken over the choices of sk_i. Although look unusual, these requirements is satisfied by the construction in Sect. 5.1. We remark that we will use the augmented notion of UHPS with these additional requirements throughout Sect. 4.3.

Now, we are ready to give a formal description of our constructions. Due to the limit of space, we only give a construction with CPA-security here and give CCA-secure ones in the full version. The presented scheme Π_3 consists of four algorithms:

- **Parameters.** Denote n as the security parameter. Let $\mathfrak{H}$ be a τ-universal λ-UHPS and $(\boldsymbol{H}, T^*) \leftarrow \mathfrak{H}.Param(1^n)$ be an instance of $\mathfrak{H}$. Assume the order of $\mathcal{K}$ is q and $ker(\mathcal{V})$ is m-decomposable. Let $Ext : \mathcal{K} \times \{0,1\}^d \rightarrow \{0,1\}^\iota$ be an average case (τ, δ)-strong extractor where δ is negligible in n and $\tau - \iota \geq 2\log(1/\delta)$. Sample $sk^* \xleftarrow{\$} ker(\mathcal{V})$ with T^*. Let l, a be positive integers. The public parameter of Π_3 is $Params = (\boldsymbol{H}, sk^*, Ext, q, m, l, a)$
- **Key Generation.** The key generation algorithm of Π_3 samples $\overline{sk} \xleftarrow{\$} \mathcal{SK}$ and evaluates $pk = \varphi(\overline{sk})$. Then it sets $PK = pk$ and $SK = [sk_1, \ldots, sk_l]^\mathsf{T}$ where $sk_i = \overline{sk} + r_i \circ sk^*$ and $r_i \xleftarrow{\$} \mathbb{Z}_q$ for $i \in [l]$.
- **Encryption.** Given a public key $PK = pk$, to encrypt a message $M \in \{0,1\}^\iota$, the encryption algorithm samples $rand \xleftarrow{\$} \{0,1\}^d$ and runs $\mathfrak{H}.VSamp(\boldsymbol{H})$ to sample $C \xleftarrow{\$} \mathcal{V}$ with a witness w. Then it evaluates $K = \mathfrak{H}.Pub(\boldsymbol{H}, pk, C, w)$, and $\Psi = Ext(K, rand) \oplus M$, Finally, it outputs $CT = (C, \Psi, rand)$ as ciphertext.
- **Decryption.** Given a secret key $SK = [sk_1, \ldots, sk_l]^\mathsf{T}$, to decrypt a ciphertext $CT = (C, \Psi, rand)$, the decryption algorithm computes $K' = \mathfrak{H}.Priv(\boldsymbol{H}, sk_1, C)$ and outputs $M' = \Psi \oplus Ext(K', rand)$.
- **Key Update.** Given a secret key $SK = [sk_1, \ldots, sk_l]^\mathsf{T}$, the update algorithm samples $\boldsymbol{A'} \xleftarrow{\$} Rk_a(\mathbb{Z}_q^{l \times l})$, computes $\boldsymbol{A}$ by setting $\boldsymbol{A}_{i,j} = \boldsymbol{A'}_{i,j}/(\sum_{k=1}^l \boldsymbol{A'}_{i,k})$,

which implies $\boldsymbol{A} \cdot [1, \dots, 1]^{\mathsf{T}} = [1, \dots, 1]^{\mathsf{T}}$, and outputs a new key $SK' = \boldsymbol{A} \circ SK$.

Correctness. Let $SK_i = \left[sk_1^{(i)}, \dots, sk_l^{(i)} \right]^{\mathsf{T}}$ be the secret key obtained by applying the update algorithm i times to the initial secret key generated by $KeyGen$ and $PK = pk$ be the public key. As shown in the proof of the correctness of Π_1, to prove the correctness of Π_3, it is sufficient to prove that for arbitrary natural number i, we have $\varphi(sk_1^{(i)}) = pk$. We first write the initial secret key SK_0 as $SK_0 = \left[sk_1, \dots, sk_l \right]^{\mathsf{T}} = \left[r_1 \circ sk^* + \overline{sk}, \dots, r_l \circ sk^* + \overline{sk} \right]^{\mathsf{T}} = \left[r_1, \dots, r_l \right]^{\mathsf{T}} \circ sk^* + \left[1, \dots, 1 \right]^{\mathsf{T}} \circ \overline{sk}$, where $r_1, \dots, r_l \in \mathbb{Z}_q$. Assume that for any positive integer j, the jth update matrix is $\boldsymbol{A}_j$, then we have

$$
\begin{aligned}
SK_i &= \boldsymbol{A}_i \cdot \boldsymbol{A}_{i-1} \dots \boldsymbol{A}_1 \circ SK_0 \\
&= \boldsymbol{A}_i \cdot \boldsymbol{A}_{i-1} \dots \boldsymbol{A}_1 \cdot \left[r_1, \dots, r_l \right]^{\mathsf{T}} \circ sk^* + \boldsymbol{A}_i \cdot \boldsymbol{A}_{i-1} \dots \boldsymbol{A}_1 \cdot \left[1, \dots, 1 \right]^{\mathsf{T}} \circ \overline{sk} \\
&= \left[r_1', \dots, r_l' \right]^{\mathsf{T}} \circ sk^* + \left[1, \dots, 1 \right]^{\mathsf{T}} \circ \overline{sk}
\end{aligned}
$$

Thus, we have $sk_1^{(i)} = r_1' \circ sk^* + \overline{sk}$ for some $r_1' \in \mathbb{Z}_q$ which can lead to the fact that $\varphi(sk_1^{(i)}) = pk$ as we need.

Security. Security of Π_3 is guaranteed by Theorem 7 stated as follows.

Theorem 7. *Π_3 is secure against chosen-plaintext attacks in the CML setting with period leakage amount $\lambda_M = \min(\lambda/2, (a - 2m - 3) \log q - \omega(\log n))$ and $\lambda_U = \lambda_M$ if $a \le l - m$.*

5   Instantiations of Updatable Hash Proof System

In this section, we give instantiations of UHPS from widely-accepted number theoretic assumptions, such as the SXDH assumption and the d-linear assumption. Interestingly, one can in fact implement our instantiations simply via modifying existing implementations of DDH-based HPS in [8], since the former are just extensions of the latter. Here, we extend the original 2-dimensional vector space to a high dimensional one; moreover, as specific secret keys will be made public when constructing PKE schemes, secret keys will be group elements rather than integers; to keep the function of secret keys, we will also base on a bilinear group instead of a normal group. Due to the limit of space, we omit the instantiation from the d-linear assumption here and give it in the full version. Besides instantiations of UHPS, in Sect. 5.2, we also consider parameters of our PKE schemes when built from concrete instantiations of UHPS.

Let $\mathbb{G}_1$, $\mathbb{G}_2$ and $\mathbb{G}_T$ be three groups of prime order q, and g, h be generators of $\mathbb{G}_1$ and $\mathbb{G}_2$ respectively. Let e be a bilinear map $e : \mathbb{G}_1 \times \mathbb{G}_2 \to \mathbb{G}_T$. Our instantiation works on the bilinear group $(\mathbb{G}_1, \mathbb{G}_2, \mathbb{G}_T, q, g, h, e)$. Let $\boldsymbol{R} = \{ r_{i,j} \}_{i \in [m], j \in [n]}$ be a matrix in $\mathbb{Z}_q^{m \times n}$, we denote by $g^{\boldsymbol{R}}$ the matrix $\{ g^{r_{i,j}} \}_{i \in [m], j \in [n]} \in \mathbb{G}_1^{m \times n}$. Similar definitions hold in $\mathbb{G}_2$ and $\mathbb{G}_T$ as well. Let $\vec{a}, \vec{b}$ be two vectors in $\mathbb{Z}_q^n$, we define $e(g^{\vec{a}}, h^{\vec{b}}) = e(g, h)^{\vec{a}^{\mathsf{T}} \cdot \vec{b}}$. This can be computed efficiently since $e(g, h)^{\vec{a}^{\mathsf{T}} \cdot \vec{b}} = e(g, h)^{\sum_{i=1}^{n} a_i b_i} = \prod_{i=1}^{n} e(g, h)^{a_i b_i} = \prod_{i=1}^{n} e(g^{a_i}, h^{b_i})$.

5.1 Instantiation from the SXDH Assumption

The instantiation Ξ is described as follows. Each instance $\boldsymbol{H}$ of Ξ works with a bilinear group $(\mathbb{G}_1, \mathbb{G}_2, \mathbb{G}_T, q, g, h, e)$. More precisely, let κ be a positive integer, then $\mathcal{C}$, $\mathcal{K}$ and $\mathcal{SK}$ in $\boldsymbol{H}$ are $\mathbb{G}_1^\kappa$, $\mathbb{G}_T$ and $\mathbb{G}_2^\kappa$ respectively. Also, for any $x = g^{\vec{\beta}}$ in $\mathcal{C}$ and $sk = h^{\vec{s}}$ in $\mathcal{SK}$, we have $\mathcal{H}_{sk}(x) = e(g^{\vec{\beta}}, h^{\vec{s}})$. Now, let $\vec{p}$ be a vector in $\mathbb{Z}_q^\kappa$. Then we define $\mathcal{V}$ to be $g^{span(\vec{p})}$ and for any $x = g^{r \cdot \vec{p}}$ in $\mathcal{V}$, the witness for $x \in \mathcal{V}$ is $r \in \mathbb{Z}_q$. We also define $\mathcal{PK}$ to be $\mathbb{G}_T$ and φ to be the function $\varphi(sk) = \mathcal{H}_{sk}(g^{\vec{p}})$. Note that for any $sk_1 = h^{\vec{s}_1}$ and $sk_2 = h^{\vec{s}_2}$ in $\mathcal{SK}$, we have $\varphi(sk_1) = \varphi(sk_2)$ if and only if $\vec{s}_1 - \vec{s}_2 \in span(\vec{p})^\perp$ if and only if $\forall x \in \mathcal{V}, \mathcal{H}_{sk_1}(x) = \mathcal{H}_{sk_2}(x)$. It is easy to check that $\mathcal{K}$ and $\mathcal{SK}$ are groups as we need. Also, for any $sk_1 = h^{\vec{s}_1}$ and $sk_2 = h^{\vec{s}_2}$ in $\mathcal{SK}$, we can evaluate $sk_3 = sk_1 + sk_2$ by setting $sk_3 = h^{\vec{s}_1 + \vec{s}_2}$, and $\forall x \in \mathcal{C}$, assuming $x = g^{\vec{\beta}}$, we have $\mathcal{H}_{sk_3}(x) = e(g^{\vec{\beta}}, h^{\vec{s}_1 + \vec{s}_2}) = e(g^{\vec{\beta}}, h^{\vec{s}_1}) \cdot e(g^{\vec{\beta}}, h^{\vec{s}_2}) = \mathcal{H}_{sk_1}(x) + \mathcal{H}_{sk_2}(x)$. For any secret key $sk = h^{\vec{s}}$, we define $span(sk) = \{h^{r \cdot \vec{s}} \mid r \in \mathbb{Z}_q\}$. It is easy to see that this is in fact the set $\{sk' \mid \forall x \in \mathcal{C}, \mathcal{H}_{sk}(x) = 0 \rightarrow \mathcal{H}_{sk'}(x) = 0\}$. For any $L \subseteq \mathcal{C}$, let $\mathcal{L}$ be the vector space spanned by exponents of all elements in L. Obviously, for any $sk = h^{\vec{s}}$ in $\mathcal{SK}$, $sk \in ker(L)$ if and only if $\vec{s} \in \mathcal{L}^\perp$, so we can set the trapdoor for L to be a basis of $\mathcal{L}$. Also, given trapdoors $T_1, T_2 \in \mathcal{T}$ (i.e. T_1 and T_2 are basis of vector spaces) for subsets $L_1, L_2 \subseteq \mathcal{C}$ respectively, we can evaluate the trapdoor T_3 for $L_1 \cup L_2$ by just evaluating a basis for $span(T_1 \cup T_2)$.

In addition, algorithms of Ξ works as follows:

- **Instance Generation.** To generate an instance of Ξ, the instance generation algorithm first samples a bilinear group $(\mathbb{G}_1, \mathbb{G}_2, \mathbb{G}_T, q, g, h, e)$ from distributions in an ensemble indexed by n where the SXDH assumption holds. Then it samples $\vec{p} \xleftarrow{\$} \mathbb{Z}_q^\kappa$ and sets public parameters as described above. The trapdoor T^* for $\mathcal{V}$ is exactly the vector $\vec{p}$.
- **Subset Sampling.** The subset sampling algorithm first samples $u \xleftarrow{\$} \mathbb{Z}_q$, then sets $w = u$ and $x = (g^{\vec{p}})^u$.
- **Complement Sampling.** The complement sampling algorithm first samples $\vec{\beta} \xleftarrow{\$} \mathbb{Z}_q^\kappa$ then sets $x = g^{\vec{\beta}}$ and $T = \vec{\beta}$. Note that x is statistically indistinguishable from a uniform element in $\mathcal{C} \backslash \mathcal{V}$.
- **Public Evaluation.** Given a public key $pk = e(g, h)^\alpha$ and an element $x \in \mathcal{V}$ with its witness $w = u$, the public evaluation algorithm sets $k = (e(g, h)^\alpha)^u$.
- **Private Evaluation.** Given a secret key $sk = h^{\vec{s}}$ and an element $x = g^{\vec{\beta}}$ in $\mathcal{C}$, the private evaluation algorithm computes $k = \mathcal{H}_{sk}(x) = e(g^{\vec{\beta}}, h^{\vec{s}})$.

Theorem 8. *Under the SXDH assumption, Ξ is a $\log(q)$-universal $((\kappa - 4)\log(q) - \omega(\log(n)))$-UHPS if $\kappa \geq 5$.*

Due to the limit of space, we give the proof to Theorem 8 in the full version.

5.2 Parameters

Now we discuss the security level and efficiency of our CML-PKE schemes from the SXDH assumption, namely, in what extent our PKE schemes can resist CML adversaries and how much they will cost when implemented in practice.

Generally, the degree of leakage resilience of a scheme can be measured by the leakage rate, which indicates the ratio of the tolerated leakage amount to the size of the secret state in each time period, i.e. the leakage rate $\rho = \lambda_M / \|sk\|$. Via simple computation, we can get the leakage rate of each scheme when instantiated with the SXDH assumption, and they are $1 - o(1)$, $\frac{1}{5} - o(1)$ and $\frac{1}{442} - o(1)$ for Π_1, Π_2 and Π_3 respectively. We observe that Π_1 can achieve a better leakage rate compared to Π_2. This is because to achieve CCA-security, we must ensure that the adversary is not able to get an authentication, which prevent the adversary from querying "bad ciphertexts", via the leakage. So the allowed leakage amount is smaller in this case. Besides, Π_3 have a much worse leakage rate compared to Π_1 and Π_2 since it has a much larger secret key.

We would also like to give an efficiency comparison between constructions of CCA-secure CML-PKE schemes based on UHPS and other known constructions. For simplicity, we only compare the best efficiency that can be achieved for each approach. Computation and communication overhead caused by operations such as signature and normal hash function are ignored as they are very low. Besides, our comparison is under a security level of 128, which means that breaking these schemes is as hard as breaking a 128-bit block cipher. The comparison is summarized in Table 1. Here, we use "NY" to denote the scheme constructed under the Naor-Yung paradigm, and the building blocks include the PKE scheme in [36], a normal Elgamal PKE scheme, and the Groth-Sahai proof system [16];[2] we use "CHK" to denote the scheme constructed by applying the CHK transform [6] to the identity-based encryption scheme in [26]; we use "LTDF" to denote the CCA-secure PKE scheme presented in [23]; we use "ours" to denote Π_2 instantiated from the SXDH assumption. We remark that the construction from CHK transform works in composite-order groups while other three constructions work in prime-order groups, so basic operations will execute slower in this case.

Table 1. Efficiency Comparison.

PKE schemes	$\|g\|$	$\|g_t\|$	CT overhead	Enc	Dec	Upd
NY	256	3072	$16\|g\| + 2\|g_t\|$	[0,24]	[0,49]	[5,0]
CHK	3072	6144	$4\|g\| + \|g_t\|$	[6,0]	[12,4]	[12,0]
LTDF	256	3072	$9\|g\|^2 + \|g\|$	$[4\|g\| + 1, 0]$	$[4\|g\| + 1, 4\|g\|]$	[4,0]
Ours	256	3072	$5\|g\| + \|g_t\|$	[11,0]	[5,5]	[5,0]

Here, $\|g\|$ and $\|g_t\|$ denote the size of group elements in $\mathbb{G}_1$ and $\mathbb{G}_T$ respectively and "CT overhead" denotes the difference between ciphertext and plaintext length. Moreover, "Enc", "Dec" and "Upd" represent computation overhead during encryption, decryption and key update respectively and an element "$[a, b]$" means there will be a exponentiations and b pairings executed in corresponding algorithm.

---

[2] This can only achieve a weaker non-adaptive CCA security, but we just compare with it for simplicity.

Acknowledgments. We appreciate the anonymous reviewers for their valuable suggestions. This work was supported by the National Natural Science Foundation of China (Grant No. 61173139, 61472416 and 61272478), and Strategic Priority Research Program of the Chinese Academy of Sciences (Grant No. XDA06010701, XDA06010703).

A   Omitted Constructions in Sect. 4.2

In this section, we present the omitted constructions of CCA-secure CML-PKE schemes discussed in Sect. 4.2, namely, the one from twin UHPS, and the one constructed from universal$_2$ UHPS plus AE. We only give the formal description of each schemes here and give their security analysis in the full version.

CCA-secure CML PKE from twin UHPS. The presented PKE scheme Π_4 consists of four algorithms:

- **Parameters.** Denote n as the security parameter. Let $\mathfrak{H}$ be a τ-universal λ-UHPS and $(\boldsymbol{H}, T^*) \leftarrow \mathfrak{H}.Param(1^n)$ be an instance of $\mathfrak{H}$. Let $Ext : \mathcal{K} \times \{0,1\}^d \to \{0,1\}^\iota$ be an average case (τ, δ)-strong extractor where δ is negligible in n and $\tau - \iota \geq 2\log(1/\delta)$. Consider a variant of $\mathfrak{H}$ which is identical to $\mathfrak{H}$ except that its hash functions will further take strings in $\{0,1\}^d$ and $\{0,1\}^\iota$ as input but these extra inputs will be ignored when evaluating hash functions. Let $\mathfrak{H}^\dagger$ be a τ-universal$_2$ UHPS constructed from this variant via the approach in [8]. Let $\boldsymbol{H}^\dagger$ be an instance of $\mathfrak{H}^\dagger$. Recall that $\boldsymbol{H}^\dagger$ can be generated with $\boldsymbol{H}$ directly and T^* is exactly the trapdoor for $\boldsymbol{H}^\dagger$. Also for any $L \in \mathcal{C}$, combining multiple secret keys of $\mathfrak{H}$ in $ker(L)$ will lead to a secret key $sk^\dagger$ of $\mathfrak{H}^\dagger$ in $ker(L \times \{0,1\}^d \times \{0,1\}^\iota)$. Assume $\mathcal{SK}^\dagger = \mathcal{SK}^\kappa$. Then sample $sk^* \xleftarrow{\$} ker(\mathcal{V})$ with T^* where sk^* is a secret key of $\mathfrak{H}$. Set $sk^{*\dagger} = (sk^*, \ldots, sk^*)$. The public parameter of Π_4 is $Params = (\boldsymbol{H}, sk^*, \boldsymbol{H}^\dagger, sk^{*\dagger}, Ext)$.
- **Key Generation.** The key generation algorithm of Π_4 samples $\overline{sk} \xleftarrow{\$} \mathcal{SK}$, $\overline{sk^\dagger} \xleftarrow{\$} \mathcal{SK}^\dagger$ and evaluates $pk = \varphi(\overline{sk})$, $pk^\dagger = \varphi^\dagger(\overline{sk^\dagger})$. Then it sets $PK = (pk, pk^\dagger)$ and $SK = (sk, sk^\dagger)$ where $sk = \overline{sk} + sk^{*\prime}$, $sk^\dagger = \overline{sk^\dagger} + sk^{*\dagger\prime}$, $sk^{*\prime} \xleftarrow{\$} span(sk^*)$, and $sk^{*\dagger\prime} \xleftarrow{\$} span(sk^{*\dagger})$.
- **Encryption.** Given a public key $PK = (pk, pk^\dagger)$, to encrypt a message $M \in \{0,1\}^\iota$, the encryption algorithm samples $rand \xleftarrow{\$} \{0,1\}^d$ and runs $\mathfrak{H}.VSamp(\boldsymbol{H})$ to sample $C \xleftarrow{\$} \mathcal{V}$ with a witness w. Then it evaluates $K = \mathfrak{H}.Pub(\boldsymbol{H}, pk, C, w)$, $\Psi = Ext(K, rand) \oplus M$, and $K^\dagger = \eta((C, rand, \Psi), \mathfrak{H}^\dagger.Pub(\boldsymbol{H}^\dagger, pk^\dagger, (C, rand, \Psi), w))$. Finally, it outputs $CT = (C, \Psi, rand, K^\dagger)$ as ciphertext.
- **Decryption.** Given a secret key $SK = (sk, sk^\dagger)$, to decrypt a ciphertext $CT = (C, \Psi, rand, K^\dagger)$, the decryption algorithm computes $K^{\dagger\prime} = \eta((C, rand, \Psi), \mathfrak{H}^\dagger.Priv(\boldsymbol{H}^\dagger, sk^\dagger, (C, rand, \Psi)))$ and checks whether $K^{\dagger\prime} = K^\dagger$. If $K^{\dagger\prime} = K^\dagger$, the decryption algorithm computes $K' = \mathfrak{H}.Priv(\boldsymbol{H}, sk, C)$ and outputs $M' = \Psi \oplus Ext(K', rand)$. Otherwise, it rejects with $\perp$.

- **Key Update.** Given a secret key $SK = (sk, sk^\dagger)$, the update algorithm samples $sk^{*\prime} \xleftarrow{\$} span(sk^*)$, $sk^{*\dagger\prime} \xleftarrow{\$} span(sk^{*\dagger})$, and outputs a new key $SK' = (sk', sk^{\dagger\prime})$ where $sk' = sk + sk^{*\prime}$ and $sk^{\dagger\prime} = sk^\dagger + sk^{*\dagger\prime}$.

Correctness of Π_4 can be proved similarly to that of Π_1 and security of Π_4 is guaranteed by Theorem 9 stated as follows.

Theorem 9. *Π_4 is secure against a posteriori chosen-ciphertext attacks in the CML setting with period leakage amount $\lambda_M = min(\lambda, \tau - \omega(\log n))$ and $\lambda_U = 0$.*

CCA-secure CML PKE from UHPS plus AE. The presented PKE scheme Π_5 consists of four algorithms:

- **Parameters.** Denote n as the security parameter. Let $\mathfrak{H}$ be a τ-universal$_2$ λ-UHPS and $(\boldsymbol{H}, T^*) \leftarrow \mathfrak{H}.Param(1^n)$ be an instance of $\mathfrak{H}$. Assume the range of η is $\mathcal{Y}$. We further require that $\tau = \log(\|\mathcal{Y}\|)$ and this can be fulfilled by our instantiated UHPS. Let $\mathfrak{AE} = (AE.Enc, AE.Dec)$ be an AE scheme. Sample $sk^* \xleftarrow{\$} ker(\mathcal{V})$ with T^*. The public parameter of Π_5 is $Params = (\boldsymbol{H}, sk^*, \mathfrak{AE})$.
- **Key Generation.** The key generation algorithm of Π_5 samples $\overline{sk} \xleftarrow{\$} \mathcal{SK}$ and evaluates $pk = \varphi(\overline{sk})$. Then it sets $PK = pk$ and $SK = \overline{sk} + sk^{*\prime}$ where $sk^{*\prime} \xleftarrow{\$} span(sk^*)$.
- **Encryption.** Given a public key $PK = pk$, to encrypt a message M, the encryption algorithm first runs $\mathfrak{H}.VSamp(\boldsymbol{H})$ to sample $C \xleftarrow{\$} \mathcal{V}$ with a witness w. Then it evaluates $K = \eta(C, \mathfrak{H}.Pub(\boldsymbol{H}, pk, C, w))$, and $\Psi = AE.Enc(K, M)$. Finally, it outputs $CT = (C, \Psi)$ as ciphertext.
- **Decryption.** Given a secret key $SK = sk$, to decrypt a ciphertext $CT = (C, \Psi)$, the decryption algorithm computes $K' = \eta(C, \mathfrak{H}.Priv(\boldsymbol{H}, sk, C))$, and outputs $M' = AE.Dec(K', \Psi)$.
- **Key Update.** Given a secret key $SK = sk$ the update algorithm samples $sk^{*\prime} \xleftarrow{\$} span(sk^*)$ and outputs a new key $SK' = sk + sk^{*\prime}$.

Correctness of Π_5 follows directly from correctness of Π_1 and security of Π_5 is guaranteed by Theorem 10 stated as follows.

Theorem 10. *Π_5 is secure against a posteriori chosen-ciphertext attacks in the CML setting with period leakage amount $\lambda_M = min(\lambda, \log(1/\epsilon) - \omega(\log n))$ and $\lambda_U = 0$ if $\mathfrak{AE}$ is ϵ-secure.*

References

1. Abe, M., Gennaro, R., Kurosawa, K., Shoup, V.: Tag-KEM/DEM: a new framework for hybrid encryption and a new analysis of kurosawa-desmedt KEM. In: Cramer, R. (ed.) EUROCRYPT 2005. LNCS, vol. 3494, pp. 128–146. Springer, Heidelberg (2005)

2. Akavia, A., Goldwasser, S., Vaikuntanathan, V.: Simultaneous hardcore bits and cryptography against memory attacks. In: Reingold, O. (ed.) TCC 2009. LNCS, vol. 5444, pp. 474–495. Springer, Heidelberg (2009)
3. Biham, E., Shamir, A.: Differential fault analysis of secret key cryptosystems. In: Kaliski Jr., B.S. (ed.) CRYPTO 1997. LNCS, vol. 1294, pp. 513–525. Springer, Heidelberg (1997)
4. Brakerski, Z., Kalai, Y.T., Katz, J., Vaikuntanathan, V.: Overcoming the hole in the bucket: public-key cryptography resilient to continual memory leakage. In: FOCS, pp. 501–510. IEEE (2010)
5. Brumley, D., Boneh, D.: Remote timing attacks are practical. In: USENIX Security Symposium, p. 1. USENIX Association (2003)
6. Canetti, R., Halevi, S., Katz, J.: Chosen-ciphertext security from identity-based encryption. In: Cachin, C., Camenisch, J.L. (eds.) EUROCRYPT 2004. LNCS, vol. 3027, pp. 207–222. Springer, Heidelberg (2004)
7. Carter, J.L., Wegman, M.N.: Universal classes of hash functions. In: STOC, pp. 106–112. ACM (1977)
8. Cramer, R., Shoup, V.: Universal hash proofs and a paradigm for adaptive chosen ciphertext secure public-key encryption. In: Knudsen, L.R. (ed.) EUROCRYPT 2002. LNCS, vol. 2332, p. 45. Springer, Heidelberg (2002)
9. Dodis, Y., Haralambiev, K., Lopez-Alt, A., Wichs, D.: Cryptography against continuous memory attacks. In: FOCS, pp. 511–520. IEEE (2010)
10. Dodis, Y., Kalai, Y.T., Lovett, S.: On cryptography with auxiliary input. In: STOC, pp. 621–630. ACM (2009)
11. Dodis, Y., Lewko, A., Waters, B., Wichs, D.: Storing secrets on continually leaky devices. In: FOCS, pp. 688–697. IEEE (2011)
12. Dodis, Y., Pietrzak, K.: Leakage-resilient pseudorandom functions and side-channel attacks on feistel networks. In: Rabin, T. (ed.) CRYPTO 2010. LNCS, vol. 6223, pp. 21–40. Springer, Heidelberg (2010)
13. Dodis, Y., Reyzin, L., Smith, A.: Fuzzy extractors: how to generate strong keys from biometrics and other noisy data. In: Cachin, C., Camenisch, J.L. (eds.) EUROCRYPT 2004. LNCS, vol. 3027, pp. 523–540. Springer, Heidelberg (2004)
14. Dziembowski, S., Pietrzak, K.: Leakage-resilient cryptography. In: FOCS, pp. 293–302. IEEE (2008)
15. Gennaro, R., Lindell, Y.: A framework for password-based authenticated key exchange. In: Biham, E. (ed.) EUROCRYPT 2003. LNCS, vol. 2656. Springer, Heidelberg (2003)
16. Groth, J., Sahai, A.: Efficient non-interactive proof systems for bilinear groups. In: Smart, N.P. (ed.) EUROCRYPT 2008. LNCS, vol. 4965, pp. 415–432. Springer, Heidelberg (2008)
17. Halderman, J.A., Schoen, S.D., Heninger, N., Clarkson, W., Paul, W., Calandrino, J.A., Feldman, A.J., Appelbaum, J., Felten, E.W.: Lest we remember: cold boot attacks on encryption keys. In: USENIX Security Symposium, pp. 45–60. USENIX Association (2008)
18. Hazay, C., López-Alt, A., Wee, H., Wichs, D.: Leakage-resilient cryptography from minimal assumptions. In: Johansson, T., Nguyen, P.Q. (eds.) EUROCRYPT 2013. LNCS, vol. 7881, pp. 160–176. Springer, Heidelberg (2013)
19. Hemenway, B., Ostrovsky, R.: Extended-DDH and lossy trapdoor functions. In: Fischlin, M., Buchmann, J., Manulis, M. (eds.) PKC 2012. LNCS, vol. 7293, pp. 627–643. Springer, Heidelberg (2012)

20. Hofheinz, D., Kiltz, E.: Secure hybrid encryption from weakened key encapsulation. In: Menezes, A. (ed.) CRYPTO 2007. LNCS, vol. 4622, pp. 553–571. Springer, Heidelberg (2007)

21. Kocher, P.C., Jaffe, J., Jun, B.: Differential power analysis. In: Wiener, M. (ed.) CRYPTO 1999. LNCS, vol. 1666, p. 388. Springer, Heidelberg (1999)

22. Kocher, P.C.: Timing attacks on implementations of Diffie-Hellman, RSA, DSS, and other systems. In: Koblitz, N. (ed.) CRYPTO 1996. LNCS, vol. 1109, pp. 104–113. Springer, Heidelberg (1996)

23. Koppula, V., Pandey, O., Rouselakis, Y., Waters, B.: Deterministic public-key encryption under continual leakage. Cryptology ePrint Archive, Report 2014/780 (2014). http://eprint.iacr.org/

24. Kurosawa, K., Desmedt, Y.G.: A new paradigm of hybrid encryption scheme. In: Franklin, M. (ed.) CRYPTO 2004. LNCS, vol. 3152, pp. 426–442. Springer, Heidelberg (2004)

25. Lewko, A., Lewko, M., Waters, B.: How to leak on key updates. In: STOC, pp. 725–734. ACM (2011)

26. Lewko, A., Rouselakis, Y., Waters, B.: Achieving leakage resilience through dual system encryption. In: Ishai, Y. (ed.) TCC 2011. LNCS, vol. 6597, pp. 70–88. Springer, Heidelberg (2011)

27. Micali, S., Reyzin, L.: Physically observable cryptography. In: Naor, M. (ed.) TCC 2004. LNCS, vol. 2951, pp. 278–296. Springer, Heidelberg (2004)

28. Naor, M., Segev, G.: Public-key cryptosystems resilient to key leakage. In: Halevi, S. (ed.) CRYPTO 2009. LNCS, vol. 5677, pp. 18–35. Springer, Heidelberg (2009)

29. Naor, M., Yung, M.: Public-key cryptosystems provably secure against chosen ciphertext attacks. In: STOC, pp. 427–437. ACM (1990)

30. Ors, S.B., Gurkaynak, F., Oswald, E., Preneel, B.: Power-analysis attack on an asic aes implementation. In: Information Technology: Coding and Computing, pp. 546–552. IEEE (2004)

31. Pietrzak, K.: A leakage-resilient mode of operation. In: Joux, A. (ed.) EURO-CRYPT 2009. LNCS, vol. 5479, pp. 462–482. Springer, Heidelberg (2009)

32. Qin, B., Liu, S.: Leakage-resilient chosen-ciphertext secure public-key encryption from hash proof system and one-time lossy filter. In: Sako, K., Sarkar, P. (eds.) ASIACRYPT 2013, Part II. LNCS, vol. 8270, pp. 381–400. Springer, Heidelberg (2013)

33. Qin, B., Liu, S.: Leakage-flexible CCA-secure public-key encryption: simple construction and free of pairing. In: Krawczyk, H. (ed.) PKC 2014. LNCS, vol. 8383, pp. 19–36. Springer, Heidelberg (2014)

34. Quisquater, J.-J., Samyde, D.: ElectroMagnetic Analysis (EMA): measures and counter-measures for smart cards. In: Attali, S., Jensen, T. (eds.) E-smart 2001. LNCS, vol. 2140, p. 200. Springer, Heidelberg (2001)

35. Sahai, A.: Non-malleable non-interactive zero knowledge and adaptive chosen-ciphertext security. In: FOCS, pp. 543–553. IEEE (1999)

36. Wichs, D.: Cryptographic resilience to continual information leakage. Ph.D. thesis, New York University (2011)

Server-Aided Revocable
Identity-Based Encryption

Baodong Qin[1,2], Robert H. Deng[1]([✉]), Yingjiu Li[1], and Shengli Liu[3]

[1] School of Information Systems, Singapore Management University,
Singapore 178902, Singapore
{robertdeng,yjli,bdqin}@smu.edu.sg
[2] Southwest University of Science and Technology, Mianyang 621010, China
[3] Department of Computer Science and Engineering, Shanghai Jiao Tong University,
Shanghai 200240, China
slliu@sjtu.edu.cn

Abstract. Efficient user revocation in Identity-Based Encryption (IBE) has been a challenging problem and has been the subject of several research efforts in the literature. Among them, the tree-based revocation approach, due to Boldyreva, Goyal and Kumar, is probably the most efficient one. In this approach, a trusted Key Generation Center (KGC) periodically broadcasts a set of key updates to all (non-revoked) users through public channels, where the size of key updates is only $O(r \log \frac{N}{r})$, with N being the number of users and r the number of revoked users, respectively; however, every user needs to keep at least $O(\log N)$ long-term secret keys and all non-revoked users are required to communicate with the KGC regularly. These two drawbacks pose challenges to users who have limited resources to store their secret keys or cannot receive key updates in real-time.

To alleviate the above problems, we propose a novel system model called *server-aided* revocable IBE. In our model, almost all of the workloads on users are delegated to an *untrusted* server which manages users' public keys and key updates sent by a KGC periodically. The server is untrusted in the sense that it does not possess any secret information. Our system model requires each user to keep just one short secret key and *does not* require users to communicate with either the KGC or the server during key updating. In addition, the system supports delegation of users' decryption keys, namely it is secure against decryption key exposure attacks. We present a concrete construction of the system that is provably secure against adaptive-ID chosen plaintext attacks under the DBDH assumption in the standard model. One application of our server-aided revocable IBE is encrypted email supporting lightweight devices (e.g., mobile phones) in which an email server plays the role of the untrusted server so that only non-revoked users can read their email messages.

Keywords: IBE · Revocation · Decryption key exposure

© Springer International Publishing Switzerland 2015
G. Pernul et al. (Eds.): ESORICS 2015, Part I, LNCS 9326, pp. 286–304, 2015.
DOI: 10.1007/978-3-319-24174-6_15

1   Introduction

Identity-Based Encryption (IBE) [26] eliminates the need for a Public Key Infrastructure (PKI) as in the traditional Public-Key Encryption (PKE) systems. In an IBE system, each user is allowed to use an arbitrary string (e.g., email address or phone number) as his/her public key. The corresponding decryption key is computed by a trusted authority, called Key Generation Center (KGC). Identity-based encryption has been thoroughly studied using pairing, e.g., [5,7,23] or other mathematical tools [6,8]. IBE has also been generalized to hierarchical IBE [12], fuzzy IBE [22] and attribute-based encryption [11]. In the IBE setting, as well as in all its generalizations, it is important and necessary to provide a means to revoke (compromised) users from the system. In the PKI setting, efficient revocation (e.g., [1,10,19,20]) is achievable via publicly available certificate revocation lists. However, realizing efficient user revocation in the IBE setting has been quit challenging.

To address the challenge of key revocation in IBE, Boneh and Franklin (BF) [5] suggested that a sender encrypts a message using a recipient's identity concatenated with the current time period, i.e., id$||$t, and the KGC issues a decryption key DK$_{\mathsf{id}||\mathsf{t}}$ for every non-revoked user and over every time period. Unfortunately, the BF approach is inefficient: the KGC must generate $O(N - r)$ new decryption keys in each time period, where N is the total number of users and r is the number of revoked users in the time period t. Hence, the workload on the KGC is proportional to N. Moreover, each non-revoked user need to maintain a secure channel with the KGC to get his/her new decryption key.

Boldyreva, Goyal and Kumar (BGK) [3] proposed and formalized the notion of revocable IBE. They presented an efficient R-IBE scheme based on the fuzzy IBE scheme of Sahai and Waters [22] and the tree-based revocation scheme of Naor et al. [19] in the selective-ID security model. In their scheme, each user keeps a tuple of long term secret keys. The KGC publicly broadcasts a set of key updates in each time period, so that only non-revoked users can compute new decryption keys from their long term secret keys and the key updates. Compared with the BF approach, the BGK approach significantly reduces the total size of key updates from linear to logarithmic (i.e., $O(r \log \frac{N}{r})$) in the number of users. Nevertheless, in practice, the BGK approach may suffer from the following two limitations: (1) all non-revoked users need to communicate with the KGC and update their decryption keys periodically; and (2) the sizes of both key updates and users' secret keys grow logarithmically in the number of users, i.e., $O(r \log \frac{N}{r})$ and $O(\log N)$, respectively. The first limitation cannot be avoided due to the system model of revocable IBE; while the second limitation, as explained in Lee et al. [21], is inherent in the tree-based revocation approach. Other revocable IBE schemes [13,17,18,21,24,25] that follow the BGK revocable IBE model also have such limitation(s). *A natural question that arises is whether the two limitations can be overcome in a new system model for revocable IBE?*

Our Contributions and Results. In this paper, we propose a novel revocable IBE system model to overcome the two limitations in the BGK approach. Our idea is based on the observation that in the BGK approach, almost all of the work-load on the user side can be delegated to an *untrusted* third party server. Our system model, referred to as Server-aided Revocable IBE (SR-IBE), is depicted in Fig. 1. Specifically, the SR-IBE system, consists of four types of parities: a KGC, senders, recipients and a server, and works as follows:

1. (Key Distribution: KGC ⟶ recipients and server) At the system setup phase, the KGC issues a long-term secret key and a corresponding tuple of long-term public keys for every recipient/user. The former is given to a recipient while the latter is given to the server.
2. (Encryption: sender ⟶ server) A sender encrypts a message for an identity and a time period. The resulting ciphertext is sent to the server.
3. (Partial Decryption: server ⟶ recipient) The server transforms the cipher-text to a partially decrypted ciphertext using a transformation key corre-sponding to the recipient's identity and the time period embedded in the ciphertext.
4. (Decryption: recipient) The recipient recovers the sender's message from the partially decrypted ciphertext using his/her long-term secret key or a dele-gated decryption key for the current time period.
5. (Key Updates: KGC ⟶ server) In each key updating period, the KGC deliv-ers a set of key updates to the server rather than to all non-revoked users. The server combines the key updates and the stored users' public keys to generate the transformation keys in the current time period for all users.

As in the standard revocable IBE, the KGC in SR-IBE is assumed to be fully trusted and cannot be compromised. However, the server in our model is assumed to be *untrusted* in the sense that it does not keep any secret data and only performs public storage and computation operations according to the system specifications. This notion of untrusted server is much weaker than the notion of *semi-trusted* third party in the literature which is normally assumed

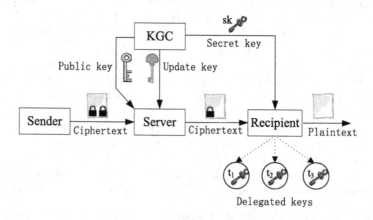

Fig. 1. System model of our server-aided revocable IBE

to hold some secret keys and cannot collude with other parties. We stress that in both cases, the server (or the third party) should perform correct operations and give correct results to the users (or the other parties). We will propose a formal security model (see Sect. 3) for RS-IBE, capturing all known threats as considered in the standard R-IBE model. We will also construct a concrete SR-IBE scheme. Remarkably, even assuming an untrusted server, our scheme achieves the following advantages simultaneously:

- It is provably secure against *both* adaptive-ID attacks and decryption exposure attacks under the Decisional Bilinear Diffie-Hellman (DBDH) assumption in the standard model, which is the refined security model for revocable IBE proposed by Seo and Emura.
- The size of every user's private key is *constant* (i.e., $O(1)$).
- *No communication* is required between users and the KGC during key update.
- The size of key updates from the KGC to the server is logarithmic (i.e., $O(r \log \frac{N}{r})$) in the number of users, as in the tree-based approach.

To show the advantages of our approach, we give a detailed comparison of our scheme with some representative non-server-aided revocable IBEs [3,5,17,18,24] and a server-aided revocable IBE [14] in Tables 1 and 2, respectively. Clearly, in our SR-IBE, non-revoked users do *not* need to communicate with the KGC or the server, while in all previous approaches, including the server-aided approach of [14], users must communicate with either the KGC or the server during every key update period. Additionally, almost all the workload on users in the previous approaches is taken over by the server in our SR-IBE while *without* sacrificing security (i.e., the scheme is still secure in the refined full security model of [24]). It is worth noting that the approach in [21] solved the second problem existed in the tree-based approach using multilinear maps, but the size of the public parameter linearly depends on the number of users and its security is proved in the selective revocation list model, which is weaker than the adaptive-ID model.

The authors of [14] showed how to delegate workload of the KGC to a semi-trusted server, which they referred to as outsourced KGC. In their approach, though the size of secret keys kept by each user is constant, the outsourced KGC must manage an outsourced master secret key and a large number of secret key shares (linear to the number of users) due to their revocation strategy of randomly splitting the master secret key for each user. Hence, the approach in [14] can not prevent collusion attacks between the outsourced KGC and revoked users, which is indicated in Table 2.

The above feature of our SR-IBE is especially attractive for lightweight user devices such as mobile phones. An excellent application scenario of the SR-IBE is secure email system in which the email server stores users' public keys, and performs key updates and partial decryptions; while email recipients only need to store their (constant size) secret keys and using them to recover email content from partially decrypted messages. In addition, the SR-IBE system supports delegation of decryption keys. When a user is away from office for a period of time, he can delegate his decryption keys over this period to his colleagues or assistants.

Table 1. Comparison with non-server-aided revocalbe IBE schemes

Schemes	BF [5]	BGK [3]	LCFZZ [18]	LV [17]	SE [24]	PLL [21]	LLP [13]	Ours 4.2	
								User	Server
PP Size	$O(1)$	$O(1)$	$O(1)$	$O(\kappa)$	$O(\kappa)$	$O(N+\kappa)$	$O(1)$		$O(\kappa)$
PK Size	-	-	-	-	-	-	-		$O(N\log N)$
SK Size	$O(1)$	$O(\log N)$	$O(1)$	$O(\log N)$	$O(\log N)$	$O(1)$	$O(\log^{1.5} N)$	$O(1)$	-
CT Size	$O(1)$	$O(1)$	$O(1)$	$O(1)$	$O(1)$	$O(1)$	$O(1)$	$O(1)$	$O(1)$
KU Size	$O(N-r)$	$O(r\log\frac{N}{r})$	$O(r)$	$O(r\log\frac{N}{r})$	$O(r\log\frac{N}{r})$	$O(1)$	$O(r)$	-	$O(r\log\frac{N}{r})$
Dec. Cost	$O(1)$	$O(1)$	$O(r)$	$O(1)$	$O(1)$	$O(1)$	$O(1)$	$O(1)$	$O(1)$
DKE Resis.	✓	✗	✗	✗	✓	✓	✓	✓	
Model	Full	Selective	Selective	Full	Full	SelectiveRL	Full	Full	
Assumption	RO, BDH	DBDH	DBDH	DBDH	DBDH	MDHE	Static	DBDH	

N is the total number of users, r is the number of revoked users and κ is the security parameter. The meanings of those abbreviations can be followed easily or found in the paper. "-" means that the item does not exist in the corresponding scheme.

Table 2. Comparison with server-aided revocable IBE schemes

Schemes	SK Size		KU Size		DKE Resis.	Model	Assumption	Collusion
	User	Server	KGC-Server	Server-User				with User
LLCJL [14]	$O(1)$	$O(N-r)$	-	$O(N-r)$	✓	Full	RO, DBDH	✗
Ours Sect. 4.2	$O(1)$	-	$O(r\log\frac{N}{r})$	-	✓	Full	DBDH	✓

Other Related Works and Discussion. Revocation with mediator [2,4,9,16] has been studied in the IBE setting, where an online semi-trusted third party (i.e., mediator) holds shares of all users' secret keys and helps users to decrypt ciphertexts. User revocation is managed by the mediator by disabling the decryption service for revoked users. As a result, this approach is subject to collusion attack between the mediator and revoked users. Our SR-IBE system model seems similar to but is inherently different from the mediator approach. In SR-IBE, user revocation is controlled by the KGC, but not the server. The server simply functions as a publicly accessible computer. Without the server, users still can decrypt their ciphertexts as they can reconstruct their transformation keys from the public keys and public key updates.

Li et al. [14] proposed an efficient method to delegate the key update workload of the trusted KGC to an outsourced semi-trusted KGC. The functionality of the outsourced KGC is similar to that of the mediator discussed earlier. For each user, the outsourced KGC splits an outsourced master secret into two shares: one is used to compute key updates and the other is used to compute the secret key for the user. To revoke a user, instead of stopping decryption service as in the mediator approach, the outsourced KGC stops sending key updates to the revoked user. So, the outsourced KGC cannot collude with revoked users and the size of key updates is linear to the number of users. Recently, Liang et al. [15] proposed a cloud-based revocable IBE with ciphertext delegation. They employed a similar secret key split technique as in [14] to achieve revocation and hence the size of key updates grows linearly with the number of system users. Besides identity revocation, they also considered ciphertext delegation through a proxy re-encryption technique so that revoked users cannot decrypt old ciphertexts.

The work in [27] combined revocable encryption with the standard IBE to directly revoke users by specifying a receiver and a set of revoked users in a ciphertext. This approach requires a sender to know the set of revoked users and hence it does not follow the notion of revocable IBE considered in this paper.

Organization. The rest of this paper is organized as follows. Section 2 introduces some basic cryptographic notions. The formal definition and security model for SR-IBE are given in Sect. 3. The main construction and security proof of our scheme are presented in Sects. 4 and 5 respectively. Summary is given in Sect. 6.

2   Preliminaries

Notations. Throughout the paper, $\mathbb{N}$ denotes the set of natural numbers and $\kappa \in \mathbb{N}$ denotes the security parameter. If S is a finite set, then $s \leftarrow_R S$ denotes the operation of picking an element s from S uniformly at random. If X is a random variable over S, then we write $x \leftarrow X$ to denote the process of sampling a value $x \in S$ according to the distribution X. We call a function negl negligible in κ, if for every positive polynomial poly$(\cdot)$ there exists an N such that for all $\kappa > N$, negl$(\kappa) < 1/$poly(κ). A probabilistic polynomial-time (PPT) algorithm A is an algorithm that on input x, computes $A(x)$ using randomness and its running time is bounded by poly(κ).

Bilinear Groups. Let $\mathbb{G}, \mathbb{G}_T$ be groups of prime order p and let g be a generator of $\mathbb{G}$. An efficiently computable map $\hat{e} : \mathbb{G} \times \mathbb{G} \to \mathbb{G}_T$ is a (symmetric) pairing if it satisfies the following two conditions:

- (Bilinearity) For all $a, b \in \mathbb{Z}_p$, we have $\hat{e}(g^a, g^b) = \hat{e}(g, g)^{ab}$;
- (Non-degeneracy) For any generator g of $\mathbb{G}$, $\hat{e}(g, g)$ is a generator of $\mathbb{G}_T$ (i.e., $\hat{e}(g, g) \neq 1$).

We denote by $\mathcal{BP}(\kappa)$ a bilinear group generator, which takes as input a security parameter κ, and outputs a description of bilinear groups $\mathcal{G} = (\mathbb{G}, \mathbb{G}_T, \hat{e}, p, g)$.

The DBDH Assumption. Let $\mathcal{G} = (\mathbb{G}, \mathbb{G}_T, \hat{e}, q, g) \leftarrow \mathcal{BP}(\kappa)$. The Decisional Bilinear Diffie-Hellman (DBDH) assumption states that, for any PPT algorithm, it is hard to distinguish the tuple $(\mathcal{G}, g^a, g^b, g^c, \hat{e}(g, g)^{abc})$ from the tuple $(\mathcal{G}, g^a, g^b, g^c, Z)$, where $a, b, c \leftarrow_R \mathbb{Z}_p$ and $Z \leftarrow_R \mathbb{G}_T$.

The Waters IBE Scheme [28]. Let $\mathbb{G}$ be a group of prime order p. For an identity id $= (b_1, \ldots, b_n) \in \{0, 1\}^n$ and $U = (u_0, u_1, \ldots, u_n) \in \mathbb{G}^{n+1}$, we denote by $F_{\mathrm{Wat}, U}(\mathrm{id}) = u_0 \cdot \prod_{i=1}^n u_i^{b_i}$ the hash function used in the IBE scheme of Waters. The Waters IBE scheme consists of the following five PPT algorithms:

$\mathsf{Sys}_{\mathrm{Wat}}(\kappa)$: On input κ, output a system parameter $\mathsf{pp}_{\mathrm{Wat}} = (\mathcal{G}, h, U)$, where $\mathcal{G} \leftarrow \mathcal{BP}(\kappa)$, $h \leftarrow_R \mathbb{G}$ and $U \leftarrow_R \mathbb{G}^{n+1}$.

$\mathsf{Setup}_{\mathrm{Wat}}(\mathsf{pp}_{\mathrm{Wat}})$: On input $\mathsf{pp}_{\mathrm{Wat}}$, output master public key $\mathsf{MPK}_{\mathrm{Wat}} = g_1 = g^\alpha$ and master secret key $\mathsf{MSK}_{\mathrm{Wat}} = h^\alpha$, where $\alpha \leftarrow_R \mathbb{Z}_p$.

$\mathsf{PrivKG}_{\mathrm{Wat}}(\mathsf{MSK}_{\mathrm{Wat}}, \mathrm{id})$: On input $\mathsf{MSK}_{\mathrm{Wat}}$ and an identity id $\in \{0, 1\}^n$, output user's secret key $\mathsf{SK}_{\mathrm{id}} = (h^\alpha \cdot F_{\mathrm{Wat}, U}(\mathrm{id})^r, g^r)$, where $r \leftarrow_R \mathbb{Z}_p$.

$\mathsf{Enc_{Wat}}(\mathsf{MPK_{Wat}}, \mathsf{id}, M)$: On input $\mathsf{MPK_{Wat}}$, $\mathsf{id} \in \{0,1\}^n$ and message $M \in \mathbb{G}$, choose $z \leftarrow_R \mathbb{Z}_p$ and output $CT_{\mathsf{id}} = (C_0, C_1, C_2)$ where $C_0 = \hat{e}(g_1, h)^z \cdot M$, $C_1 = g^z$, $C_2 = F_{\mathsf{Wat},U}(\mathsf{id})^z$.

$\mathsf{Dec_{Wat}}(\mathsf{SK_{id}}, CT_{\mathsf{id}})$: On input $\mathsf{SK_{id}} = (d_1, d_2)$ and $CT_{\mathsf{id}} = (C_0, C_1, C_2)$, output $M = C_0 \cdot K^{-1}$, where $K = \hat{e}(d_1, C_1) \cdot \hat{e}(d_2, C_2)^{-1}$.

We adopt the standard (adaptive) ID-CPA security of IBE as defined, e.g., in [5]. From [28], we have the following theorem.

Theorem 1 (Security of the Waters IBE [28, Theorem 1]**).** *Under the DBDH assumption, the Waters IBE scheme is ID-CPA secure and the security proof induces to a factor of $O(nQ)$ reduction loss, where Q is the number of private key queries.*

3   Definition and Security of SR-IBE

Definition 1 (SR-IBE). *A SR-IBE scheme involves four parties: a key generation center (KGC), sender, recipient and a third party (i.e., a server). Algorithms among these parties are defined as follows:*

$\mathsf{pp} \leftarrow \mathsf{Sys}(\kappa)$: *This is the system parameter generation algorithm run by the KGC. It takes as input a security parameter κ and outputs a system parameter pp, shared by all parities.*

$(\mathsf{MPK}, \mathsf{MSK}, \mathsf{RL}, \mathsf{ST}) \leftarrow \mathsf{Setup}(\mathsf{pp}, N)$: *This is the setup algorithm run by the KGC. It takes as input the system parameter pp and a maximal number of users N, and outputs a master public key MPK, a master secret key MSK, an initial revocation list RL and state ST.*

$(\mathsf{PK_{id}}, \mathsf{ST}) \leftarrow \mathsf{PubKG}(\mathsf{MSK}, \mathsf{id}, \mathsf{ST})$: *This is the public key generation algorithm run by the KGC. It takes as input a master secret key MSK, the recipient's identity id and state ST, and outputs a public key $\mathsf{PK_{id}}$ for the recipient, and an updated state ST. The public key $\mathsf{PK_{id}}$ is sent to the server (through a public channel).*

$(\mathsf{KU_{TK,t}}, \mathsf{ST}) \leftarrow \mathsf{TKeyUp}(\mathsf{MSK}, \mathsf{t}, \mathsf{RL}, \mathsf{ST})$: *This is the transformation key update generation algorithm run by the KGC. It takes as input a master secret key MSK, a time period t, a revocation list RL and a state ST, and outputs a transformation key update $\mathsf{KU_{TK,t}}$ and an updated state ST. The key update $\mathsf{KU_{TK,t}}$ is sent to the server (through a public channel).*

$\mathsf{TK_{id,t}} \leftarrow \mathsf{TranKG}(\mathsf{PK_{id}}, \mathsf{KU_{TK,t}})$: *This is the transformation key generation algorithm run by the server. It takes as input a public key $\mathsf{PK_{id}}$ for identity id and a transformation key update $\mathsf{KU_{TK,t}}$ for time period t, and outputs a transformation key $\mathsf{TK_{id,t}}$.*

$\mathsf{SK_{id}} \leftarrow \mathsf{PrivKG}(\mathsf{MSK}, \mathsf{id})$: *This is the private key generation algorithm run by the KGC. It takes as input a master secret key MSK and the recipient's identity id, and outputs a private key $\mathsf{SK_{id}}$ for the recipient. The private key must be sent to the recipient through a secure channel.*

$\mathsf{DK}_{\mathsf{id},\mathsf{t}} \leftarrow \mathsf{DecKG}(\mathsf{SK}_{\mathsf{id}},\mathsf{t})$: *This is the decryption key generation algorithm run by the recipient himself. It takes as input his private key* $\mathsf{SK}_{\mathsf{id}}$ *and a time period* t, *and outputs a decryption key* $\mathsf{DK}_{\mathsf{id},\mathsf{t}}$ *for time period* t.

$CT_{\mathsf{id},\mathsf{t}} \leftarrow \mathsf{Enc}(\mathsf{MPK},\mathsf{id},\mathsf{t},M)$: *This is the encryption algorithm run by the sender. It takes as input a master public key* MPK, *the recipient's identity* id, *a time period* t *and a message* M, *and outputs a ciphertext* $CT_{\mathsf{id},\mathsf{t}}$. *The ciphertext is sent into the server.*

$CT'_{\mathsf{id},\mathsf{t}} \leftarrow \mathsf{Transform}(\mathsf{TK}_{\mathsf{id},\mathsf{t}}, CT_{\mathsf{id},\mathsf{t}})$: *This is the ciphertext transformation algorithm run by the server. It takes as input a transformation key* $\mathsf{TK}_{\mathsf{id},\mathsf{t}}$ *and a ciphertext* $CT_{\mathsf{id},\mathsf{t}}$, *and outputs a partially decrypted ciphertext* $CT'_{\mathsf{id},\mathsf{t}}$. *The partially decrypted ciphertext* $CT'_{\mathsf{id},\mathsf{t}}$ *is publicly sent to the recipient.*

$M/\perp \leftarrow \mathsf{Dec}(\mathsf{DK}_{\mathsf{id},\mathsf{t}}, CT'_{\mathsf{id},\mathsf{t}})$: *This is the decryption algorithm run by the recipient. It takes as input a decryption key* $\mathsf{DK}_{\mathsf{id},\mathsf{t}}$ *and a partially decrypted ciphertext* $CT'_{\mathsf{id},\mathsf{t}}$, *and outputs a message* M *or the special symbol* $\perp$.

$\mathsf{RL} \leftarrow \mathsf{Revoke}(\mathsf{id},\mathsf{t},\mathsf{RL},\mathsf{ST})$: *This is the revocation algorithm run by the KGC. It takes as input an identity* id, *a time period* t, *a revocation list* RL *and state* ST, *and outputs an updated revocation list* RL.

Correctness. The *correctness* requires that for all security parameter κ and all message M, if the recipient is not revoked at time period t and if all parties follow the prescribed algorithms, then we have $\mathsf{Dec}(\mathsf{DK}_{\mathsf{id},\mathsf{t}}, CT'_{\mathsf{id},\mathsf{t}}) = M$.

Next, we give the semantic security against adaptive IDentity Chosen Plaintext Attacks for Server-aided Revocable IBE scheme (shorted as SR-ID-CPA security). We begin by introducing the oracles that can be accessed adaptively and repeatedly by an adversary.

- (Public Key Oracle) $\mathcal{O}^{\mathrm{sr-ibe}}_{\mathsf{PubKG}}(\cdot)$: On input an identity id, it outputs a public key $\mathsf{PK}_{\mathsf{id}}$ by running $\mathsf{PubKG}(\mathsf{MSK},\mathsf{id},\mathsf{ST})$.
- (Transformation Key Update Oracle) $\mathcal{O}^{\mathrm{sr-ibe}}_{\mathsf{TKeyUp}}(\cdot)$: On input a time period t, it outputs $\mathsf{KU}_{\mathsf{TK},\mathsf{t}}$ by running $\mathsf{TKeyUp}(\mathsf{MSK},\mathsf{t},\mathsf{RL},\mathsf{ST})$.
- (Private Key Oracle) $\mathcal{O}^{\mathrm{sr-ibe}}_{\mathsf{PrivKG}}(\cdot)$: On input an identity id, it outputs a private key $\mathsf{SK}_{\mathsf{id}}$ through running $\mathsf{PrivKG}(\mathsf{MSK},\mathsf{id})$.
- (Decryption Key Oracle) $\mathcal{O}^{\mathrm{sr-ibe}}_{\mathsf{DecKG}}(\cdot,\cdot)$: On input an identity id and a time period t, it outputs $\mathsf{DK}_{\mathsf{id},\mathsf{t}}$ by running $\mathsf{DecKG}(\mathsf{SK}_{\mathsf{id}},\mathsf{t})$, where $\mathsf{SK}_{\mathsf{id}}$ is obtained via $\mathsf{PrivKG}(\mathsf{MSK},\mathsf{id})$.
- (Revocation Oracle) $\mathcal{O}^{\mathrm{sr-ibe}}_{\mathsf{Revoke}}(\cdot,\cdot)$: On input an identity id and a time period t, it outputs an updated revocation list RL by running $\mathsf{Revoke}(\mathsf{id},\mathsf{t},\mathsf{RL},\mathsf{ST})$.

Definition 2 (SR-ID-CPA Security). *Let* $\mathcal{O}^{\mathrm{ibe}}_{\mathrm{sr}}$ *denote the family of the oracles defined above. We say a SR-IBE scheme is SR-ID-CPA secure, if for any PPT adversary* $\mathcal{A}$, *the function* $\mathsf{Adv}^{\mathrm{sr-id-ibe}}_{\mathrm{SR-IBE},\mathcal{A}}(\kappa)$ *is negligible in* κ, *where*

$$\mathsf{Adv}^{\mathrm{sr-id-cpa}}_{\mathrm{SR-IBE},\mathcal{A}}(\kappa) := \left| \Pr\left[b' = b : \begin{array}{l} \mathsf{pp} \leftarrow \mathsf{Sys}(\kappa) \\ (\mathsf{MPK},\mathsf{MSK},\mathsf{RL},\mathsf{ST}) \leftarrow \mathsf{Setup}(\mathsf{pp}) \\ (\mathsf{id}^*,\mathsf{t}^*,M_0,M_1) \leftarrow \mathcal{A}^{\mathcal{O}^{\mathrm{ibe}}_{\mathrm{sr}}}(\mathsf{MPK}) \\ b \leftarrow_R \{0,1\} \\ CT_{\mathsf{id}^*,\mathsf{t}^*} \leftarrow \mathsf{Enc}(\mathsf{MPK},\mathsf{id}^*,\mathsf{t}^*,M_b) \\ b' \leftarrow \mathcal{A}^{\mathcal{O}^{\mathrm{ibe}}_{\mathrm{sr}}}(CT_{\mathsf{id}^*,\mathsf{t}^*}) \end{array} \right] - \frac{1}{2} \right|.$$

In the above definition, the following conditions must hold:

1. $M_0, M_1 \in \mathcal{M}$ and $|M_0| = |M_1|$, where $\mathcal{M}$ is the message space.
2. $\mathcal{O}^{sr-ibe}_{TKeyUp}(\cdot)$ and $\mathcal{O}^{sr-ibe}_{Revoke}(\cdot, \cdot)$ can be queried only in non-decreasing order of time.
3. $\mathcal{O}^{sr-ibe}_{Revoke}(\cdot, \cdot)$ can not be queried on time t if $\mathcal{O}^{sr-ibe}_{TKeyUp}(\cdot)$ has been queried on time t.
4. If the private key generation oracle $\mathcal{O}^{sr-ibe}_{PrivKG}(\cdot)$ is queried on the challenge identity id^*, the revocation oracle $\mathcal{O}^{sr-ibe}_{Revoke}(\cdot, \cdot)$ must be queried on (id^*, t) for any $t \leq t^*$.
5. If id^* is not revoked at time t^*, $\mathcal{O}^{sr-ibe}_{DecKG}(\cdot, \cdot)$ can not be queried on (id^*, t^*).

The above security notion essentially captures the following scenarios: (1) a revoked user cannot access ciphertexts encrypted under a future time period; (2) a compromised decryption key for (id, t) only endangers the privacy of ciphertexts encrypted under (id, t); (3) Except the KGC, all other parities can collude. A user's decryption key is updated by the user himself; hence, no communication is required between the user and the KGC once the user's private key was distributed. Moreover, all communications between the KGC and the server take place over a public channel which can be accessed by the adversary. The server does not hold any secret data, it simply functions as a computing device.

4   Construction of SR-IBE Scheme

4.1   The Node Selection Algorithm: KUNodes

In this subsection, we recall the node selection algorithm KUNodes as in previous revocable IBE systems [3,24]. This algorithm computes a minimal set Y of nodes for which transformation key updates have to be published so that the server can generate the transformation keys corresponding to non-revoked users.

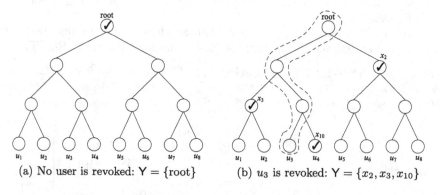

(a) No user is revoked: $Y = \{root\}$ (b) u_3 is revoked: $Y = \{x_2, x_3, x_{10}\}$

Fig. 2. Illustration of KUNodes Algorithm

We employ similar notations as in [3]. For a binary tree BT with N leaves, corresponding to N users, we denote by root the root node of the tree BT. If θ is a leaf node, we let Path(θ) stand for the set of nodes on the path from θ to root (both θ and root are inclusive). If θ is a non-leaf node, then θ_l and θ_r denote left and right children of θ. The node selection algorithm KUNodes takes as input the binary tree BT, the revocation list RL and a revocation time t, and works as follows: it first marks all ancestors of users that were revoked by revocation time t as revoked nodes. Then, it outputs all the non-revoked children of revoked nodes. A simple pictorial depiction of KUNodes is given in Fig. 2. Below is the formal definition.

> KUNodes(BT, RL, t) //Node selection algorithm
> $\quad$ X, Y $\leftarrow \emptyset$
> $\quad \forall (\theta_i, t_i) \in$ RL, if $t_i \leq$ t, then add Path(θ_i) to X
> $\quad \forall x \in$ X, if $x_l \notin$ X, then add x_l to Y; if $x_r \notin$ X, then add x_r to Y
> $\quad$ If Y $= \emptyset$, then add root to Y
> $\quad$ Return Y

4.2 The Construction

We assume that the identity space is $\{0,1\}^n$ and the time space is $\mathcal{T}$. The message space $\mathcal{M}$ is the same as that of the underlying group. Our SR-IBE scheme consists of the following algorithms:

Sys(κ): On input a security parameter κ, the KGC does the following:

1. Choose $\mathcal{G} = (\mathbb{G}, \mathbb{G}_T, p, g, \hat{e}) \leftarrow \mathcal{BP}(\kappa)$.
2. Choose a random element $h \leftarrow_R \mathbb{G}$.
3. Choose a random $n+1$-dimensional vector $U = (u_0, u_1, \ldots, u_n) \leftarrow_R \mathbb{G}^{n+1}$ and a random 2-dimensional vector $(v_0, v_1) \leftarrow_R \mathbb{G}^2$.
4. Define and return pp $= (\mathcal{G}, h, U, v_0, v_1)$.

Setup(pp, N): On input pp and a maximal number of users N, the KGC does the following:

1. Choose two random exponents $\alpha, \beta \leftarrow_R \mathbb{Z}_p$ and set $g_1 = g^{\alpha+\beta}$.
2. Initialize the revocation list RL $= \emptyset$ and the state ST $:=$ BT, where BT is a binary tree with N leaves.
3. Define MPK $= g_1$ and MSK $= (h^\alpha, h^\beta)$.
4. Return (MPK, MSK, RL, ST).

PubKG(MSK, id, ST): Parse MSK as (h^α, h^β) and ST as BT. The KGC does the following:

1. Pick an unassigned leaf note θ from BT and store id in this node.
2. For each node $x \in$ Path(θ), it does the following:
   (a) Recall $g_{x,1}$ from BT. If it is undefined, choose $g_{x,2} \leftarrow_R \mathbb{G}$, set $g_{x,1} = h^\alpha/g_{x,2}$ and store the pair $(g_{x,1}, g_{x,2})$ in node x.

    (b) Choose $r_x \leftarrow_R \mathbb{Z}_p$.

    (c) Compute $(P_{x,1}, P_{x,2}) = (g_{x,1} \cdot F_{\mathsf{Wat},U}(\mathsf{id})^{r_x}, g^{r_x})$.

3. Return $\mathsf{PK}_{\mathsf{id}} = \{(x, P_{x,1}, P_{x,2})\}_{x \in \mathsf{Path}(\theta)}$ and an updated state ST.

TKeyUp(MSK, t, RL, ST): Parse MSK as (h^α, h^β) and ST as BT. For all $x \in$ KUNodes(BT, RL, t), the KGC does the following:

1. Fetch $g_{x,2}$ from BT. If it is not defined, similar as in the public key generation algorithm, choose $(g_{x,1}, g_{x,2}) \in \mathbb{G} \times \mathbb{G}$ such that $g_{x,1} \cdot g_{x,2} = h^\alpha$ and store it in the node x.
2. Choose $s_x \leftarrow_R \mathbb{Z}_p$.
3. Compute $(Q_{x,1}, Q_{x,2}) = (g_{x,2} \cdot (v_0 v_1^t)^{s_x}, g^{s_x})$.
4. Return $\mathsf{KU}_{\mathsf{TK},t} = \{(x, Q_{x,1}, Q_{x,2})\}_{x \in \mathsf{KUNodes}(\mathsf{BT},\mathsf{RL},t)}$ to the server.

TranKG($\mathsf{PK}_{\mathsf{id}}$, $\mathsf{KU}_{\mathsf{TK},t}$): On input $\mathsf{PK}_{\mathsf{id}}$ and $\mathsf{KU}_{\mathsf{TK},t}$, the server generates a transformation key for (id, t) as follows: Parse $\mathsf{PK}_{\mathsf{id}}$ as $\{(x, P_{x,1}, P_{x,2})\}_{x \in I}$ and $\mathsf{KU}_{\mathsf{id},t}$ as $\{(x, Q_{x,1}, Q_{x,2})\}_{x \in J}$ for some sets of nodes I, J. If $I \cap J = \emptyset$ (i.e., no pair $(i,j) \in I \times J$ such that $i = j$), return $\perp$; else choose an arbitrary $x \in I \cap J$ and $r'_x, s'_x \leftarrow_R \mathbb{Z}_p$, compute and return $\mathsf{TK}_{\mathsf{id},t} = (TK_1, TK_2, TK_3)$, where

$$
\begin{cases}
TK_1 = P_{x,1} \cdot Q_{x,1} \cdot F_{\mathsf{Wat},U}(\mathsf{id})^{r'_x} \cdot (v_0 v_1^t)^{s'_x} & (= h^\alpha \cdot F_{\mathsf{Wat},U}(\mathsf{id})^{r_x + r'_x} \cdot (v_0 v_1^t)^{s_x + s'_x}) \\
TK_2 = P_{x,2} \cdot g^{r'_x} & (= g^{r_x + r'_x}) \\
TK_3 = Q_{x,2} \cdot g^{s'_x} & (= g^{s_x + s'_x})
\end{cases}.
$$

PrivKG(MSK, id): Parse MSK as (h^α, h^β), the KGC does the following:

1. Choose $r_{\mathsf{id}} \leftarrow_R \mathbb{Z}_p$.
2. Compute $(D_{\mathsf{id},1}, D_{\mathsf{id},2}) = (h^\beta \cdot F_{\mathsf{Wat},U}(\mathsf{id})^{r_{\mathsf{id}}}, g^{r_{\mathsf{id}}})$.
3. Return $\mathsf{SK}_{\mathsf{id}} = (D_{\mathsf{id},1}, D_{\mathsf{id},2})$.

DecKG($\mathsf{SK}_{\mathsf{id}}$, t): Parse $\mathsf{SK}_{\mathsf{id}}$ as $(D_{\mathsf{id},1}, D_{\mathsf{id},2})$. The user chooses $r'_{\mathsf{id}}, s'_t \leftarrow_R \mathbb{Z}_p$, and then computes and returns $\mathsf{DK}_{\mathsf{id},t} = (D_1, D_2, D_3)$, where

$$
\begin{cases}
D_1 = D_{\mathsf{id},1} \cdot F_{\mathsf{Wat},U}(\mathsf{id})^{r'_{\mathsf{id}}} \cdot (v_0 v_1^t)^{s'_t} & (= h^\beta \cdot F_{\mathsf{Wat},U}(\mathsf{id})^{r_{\mathsf{id}} + r'_{\mathsf{id}}} \cdot (v_0 v_1^t)^{s'_t}) \\
D_2 = D_{\mathsf{id},2} \cdot g^{r'_{\mathsf{id}}} & (= g^{r_{\mathsf{id}} + r'_{\mathsf{id}}}) \\
D_3 = g^{s'_t} & (= g^{s'_t})
\end{cases}.
$$

Encrypt(MPK, id, t, M): To encrypt a message M under identity id and time period t, the sender chooses $z \leftarrow_R \mathbb{Z}_p$ and sets $CT = (C_0, C_1, C_2, C_3)$, where

$$
C_0 = \hat{e}(g_1, h)^z \cdot M \qquad C_1 = g^z \qquad C_2 = F_{\mathsf{Wat},U}(\mathsf{id})^z \qquad C_3 = (v_0 v_1^t)^z.
$$

It returns $CT_{\mathsf{id},t} = (\mathsf{id}, t, CT)$ to the server.

Transform($\mathsf{TK}_{\mathsf{id},t}$, $CT_{\mathsf{id},t}$): Parse $\mathsf{TK}_{\mathsf{id},t}$ as (TK_1, TK_2, TK_3) and $CT_{\mathsf{id},t}$ as $(\mathsf{id}, t, C_0, C_1, C_2, C_3)$. It computes

$$
K_1 = \frac{\hat{e}(C_1, TK_1)}{\hat{e}(C_2, TK_2) \cdot \hat{e}(C_3, TK_3)} \qquad \left(= \hat{e}(g^\alpha, h)^z\right)
$$

Then, it sets $C'_0 = C_0 / K_1$ and returns $CT'_{\mathsf{id},t} = (\mathsf{id}, t, C'_0, C_1, C_2, C_3)$ to the recipient.

Decrypt($\mathsf{DK}_{\mathsf{id},\mathsf{t}}, CT'_{\mathsf{id},\mathsf{t}}$): Parse $\mathsf{DK}_{\mathsf{id},\mathsf{t}}$ as (D_1, D_2, D_3) and $CT'_{\mathsf{id},\mathsf{t}}$ as (id, t, $(C'_0, C_1,$ $C_2, C_3))$. It computes

$$K_2 = \frac{\hat{e}(C_1, D_1)}{\hat{e}(C_2, D_2) \cdot \hat{e}(C_3, D_3)} \quad \left(= \frac{\hat{e}(g^z, h^\beta \cdot F_{\mathsf{Wat},U}(\mathsf{id})^{r_{id}+r'_{id}} \cdot (v_0 v_1^t)^{s_t+s'_t})}{\hat{e}(F_{\mathsf{Wat},U}(\mathsf{id})^z, g^{r_{id}+r'_{id}}) \cdot \hat{e}((v_0 v_1^t)^z, g^{s_t+s'_t})} = \hat{e}(g^\beta, h)^z \right)$$

and returns $M = C'_0/K_2$.

5   Security Proof

Correctness of the scheme can be verified by direct calculation. We omit it here and only focus on its security proof below.

Theorem 2. *If there exists a PPT adversary $\mathcal{A}$ breaking the SR-ID-CPA security of the proposed SR-IBE scheme, then we can construct a PPT adversary $\mathcal{B}$ breaking the ID-CPA security of the Waters IBE scheme. Moreover,*

$$\mathsf{Adv}^{\mathsf{sr-id-cpa}}_{\mathsf{SR-IBE},\mathcal{A}}(\kappa) \leq 2Q|\mathcal{T}| \cdot \mathsf{Adv}^{\mathsf{id-cpa}}_{\mathsf{IBE_{Wat}},\mathcal{B}}(\kappa)$$

where Q is the maximal number of oracle queries issued by the adversary $\mathcal{A}$ and $\mathcal{T}$ is the set of revocation time periods.

Proof Outline. Here, we only highlight the center idea of proof. We refer the interested reader to Appendix A for the formal proof.

At a high level, we can view our scheme as a combination of a traditional revocable IBE scheme of Seo and Emura [24] (with master secret key h^α) and a two-level HIBE scheme derived from the Waters IBE scheme [28] (with master secret key h^β). The first component is again built from the Waters IBE scheme. The long-term private keys, hold by users in RIBE, are now publicly delegated to the server. Each user actually holds one of the first level secret keys of the underlying two-level HIBE scheme as his long-term private key. In the proof, we divide the adversaries into the following two distinct types.

Type I Adversary: The adversary issues a query to the private key oracle $\mathcal{O}^{\mathsf{sr-ibe}}_{\mathsf{PrivKG}}(\cdot)$ with the challenge identity id*. So, the identity id* must be revoked before the challenge time t*.

Type II Adversary: The adversary *never* issues a query to the private key oracle $\mathcal{O}^{\mathsf{sr-ibe}}_{\mathsf{PrivKG}}(\cdot)$ with the challenge identity id*, but it may query the decryption key oracle $\mathcal{O}^{\mathsf{sr-ibe}}_{\mathsf{DecKG}}(\cdot, \cdot)$ with (id*, t) as long as t $\neq$ t*.

We can view our proof as a reduction to either the security of the underlying revocable IBE scheme or the security of the HIBE scheme according to which type of adversaries our scheme is faced with. For the first type of adversary, it can obtain the challenge first-level secrete key of the HIBE scheme, and hence any decryption key. So, we cannot reduce our security to the underlying HIBE. Instead, we reduce it to the security of the underlying RIBE. The RIBE oracle can answer all public key queries and transformation key update queries issued by

298   B. Qin et al.

the adversary since the challenge identity must be revoked before the challenge time. For the second type of adversary, the adversary does not query the private key of the challenge identity, so it can query for long-term public keys and key updates even for challenge identity and time period. In this case, it is possible to reduce our security to that of the underlying HIBE since the adversary is forbidden to query the decryption key for challenge identity and time period.

6 Conclusion

In this paper, we proposed a new system model for revocable IBE, named server-aided revocable IBE (SR-IBE). The model has two desirable features which make it especially suitable for users with limited computation, communication, and storage capabilities. First, SR-IBE delegates almost all of the workload imposed on users in previous non-server aided revocable IBE systems to an untrusted third party server. Second, SR-IBE only requires each user to store a short long-term private key such that a user can update decryption keys all by himself, without having to communicate with either the KGC or the third party server. We also presented a concrete SR-IBE scheme and proved that it is secure against both adaptive-ID attacks and decryption exposure attacks under the decisional Bilinear Diffie-Hellman assumption in the standard model. An ideal application of the SR-IBE is secure Email systems supporting mobile users in which Email servers could naturally double as the untrusted third party server.

Acknowledgments. We thank the anonymous reviewers for their helpful comments. The work of Robert H. Deng was supported by Singapore Ministry of Education Academic Research Fund Tier 1 under the research grant 14-C220-SMU-06. The work of Shengli Liu was supported by the National Natural Science Foundation of China (NSFC Grant No. 61170229 and 61373153), the Specialized Research Fund for the Doctoral Program of Higher Education (Grant No. 20110073110016), and the Scientific innovation projects of Shanghai Education Committee (Grant No. 12ZZ021).

A Proof of Theorem 2

Proof. Let $\mathcal{A}$ be the adversary that breaks the SR-ID-CPA security of the above SR-IBE scheme. We construct an adaptive ID-CPA adversary (simulator) of the Waters IBE scheme using $\mathcal{A}$ as a subroutine.

The simulator is given a challenge instance of the Waters IBE scheme, including a system parameter $pp_{Wat} = (\mathcal{G}, h, U)$, a master public key $MPK_{Wat} = g^{\gamma^*}$ for some unknown exponent γ^*, private key generation oracle $\mathcal{O}^{ibe}_{PrivKG_{Wat}}(\cdot)$ and an encryption oracle $\mathcal{O}^{ibe}_{Enc_{Wat}}(\cdot, \cdot, \cdot)$[1]. The simulator first randomly guesses the challenge revocation time period $t^* \leftarrow_R \mathcal{T}$.

In the proof, the simulator has to randomly guess which type of adversaries (as described in Sect. 5) is going to be.

---
[1] The encryption oracle is defined as follows: on input (id, M_0, M_1), output $CT^{Wat}_{id} = (C_0, C_1, C_2) \leftarrow Enc_{Wat}(id, M_b)$, where $b \leftarrow_R \{0, 1\}$.

Proof (Proof of Type I Adversary). Let Q be the maximal number of queries issued by the adversary. The simulator randomly guesses $i^* \leftarrow_R \{1, \ldots, Q\}$, assuming that id^* firstly appears in the i^*-th query among all queries issued by the adversary. We show at the end of the proof that the guess holds with probability $1/Q$. Additionally, the simulator randomly chooses an unassigned leaf node θ^* for storing the challenge identity id^*.

The simulator simulates the SR-ID-CPA game as follows:

System Parameter: The simulator chooses random exponents $a, b \leftarrow_R \mathbb{Z}_p$ and sets $v_0 = h^{t^*} \cdot g^a$, $v_1 = h^{-1} \cdot g^b$. The simulator returns $\mathsf{pp} = (\mathsf{pp}_{\mathsf{Wat}}, v_0, v_1)$ to the adversary and holds (a, b).

Setup: The simulator chooses a random exponent $\beta \leftarrow_R \mathbb{Z}_p$. It sets $\mathsf{MPK} = g_1 = \mathsf{MPK}_{\mathsf{Wat}}$ and $\mathsf{MSK} = (h^{\gamma^* - \beta}, h^\beta)$, where $\gamma^* - \beta = \alpha$ is unknown to the simulator. The simulator sends MPK to the adversary. It holds h^β, an empty revocation list RL and an initial state of a binary tree $\mathsf{ST} := \mathsf{BT}$.

Private Key Oracle and Decryption Key Oracle: Since the simulator knows the master secret key part h^β, it can answer all queries issued by the adversary to these two oracles. If the i^*-th query appears among the queries issued to these two oracles, the simulator knows the challenge identity id^* and stores it in the pre-assigned leaf node θ^*.

Transformation Key Update Oracle: When $\mathcal{A}$ issues a transformation key update generation query on time period t, the simulator does the following:

1. For all $x \in \mathsf{KUNodes}(\mathsf{BT}, \mathsf{RL}, t)$, fetch η_x from node x of BT if it is defined. Otherwise, randomly choose $\eta_x \in \mathbb{G}$ and store it in the node x.
2. Choose $s_x \leftarrow_R \mathbb{Z}_p$.
3. Compute $(x, Q_{x,1}, Q_{x,2})$ as follows:

$$(Q_{x,1}, Q_{x,2}) = \begin{cases} (\eta_x^{-1} \cdot h^{-\beta} \cdot (v_0 v_1^t)^{s_x}, g^{s_x}) & \text{If } x \notin \mathsf{Path}(\theta^*) \\ (\eta_x^{-1} \cdot h^{-\beta} \cdot h^{(t^* - t)s_x} \cdot g_1^{\frac{a+bt}{t-t^*}} \cdot g^{(a+bt)s_x}, g_1^{\frac{1}{t-t^*}} \cdot g^{s_x}) & \text{Otherwise} \end{cases}.$$

4. Return $\mathsf{KU}_{\mathsf{TK},t} = \{(x, Q_{x,1}, Q_{x,2})\}_{x \in \mathsf{KUNodes}(\mathsf{BT}, \mathsf{RL}, t)}$ to the adversary.

Remark 1. For all $x \in \mathsf{Path}(\theta^*)$, if $t \neq t^*$, $(Q_{x,1}, Q_{x,2})$ can be rewritten in the form $(Q_{x,1}, Q_{x,2}) = \left(\eta_x^{-1} \cdot h^{\gamma^* - \beta} \cdot (v_0 v_1^t)^{s_x'}, g^{s_x'} \right)$ for some unknown exponent $s_x' = -\frac{\gamma^*}{t^* - t} + s_x$.

Public Key Oracle: Let j_{PK} denote $\mathcal{A}$'s j_{PK}-th query issued to the public key oracle. When $\mathcal{A}$ issues a public key generation query on identity id, if the identity id firstly appears in $\mathcal{A}$'s queries, the simulator randomly chooses an unassigned leaf node θ and stores id in θ. We consider the following three cases:

Case 1: $j_{\mathsf{PK}} < i^*$. In this case, $id \neq id^*$. So, the simulator can query the Waters user key generation oracle $\mathcal{O}_{\mathsf{PrivKGWat}}^{\mathsf{ibe}}(\cdot)$ on identity id and obtain a

Waters "private key" (d_1, d_2) for identity id. For each node $x \in \mathsf{Path}(\theta)$, the simulator recalls η_x if it is defined. If not, it chooses $\eta_x \leftarrow_R \mathbb{G}$ and stores η_x in node x. Then, it chooses $r_x \leftarrow_R \mathbb{Z}_p$ and computes $(x, P_{x,1}, P_{x,2})$ as follows

$$(P_{x,1}, P_{x,2}) = \begin{cases} (\eta_x \cdot d_1 \cdot F_{\mathsf{Wat},U}(\mathsf{id})^{r_x}, d_2 \cdot g^{r_x}) & \text{If } x \notin \mathsf{Path}(\theta^*) \\ (\eta_x \cdot F_{\mathsf{Wat},U}(\mathsf{id})^{r_x}, g^{r_x}) & \text{Otherwise} \end{cases}.$$

The simulator returns $\mathsf{PK_{id}} = \{(x, P_{x,1}, P_{x,2})\}_{x \in \mathsf{KUNodes(BT,RL,t)}}$ to the adversary.

Case 2: $j_{\mathsf{PK}} = i^*$. In this case, the simulator knows the challenge identity id^* and stores it in the pre-assigned leaf node θ^*. For each $x \in \mathsf{Path}(\theta^*)$, the simulator recalls η_x if it is defined. If not, it chooses $\eta_x \leftarrow_R \mathbb{G}$ and stores η_x in node x. It then chooses $r_x \leftarrow_R \mathbb{Z}_p$ and computes $(x, P_{x,1}, P_{x,2})$ as follows

$$(P_{x,1}, P_{x,2}) = (\eta_x \cdot F_{\mathsf{Wat},U}(\mathsf{id}^*)^{r_x}, g^{r_x}).$$

The simulator returns $\mathsf{PK_{id^*}} = \{(x, P_{x,1}, P_{x,2})\}_{x \in \mathsf{Path}(\theta^*)}$ to the adversary.

Case 3: $j_{\mathsf{PK}} > i^*$. In this case, the simulator knows the challenge identity id^{*2}. If $\mathsf{id} \neq \mathsf{id}^*$, the simulator does the same process as in Case 1. Otherwise, it does the same process as in Case 2.

Remark 2. Observe that for each node $x \in \mathsf{BT}$, the pair of values $(g_{x,1}, g_{x,2})$ is well defined. For example, if $x \notin \mathsf{Path}(\theta^*)$, the simulator in fact implicitly defined $g_{x,1} = \eta_x \cdot h^{\gamma^*}$ and $g_{x,2} = \eta_x^{-1} \cdot h^{-\beta}$ so that $g_{x,1} \cdot g_{x,2} = h^{\gamma^* - \beta}$. So, from the above constructions of transformation key updates and public keys, if an identity id is not revoked at time period t, the transformation key $\mathsf{TK_{id,t}}$ always has the form $\mathsf{TK_{id,t}} = (h^{\gamma^* - \beta} \cdot F_{\mathsf{Wat},U}(\mathsf{id})^{r_x} \cdot (v_0 v_1^t)^{s_x}, g^{r_x}, g^{s_x})$ for some random exponents $r_x, s_x \leftarrow_R \mathbb{Z}_p$.

Challenge Ciphertext: When $\mathcal{A}$ issues a challenge ciphertext query $(\mathsf{id}^*, \mathsf{t}^*, M_0, M_1)$, the simulator submits $(\mathsf{id}^*, M_0, M_1)$ to the Waters encryption oracle $\mathcal{O}^{\mathsf{ibe}}_{\mathsf{EncWat}}(\cdot, \cdot, \cdot)$ and obtains the Waters challenge ciphertext $CT^{\mathsf{Wat}}_{\mathsf{id}^*} = (C_0^{\mathsf{Wat}}, C_1^{\mathsf{Wat}}, C_2^{\mathsf{Wat}})$ where

$$C_0^{\mathsf{Wat}} = \hat{e}(\mathsf{MPK_{Wat}}, h)^z \cdot M_b \qquad C_1^{\mathsf{Wat}} = g^z \qquad C_2^{\mathsf{Wat}} = F_{\mathsf{Wat},U}(\mathsf{id}^*)^z$$

for some unknown random exponent $z \leftarrow_R \mathbb{Z}_p$. The simulator computes $C_3 = (C_1^{\mathsf{Wat}})^{a+bt^*}$ and returns $CT_{\mathsf{id}^*, \mathsf{t}^*} = (C_0^{\mathsf{Wat}}, C_1^{\mathsf{Wat}}, C_2^{\mathsf{Wat}}, C_3)$ to $\mathcal{A}$.

Guess: Finally, $\mathcal{A}$ outputs a bit b'. The simulator forwards it to its own challenger.

Discussion 1. Since the simulated master public key $\mathsf{MPK} = \mathsf{MPK_{Wat}}$ and $C_3 = C_1^{a+bt^*} = (v_0 v_1^{t^*})^z$, the simulated challenge ciphertext has the right distribution as that in the original SR-ID-CPA game. Recall that all the oracles are also well

---

[2] It may be obtained from previous queries issued to other oracles.

simulated. So, if the simulator correctly guesses the challenge time period t^* *and the index* i^*, *the simulator perfectly simulates Type I adversary* $\mathcal{A}$'s *environment in the SR-ID-CPA game. Recall that all guesses are randomly and independently chosen from the corresponding sets and the simulated SR-ID-CPA game only depends on the simulator's guesses, not depending on the adversary's behaviour. So, the simulator successfully simulates the SR-ID-CPA game with probability at least* $1/(Q|\mathcal{T}|)$, *i.e.,* $\mathsf{Adv}_{SR-IBE,\mathcal{A}}^{sr-id-cpa}(\kappa) \le Q|\mathcal{T}| \cdot \mathsf{Adv}_{Wat,\mathcal{B}}^{id-cpa}(\kappa)$, *where* $\mathcal{B}$ *is an adversary (the simulator) attacking the Waters IBE scheme.*

Proof (Proof of Type II Adversary). The simulator simulates the SR-ID-CPA game for Type II adversary as follows:

System Parameter: The simulator chooses $a, b \leftarrow_R \mathbb{Z}_p$ and sets $v_0 = h^{t^*} \cdot g^a$, $v_1 = h^{-1} \cdot g^b$. It returns $\mathsf{pp} = (\mathsf{pp}_{Wat}, v_0, v_1)$ to the adversary and holds (a, b).

Setup: The simulator chooses $\alpha \leftarrow_R \mathbb{Z}_p$ and implicitly sets $\beta = \gamma^* - \alpha$. It defines $\mathsf{MPK} = \mathsf{MPK}_{Wat}$ and $\mathsf{MSK} = (h^\alpha, h^\beta)$, where $h^\beta = h^{\gamma^* - \alpha}$ is unknown. The simulator sends MPK to the adversary, and holds h^α, an empty revocation list RL and a state of a binary tree $\mathsf{ST} := \mathsf{BT}$.

Public Key Oracle and Transformation Key Update Oracle: Note that, the simulator knows the master secret key part h^α. So, it can answer all the queries issued by the adversary to these two oracles.

Private Key Oracle: Recall that a Type II adversary does not query the private key SK_{id^*}. When the adversary issues a private key generation query for identity id, the simulator can answer it as follows:

1. Forward id to the Waters private key oracle $\mathcal{O}_{PrivKG_{Wat}}^{ibe}(\cdot)$ and obtain a Waters private key (d_1, d_2) for identity id.
2. Set $D_{id,1} = h^{-\alpha} \cdot d_1$ and $D_{id,2} = d_2$.
3. Return $\mathsf{SK}_{id} = (D_{id,1}, D_{id,2})$ to $\mathcal{A}$.

Decryption Key Oracle: When $\mathcal{A}$ issues a decryption key generation query on (id, t), the simulator first checks whether $t = t^*$. If so, we must have $id \ne id^*$. The simulator first involves private key oracle with id to obtain private key SK_{id} and thereby the decryption key DK_{id,t^*}. Otherwise (i.e., $t \ne t^*$), the simulator does the following:

1. Choose $r_{id}, s_t \leftarrow_R \mathbb{Z}_p$.
2. Compute $D_1 = h^{-\alpha} \cdot F_{Wat,U}(id)^{r_{id}} \cdot h^{(t^*-t)s_t} \cdot (g^{\beta^*})^{-\frac{a+bt}{t^*-t}} \cdot g^{(a+bt)s_t}$, $D_2 = g^{r_{id}}$ and $D_3 = (g^{\beta^*})^{-\frac{1}{t^*-t}} \cdot g^{s_t}$.
3. Return $\mathsf{DK}_{id,t} = (D_1, D_2, D_3)$ to $\mathcal{A}$.

Challenge Ciphertext Oracle: When $\mathcal{A}$ issues a challenge ciphertext query with (id^*, t^*, M_0, M_1), the simulator does the following:

1. Forward (id^*, M_0, M_1) to the Waters encryption oracle $\mathcal{O}_{EncWat}^{ibe}(\cdot, \cdot, \cdot)$, which will outputs a challenge ciphertext of the Waters IBE scheme $CT_{id^*}^{Wat} = (C_0^{Wat}, C_1^{Wat}, C_2^{Wat})$.
2. Compute $C_3 = (C_1^{Wat})^{a+bt^*}$.
3. Define $(C_0, C_1, C_2) = (C_0^{Wat}, C_1^{Wat}, C_2^{Wat})$.

4. Return $CT_{id^*,t^*} = (C_0, C_1, C_2, C_3)$ to $\mathcal{A}$.

Guess: Finally, the adversary outputs a guess bit b', which is also the guess bit of the simulator.

Discussion 2 *Similar to previous analysis, the challenge ciphertext is well distributed. Recall that a valid Waters private key for identity* id *is of the form* $\mathsf{SK}_{id}^{\mathsf{Wat}} = (d_1, d_2) = (h^{\gamma^*} \cdot F_{\mathsf{Wat},U}(id)^{r_{id}}, g^{r_{id}})$, *where* $r_{id} \leftarrow_R \mathbb{Z}_p$. *So,*

$$(D_{id,1}, D_{id,2}) = (h^{-\alpha} \cdot d_1, d_2) = (h^{\beta} \cdot F_{\mathsf{Wat},U}(id)^{r_{id}}, g^{r_{id}})$$

is a valid SR-IBE private key for identity id. *For decryption key generation oracle, if* $t = t^*$, *we must have* id $\neq$ id* *and hence the decryption key is well defined. If* $t \neq t^*$, *the decryption key* $\mathsf{DK}_{id,t}$ *can be rewritten as the form* $(D_1, D_2, D_3) = (h^{\gamma^* - \alpha} \cdot F_{\mathsf{Wat},U}(id)^{r_{id}} \cdot (v_0 v_1^t)^{s'_t}, g^{r_{id}}, g^{s'_t})$ *for some unknown exponent* $s'_t = -\frac{\gamma^*}{t^* - t} + s_t$. *So, in this case, the decryption key oracle is also well defined. To conclude, if the simulator correctly guesses the challenge revocation time, the simulator perfectly simulates the SR-ID-CPA game for the Type II adversary* $\mathcal{A}$. *Since the guess is independent of the adversary's behaviour, we have* $\mathsf{Adv}_{\mathsf{SR-IBE},\mathcal{A}}^{\mathsf{sr-id-cpa}}(\kappa) \leq |\mathcal{T}| \cdot \mathsf{Adv}_{\mathsf{IBE}_{\mathsf{Wat}},\mathcal{B}}^{\mathsf{id-cpa}}(\kappa)$, *where* $\mathcal{B}$ *is an adversary (i.e., the simulator) attacking the Waters IBE scheme.*

Finally, we discuss the probability of the events that the simulator correctly guess the type of adversary. Since the adversary's behaviour is independent of the simulator's guess, with probability exactly $1/2$ the guess is correct. So,

$$\mathsf{Adv}_{\mathsf{SR-IBE},\mathcal{A}}^{\mathsf{sr-id-cpa}}(\kappa) \leq 2 \cdot \max(Q \cdot |\mathcal{T}| + |\mathcal{T}|) \cdot \mathsf{Adv}_{\mathsf{IBE}_{\mathsf{Wat}},\mathcal{B}}^{\mathsf{id-cpa}}(\kappa) = 2Q|\mathcal{T}| \cdot \mathsf{Adv}_{\mathsf{IBE}_{\mathsf{Wat}},\mathcal{B}}^{\mathsf{id-cpa}}(\kappa).$$

So, the reduction loss in our security proof is $2Q|\mathcal{T}|$. Since the Waters IBE scheme has been proven secure under the DBDH assumption with reduction loss $O(nQ)$, our SR-IBE scheme is secure under the DBDH assumption with $O(nQ^2|\mathcal{T}|)$ reduction loss, which is the same as in previous revocable IBE schemes [17,24]. This completes the proof of Theorem 2. □

References

1. Aiello, W., Lodha, S.P., Ostrovsky, R.: Fast digital identity revocation. In: Krawczyk, H. (ed.) CRYPTO 1998. LNCS, vol. 1462, pp. 137–152. Springer, Heidelberg (1998)
2. Baek, J., Zheng, Y.: Identity-based threshold decryption. In: Bao, F., Deng, R., Zhou, J. (eds.) PKC 2004. LNCS, vol. 2947, pp. 262–276. Springer, Heidelberg (2004)
3. Boldyreva, A., Goyal, V., Kumar, V.: Identity-based encryption with efficient revocation. In: Ning, P., Syverson, P.F., Jha, S. (eds.) CCS 2008, pp. 417–426. ACM (2008)
4. Boneh, D., Ding, X., Tsudik, G., Wong, C.: A method for fast revocation of public key certificates and security capabilities. In: Wallach, D.S. (ed.) 10th USENIX Security Symposium, Washington, D.C., USA, 13–17 August 2001. USENIX (2001)

5. Boneh, D., Franklin, M.: Identity-based encryption from the weil pairing. In: Kilian, J. (ed.) CRYPTO 2001. LNCS, vol. 2139, pp. 213–229. Springer, Heidelberg (2001)

6. Boneh, D., Gentry, C., Hamburg, M.: Space-efficient identity based encryption without pairings. In: FOCS 2007, pp. 647–657. IEEE Computer Society (2007)

7. Canetti, R., Halevi, S., Katz, J.: A forward-secure public-key encryption scheme. In: Biham, E. (ed.) EUROCRYPT 2003. LNCS, vol. 2656, pp. 255–271. Springer, Heidelberg (2003)

8. Cocks, C.: An identity based encryption scheme based on quadratic residues. In: Honary, B. (ed.) Cryptography and Coding 2001. LNCS, vol. 2260, pp. 360–363. Springer, Heidelberg (2001)

9. Ding, X., Tsudik, G.: Simple identity-based cryptography with mediated RSA. In: Joye, M. (ed.) CT-RSA 2003. LNCS, vol. 2612, pp. 193–210. Springer, Heidelberg (2003)

10. Gentry, C.: Certificate-based encryption and the certificate revocation problem. In: Biham, E. (ed.) EUROCRYPT 2003. LNCS, vol. 2656, pp. 272–293. Springer, Heidelberg (2003)

11. Goyal, V., Pandey, O., Sahai, A., Waters, B.: Attribute-based encryption for fine-grained access control of encrypted data. In: Juels, A., Wright, R.N., di Vimercati, S.D.C. (eds.) CCS 2006, pp. 89–98. ACM (2006)

12. Horwitz, J., Lynn, B.: Toward hierarchical identity-based encryption. In: Knudsen, L.R. (ed.) EUROCRYPT 2002. LNCS, vol. 2332, pp. 466–481. Springer, Heidelberg (2002)

13. Lee, K., Lee, D.H., Park, J.H.: Efficient revocable identity-based encryption via subset difference methods. IACR Cryptology ePrint Arch. **2014**, 132 (2014)

14. Li, J., Li, J., Chen, X., Jia, C., Lou, W.: Identity-based encryption with outsourced revocation in cloud computing. IEEE Trans. Comput. 99(PrePrints), 1 (2013)

15. Liang, K., Liu, J.K., Wong, D.S., Susilo, W.: An efficient cloud-based revocable identity-based proxy re-encryption scheme for public clouds data sharing. In: Kutyłowski, M., Vaidya, J. (eds.) ESORICS 2014, Part I. LNCS, vol. 8712, pp. 257–272. Springer, Heidelberg (2014)

16. Libert, B., Quisquater, J.: Efficient revocation and threshold pairing based cryptosystems. In: Borowsky, E., Rajsbaum, S. (eds.) PODC 2003, pp. 163–171. ACM (2003)

17. Libert, B., Vergnaud, D.: Adaptive-ID secure revocable identity-based encryption. In: Fischlin, M. (ed.) CT-RSA 2009. LNCS, vol. 5473, pp. 1–15. Springer, Heidelberg (2009)

18. Lin, H., Cao, Z., Fang, Y., Zhou, M., Zhu, H.: How to design space efficient revocable IBE from non-monotonic ABE. In: Cheung, B.S.N., Hui, L.C.K., Sandhu, R.S., Wong, D.S. (eds.) ASIACCS 2011, pp. 381–385. ACM (2011)

19. Naor, D., Naor, M., Lotspiech, J.: Revocation and tracing schemes for stateless receivers. In: Kilian, J. (ed.) CRYPTO 2001. LNCS, vol. 2139, pp. 41–62. Springer, Heidelberg (2001)

20. Naor, M., Nissim, K.: Certificate revocation and certificate update. IEEE J. Sel. Areas Commun. **18**(4), 561–570 (2000)

21. Park, S., Lee, K., Lee, D.H.: New constructions of revocable identity-based encryption from multilinear maps. IACR Cryptology ePrint Arch. **2013**, 880 (2013)

22. Sahai, A., Waters, B.: Fuzzy identity-based encryption. In: Cramer, R. (ed.) EUROCRYPT 2005. LNCS, vol. 3494, pp. 457–473. Springer, Heidelberg (2005)

23. Sakai, R., Ohgishi, K., Kasahara, M.: Cryptosystems based on pairing. In: The 2000 Symposium on Cryptography and Information Security, Okinawa, Japan, pp. 135–148 (2000)
24. Seo, J.H., Emura, K.: Revocable identity-based encryption revisited: security model and construction. In: Kurosawa, K., Hanaoka, G. (eds.) PKC 2013. LNCS, vol. 7778, pp. 216–234. Springer, Heidelberg (2013)
25. Seo, J.H., Emura, K.: Revocable identity-based cryptosystem revisited: security models and constructions. IEEE Trans. Inf. Forensics Secur. $9(7)$, 1193–1205 (2014)
26. Shamir, A.: Identity-based cryptosystems and signature schemes. In: Blakely, G.R., Chaum, D. (eds.) CRYPTO 1984. LNCS, vol. 196, pp. 47–53. Springer, Heidelberg (1985)
27. Su, L., Lim, H.W., Ling, S., Wang, H.: Revocable IBE systems with almost constant-size key update. In: Cao, Z., Zhang, F. (eds.) Pairing 2013. LNCS, vol. 8365, pp. 168–185. Springer, Heidelberg (2014)
28. Waters, B.: Efficient identity-based encryption without random oracles. In: Cramer, R. (ed.) EUROCRYPT 2005. LNCS, vol. 3494, pp. 114–127. Springer, Heidelberg (2005)

Efficient Zero-Knowledge Proofs for Commitments from Learning with Errors over Rings

Fabrice Benhamouda[1], Stephan Krenn[2(✉)], Vadim Lyubashevsky[3], and Krzysztof Pietrzak[4]

[1] ENS, CNRS, INRIA, and PSL, Paris, France
fabrice.ben.hamouda@ens.fr
[2] AIT Austrian Institute of Technology GmbH, Vienna, Austria
stephan.krenn@ait.ac.at
[3] ENS, INRIA, Paris, France
lyubash@di.ens.fr
[4] IST Austria, Klosterneuburg, Austria
pietrzak@ist.ac.at

Abstract. We extend a commitment scheme based on the learning with errors over rings (RLWE) problem, and present efficient companion zero-knowledge proofs of knowledge. Our scheme maps elements from the ring (or equivalently, n elements from $\mathbb{F}_q$) to a small constant number of ring elements. We then construct Σ-protocols for proving, in a zero-knowledge manner, knowledge of the message contained in a commitment. We are able to further extend our basic protocol to allow us to prove additive and multiplicative relations among committed values.

Our protocols have a communication complexity of $\mathcal{O}(Mn \log q)$ and achieve a negligible knowledge error in one run. Here M is the constant from a rejection sampling technique that we employ, and can be set close to 1 by adjusting other parameters. Previously known Σ-protocols for LWE-related languages only achieved a noticeable or even constant knowledge error (thus requiring many repetitions of the protocol), or relied on "smudging" out the error (which necessitates working over large fields, resulting in poor efficiency).

Keywords: Commitment schemes · Ring learning with errors · Zero-Knowledge Proofs of Knowledge

1 Introduction

Commitment schemes are among the most widely used cryptographic primitives. They allow one party, the committer, to *commit* to a message m to another

---

This work was done while the second author was at IBM Research – Zurich. This work was partly funded by the ERC Grants 321310–PERCY and 259668–PSPC, and by the French ANR-13-JS02-0003 JCJC Project CLE.

© Springer International Publishing Switzerland 2015
G. Pernul et al. (Eds.): ESORICS 2015, Part I, LNCS 9326, pp. 305–325, 2015.
DOI: 10.1007/978-3-319-24174-6_16

party. At a later point in time, the committer may reveal m by *opening* the commitment c. The scheme is said to be secure if it is *binding* and *hiding*. The former property says that the committer cannot open c to a message different from m, and the latter ensures that only knowing c gives no information about m to the receiver.

In higher-level protocols, commitments are often used to link different building blocks, e.g., encryption-, signature-, and revocation schemes in constructions of group signatures or anonymous credentials [CKL+14]. In such situations, it is often necessary to prove properties of a message m contained in a commitment, without revealing any additional information about m. This is done via so-called *zero-knowledge proofs of knowledge* (ZK-PoK). These are two-party protocols which allow a *prover* to convince a *verifier* that it knows some secret piece of information, without revealing anything else than what is already revealed by the claim itself [GMR85]. As the efficiency of ZK-PoKs of commitments directly affects the efficiency of many higher-level systems, generic constructions such as [GMW86, GMR85] are too inefficient for practical use. A large amount of research effort has therefore been expended in improving the efficiency of such protocols for concrete proof goals. We continue this direction by presenting the so far most efficient ZK-PoKs for lattice-based commitment schemes.

Our constructions are proved secure under the *learning with errors over rings* (RLWE) assumption. Informally, it says that tuples $(a, a.s + e) \in R_q^2$ are computationally indistinguishable from $(a, u) \in R_q^2$, where a, s, u are uniformly random in R_q and e is drawn according to some low-weight distribution χ. We use $R_q = \mathbb{Z}_q[x]/\langle x^n + 1 \rangle$, which as a vector space is isomorphic to $\mathbb{Z}_q^n$ (one can identify $a = a_1 + a_2 x + \cdots + a_n x^{n-1} \in R_q$ with $(a_1, \ldots, a_n) \in \mathbb{Z}_q^n$). For appropriately chosen parameters there exists a quantum reduction from certain worst-case problems on ideal lattices to the RLWE-problem [LPR10].

1.1 Our Contributions

In this paper is to construct efficient commitments and zero-knowledge proofs from the RLWE-assumption. To the best of our knowledge, our protocols are the first to achieve a negligible knowledge error in one run for lattice-based crypto systems.

In detail, our contributions are as follows:

- **Efficient Commitment Schemes from RLWE.** We first construct a perfectly binding and computationally hiding string commitment scheme. Committing to a message is done as in Xie et al. [XXW13], but we relax requirements on valid openings to be able to realize better ZK proofs while still preserving the binding property of the scheme.
- **Efficient ZK-PoK for Committed Values.** We then give a simple and efficient zero-knowledge protocol for proving knowledge of committed values. The protocol differs substantially from previous protocols for RLWE, and improves over them in the following ways: On the one hand, our protocol

already achieves a negligible knowledge error in a single run. Previous protocols only achieved a noticeable knowledge error, e.g., Ling et al. [LNSW13] or Xie et al. [XXW13], and thus many repetitions are required to get meaningful security, resulting in a low efficiency. On the other hand, we only require that the modulus is polynomially larger than the error in the RLWE problem. The construction of Asharov et al. [AJLA+12], which achieves a knowledge error of $1/2$, relied on "smudging out" (or "drowning") the error, which required stronger assumptions as the modulus-error ratio had to be super-polynomial. Our protocols can be turned into concurrently zero-knowledge arguments of knowledge without any additional computational costs.

- **Efficient ZK-PoK for Relations.** Starting from our basic ZK-PoK we then construct protocols for proving that committed values $m_1, m_2, m_3 \in R_q$ satisfy $m_3 = m_1 + m_2$ as well as $m_3 = m_1 m_2$.

1.2   Related Work

At Asiacrypt'12, Jain et al. [JKPT12] presented a commitment scheme whose hiding property relies on the learning parity with noise (LPN) assumption, which is defined like LWE but over bits, i.e., for $q = 2$. Similar to our work, they give a Σ-protocol to prove any relation among committed values. A single run of their preimage proof requires $\mathcal{O}(n \log n)$ bits of communication, where each committed message is from $\{0, 1\}^n$. However, their protocols only achieve a knowledge error of $2/3$, and thus reaching a success probability of a malicious prover negligible in k, requires $\mathcal{O}(kn \log n)$ bits of communication. The main open problem of [JKPT12] was to find a commitment scheme and protocols whose security is based on LPN or a related problem, and which avoids the dependency on k.

Xie et al. [XXW13] generalized the commitment scheme from Jain et al. [JKPT12] from LPN to RLWE, and gave companion protocols for their scheme. However, their zero-knowledge proofs still require Stern-like techniques [Ste93], and therefore only achieve a knowledge error of $2/3$. Our commitment scheme is closely related to theirs and may be seen as a generalization as we relax the requirements on valid openings. In their construction, a commitment c to a message m can be opened by revealing r and a short e such that $c = am + br + e$, where $a, b, c, e \in R_q^k$ and $m, r \in R_q$. Getting a bit ahead, we relax the openings such that we also accept openings of the form $c = am + br + f^{-1}e$, where $f \in R_q$ is an additional small polynomial. We will prove that commitments are still binding, and show that this relaxation allows us to overcome the constant knowledge-error "barrier" for the commitment scheme by employing rejection sampling techniques introduced by Lyubashevsky [Lyu09, Lyu12].

Recently, Benhamouda et al. [BCK+14] improved the efficiency of ZK-PoKs for RLWE-based encryption schemes. As encryption schemes can also be seen as commitment schemes, it is worthwhile comparing their result to ours. They give a protocol for proving relations of the form $y = as + e$ (for $y, a, s, e \in R_q$ and s, e short) that has a knowledge error of $1/(2n)$, where n is the dimension of the ring, and thus also overcomes the above barrier. However, their protocol has a soundness gap in the sense that it only proves that the prover knows a valid representation of $2y$, not of y itself, which is still sufficient for many applications as illustrated in their work. We improve over their results by reaching a negligible knowledge error already in one run of the protocol (compared to $1/(2n)$) and by not having such a soundness gap. On the other hand, our protocol requires the ring R_q to have a large subring that is a field, whereas the protocol in [BCK+14] does not require such a property.

Asharov et al. [AJLA+12] constructed Σ-protocols for several specific languages related to the standard LWE-problem. However, they do not give (efficient, i.e., direct) constructions for proving relations among LWE-secrets. Furthermore, their protocols have a super-polynomial knowledge-gap, i.e., the norm of the error known to a potentially malicious prover can only be guaranteed to be super-polynomially larger than that known to an honest party, while this gap is only polynomial in our case. This allows us to prove the security of our scheme under weaker assumptions, and to use a smaller modulus in the RLWE-problem, giving better efficiency.

Apart from these very closely related works, a large number of cryptographic applications based on the LWE-assumption has been proposed, starting with the work of Regev [Reg05]. This includes (fully homomorphic) encryption [BV11a, Gen09, LP11, LPR10, Reg05], signature schemes [DDLL13, GPV08, Lyu09, Lyu12, Rüc10], pseudorandom functions [BPR12] and hash functions [KV09, PR06]. Similarly, efficient (non-)interactive zero-knowledge proofs and arguments have been a vivid topic of research, see, e.g., [AJLA+12, BDP00, CD97, CD98, CD09, DPSZ12, GS08, IKOS07, KR06, KMO90, KP98] and the references therein. Finally, starting with a different motivation, the idea of committing to the first message in a Σ-protocol was also used by Damgård [Dam00], where it was shown how to obtain concurrent zero-knowledge for any Σ-protocol. We commit to the first message to get zero-knowledge in the first place, and we will discuss how the concurrency results also apply to our constructions in Sect. 4.1.

1.3   Roadmap

In Sect. 2 we recap some basic definitions on ZK proofs and LWE. Then, in Sect. 3 we present our commitment scheme, and give protocols for proving knowledge of, and relations among, the contents of commitments in Sect. 4. We finally briefly conclude in Sect. 5.

2   Preliminaries

We denote vectors by bold lower-case letters $(a, b, \ldots)$ and algorithms by sans-serif letters $(A, B, \ldots)$. We write $a \xleftarrow{\$} A$ for a set A if a was uniformly drawn from A, $a \xleftarrow{\$} D$ for a distribution D if a was drawn according to D, and $a \xleftarrow{\$} A$ if a is the output of a randomized algorithm A.

For two distributions D, E, we write $D \overset{c}{\sim} E$, if D and E are computationally indistinguishable. Furthermore, we use the notation $\Pr[\mathcal{E} : \Omega]$ to denote the probability of event $\mathcal{E}$ over the probability space Ω. For instance, $\Pr[x = y : x, y \xleftarrow{\$} D]$ denotes the probability that $x = y$ if x, y were drawn according to a distribution D.

The language induced by a binary relation $\mathcal{R}$ is defined as

$$\mathcal{L}(\mathcal{R}) = \{c : \exists w \text{ such that } (c, w) \in \mathcal{R}\}.$$

We finally assume that elements of $\mathbb{Z}_q$ (q odd) are represented by elements from $\{-\frac{q-1}{2}, \ldots, \frac{q-1}{2}\}$.

2.1 Commitment Schemes

We now formally define commitment schemes.

Definition 2.1. *A* commitment scheme *consists of three algorithms* (KGen, Com, Ver) *such that:*

- *On input 1^ℓ, the key generation algorithm* KGen *outputs a public commitment key pk.*
- *The commitment algorithm* Com *takes as inputs a message m from a message space $\mathcal{M}$ and a commitment key pk, and outputs a commitment/opening pair (c, d).*
- *The verification algorithm* Ver *takes a key pk, a message m, a commitment c and an opening d and outputs* accept *or* reject.

A commitment scheme has to satisfy the following security requirements:

- *Correctness*: Ver outputs accept whenever the inputs were computed by an honest party, i.e.,

$$\Pr[\mathsf{Ver}(pk, m, c, d) = \mathsf{accept} : m \in \mathcal{M}, (c, d) \xleftarrow{\$} \mathsf{Com}(m, \mathsf{KGen}(1^\ell))] = 1.$$

- *Binding*: A commitment cannot be opened to different messages. A scheme is said to be *perfectly binding* if this holds unconditionally, i.e., with overwhelming probability over the choice of the public key $pk \xleftarrow{\$} \mathsf{KGen}(1^\ell)$ we have that:

$$((\mathsf{Ver}(pk, m, c, d) = \mathsf{accept}) \wedge (\mathsf{Ver}(pk, m', c, d') = \mathsf{accept})) \Rightarrow m = m'.$$

On the other hand, a scheme is said to be *computationally binding* if no PPT adversary can come up with a commitment and two different openings, i.e., for every PPT adversary A there exists a negligible function negl such that:

$$\Pr\Big[\mathsf{Ver}(pk, m, c, d) = \mathsf{Ver}(pk, m', c, d') : pk \xleftarrow{\$} \mathsf{KGen}(1^\ell),$$

$$(c, m, d, m', d') \xleftarrow{\$} \mathsf{A}(pk)\Big] \leq \mathsf{negl}(n).$$

310 F. Benhamouda et al.

– *Computational hiding*: A commitment computationally hides the committed message: for every probabilistic polynomial time (PPT) adversary A there is a negligible function negl such that:

$$\Pr\left[b = b' : \begin{array}{l} pk \overset{\$}{\leftarrow} \mathsf{KGen}(1^\ell), (m_0, m_1, \mathsf{aux}) \overset{\$}{\leftarrow} A_1(pk), \\ b \overset{\$}{\leftarrow} \{0,1\}, (c,d) = \mathsf{Com}(m_b, pk), b' \overset{\$}{\leftarrow} A_2(c, \mathsf{aux}) \end{array}\right] \leq \frac{1}{2} + \mathsf{negl}(n).$$

A scheme is called a *trapdoor commitment scheme*, if KGen additionally outputs a trapdoor td for the public key, such that there exists an efficient algorithm taking $(c,d) = \mathsf{Com}(m, pk)$, m, td and $m' \in \mathcal{M}$ as inputs, that outputs d' such that $\mathsf{Ver}(pk, m', c, d') = \mathsf{accept}$. Note that trapdoor commitment schemes can only be computationally binding. See, e.g., Fischlin [Fis01] for a detailed discussion of such schemes.

For the sake of simplicity, we will not state pk explicitly as an input in the following.

2.2 Zero-Knowledge Proofs and Σ-Protocols

Informally, a zero-knowledge proof of knowledge is a two party protocol between a prover and a verifier, which allows the former to convince the latter that it knows some secret piece of information, without revealing anything about the secret apart from what the claim itself already reveals. For a formal definition we refer to Bellare and Goldreich [BG93]. The ZK proofs constructed in this paper will be instantiations of the following definition, which is a straightforward generalization of the standard notion of Σ-protocols [Cra97, Dam10]:

Definition 2.2. *Let* (P, V) *be a two-party protocol, where* V *is PPT, and let* $\mathcal{R}, \mathcal{R}'$ *be a binary relation such that* $\mathcal{R} \subseteq \mathcal{R}'$. *Then* (P, V) *is called a* Σ'_m-*protocol for* $\mathcal{R}, \mathcal{R}'$ *with challenge set* $\mathcal{C}$, *public input* c *and private input* w, *if and only if it satisfies the following conditions:*

– **3-move form:** *The protocol is of the following form:*
  • *The prover* P *computes a commitment* t *and sends it to* V.
  • *The verifier* V *draws a challenge* $d \overset{\$}{\leftarrow} \mathcal{C}$ *and sends it to* P.
  • *The prover sends a response* s *to the verifier.*
  • *Depending on the protocol transcript* (t, d, s), *the verifier accepts or rejects the proof.*
  The protocol transcript (t, d, s) *is called* accepting, *if the verifier accepts the protocol run.*
– **Completeness:** *Whenever* $(c, w) \in \mathcal{R}$, *the verifier* V *accepts with probability at least* $1 - \alpha$.
– **Special soundness:** *There exists a PPT algorithm* E *(the* knowledge extractor*) which takes* m *accepting transcripts* $(t, d_1, s_1), \ldots, (t, d_m, s_m)$ *satisfying* $d_i \neq d_j$ *for* $i \neq j$ *as inputs, and outputs* w' *such that* $(c, w') \in \mathcal{R}'$.
– **Special honest-verifier zero-knowledge:** *There exists a PPT algorithm* S *(the* simulator*) taking* $c \in \mathcal{L}(\mathcal{R})$ *and* $d \in \mathcal{C}$ *as inputs, that outputs triples* (t, d, s) *whose distribution is (computationally) indistinguishable from accepting protocol transcripts generated by real protocol runs.*

We now discuss some additional points regarding Definition 2.2. First, the standard definition for Σ-protocols found in the literature considers the case where $m = 2$, $\mathcal{R} = \mathcal{R}'$ and $\alpha = 0$. In this case, it is well known that the protocol is also a proof of knowledge for the same relation $\mathcal{R}$ with knowledge error $1/|\mathcal{C}|$ [Dam10]. However, it can be seen that the proof given there also generalizes to other constants m with a knowledge error of $(m-1)/|\mathcal{C}|$ if $1 - \alpha > (m-1)/|\mathcal{C}|$, and special cases of this result were already used implicitly in previous work, e.g., [JKPT12, Ste93]. Second, the modification that $\mathcal{R} \subseteq \mathcal{R}'$ means that the protocol is honest-verifier zero-knowledge and complete whenever the prover uses a secret witness w such that $(c, w) \in \mathcal{R}$, but the verifier is only assured that the prover supplied a witness w' such that $(c, w') \in \mathcal{R}'$. For many interesting relations this gap allows for much more efficient protocols, e.g., Fujisaki et al. [FO97, DF02] or Benhamouda et al. [BCK+14]. If this gap is reasonably small, as is the case in the protocols we present, one still obtains sufficient security guarantees from the protocol. Finally, the above definition only guarantees privacy to the prover against honest-but-curious verifiers, i.e., verifiers not deviating from the protocol. This issue can be solved generically using techniques of, e.g., Damgård et al. [DGOW95] or Fiat and Shamir [FS87]; furthermore, for our concrete protocols it can be solved without any extra costs, cf. Lemma 4.3.

2.3 Learning with Errors

The learning with errors (LWE) problems was first introduced by Regev [Reg05]. Informally, it asks to distinguish slightly perturbed random linear equations from truly random ones. LWE has been shown to be as hard as certain worst-case problems on lattices, and has served as a basis for a large variety of cryptographic schemes. Unfortunately, schemes built upon LWE are inherently inefficient due to a large overhead in the use of the problem. This drawback has been resolved by Lyubashevsky et al. [LPR10] by introducing the ring learning with noise problem, which still enjoys strong hardness guarantees. The following formulation is a special case of the problem restricted to the ring $\mathbb{Z}[x]/\langle x^n + 1 \rangle$, with n a power of two:

Definition 2.3. *Let $R = \mathbb{Z}[x]/\langle x^n + 1 \rangle$ and $R_q = R/qR$, and let χ be a distribution over R.*

The (decisional) ring learning with errors assumption (denoted by $\mathsf{RLWE}_{q,\chi}$) states that:

$$\{(a_i, a_i \cdot s + e_i)\} \overset{c}{\sim} \{(a_i, u_i)\},$$

for any polynomial number of samples, where $a_i \overset{\$}{\leftarrow} R_q$, $e_i \overset{\$}{\leftarrow} \chi$, $u_i \overset{\$}{\leftarrow} R_q$, and $s \overset{\$}{\leftarrow} R_q$ is secret.

We further recapitulate the definition of Normal distributions:

Definition 2.4. *The* continuous Normal distribution *on* $\mathbb{R}^m$ *centered at* $\boldsymbol{v}$ *with standard deviation* σ *is defined by the density function*

$$\rho_{\boldsymbol{v},\sigma}^m(\boldsymbol{x}) = \left(\frac{1}{\sqrt{2\pi}\sigma}\right)^m e^{-\frac{\|\boldsymbol{x}-\boldsymbol{v}\|^2}{2\sigma^2}}.$$

We avoid the subscript $\boldsymbol{v}$ *if* $\boldsymbol{v} = 0^m$.

The discrete Normal distribution *on* $\mathbb{Z}^m$ *centered at* $\boldsymbol{v}$ *with standard deviation* σ *is defined by the density function* $D_{\boldsymbol{v},\sigma}^m(\boldsymbol{x}) = \rho_{\boldsymbol{v},\sigma}^m(\boldsymbol{x})/\rho_\sigma(\mathbb{Z}^m)$, *where* $\rho_\sigma(\mathbb{Z}^m) = \sum_{\boldsymbol{z}\in\mathbb{Z}^m} \rho_\sigma^m(\boldsymbol{z})$ *is the scaling factor required to obtain a probability distribution.*

For convenience, sampling the normal distribution over a ring R, we will still write $D_{\boldsymbol{v},\sigma}$ even though it is not a 1-dimensional distribution. Lyubashevsky et al. [LPR10] showed the search and the decisional version of $\mathsf{RLWE}_{q,\chi}$ are polynomially related, and that there exists a quantum reduction from the worst-case approximate shortest vector problem on ideal lattices to $\mathsf{RLWE}_{q,\chi}$.[1]

2.4 Rejection Sampling

For proving the zero-knowledge property of our protocol, it is essential that all the responses of the prover can be simulated without knowing the secret key. We thus need that the response elements are from a distribution which is *independent* of the secret key. In our protocol, however, all the potential responses will be from a shifted distribution $D_{\boldsymbol{v},\sigma}^\ell$ for $\ell = kn$ and some vector $\boldsymbol{v}$ depending on the secret key. To correct for this, we employ rejection sampling [Lyu09,Lyu12], where a potential response is only output with a certain probability, and otherwise the protocol is aborted.

Informally, the following theorem states that if $\sigma \in \tilde{\Theta}(\|\boldsymbol{v}\|)$, then the rejection sampling procedure will result in a distribution statistically close to D_σ^ℓ, which is independent of $\boldsymbol{v}$ as required. The technique only requires a constant number of iterations before a value is output, and furthermore the output is also statistically close for every $\boldsymbol{v}'$ with norm at most $\|\boldsymbol{v}\|$. For concrete parameters we refer to the original work of Lyubashevsky [Lyu12].

Theorem 2.5 ([Lyu12]). *Let V be a subset of $\mathbb{Z}^\ell$ in which all elements have norms less than T, and let h be a probability distribution over V. Then, for any constant M, there exists a $\sigma = \tilde{\Theta}(T)$ such that the output distributions of the following algorithms* A, F *are statistically close:*

A:

$\boldsymbol{v} \xleftarrow{\$} h; \quad \boldsymbol{z} \xleftarrow{\$} D_{\boldsymbol{v},\sigma}^\ell;$

output $(\boldsymbol{z}, \boldsymbol{v})$ with probability $\min\left(\exp\left(\frac{-2\langle\boldsymbol{z},\boldsymbol{v}\rangle+\|\boldsymbol{v}\|^2}{2\sigma^2}\right), 1\right)$

F:

$\boldsymbol{v} \xleftarrow{\$} h; \quad \boldsymbol{z} \xleftarrow{\$} D_\sigma^\ell;$

output $(\boldsymbol{z}, \boldsymbol{v})$ with probability $\frac{1}{M}$

Moreover, the probability that A *outputs something is exponentially close to that of* F*, i.e.,* $1/M$.

---

[1] The work of [LPR10] showed the hardness for decisional RLWE only for rings where $x^n + 1$ splits completely modulo q. Employing the modulus switching technique from [BV11b], it was shown in [BLP+13] that the problem remains hard for any q.

In [Lyu12], it is also shown that if $\sigma = \alpha T$ for a positive α, then $M = e^{12/\alpha + 1/(2\alpha^2)}$, the output of A is within a statistical distance of $\frac{2^{-100}}{M}$ of the output of F, and the probability that A outputs something is at least $\frac{1 - 2^{-100}}{M}$.

3 Commitments from Ring-LWE

In the following we describe our commitment scheme. Table 1 lists the parameters being used and the requirements we pose on them.

- KGen: The public commitment key $pk = (\boldsymbol{a}, \boldsymbol{b})$ is computed as $\boldsymbol{a}, \boldsymbol{b} \xleftarrow{\$} (\mathbb{Z}_q[x]/\langle x^n + 1\rangle)^k$, where $q \equiv 3 \bmod 8$ is prime, and n is a power of 2.
- Com: To commit to a message $m \in \mathbb{Z}_q[x]/\langle x^n + 1\rangle$, the commitment algorithm draws $r \xleftarrow{\$} \mathbb{Z}_q[x]/\langle x^n + 1\rangle$ and $\boldsymbol{e} \xleftarrow{\$} D_{\sigma_e}^k$ conditioned on $\|\boldsymbol{e}\|_\infty \le n$, and outputs

$$\boldsymbol{c} = \boldsymbol{a}m + \boldsymbol{b}r + \boldsymbol{e},$$

and the opening information for $\boldsymbol{c}$ is given by $(m, r, \boldsymbol{e}, 1)$.
- Ver: Given a commitment $\boldsymbol{c}$, a message m', a randomness r', as well as $\boldsymbol{e}'$ and f', the verifier accepts, if and only if

$$\boldsymbol{a}m' + \boldsymbol{b}r' + f'^{-1}\boldsymbol{e}' = \boldsymbol{c} \wedge \|\boldsymbol{e}'\|_\infty < \left\lfloor \frac{n^{4/3}}{2} \right\rfloor \wedge \|f'\|_\infty \le 1 \wedge \deg f' < \frac{n}{2}.$$

The scheme above is a generalization of that by Xie et al. [XXW13], as we allow for the additional small polynomial f in valid openings. While an honest party can always set $f = 1$ when opening $\boldsymbol{c}$ and therefore the completeness property is not affected by this relaxation, the immediate question arises whether the given construction is still binding, i.e., whether a malicious user still cannot

Table 1. Overview of parameters used in this document.

Parameter	Semantics/Restrictions
n	degree of polynomial, power of 2, typical values are 2^9 or 2^{10}
γ	integer parameter controlling the size of the modulus
q	prime number, $\equiv 3 \bmod 8$ and $\ge n^\gamma$
k	multiplicative overhead of commitment size
σ_e	standard deviation of the error in the commitment scheme; $\tilde{\mathcal{O}}(n^{3/4})$
κ	integer, where $1/|\mathcal{C}| = 1/\binom{n/2}{\kappa}$ bounds the knowledge error of our proofs; for instance, $n = 2^9$, $\kappa = 21$ or $n = 2^{10}$, $\kappa = 17$ give a knowledge error of less than 2^{-100}
$\mathcal{C}$	domain of challenges; $\mathcal{C} = \{d \in \{0,1\}^n : \|d\|_1 \le \kappa \wedge \deg d < n/2\}$
σ_η	standard deviation of the randomness for $\boldsymbol{e}$ in the protocols; $\tilde{\mathcal{O}}(n^{5/4})$

open a commitment to two different messages. We give a formal security proof in the following.

We want to stress that the above modification will be at the heart for the construction of efficient zero-knowledge proofs of the contained message in Sect. 4.

Theorem 3.1. *Let* $\gamma > 6$ *and* q, k *be polynomial in* n *such that the following is satisfied:*

$$q \geq n^\gamma \geq n^6 \quad and \quad k > \frac{18\gamma}{3\gamma - 16}. \tag{1}$$

Then, under the RLWE*-assumption, the above scheme is a computationally hiding and perfectly binding commitment scheme with overwhelming probability over the choices of the public commitment key.*

Proof. Correctness is trivial to see.

Computational Hiding. First note that by, e.g., [Lyu12, Lemma 4.4], the probability that $e \xleftarrow{\$} D_{\sigma_e}^k$ has $\|e\|_\infty > n$ is negligible, and thus the conditional distribution of e in Com is statistically close to a discrete Normal distribution. Now, by the RLWE-assumption, $br + e$ is pseudorandom, and thus so is c.

Binding. For the binding property, we have to show that

$$c = am' + br' + f'^{-1}e' = am'' + br'' + f''^{-1}e''$$

implies that $m' = m''$, if $\|e'\|_\infty, \|e''\|_\infty < n^{4/3}/2$, $\|f'\|_\infty, \|f''\|_\infty \leq 1$, and $\deg f', \deg f'' < n/2$, or, alternatively, that

$$am + br = f'^{-1}e' - f''^{-1}e''$$

implies that $m = 0$ with overwhelming probability over the choices of a, b.

Assume by contradiction that this holds for some fixed m, r, e', e'', f', f'' with $m \neq 0$ and e', e'', f', f'' being sufficiently small. Because of the assumption on n and q, we have that $x^n + 1$ splits into two irreducible factors $\alpha(x), \beta(x)$ [SSTX09, Lemma 3]. Now, since $m \neq 0 \mod (x^n + 1)$, we also have that $m \neq 0 \mod \alpha(x)$ or $m \neq 0 \mod \beta(x)$, and thus $a_i m$ takes at least $q^{n/2}$ different values. We then have that

$$\Pr\left[\begin{pmatrix} a_1 m + b_1 r \\ \vdots \\ a_k m + b_k r \end{pmatrix} = \begin{pmatrix} f'^{-1}e_1' - f''^{-1}e_1'' \\ \vdots \\ f'^{-1}e_k' - f''^{-1}e_k'' \end{pmatrix} : a, b \xleftarrow{\$} (\mathbb{Z}_q[x]/\langle x^n + 1 \rangle)^k \right] \leq \frac{1}{q^{kn/2}}.$$

Now, taking a union bound over all m, r, e', e'', f', f'' we get that the overall probability that there exists such an $m \neq 0$ is at most

$$\frac{q^{2n}(n^{4/3})^{2kn}3^{2n/2}}{q^{kn/2}} \leq \frac{q^{2n}(q^{4/(3\gamma)})^{2kn}3^{2n/2}}{q^{kn/2}} = 3^n q^{(2+(\frac{8}{3\gamma}-\frac{1}{2})k)n}.$$

This is negligible in n if $3q^{2+(8/(3\gamma)-1/2)k} \leq 1/2$, which holds if the requirements from (1) are satisfied. □

4 Zero-Knowledge of Proofs of Knowledge

In this section we first present a protocol for proving knowledge of valid openings of commitments as defined in the previous section. We then give protocols which allow one to prove that the messages m_1, m_2, m_3 contained in commitments c_1, c_2, c_3 satisfy $m_3 = m_1 + m_2$ or $m_3 = m_1 m_2$, respectively. Together this allows one to prove knowledge of arbitrary algebraic circuits.

In this entire section we let (aKGen, aCom, aVer) be an arbitrary auxiliary string commitment scheme. For simplicity, the reader may think of it as the scheme from Sect. 3, or as well just as a random oracle. We write $(c_{\mathsf{aux}}, d_{\mathsf{aux}}) = \mathsf{aCom}(s)$, where c_{aux} is the commitment and d_{aux} is the opening of c_{aux}.

4.1 Preimage Proofs

Protocol 4.1 is a Σ_2'-protocol for showing knowledge of a valid opening for a single commitment. It is honest-verifier zero-knowledge whenever the commitment was honestly computed, and is sound with respect to valid openings. In particular, whenever a potentially malicious prover can make the verifier accept with more than negligible probability, it must know a valid opening of c. We stress that this gap between the zero-knowledge and the soundness property is in line with previous protocols, e.g., for discrete logarithms in groups of hidden order [DF02], where the prover is also guaranteed security only for a subset of valid openings. However, this gap is meaningful, as our commitment scheme is still perfectly binding also for the larger set of valid openings, and so the proof still guarantees knowledge of the *unique* valid opening of c.

Theorem 4.2. *If the auxiliary commitment scheme is perfectly binding, then Protocol 4.1 is an honest-verifier zero-knowledge proof of knowledge with knowledge error* $1/\binom{n/2}{\kappa}$ *for the following relations:*

$$\mathcal{R}_{LWE} = \{((\boldsymbol{a}, \boldsymbol{b}, \boldsymbol{c}), (m, r, \boldsymbol{e})) : \boldsymbol{c} = \boldsymbol{a}m + \boldsymbol{b}r + \boldsymbol{e} \ \wedge \ \|\boldsymbol{e}\|_\infty \leq n\} \quad and$$

$$\mathcal{R}_{LWE}' = \Big\{ ((\boldsymbol{a}, \boldsymbol{b}, \boldsymbol{c}), (m, r, \boldsymbol{e}, f)) : \boldsymbol{c} = \boldsymbol{a}m + \boldsymbol{b}r + f^{-1}\boldsymbol{e} \ \wedge \ \|\boldsymbol{e}\|_\infty \leq \lfloor n^{4/3}/2 \rfloor, \\ \|f\|_\infty \leq 1, \deg f < \frac{n}{2} \Big\}.$$

Proof. The theorem is proved by showing that the protocol is a Σ_2'-protocol for the given relation. The claim then follows directly from the discussion in Sect. 2.2.

The 3-move-form is obvious.

Completeness. An honest prover responses with a probability close to $\frac{1}{M}$. In this case we get:

$$\boldsymbol{t} + d\boldsymbol{c} = \boldsymbol{a}\mu + \boldsymbol{b}\rho + \boldsymbol{\eta} + d\boldsymbol{a}m + d\boldsymbol{b}r + d\boldsymbol{e}$$
$$= \boldsymbol{a}(\mu + dm) + \boldsymbol{b}(\rho + dr) + (\boldsymbol{\eta} + d\boldsymbol{e}) = \boldsymbol{a}s_m + \boldsymbol{b}s_r + s_e.$$

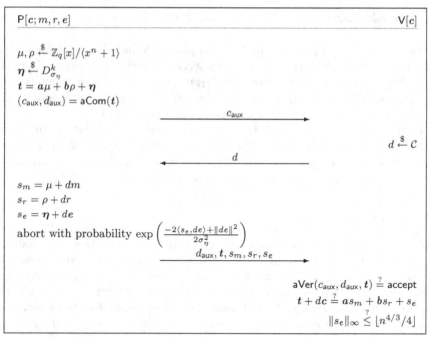

Protocol 4.1: Simple preimage proof. The verifier accepts, iff all conditions marked with "?" are satisfied.

Furthermore, we have that with overwhelming probability

$$\|s_e\|_\infty = \|\boldsymbol{\eta} + d\boldsymbol{e}\|_\infty \le \|\boldsymbol{\eta}\|_\infty + \kappa \|\boldsymbol{e}\|_\infty \le \lfloor n^{4/3}/4 \rfloor,$$

as the standard deviations of $D_{\sigma_e}, D_{\sigma_\eta}$ are significantly smaller than $n^{4/3}$.

Special Soundness. Let the extractor E be given two accepting protocol transcripts $(c_{\mathsf{aux}}, d', (d'_{\mathsf{aux}}, t', s'_m, s'_r, s'_e))$ and $(c_{\mathsf{aux}}, d'', (d''_{\mathsf{aux}}, t'', s''_m, s''_r, s''_e))$, where $d' \ne d''$. By the perfect binding property of aCom we get that $t' = t'' = t$. By subtracting the verification equations performed by the verifier we then obtain:

$$\Delta_d c = a \Delta_m + b \Delta_r + \Delta_e,$$

where we set $\Delta_d = d' - d''$, $\Delta_m = s'_m - s''_m$, $\Delta_r = s'_r - s''_r$ and $\Delta_e = s'_e - s''_e$. As $\deg \Delta_d < n/2$, we also have that Δ_d is invertible in R_q. We get the witness $(\Delta_d^{-1} \Delta_m, \Delta_d^{-1} \Delta_r, \Delta_d, \Delta_e)$, where $\|\Delta_d\|_\infty \le 1$ and $\|\Delta_e\| \le \lfloor n^{4/3}/2 \rfloor$.

Honest-Verifier Zero-Knowledge. Taking a challenge d as an input, the simulator first draws uniformly random elements $s'_m, s'_r \xleftarrow{\$} \mathbb{Z}_q[x]/\langle x^n + 1 \rangle$, and s'_e to be $\bot$ with probability $1 - 1/M$ and distributed according to D_{σ_η} with probability $1/M$. If $s'_e \ne \bot$, it computes $(c'_{\mathsf{aux}}, d'_{\mathsf{aux}}) = \mathsf{aCom}(t' = a s'_m + b s'_r + s'_e - d c)$ and outputs $(c'_{\mathsf{aux}}, d, (d'_{\mathsf{aux}}, t', s'_m, s'_r, s'_e))$. (Note that s'_i and d uniquely determine t' in the protocol and in the simulation.) Otherwise the simulator sets $(c'_{\mathsf{aux}}, d'_{\mathsf{aux}}) = \mathsf{aCom}(0)$ and outputs $(c'_{\mathsf{aux}}, d, \perp)$.

It follows from Theorem 2.5 that the distribution conditioned on the prover not outputting $\perp$ is indistinguishable from real protocol runs. From the same theorem, it follows that aborts occur with probability $1 - 1/M$ for every value of de. In case of an abort, the indistinguishability follows from the hiding property of aCom and the fact that for every d, there is an equal chance of an abort happening. □

Lemma 4.3. *If the auxiliary commitment scheme is a trapdoor commitment scheme, then Protocol 4.1 is a concurrently secure zero-knowledge argument of knowledge with knowledge error $1/\binom{n/2}{\kappa}$ for the relation specified in Theorem 4.2.*

The proof is similar to Damgård [Dam00] who gives a generic construction to achieve concurrent ZK for any Σ-protocol. However, our technique had a slightly different origin as our protocols are inherently based on the auxiliary commitment scheme to achieve honest-verifier zero-knowledge. The lemma literally also applies for the subsequent protocols.

On the Abort Probability. From Theorem 2.5 and [Lyu12] it follows that the probability that the prover does not abort is exponentially close to $\frac{1}{M}$, where $M \in \mathcal{O}(\exp(\frac{\|de\|}{\sigma_\eta}))$. Thus, on average M repetitions of the protocol are required. By choosing σ_η sufficiently large, M can be made arbitrarily small at the cost of requiring larger parameters, see also Lyubashevsky [Lyu12].

Number of Rounds. By nesting the executions, the expected number of rounds until a successful protocol run is about $2M$. Alternatively, when only aiming for *arguments* of knowledge, one can also use the idea of Damgård et al. [DPSZ12], who compute many independent first messages and send a Merkle-tree commitment of those in the first step. While on average requiring more computation on the prover side, this approach gives a constant 3-round protocol.

4.2 Proving Linear Relations

Protocol 4.4 allows one to prove knowledge of messages m_1, m_2, m_3 contained in c_1, c_2, c_3, where the m_i additionally satisfy a linear relation of the form $m_3 = x_1 m_1 + x_2 m_2$ for arbitrary public $x_i \in \mathbb{Z}_q[x]/\langle x^n + 1 \rangle$. The construction uses a standard technique: Three instances of Protocol 4.1 are run in parallel for m_1, m_2, m_3 using the same challenge, but instead of choosing the randomness μ_3 for m_3 in the prover's first step at random, it is computed such that μ_1, μ_2, μ_3 satisfy the claimed linear relation. Verifying now whether the s_{m_i} also satisfy that linear relation is enough for the verifier to be guaranteed that the supplied messages have the correct form.

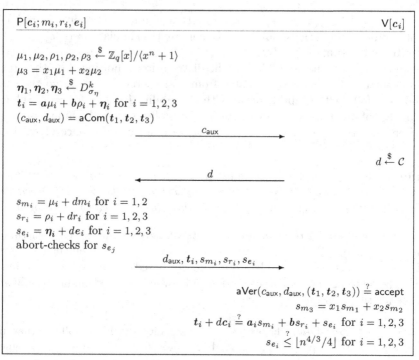

Protocol 4.4: Proving linear relations. The abort-checks are as in Protocol 4.1 and Theorem 2.5.

Theorem 4.5. *If the auxiliary commitment scheme is perfectly binding, then Protocol 4.4 is an honest-verifier zero-knowledge proof of knowledge with knowledge error* $1/\binom{n/2}{\kappa}$ *for the following relations:*

$$\mathcal{R}_{LLWE} = \left\{ ((a, b, x_1, x_2, c_1, c_2, c_3), (m_1, m_2, m_3, r_1, r_2, r_3, e_1, e_2, e_3)) : \right.$$

$$\left. \bigwedge_{i=1}^{3} (c_i = am_i + br_i + e_i \wedge \|e_i\|_\infty \le n) \wedge m_3 = x_1 m_1 + x_2 m_2 \right\},$$

and $\mathcal{R}'_{LLWE}$ *is defined accordingly.*

Proving Inhomogeneous Relations. As for, e.g., DLOG based protocols, inhomogeneous relations like $m_3 = x_1 m_1 + x_2 m_2 + x_3$ can be proved by first removing the inhomogeneity: If c_i is a commitment to m_i, both parties first compute $c'_3 = c_3 - ax_3$, and the prover sets $m'_3 = m_3 - x_3$. The parties then perform Protocol 4.4 for c_1, c_2, c'_3 and m_1, m_2, m'_3 and the homogeneous linear relation $m'_3 = x_1 m_1 + x_2 m_2$.

4.3 Proving Multiplicative Relations

In this section we show how one can prove knowledge of $m_i, r_i, e_i,\ i = 1, 2, 3$ such that $c_i = am_i + br_i + e_i$, and additionally $m_3 = m_1 \cdot m_2$. We begin by giving the intuition behind the protocol.

(i) The prover first proves knowledge of the contents of c_1, c_2, c_3 by running 3 instances of Protocol 4.1 in parallel.

(ii) Similar to Protocol 4.4, the verifier will check the multiplicative relation by combining the responses for m_1, m_2, m_3 accordingly. Unfortunately, in contrast to linear proofs where we have $s_{m_1} + s_{m_2} = s_{m_3}$ for an honest prover, we have that $s_{m_1} s_{m_2} \neq s_{m_3}$. We tackle this problem by letting the prover commit to the arising cross-terms $\mu_1 m_2 + \mu_2 m_1$ and $\mu_1 \mu_2$ in a second part. The according commitments are denoted by c_+ and $c_\times$. Again using two instances of Protocol 4.1, the prover now proves that it knows the openings of those two commitments.

(iii) The third part of the proof now establishes the multiplicative relation. It is based on the following observation: from (i) and (ii) it follows that:

$$\begin{aligned}
\tilde{c} = {}& as_{m_1} s_{m_2} - d^2 c_3 - c_\times - dc_+ \\
= {}& a\left(\mu_1 \mu_2 - m_\times + d(\mu_1 m_2 + \mu_2 m_1 - m_+) + d^2(m_1 m_2 - m_3)\right) \\
& + b(-d^2 r_3 - r_\times - dr_+) + (-d^2 e_3 - e_\times - de_+),
\end{aligned}$$

for some $m_\times, m_+$. Note here that the error term $(-d^2 e_3 - e_\times - de_+)$ of $\tilde{c}$ has small norm, because $e_3, e_\times, e_+$ have small norm and $\|d\|_1 \le \kappa$.

Now, for an honest prover it can easily be seen that $\tilde{c} = b\tilde{r} + \tilde{e}$ for $\tilde{r}$ and $\tilde{e}$ as defined in the protocol, i.e., $\tilde{c}$ is a commitment to 0. On the other hand, if a prover can prove that for at least three different challenges d, the multiplicative relation follows. This can be seen as follows. If

$$\mu_1 \mu_2 - m_\times + d(\mu_1 m_2 + \mu_2 m_1 - m_+) + d^2(m_1 m_2 - m_3) = 0,$$

for three different values of d, this coefficient must be the zero-polynomial (in the indeterminate d), and thus $m_3 = m_1 m_2$. This is because a quadratic polynomial in R_q can only have at most two distinct roots in $\mathcal{C}$. The proof of this claim is straightforward and thus omitted.

Theorem 4.6. *If the auxiliary commitment scheme is perfectly binding, then Protocol 4.7 is an honest-verifier zero-knowledge proof of knowledge with knowledge error $2/\binom{n/2}{\kappa}$ for the following relations:*

$$\mathcal{R}_{MLWE} = \Bigg\{ ((\boldsymbol{a}, \boldsymbol{b}, x_1, x_2, \boldsymbol{c}_1, \boldsymbol{c}_2, \boldsymbol{c}_3), (m_1, m_2, m_3, r_1, r_2, r_3, e_1, e_2, e_3)) :$$

$$\bigwedge_{i=1}^{3} (\boldsymbol{c}_i = \boldsymbol{a}m_i + \boldsymbol{b}r_i + e_i \ \wedge \ \|e_i\|_\infty \le n) \ \wedge \ m_3 = m_1 m_2 \Bigg\},$$

and $\mathcal{R}'_{MLWE}$ is defined accordingly.

P$[c_i; m_i, r_i, e_i]$ V$[c_i]$

(i) $\mu_1, \mu_2, \mu_3, \rho_1, \rho_2, \rho_3 \xleftarrow{\$} \mathbb{Z}_q[x]/\langle x^n + 1 \rangle$

     $\boldsymbol{\eta}_1, \boldsymbol{\eta}_2, \boldsymbol{\eta}_3 \xleftarrow{\$} D^k_{\sigma_\eta}$

     $t_i = a\mu_i + b\rho_i + \boldsymbol{\eta}_i$ for $i = 1, 2, 3$

(ii) $m_+ = \mu_1 m_2 + \mu_2 m_1$

     $m_\times = \mu_1 \mu_2$

     $r_+, r_\times \xleftarrow{\$} \mathbb{Z}_q[x]/\langle x^n + 1 \rangle$

     $e_+, e_\times \xleftarrow{\$} D^k_{\sigma_e}$

     $c_+ = am_+ + br_+ + e_+$

     $c_\times = am_\times + br_\times + e_\times$

     $\mu_+, \mu_\times, \rho_+, \rho_\times \xleftarrow{\$} \mathbb{Z}_q[x]/\langle x^n + 1 \rangle$

     $\boldsymbol{\eta}_+, \boldsymbol{\eta}_\times \xleftarrow{\$} D^k_{\sigma_\eta}$

     $t_+ = a\mu_+ + b\rho_+ + \boldsymbol{\eta}_+$

     $t_\times = a\mu_\times + b\rho_\times + \boldsymbol{\eta}_\times$

(iii) $\tilde{\rho} \xleftarrow{\$} \mathbb{Z}_q[x]/\langle x^n + 1 \rangle$

     $\tilde{\boldsymbol{\eta}} \xleftarrow{\$} D^k_{\sigma_\eta}$

     $\tilde{t} = b\tilde{\rho} + \tilde{\boldsymbol{\eta}}$

     $(c_{\mathsf{aux}}, d_{\mathsf{aux}}) = \mathsf{aCom}(t_+, t_\times, t_i, \tilde{t}, c_+, c_\times)$

$$\xrightarrow{\hspace{2cm} c_{\mathsf{aux}} \hspace{2cm}}$$

                                                                 $d \xleftarrow{\$} C$

$$\xleftarrow{\hspace{2cm} d \hspace{2cm}}$$

$(i) + (ii)$ $s_{m_i} = \mu_i + dm_i$ for $i = 1, 2, 3, +, \times$

         $s_{r_i} = \rho_i + dr_i$ for $i = 1, 2, 3, +, \times$

         $s_{e_i} = \boldsymbol{\eta}_i + de_i$ for $i = 1, 2, 3, +, \times$

(iii) $s_{\tilde{r}} = \tilde{\rho} + d\tilde{r}$

         $\tilde{e} = -d^2 e_3 - e_\times - de_+$

         $\tilde{r} = -d^2 r_3 - r_\times - dr_+$

         $s_{\tilde{e}} = \tilde{\boldsymbol{\eta}} + d\tilde{e}$

         abort-checks for $s_{\tilde{e}}, s_{e_j}$

$$\xrightarrow{\hspace{0.5cm} d_{\mathsf{aux}}, t_+, t_\times, t_i, \tilde{t}, c_+, c_\times, s_{m_i}, s_{r_i}, s_{e_i}, s_{\tilde{r}}, s_{\tilde{e}} \hspace{0.5cm}}$$

                    $\mathsf{aVer}(c_{\mathsf{aux}}, d_{\mathsf{aux}}, (t_+, t_\times, t_i, \tilde{t}, c_+, c_\times)) \overset{?}{=} \mathsf{accept}$

$(i) + (ii)$ $t_i + dc_i \overset{?}{=} a_i s_{m_i} + b s_{r_i} + s_{e_i}$ for $i = 1, 2, 3, +, \times$

                           $s_{e_i} \overset{?}{\le} \lfloor n^{4/3}/4 \rfloor$ for $i = 1, 2, 3, +, \times$

            (iii) $\tilde{c} = as_{m_1} s_{m_2} - d^2 c_3 - c_\times - dc_+$

                                 $\tilde{t} + d\tilde{c} \overset{?}{=} bs_{\tilde{r}} + s_{\tilde{e}}$

                                     $s_{\tilde{e}} \overset{?}{\le} \lfloor n^{4/3}/4 \rfloor$

Protocol 4.7: Proving multiplicative relations. The abort-checks are as in Protocol 4.1 and Theorem 2.5

5   Conclusion

We presented a simple and efficient string commitment scheme whose security is based on the hardness of the RLWE-problem, or, equivalently, on the hardness of solving certain problems on ideal lattices. Additionally we gave constructions for zero-knowledge proofs of knowledge of valid openings of such commitments, and for proving arbitrary relations among such messages. By achieving a negligible knowledge error in our protocols, we solve an open problem stated in previous work, e.g., Jain et al. [JKPT12].

A   Proofs

A.1   Proofs of Theorem 4.5

The theorem is proved by showing that the protocol is a Σ_2'-protocol for the given relation. The claim then follows directly from the discussion in Sect. 2.2.

The proof is essentially a straightforward adaption of that of Theorem 4.2.

Completeness. This follows directly from the completeness of Protocol 4.1 and:

$$x_1 s_{m_1} + x_2 s_{m_2} = x_1(\mu_1 + dm_1) + x_2(\mu_2 + dm_2)$$
$$= (x_1\mu_1 + x_2\mu_2) + d(x_1 m_1 + x_2 m_2) = \mu_3 + dm_3 = s_{m_3},$$

Special Soundness. Given two accepting transcripts, we can extract witnesses $(\Delta_{m_i}, \Delta_{r_i}, \Delta_d, \Delta_{e_i})$ for c_i ($i = 1, 2, 3$) analogously to Theorem 4.2. The only thing that remains to show is that the linear relation $\Delta_{m_3} = x_1 \Delta_{m_1} + x_2 \Delta_{m_2}$ is indeed satisfied. This can be seen as follows:

$$\Delta_{m_3} = s'_{m_3} - s''_{m_3} = (x_1 s'_{m_1} + x_2 s'_{m_2}) - (x_1 s''_{m_1} + x_2 s''_{m_2})$$
$$= x_1(s'_{m_1} - s''_{m_1}) + x_2(s'_{m_2} - s''_{m_2}) = x_1 \Delta_{m_1} + x_2 \Delta_{m_2}.$$

Special Honest-Verifier Zero-Knowledge. The simulator is essentially given by three independent instances of that for Protocol 4.1, except that $s'_{m_3} = x_1 s'_{m_1} + x_2 s'_{m_2}$. The correctness of this simulation is shown by a standard argument, cf., e.g., [BGK+09, JKPT12].

A.2   Proofs of Theorem 4.6

The theorem is proved by showing that the protocol is a Σ_3'-protocol for the given relation. The claim then follows directly from the discussion in Sect. 2.2.

Completeness. It is easy to see that V accepts with overwhelming probability when P does not abort.

Special Soundness. This follows from the soundness of Protocol 4.1 and 4.4 and the above considerations.

Special Honest-Verifier Zero-Knowledge. The intuition is the following: By the hiding property of our commitment scheme, c_+ and $c_\times$ computationally do not reveal any information about the secrets. Furthermore, as Protocol 4.1 is zero-knowledge, s_{m_1}, s_{m_2} and consequently $\tilde{c}$ do not reveal anything to the verifier either. The claim then follows from the proof of Theorem 4.2.

More formally, the simulator first computes $\tilde{c}'$ as a commitment to 0, and similarly for c'_+. It then runs the simulator for c_1, c_2, c_3 and, assuming that no aborts happened, computes $c'_\times = \tilde{c}' + d^2 c_3 - a s'_{m_1} s'_{m_2} + d c_+$. It now runs the simulator for $c'_\times, c'_+, \tilde{c}'$, and, again assuming no aborts, computes an auxiliary commitment, and outputs a transcript by appropriately arranging the messages. If in any step an abort occurred, it sets $(c'_{\mathsf{aux}}, d'_{\mathsf{aux}}) = \mathsf{aCom}(0)$ and returns $(c'_{\mathsf{aux}}, d, \perp)$. It can now be shown that the simulator outputs transcripts that are computationally indistinguishable from real protocol runs. Note therefore that even though the error distributions of $\tilde{c}'$ and $\tilde{c}$ (and of $c'_\times$ and $c_\times$, respectively) are not identical, the resulting commitments cannot be distinguished under the RLWE-assumption.

References

[AJLA+12] Asharov, G., Jain, A., López-Alt, A., Tromer, E., Vaikuntanathan, V., Wichs, D.: Multiparty computation with low communication, computation and interaction via threshold FHE. In: Pointcheval, D., Johansson, T. (eds.) EUROCRYPT 2012. LNCS, vol. 7237, pp. 483–501. Springer, Heidelberg (2012)

[BCK+14] Benhamouda, F., Camenisch, J., Krenn, S., Lyubashevsky, V., Neven, G.: Better zero-knowledge proofs for lattice encryption and their application to group signatures. In: Sarkar, P., Iwata, T. (eds.) ASIACRYPT 2014. LNCS, vol. 8873, pp. 551–572. Springer, Heidelberg (2014)

[BDP00] Boyar, J., Damgård, I., Peralta, R.: Short non-interactive cryptographic proofs. J. Cryptology **13**(4), 449–472 (2000)

[BG93] Bellare, M., Goldreich, O.: On defining proofs of knowledge. In: Brickell, E.F. (ed.) CRYPTO 1992. LNCS, vol. 740, pp. 390–420. Springer, Heidelberg (1993)

[BGK+09] Bangerter, E., Ghadafi, E., Krenn, S., Sadeghi, A.-R., Schneider, T., Smart, N.P., Tsay, J.-K., Warinschi, B.: Final Report on Unified Theoretical Framework of Efficient Zero-Knowledge Proofs of Knowledge. CACE Project Deliverable (2009)

[BLP+13] Brakerski, Z., Langlois, A., Peikert, C., Regev, O., Stehlé, D.: Classical Hardness of Learning with Errors. In: Boneh, D., Roughgarden, T., Feigenbaum, J. (eds.) STOC 2009, pp. 575–584. ACM (2013)

[BPR12] Banerjee, A., Peikert, C., Rosen, A.: Pseudorandom functions and lattices. In: Pointcheval, D., Johansson, T. (eds.) EUROCRYPT 2012. LNCS, vol. 7237, pp. 719–737. Springer, Heidelberg (2012)

[BV11a] Brakerski, Z., Vaikuntanathan, V.: Fully homomorphic encryption from Ring-LWE and security for key dependent messages. In: Rogaway, P. (ed.) CRYPTO 2011. LNCS, vol. 6841, pp. 505–524. Springer, Heidelberg (2011)

[BV11b] Brakerski, Z., Vaikuntanathan, V.: Efficient fully homomorphic encryption from (standard) LWE. In: FOCS (2011)

[CD97] Cramer, R., Damgård, I.: Linear zero-knowledge - a note on efficient zero-knowledge proofs and arguments. In: Leighton, F.T., Shor, P.W. (eds.) STOC 97, pp. 436–445. ACM (1997)

[CD98] Cramer, R., Damgård, I.B.: Zero-knowledge proofs for finite field arithmetic or: can zero-knowledge be for free? In: Krawczyk, H. (ed.) CRYPTO 1998. LNCS, vol. 1462, pp. 424–441. Springer, Heidelberg (1998)

[CD09] Cramer, R., Damgård, I.: On the amortized complexity of zero-knowledge protocols. In: Halevi, S. (ed.) CRYPTO 2009. LNCS, vol. 5677, pp. 177–191. Springer, Heidelberg (2009)

[CKL+14] Camenisch, J., Krenn, S., Lehmann, A., Mikkelsen, G.L., Neven, G., Pedersen, M.Ø.: Formal treatment of privacy-enhancing credential systems. Cryptology ePrint Archive, Report 2014/708 (2014). http://eprint.iacr.org/

[Cra97] Cramer, R.: Modular Design of Secure yet Practical Cryptographic Protocols. Ph.D. thesis, CWI and University of Amsterdam (1997)

[Dam00] Damgård, I.B.: Efficient concurrent zero-knowledge in the auxiliary string model. In: Preneel, B. (ed.) EUROCRYPT 2000. LNCS, vol. 1807, pp. 418–430. Springer, Heidelberg (2000)

[Dam10] Damgård, I.: On Σ-Protocols, Lecture on Cryptologic Protocol Theory, Faculty of Science. University of Aarhus (2010)

[DPSZ12] Damgård, I., Pastro, V., Smart, N., Zakarias, S.: Multiparty computation from somewhat homomorphic encryption. In: Safavi-Naini, R., Canetti, R. (eds.) CRYPTO 2012. LNCS, vol. 7417, pp. 643–662. Springer, Heidelberg (2012)

[DDLL13] Ducas, L., Durmus, A., Lepoint, T., Lyubashevsky, V.: Lattice signatures and bimodal gaussians. In: Canetti, R., Garay, J.A. (eds.) CRYPTO 2013, Part I. LNCS, vol. 8042, pp. 40–56. Springer, Heidelberg (2013)

[DF02] Damgård, I.B., Fujisaki, E.: A statistically-hiding integer commitment scheme based on groups with hidden order. In: Zheng, Y. (ed.) ASIACRYPT 2002. LNCS, vol. 2501, pp. 125–142. Springer, Heidelberg (2002)

[DGOW95] Damgård, I.B., Goldreich, O., Okamoto, T., Wigderson, A.: Honest verifier vs dishonest verifier in public coin zero-knowledge proofs. In: Coppersmith, D. (ed.) CRYPTO 1995. LNCS, vol. 963, pp. 325–338. Springer, Heidelberg (1995)

[Fis01] Fischlin, M.: Trapdoor Commitment Schemes and Their Applications. Ph.D. thesis, Johann Wolfgang Goethe-Universität Frankfurt am Main (2001)

[FO97] Fujisaki, E., Okamoto, T.: Statistical zero knowledge protocols to prove modular polynomial relations. In: Kaliski Jr., B.S. (ed.) CRYPTO 1997. LNCS, vol. 1294, pp. 16–30. Springer, Heidelberg (1997)

[FS87] Fiat, A., Shamir, A.: How to prove yourself: practical solutions to identification and signature problems. In: Odlyzko, A.M. (ed.) CRYPTO 1986. LNCS, vol. 263, pp. 186–194. Springer, Heidelberg (1987)

[Gen09] Gentry, C.: Fully homomorphic encryption using ideal lattices. In: Mitzenmacher, M. (eds.) STOC 2009, pp. 169–178. ACM (2009)

[GMR85] Goldwasser, S., Micali, S., Rackoff, C.: The knowledge complexity of interactive proof-systems (extended abstract). In: STOC, pp. 291–304 (1985)

[GMW86] Goldreich, O., Micali, S., Wigderson, A.: How to prove all NP-statements in zero-knowledge and a methodology of cryptographic protocol design. In: Odlyzko, A.M. (ed.) CRYPTO 1986. LNCS, vol. 263, pp. 171–185. Springer, Heidelberg (1987)

[GPV08] Gentry, C., Peikert, C., Vaikuntanathan, V.: Trapdoors for hard lattices and new cryptographic constructions. In: Dwork, C. (eds.) STOC 2008, pp. 197–206. ACM (2008)

[GS08] Groth, J., Sahai, A.: Efficient non-interactive proof systems for bilinear groups. In: Smart, N.P. (ed.) EUROCRYPT 2008. LNCS, vol. 4965, pp. 415–432. Springer, Heidelberg (2008)

[IKOS07] Ishai, Y., Kushilevitz, E., Ostrovsky, R., Sahai, A.: Zero-knowledge from secure multiparty computation. In: Johnson, D.S., Feige, U. (eds.) STOC 2007, pp. 21–30. ACM (2007)

[JKPT12] Jain, A., Krenn, S., Pietrzak, K., Tentes, A.: Commitments and efficient zero-knowledge proofs from learning parity with noise. In: Wang, X., Sako, K. (eds.) ASIACRYPT 2012. LNCS, vol. 7658, pp. 663–680. Springer, Heidelberg (2012)

[KMO90] Kilian, J., Micali, S., Ostrovsky, R.: Minimum resource zero-knowledge proofs. In: Brassard, G. (ed.) CRYPTO 1989. LNCS, vol. 435, pp. 545–546. Springer, Heidelberg (1990)

[KP98] Kilian, J., Petrank, E.: An efficient noninteractive zero-knowledge proof system for NP with general assumptions. J. Cryptology 11(1), 1–27 (1998)

[KR06] Kalai, Y.T., Raz, R.: Succinct non-interactive zero-knowledge proofs with preprocessing for LOGSNP. In: FOCS 2006, pp. 355–366. IEEE Computer Society (2006)

[KV09] Katz, J., Vaikuntanathan, V.: Smooth projective hashing and password-based authenticated key exchange from lattices. In: Matsui, M. (ed.) ASIACRYPT 2009. LNCS, vol. 5912, pp. 636–652. Springer, Heidelberg (2009)

[LNSW13] Ling, S., Nguyen, K., Stehlé, D., Wang, H.: Improved zero-knowledge proofs of knowledge for the ISIS problem, and applications. In: Kurosawa, K., Hanaoka, G. (eds.) PKC 2013. LNCS, vol. 7778, pp. 107–124. Springer, Heidelberg (2013)

[LP11] Lindner, R., Peikert, C.: Better key sizes (and attacks) for LWE-based encryption. In: Kiayias, A. (ed.) CT-RSA 2011. LNCS, vol. 6558, pp. 319–339. Springer, Heidelberg (2011)

[LPR10] Lyubashevsky, V., Peikert, C., Regev, O.: On ideal lattices and learning with errors over rings. In: Gilbert, H. (ed.) EUROCRYPT 2010. LNCS, vol. 6110, pp. 1–23. Springer, Heidelberg (2010)

[Lyu09] Lyubashevsky, V.: Fiat-shamir with aborts: applications to lattice and factoring-based signatures. In: Matsui, M. (ed.) ASIACRYPT 2009. LNCS, vol. 5912, pp. 598–616. Springer, Heidelberg (2009)

[Lyu12] Lyubashevsky, V.: Lattice signatures without trapdoors. In: Pointcheval, D., Johansson, T. (eds.) EUROCRYPT 2012. LNCS, vol. 7237, pp. 738–755. Springer, Heidelberg (2012)

[PR06] Peikert, C., Rosen, A.: Efficient collision-resistant hashing from worst-case assumptions on cyclic lattices. In: Halevi, S., Rabin, T. (eds.) TCC 2006. LNCS, vol. 3876, pp. 145–166. Springer, Heidelberg (2006)

[Reg05] Regev, O.: On lattices, learning with errors, random linear codes, and cryptography. In: STOC 2005, pp. 84–93. ACM (2005)

[Rüc10] Rückert, M.: Lattice-based blind signatures. In: Abe, M. (ed.) ASIACRYPT 2010. LNCS, vol. 6477, pp. 413–430. Springer, Heidelberg (2010)

[SSTX09] Stehlé, D., Steinfeld, R., Tanaka, K., Xagawa, K.: Efficient public key encryption based on ideal lattices. In: Matsui, M. (ed.) ASIACRYPT 2009. LNCS, vol. 5912, pp. 617–635. Springer, Heidelberg (2009)

Efficient Zero-Knowledge Proofs for Commitments from Ring-LWE   325

[Ste93] Stern, J.: A new identification scheme based on syndrome decoding. In: Stinson, D.R. (ed.) CRYPTO 1993. LNCS, vol. 773, pp. 13–21. Springer, Heidelberg (1994)
[XXW13] Xie, X., Xue, R., Wang, M.: Zero knowledge proofs from Ring-LWE. In: Abdalla, M., Nita-Rotaru, C., Dahab, R. (eds.) CANS 2013. LNCS, vol. 8257, pp. 57–73. Springer, Heidelberg (2013)

Making *Any* Identity-Based Encryption
Accountable, Efficiently

Aggelos Kiayias[1] and Qiang Tang[2](✉)

[1] National and Kapodistrian University of Athens, Athens, Greece
aggelos@di.uoa.gr
[2] University of Connecticut, Storrs, USA
qtang84@gmail.com

Abstract. Identity-Based Encryption (IBE) provides a compelling solution to the PKI management problem, however it comes with the serious privacy consideration that a trusted party (called the PKG) is required to generate (and hence also know) the secret keys of all users. This inherent key escrow problem is considered to be one of the major reasons hindering the wider utilization of IBE systems. In order to address this problem, Goyal [20] introduced the notion of accountable authority IBE (A-IBE), in which a judge can differentiate the PKG from the user as the source of a decryption software. Via this "tracing" mechanism, A-IBE deters the PKG from leaking the user's secret key and hence offers a defense mechanism for IBE users against a malicious PKG.

All previous works on A-IBE focused on specialized constructions trying to achieve different properties and efficiency enhancements. In this paper for the first time we show how to add accountability to *any* IBE scheme using oblivious transfer (OT), with almost the same ciphertext efficiency as the underlying IBE. Furthermore, we extend our generic construction to support identity reuse without losing efficiency. This property is desirable in practice as users may accidentally lose their secret keys and they -naturally- prefer not to abandon their identities. How to achieve this property was open until our work. Along the way, we first modify the generic construction and develop a new technique to provide public traceability generically.

1 Introduction

Identity-Based Encryption (IBE) was introduced by Shamir [31], to remove the need for maintaining a certificate based public-key infrastructure (PKI). Long time after the concept was proposed, Boneh and Franklin constructed the first practical IBE [8] in the random oracle model [4]. Since then, IBE has gotten more attention and a lot of alternative schemes have emerged with an extended set of properties, cf. [5,6,11,19,22,29,32,33].

Although significant progress has been made in constructing secure and efficient IBE schemes, a critical problem of IBE is that a trusted authority, called PKG, is required to generate secret keys for all users. The possibility of the corruption of this authority (or just her temporary misbehavior due to an insider

© Springer International Publishing Switzerland 2015
G. Pernul et al. (Eds.): ESORICS 2015, Part I, LNCS 9326, pp. 326–346, 2015.
DOI: 10.1007/978-3-319-24174-6_17

attack) is considered one of the most important reasons hindering the deployment of IBE systems in practice [1,18,21]. The problem is inherent since there is no user-side secret that is used when generating the secret key corresponding to an arbitrarily formed identity; it follows that there is no *built-in* incentive for the PKG in a standard IBE system to protect the users' secret information.

Beyond the obvious privacy problem (the unavoidable fact that the PKG can decrypt all users' ciphertexts) there is also a more serious attack that can take place: the PKG may share the users' secret keys. One may address this by arguing that such malicious behavior can be detectable by the user: for instance, a decryption program B leaked to the public (e.g., uploaded on a public forum) can be noticed by the user. In such case, the user could conceivably bring the program to court and sue the PKG, thus the PKG would be deterred from such behavior. However, notice that both user and PKG are capable of producing B thus the device itself can not be used as conclusive proof about who is at fault.

In order to make the above detect-then-punish mechanism effective, Goyal introduced the concept of accountable authority IBE, (A-IBE in short) [20], where a convincing proof can be provided from which a judge can make a decision about who is at fault. In order to achieve this characteristic, every identity must be corresponded with super-polynomially many secret keys, and the PKG and the user jointly generate a secret key for the user so that the PKG does not know which key is chosen by the user. Using the secret key received by the user, any third party, a judge for example, can tell whether the decryption device is made from the user secret key or not, thus the judge (and the public) can identify unequivocally the creator of the device. A number of works followed up this seminal result, [21,25,26,28,34], further refining the notion of A-IBE.

Still, the adoption of A-IBE in practice is hindered by a couple of facts. First, many constructions are inefficient (in the sense that they require linear in the security parameter number of group elements, cf. Fig. 1) or that the designs are incompatible with existing practical deployments such as RFC 5091 [12]. Second, when a user accidentally loses his key, in all existing A-IBE schemes, the user and the PKG have to discard this identity and generate a new key for the user using a different identity (otherwise, it enables malicious users to frame the PKG). This artifact brings users annoying inconvenience. These put forth the main motivations in our work: is it possible to add accountability to *any* existing (that is potentially already deployed, e.g., RFC 5091) IBE system, with a minimum cost? furthermore, we ask whether such generic transformation can be extended to allow identity reuse, without losing efficiency? If such transformation exists, users may choose to "upgrade" their IBE scheme to be accountable without requiring a modification to the basic algorithms of the underlying IBE.

Our Contributions. In this work, we address both problems listed above. First, we propose a generic construction of an A-IBE (in the so-called weak black-box model with full security against malicious users, see definition in Appendix A) that uses any existing IBE in a black-box way. And this generic construction has ciphertext size only 2 times the underlying IBE ciphertext size. (we call this construction S-I). The key observation behind our construction is that users can choose from a set of secret-keys that are based on an extended form of their identity. When encrypting messages it is possible for the sender to use only two ciphertexts to guarantee an honest user to decrypt. However, it is also possible to generate a set of tracing ciphertexts that can reveal part of the "fingerprint" of the secret-key that was assigned obliviously to the user by the PKG. The presence of the partial fingerprint in a user decoder that is found publicly incriminates the user, otherwise, incriminates the PKG.

We then consider how to allow identity reuse. This property is not known whether achievable before, even with specifically tailored constructions. We achieve it while maintaining the generic nature and the small size ciphertext. The main challenge for achieving identity reuse in A-IBE setting is that a malicious user can obtain multiple secret keys corresponding to the same identity by claiming to the PKG that she lost the key. Such malicious user could then implement a pirate box B using one key, and reveal another key to the judge. A secret key tracing algorithm may erroneously accuse the PKG, as, by definition, the key used to implement B is different to the key that the user is currently using.

Our strategy is to add public traceability to our generic construction that will enable the judge to differentiate among all the secret keys that were ever obtained by a user for the same identity. Note that in S-I, part of the user fingerprint is recovered, if there is a public reference for the user fingerprint, it might be possible for the judge to check whether the recovered string matches. In order to implement this idea, we improve the generic construction S-I to allow the tracing algorithm to recover the *whole* "fingerprint" while maintaining the ciphertext size still to be small (at most logarithmic overhead, and we call it S-II). With this new feature of S-II we developed, it is possible to deposit the fingerprint (using a one way function) that the user chooses for selecting the secret key to the PKG in a secure way so that: (i) it enables the judge to use a public tracing key T to determine whether a recovered fingerprint matches the fingerprint, and (ii) it prevents a malicious PKG from producing a pirate box without being traced with the help of T. The main technical part is to design a proper one way function for the secure deposit of the bitstring, together with an efficient zero-knowledge proof for the consistency between the privately deposited fingerprint and that used in the OT protocol, bit by bit.

The intuition for S-II follows from the observation that if the "fingerprint" is generated from an error correcting code, a linear fraction of it could be enough to reveal the whole string. With a careful probabilistic analysis, we see that with slightly longer ciphertexts, one is able to retrieve a larger fraction of the fingerprint from a pirate box. (this new mechanism also allows the length of the fingerprint to be reduced asymptotically, so as the secret key size). This feature of S-II makes it a steppingstone for further allowing identity re-use and public traceability. Our A-IBE tracing mechanisms are inspired by previous works related to traitor tracing [10] and leakage-deterring cryptosystems [24].

With such public traceability, the scheme can be further extended to support identity reuse. Each identity now will have multiple extended forms (instead of one in S-II), and for each extended form indexed by a state, the user can use

	G-I	G-II	GLSW08	LV09	SS11	LDZW13	YCZY14	S-I	S-III
Generic	no	no	no	no	no	no	no	yes	yes
Ciphertext size	$O(\lambda)$	$O(\lambda)$	$O(\lambda)$	$O(1)$	$O(\lambda)$	$O(1)$	$O(1)$	$O(1)$	$O(1)$
Malicious User	s	s	s	a	a	a	a	a	a
Malicious PKG	w	bb_0	bb_1	bb_0	bb_1	bb_0	bb_1	bb_0	bb_0
Public Traceable	no	no	no	no	no	yes	no	no	yes
ID Reuse	no	no	no	no	no	no	no	no	yes

Fig. 1. Comparisons of all existing A-IBEs, ciphertext size means the number of group elements; 's' means selective, 'a' means adaptive; w, bb_0, bb_1 mean white box, weak black-box and full black-box traceability respectively; S-I, S-III are our constructions.

an independent string as a fingerprint to request one secret key. During the i-th key generation protocol for an identity, the PKG will store a public tracing key T_i and the updated state about the current version of the extended form for each identity in a public directory. The encryption algorithm will use the current version of the extended form of identity. The tracing algorithm will run on all versions of the extended form of the identity, extract (potentially multiple) fingerprints; subsequently, it will check whether they match the public tracing keys. In this way, the tracing algorithm can decide that the key inside the pirate box is the one the user is currently using or whether it is one of the keys claimed to be lost, or is a key originating from the PKG. A malicious user can never frame the PKG using a key claimed to be lost, and a PKG can not evade the tracing algorithm if she ever leaks a decryption box for the user identity (even for previous versions of extended form of identity).

Note that after adding public traceability and id-reuse to our generic construction, the ciphertext efficiency and the generic nature are still the same as in S-II. The model that T has to be stored for each user is the same as the only existing paper [25] (that was based on Gentry IBE [19]) providing public traceability.[1] Finally it is worth to point out that our construction allows these two properties to be optional services by the PKG and the user may opt-in or opt-out to such properties at will when she requests a key from the PKG.

We remark that our generic transformations can go beyond IBE and can be easily adapted to apply to more advanced systems like attribute based encryption [22,29]. The performance comparison of all A-IBE schemes (including ours) is summarized in Fig. 1.

Related Work. In [20], Goyal proposed the notion of A-IBE and gave two constructions. The first one is traceable only in the white-box model (requires the key material of the pirate box) while the second one is in the weak black-box model. We call those constructions G-I, G-II and both have ciphertext size that includes a linear number of group elements. In the following work of [21], Goyal et al. proposed a construction having traceability in the full black-box model, but at the price of having (i) secret key and ciphertext size that has linear in the security parameter

---

[1] In fact, it is not hard to see (explained in Sect. 3.1) that the size of the public tracing key has to grow linearly with the number of users.

number of group elements, (ii) security against malicious users only in a selective model (where the adversary needs to commit to its move ahead at the beginning of the game). Libert and Vergnaud [26] made an improvement on G-I, and they gave an A-IBE with constant group elements in the ciphertext that is proven traceable in the weak black box model. Sahai and Seyalioglu [28] improved the security against dishonest users, and achieved full security against dishonest users, but their construction still has a linear size ciphertext. Lai et al. [25] proposed the first scheme with public traceability that the authority is required to store a public tracing key for each user which is later used to generate tracing ciphertext, and it is also traceable in the weak black-box model. Our public traceability can be based on any IBE and uses a different tracing technique that we can directly compare whether a recovered fingerprint matches the one contained in the public tracing key. Concurrent to our work an E-print technical report [34] proposed an A-IBE with traceability in the full black-box model, adaptive security against malicious user and constant size ciphertext under non-standard assumptions. All these works rely on a highly specific structure, specifically, Gentry IBE [19] as in [20, 25, 26, 34] or fuzzy IBE [29] as in [20, 21, 28]; their techniques for accountability do not adapt in other settings straightforwardly (and specifically none can be applied to current real world IBE's such as those of RFC5091 directly). Also, none of those works allows public traceability (except [25]) or identity reuse.

There are also other proposals to deal with the key escrow problem in IBE. In [8], Boneh and Franklin gave a simple solution where multiple authorities distributively produce the PKG master secret key. However, in principle, those PKGs still may collude to leak user's secret leaving the user defenseless; Al-Riyami and Paterson proposed the concept of certificateless public key cryptography [1], and attempted to combine both the advantages of certificate-based PKI and IBE. The authority only has a partial secret key k_1, and it jointly generates secret key together with the user who has her own secret k_2. However, part of the public key must be in a specific form corresponding to k_2 and thus it can not be as expressive as IBE. Hence such systems may be of more narrow applicability compared to proper IBE schemes. Au et al. [2] proposed the notion of retrievability that from two secret keys of a user, one can compute the master secret key. The notion of retrievability is interesting but it is achieved only in the white box model. Chow [14] considers the notion of anonymous ciphertext indistinguishability, which requires that the PKG cannot learn the recipient identity from a ciphertext, thus hoping that the authority is not able to figure out which secret key to use to decrypt. This is an interesting notion as well, but only meaningful in an IBE system with an extremely large number of users; furthermore it does not protect against a PKG that targets a specific user and publishes the decryption algorithm (which is the main defense objective of A-IBE).

2 Generic Construction of A-IBE with Constant Size Ciphertext

Due to space limit, we refer the definitions and security models for A-IBE to Appendix A. In this section, we give a generic construction of A-IBE secure in the weak dishonest-PKG model from any IBE scheme using 1-out-of-2 OT, and it only has ciphertext size two times the underlying IBE scheme.

The intuition behind this generic transformation is that for each identity ID, there are exponentially many secret keys, each of which has a unique "fingerprint". Each user will select his key with a random "fingerprint" using an OT protocol. Given only an oracle access to a decryption box B implemented using one key, part of the fingerprint can be retrieved. When a decryption box is found, the recovered partial "fingerprint" is able to reveal the source of the box.

Specifically, 2ℓ identities $(ID||1||0, ID||1||1), \ldots, (ID||\ell||0, ID||\ell||1)$ are all considered as the same user with identity ID.[2] During **KeyGen**, for each pair of secret keys corresponding to identities $ID||i||0$, and $ID||i||1$, user randomly selects one of them using a 1-out-of-2 OT.[3] The "fingerprint" of the user selected key corresponds to the bit string of length ℓ he uses in the OT protocols. **Enc** randomly selects an index r, and simply encrypts the same message under both $ID||r||0, ID||r||1$, thus sender does not need to know the fingerprint of the user with ID. Note the user has one key per location, i.e., one key corresponding to the identity $ID||r||0$ or $ID||r||1$ for each r, thus he can decrypt. Also **Trace** can attempt to recover each bit of the fingerprint from a decryption box by feeding ciphertexts containing different messages for the location, i.e., for an index i, c_0, c_1 are fed, where $c_b = \mathbf{Enc}(ID||i||b, mpk, m_b)$. The semantic security of the underlying IBE suggests that the box will not distinguish these tracing ciphertexts from regular ciphertexts, and the answer m_b reveals the i−th bit of the user fingerprint. Whenever λ bits are recovered, and all of them equal to the corresponding bits in the user "fingerprint", the user will be accused, otherwise the PKG will be accused. Essentially, a malicious PKG can evade the tracing algorithm only if she guesses correctly λ random bits.

One may notice that a malicious user may put as few keys as possible, e.g., only one key corresponding to $ID||t||b_t$ for some t, into a pirate box B and thus for the other indices, there is no hope to recover the fingerprint bits. However, since B has to provide some minimum functionality, i.e., answering correctly with some noticeable probability δ, (formally, $\Pr[B(\mathbf{Enc}(m, ID, mpk)) = m] \geq \delta$), if we choose ℓ large enough (λ/δ through our probabilistic analysis), there must be at least λ keys contained in the pirate box to maintain the δ-correctness. In particular, we can argue that there exist at least λ indices, the box decrypts ciphertext generated using those indices, with probability at least δ/λ. Then as elaborated above, once a key is used, we can recover the corresponding bit.

2.1 Detailed Construction

We call this generic construction S-I, for an IBE scheme (`Setup`, `KeyGen`, `Enc`, `Dec`), the details of S-I are as follows:

---

[2] Doing above may reduce the original identity space, however, this problem can be easily addressed by extending the identity string $O(\log \ell)$ bits longer.

[3] Unlike ABE schemes, our generic construction does not have to provide collusion-resistance, as for each index, a user can obtain only one key.

- **Setup**(λ, δ): This algorithm inputs the security parameter λ and the correctness parameter δ, it runs the Setup algorithm of the underlying IBE and outputs master key pair (mpk, msk), and a parameter $\ell = \lambda/\delta$.
- **KeyGen** This is a protocol between PKG and a user A with identity ID,
    1. PKG generates 2ℓ secret keys $\{k_{i,b}\}_{i=1,\ldots,\ell,b=0,1}$, using KeyGen of the underlying IBE, where $k_{i,b} = \text{KeyGen}(msk, ID\|i\|b)$.
    2. User A randomly chooses a bit string $\bar{b} = b_1, \ldots, b_\ell$ with length ℓ.
    3. A executes ℓ (1,2)-OT protocols with the PKG in parallel. In the i-th execution, A inputs b_i, PKG inputs $k_{i,0}, k_{i,1}$ and A receives k_{i,b_i}.
    The protocol ends with A outputting $sk_{ID} = \{sk_i = (b_i, k_{i,b_i})\}_{i=1,\ldots,\ell}$.
- **Enc**(ID, mpk, m): To encrypt a message m for user A, the algorithm randomly chooses an index $r \in \{1, \ldots, \ell\}$ and outputs ciphertext $C = (r, c_{r,0}, c_{r,1})$, where for $b \in \{0,1\}$, $c_{r,b} = \text{Enc}(ID\|r\|b, mpk, m)$.
- **Dec**(C, sk_{ID}): On input ciphertext C and the secret keys of user A, the decryption algorithm parses the ciphertext and runs the underlying IBE decryption algorithm, it returns $m = \text{Dec}(c_{r,b_r}, sk_r)$.
- **Trace**$^B(ID, \delta, \{b_i\})$ This is a two stage protocol. In the first stage, the judge $\mathcal{J}$ interacts with user A[4] to get his secret string and verify its validity.
    1. A sends $\bar{b}$ and a pirate decryption box B to $\mathcal{J}$.
    2. $\mathcal{J}$ parses $\bar{b}$, and then randomly selects 2ℓ messages $\{r_{i,0}, r_{i,1}\}_{i=1,\ldots,\ell}$, and asks A to decrypt one of the ciphertext $\{c_{i,0}, c_{i,1}\}$, where $c_{i,b} = \text{Enc}(ID\|i\|b, mpk, r_{i,b})$ for $i = 1, \ldots, \ell$. A decrypts $\{c_{i,b_i}\}$ and sends back $\{r'_{i,b_i}\}$, $\mathcal{J}$ then checks $r_{i,b_i} \overset{?}{=} r'_{i,b_i}$ for all $i \in \{1, \ldots, \ell\}$.

If not, $\mathcal{J}$ outputs "user"; otherwise, $\mathcal{J}$ runs the following algorithm:

1. For each $i \in \{1, \ldots, \ell\}$, $\mathcal{J}$ repeats the following N times (the exact number of N will be specified in the analysis) to define a bit s_i. In each run, $\mathcal{J}$ randomly selects m_0, m_1, and feeds B with $(i, c_{i,0}, c_{i,1})$, where $c_{i,b} = \text{Enc}(ID\|i\|b, mpk, m_b)$ for $b = 0, 1$. $\mathcal{J}$ records a b for s_i if B returns m_b, otherwise, $\mathcal{J}$ records a $\perp$.
2. After the repetitions for each i, $\mathcal{J}$ takes the majority of the non-$\perp$ records as the value for s_i; if all records are $\perp$, then s_i is undefined.
3. Suppose $s_{i_1}, \ldots, s_{i_t}$ are the defined bits. If $s_{i_j} = b_{i_j}$ for all $j \in \{1, \ldots, t\}$ and $t \geq \lambda$, $\mathcal{J}$ returns "user"; otherwise, $\mathcal{J}$ returns "PKG".

Remark. Our tracing algorithm is conditioned on the fact that the box has a noticeable correctness δ for random messages, and the box is resettable.

A Note about Fully Black-Box Traceability. We can see from the tracing algorithm of S-I that given access to a decryption oracle, the PKG learns the bit string that the user chose to select the secret keys, thus further learns the chosen secret keys of the user. One possible remedy is to introduce a mechanism that only the judge can create a valid tracing ciphertext, i.e., regular ciphertext pair is augmented with a ZK proofs of the statement that "either they contain equal plaintexts or I am the judge". This prevents the PKG from learning any

---

[4] It can be easily made non-interactive if the user proves that he has the right keys.

information about the user fingerprint via access to a decryption oracle, but also at the same time enables the judge to trace. One downside of this mechanism is that the judge needs to keep some private state thus we will have to work on a slightly weaker model. Due to lack of space, we defer the details of achieving fully black-box recoverability in this model to the full version. We will focus on the other advanced properties, e.g., identity reuse, which is not known whether achievable before in the standard model of A-IBE in the rest of the paper.

2.2 Security Analysis

We will give intuitions about the security properties of S-I and for the proof, we mainly focused on the most involved part dealing with malicious users.

IND-ID-CPA Security. $ID||i||0, ID||i||1$ are considered two different identities and thus our generic construction S-I is simply a double encryption of a same message using two different identities. It follows easily that a double encryption is as secure as the underlying IBE.

Security in the Weak Dishonest-PKG Game. Note that the **Trace** algorithm does not outputs "PKG" only when the recovered string is composed of two parts: an all-$\bot$ part, and a bitstring which is at least λ bits long and matches the corresponding substring of the user secret string. All other cases, including an all-$\bot$ string is recovered, or any single bit recovered is different with the corresponding bit of the user "fingerprint", the PKG is accused.

The receiver security of the OT protocol executed in **KeyGen** guarantees that a malicious PKG can only guess each bit of the secret string, thus she can fools the **Trace** algorithm with probability negligibly close to $2^{-\lambda}$. Specifically, in the execution of the i-th OT protocol, the malicious PKG can not distinguish the transcript created by an user inputting a random bit r from the transcript created using the selected bit b_i. We can do a sequence of game changes and end up with a game that all OT transcripts are created using independently selected random bits $\bar{r} = r_1, \ldots, r_\ell$. In the last game, since $\bar{b} = b_1, \ldots, b_\ell$ are independent of the transcripts, we can let the malicious PKG output a box and the judge recovers a substring with length at least λ first, and then select $\bar{b}$. It follows easily that the corresponding substring of $\bar{b}$ matches the recovered substring of $\bar{r}$, with probability at most $2^{-\lambda}$.

Security in the Adaptive Dishonest-User Game. Our main observation that if the box is leaked by a user, the judge will always be able to accuse her, relies on the following reasons. First, since the user has only one key for each location, due to the semantic security of the underlying IBE (and the OT sender security), the user has to report to the judge honestly her secret string. Furthermore, the box B is not able to tell a tracing ciphertext (the pair of the ciphertext encrypting different messages) from a normal ciphertext, thus B will have δ-correctness during tracing. We will analyze that the box has to decrypt using the keys with probability δ/λ for at least λ indices to maintain such correctness. Again, for each index i, B can never succeed in decrypting

m_{1-b} if only $k_{i,b}$ is inside, thus for the indices it responds, it has to reveal the correct bits after enough repetitions.

Theorem 1. *(1). S-I is IND-ID-CPA secure if the underlying IBE scheme is IND-ID-CPA secure; (2). S-I is secure in the* **weak dishonest-PKG** *game if the underlying 1-out-of-2-OT protocol satisfies the receiver security; (3). S-I is secure in the adaptive* **dishonest-user** *game if the underlying IBE is IND-ID-CPA secure, and the 1-out-of-2-OT protocol satisfies the (simulatable) sender security.*

Proof. The security properties (1) and (2) follow easily from the explanation above, we will focus on property (3).

First, it is not hard to see that in the first phase of the **Trace** protocol, the user has to submit the same string she selected. This can be shown via a sequence of game changes. In the original game, the adversary $\mathcal{A}$ runs the OT protocols one by one for ℓ times (or in parallel), during the **KeyGen** protocol, and answers the decryption queries during the first phase of the **Trace** algorithm. In the modified ℓ games, the OT protocols are replaced with an oracle (one by one) that on inputting a bit, outputting the corresponding secret key. The indistinguishability of these game changes are ensured by the (simulatable) sender security of the OT protocol (see the composition lemma of Canetti [13]).

In the last game, during **KeyGen** $\mathcal{A}$ has only oracle access to the OT instances, which can be "controlled" by a simulator. Now suppose the adversary answers correctly for the decryption request $c_{i,1-b_i}$ at some index i with probability Δ_i, there exists a simulator $\mathcal{S}$ playing the role of PKG with $\mathcal{A}$ as a user, can break the IND-ID-CPA security of the underlying IBE. $\mathcal{S}$ can answer all the OT queries perfectly with the corresponding secret keys, (which can be asked to the IND-ID-CPA game challenger directly). $\mathcal{S}$ simply uses $ID||i||1-b_i$ as the challenge identity. $\mathcal{S}$ selects m_0, m_1 as the challenge message, and forwards the challenge ciphertexts to the adversary. If $\mathcal{A}$ answers m_b, $\mathcal{S}$ answers b, otherwise, a random bit. It is straightforward that $\mathcal{S}$ breaks the IND-ID-CPA security with advantage $\frac{\Delta_i}{2}$ (which can be derived as follows: $\Delta_i \cdot 1 + (1 - \Delta_i)\frac{1}{2} - \frac{1}{2}$).

Let $\delta_i = \Pr[B$ decrypts correctly $\mid i$ is selected]. We divide the indices $i \in \{1, \ldots, \ell\}$ in two sets, Bad and Good, we define $i \in$ Good if and only if $\delta_i \geq \delta_0$, where $\delta_0 = \delta/\lambda$. Next, we lower bound $n = |$Good$|$. If $n < \lambda$, then:

$$\Pr[B \text{ works correctly}] = \sum_{i=1}^{\ell} \Pr[B \text{ works correctly}|i \text{ is selected}] \Pr[i \text{ is selected}]$$

$$\leq [1 \cdot (\lambda - 1) + \delta_0 \cdot (\ell - n + 1)]\frac{1}{\ell} = \frac{\lambda - 1}{\ell} + \frac{\delta(\ell - n + 1)}{\ell\lambda} \leq \frac{\lambda - 1}{\ell} + \frac{\delta}{\lambda} = \frac{\lambda}{\ell} = \delta$$

thus, we can conclude that for at least λ indices, the box will answer correctly with probability at least δ/λ.

Next, similar to the analysis for the first stage of the protocol, we can show that the probability that B decrypts to the other message selected in the **Trace** algorithm (m_{1-b_i}, which is with high entropy) will be a negligible function. Following the standard Chernoff bound, we can see that if we run the **Trace** algorithm with the a number of $N = O(\delta_0^{-2} \log^2 \lambda)$ repetitions, the correct value of b_i would form a majority of the non-$\perp$ records for s_i.

Summarizing the above facts, if a box B implemented using one key from the user and it has δ-correctness, there will be at least λ indices that the **Trace** algorithm recovers the correct bits, ($\perp$ for all other indices), it returns "user". $\square$

3 Generic Construction of A-IBE Allowing Public Traceability and Identity Reuse

In this section, we consider how to add advanced properties of A-IBE generically, without influencing the ciphertext efficiency much. And for a general definition and security models capturing the advanced properties, we refer to Appendix A.

3.1 A General Framework Allowing Identity Re-use

As elaborated in the introduction, a user may accidentally lose his secret key, in all previous works, the user has to change a different identity to request a new key. Allowing identity re-use in such cases is highly desirable. The main difficulty for achieving id reuse lies in the fact that a malicious user can obtain multiple keys (for a same ID) by claiming to the PKG that she lost her key. Then she will implement a pirate box using one key and reveal a different key to the judge for the tracing algorithm, trying to frame the PKG.

Necessity of Public Traceability and Linear Size Tracing Key. To defend against the above attack, a correct tracing algorithm on inputting two keys requested using the same identity should not always output "PKG". It follows that the judge has to be able to identify a "lost" key using some public information, which in turn "implies" public traceability.

Note that in S-I, each user chooses a "fingerprint" $b_1 \ldots b_\ell$ when requesting a key. If the **Trace** algorithm is able to recover the whole "fingerprint" from the pirate box, and there is a public reference, e.g., a value $T = f(b_1 \ldots b_\ell)$ for a one way function f, then the judge can publicly check whether the pirate box is from the user or not. In particular, T is generated by the user during the key generation, and he proved in zero-knowledge that the bits of the pre-image of T are consistent with those used in the OT protocols. We will first revise S-I to enable the tracing algorithm to recover the whole fingerprint, and explain in detail in the next section about the one way function and the ZK proofs.

Before we go into technical details of constructions, we first argue that the public tracing key has to grow linear to the number of the identities. To see this, suppose there are N different identities, d_i is the binary random variable that denotes the judge output when seeing a key k_{ID_i} for identity ID_i, and T is the public tracing key. It is obvious that without the tracing key, each d_i is a uniformly random bit (and they are mutually independent), thus $H(d_1, \ldots, d_N) = N$; while given T, all $\{d_i\}$ will be determined, thus $H(d_1, \ldots, d_N | T) = 0$, from the chain rule, we can see $H(T) = H(d_1, \ldots, d_N, T) \geq H(d_1, \ldots, d_N) = N$. Thus the length of T grows linearly to the number of identities used in the system.

Recovering All Bits of Each User Fingerprint. As one may notice, the **Trace** algorithm of S-I can recover only λ bits, thus for the above public tracing strategy to work, we have to improve the construction of S-I so that one can publicly recover the user "fingerprint" perfectly. A simple observation is that if one can recover a larger fraction of bits, e.g., a linear fraction of ℓ, one may use an error correcting code to generate the fingerprint and recover the whole string by decoding a string having a linear fraction of correct bits. However, the probabilistic analysis of S-I will not hold if we set $n = |\mathsf{Good}|$ to be $O(\ell)$. We further observe that if we use slightly more indices for encryption, (splitting the message, and using the S-I encryption algorithm at each index for the shares), the pirate box has to contain more keys to maintain the δ-correctness. Through a careful analysis, if we use $t = 5\ln\frac{2}{\delta}$ pairs of identities for encryption, B has to include at least $\frac{4}{5}$ fraction of the keys to maintain δ-correctness. Interestingly, the secret key length of is reduced to $O(\log\frac{1}{\delta})$. We present here the modified generic construction, (named S-II) with only the difference with S-I. We will show how to augment S-II to allow id-reuse and analyze the security in the next sections.

- **Setup**(λ, δ): Same as S-I, except $\ell = O(\log\frac{1}{\delta})$, and it also generates an error correcting code ECC : $\{0,1\}^{\ell_0} \to \{0,1\}^{\ell}$, (e.g., [23].) which corrects at least $\frac{\ell}{5}$-bit errors.
- **KeyGen**: Same as S-I, except that the bitstring of user A is generated by first selecting a random bitstring $\bar{r}$ with length ℓ_0, then applying the ECC to $\bar{r}$ and produces $\bar{b} = b_1, \ldots, b_\ell$.
- **Enc**(ID, mpk, m, δ): To encrypt a message m for user A, the algorithm first randomly chooses a subset $S = \{s_1, \ldots, s_t\} \subset \{1, \ldots, \ell\}$ with size $t(\delta) = 5\ln\frac{2}{\delta}$. It then chooses $t-1$ random messages $m_2, \ldots, m_t$ and computes $m_1 = m - \sum_{i=2}^{t} m_i$ and uses the Enc algorithm of the underlying IBE to encrypt each m_i. The algorithm outputs ciphertext $C = \{(s_i, c_{i,0}, c_{i,1})\}_{i=1,\ldots,t}$, where for $b \in \{0,1\}$, $c_{i,b} = \mathsf{Enc}(ID||s_i||b, mpk, m_i)$.
- **Dec**(C, sk_{ID}): On input ciphertext C and the secret key of user A, the decryption algorithm parses the ciphertext and then runs the underlying IBE decryption algorithm, and it selects the secrect keys corresponding to s_i and returns $m = \sum_{i=1}^{t} m_i$, where $m_i = \mathsf{Dec}(sk_{s_i}, c_{i,b_i})$.
- **Trace**$^B(ID, \delta, \{b_i\})$ The first stage is the same as that of S-I except that the user submits $\bar{r}$ and the judge $\mathcal{J}$ applies the ECC to get $\bar{b}$ himself. If $\mathcal{J}$ does not output "user" in the first stage, it runs the following:
  1. For each $i \in \{1, \ldots, \ell\}$, $\mathcal{J}$ randomly selects a subset $S \subset \{1, \ldots, \ell\}$ of size t until $i \in S$, and let us denote $S = \{s_1, \ldots, s_t\}$ and $i = s_k$; $\mathcal{J}$ randomly samples m, m' and other $t-1$ messages $m_1, \ldots, m_{k-1}, m_{k+1}, \ldots, m_t$ uniformly, and he computes $m_{k,0} = m - \sum_{j\neq k} m_j, m_{k,1} = m' - \sum_{j\neq k} m_j$. For $j = 1, \ldots, t$, $\mathcal{J}$ feeds the box B with $\{(s_j, c_{j,0}, c_j^1)\}$, where for $j \neq k$, $c_{j,b} = \mathsf{Enc}(ID||s_j||b, m_j)$, and $c_{k,b}$ is encryption of $m_{k,b}$, i.e., $c_{k,b} = \mathsf{Enc}(ID||s_k||b, m_{k,b})$ for both $b = 0, 1$. $\mathcal{J}$ records a 0 for b_i if the box returns m, 1 if the box returns m' and $\perp$ otherwise.

2. After repeating the above N times (the exact number of N will be specified in the analysis), $\mathcal{J}$ takes the majority of the non-$\perp$ symbols in the records as the value for b_i. If b_i is not defined, let $b_i = 0$.
3. $\mathcal{J}$ runs the decoding algorithm of ECC on $\bar{b}$, and gets a bitstring $\bar{r}'$ or $\perp$. If $\bar{r} = \bar{r}'$, $\mathcal{J}$ returns "user", otherwise, it returns "PKG".

Allowing Identity Re-Use. Now with the above briefly explained intuition of public traceability, a user can use different secret string $\{b_1^k, \ldots, b_\ell^k\}$ to choose the k-th secret key. The PKG keeps different public tracing key for each string, and the judge can indeed differentiate among the keys of the same identity and the PKG as long as he can extract the "fingerprints" correctly. (For detailed construction, see Sect. 3.3). To provide some collision resilience to the generic construction S-II, we extend it further to keep a state st_{ID} for each identity, so that each secret key request for a same identity can actually correspond to different extended identities. In more detail, in S-II, an identity ID is represented using a group of identities $\{ID||i||b_i\}_{i=1,\ldots,\ell, b_i=0,1}$. With a state st_{ID} denoting the number of key requested for ID, the modified extended identities would be $\{ID||st_{ID}||i||b_i^k\}_{i=1,\ldots,\ell; b_i^k=0,1; k=st_{ID}}$.

For the k-th time the user requests a key using $b_1^k, \ldots, b_\ell^k$, the PKG adds a new public tracing key $T_k = f_k(b_1^k, \ldots, b_\ell^k)$ to the public directory, and also updates st_{ID} to be $k + 1$.[5] The sender first figures out the state, then he can simply run **Enc** of S-II using $ID||st_{ID}$ as identity. The **Trace** algorithm runs the S-II tracing algorithm on all $ID||1, \ldots, ID||st_{ID}$, with a smaller correctness parameter δ/st_{ID}, and extracts fingerprints (potentially more than one). If all of the fingerprints match the corresponding public tracing keys (except the st_{ID}-th one), they are considered as lost keys then no one will be accused; If the one that the user is using (the st_{ID}-th key) matches $T_{st_{ID}}$, the user would be accused, otherwise the PKG will be accused.[6]

We can see that we use the underlying IBE as a black-box, thus this improved construction (named S-III) is still a general transformation from IBE to A-IBE.

3.2 Building Blocks for Public Traceability

OT Instantiation. We choose the Bellare-Micali OT [3] as an example, and construct efficent zero-knowledge proofs for the consistency. (In principle any OT is applicable if we do not insist on efficient ZK proofs). The sender S (the PKG in our setting) sets up the system parameters (including a prime q, group G_q with a random generator g, and a random value $C \in Z_q$). The receiver R(with input b) randomly chooses $PK_b = g^x$ and computes $PK_{1-b} = C/PK_b$, then R sends PK_0 to S; the sender computes $PK_1 = C/PK_0$ and encrypts the messages m_0, m_1 to be transmitted, using ElGamal encryption [17] with PK_0, PK_1 as

[5] A malicious PKG may put different public tracing keys, however this is trivially detectable by the user and proves to the judge.
[6] Note that if the recovered fingerprint corresponds to one of the lost keys, it is impossible to decide whether it is from the user or from someone else who gets the lost key, not erroneously accusing the PKG is the best possible security in this case.

public keys respectively, i.e., $\{(g^{r_b}, H(PK_b^{T_b}) \oplus m_b)\}_{b=0,1}$ are returned to R, where H is modeled as a random oracle. It is well-known that this OT protocol satisfies information theoretic receiver security, and simulatable sender security under the CDH assumption [27].

Public Tracing Key Generation. We first describe the one way function tailored for our A-IBE scheme. Suppose $\bar{g} = (g_{1,0}, g_{1,1}), \ldots, (g_{\ell,0}, g_{\ell,1}) \in G^{2\ell}$, for each i, $g_{i,0} \cdot g_{i,1} = C$ for a random group element C, and $\bar{b} = b_1 \ldots b_\ell \in \{0,1\}^\ell$, we define $f_{\bar{g}}(b_1 \ldots b_\ell) = \prod_{i=1}^{\ell} g_{i,b_i}$. We will show that $f_{\bar{g}}(\cdot)$ is one way. Let us first look at a related one way function, suppose $\tilde{g} = (g_1, \ldots, g_\ell) \in G^\ell$ and for $b_1 \ldots b_\ell \in \{0,1\}^\ell$, $\tilde{f}_{\tilde{g}}(b_1 \ldots b_\ell)$ is defined by $\prod_{i=1}^{\ell} g_i^{b_i}$. It is implicit that $\tilde{f}_{\tilde{g}}(\cdot)$ is one way in a couple of papers, e.g., in [9], $b_1 \ldots b_\ell$ is the secret key and $\tilde{g}, h = \tilde{f}_{\tilde{g}}(b_1 \ldots b_\ell)$ are the public keys for their circular secure encryption scheme. We will omit the proof of one-wayness for $\tilde{f}$, and we prove the one-wayness of our function f in the following lemma.

Lemma 1. *If there exists a PPT adversary $\mathcal{A}$ breaks the one way security of f with advantage δ, then there exists another PPT adversary $\mathcal{B}$ breaks the one way security of $\tilde{f}$ with advantage δ/ℓ.*

Proof. When $\mathcal{B}$ receives the public keys $\tilde{g} = g_1, \ldots, g_\ell$ from the $\tilde{f}$ challenger $\mathcal{C}$, $\mathcal{B}$ selects a random C and prepares $g_{1,0}, \ldots, g_{\ell,0}$ such that for each i, $g_{i,0} = g_i$, he also prepares $g_{1,1}, \ldots, g_{\ell,1}$ in a way that $g_{i,1} = C/g_{i,0}$ for all i. $\mathcal{B}$ sends $\mathcal{A}$ $C, \bar{g} = (g_{1,0}, g_{1,1}), \ldots, (g_{\ell,0}, g_{\ell,1})$ as public keys.

Once $\mathcal{B}$ receives the challenge $X = \tilde{f}_{\tilde{g}}(b_1 \ldots b_\ell)$ for some $b_1 \ldots b_\ell$, $\mathcal{B}$ selects a random $t \in \{1, \ldots, \ell\}$, computes $Y = C^{\ell-t} \cdot \prod_{i=1}^{\ell} g_i \cdot X^{-2}$ and sends Y to $\mathcal{A}$. $\mathcal{B}$ forwards the bit string $b_1' \ldots b_\ell'$ returned by $\mathcal{A}$ as her answer to the challenger $\mathcal{C}$.

Note that if the bitstring $b_1 \ldots b_\ell$ has Hamming weight $\ell - t$, i.e., t of them are 0, then $Y = \prod_{i=1}^{\ell} g_{i,b_i}$. To see this, suppose $S = \{i | b_i = 0\}$, and $|S| = t$, $Y = C^{\ell-t} \cdot \prod_{i=1}^{\ell} g_i / \prod_{i=1}^{\ell} g_i^{2b_i} = \prod_{i \in S} g_i \cdot \prod_{i \notin S}(C/g_i)$. Thus with probability $1/\ell$, $\mathcal{B}$ guesses t correctly, and in turn, $\mathcal{B}$ produces a valid value of $f_{\bar{g}}(b_1 \ldots b_\ell)$. In this case under our assumption, $\mathcal{A}$ will invert correctly with probability δ. We can conclude that $\mathcal{B}$ breaks the one way security of $\tilde{f}$ with probability δ/ℓ.   □

The public tracing key T will be $h = f_{\overline{PK}}(b_1 \ldots b_\ell)$, together with $\overline{PK}$ which are $\{(PK_{1,0}, PK_{1,1}) \ldots, (PK_{\ell,0}, PK_{\ell,1})\}$ used in the OT protocols.

Efficient Zero-Knowledge Proof for Consistency. Next, we provide an efficient zero-knowledge proof protocol for the consistency between the public tracing key and the bit string selected by the user in the OT protocol. Essentially, we need to prove that each bit of the pre-image of the public tracing key is used for selecting one secret key in each call of the OT protocol. For the public tracing key h, the user first commits $\{PK_{i,b_i}\}$ to be $\{c_i\}$, and proves in zero-knowledge for the following statements, $\exists g_1, \ldots, g_\ell$:

$$h = \prod_{i=1}^{\ell} g_i \wedge_{i=1}^{\ell} [c_i \text{ opens to } g_i \wedge (g_i = PK_{i,0} \vee g_i = PK_{i,1})] \wedge \text{PoK for } \log_g h.$$

Before we describe the detailed ZK proofs, we first explain how we can prove a commitment opens to a value. We will use a homomorphic commitment scheme from the BBS encryption [7]. It has the public keys in the form of (g, u, v, w), where $u^x = v^y = w$, and x, y are private keys. The ciphertext (which is a commitment as well) for m is $\bar{C} = (C_1, C_2, C_3)$ where $C_1 = u^{r_1}, C_2 = v^{r_2}, C_3 = w^{r_1+r_2}m$. One can easily prove a BBS commitment $\bar{C}$ opens to a message m in zero-knowledge using the following $\Sigma-$protocol: the proof is in the form of (a_1, a_2, c, z_1, z_2), where $a_1 = C_1^{t_1}, a_2 = C_2^{t_2}$ are the first round messages sent by the prover, a random value c is returned by the verifier and $z_1 = t_1 + cx, z_2 = t_2 + cy$ are calculated by the prover, The verifier checks $C_1^{z_1} \cdot C_2^{z_2} = a_1 \cdot a_2 \cdot (C_3/m)^c$.

Now we are ready to construct the efficient ZK proofs. (1). Prove the first clause, which is equivalent to prove $\prod_{i=1}^{\ell} c_i$ opens to h. (2). Prove c_i opens to either $PK_{i,0}$ or $PK_{i,1}$. This can be done easily using the OR proof [15] of the two $\Sigma-$protocol. More specifically, suppose $b_i = 1$, the proof is in the form of $(a_{1,0}, a_{2,0}, a_{1,1}, a_{2,1}, c, z_{1,0}, z_{2,0}, z_{1,1}, z_{2,1})$, where $(a_{1,0}, a_{2,0}, c_0, z_{1,0}, z_{2,0})$ is simulated and using $c_1 = c - c_0$, and generates the proof of $(a_{1,1}, a_{2,1}, c_1, z_{1,1}, z_{2,1})$. The verifier checks $C_1^{z_{1,0}+z_{1,1}} \cdot C_2^{z_{2,0}+z_{2,1}} = a_{1,0} \cdot a_{1,1} \cdot a_{2,0} \cdot a_{2,1} \cdot (C_3/m)^c$. (3) Repeat step (2) for each commitment c_i to do an "And" proof. (4) Do a regular proof of knowledge about the exponent of h using e.g., Schnorr proof [30].

All these $\Sigma-$protocols can be made zero-knowledge following the standard technique, e.g., let the verifier commits to the challenge value c first, and they can be made non-interactive by applying the FS heuristic [16].

Finally, let us check whether the soundness is enough for ensuring h is generated in the honest way, i.e. $h = \prod_{i=1}^{\ell} PK_{i,b_i}$. Suppose there is an adversary $\mathcal{A}$ convinces the verifier and uses one $PK_{i,1-b_i}$ when generating h. We can see that $\mathcal{A}$ can be separated into two independent parts $(\mathcal{A}_1, \mathcal{A}_2)$. $\mathcal{A}_1$ prepares $\{PK_{i,0}, PK_{i,1}\}$ and the corresponding exponents, and $\mathcal{A}_2$ finishes the ZK proofs. It follows that if we replace $\mathcal{A}_1$ with another algorithm $\mathcal{A}_1'$ which simply receives $\{PK_{i,0}, PK_{i,1}\}$ and the corresponding exponents from an oracle, the modified adversarial algorithm $\mathcal{A}' = (\mathcal{A}_1', \mathcal{A}_2)$ behaves identically as $\mathcal{A}$.

According to the special soundness of the proof of knowledge part, a simulator can run $\mathcal{A}'$ ($\mathcal{A}_2$ part) to extract $\log_g h = \sum_{j \neq i} \alpha_{j,b_j} + \alpha_{i,1-b_i}$, where $\alpha_{j,b} = \log_g PK_{j,b}$ for $j \in \{1, \dots, \ell\}$ and $b = 0, 1$. As the simulator can "control" the oracle of $\mathcal{A}_1'$, and prepare $\{PK_j\}_{j \neq i}$ accordingly for $\mathcal{A}_1'$, thus he knows the exponents $\{\alpha_{j,b_j}\}$ and recovers $\alpha_{i,1-b_i}$ and further $\log_g C = \alpha_{i,b_i} + \alpha_{i,1-b_i}$ thus breaks the discrete log assumption, where C is the system parameter in the OT protocol. (for the case that more than one PK_{i,b_i} are used in generating h, a similar argument can be made to recover $\log_g C$).

3.3 Concrete Construction and Security Analysis

With the building blocks we developed above, we now describe the concrete algorithms of our generic A-IBE construction allowing public traceability and identity reuse (named S-III). We only describe the difference with S-II here.

– **Setup**(λ, δ): Same as S-II.

- **KeyGen**: For the k-th key requests from user A for an identity ID, the **Key-Gen** protocol of S-II is run for identity $ID\|k$, and user returns $sk_{ID,k}$. During the **KeyGen**, the OT described above [3] is utilized to transmit secret keys. Suppose $\overline{PK}_k = \{(PK_{i,0}^k, PK_{i,1}^k)\}$ are the first round messages of the user. After the OT protocols are done, A sends the PKG his public tracing key $h_k = \prod_{i=1}^{\ell} PK_{i,b_i}^k$ and proves in zero-knowledge (we call this proof π_k) for the consistency using protocol described in Sect. 3.2. The PKG outputs a new public tracing key $T_k = (h_k, \overline{PK}_k)$, adds them to the list of public tracing keys T_{ID} for ID and updates the st_{ID} to be k. The PKG outputs (T_{ID}, st_{ID}) and the user outputs secret key $sk_{ID,k}$.
- **Enc**$(ID, mpk, m, st_{ID}, \delta)$: It runs the **Enc** of S-II with identity $ID\|st_{ID}$.
- **Dec**$(C, sk_{ID,st_{ID}})$: It runs the **Dec** of S-II with identity $ID\|st_{ID}$.
- **Trace**$^B(ID, \delta/st_{ID}, T_{ID})$: The first stage is the same as S-II using $ID\|st_{ID}$. If the judge does not output "user", the following is run. The second stage of the **Trace** algorithm of S-II is repeated for all identities from $ID\|1$ to $ID\|st_{ID}$. For $ID\|k$, the algorithm recovers a bitstring $b_1^k, \ldots, b_\ell^k$ or $\bot$, and it records a flag t_k for this run. For $k = 1, \ldots, st_{ID} - 1$, if the recovered string is $\bot$ or $f_{\overline{PK}_k}(b_1^k, \ldots, b_\ell^k) = h_k$, where $h_k, \overline{PK}_k$ are from T_k, then $t_k = 0$; otherwise $t_k = 2$. For $k = st_{ID}$, if no string is extracted, $t_{st_{ID}} = 0$; if $f_{\overline{PK}_{st_{ID}}}(b_1^{st_{ID}}, \ldots, b_\ell^{st_{ID}}) = h_{st_{ID}}$, then $t_{st_{ID}} = 1$; otherwise, $t_{st_{ID}} = 2$. The algorithm returns $\bot$ if for all $k = 1, \ldots, st_{ID}$, $t_k = 0$; it returns "user" if $t_{st_{ID}} = 1$; it returns "PKG", otherwise.

Remark that using δ/st_{ID} for tracing is necessary, as from our definition of δ−correctness in this case is only for a random state (see Appendix A).

Security Analysis of S-III. Due to lack of space, we provide here only some high-level intuition for S-III, and mainly on the difference with S-I.

IND-ID-CPA Security. This is very similar to that of S-I, except that there are extra public tracing keys T_{ID}, while they are only related with the bit strings for selecting the keys, thus independent with the real secret keys. Also S-III uses multiple extended form of identities, but all of them can be seen as different identities of the underlying IBE scheme. The semantic security is not influenced.

Security in the Weak Dishonest-PKG Game. Note that a malicious PKG can evade the **Trace** algorithm only when the recovered string matches one of the fingerprints contained in the public tracing key. The difference with S-I is that the malicious PKG receives extra public tracing keys $\{T_i = (h_i, \overline{PK}_i)\}$, and ZK proof transcripts $\{\pi_i\}$. If an adversary $\mathcal{A}$ (malicious PKG) is able to produce a pirate box which fools the **Trace** algorithm, it can be easily turned to an algorithm that breaks the OT receiver security or the one-wayness of f.

In more detail, we can argue the security via a sequence of game changes by first replacing each OT transcript with one generated using a random bit r. The indistinguishability can be guaranteed by the information theoretic receiver security of the Bellare-Micali OT. In the next game changes, the ZK proofs will be replaced with simulated transcripts, and the indistinguishability can be guaranteed by the zero-knowledge property of the proofs. Now in the last game, what the adversary sees are only simulated transcripts (OT and ZK proofs) which are independent with the actual fingerprints, there exists a simulator $\mathcal{S}$ who can use $\mathcal{A}$ to break the one-way security of f. In particular, $\mathcal{S}$ randomly picks an one way function instance, i.e., $\mathcal{S}$ embeds the public keys and a value h received from the one way security challenger and sets it to be the i-th public tracing key, and sends them (together with a simulated proof) to $\mathcal{A}$. Then from the pirate box outputted by $\mathcal{A}$, with probability $1/st_{ID}$, the recovered string is the pre-image of h, thus $\mathcal{S}$ breaks the one way security.

Security in the Adaptive Dishonest User Game. A malicious user may try to frame the PKG by outputting a box with recovered fingerprint not matching any of the public tracing keys for the target identity, and it is possible unless one of the following events happens: for at least one index i, the adversary $\mathcal{A}$, (1). learns the secret key of $ID||i||1 - b_i$ during the OT protocol; (2). is able to decrypt ciphertext under $ID||i||1 - b_i$ for which she does not have the secret key; (3). cheats in the ZK proof of consistency during **KeyGen**. We can similarly do a sequence of game changes that first replace the OT instance to be oracle, the indistinguishability is guaranteed by the simulatable sender security of OT. We then argue from a box, the tracing algorithm must extract one of the whole fingerprints of the keys. This is similar to the proof of Theorem 1, we will focused on the main difference about the probabilistic argument. We can see that if the sender splits the message into $t(\delta) = 5\ln\frac{2}{\delta}$ pieces, the user has to put at least $\frac{4}{5}$ fraction of keys for each state into the box B to ensure δ-correctness, and this fraction is enough for the ECC decoding to recover the whole original fingerprint.
The probabilistic argument. Let $\delta_i = \Pr[B$ decrypts correctly $\mid i \in S]$. We divide the indices $i \in \{1, \ldots, \ell\}$ in two sets, Bad and Good, we define $i \in$ Good if and only if $\delta_i \geq \delta_0$, where $\delta_0 = \delta/\ell^2$. In order to upper bound the size of Bad consider the following. Let D be the event of correct decryption,

$$\Pr[D] = \Pr[D \mid S \cap \text{Bad} = \emptyset] \cdot \Pr[S \cap \text{Bad} = \emptyset] + \Pr[D \mid S \cap \text{Bad} \neq \emptyset] \cdot \Pr[S \cap \text{Bad} \neq \emptyset],$$

Regarding $\Pr[S \cap \text{Bad} = \emptyset]$ observe that if $k = |\text{Bad}|$, this probability is bounded by $p(k, t) = C_{\ell-k}^t/C_\ell^t = \prod_{i=0}^{t-1}(1 - \frac{k}{\ell-i}) \leq (1 - \frac{k}{\ell})^t$. From inequality $e^x \geq 1 + x$, we can get $p(k, t) \leq e^{-kt\ell}$. Regarding $\Pr[D \mid S \cap \text{Bad} \neq \emptyset]$, note that it is bounded by $\sum_{i \in \text{Bad}} \delta_i \leq \ell\delta_0 = \delta/\ell$ (This follows from the fact that $\Pr[F \mid \cup_{i=1}^n A_i] \leq \sum_{i=1}^n \Pr[F \mid A_i]$, for any event F, A_i). We can now derive the following, $\delta \leq \Pr[D] \leq e^{-tk/\ell} + \delta/\ell$, from which we obtain the upper bound $k \leq \frac{\ell}{t} \cdot \ln(\delta - \delta/\ell)^{-1}$, since $\delta - \delta/\ell \geq \delta/2$, when we set $t = 5\ln(2\delta^{-1})$ into the above bound for k, and in this case $k \leq \ell/5$.

Now in the last game, the adversary has only oracle access to OT which can be controlled by the simulator if from the outputted box, the simulator recovers a different fingerprint, the simulator can break the one way security using the extractor as explained at the end of Sect. 3.2.

Public traceability is obvious, and identity reuse follows also straightforwardly as for each state, the identities are considered as independent "user", the above argument implicitly captures this property. We summarize the security properties of S-III in the following theorem:

Theorem 2. *(1). S-III is secure in the* IND–ID–CPA *model if the underlying IBE is IND-ID-CPA secure. (2). S-III is secure in the* weak dishonest PKG *game if the proof π is zero-knowledge, f is one way and the OT has receiver security. (3). S-III is secure in the* adaptive dishonest user *game, if the underlying IBE is IND-ID-CPA secure, the proof π is sound, and the CDH assumption holds.*

4   Conclusions and Open Problems

We presented a generic transformation from IBE to A-IBE, with ciphertext size to be only twice large as the underlying IBE. We further refine the generic construction, and for the first time achieve identity reuse. We believe that the efficient generic transformations with preferable advanced properties can be an important step towards a wider deployment of A-IBE thus may potentially stimulate the adoption of IBE schemes in practice.

There are still several interesting open problems relating to the authority accountability in IBE schemes. One is to consider efficient generic construction of A-IBE with fully blackbox traceability directly, the other is to do a systematic study about proactive deterring mechanisms for IBE schemes.

Acknowledgements.. We thank Hong-Sheng Zhou for the early discussions. We thank the anonymous reviewer to point out the simplification for S-I. The authors were supported by the ERC project CODAMODA.

A   Preliminaries

1-out-of-2 Oblivious Transfer Protocol. Briefly speaking, a 1-out-of-2 OT protocol [27] is between a sender S and a receiver R. S has two messages (m_0, m_1) as input, and R chooses one of them according to a bit b. S should not know b, while R should not have any knowledge of m_{1-b}.

We only provide a half simulation type of definition (cf. [27]). For sender security, we make a comparison to the ideal implementation in which there is a trusted party receiving m_0, m_1 from S and b from R, and sends R the message m_b. We require that $\forall m_0, m_1$ and any efficient adversary $\mathcal{A}$ as the receiver, there is a simulator plays as the receiver in the ideal world that, the output distribution of the simulator and $\mathcal{A}$ are computationally indistinguishable. For receiver security, suppose t_0, t_1 represent the trascript sent by the receiver w.r.t input 0 and 1 respectively, we require that the sender can not distinguish the distribution of t_0 and t_1.

Accountable authority identity-based encryption. Here we provide a general definition for an A-IBE scheme, it is composed of the following algorithms:

- **Setup**(λ, δ) This algorithm takes the security parameter λ and the correctness parameter δ as input and outputs master key pair (mpk, msk) and the system parameters $t(\delta), \ell(\delta)$.
- **KeyGen** This is a stateful protocol between a user and the PKG in which the user has an identity ID and mpk, and the PKG has mpk, msk, ID as inputs respectively. It ends with the user outputting her secret key sk_{ID} or $\perp$ if the secret-keys are malformed, and the PKG output a tracing key T_{ID} and a current state st_{ID}.
- **Enc**(ID, mpk, m, st_{ID}) This algorithm inputs a receiver identity(ID), master public key mpk, the message m and potentially a public state st_{ID}, and outputs the ciphertext C.
- **Dec**(C, sk_{ID}) This algorithm takes ciphertext C and user secret key sk_{ID} as input, and outputs the plaintext m.
- **Trace**$^B(ID, \delta, T_{ID})$. This algorithm inputs a pirate decryption box B for ID, correctness parameter δ and a tracing key T_{ID} as input, it outputs "user", "PKG" or "$\perp$".

Note that the algorithms can be stateless as usual if identity reuse is not required. When T_{ID} is public, then the A-IBE scheme has public traceability.

δ-**correctness** of a decryption device B, for regular A-IBE schemes, it is defined as $\Pr[B(C) = m : C = \mathbf{Enc}(ID, mpk, m)] \geq \delta$; while for A-IBE schemes allowing identity re-use, the box might contain a couple of keys for one identity corresponding to different states, we require that for a randomly selected state, it works with δ correctness, thus the δ-correctness in this case is defined as $\Pr[B(C) = m : C = \mathbf{Enc}(ID, mpk, m, i) \wedge i \leftarrow \{1, \ldots, st_{ID}\}] \geq \delta$. Note that according to the pigeonhole principle, there exists at least one state j, $\Pr[B(C) = m : C = \mathbf{Enc}(ID, mpk, m, j)] \geq \delta/st_{ID}$, and this is important for the tracing algorithm of S-III.

IND-ID-CPA security. This is similar to the standard semantic security for IBE schemes. Consider the following game between the adversary $\mathcal{A}$ and the challenger $\mathcal{C}$:

- **Setup** $\mathcal{C}$ runs **Setup**, and sends $\mathcal{A}$ the system public key: mpk.
- **Phase 1** $\mathcal{A}$ runs the **KeyGen** protocol with the challenger for several distinct adaptively chosen identities $ID_1, .., ID_q$ and gets the decryption keys $sk_{ID_1}, .., sk_{ID_q}$.
- **Challenge** $\mathcal{A}$ submits two equal length messages m_0, m_1 and an identity ID that is not appearing in the queries of Phase 1. $\mathcal{C}$ flips a random coin b and encrypts m_b with ID. The ciphertext C is passed on to $\mathcal{A}$.
- **Phase 2** This is identical to Phase 1 and $\mathcal{A}$ is not allowed to query for ID.
- **Guess** The adversary outputs a guess b' of b.

The advantage of the adversary $\mathcal{A}$ is defined as $|\Pr[b' = b] - 1/2|$; we say an A-IBE is IND-ID-CPA secure if $\mathcal{A}$'s advantage is negligible.

Note that for A-IBE schemes with public traceability, the adversary also gets the public tracing key T.

Besides standard semantic security, for an A-IBE scheme, there are two additional security properties that have to be considered. The first is security against a malicious PKG. Any A-IBE scheme, should prevent the PKG from learning useful information which can help her to leak a decryption program B (we will also call it a decryption "box") on behalf of a certain identity and evade the tracing algorithm. The second is security against malicious users. In this perspective, a group of colluding users should not be able to make a working box B that frames the PKG. Depending of the form of B, one may consider various models for the tracing algorithm. Specifically, if the tracing algorithm only needs oracle access to B, we call it traceable in the black-box model. Common variants of the black-box model exist depending on whether the PKG is given access to the decryption oracle that corresponds to the secret key the user gets (called the "fully black-box model" if yes, and the "weak black-box model" otherwise).

Weak (Black-Box) Dishonest-PKG Game. Consider the following game between a PPT adversary $\mathcal{A}$ and a PPT challenger $\mathcal{C}$:

- **Setup**: The adversary acts as a malicious PKG, generates system public keys and sends $\mathcal{C}$ mpk. Also $\mathcal{A}$ specifies an identity ID.
- **KeyGen**: $\mathcal{C}$ and $\mathcal{A}$ then engage in the **KeyGen** protocols of A-IBE acting as a user and PKG respectively. In each run, they jointly generate a decryption key and a tracing key T_{ID} and state st_{ID} for the identity ID. If neither party aborts, then $\mathcal{C}$ gets a decryption key sk_{ID} for user ID as output.
- **Create Decryption Box**: The adversary outputs a decryption box B.

The adversary $\mathcal{A}$ wins the game if the following conditions hold true:

$$B \text{ has } \delta\text{-correctness} \wedge \mathbf{Trace}^B(ID, sk_{ID}) \neq \text{``PKG''}.$$

In a *full* dishonest-PKG game, $\mathcal{A}$ is also allowed to ask decryption queries. In other weaker (non-black-box) models, the tracing algorithm might have non-black-box access to the pirate box B.

Adaptive Dishonest-User Game. In this game, a set of malicious users collude to create a decoder box, trying to frame the PKG.

- **Setup** $\mathcal{C}$ runs the A-IBE **Setup** algorithm, and sends $\mathcal{A}$ mpk;
- **Secret Key Queries** The adversary runs the **KeyGen** protocols with $\mathcal{C}$, playing the role of different users and PKG respectively, for adaptively chosen identities $ID_1, .., ID_q$ for different times. $\mathcal{A}$ gets the corresponding secret keys $\{sk_{ID_1}\}, .., \{sk_{ID_q}\}$ and $\mathcal{C}$ outputs the corresponding tracing keys $T_{ID_1}, \ldots, T_{ID_q}$ and the states $st_{ID_1}, \ldots, st_{ID_q}$.
- **Create Decryption Box** The adversary outputs an identity ID together with a decryption box B for ID.

The adversary wins if the followings hold true:

$$B \text{ has } \delta\text{-correctness} \wedge \mathbf{Trace}^B(ID, sk_{ID}) = \text{``PKG''}.$$

Weaker model also exists, i.e., in the selective dishonest-user game, the adversary is required to declare the ID to be attacked at the beginning.

References

1. Al-Riyami, S.S., Paterson, K.G.: Certificateless public key cryptography. In: Laih, C.-S. (ed.) ASIACRYPT 2003. LNCS, vol. 2894, pp. 452–473. Springer, Heidelberg (2003)
2. Au, M.H., Huang, Q., Liu, J.K., Susilo, W., Wong, D.S., Yang, G.: Traceable and retrievable identity-based encryption. In: Bellovin, S.M., Gennaro, R., Keromytis, A.D., Yung, M. (eds.) ACNS 2008. LNCS, vol. 5037, pp. 94–110. Springer, Heidelberg (2008)
3. Bellare, M., Micali, S.: Non-interactive oblivious transfer and applications. In: Brassard, G. (ed.) CRYPTO 1989. LNCS, vol. 435, pp. 547–557. Springer, Heidelberg (1989)
4. Bellare, M., Rogaway, P.: Random oracles are practical: Aa paradigm for designing efficient protocols. In: ACM Conference on Computer and Communications Security, pp. 62–73 (1993)
5. Boneh, D., Boyen, X.: Efficient selective-ID secure identity-based encryption without random oracles-. In: Cachin, C., Camenisch, J.L. (eds.) EUROCRYPT 2004. LNCS, vol. 3027, pp. 223–238. Springer, Heidelberg (2004)
6. Boneh, D., Boyen, X.: Secure identity based encryption without random oracles. In: Franklin, M. (ed.) CRYPTO 2004. LNCS, vol. 3152, pp. 443–459. Springer, Heidelberg (2004)
7. Boneh, D., Boyen, X., Shacham, H.: Short group signatures. In: Franklin, M. (ed.) CRYPTO 2004. LNCS, vol. 3152, pp. 41–55. Springer, Heidelberg (2004)
8. Boneh, D., Franklin, M.: Identity-based encryption from the weil pairing. In: Kilian, J. (ed.) CRYPTO 2001. LNCS, vol. 2139, p. 213. Springer, Heidelberg (2001)
9. Boneh, D., Halevi, S., Hamburg, M., Ostrovsky, R.: Circular-secure encryption from decision Diffie-Hellman. In: Wagner, D. (ed.) CRYPTO 2008. LNCS, vol. 5157, pp. 108–125. Springer, Heidelberg (2008)
10. Boneh, D., Naor, M.: Traitor tracing with constant size ciphertext. In: ACM Conference on Computer and Communications Security, pp. 501–510 (2008)
11. Boneh, D., Sahai, A., Waters, B.: Functional encryption: definitions and challenges. In: Ishai, Y. (ed.) TCC 2011. LNCS, vol. 6597, pp. 253–273. Springer, Heidelberg (2011)
12. Boyen, X., Martin, L.: Identity-Based Cryptography Standard (IBCS) #1: Supersingular Curve Implementations of the BF and BB1 Cryptosystems. RFC 5091 (Informational), December (2007)
13. Canetti, R.: Security and composition of multiparty cryptographic protocols. J. Cryptol. 13(1), 143–202 (2000)
14. Chow, S.S.M.: Removing escrow from identity-based encryption. In: Jarecki, S., Tsudik, G. (eds.) PKC 2009. LNCS, vol. 5443, pp. 256–276. Springer, Heidelberg (2009)
15. Cramer, R., Damgård, I., Schoenmakers, B.: Proofs of partial knowledge and simplified design of witness hiding protocols. In: Desmedt, Y.G. (ed.) CRYPTO 1994. LNCS, vol. 839, pp. 174–187. Springer, Heidelberg (1994)
16. Fiat, A., Shamir, A.: How to prove yourself: practical solutions to identification and signature problems. In: Odlyzko, A.M. (ed.) CRYPTO 1986. LNCS, vol. 263, pp. 186–194. Springer, Heidelberg (1987)
17. Gamal, T.E.: A public key cryptosystem and a signature scheme based on discrete logarithms. IEEE Trans. Inf. Theory 31(4), 469–472 (1985)

18. Gentry, C.: Certificate-based encryption and the certificate revocation problem. In: Biham, E. (ed.) EUROCRYPT 2003. LNCS, vol. 2656, pp. 272–293. Springer, Heidelberg (2003)
19. Gentry, C.: Practical identity-based encryption without random oracles. In: Vaudenay, S. (ed.) EUROCRYPT 2006. LNCS, vol. 4004, pp. 445–464. Springer, Heidelberg (2006)
20. Goyal, V.: Reducing trust in the PKG in identity based cryptosystems. In: Menezes, A. (ed.) CRYPTO 2007. LNCS, vol. 4622, pp. 430–447. Springer, Heidelberg (2007)
21. Goyal, V., Lu, S., Sahai, A., Waters, B.: Black-box accountable authority identity-based encryption. In: ACM Conference on Computer and Communications Security, pp. 427–436 (2008)
22. Goyal, V., Pandey, O., Sahai, A., Waters, B.: Attribute-based encryption for fine-grained access control of encrypted data. In: ACM Conference on Computer and Communications Security, pp. 89–98 (2006)
23. Guruswami, V., Indyk, P.: Expander-based constructions of efficiently decodable codes. FOCS **2001**, 658–667 (2001)
24. Kiayias, A., Tang, Q.: How to keep a secret: leakage deterring public-key cryptosystems. In: ACM Conference on Computer and Communications Security, pp. 943–954 (2013)
25. Lai, J., Deng, R.H., Zhao, Y., Weng, J.: Accountable authority identity-based encryption with public traceability. In: Dawson, E. (ed.) CT-RSA 2013. LNCS, vol. 7779, pp. 326–342. Springer, Heidelberg (2013)
26. Libert, B., Vergnaud, D.: Towards black-box accountable authority ibe with short ciphertexts and private keys. In: Jarecki, S., Tsudik, G. (eds.) PKC 2009. LNCS, vol. 5443, pp. 235–255. Springer, Springer (2009)
27. Naor, M., Pinkas, B.: Efficient oblivious transfer protocols. In: SODA, pp. 448–457 (2001)
28. Sahai, A., Seyalioglu, H.: Fully secure accountable-authority identity-based encryption. In: Catalano, D., Fazio, N., Gennaro, R., Nicolosi, A. (eds.) PKC 2011. LNCS, vol. 6571, pp. 296–316. Springer, Heidelberg (2011)
29. Sahai, A., Waters, B.: Fuzzy Identity-based encryption. In: Cramer, R. (ed.) EUROCRYPT 2005. LNCS, vol. 3494, pp. 457–473. Springer, Heidelberg (2005)
30. Schnorr, C.-P.: Efficient identification and signatures for smart cards. In: Brassard, G. (ed.) CRYPTO 1989. LNCS, vol. 435, pp. 239–252. Springer, Heidelberg (1990)
31. Shamir, A.: Identity-based cryptosystems and signature schemes. In: Blakely, G.R., Chaum, D. (eds.) CRYPTO 1984. LNCS, vol. 196, pp. 47–53. Springer, Heidelberg (1985)
32. Waters, B.: Efficient identity-based encryption without random oracles. In: Cramer, R. (ed.) EUROCRYPT 2005. LNCS, vol. 3494, pp. 114–127. Springer, Heidelberg (2005)
33. Waters, B.: Dual system encryption: realizing fully secure IBE and HIBE under simple assumptions. In: Halevi, S. (ed.) CRYPTO 2009. LNCS, vol. 5677, pp. 619–636. Springer, Heidelberg (2009)
34. Yuen, T.H., Chow, S.S.M., Zhang, C., Yiu, S.-M.: Exponent-inversion signatures and ibe under static assumptions. IACR Cryptol. ePrint Arch. **2014**, 311 (2014)

Practical Threshold Password-Authenticated Secret Sharing Protocol

Xun Yi[1]([✉]), Feng Hao[2], Liqun Chen[3], and Joseph K. Liu[4]

[1] School of CS and IT, RMIT University, Melbourne, Australia
`Xun.yi@rmit.edu.au`
[2] School of Computing Science, Newcastle University, Newcastle upon Tyne, UK
[3] Hewlett-Packard Laboratories, Bristol, UK
[4] Faculty of Information Technology, Monash University, Melbourne, Australia

Abstract. Threshold password-authenticated secret sharing (TPASS) protocols allow a client to secret-share a secret s among n servers and protect it with a password pw, so that the client can later recover s from any subset of t of the servers using the password pw, but so that no coalition smaller than t learns anything about s or can mount an offline dictionary attack on the password pw. Some TPASS protocols have appeared in the literature recently. The protocol by Bagherzandi et al. (CCS 2011) leaks the password if a client mistakenly executes the protocol with malicious servers. The first t-out-of-n TPASS protocol for any $n > t$ that does not suffer from this shortcoming was given by Camenisch et al. (CRYPTO 2014). This protocol, proved to be secure in the UC framework, requires the client to involve in many communication rounds so that it becomes impractical for the client. In this paper, we present a practical TPASS protocol which is in particular efficient for the client, who only needs to send a request and receive a response. In addition, we have provided a rigorous proof of security for our protocol in the standard model.

Keywords: Threshold password-authenticated secret sharing protocol · ElGamal encryption scheme · Shamir secret sharing scheme · Diffie-Hellman problems

1 Introduction

Threshold password-authenticated secret sharing (TPASS) protocols consider a scenario [5], inspired by the movie "Memento" in which the main character suffers from short-term memory loss, leads to an interesting cryptographic problem, can a user securely recover his secrets from a set of servers, if all the user can or wants to remember is a single password and all of the servers may be adversarial? In particular, can he protect his previous password when accidentally trying to run the recovery with all-malicious servers? A solution for this problem can act as a natural bridge from human-memorisable passwords to strong keys for cryptographic tasks. Practical applications include secure password managers (where the shared secret is a list of strongly random website passwords) and encrypting

© Springer International Publishing Switzerland 2015
G. Pernul et al. (Eds.): ESORICS 2015, Part I, LNCS 9326, pp. 347–365, 2015.
DOI: 10.1007/978-3-319-24174-6_18

data in the cloud (where the shared secret is the encryption key) based on a single master password.

The first TPASS protocol was given by Bagherzandi et al. [1]. It is built on the PKI model, secure under the decisional Diffie-Hellman assumption, using non-interactive zero-knowledge proofs. The basic idea is: The client initially generates an ElGamal public and private key pairs $(sk, pk = g^{sk})$ [7] and secret-shares sk among servers using an t-out-of-n secret sharing [15] and outputs public parameters including the public key pk and the encryptions $E(g^{pw}, pk)$ and $E(s, pk)$ of password pw and secret s, respectively, under the public key pk. When retrieving the secret from the servers, the client encrypts the password pw' he remembers and sends the encryption $E(g^{pw'}, pk)$ to the servers, each of which computes and returns $A_i = [E(g^{pw}, pk)/E(g^{pw'}, pk)]^{t_i} = E(g^{t_i(pw-pw')}, pk)$. The client then computes $A = \prod_{i=1}^{n} A_i$ and sends it to the servers. In the end, t servers cooperate to decrypt $B = E(s, pk)A = E(sg^{\sum t_i(pw-pw')}, pk)$ and sends partial decryptions to the client through secure channels, respectively. When pw' = pw, the client is able to retrieve the secret s by combining t partial decryptions. This protocol is secure against honest-but-curious adversaries but not malicious adversaries. A protocol against malicious adversaries was also given by Bagherzandi et al. [1] using non-interactive zero-knowledge proofs.

In Bagherzandi et al. protocol, it is easy to see that the client must correctly remember the public key pk and the exact set of servers, as he sends out an encryption of his password attempt pw' he remembers. If pk can be tampered with and changed so that the adversary knows the decryption key, then the adversary can decrypt pw'. Although the protocol actually encrypt $g^{pw'}$, the malicious servers can perform an offline dictionary attack on $g^{pw'}$ to obtain the password pw'.

Authenticating to the wrong servers is a common scenario when users are tricked in phishing attacks. To overcome this shortcoming, Camenisch et al. [5] proposed the first t-out-of-n TPASS protocol for any $n > t$ that does not require trusted, user-specific state information to be carried over from the setup phase. The protocol requires the client to only remember a username and a password, assuming that a PKI is available. If the client misremember his list of servers and tries to retrieve his secret from corrupt servers, the protocol prevents the servers from learning anything about the password or secret, as well as from planting a different secret into the user's mind than the secret that he stored earlier.

The construction of Camenisch et al. protocol is inspired by Bagherzandi et al. protocol based on a homomorphic threshold encryption scheme, but the crucial difference is that in the retrieval protocol of Camenisch et al., the client never sends out an encryption of his password attempt. Instead, the client derives an encryption of the (randomised) quotient of the password used at setup and the password attempt. The servers then jointly decrypt the quotient and verify whether it yields "1", indicating that both passwords matched. In case the passwords were not the same, all the servers learn is a random value.

Camenisch et al. protocol, proved to be secure in the UC framework, requires the client to involve in many communication rounds so that it becomes impractical for the client. The client has to do $5n + 15$ exponentiations in $\mathbb{G}$ for the setup protocol and $14t + 24$ exponentiations in the retrieval protocol. Each server has to perform $n + 18$ and $7t + 28$ exponentiations in these respective protocols.

Our Contribution. We provide a practical t-out-of-n TPASS protocol for any $n > t$. The basic idea is: The client initially secret-shares a password, a secret and the digest of the secret with n servers, such as t out of the n servers can recover the secret. When retrieving the secret from the servers, the client submits to the servers $A = g_1^r g_2^{\mathsf{pw}_C}$, where r is randomly chosen and pw_C is the password, and then t servers cooperate to generate and return an ElGamal encryption of the secret and an ElGamal encryption of the digest of the secret, both under the public key g_1^r. In the end, the client then decrypts the two ciphertexts and accepts the secret if one decrypted value is another's digest.

Our protocol is significantly more efficient than Camenisch et al. protocol [5] in terms of communication rounds for the client and computation and communication complexities as well. In our protocol, the client only needs to send a request and receive a response. In addition, the client needs to do $3n$ evaluations of polynomials of degree $t - 1$ in $\mathbb{Z}_q$ for the initialization and 7 exponentiations for the retrieval protocol. Each server only needs to do $t + 10$ exponentiations in the retrieval protocol. The computation and communication complexities for the client are independent of the number of the servers n and the threshold t.

We have provided a rigorous proof of security for our protocol in the standard model. Like Camenisch et al. protocol [5], our protocol can protect the password of the client even if he communicates with all-malicious servers by mistake. In addition, it prevents the servers from planting a different secret into the user's mind than the secret that he stored earlier.

Related Work. A close work related to TPASS is threshold password - authenticated key exchange (TPAKE), which lets the client agree on a fresh session key with each of the servers, but does not allow the client to store and recover a secret. Depending on the desired security properties, one can build a TPASS scheme from a TPAKE scheme by using the agreed-upon session keys to transmit the stored secret shares over secure channels [1].

The first TPAKE protocols, due to Ford and Kaliski [8] and Jablon [9], were not proved secure. The first provably secure TPAKE protocol, a t-out-of-n protocol in a PKI setting, was proposed by MacKenzie et al. [12]. The 1-out-of-2 protocol of Brainard et al. [3] is implemented in EMC's RSA Distributed Credential Protection [14]. Both protocols either leak the password or allow an offline dictionary attack when the retrieval is performed with corrupt servers. The t-out-of-n TPAKE protocols by Di Raimondo and Gennaro [13] and the 1-out-of-2 protocol by Katz et al. [11] are proved secure in a hybrid password-only/PKI setting, where the user does not know any public keys, but the servers and an intermediate gateway do have a PKI. These protocols actually remain secure when executed with all-corrupt servers, but are restricted to the cases that $n > 3t$ and $(t, n) = (1, 2)$. Based on identity-based encryption (IBE), an 1-out-of-2 protocol where the client is required to remember the identities of the two servers besides his password, was proposed by Yi et al. [17]. In case that the public parameters for IBE can be tampered and changed by the adversary, the protocol leaks the password.

In addition, the 1-out-of-2 TPASS by Camenisch et al. [4] leaks the password when the client tries to retrieve his secret from a set of all-malicious servers.

2   Definition of Security

In this section, we define the security for TPASS protocol on the basis of the security models for PAKE [2,10].

Participants, Initialization, Passwords, Secrets. A TPASS protocol involves three kinds of protocol participants: (1) A group of clients (denoted as Client), each of which requests TPASS services from t servers on the network; (2) A group of n servers $S_1, S_2, \cdots, S_n$ (denoted as Server $= \{S_1, S_2, \cdots, S_n\}$), which cooperate to provide TPASS services to clients on the network; (3) A gateway (GW), which coordinates TPASS. We assume that User $=$ Client $\bigcup$ Server and Client $\bigcap$ Server $= \emptyset$. When the gateway GW coordinates TPASS, it simply forwards messages between a client and t servers.

Prior to any execution of the protocol, we assume that an initialization phase occurs. During initialization, the n servers cooperate to generate public parameters for the protocol, which are available to all participants.

We assume that the client C chooses its password pw_C independently and uniformly at random from a "dictionary" $\mathsf{D} = \{\mathsf{pw}_1, \mathsf{pw}_2, \cdots, \mathsf{pw}_N\}$ of size N, where N is a fixed constant which is independent of any security parameter. The client then secretly shares the password with the n servers such that any t servers can restore the password.

In addition, we assume that the client C chooses its secret s_C independently and uniformly at random from $\mathbb{Z}_q^*$, where q is a public parameter. The client then secretly shares the secret with the n servers such that any t servers can recover the secret.

We assume that at least $n-t+1$ servers are trusted not to collude to determine the password and the secret of the client. The client C needs to remember pw_C only to retrieve its secret s_C.

Execution of the Protocol. In the real world, a protocol determines how users behave in response to input from their environments. In the formal model, these inputs are provided by the adversary. Each user is assumed to be able to execute the protocol multiple times (possibly concurrently) with different partners. This is modeled by allowing each user to have unlimited number of instances with which to execute the protocol. We denote instance i of user U as U^i. A given instance may be used only once. The adversary is given oracle access to these different instances. Furthermore, each instance maintains (local) state which is updated during the course of the experiment. In particular, each instance U^i is associated with the following variables, initialized as NULL or FALSE (as appropriate) during the initialization phase.

- sid_U^i is a variable containing the session identity for an instance U^i. The session identity is simply a way to keep track of the different executions of a particular user U. Without loss of generality, we simply let this be the (ordered) concatenation of all messages sent and received by instance U^i.
- s_C^i is a variable containing the secret s_C for a client instance C^i. Retrieval of the secret is, of course, the ultimate goal of the protocol.
- acc_U^i and term_U^i are boolean variables denoting whether a given instance U^i has been accepted or terminated, respectively. Termination means that the given instance has done receiving and sending messages, acceptance indicates successful termination. When an instance U^i has been accepted, sid_U^i is no longer NULL. When a client instance C^i has been accepted, s_C^i is no longer NULL.
- state_U^i records any state necessary for execution of the protocol by U^i.
- used_U^i is a boolean variable denoting whether an instance U^i has begun executing the protocol. This is a formalism which will ensure each instance is used only once.

The adversary $\mathcal{A}$ is assumed to have complete control over all communications in the network (between the clients and servers, and between servers and servers) and the adversary's interaction with the users (more specifically, with various instances) is modelled via access to oracles. The state of an instance may be updated during an oracle call, and the oracle's output may depend upon the relevant instance. The oracle types include:

- Send(C, i, M) – This sends message M to a client instance C^i. Assuming $\mathsf{term}_C^i = \mathsf{FALSE}$, this instance runs according to the protocol specification, updating state as appropriate. The output of C^i (i.e., the message sent by the instance) is given to the adversary, who receives the updated values of sid_C^i, acc_C^i, and term_C^i. This oracle call models an active attack to the protocol. If M is empty, this query represents a prompt for C to initiate the protocol.
- Send(S, j, U, M) – This sends message M to a server instance S^j, supposedly from a user U (either a client or a server) or even a set of servers. Assuming $\mathsf{term}_S^j = \mathsf{FALSE}$, this instance runs according to the protocol specification, updating state as appropriate. The output of S^j (i.e., the message sent by the instance) is given to the adversary, who receives the updated values of sid_S^j, acc_S^j, and term_S^j. If S is corrupted, the adversary also receives the entire internal state of S. This oracle call also models an active attack to the protocol.
- Execute($C, i, \mathbb{S}$) – If the client instance C^i and t server instances, denoted as $\mathbb{S}$, have not yet been used, this oracle executes the protocol between these instances and outputs the transcript of this execution. This oracle call represents passive eavesdropping of a protocol execution. In addition to the transcript, the adversary receives the values of sid, acc, and term for client and server instances, at each step of protocol execution. In addition, if any server in $\mathbb{S}$ is corrupted, the adversary is given the entire internal state of the server.
- Corrupt(S) – This sends the password and secret shares of all clients stored in the server S to the adversary. This oracle models possible compromising of a server due to, for example, hacking into the server.

- Corrupt(C) – This query allows the adversary to learn the password of the client C and then the secret of the client, which models the possibility of subverting a client by, for example, witnessing a user typing in his password, or installing a "Trojan horse" on his machine.
- Test(C, i) – This oracle does not model any real-world capability of the adversary, but is instead used to define security. If $\mathsf{acc}_C^i = \mathsf{TRUE}$, a random bit b is generated. If $b = 0$, the adversary is given s_C^i, and if $b = 1$ the adversary is given a random number. The adversary is allowed only a single Test query, at any time during its execution.

Correctness. To be viable, a TPASS protocol must satisfy the following notion of correctness: If a client instance C^i and t server instances $\mathbb{S}$ runs an honest execution of the protocol with no interference from the adversary, then $\mathsf{acc}_C^i = \mathsf{acc}_S^j = \mathsf{TRUE}$ for any server instance S^j in $\mathbb{S}$.

Freshness. To formally define the adversary's success we need to define a notion of freshness for a secret of a client, where freshness of the secret is meant to indicate that the adversary does not trivially know the value of the secret. We say a secret s_C^i is fresh if (1) C is not corrupted and (2) at least $n - t + 1$ out of n servers are not corrupted.

Advantage of the Adversary. Informally, the adversary succeeds if it can guess the bit b used by the Test oracle. We say an adversary $\mathcal{A}$ succeeds if it makes a single query Test(C, i) to a fresh client instance C^i, with $\mathsf{acc}_C^i = \mathsf{TRUE}$ at the time of this query, and outputs a single bit b' with $b' = b$ (recall that b is the bit chosen by the Test oracle). We denote this event by Succ. The advantage of adversary $\mathcal{A}$ in attacking protocol P is then given by

$$\mathsf{Adv}_{\mathcal{A}}^P(k) = 2 \cdot \mathsf{Pr}[\mathsf{Succ}] - 1$$

where the probability is taken over the random coins used by the adversary and the random coins used during the course of the experiment (including the initialization phase).

An adversary can always succeed by trying all passwords one-by-one in an on-line impersonation attack. A protocol is secure if this is the best an adversary can do. The on-line attacks correspond to Send queries. Formally, each instance for which the adversary has made a Send query counts as one on-line attack. Instances with which the adversary interacts via Execute are not counted as on-line attacks. The number of on-line attacks represents a bound on the number of passwords the adversary could have tested in an on-line fashion.

Definition 1. Protocol P is a secure TPASS protocol if, for all dictionary size N and for all PPT adversaries $\mathcal{A}$ making at most $Q(k)$ on-line attacks, there exists a negligible function $\varepsilon(\cdot)$ such that for a security parameter k,

$$\mathsf{Adv}_{\mathcal{A}}^P(k) \leq Q(k)/N + \varepsilon(k)$$

3 Our TPASS Protocol

3.1 Description of Our Protocol

Initialization. Given a security parameter $k \in \mathbb{Z}^*$, the initialization includes:

Parameter Generation: On input k, the n servers agree on a cyclic group $\mathbb{G}$ of large prime order q with a generators g_1 and a hash function $H : \{0,1\}^* \to \mathbb{Z}_q$. Then the n servers cooperate to generate g_2, like [16], such that none knows the discrete logarithm of g_2 based on g_1 if one out of the n server is honest. The public parameters for the protocol is $\mathsf{params} = \{\mathbb{G}, q, g_1, g_2, H\}$.

Password Generation: On input params, each client $C \in \mathsf{Client}$ with identity ID_C uniformly draws a string pw_C, the password, from the dictionary $\mathsf{D} = \{\mathsf{pw}_1, \mathsf{pw}_2, \cdots, \mathsf{pw}_N\}$. The client then randomly chooses a polynomial $f_1(x)$ of degree $t - 1$ over $\mathbb{Z}_q$ such that $\mathsf{pw}_C = f_1(0)$, and distributes $\{ID_C, i, f_1(i)\}$ to the server S_i via a secure channel, where $i = 1, 2, \cdots, n$.

Secret Sharing: On input params, each client $C \in \mathsf{Client}$ randomly chooses s from $\mathbb{Z}_q^*$. The client then randomly chooses two polynomials $f_2(x)$ and $f_3(x)$ of degree $t - 1$ over $\mathbb{Z}_q$ such that $s = f_2(0)$ and $H(g_2^s) = f_3(0)$, and distributes $\{ID_C, i, f_2(i), f_3(i)\}$ to the server S_i via a secure channel, where $i = 1, 2, \cdots, n$. We define the secret s_C as g_2^s.

Protocol Execution. Given the public $\mathsf{params} = \{\mathbb{G}, q, g_1, g_2, H\}$, the client C (knowing its identity ID_C and password pw_C) runs TPASS protocol P with t servers (each server knowing $\{ID, i, f_1(i), f_2(i), f_3(i)\}$) to retrieve the secret s_C as shown in Fig. 1.

In Fig. 1, TPASS protocol is executed in three phases as follows.

Retrieval Request. Given the public parameters $\{\mathbb{G}, g_1, g_2, q, H\}$, the client C with the identity ID_C validates if q is a large prime and $g_1^q = g_2^q = 1$. If so, the client, who remembers the password pw_C, randomly chooses r from $\mathbb{Z}_q^*$ and computes

$$A = g_1^r g_2^{-\mathsf{pw}_C}.$$

Then the client submits $\mathsf{msg}_C = \langle ID_C, A \rangle$ to the gateway GW for the n servers.

Remark. The purpose for the client to validate the public parameters is to ensure that the discrete logarithm over $\{\mathbb{G}, q, g_1, g_2\}$ is hard in case that the adversary can change the public parameters.

Retrieval Response. After receiving the request msg_C from the client C, the gateway GW forwards it to t available servers to response the request. Without loss of generality, we assume that the first t servers, denoted as $\mathbb{S} = \{\mathsf{S}_1, \mathsf{S}_2, \cdots, \mathsf{S}_t\}$, cooperate to generate a response as follows.

Based on the identity ID_C of the client, each server S_i ($i = 1, 2, \cdots, t$) randomly chooses r_i, c_i, d_i from $\mathbb{Z}_q^*$ and computes

$$B_i = g_1^{r_i} g_2^{a_i f_1(i)}, C_i = g_1^{c_i}, D_i = g_1^{d_i}, \delta_i = g_1^{H(ID_C, A, B_i, C_i, D_i)}$$

Public: $\mathbb{G}, q, g_1, g_2, H$

Client C

ID_C, pw_C

Server S_i

$\{ID_C, i, f_1(i), f_2(i), f_3(i)\}$
$i = 1, 2, \cdots, t$

$r \xleftarrow{R} \mathbb{Z}_q^*$
$A = g_1^r g_2^{-\mathsf{pw}_C}$

$\xrightarrow{\quad \mathsf{msg}_C = \langle ID_C, A \rangle \quad}$ Gateway
GW $\xrightarrow{\quad \mathsf{msg}_C = \langle ID_C, A \rangle \quad}$
$\mathbb{S} = \{\mathsf{S}_1, \mathsf{S}_2, \cdots, \mathsf{S}_t\}$

$r_i, c_i, d_i \xleftarrow{R} \mathbb{Z}_q^*, a_i = \prod_{1 \le j \le t, j \ne i} \frac{j}{j-i}$
$B_i = g_1^{r_i} g_2^{a_i f_1(i)}$
$C_i = g_1^{c_i}, D_i = g_1^{d_i}$
$\delta_i = g_1^{H(ID_C, A, B_i, C_i, D_i)}$
$\mathsf{msg}_i = \langle ID_C, \delta_i, B_i, C_i, D_i \rangle \to \mathbb{S}$

$\langle ID_C, \delta_i \rangle, i = 1, 2, \cdots, t$
$\xrightarrow{\qquad\qquad\qquad\qquad\qquad}$
S_i broadcasts commit in $\mathbb{S}$

$\langle ID_C, B_i, C_i, D_i \rangle, i = 1, 2, \cdots, t$
$\xrightarrow{\qquad\qquad\qquad\qquad\qquad}$
S_i broadcasts opening in $\mathbb{S}$

if $\delta_j = g_1^{H(ID_c, A, B_j, C_j, D_j)} \ (1 \le j \le t)$
$C = \prod_{j=1}^t C_j, D = \prod_{j=1}^t D_j$
$h_i = H(ID_C, A, C, D)$
$E_i = g_2^{a_i f_2(i) h_i} C^{-r_i} (A \prod_{j=1}^t B_j)^{c_i}$
$F_i = g_2^{a_i f_3(i) h_i} D^{-r_i} (A \prod_{j=1}^t B_j)^{d_i}$
$\mathsf{acc}_{\mathsf{S}_i} = \mathsf{TRUE}$
else return $\perp$

Gateway $\xleftarrow{\quad \mathsf{msg}_i^* = \langle ID_C, C, D, E_i, F_i \rangle \quad}$
GW

$E = \prod_{i=1}^t E_i$
$F = \prod_{i=1}^t F_i$

$\xleftarrow{\quad \mathsf{msg}_S = \langle ID_C, C, D, E, F \rangle \quad}$

$h = H(ID_C, A, C, D)$
$S = (E/C^r)^{h^{-1}}$
$T = (F/D^r)^{h^{-1}}$
if $T = g_2^{H(S)}$, $\mathsf{acc}_C = \mathsf{TRUE}$
else return $\perp$

Fig. 1. Our TPASS protocol P

where $a_i = \prod_{1 \le j \le t, j \ne i} \frac{j}{j-i}$.

Then S_i broadcasts $\mathsf{msg}_i = \langle ID_C, \delta_i, B_i, C_i, D_i \rangle$ in $\mathbb{S}$ in two phases. In the commit phase, S_i broadcasts its commitment $\langle ID_C, \delta_i \rangle$. After receiving all commitments $\langle ID_C, \delta_j \rangle$ $(1 \le j \le t)$, S_i broadcasts its opening $\langle ID_C, B_i, C_i, D_i \rangle$ in the reveal phase.

Each server S_i verifies if $\delta_j = g_1^{H(ID_C, A, B_j, C_j, D_j)}$ for all $j \ne i$. If so, based on the identity ID_C of the client, S_i computes

$$C = \prod_{j=1}^{t} C_j, D = \prod_{j=1}^{t} D_j, h_i = H(ID_C, A, C, D)$$

$$E_i = g_2^{a_i f_2(i) h_i} C^{-r_i} (A \prod_{j=1}^{t} B_j)^{c_i}, F_i = g_2^{a_i f_3(i) h_i} D^{-r_i} (A \prod_{j=1}^{t} B_j)^{d_i}$$

and sets $\mathsf{accs}_i = \mathsf{TRUE}$.

Then S_i sends $\mathsf{msg}_i^* = \{ID_C, C, D, E_i, F_i\}$ to the gateway GW. The gateway GW computes

$$E = \prod_{i=1}^{t} E_i, F = \prod_{i=1}^{t} F_i$$

and returns to the client with $\mathsf{msg}_S = \{ID_C, C, D, E, F\}$.

Secret Retrieval. After receiving the response $\mathsf{msg}_S = \{ID_C, C, D, E, F\}$ from the gateway, the client computes

$$h = H(ID_C, A, C, D), S = (E/C^r)^{h^{-1}}, T = (F/D^r)^{h^{-1}}$$

and verifies if $T = g_2^{H(S)}$. If so, the client sets $\mathsf{acc}_C = \mathsf{TRUE}$ and $\perp$ otherwise.

3.2 Correctness and Efficiency

Correctness. Assume that a client instance C^i and t server instances $\mathbb{S}$ run an honest execution of our TPASS protocol P with no interference from the adversary. With reference to Fig. 1, it is obvious that $\mathsf{accs}_j = \mathsf{TRUE}$ for $1 \le j \le t$. In addition, we have

$$C = \prod_{j=1}^{t} C_j = g_1^{\sum_{j=1}^{t} c_j}$$

$$D = \prod_{j=1}^{t} D_j = g_1^{\sum_{j=1}^{t} d_j}$$

$$E_i = g_2^{a_i f_2(i) h_i} C^{-r_i} (A \prod_{j=1}^{t} B_j)^{c_i}$$

$$= g_2^{a_i f_2(i) h_i} g_1^{-r_i \sum_{j=1}^{t} c_j} (g_1^r g_2^{-\text{pw}_C} g_1^{\sum_{j=1}^{t} r_j} g_2^{\text{pw}_C})^{c_i}$$

$$= g_2^{a_i f_2(i) h_i} g_1^{-r_i \sum_{j=1}^{t} c_j} g_1^{c_i \sum_{j=1}^{t} r_j} g_1^{c_i r}$$

$$F_i = g_2^{a_i f_3(i) h_i} D^{-r_i} (A \prod_{j=1}^{t} B_j)^{d_i}$$

$$= g_2^{a_i f_3(i) h_i} g_1^{-r_i \sum_{j=1}^{t} d_j} (g_1^r g_2^{-\text{pw}_C} g_1^{\sum_{j=1}^{t} r_j} g_2^{\text{pw}_C})^{d_i}$$

$$= g_2^{a_i f_3(i) h_i} g_1^{-r_i \sum_{j=1}^{t} d_j} g_1^{d_i \sum_{j=1}^{t} r_j} g_1^{d_i r}$$

$$h = h_1 = h_2 = \cdots = h_t$$

$$= H(ID_C, A, C, D)$$

$$E = \prod_{i=1}^{t} E_i = \prod_{i=1}^{t} g_2^{a_i f_3(i) h} g_1^{-r_i \sum_{j=1}^{t} d_j} g_1^{d_i \sum_{j=1}^{t} r_j} g_1^{d_i r}$$

$$= g_2^{sh} g_1^{-\sum_{i=1}^{t} r_i \sum_{j=1}^{t} c_j} g_1^{\sum_{i=1}^{t} c_i \sum_{j=1}^{t} r_j} g_1^{r \sum_{i=1}^{t} c_i}$$

$$= g_2^{sh} C^r$$

$$F = \prod_{i=1}^{t} F_i = \prod_{i=1}^{t} g_2^{a_i f_3(i) h} g_1^{-r_i \sum_{j=1}^{t} d_j} g_1^{d_i \sum_{j=1}^{t} r_j} g_1^{d_i r}$$

$$= g_2^{H(g_2^s) h} g_1^{-\sum_{i=1}^{t} r_i \sum_{j=1}^{t} d_j} g_1^{\sum_{i=1}^{t} d_i \sum_{j=1}^{t} r_j} g_1^{r \sum_{i=1}^{t} d_i}$$

$$= g_2^{H(g_2^s) h} D^r$$

We can see that (C, E) and (D, F) are in fact the EGamal encryptions of g_2^{sh} and $g_2^{H(g^s) h}$ under the public key g_1^r, respectively. Therefore, we have $\text{acc}_C = \text{TRUE}$ because

$$h = H(ID_C, A, C, D)$$

$$S = (E/C^r)^{h^{-1}} = (g_2^{sh})^{h^{-1}} = g_2^s$$

$$T = (F/D^r)^{h^{-1}} = (g_2^{H(g_2^s) h})^{h^{-1}} = g_2^{H(g_2^s)}$$

$$T = g_2^{H(S)}.$$

In summary, our TPASS protocol has correctness.

Efficiency. In our TPASS protocol, the client needs to compute 7 exponentiations in $\mathbb{G}$ and send or receive 5 group elements in $\mathbb{G}$. Each server needs to compute $t + 10$ exponentiations in $\mathbb{G}$ and send or receive $4t + 5$ group elements in $\mathbb{G}$.

The client involves only two communication rounds with the gateway, i.e., sending msg_C to the gateway and receiving msg_S from the gateway. Each server S_i participates in six communication rounds with other servers and the gateway, i.e., receiving msg_C from the gateway, broadcasting the commitment $\langle ID_C, \delta_i \rangle$ to other servers, receiving $\langle ID_C, \delta_j \rangle$ for all $j \neq i$ from other servers, broadcasting $\langle ID_C, B_i, C_i, D_i \rangle$, receiving $\langle ID_C, B_j, C_j, D_j \rangle$ for all $j \neq i$, and finally sending msg_i^* to the gateway.

The performance comparison of Camenisch et al. protocol [5] and our protocol can be shown in Table 1.

Table 1. Performance comparison of Camenisch et al. protocol and our protocol

	Camenisch et al. protocol [5]	Our protocol
Public keys	Client: username	Client: username
	Server S_i: epk_i, spk_i, tpk_i	Server S_i: none
Private keys	Client: pw_C	Client: pw_C
	Server S_i: esk_i, ssk_i, tsk_i	Server S_i: $f_1(i), f_2(i), f_3(i)$ where
	$E(pw_C, pk), E(s, pk), pk = \prod epk_i$	$\sum a_i f_1(i) = pw_C, \sum a_i f_2(i) = s$
	$E(pw_C, tpk), E(s, tpk), tpk = \prod tpk_i$	and $\sum a_i f_3(i) = H(g_2^s)$
Setup Comp.	Client: $5n + 15$ (exp.)	Client: $3n$ polynomial evaluations
Complexity	Server: $n + 18$ (exp.)	Server: none
Setup Comm.	$n(2.5n + 18.5)\|g\|$	Client: $3n\|q\|$
Complexity		Server: $3\|q\|$
Setup Comm.	4	Client: 1
Round		Server: 1
Retrieve Comp.	Client: $14t + 24$ (exp.)	Client: 7 (exp.)
Complexity	Server: $7t + 28$ (exp.)	Server: $t + 10$ (exp.)
		Gateway: 0 (exp.)
Retrieve Comm.	$(t + 1)(36.5 + 2.5n$	Client: $5\|g\|$
Complexity	$+10.5t(t + 1))\|g\|$	Server: $(4t + 5)\|g\|$
		Gateway: $(4t + 5)\|g\|$
Retrieve Comm.	10	Client: 2/Server: 6
Rounds		Gateway: 4

In Table 1, exp. represent the computation complexity of a modular exponentiation, $|g|$ is the size of a group element in $\mathbb{G}$ and $|q|$ is the size of a group element in $\mathbb{Z}_q$. In Camenisch et al. protocol [5], a hash value is counted as half a group element.

In our initialization, the client secret-shares the password, secret and the digest of the secret with the n servers via n secure channels which may be established with PKI. In the setup protocol of Camenisch et al., the client setups the shares with the n servers based on PKI. Our retrieval protocol does not rely on PKI, but the retrieval protocol of Camenisch et al. still requires PKI. In view of this, our retrieval protocol can be implemented easier than Camenisch et al. retrieval protocol.

From Table 1, we can see that our retrieval protocol is significantly more efficient than the retrieval protocol of Camenisch et al. not only in communication rounds for client but also in computation and communication complexities. In particular, the performance of the client in our retrieval protocol is independent of the number of the servers and the threshold.

4   Security Analysis

Based on the security model defined in Sect. 2, we have the following theorem:

Theorem 1. Assuming that the decisional Diffie-Hellman (DDH) problem [6] is hard over $\{\mathbb{G}, q, g_1\}$ and H is a collision-resistant hash function, then our TPASS protocol P illustrated in Fig. 1 is secure according to Definition 1.

Proof. In the security analysis, we consider the worst case where $t - 1$ servers have been corrupted and only one server is honest in our protocol as shown in Fig. 1. Without loss of generality, we assume that the first server S_1 is honest and the rest have been corrupted.

Given an adversary $\mathcal{A}$ attacking the protocol, we imagine a simulator $\mathcal{S}$ that runs the protocol for $\mathcal{A}$.

First of all, the simulator $\mathcal{S}$ initializes the system by generating public parameters params $= \{\mathbb{G}, q, g_1, g_2, H\}$. Next, Server $= \{S_1, S_2, \cdots, S_n\}$ and Client sets are determined. For each $C \in$ Client, a password pw_C and a secret s_C are chosen at random and then secret-shared with the n servers. In addition, the digest of the secret $H(s_C)$ is also secret-shared with the n servers.

The public parameters params and the shares $\{ID_C, i, f_1(i), f_2(i), f_3(i)\}$ for $i = 2, 3, \cdots, t$ are provided to the adversary. When answering to any oracle query, the simulator $\mathcal{S}$ provides the adversary $\mathcal{A}$ with the internal state of the corrupted servers S_i $(i = 2, 3, \cdots, t)$.

We view the adversary's queries to its Send oracles as queries to four different oracles as follows:

- Send(C, i) represents a request for instance C^i of client C to initiate the protocol. The output of this query is $msg_C = \langle ID_C, A \rangle$.
- Send(S_1, j, C, msg_C) represents sending message msg_C to instance S_1^j of the server S_1, supposedly from the client C. The input of this query is $msg_C = \langle ID_C, A \rangle$ and the output of this query is $msg_1 = \langle ID_C, \delta_1, B_1, C_1, D_1 \rangle$.
- Send$(S_1, j, S_2, S_3, \cdots, S_t, M)$ represents sending message M to instance S_1^j of the server S_1, supposedly from the servers $S_2, S_3, \cdots, S_t$. The input of this query is $M = msg_2 \| msg_3 \| \cdots \| msg_t$ and the output of this query is $msg_1^* = \langle ID_C, C, D, E_1, F_1 \rangle$ or $\perp$.
- Send(C, i, msg_S) represents sending the message msg_S to instance C^i of the client C. The input of this query is $msg_S = \langle ID_C, C, D, E, F \rangle$ and the output of this query is either $acc_C^i = $ TRUE or $\perp$.

When $\mathcal{A}$ queries the Test oracle, the simulator $\mathcal{S}$ chooses a random bit b. When the adversary completes its execution and output a bit b', the simulator can tell whether the adversary succeeds by checking if (1) a single Test query was made regarding some fresh client session, and (2) $b' = b$. Success of the adversary is denoted by event Succ. For any experiment P, we denote $\mathsf{Adv}_{\mathcal{A}}^P = 2 \cdot \mathsf{Pr}[\mathsf{Succ}] - 1$, where $\mathsf{Pr}[\cdot]$ denotes the probability of an event when the simulator interacts with the adversary in accordance with experiment P.

We will use some terminology throughout the proof. A given message is called oracle-generated if it was output by the simulator in response to some oracle query. The message is said to be adversarially-generated otherwise. An adversarially-generated message must not be the same as any oracle-generated message.

We refer to the real execution of the experiment, as described above, as P_0. We introduce a sequence of transformations to the experiment P_0 and bound the effect of each transformation on the adversary's advantage. We then bound the adversary's advantage in the final experiment. This immediately yields a bound on the adversary's advantage in the original experiment.

As shown in the appendix, we have $\mathsf{Adv}_{\mathcal{A}}^{P_0}(k) \leq Q(k)/N + \varepsilon(k)$ for some negligible function $\varepsilon(\cdot)$. This completes the proof of the theorem. $\triangle$

In our retrieval protocol, the client sends out one message $A = g_1^r g_2^{\mathsf{pw}_C}$ only after validating the public parameters $\{\mathbb{G}, q, g_1, g_2\}$. Even if the client communicates with all malicious servers by mistake and the adversary can change the public parameters, our retrieval protocol does not leak the password because r in A is randomly chosen from $\mathbb{Z}_q^*$ by the client.

In addition, in the appendix, we have modified the definition of the security in order to take into account the attack where the adversary attempts to plant a different secret into the user's mind than the secret that he stored earlier. This attack is restricted to online dictionary attack.

5   Conclusion

In this paper, we have presented a practical t-out-of-n TPASS protocol for any $n > t$ that protects the password of the client when he tries to retrieve his secret from all corrupt servers as well as prevents the adversary from planting a different secret into the user's mind than the secret that he stored earlier. Our protocol is significantly more efficient than existing TPASS protocols. Furthermore, we have provide a rigorous proof of security for our protocol in the standard model.

Our future work will study how efficiently to detect the corrupted servers and implement our protocol in light-weight mobile devices to support cloud-based services/management.

Appendix: Security Proof

Experiment P_1: In this experiment, the simulator interacts with the adversary as P_0 except that the adversary does not succeed, and the experiment is aborted, if any of the following occurs:

1. At any point during the experiment, an oracle-generated message (e.g., msg_C, msg_i, msg_i^*, or msg_S) is repeated.

2. At any point during the experiment, a collision occurs in the hash function H (regardless of whether this is due to a direct action of the adversary, or whether this occurs during the course of the simulator's response to an oracle query).

It is immediate that events 1 occurs with only negligible probability, event 2 occurs with negligible probability assuming H as collision-resistant hash functions. Put everything together, we are able to see that

Claim 1. If H is a collision-resistant hash function, $|\mathsf{Adv}_{\mathcal{A}}^{P_0}(k) - \mathsf{Adv}_{\mathcal{A}}^{P_1}(k)|$ is negligible.

Experiment P_2: In this experiment, the simulator interacts with the adversary $\mathcal{A}$ as in experiment P_1 except that the adversary's queries to Execute oracles are handled differently: in any Execute$(C, i, \mathbb{S})$, where the adversary $\mathcal{A}$ has not queried corrupt(C), the password pw_C in $\mathsf{msg}_C = \langle ID_C, A \rangle$ where $A = g_1^r g_2^{\mathsf{pw}_C}$ is replaced with a random number pw in $\mathbb{Z}_q^*$.

Because r in $A = g_1^r g_2^{\mathsf{pw}_C}$ is randomly chosen from $\mathbb{Z}_q^*$ by the simulator, the adversary cannot distinguish $g_1^r g_2^{\mathsf{pw}_C}$ with $g_1^r g_2^{\mathsf{pw}}$. Therefore, we have

Claim 2. $|\mathsf{Adv}_{\mathcal{A}}^{P_1}(k) - \mathsf{Adv}_{\mathcal{A}}^{P_2}(k)|$ is negligible.

Experiment P_3: In this experiment, the simulator interacts with the adversary $\mathcal{A}$ as in experiment P_2 except that: for any Execute$(C, i, \mathbb{S})$ oracle, where the adversary $\mathcal{A}$ has not queried corrupt(C) and corrupt(S_1), $a_1 f_1(1)$ in $\mathsf{msg}_1 = \langle ID_C, \delta_1, B_1, C_1, D_1 \rangle$ where $B_1 = g_1^{r_1} g_2^{a_1 f_1(1)}$ is replaced by a random number in $\mathbb{Z}_q^*$.

Although the adversary who has corrupted $\mathsf{S}_2, \mathsf{S}_3, \cdots, \mathsf{S}_t$ can obtain $B_1' = B_1 g_2^{a_2 f_1(2) + \cdots + a_t f_1(t)} = g_1^{r_1} g_2^{\mathsf{pw}_C}$ for B_1, he cannot distinguish $g_1^{r_1} g_2^{\mathsf{pw}_C}$ with $g_1^{r_1} g_2^{\mathsf{pw}}$ for a randomly chosen pw because r_1 is randomly chosen by the simulator. This leads that he cannot distinguish $g_1^{r_1} g_2^{a_1 f_1} = g_1^{r_1} g_2^{\mathsf{pw}_C - a_2 f_1(2) - \cdots - a_t f_1(t)}$ with $g_1^{r_1} g_2^{\mathsf{pw} - a_2 f_1(2) - \cdots - a_t f_1(t)}$ for a randomly chosen pw. Therefore, we have

Claim 3. $|\mathsf{Adv}_{\mathcal{A}}^{P_2}(k) - \mathsf{Adv}_{\mathcal{A}}^{P_3}(k)|$ is negligible.

Experiment P_4: In this experiment, the simulator interacts with the adversary $\mathcal{A}$ as in experiment P_3 except that: for any Execute$(C, i, \mathbb{S})$ oracle, where the adversary $\mathcal{A}$ has not queried corrupt(C) and corrupt(S_1), E_1 in $\mathsf{msg}_1^* = \langle ID_C, C, D, E_1, F_1 \rangle$ is replaced with a random element in the group $\mathbb{G}$.

The difference between the current experiment and the previous one is bounded by the probability to solve the decisional Diffie-Hellman (DDH) problem over $\{\mathbb{G}, q, g_1\}$. More precisely, we have

Claim 4. If the decisional Diffie-Hellman (DDH) problem over $\{\mathbb{G}, q, g_1\}$ is hard, $|\mathsf{Adv}_{\mathcal{A}}^{P_3}(k) - \mathsf{Adv}_{\mathcal{A}}^{P_4}(k)|$ is negligible.

If $|\mathsf{Adv}_{\mathcal{A}}^{P_3}(k) - \mathsf{Adv}_{\mathcal{A}}^{P_4}(k)|$ is non-negligible, we show that the simulator can use $\mathcal{A}$ as a subroutine to solve the DDH problem with non-negligible probability as follows.

Given a DDH problem (g_1^x, g_1^y, Z), where x, y are randomly chosen from $\mathbb{Z}_q^*$ and Z is either g_1^{xy} or a random element z from $\mathbb{G}$, the simulator replaces g_1^r in $A = g_1^r g_2^{\mathsf{pw}_C}$ with g_1^x, $C_1 = g_1^{c_1}$ with g_1^y, and $(g_1^{c_1}, g_1^{c_1 r})$ in

$$E_1 = g_2^{a_1 f_2(1) h_1} g_1^{-r_1 \sum_{j=1}^{t} c_j} g_1^{c_1 \sum_{j=1}^{t} r_j} g_1^{c_1 r}$$

with g_1^y, Z, respectively, where r_j $(j = 1, 2, \cdots, t)$ and c_j $(j = 2, 3, \cdots, t)$ are randomly chosen by the simulator. When $Z = g^{xy}$, the experiment is the same as the experiment P_3. When Z is a random element z in $\mathbb{G}$, the experiment is the same as the experiment P_4. If the adversary can distinguish the experiments P_3 and P_4 with non-negligible probability, the simulator can solve the DDH problem with non-negligible probability.

Experiment P_5: In this experiment, the simulator interacts with the adversary $\mathcal{A}$ as in experiment P_4 except that: for any $\mathsf{Execute}(C, i, \mathbb{S})$ oracle, where the adversary $\mathcal{A}$ has not queried $\mathsf{corrupt}(C)$ and $\mathsf{corrupt}(\mathsf{S}_1)$, F_1 in $\mathsf{msg}_1^* = \langle ID_C, C, D, E_1, F_1 \rangle$ is replaced with a random element in the group $\mathbb{G}$.

Like the experiment P_4, we have

Claim 5. If the decisional Diffie-Hellman (DDH) problem is hard over $\{\mathbb{G}, q, g_1\}$, $|\mathsf{Adv}_{\mathcal{A}}^{P_4}(k) - \mathsf{Adv}_{\mathcal{A}}^{P_5}(k)|$ is negligible.

Experiment P_6: In this experiment, the simulator interacts with the adversary $\mathcal{A}$ as in experiment P_5 except that: for any $\mathsf{Execute}(C, i, \mathbb{S})$ oracle, where the adversary $\mathcal{A}$ has not queried $\mathsf{corrupt}(C)$ and $\mathsf{corrupt}(\mathsf{S}_1)$, the secret s_C of the client is replaced with a random element in the group $\mathbb{G}$.

Given a DDH problem (g_1^x, g_1^y, Z), where x, y are randomly chosen from $\mathbb{Z}_q^*$ and Z is either g_1^{xy} or a random element z from $\mathbb{G}$, the simulator replaces g_1^r in $A = g_1^r g_2^{\mathsf{pw}_C}$ with g_1^x, $C_1 = g_1^{c_1}$ with g_1^y, and $(g_1^r, g_1^{c_1 r})$ in

$$s_C = (E/C^r)^{h^{-1}} = (E/g_1^{r \sum_{i=1}^{t} c_i})^{h^{-1}} = (E/(g_1^{r \sum_{i=2}^{t} c_i} g_1^{r c_1}))^{h^{-1}}$$

with g_1^x, Z, respectively, where $h = H(ID_C, A, C, D)$, c_j $(j = 2, 3, \cdots, t)$ are randomly chosen by the simulator. When $Z = g^{xy}$, the experiment is the same as the experiment P_5. When Z is a random element z in $\mathbb{G}$, the experiment is the same as the experiment P_6. If the adversary can distinguish the experiments P_5 and P_6 with non-negligible probability, the simulator can solve the DDH problem with non-negligible probability. Therefore, we have

Claim 6. If the decisional Diffie-Hellman (DDH) problem is hard over $\{\mathbb{G}, q, g_1\}$, $|\mathsf{Adv}_{\mathcal{A}}^{P_5}(k) - \mathsf{Adv}_{\mathcal{A}}^{P_6}(k)|$ is negligible.

In experiment P_6, the adversary's probability of correctly guessing the bit b used by the Test oracle is exactly $1/2$ when the Test query is made to a fresh client instance C^i invoked by an Execute$(C, i, \mathbb{S})$ oracle. This is so because the secret s_C is chosen at random from $\mathbb{G}$, and hence there is no way to distinguish whether the Test oracle outputs a random secret or the "actual" secret (which is a random element, anyway). Therefore, all passive adversaries cannot win the game.

The rest of the proof concentrates on the instances invoked by Send oracles.

Experiment P_7: In this experiment, the simulator interacts with the adversary $\mathcal{A}$ as in experiment P_6 except that the adversary's queries to Send(C, i) oracles are handled differently: in any Send(C, i), where the adversary $\mathcal{A}$ has not queried corrupt(C), the password pw$_C$ in msg$_C = \langle ID_C, A \rangle$ where $A = g_1^r g_2^{\text{pw}_C}$ is replaced with a random number pw in $\mathbb{Z}_q^*$.

Like the experiment P_2, we have

Claim 7. $|\mathsf{Adv}_{\mathcal{A}}^{P_6}(k) - \mathsf{Adv}_{\mathcal{A}}^{P_7}(k)|$ is negligible.

Experiment P_8: In this experiment, the simulator interacts with the adversary $\mathcal{A}$ as in experiment P_7 except that the adversary's queries to Send$(S_1, j, C, \text{msg}_C)$ oracles are handled differently: in any Send$(S_1, j, C, \text{msg}_C)$, where the adversary $\mathcal{A}$ has not queried corrupt(C) and corrupt(S_1), $a_1 f_1(1)$ in msg$_1 = \langle ID_C, B_1, C_1, D_1 \rangle$ where $B_1 = g_1^{r_1} g_2^{a_1 f_1(1)}$ is replaced by a random number in $\mathbb{Z}_q^*$.

Like the experiment P_3, we have

Claim 8. $|\mathsf{Adv}_{\mathcal{A}}^{P_7}(k) - \mathsf{Adv}_{\mathcal{A}}^{P_8}(k)|$ is negligible.

Experiment P_9: In this experiment, the simulator interacts with the adversary $\mathcal{A}$ as in experiment P_8 except that the adversary's queries to Send$(S_1, j, S_2, \cdots, S_t, \text{msg}_2 \| \cdots \| \text{msg}_t)$ oracles are handled differently: in any Send$(S_1, j, S_2, \cdots, S_t, \text{msg}_2 \| \cdots \| \text{msg}_t)$, where $\mathcal{A}$ has not queried corrupt(C) and corrupt(S_1), E_1 in msg$_1^* = \langle ID_C, C, D, E_1, F_1 \rangle$ is replaced with a random element in the group $\mathbb{G}$.

If msg$_C$, msg$_2$, msg$_3$, $\cdots$, msg$_t$ are all oracle-generated, we can replace E_1 with a random element in $\mathbb{G}$ as in the experiment P_4.

If some of msg$_C$, msg$_2$, msg$_3$, $\cdots$, msg$_t$ are adversarially-generated, the adversary $\mathcal{A}$ cannot produce $A, (B_j, C_j, D_j)$ $(j = 2, 3, \cdots, t)$, such as $A \prod_{j=1}^{t} B_j$ excludes B_1 and $\delta_j = g_1^{H(ID_C, A, B_j, C_j, D_j)}$ for $j = 2, 3, \cdots, t$ still hold because A and the commitments δ_j $(j = 2, 3, \cdots, t)$ must be broadcast and received by the server S_1 at first and H is a collision-resistant hash function.

Because $B_1 = g_1^{r_1} g_2^{a_1 f_1(1)}$, we have

$$E_1 = g_2^{a_1 f_2(1) h_1} C^{-r_1} (A \prod_{j=1}^{t} B_j)^{c_i}$$

$$= g_2^{a_1 f_2(1) h_1} C^{-r_1} (A \prod_{j=2}^{t} B_j)^{c_i} g_1^{c_1 r_1} (g_2^{c_1})^{a_1 f_1(1)}.$$

Given a DDH problem (g_1^x, g_1^y, Z), where x, y are randomly chosen from $\mathbb{Z}_q^*$ and Z is either g_1^{xy} or a random element z from $\mathbb{G}$, the simulator replaces g_2 with g_1^x, $C_1 = g_1^{c_1}$ with g_1^y, and $(g_1^{c_1}, g_2^{c_1})$ in the above E_1 with g_1^y, Z, respectively, where r_1 is randomly chosen by the simulator. When $Z = g^{xy}$, the experiment is the same as the experiment P_8. When Z is a random element z in $\mathbb{G}$, the experiment is the same as the experiment P_9. If the adversary can distinguish the experiments P_8 and P_9 with non-negligible probability, the simulator can solve the DDH problem with non-negligible probability. Therefore, we have

Claim 9. If the decisional Diffie-Hellman (DDH) problem is hard over $\{\mathbb{G}, q, g_1\}$, $|\mathsf{Adv}_{\mathcal{A}}^{P_8}(k) - \mathsf{Adv}_{\mathcal{A}}^{P_9}(k)|$ is negligible.

Experiment P_{10}: In this experiment, the simulator interacts with the adversary $\mathcal{A}$ as in experiment P_9 except that the adversary's queries to $\mathsf{Send}(\mathsf{S}_1, j, \mathsf{S}_2, \cdots, \mathsf{S}_t, \mathsf{msg}_2 \| \cdots \| \mathsf{msg}_t)$ oracles are handled differently: in any $\mathsf{Send}(\mathsf{S}_1, j, \mathsf{S}_2, \cdots, \mathsf{S}_t, \mathsf{msg}_2 \| \cdots \| \mathsf{msg}_t)$, where $\mathcal{A}$ has not queried $\mathsf{corrupt}(C)$ and $\mathsf{corrupt}(\mathsf{S}_1)$, F_1 in $\mathsf{msg}_1^* = \langle ID_C, C, D, E_1, F_1 \rangle$ is replaced with a random element in the group $\mathbb{G}$.

Like the experiment P_9, we have

Claim 10. If the decisional Diffie-Hellman (DDH) problem is hard over $\{\mathbb{G}, q, g_1\}$, $|\mathsf{Adv}_{\mathcal{A}}^{P_9}(k) - \mathsf{Adv}_{\mathcal{A}}^{P_{10}}(k)|$ is negligible.

Experiment P_{11}: In this experiment, the simulator interacts with the adversary $\mathcal{A}$ as in experiment P_{10} except that we change the definition of the adversary's success as follows: (1) If the adversary queries $\mathsf{Send}(\mathsf{S}_1, j, C, \mathsf{msg}_C)$ oracle to a fresh client instance C^i for adversarially-generated $\mathsf{msg}_C = \langle ID_C, A' \rangle$ where $A' = g_1^{r'} g_2^{\mathsf{pw}'_C}$, which results in $T' = g_2^{H(S')}$ where $h' = H(ID_C, A', C', D')$, $S' = (E'/C'^{r'})^{h'-1}, T' = (F'/D'^{r'})^{h'-1}$ and C', D', E', F' are generated by t honest servers and the honest gateway according the protocol, the simulator halts and the adversary succeeds (let Succ_1 denote this event); (2) If the adversary ever queries $\mathsf{Send}(C, i, \mathsf{msg}_S)$ oracle to a fresh client instance C^i for adversarially-generated $\mathsf{msg}_S = \langle ID_C, C', D', E', F' \rangle$, which results in $\mathsf{acc}_C^i = \mathsf{TRUE}$, the simulator halts and the adversary succeeds (let Succ_2 denote this event); Otherwise the adversary's success is determined as in experiment P_{10}.

The distribution on the adversary's view in experiments P_{10} and P_{11} are identical up to the point when either Succ_1 or Succ_2 occurs. If both Succ_1 and Succ_2 never occur, the distributions on the view are identical. Therefore, we have

Claim 11. $\mathsf{Adv}_{\mathcal{A}}^{P_{10}}(k) \leq \mathsf{Adv}_{\mathcal{A}}^{P_{11}}(k)$.

Remark. The modified definition of security takes into account the attack where the adversary attempts to plant a different secret into the user's mind than the secret that he stored earlier.

In experiment P_{11}, msg_C, msg_1, msg_1^* in Execute and Send oracles have become independent of the password pw_C used by the client C and the secret s_C and $g_2^{H(s_C)}$ in the view of the adversary $\mathcal{A}$, if $\mathcal{A}$ has not require $\mathsf{Corrupt}(C)$ and $\mathsf{Corrupt}(\mathsf{S}_1)$. In view of this, any off-line dictionary attack cannot succeed.

The adversary $\mathcal{A}$ succeeds only if one of the following occurs: (1) Succ_1 occurs; (2) Succ_2 occurs; (3) neither Succ_1 nor Succ_2 occurs, the adversary wins the game by a Test query to a fresh instance C^i.

To evaluate $\Pr[\mathsf{Succ}_1]$ and $\Pr[\mathsf{Succ}_2]$, we consider three cases as follows.

Case 1. The adversary $\mathcal{A}$ forges $\mathsf{msg}'_C = \langle ID_C, A' \rangle$ where $A' = g_1^{r'} g_2^{\mathsf{pw}'_C}$ by choosing his own r' from $\mathbb{Z}_q^*$ and pw'_C from the dictionary D. In this case, if Succ_1 occurs, the adversary can conclude that the password used by the client is pw'_C. Therefore, the probability $\Pr[\mathsf{Succ}_1] = Q_1(k)/N$, where $Q_1(k)$ denotes the number of queries to $\mathsf{Send}(S_1, j, C, \mathsf{msg}_C)$ oracle.

Case 2. Given $\mathsf{msg}_C = \langle ID_C, A \rangle$, the adversary $\mathcal{A}$ forges $\mathsf{msg}_S = \langle ID_C, C', D', E', F' \rangle$ by choosing his own s', c', d' from $\mathbb{Z}_q^*$ and pw'_C from the dictionary D and computing $C' = g_1^{c'}, D' = g_1^{d'}, E' = g_2^{s'h'}(Ag_2^{\mathsf{pw}'_C})^{c'}, F' = g_2^{H(g_2^{s'})h'}(Ag_2^{\mathsf{pw}'_C})^{d'}$ where $h' = H(ID_C, A, C', D')$. When $\mathsf{pw}_C = \mathsf{pw}'_C$, we have $\mathsf{acc}_C^i = \mathsf{TRUE}$. Therefore, in this case, the probability $\Pr[\mathsf{Succ}_2] = Q_2(k)/N$, where $Q_2(k)$ denotes the number of queries to $\mathsf{Send}(C, i, \mathsf{msg}_S)$ oracle.

Case 3. Given $\mathsf{msg}_C = \langle ID_C, A \rangle$, the adversary $\mathcal{A}$ forwards msg_C to t servers twice to get two responses $\mathsf{msg}_S = \langle ID_C, C, D, E, F \rangle$ and $\mathsf{msg}'_S = \langle ID_C, C', D', E', F' \rangle$. Then the adversary $\mathcal{A}$ sends to the client a forged message $\mathsf{msg}_S = \langle ID_C, C'/C, D'/D, g_2^{s^*h^*}E'/E, g_2^{H(g_2^{s^*}h^*)}F'/F \rangle$, where $E'/E = g_1^{s(h'-h)}(C'/C)^r$, $F'/F = g_1^{H(g_1^s)(h'-h)}(D'/D)^r$, $h = H(ID_C, A, C, D)$, $h' = H(ID_C, A, C', D')$, $h^* = H(ID_C, A, C'/C, D'/D)$ and s^* is chosen from $\mathbb{Z}_q^*$ by the adversary. The client accepts msg_S if and only if $h' = h$. Because H is a collision-resistant hash function, the probability $\Pr[\mathsf{Succ}_2]$ is negligible in this case.

In summary, $\Pr[\mathsf{Succ}_1 \vee \mathsf{Succ}_2] = Q(k)/N$, where $Q(k)$ denotes the number of on-line attacks.

In experiment P_{11}, the adversary's probability of success when neither Succ_1 nor Succ_2 occurs is $1/2$. The preceding discussion implies that

$$Pr_{\mathcal{A}}^{P_{11}}[\mathsf{Succ}] \leq Q(k)/N + 1/2 \cdot (1 - Q(k)/N)$$

and thus the adversary's advantage in experiment P_{11}

$$\begin{aligned}
\mathsf{Adv}_{\mathcal{A}}^{P_{11}}(k) &= 2Pr_{\mathcal{A}}^{P_{11}}[\mathsf{Succ}] - 1 \\
&\leq 2Q(k)/N + 1 - Q(k)/N - 1 \\
&= Q(k)/N
\end{aligned}$$

The sequence of claims proved above show that

$$\mathsf{Adv}_{\mathcal{A}}^{P_0}(k) \leq \mathsf{Adv}_{\mathcal{A}}^{P_{11}}(k) + \varepsilon(k) \leq Q(k)/N + \varepsilon(k)$$

for some negligible function $\varepsilon(\cdot)$. This completes the proof of the theorem.

References

1. Bagherzandi, A., Jarecki, S., Saxena, N., Lu, Y.: Password-protected secret sharing. In: ACM CCS 2011, pp. 433–444 (2011)

2. Bellare, M., Pointcheval, D., Rogaway, P.: Authenticated key exchange secure against dictionary attacks. In: Eurocrypt 2000, pp. 139–155 (2000)
3. Brainard, J., Juels, A., Kaliski, B., Szydlo, M.: Nightingale: a new two-server approach for authentication with short secrets. In: 12th USENIX Security Symposium, pp. 201–213 (2003)
4. Camenisch, J., Lysyanskaya, A., Neven, G.: Practical yet universally composable two-server password-authenticated secret sharing. In: ACM CCS 2012, pp. 525–536 (2012)
5. Camenisch, J., Lysyanskaya, A., Lysyanskaya, A., Neven. G.: Memento: How to reconstruct your secrets from a single password in a hostile environment. In: Crypto 2014, pp. 256–275 (2014)
6. Diffie, W., Hellman, M.: New directions in cryptography. IEEE Trans. Inf. Theory **32**(2), 644–654 (1976)
7. ElGamal, T.: A public-key cryptosystem and a signature scheme based on discrete logarithms. IEEE Trans. Inf. Theory **31**(4), 469–472 (1985)
8. Ford, W., Kaliski, B.S.: Server-assisted generation of a strong secret from a password. In: 5th IEEE International Workshop on Enterprise Security (2000)
9. Jablon, D.: Password authentication using multiple servers. In: CT-RSA 2001, pp. 344–360 (2001)
10. Katz, J., Ostrovsky, R., Yung, M.: Efficient password-authenticated key exchange using human-memorable passwords. In: Eurocrypt 2001, pp. 457–494 (2001)
11. Katz, J., MacKenzie, P., Taban, G., Gligor, V.: Two-server password-only authenticated key exchange. In: ACNS 2005, pp. 1–16 (2005)
12. MacKenzie, P., Shrimpton, T., Jakobsson, M.: Threshold password-authenticated key exchange. J. Cryptol. **19**(1), 27–66 (2006)
13. Di Raimondo, M., Gennaro, R.: Provably secure threshold password-authenticated key exchange. J. Comput. Syst. Sci. **72**(6), 978–1001 (2006)
14. RSA, The Security Division of EMC: New RSA innovation helps thwart "smash-and-grab" credential theft. Press release (2012)
15. Shamir, A.: How to share a secret. Commun. ACM **22**(11), 612–613 (1979)
16. Yi, X., Ling, S., Wang, H.: Efficient two-server password-only authenticated key exchange. IEEE Trans. Parallel Distrib. Syst. **24**(9), 1773–1782 (2013)
17. Yi, X., Hao, F., Bertino, E.: ID-based two-server password-authenticated key exchange. In: ESORICS 2014, pp. 257–276 (2014)

On Security of Content-Based Video Stream Authentication

Swee-Won Lo$^{(\boxtimes)}$, Zhuo Wei, Robert H. Deng, and Xuhua Ding

School of Information Systems,
Singapore Management University, Singapore, Singapore
{sweewon.lo.2009,robertdeng,xhding}@smu.edu.sg

Abstract. Content-based authentication (CBA) schemes are used to authenticate multimedia streams while allowing content-preserving manipulations such as bit-rate transcoding. In this paper, we survey and classify existing transform-domain CBA schemes for videos into two categories, and point out that in contrary to CBA for images, there exists a common design flaw in these schemes. We present the principles (based on video coding concept) on how the flaw can be exploited to mount semantic-changing attacks in the transform domain that cannot be detected by existing CBA schemes. We show attack examples including content removal, modification and insertion attacks. Noting that these CBA schemes are designed at the macroblock level, we discuss, from the attacker's point of view, the conditions in attacking content-based authenticated macroblocks.

Keywords: Content-based authentication · Attack · H.264/AVC

1 Introduction

Video editing tools widely used for synthesizing videos are often being used to maliciously manipulate content of videos for commercial or political purposes, or with the intention to evade law (e.g. surveillance streams). Without an authentication mechanism in place, both the sending and receiving entities could not verify the integrity of a video transmitted through open and insecure networks.

There are two general approaches for multimedia authentication [36], namely Cryptographic-Based Authentication (CrBA) and Content-Based Authentication (CBA). As its name suggests, CrBA schemes (e.g. [8,43]) use cryptographic techniques such as hash function and digital signature algorithm to compute authentication data for the multimedia object. To verify its integrity, a verifier recomputes the hash of the object and verifies it against the digital signature. One of the shortcomings of CrBA schemes is that they are sensitive to random errors due to lossy networks; they are also unable to authenticate objects that usually undergo content-preserving manipulations such as bit-rate transcoding. A CBA scheme (e.g., [5,32,41]) authenticates the semantic meaning of a multimedia object by extracting an invariant *feature* from the object and computing

G. Pernul et al. (Eds.): ESORICS 2015, Part I, LNCS 9326, pp. 366–383, 2015.
DOI: 10.1007/978-3-319-24174-6_19

authentication data (using keyed-hash function or digital signature algorithm) on the feature. The integrity of the object can be verified as long as its feature (i.e., semantic meaning) is unchanged. Hence, CBA schemes are more error-tolerant as compared to CrBA schemes and they allow content-preserving manipulations on the object; some also have the ability to localize tampered regions.

Existing CBA schemes for videos may perform feature extraction in either the pixel, transform or bitstream domain. In this paper, we focus on transform-domain CBA schemes for the following reasons: Although pixel-domain feature extraction is robust to content-preserving manipulations and random errors, it is more computational intensive since the verifier needs to fully decode the video before verification. In retrospect, bitstream-domain feature extraction is more efficient, but it is sensitive to random errors and content-preserving manipulations; since the authentication data is embedded at the bitstream level, it also affects the video quality. Transform-domain CBA schemes are designed to trade off between efficiency, error-tolerance and video quality. In a nutshell, in a transform-domain CBA scheme, the authenticator extracts an invariant transform-domain feature and computes the authentication data, which is embedded back to the video as a watermark. During verification, a verifier extracts feature from the received video, and verifies it against the extracted authentication data (i.e., watermark). Thus, both feature extraction and watermark extraction are pivotal in a CBA scheme to ensure that a video can be securely authenticated.

It is worth noting that earlier work on CBA first focused on the authentication of still images. For example in [2] and [11], the CBA scheme extracts and authenticates feature from the transform coefficients of JPEG and JPEG 2000 images, respectively. These schemes have been proven to be highly efficient and are able to detect semantic-changing attacks. Since video is a sequence of frames, and each frame is essentially a still image, many existing CBA schemes for video adopt a similar design convention as that for images. The work of [5,14,32], for example, extract a transform-domain feature from the frame's coefficients (hereinafter called the *payload*), and show that the feature can detect semantic-changing attacks while remain unchanged under bit-rate transcoding. For applications such as surveillance videos that may lose vital details if transcoded, the work of [10,25] extract a fragile feature from the frame *header* and show that both semantic-changing attacks and bit-rate transcoding cause an avalanche change on the header parameters that inevitably destroys the feature.

The work of [7] summarizes three most common security problems in CBA schemes for images, namely undetected modifications, information leakage and protocol weakness. For example, in [9], the authors point out that due to independent pixel-/block-wise feature and watermark extraction, the schemes in [37] and [40] are vulnerable to *collage attacks*; an attacker can swap pixels or blocks within an image (or among database of images authenticated using the same secret key) to produce a counterfeit image. To thwart this attack, [18] proposes to extract feature from one block and embed its watermark into another randomly selected block. However, due to information leakage in watermark generation, the secret block relationship graph can be exposed by an attacker [3]. A similar flaw in [16,17] has also been exploited by [38] to expose the secret relationship graph via a *verification device attack* [7]. While there are many studies on security of CBA schemes for images, not many have been done for videos. To the best of our knowledge, the work that addresses security of CBA schemes for video is that of [34], where a flaw in watermark generation in [28] is identified.

The main focus of this paper is to study the security of existing transform-domain CBA schemes as a mean to integrity-protect videos transmitted through open and insecure network. We first survey and categorize existing transform-domain CBA schemes into two categories, namely header- and payload-protected CBA schemes, and we point out a common design flaw in these schemes: the transform-domain feature extracted and authenticated in these schemes is insufficient to securely authenticate a video. We note that while both categories of schemes are able to detect semantic-changing attacks performed in the pixel domain, they are unable to detect attacks performed in the transform domain. We show that unlike images, where the payload (coefficients) represent its overall semantic meaning, the payload and the header of a video have a strong inter-dependency relationship. This relationship, when maliciously exploited, changes the semantic meaning of the final, decoded video to a similar effect as attacks in the pixel domain, and these attacks cannot be detected by the CBA schemes. We discuss the ways that the relationship can be exploited and we show several attack examples (some of which were given in [19]). Finally, we discuss in depth the attacks that manipulate the header of a video, and the conditions of the attack, given the attacker's desired attack content. Note that although our attacks are performed on H.264/AVC-encoded videos, they are also applicable to CBA-protected videos encoded by other standards such as MPEG-2, MPEG-4 and H.264/SVC due to the same underlying video coding concept.

2   The H.264 Video Coding Standard

Most video coding standards including MPEG-2, MPEG-4 and H.264 achieve compression by identifying similarities in the spatial (within frame) and the temporal (between frames) dimensions. In the H.264 standard, a prediction model takes as input a raw video frame and outputs a residual frame. The raw frame is first partitioned into units (each of size 16×16 pixels) called macroblocks, which may be further partitioned into 16 (4×4)-blocks. Given a raw macroblock Ori, the prediction model searches for the most perceptually similar macroblock within a *searchable region*, i.e., neighbouring macroblocks in the same frame (intra prediction) or in adjacent frames (inter-prediction), and uses the most similar macroblock as reference to generate a prediction macroblock Pred. The prediction macroblock is (pixel-wise) subtracted from the raw macroblock to obtain the residual macroblock Res as in (1). The residual macroblock is then transformed, quantized and entropy encoded to the bitstream domain.

Figure 1 shows the syntax of a H.264 macroblock. In this figure, parameter *type* indicates whether the macroblock is intra- or inter-predicted.

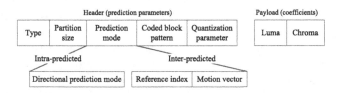

Fig. 1. The syntax elements of a H.264 macroblock.

Each (intra/inter) macroblock can be partitioned into sub-blocks of different sizes, which is conveyed by the parameter *partition size*. For an intra macroblock, *prediction mode* conveys the Directional Prediction Mode (DPM) indicating the location of reference macroblock(s) and the method of generating prediction macroblock; for an inter macroblock, this parameter conveys the reference frame index pointing to a previously-decoded frame and the Motion Vector (MV) indicating the displacement of the reference macroblocks from the raw macroblock. *Coded Block Pattern* (CBP) indicates the existence of non-zero coefficients in the macroblock, followed by the *Quantization parameter* (QP). We collectively refer these prediction parameters as the macroblock *header*. The quantized luma and chroma coefficients are referred to as the macroblock *payload*.

At the decoder, the decoded macroblock Dec is obtained as in (2) after reconstructing the prediction macroblock Pred* (using the macroblock header) and the residual macroblock Res* (using the macroblock payload). Note that for a non-tampered macroblock, the quantity α is due to lossy compression and is negligible, and Dec is perceptually similar to Ori. We can also observe an interdependent relationship between the macroblock header and payload from (2).

$$\text{Encoder: } \mathsf{Res} = \mathsf{Ori} - \mathsf{Pred} \tag{1}$$
$$\text{Decoder: } \mathsf{Dec} = \mathsf{Pred}^* + \mathsf{Res}^* = \mathsf{Ori} + \alpha \tag{2}$$

In the next section, we show the attacks that can be performed on each category by exploiting the relationship between macroblock header and its payload.

3 Common Design Flaw in Existing Content-Based Video Authentication Schemes

We describe a generic CBA model which is followed by most of the CBA schemes in the literature and classify existing schemes based on the domain of feature extraction in Sects. 3.1 and 3.2, respectively. The design flaw of the CBA schemes is described in detail in Sect. 3.3 and we show how the flaw can be exploited to achieve semantic-changing attacks without being detected by the CBA schemes.

3.1 Content-Based Authentication Model

A transform-domain CBA scheme for video works at the *macroblock* level, in compatible with video coding standards such as MPEG-2, MPEG-4 and H.264

370 S.-W. Lo et al.

that use block-based coding. Given a macroblock in the transform domain, a CBA scheme first identifies the feature extraction domain and the prediction parameter(s) or coefficients to extract feature F from. The feature F, together with the authenticator's private key sk, serve as inputs to the feature authentication phase that outputs a watermark W_F. In the watermark embedding phase, a different secret key k is used to identify a set of embedding locations and W_F is embedded into the macroblock following a set of embedding rules. The watermarked macroblock is then entropy encoded into a bitstream and transmitted to a verifier. Upon receiving the bitstream, the verifier performs entropy-decoding and watermark extraction by identifying the extraction domain, locations and extraction rules to output the watermark W_F. The verifier then performs the same feature extraction operation to output a feature F' of the macroblock and verifies it against W_F using the authenticator's public key pk (which corresponds to the authenticator's private key sk) in the feature verification phase. Upon successful verification, the verifier proceeds to decode the macroblock.

3.2 Classification of Existing Schemes

We classify existing CBA schemes for video into two categories, namely payload- and header-protected CBA schemes.

Payload-Protected Schemes. Payload-protected schemes extract and authenticate a feature from the macroblock payload (i.e., coefficients) that is able to detect semantic-changing attacks and survive bit-rate transcoding. The watermark computed from the feature is embedded back into the coefficients in the payload, or into the prediction parameters in the header. For embedding into payload, the rule of evaluating LSB [5,32,35,41], zero/non-zero coefficients [42] or energy relationship between coefficients [4,35] are used, whereas for embedding into header, the rule of evaluating LSB [14,28] of MVs is used.

Header-Protected Schemes. In the work of [10,25], a feature is extracted, respectively, from the DPMs of intra frames and the partition sizes of macroblocks. Their schemes are shown to reliably detect semantic-changing attacks as well as unauthorized bit-rate transcoding due to the fragile nature of header parameters. The watermark is embedded into the payload using the LSB evaluation rule due to limited embedding capacity in the header.

Remark. We note that there are several CBA schemes that extract feature from the payload *and* motion vectors [15,30,41] in the header. For clarity sake, we do not classify them but as we will discuss and show in the remainder of the paper, almost all prediction parameters in the header have interdependent relationship with the payload that can be exploited to achieve semantic-changing attacks; these schemes are still susceptible to our attacks in the transform domain.

3.3   The Design Flaw and Its Exploitation

The common flaw of existing transform-domain CBA schemes is that the feature extracted is insufficient to truly represent the video semantic. This is because they did not take into account the interdependent relationship between prediction parameters in the macroblock header with the coefficients in the macroblock payload. By exploiting this relationship, attacks performed in the transform domain can not only change the video semantic, they are also undetectable by the CBA schemes.

Exploiting the Flaw in Payload-Protected Schemes. Unlike images where image pixels were directly transformed and quantized [31], a video's macroblock coefficients convey the *relationship* between the macroblock pixel content and its prediction macroblock, i.e., the residual macroblock Res. If an attacker finds an *attack prediction macroblock* Pred' to replace the *original prediction macroblock* Pred*, the targeted macroblock Dec could be modified to the attacker's desired attack macroblock Dec' (see (2)). Hereafter, we base our discussion at the (4 × 4)-block level since it is the smallest coding unit.

To find an attack prediction block, an attacker proceeds as follow. Firstly, identify the "searchable region" and the candidate reference blocks that generate the suitable Pred' to obtain Dec'. In intra-prediction, the searchable region is the four neighbouring blocks (left, above-and-to-the-left, above, and above-and-to-the-right of) the targeted block whereas in inter-prediction, the searchable region is within an area centering on the targeted block [44]. To replace Pred* with Pred', modify the *prediction mode* (e.g., DPM, MV and reference frame index) of the targeted block Dec.

Depending on the video content, it is possible that a suitable Pred' is unavailable. If so, a workaround that indirectly modifies the residual block Res without being detected by payload-protected schemes can be performed using the effect of QP. At the encoder, a larger QP in forward quantization removes insignificant coefficients. At the decoder, given a set of coefficients, a larger QP in inverse quantization magnifies the residual samples whereas a smaller QP suppresses the samples. If a decoder receives a corrupted QP, inverse quantization results in a different set of coefficients that may misrepresent the residual samples in Res. Note that this cannot be detected by payload-protected schemes because the magnifying/suppressing happens during the decoding process, which is only executed *after* integrity verification. Having different QPs across macroblocks in a frame is not uncommon; macroblock-layer rate control in H.264 has been proven to improve coding efficiency [21] whereas earlier standards (e.g., MPEG-4) and the H.264 High Profile allow different QPs for DC and AC coefficients [6,27].

If the targeted macroblock spans across targeted and non-targeted content, it is more complicated to modify its prediction mode because the attacker needs to find a suitable attack prediction macroblock of the same size that changes only the targeted content while keeping the non-targeted content intact. By modifying the macroblock *partition size*, the targeted macroblock can be partitioned into sub-blocks, such that the targeted content is isolated in a sub-block, and then perform a search for the suitable attack prediction sub-block thereof.

Remarks. Attacks on payload-protected schemes involve replacing the original prediction block with an attack prediction block in order to change the content of a targeted block. Given the searchable region which is constrained in one frame (intra frames) or within the same video (inter frames), arbitrary content insertion attacks cannot be realized. However, content removal and modification attacks are possible as will be shown in Sect. 4. We also note that prediction mode parameters such as DPM, MV and reference frame index are coded differentially between successive blocks. If these parameters are changed, it may affect the corresponding parameter of subsequent (targeted/non-targeted) blocks, causing them to use a wrong/different prediction block for decoding. This may result in error propagation that occur in the form of visual distortion on the decoded frame. In Sect. 4, we show an example of such error propagation, and show that the visual distortion can be corrected to a certain degree by either restoring the prediction mode of affected blocks, or by restricting their choice of prediction block to a more suitable one.

Exploiting the Flaw in Header-Protected Schemes. Although header-protected schemes can detect both content-preserving and semantic-changing manipulations, they are more insecure compared to payload-protected schemes. Since the payload represents the residual block with samples that are integers ranging from -255 to $+255$, an attacker can perform a simple but powerful attack using reverse engineering. Since the verifier has no prior information about the original block, an attacker can replace them with a new block with different content Dec$'$ and compute the new residual block Res$'$ such that Res$' =$ Dec$' -$ Pred, where Pred is the original prediction block. The attacker then performs forward transform and quantization to obtain a new set of transform coefficients, replacing the original coefficients in the payload.

Complying with Watermark Extraction. Apart from ensuring that the transform-domain attacks do not alter the authenticated feature, it is also vital to ensure that the tampered data obeys the watermark extraction rule. Watermark extraction includes: extract location identification and extraction based on extraction rules. Although random extraction locations is deemed vital for security reason [22], we argue that it is more important for copyright protection where the attack objective is to find and destroy the watermark; a successful attack in our approach depends more heavily on complying with the watermark extraction rules. For verification efficiency, existing CBA schemes perform extraction by evaluating either the LSB or zero/non-zero coefficients as mentioned in Sect. 3.2. Such characteristics can always be engineered in the coefficients or MVs. Since DPMs can be categorized into sets generating similar prediction blocks [24], an attacker can select DPMs within the same set to satisfy the even/odd evaluation.

4   Attack Examples on Existing CBA Schemes

In this section, we demonstrate transform-domain attack examples[1] that can be applied on each category of CBA schemes as discussed in Sect. 3.3. More specifically, we show content removal and content modification attacks on payload-protected schemes, and content insertion attack on header-protected schemes. Our attacks are implemented using the JM reference software [12]. We emulate the attacker's interception and replacement of macroblock stream by modifying the decoder's 'read' data. The video sequences used in our attacks are the 352 × 288 News, Bridge and Waterfall sequences [1] and a 384 × 288 surveillance sequence [33], all encoded in IBBBBBBBP format with QP = 28 for intra frames and QP = 30 for inter frames.

4.1   Content Removal Attacks

A content removal attack is the act of replacing an object with its background information.

Figure 2a, b, c, d, and e show the first five frames of the original News sequence, where Fig. 2a is an intra frame and Fig. 2b, c, d, and e are inter frames. The aim of the attack is to remove content of the targeted blocks, i.e., the ballerina, by finding new attack prediction blocks such that the end result is a set of attacked blocks that convey the background information, i.e., the walls. Notice that in Fig. 2a, the targeted blocks are surrounded by reference blocks conveying similar content, i.e., the walls. This is an example where the attack prediction blocks *are* the original prediction blocks and it implies that the samples in the (targeted) residual blocks have high magnitude since they do not have similar prediction blocks to be used for compression (see (1)). Hence, the workaround by manipulating QP of the targeted blocks to suppress their residual samples is executed. Subsequently, if necessary, the DPMs of the targeted blocks (e.g., torso of the ballerina) are modified to use background blocks as attack prediction blocks.

Since intra frames are used as (one of the) reference frame(s) to generate prediction blocks for the subsequent inter frames, the content of the attacked intra frame will "propagate" to the inter frames during decoding. The residuals of the original content in inter frames were completely removed by modifying the MV of targeted blocks in the inter frames. The final result of the removal attack is shown in Fig. 2f, g, h, i, and j.

Due to differential coding of prediction mode parameters, there is a risk of error propagation after one is manipulated. Figure 3a shows an example of error propagation due to erroneous DPM decoding in an intra frame, which is resolved by correcting the DPM of the affected block(s) to use a *more* suitable prediction block for decoding. The result of this correction is shown in Fig. 3b.

There are also cases where QP manipulation is not needed. Figure 4a shows the first frame of the Bridge sequence. In this example, it is sufficient to modify

---

[1] Source files can be viewed at https://sites.google.com/site/smusvc/Authentication.

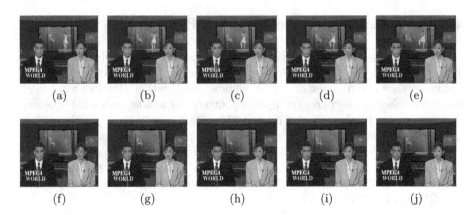

Fig. 2. Content removal attack on News sequence, with the original frames shown in (a)–(e) and attack frames in (f)–(j).

(a) Distorted frame   (b) Corrected frame

Fig. 3. An example of visual distortion due to DPM decoding error and its corrected version.

(a) Original frame   (b) Attacked frame

Fig. 4. Content removal attack on Bridge sequence.

the DPMs of targeted blocks, i.e., the left pier, to use the background information, i.e., the river, as attack prediction blocks. The result of the removal attack is shown in Fig. 4b. In this case, QP manipulation is not needed because the original prediction blocks are obtained from the top of the targeted blocks and they are semantically similar, thus, the residual blocks have samples of small magnitude. Replacing the original prediction blocks with the attack prediction blocks on the left (i.e., the river) replaces the content of the targeted blocks with the content of the attack prediction blocks.

(a) Original frame   (b) Attacked frame

Fig. 5. Content replacement attack on Waterfall sequence.

(a) Original frame   (b) Original timing   (c) Attacked timing

Fig. 6. Content replacement attack on a surveillance sequence.

4.2   Content Modification Attacks

In this subsection, we show two examples of content modification attacks on payload-protected schemes that includes content replacement and content relocation attacks.

Content replacement is the act of replacing (or "overwriting") the content of a targeted block with that of its desired attack block. In our first example, we perform content replacement attack on the intra frame of the Waterfall sequence. As shown in Fig. 5, the DPMs of a large set of targeted blocks are modified to "extend" the effect of attack prediction blocks, i.e., the trees, such that they cover the original blocks, i.e., the waterfall.

In the second example, the reference frame index is modified to achieve content replacement in inter frames. In addition, the partition size parameter is also modified to facilitate the attack. Figure 6b shows the timing information extracted from a surveillance frame in Fig. 6a. This timing information is encoded using 16×16 macroblocks, where the upper half of each macroblock covers the timing information (targeted) while the lower half covers the surveillance background (non-targeted). Tampering with the reference frame index will affect *both* the timing information and the surveillance background. By manipulating the *partition size* parameter such that each targeted 16×16 macroblock is partitioned into sixteen 4×4 blocks, the targeted content is isolated from the non-targeted content. The reference frame index of the targeted blocks can then be modified independently without affecting the non-targeted blocks. Figure 6c shows the result of this attack; when the attacked frames are inserted into the video sequence, a scrambled timing information is observed.

(a) Original frame   (b) Tampered frame

Fig. 7. Content relocation attack on a surveillance sequence.

Fig. 8. Content insertion attack on header-protected CBA schemes.

Content relocation is the act of changing the position of an object from one location to another. This attack is typically difficult to achieve on intra frames because each intra block is predicted from its neighbouring blocks; to perform a meaningful content relocation that is affected by, and will be affecting, neighbouring blocks is intuitively hard. For an inter block, however, this attack can be achieved by modifying the MV using a concept similar to content removal. Figure 7a shows a frame extracted from the surveillance sequence. In this attack, the MVs of the targeted blocks, i.e., the dustbin, are modified such that they use a new content, i.e., the man, as attack prediction blocks. Subsequently, the blocks containing the man is removed using the content removal attack methodology presented in the previous subsection. The result of this attack is shown in Fig. 7b.

4.3   Content Insertion Attacks

For completeness, we show an example of content insertion attack on header-protected schemes since this attack is not possible on payload-protected schemes. Figure 8 shows an example of content insertion attack on header-protected CBA schemes, where the original frame is shown in Fig. 6a. Taking the samples of arbitrary image of a clock, the residual blocks are obtained by subtracting the original prediction blocks from the samples. The residual blocks are then transformed and quantized, and inserted into the macroblock payload.

4.4   Summary and Remarks

In summary, we showed that contrary to images, the video header and payload must be simultaneously integrity protected since their interdependency relationship can be exploited by attacks performed in the transform domain. For attacks on payload-protected schemes, DPM, MV and reference frame index affect the generation of prediction block, which when combined with the residual block could semantically change the targeted block. While DPM selects prediction blocks from neighbouring blocks, MV and reference frame index select them from a wider search range. An advanced attacker may modify the macroblock type (intra/inter) and remove or insert bogus prediction mode relevant to the new macroblock type; we leave attacks of such nature as future work. Additionally, the QP is a header parameter that can be used as a workaround to inexplicitly modify the residual block while the partition size can be modified to facilitate search for a suitable prediction block. For attacks on header-protected schemes, it is vital that the distribution of tampered coefficients tallies with the coded block pattern (CBP) in the header, otherwise a decoding error may occur. We acknowledge that authenticating the CBP in the header will impose a higher level of difficulty on the attacks, however, in existing header-protected schemes, this parameter is often left unprotected. In the literature, there are also CBA schemes that authenticate both the payload and the MVs in the header [15,30,41]. However, as we have shown in our attack examples, these schemes are still vulnerable to attacks such as DPM attacks on intra blocks, reference frame index and/or partition size attacks on inter blocks.

We also note some interesting observations on H.264/SVC - the scalable extension of H.264/AVC that is used to encode the sequences used in this study. In SVC, a mandatory base layer (BL) that is backward compatible with AVC is encoded. Using BL as reference to generate prediction, one or more enhancement layers (ELs) that gradually improve the resolution or quality of the video are encoded. If header-protected CBA schemes are applied on an SVC stream, attacks on the payload of BL and ELs are possible (and powerful). On the other hand, if coefficients-protected CBA schemes are applied, our attacks are applicable to the BL and the effect could propagate to the ELs. Thus, noting the importance of the BL, the work of [36] cryptographically protects the BL to prevent any form of malicious tampering[2]. Although there are minimal header parameters in the ELs [29], we observe the following important parameters, e.g., the *motion prediction flag* and *residual prediction flag*. For the ELs, a motion prediction flag of '1' indicates that the EL directly uses header parameters of its reference (base) layer; otherwise, it carries its own header parameters. A residual prediction flag of '1', on the other hand, indicates that the EL's payload R'_{EL} is obtained by subtracting the upsampled BL payload R_{BL} from the payload obtained via AVC-like encoding R_{EL}; otherwise, $R'_{EL} = R_{EL}$. An advanced attacker could then opt to modify these flags and to manipulate the video semantic. In short, content-based authentication for SVC present several interesting research problems to be explored.

---

[2] Pixel-domain CBA scheme is used in [36] to protect the ELs and thus is out of the scope of study for this paper.

5   Discussions

We have shown that semantic-changing attacks on videos authenticated by payload- or header-protected CBA schemes are possible by modifying, respectively, the header or the payload of the targeted block(s). Moreover, these attacks cannot be detected by the respective CBA schemes.

Since the attacks on header-protected schemes are relatively straightforward, we focus the following discussions on the attacks on *payload-protected schemes*. As shown in Sect. 4, a targeted block will convey a semantically different content as compared to its original content if a *suitable* attack prediction block is found from the searchable region. In this section, we analyze (from an attacker's point of view) that given the desired attack block and the unmodifiable residual block, whether it is possible for an attacker to obtain the suitable attack prediction block. Our analysis is performed on a 4×4-block level, where a macroblock M is represented as follow:

$$M = \begin{array}{|c|c|c|c|} \hline M(B_0) & M(B_1) & M(B_4) & M(B_5) \\ \hline M(B_2) & M(B_3) & M(B_6) & M(B_7) \\ \hline M(B_8) & M(B_9) & M(B_{12}) & M(B_{13}) \\ \hline M(B_{10}) & M(B_{11}) & M(B_{14}) & M(B_{15}) \\ \hline \end{array}$$

where $M(B_i)$ denotes the i-th (4×4)-block of M, and can be represented by a 4×4 matrix. Using the same convention, an original and prediction macroblock (denoted Dec and Pred respectively), are made up of $Dec(B_i)$ and $Pred(B_i)$ for $i = 0, \cdots, 15$. The list of notations is shown in Table 1.

Generally, the average value of a 4×4-block is a good approximation of the block's samples [20,23,39] due to the high correlation between samples in the block. Since the residual block may consist of positive and negative integers, we

Table 1. List of notations

Notations	Descriptions
Dec, Res, Pred	Original decoded, residual and prediction macroblock, respectively, each containing 16 4×4-blocks
Dec(B), Res(B), Pred(B)	Original decoded, residual and prediction 4×4-block, respectively
$\bar{d}(B)$, $\bar{p}(B)$	Average of the samples in Dec(B) and Pred(B), respectively
$\hat{r}(B)$	Median of residual samples in Res(B)
Dec$'$(B), Res$'$(B), Pred$'$(B)	An attack decoded, residual and prediction 4×4-block, respectively
$\bar{d}'(B)$, $\hat{r}'(B)$, $\bar{p}'(B)$	Average of the samples in Dec$'$(B), Res$'$(B), Pred$'$(B), respectively
$E(Res) = \sum_{i,j=0}^{3} \frac{r_{i,j}}{16}$	Energy of the residual samples in Res(B), where $r_{i,j}$ is the residual sample at position (i,j) in Res(B)
$\oplus$, $\ominus$	Pixel-/Sample-wise addition and subtraction, respectively

use the median of the residual samples to indicate the relationship between the original block and the original prediction block. In other words, if $\hat{r}(B) > 0$, then $\mathsf{Dec}(B)$ is perceptually brighter than $\mathsf{Pred}(B)$; otherwise, $\mathsf{Dec}(B)$ is perceptually darker than $\mathsf{Pred}(B)$. In addition, we let $\mathsf{E}(\mathsf{Res})$ be the energy of the residual samples in $\mathsf{Res}(B)$ as defined in Table 1.

Given an original (targeted) block $\mathsf{Dec}(B)$ with $\bar{d}(B)$ and the residual block $\mathsf{Res}(B)$ having a median $\hat{r}(B)$, we discuss the conditions on the desired attack block $\mathsf{Dec}'(B)$ in terms of $\bar{d}'(B)$ such that the attacker can find an attack prediction block $\mathsf{Pred}'(B)$, where $\mathsf{Dec}'(B) = \mathsf{Pred}'(B) \oplus \mathsf{Res}(B)$. The following analysis can be applied to the attacks on both intra and inter blocks.

Case 1A. When most of the residual samples are positive, i.e., $\hat{r}(B) > 0$, it implies that the original (targeted) block $\mathsf{Dec}(B)$ is perceptually brighter than the original prediction block $\mathsf{Pred}(B)$, i.e., $\bar{d}(B) > \bar{p}(B)$. If the desired attack block $\mathsf{Dec}'(B)$ is to be perceptually brighter than $\mathsf{Dec}(B)$, we say that an attacker finds an attack prediction block $\mathsf{Pred}'(B)$ if and only if $\bar{d}'(B) \geq \bar{d}(B) + 2\hat{r}(B)$.

To prove this, suppose $\bar{d}(B) < \bar{d}'(B) < \bar{d}(B) + 2\hat{r}(B)$. Substituting (2):

$$\bar{p}(B) + \hat{r}(B) < \bar{p}'(B) + \hat{r}(B) < \bar{p}(B) + \hat{r}(B) + 2\hat{r}(B)$$
$$\bar{p}(B) < \qquad \bar{p}'(B) \quad < \bar{p}(B) + 2\hat{r}(B) \qquad (3)$$

Referring to (3), we say that an attack prediction block $\mathsf{Pred}'(B)$ with $\bar{p}'(B)$ cannot be found. Otherwise, by computing $\mathsf{Res}'(B) = \mathsf{Dec}(B) \ominus \mathsf{Pred}'(B)$, the upper and lower bound of $\hat{r}'(B)$ is:

$$\hat{r}'(B)_{UB} = \bar{d}(B) - \bar{p}(B) = \hat{r}(B), \text{ and}$$
$$\hat{r}'(B)_{LB} = \bar{d}(B) - (\bar{p}(B) + 2\hat{r}(B)) = -\hat{r}(B)$$

In other words, $-\hat{r}(B) < \hat{r}'(B) < \hat{r}(B)$. This implies that compared to the original prediction block $\mathsf{Pred}(B)$, the attack prediction block $\mathsf{Pred}'(B)$ generates smaller residual samples if it is used to encode $\mathsf{Dec}(B)$. This contradicts the video coding rule, where $\mathsf{Pred}(B)$ is initially chosen to encode $\mathsf{Dec}(B)$ because it generates the smallest Sum of Absolute Errors, $\mathsf{SAE} = \sum_{i,j=0}^{3} |d_{i,j} - p_{i,j}|$, where $d_{i,j}$ is the sample of $\mathsf{Dec}(B)$ at position (i,j) and $p_{i,j}$ is the sample of $\mathsf{Pred}(B)$ at position (i,j), compared to all other candidate prediction blocks in the searchable region [27]. This case can be demonstrated in the attack shown in Fig. 4b. If $\mathsf{Pred}'(B)$ cannot be found, the workaround by manipulating QP can be implemented to suppress the residual samples so that the available candidate prediction blocks can be used to obtain $\mathsf{Dec}'(B)$.

Case 1B. When most of the residual samples are positive, i.e., $\hat{r}(B) > 0$, but the desired attack block $\mathsf{Dec}'(B)$ is to be perceptually darker than the original block $\mathsf{Dec}(B)$, then the minimum value for a sample $d'_{i,j}$ in $\mathsf{Dec}'(B)$ must be equal to the residual sample $r_{i,j}$ in $\mathsf{Res}(B)$. This is because the minimum sample for $\mathsf{Dec}'(B)$ is when $\mathsf{Pred}'(B) = 0$ (see (2)), otherwise, if $\bar{d}'(B) < \hat{r}(B)$, then by substituting (2),

Table 2. Summary of Cases 1A, 1B, 2A and 2B.

	$\hat{r}(\mathsf{B}) > 0$	$\hat{r}(\mathsf{B}) < 0$
Dec'(B) is perceptually brighter than Dec(B)	**Case 1A** $\bar{d}'(\mathsf{B}) - \bar{d}(\mathsf{B}) \geq 2\hat{r}(\mathsf{B})$	**Case 2A** $\bar{d}(\mathsf{B}) < \bar{d}'(\mathsf{B}) \leq 255 - |\hat{r}(\mathsf{B})|$
Dec'(B) is perceptually darker than Dec(B)	**Case 1B** $\hat{r}(\mathsf{B}) \leq \bar{d}'(\mathsf{B}) < \bar{d}(\mathsf{B})$	**Case 2B** $\bar{d}'(\mathsf{B}) - \bar{d}(\mathsf{B}) \leq -2|\hat{r}(\mathsf{B})|$

we get $\bar{p}'(\mathsf{B}) + \hat{r}(\mathsf{B}) < \hat{r}(\mathsf{B})$ and the samples in the attack prediction block is less than zero, which is not feasible. Thus, we write, in approximation, $\hat{r}(\mathsf{B}) \leq \bar{d}'(\mathsf{B}) < \bar{d}(\mathsf{B})$. This condition is demonstrated in the attack shown in Fig. 2, where the background information (the walls) is perceptually darker than the targeted blocks (the ballerina), but the residuals samples are too large for Dec'(B) to satisfy this condition. The QP can then be manipulated to suppress/magnify the residual samples as deemed necessary.

Case 2A. When most of the residual samples are negative, i.e., $\hat{r}(\mathsf{B}) < 0$, the original block Dec(B) is perceptually darker than the original prediction block Pred(B). Suppose the desired attack block Dec'(B) is to be perceptually brighter than Dec(B), we say that a sample $d'_{i,j}$ in Dec'(B) is upper bounded by $255 - |r_{i,j}|$ in Res(B) as dictated by (2). Thus, we can write in approximation that $\bar{d}(\mathsf{B}) < \bar{d}'(\mathsf{B}) \leq 255 - |\hat{r}(\mathsf{B})|$. A similar analysis to Case 1B can be applied, where if $\bar{d}'(\mathsf{B}) > 255 - |\hat{r}(\mathsf{B})|$, then the attacker must find an attack prediction block Pred'(B) where $\bar{p}'(\mathsf{B}) > 255$, which is not possible. This condition can be observed in the attack shown in Fig. 5b.

Case 2B. When most of the residual samples are negative, i.e., $\hat{r}(\mathsf{B}) < 0$, but the desired attack block Dec'(B) is to be perceptually darker than the original block Dec(B), then we say that an attacker can find an attack prediction block Pred'(B) if and only if $\bar{d}'(\mathsf{B}) \leq \bar{d}(\mathsf{B}) - 2|\hat{r}(\mathsf{B})|$. This condition can be obtained by a similar prove by contradiction as in Case 1A, whereas an illustration example is shown in the upper torso, especially the head of the ballerina in Fig. 2a.

Table 2 summarizes the conditions for the above cases. When the attack block Dec'(B) cannot satisfy the conditions in any of the cases above, then the attacker cannot find an attack prediction block Pred'(B) such that Dec'(B) = Pred'(B) $\oplus$ Res(B). A workaround can then be performed by modifying the unprotected QP to suppress or magnify the residual samples depending on the available candidate attack prediction blocks.

6   Conclusions and Future Work

We have shown that existing content-based authentication (CBA) schemes designed for videos are insecure due to insufficient feature extraction. The overlooked interdependent relationship between the header and payload parameters can be exploited to perform semantic-changing attacks in the transform domain. We showed several semantic-changing attack examples that are performed in the transform domain and our attacks cannot be detected by the schemes. We discussed in detail the conditions at which an attack on payload-protected CBA schemes can succeed given a desired attack content and the unmodifiable payload, and if not, a workaround for it.

A possible countermeasure to our attacks is to use more complicated watermark extraction rules. However, unlike images, real-time extraction is vital for video authentication [26] which makes straight-forward watermark extraction rules such as those surveyed in this paper highly preferred. Another possible countermeasure is to extract and authenticate features from both the header and payload domains. In practical applications, transcoding requires full decoding of intra frames and partial decoding of inter frames. The transcoding of intra frames drastically changes the header and payload [13], and to the best of our knowledge, there is no work that addresses this problem. Transcoding inter frames changes the payload while the remaining data in the header remains unchanged. Although existing payload-domain schemes are able to extract a stable feature from the coefficients, but sparsely-distributed coefficients in inter frames (especially after transcoding) are commonly overlooked, thereby leaving them vulnerable to tampering. Thus far, we observed a stable feature from the header of intra frames and we are working on extracting a stable feature from the header of inter frames. Our future research is to design a secure and efficient authentication scheme that overcomes the vulnerability of existing schemes and is robust against bit-rate transcoding (performed by semi-trusted intermediary proxies) as described above.

Acknowledgement. This work was partly supported by National Natural Science Funds of China (Grant No. 61402199).

References

1. Arizona State University: Video trace library. http://trace.eas.asu.edu/index.html
2. Bianchi, T., Rosa, A.D., Piva, A.: Improved DCT coefficient analysis for forgery localization in JPEG images. In: IEEE International Conference on Acoustics, Speech and Signal Processing (ICASSP 2011), pp. 2444–2447 (2011)
3. Chang, C., Fan, Y., Tai, W.: Four-scanning attack on hierarchical digital watermarking method for image tamper detection and recovery. Pattern Recogn. **41**(2), 654–661 (2008)
4. Dai, Y., Thiemert, S., Steinebach, M.: Feature-based watermarking scheme for MPEG-I/II video authentication. In: SPIE Security, Steganography, and Watermarking of Multimedia Contents VI, vol. 5306, pp. 325–335 (2004)
5. Du, R., Fridrich, J.: Lossless authentication of MPEG-2 video. In: 2002 International Conference on Image Processing (ICIP), vol. 2, pp. II-893–II-896 (2002)
6. Ebrahimi, T., Horne, C.: MPEG-4 natural video coding - an overview. Signal Process. Image Commun. **15**(4–5), 365–385 (2000)
7. Fridrich, J.: Security of fragile authentication watermarks with localization. In: SPIE, Security and Watermarking of Multimedia Contents IV, vol. 4675, pp. 691–700 (2002)

8. Hefeeda, M., Mokhtarian, K.: Authentication schemes for multimedia streams: quantitative analysis and comparison. ACM Trans. Multimedia Comput. Commun. Appl. **6**(1), 1–24 (2010)
9. Holliman, M., Memon, N.: Counterfeiting attacks on oblivious block-wise independent invisible watermarking schemes. IEEE Trans. Image Process. **9**(3), 432–442 (2000)
10. Horng, S.J., Farfoura, M.E., Fan, P., Wang, X., Li, T., Guo, J.M.: A low cost fragile watermarking scheme in H.264/AVC compressed domain. Multimedia Tools Appl. **72**(3), 2469–2495 (2014)
11. Hu, H.T., Hsu, L.Y.: Exploring DWT-SVD-DCT feature parameters for robust multiple watermarking against JPEG and JPEG2000 compression. Comput. Electr. Eng. **41**, 52–63 (2015)
12. Joint Video Team (JVT) of ISO/IEC MPEG & ITU-T VCEG (ISO/IEC JTC1/SC29/WG11 and ITU-T SG16 Q.6).: JM Reference Software Manual (2009)
13. Kim, D., Choi, Y., Kim, H., Yoo, J., Choi, H., Seo, Y.: The problems in digital watermarking into intra-frames of H.264/AVC. Image Vis. Comput. **28**(8), 1220–1228 (2010)
14. Kuo, T.Y., Lo, Y.C., Lin, C.I.: Fragile video watermarking technique by motion field embedding with rate-distortion minimization. In: International Conference on Intelligent Information Hiding and Multimedia Signal Processing (IIHMSP), pp. 853–856 (2008)
15. Lin, C.Y., Chang, S.F.: Issues and solutions for authenticating MPEG video. In: SPIE International Conference on Security and Watermarking of Multimedia Contents, vol. 3657, pp. 54–56 (1999)
16. Lin, C.Y., Chang, S.F.: Semi-fragile watermarking for authenticating JPEG visual content. In: SPIE Security and Watermarking of Multimedia Contents, pp. 140–151 (2000)
17. Lin, C.Y., Chang, S.F.: A robust image authentication method distinguishing JPEG compression from malicious manipulation. IEEE Trans. Circuits Syst. Video Technol. **11**(2), 153–168 (2001)
18. Lin, P., Hsieh, C., Huang, P.: A hierarchical digital watermarking method for image tamper detection and recovery. Pattern Recogn. **38**(12), 2519–2529 (2005)
19. Lo, S.W., Wei, Z., Deng, R.H., Ding, X.: Generic attacks on content-based video stream authentication. In: IEEE International Conference on Multimedia and Expo Workshops (ICMEW), pp. 1–6 (2014)
20. Luo, Z., Song, L., Zheng, S., Ling, N.: H.264 advanced video control perceptual optimization coding based on JND-directed coefficient suppression. IEEE Trans. Circuits Syst. Video Technol. **23**(6), 935–948 (2013)
21. Ma, S., Gao, W., Zhao, D., Lu, Y.: A study on the quantization scheme in H.264/AVC and its application to rate control. In: Advances in Multimedia Information Processing, PCM, pp. 192–199 (2004)
22. Mansouri, A., Aznaveh, A.M., Torkamani-Azar, F., Kurugollu, F.: A low complexity video watermarking in H.264 compressed domain. IEEE Trans. Inf. Forensics Secur. **5**(4), 649–657 (2010)
23. Naccari, M., Pereira, F.: Advanced H.264/AVC-based perceptual video coding: architecture, tools and assessment. IEEE Trans. Circuits Syst. Video Technol. **21**(6), 806–819 (2011)
24. Park, J.S., Song, H.J.: Selective intra prediction mode decision for H.264/AVC encoders. World Acad. Sci. Eng. Technol. **13**, 51–55 (2006)
25. Park, S.W., Shin, S.: Authentication and copyright protection scheme for H.264/AVC and SVC. J. Inf. Sci. Eng. **27**(1), 129–142 (2011)

26. Podilchuk, C.I., Delp, E.J.: Digital watermarking: algorithms and applications. IEEE Signal Process. Mag. **18**(4), 33–46 (2001)
27. Richardson, I.E.: The H.264 Advanced Video Compression Standard, 2nd edn. Wiley, Chichester (2010)
28. Saadi, K.A., Bouridane, A., Guessoum, A.: Combined fragile watermark and digital signature for H.264/AVC video authentication. In: 17th European Signal Processing Conference, pp. 1799–1803 (2009)
29. Schwarz, H., Merpe, D., Wiegand, T.: Overview of the scalable video coding extension of the H.264/AVC standard. IEEE Trans. Circuits Syst. Video Technol. **17**(9), 1103–1120 (2007)
30. Shahabuddin, S., Iqbal, R., Shirmohammadi, S., Zhao, J.: Compressed-domain temporal adaptation-resilient watermarking for H.264 video authentication. In: IEEE International Conference on Multimedia and Expo (ICME), pp. 1752–1755 (2009)
31. Skodras, A., Christopoulos, C., Ebrahimi, T.: The JPEG 2000 still image compression standard. IEEE Signal Process. Mag. **18**(5), 36–58 (2001)
32. Sun, Q., He, D., Tian, Q.: A secure and robust authentication scheme for video transcoding. IEEE Trans. Circuits Syst. Video Technol. **16**(10), 1232–1244 (2006)
33. The CAVIAR team: EC funded CAVIAR project/IST 2001 37540. http://homepages.inf.ed.ac.uk/rbf/CAVIAR/
34. Ting, G.C., Goi, B.M., Lee, S.W.: Cryptanalysis of a fragile watermark based H.264/AVC video authentication scheme. Appl. Mech. Mater. **145**, 552–556 (2011)
35. Wang, Y., Pearmain, A.: Blind MPEG-2 video watermarking robust against geometric attacks: a set of approaches in DCT domain. IEEE Trans. Image Process. **15**(6), 1536–1543 (2006)
36. Wei, Z., Wu, Y., Deng, R., Ding, X.: A hybrid scheme for authenticating scalable video codestreams. IEEE Trans. Inf. Forensics Secur. **9**(4), 543–553 (2014)
37. Wong, P.: A watermark for image integrity and ownership verification. In: IS and TS PICS Conference, pp. 374–379 (1998)
38. Wu, Y., Xu, C.: A fault-induced attack to semi-fragile image authentiation schemes. In: SPIE on Visual Communications and Image Processing, vol. 5150, pp. 1875–1883 (2003)
39. Yang, X., Lin, W., Lu, Z., Ong, E., Yao, S.: Motion-compensated residue preprocessing in video coding based on just-noticeable-distortion profile. IEEE Trans. Circuits Syst. Video Technol. **15**(6), 742–752 (2005)
40. Yeung, M., Mintzer, F.: An invisible watermarking technique for image verification. In: International Conference on Image Processsing (ICIP), pp. 680–683 (1997)
41. Yin, P., Yu, H.H.: A semi-fragile watermarking system for MPEG video authentication. In: IEEE International Conference on Acoustics, Speech, and Signal Processing (ICASSP), vol. 4, pp. IV-3461–IV-3464 (2002)
42. Zhang, W., Zhang, R., Liu, X., Wu, C., Niu, X.: A video watermarking algorithm of H.264/AVC for content authentication. J. Networks **7**(8), 1150–1154 (2012)
43. Zhao, Y., Lo, S.W., Deng, R.H., Ding, X.: An improved authentication scheme for H.264/SVC and its performance evaluation over non-stationary wireless mobile networks. In: 6th International Conference on Network and System Security (NSS), pp. 192–206 (2012)
44. Zhao, Z., Liang, P.: A statistical analysis of H.264/AVC FME mode reduction. IEEE Trans. Circuits Syst. Video Technol. **21**(1), 53–61 (2011)

Oblivious Maximum Bipartite Matching Size Algorithm with Applications to Secure Fingerprint Identification

Marina Blanton$^{(\boxtimes)}$ and Siddharth Saraph

Department of Computer Science and Engineering, University of Notre Dame,
Notre Dame, IN, USA
{mblanton,ssaraph}@nd.edu

Abstract. The increasing availability and use of biometric data leads to situations when sensitive biometric data is to be handled by entities who may not be fully trusted or otherwise are not authorized to have full access to such data. This calls for mechanisms of provably protecting biometric data while still allowing the computation to take place. Our focus is on privacy-preserving matching of two fingerprints (authentication or identification purposes) using traditional minutia-based representation of fingerprints that leads to the most discriminative fingerprint comparisons. Unlike previous work in the security literature, we would like to focus on algorithms that are guaranteed to find the maximum number of minutiae that can be paired together between two fingerprints leading to more accurate comparisons. To address this problem, we formulate it as a flow network problem and reduce it to finding maximum matching size in bipartite graphs. The resulting problem is in turn reduced to computing the rank of a (non-invertible) matrix, formed as a randomized adjacency matrix of the bipartite graph. We then provide data-oblivious algorithms for matrix rank computation and consecutively finding maximum matching size in a bipartite graph and also extend the algorithms to solve the problem of accurate fingerprint matching. These algorithms lead to their secure counterparts using standard secure two-party or multi-party techniques. Lastly, we implement secure fingerprint matching in the secure two-party computation setting using garbled circuit evaluation. Our experimental results demonstrate that the techniques are efficient, leading to performance similar to that of other fastest secure fingerprint matching techniques, despite higher complexity of our solution that higher accuracy demands.

1 Introduction

The motivation for this work comes from the need to protect sensitive biometric data when it is being used in a growing range of applications. In particular, biometric authentication and other uses of biometric data are becoming more prevalent today in a variety of applications, which was prompted in part by recent advances in biometric recognition. Large-scale collections of biometric data in

© Springer International Publishing Switzerland 2015
G. Pernul et al. (Eds.): ESORICS 2015, Part I, LNCS 9326, pp. 384–406, 2015.
DOI: 10.1007/978-3-319-24174-6_20

use today include fingerprint, face, and iris images collected by the US Department of Homeland Security (DHS) from visitors [44]; fingerprint and iris images collected by the government of India from (more than billion) citizens [41]; iris, fingerprint, and face images collected by the United Arab Emirates (UAE) Ministry of Interior from visitors [43]; and adoption of biometric passports in several countries. It is evident that biometric authentication and identification have advantages over alternative mechanisms such as good accuracy and unforgeability of biometry. Biometric data, however, is highly sensitive and, once leaked, cannot be revoked or replaced. This calls for stringent protection of biometric data while at rest and when used in applications.

The above means that biometric data cannot be easily shared between organizations or agencies, but there are often legitimate reasons for computing with biometric data that belong to different entities. As an example, a private investigator can be interested in knowing whether a biometric she captured appears in the government's criminal database, but without disclosing the biometric if no matches are found. Similarly, two organizations or collaborating governments might want to determine which individuals, if any, appear simultaneously in their respective databases without revealing any additional information. A solution to enabling such computation while protecting privacy of the data is to employ secure multi-party computation techniques, which compute the result without disclosing any additional information.

In this work we would like to specifically treat the problem of secure computation with fingerprint data due to popularity and good accuracy of this type of biometry. We would like to cover as many settings where biometric data may used in computation by not fully trusted entities (or data sharing is restricted by law or other provisions) as possible. At the most basic level the problem is formulated as having one party A who possesses private input (fingerprint X) and another party B who possesses another private input (fingerprint Y). The parties would like to compute a function of their private inputs without disclosing any information other than the agreed-upon computation output. In the context of fingerprint matching, this can correspond to biometric authentication (comparing X and Y) and also biometric identification (when one party, e.g., B has a biometric database D and the computation consists of securely comparing X to all $Y \in D$ and identifying all biometrics that matched (if any) or determining the closest match). Another setting in which secure processing of biometric data is relevant is that of computation outsourcing by one or more data owners. In such a case, the computation still consists of comparing two biometrics to each other, but the security requirements are such that the servers that carry out the computation must learn no information about the data they process. Regardless of the setting, the core of the computation consists of comparing two fingerprints to each other, which is what we are to address. When standard secure computation techniques are used for implementing this computation, other described variants can be easily realized.

Prior literature [3,9,10,36] already contains solutions for secure fingerprint matching. All such publications introduce secure two-party computation protocols for fingerprint comparisons after feature extraction and fingerprint alignment (if any). From this list, [9,10,36] offer solutions for minutia-based representations of fingerprints, which have the most discriminative power and are the only type of fingerprint representation suitable for biometric identification. What, however, we aim in this work is improving the precision of the matching step while maintaining efficiency of the algorithm. In particular, a minutia-based fingerprint representation consists of a number of minutiae in a two-dimensional space.[1] Roughly speaking, matching of minutiae from one fingerprint with minutiae from another fingerprint consists of computing distances between the minutiae and marking two minutiae as a possible match if the corresponding distances are within certain thresholds. The next step consists of pairing points from X with "possible match" points from Y and the number of points that could be paired together determines whether the fingerprints were a match or not. A simple way to determine the pairing is to associate a point from X to the closest point from Y that has not already been paired with another point from X. A more involved algorithm (as suggested in the fingerprint literature), on the other hand, would try to find a pairing of the largest possible size, where a point from X is paired with a "possible match" point from Y, but not necessarily the closest to it. This results in more accurate matching of two fingerprints [16,24,45], but incurs higher computational cost.

The latter approach has not been explored in the security literature and requires new techniques for secure processing of the data. We note that the new techniques are necessary even if a general-purpose mechanism for securing computation (such as garbled circuits or secret sharing) are to be used. In this work, we reduce the problem to that of computing the size of the maximum flow in a bipartite graph and build techniques for solving it in secure computation context. Thus, the main contribution of this work consists of the design of a data-oblivious algorithm for maximum matching size of a bipartite graph, which proceeds by computing the rank of a randomized adjacency matrix of the graph and has complexity $O(|V|^3 \log(|V|))$. Data-oblivious execution is defined as consisting of instructions and accessing memory locations independent of the data, which makes such algorithms suitable for secure computation and outsourcing. To the best of our knowledge, data-oblivious or privacy-preserving algorithms that protect the structure of the graph for the problem of maximum matching in a flow network have been treated in the literature only for general graphs and the available algorithms have complexities $O(|V|^4)$ and higher. Beyond the application of the solution to fingerprint matching, the algorithm may be applicable to other domains and be of independent interest. When the solution is used for fingerprint matching, despite higher complexity of the algorithm than earlier

---

[1] In what follows, we refer to a single element of fingerprint representation as a minutia, which typically consists of coordinates in a two-dimensional space, orientation, and optionally minutia type. The fingerprint representation may also be expanded with additional information or extra fields associated with each minutia, which are the result of fingerprint pre-processing.

techniques, we show through experimental evaluation that the solution nevertheless offers good performance.

2   Related Work

Secure Multi-party Computation (SMC). Work on SMC was initiated by Yao's [46] who showed that any function can be securely evaluated by representing it as a boolean circuit. Since then a large number of both general and special-purpose techniques followed and their overview is beyond the scope of this work. We only mention that there are a number of tools and compilers (Fairplay [30], VIFF [14], Sharemind [13], PICCO [47], etc.) that can securely evaluate functions on private data in several settings.

Secure Computation with Biometric Data. In the context of biometric matching, results available today include work on secure face recognition ([15,35] and others), DNA matching ([7,42], and others), iris code comparisons ([8,9]), fingerprint comparisons ([3,10,36]), and speaker authentication ([1,34]). Each biometric type has a unique representation and the corresponding algorithm for comparing two biometrics, which prompted the need to design separate solutions for different biometric modalities.

The first privacy-preserving protocol for fingerprint identification is due to Barni et al. [3] who utilize the so-called FingerCode approach [23] for comparing two fingerprints and built a solution using a homomorphic encryption scheme. FingerCode-based algorithm is not as discriminative as minutia-based matching and is not suitable for biometric identification, despite offering computational advantages.

Blanton and Gasti [9,10] provide privacy-preserving protocols for both FingerCode and minutia-based fingerprint representations. Their solution utilizes homomorphic encryption and garbled circuit evaluation. To compare fingerprints X and Y consisting of m_X and m_Y minutiae, respectively, the solution in [10] proceeds by first computing the adjacency matrix of size $m_X m_Y$, which indicates which points from X and Y are a possible match. That is, the cell at row i and column j is set if the spatial (Euclidean) distance between point i in X and point j in Y as well as the difference in their orientation are within specific thresholds. Then the algorithm considers each minutia i of X in turn matching it with the closest unmatched minutia j in Y among its possible matches in the adjacency matrix. At the end, the size of the computed matching is compared to the threshold to determine whether the fingerprints are related. As mentioned earlier, this approach may fail to find the best matching for the input fingerprints, and we use it as the starting point for our solution. The protocol's complexity is $O(m_X m_Y)$.

Lastly, Shahandashti et al. [36] design a privacy-preserving protocol for minutia-based fingerprint matching using homomorphic encryption. The computation is based on evaluation of polynomials in encrypted form and a pair of minutiae $i \in X$ and $j \in Y$ are added to the matching if they are a possible match. Note that the computation introduces an error every time a minutia from X or Y has more than one possible match. The complexity of the solution is dominated by $O(m_X m_Y(|T| + |D_E| + |D_a|))$ cryptographic operations, where $|T|$ is the number of minutia types, $|D_E|$ is the number of all possible squared Euclidean distances between two points and $|D_a|$ is the number of all possible squared angular distances between point orientations. Because the complexity is quadratic in the domain size of point location values, this approach is substantially slower than others for a typical set of parameters.

Data-Oblivious Protocols. Data-oblivious algorithms and their use in secure computation are receiving an increasing amount of attention. When a data-oblivious algorithm is implemented using secure multi-party computation techniques, where each operation is properly secured, the overall algorithm is guaranteed to leak no information about the data (through its structure or accessed memory locations). In addition to advances in the performance of secure multi-party computation techniques that make performance of complex algorithms practical, the emergence of cloud computing also facilitated work on data-oblivious algorithms suitable for computation outsourcing.

To the best of our knowledge, secure data-oblivious algorithms for maximum flow have appeared in [2,12]. The complexity of the algorithm from [2] that protects the structure of the graph is $O(|V|^5)$ based on Edmonds-Karp algorithm and $O(|V|^4)$ based on Push-Relabel algorithm, where $|V|$ is the number of nodes in the graph. The oblivious algorithm proposed in [12] provides a solution of complexity $O(|V|^3 |E| \log(|V|))$ based on Ford-Fulkerson algorithm, where $|E|$ is the number of edges in the graph.

Oblivious RAM (ORAM). ORAM techniques ([19,39] and others) were designed to hide memory access patterns from the external server where the memory resides and are applicable to the secure multi-party computation framework. In our setting, they can be used to protect information about what data item needs to be read (e.g., a specific vertex or edge of the graph) and thus can be applied to make any algorithm data-oblivious. Each ORAM access (reading or writing a data block) has complexity at least $O(\log n^2)$, where n is the total memory size. ORAM constructions assume there is a single client with a small amount of trusted memory who knows what block it needs to read or write. When a non-oblivious algorithm is securely evaluated by a number of computational parties, there is no such client and it now needs to be obliviously simulated by the computational parties. Currently, there are still challenges for efficiently realizing ORAM techniques within the secure computation framework. The publications we are aware on this topic are [29] in the two-party and [25] in the multi-party settings, where the cost of a single ORAM access increases by a factor of $O(\log n)$. This work is complementary to ORAM as it provides an alternative mechanism for achieving data-obliviousness of a number of algorithms (and consecutively their secure versions). Because the benefits of ORAM become significant only for large input sizes [25], in our problem domain alternative techniques will be preferred as providing faster performance (e.g., [25] compares ORAM-based techniques for SMC to a naive oblivious array implementation that touches all elements of the array to retrieve an item at a private location and suggests that ORAM techniques are faster only when the size of the data is over 1000 items).

3   Security Model

In this work, we use standard security models for secure multi-party computation. We primarily focus on security in presence of semi-honest participants (also known as honest-but-curious or passive), who follow the prescribed behavior, but might try to compute additional information from the information obtained during protocol execution. The protocols, however, can be extended to achieve stronger security in presence of fully malicious (also known as active) adversaries who can arbitrary deviate from the prescribed computation. Regardless of the model, it is required that the participants do not learn anything about private input data beyond the agreed-upon output. Consequently, security is defined using simulation argument, which we provide in Appendix A due to space considerations. We choose to use a general setup with n parties carrying out the computation. For the problem we study, the most common setting is going to be $n = 2$, but we also would like to offer a solution that works for $n > 2$ and is also suitable for outsourcing to multiple computational nodes.

Because this work treats a graph problem, where the graph is derived from private data, the graph structure graph (e.g., node connectivity) is sensitive information that cannot be revealed to the participants. For that reason, any solution must be data-independent or oblivious, in which the sequence of executed instructions and accessed memory locations must be independent of the data. Achieving data-obliviousness can be realized by using a randomized algorithm (as in ORAM) where these sequences must be indistinguishable for different inputs or a deterministic algorithm where the sequences are the same for all possible inputs. In this work, we pursue the second option.

4   Fingerprint Background

To understand how the solution we develop for maximum matching in bipartite graphs is used to address the problem of fingerprint matching, we present the background related to fingerprint representations and comparisons before moving to the algorithm itself.

Fingerprint identification is a well-studied area with many available approaches [31]. The most popular and widely used techniques extract information about minutiae from a fingerprint and store it as a set of points in the two-dimensional plane. Fingerprint matching normally consists of finding a matching between two sets of points so that the number of minutiae pairings is maximized. In more detail, a biometric X is often represented as a set of m_X points $X = \langle (x_1, y_1, \alpha_1), \ldots, (x_{n_X}, y_{n_X}, \alpha_{n_X}) \rangle$, where x_i and y_i denote the coordinates of minutia i and α_i denotes minutia's orientation. Optionally, a minutia can also have its type included in the fingerprint representation and biometric X might also include secondary features. A minutia $X_i = (x_i, y_i, \alpha_i)$ in X and minutia $Y_j = (x'_j, y'_j, \alpha'_j)$ in Y are considered matching if the spatial distance (normally Euclidean distance) between them is smaller than a given threshold d_0 and the orientation difference between them is smaller than a given threshold α_0. In other words, the matching condition for minutiae X_i and Y_j is computed as:

$$\sqrt{(x'_j - x_i)^2 + (y'_j - y_i)^2} < d_0 \quad \wedge \quad \min(|\alpha'_j - \alpha_i|, 360° - |\alpha'_j - \alpha_i|) < \alpha_0. \quad (1)$$

The tolerance values d_0 and α_0 are necessary to account for errors introduced by feature extraction algorithms (e.g., quantizing) and small skin distortions. Two points within a single fingerprint are also assumed to lie within at least distance d_0 of each other.

Before fingerprint matching is performed, the two fingerprints need to be aligned, which maximizes the number of matching minutiae. Alignment can be either absolute (each fingerprint is pre-aligned independently using the core point or other information) or relative (fingerprint features are used to guide fingerprint alignment relative to each other). Relative alignment is more accurate that absolute, while absolute alignment is performed much faster in the context of secure computation. In particular, with absolute alignment, each fingerprint is aligned independently and locally without secure computation. To increase the accuracy of matching when absolute alignment is used, a fingerprint can be stored using a small number of slightly different alignments, all of which are compared to another fingerprint, and the result of the comparison is a match if at least one representation matches the second biometric. To the best of our knowledge, relative alignment has not been investigated in secure multi-party computation literature and we leave it as a direction for future research. The matching step, however, always needs to be performed, and this constitutes the focus of this work.

A simple way to determine a pairing between minutiae of fingerprints X and Y consists of considering each minutia X_i from X in turn and pairing it with the closest minutia Y_j in Y that satisfies the matching predicate in Eq. 1 and which has not already been paired with another minutia from X. If no such minutia Y_j from Y exists, X_i is not added to the pairing. We denote the result of applying the minutia matching predicate in Eq. 1 to minutiae X_i and Y_j by $mm(X_i, Y_j)$.

This approach was used in prior secure fingerprint matching solutions, but it does not find the optimum assignment (i.e., the one that maximizes the number of mates). That is, sometimes minutia X_i should be paired with another minutia Y_j, which is not the closest to X_i, to result in an assignment of the largest size. According to fingerprint literature [24,45], the optimum pairing can be achieved by formulating the problem as an instance of maximum flow, where fingerprints X and Y are used to create a flow network. In particular, we form a bipartite graph in which minutia points from X and Y form the nodes of the first and second partitions, respectively. The edges are created as follows: there is an edge from node $X_i \in X$ to $Y_j \in Y$ iff $mm(X_i, Y_j) = 1$. To use the resulting bipartite graph as a flow network, we create an additional source node s and connect it to all nodes from X using (directional) edges of capacity 1. Similarly, we create a sink node and connect each node from Y to the sink node t using edges of capacity 1. Then each edge from X_i to Y_j also has capacity 1 (in one direction only). We refer the reader to [24,45] for additional detail.

The problem of fingerprint matching in the maximum flow formulation can be solved using one of the known algorithms such as Ford-Fulkerson [17] and others. For n-minutia fingerprints, the optimal pairing can be found in $O(n^2)$ time using Ford-Fulkerson algorithm because each node X_i is connected to at most a constant number of nodes from Y. In a privacy-preserving setting, however, when information about connections between minutiae in X and Y (and thus the structure of the graph) must remain private, the complexity of this algorithm increases at least by a factor n. Finding a pairing of optimal size was considered impractical in [10], but in this work we show that with the techniques we develop, performance of fingerprint matching can be comparable to or even faster than performance of simpler and not as accurate matching in [10] (which is currently the fastest secure minutia-based fingerprint matching).

In this work, we assume that fingerprints X and Y result in a match if the number of paired minutiae exceeds a fixed (known to all parties) threshold T (T can be a function of the number of minutiae in X and Y, but is fixed once the sizes are known).[2]

5 Working Toward the Solution

Our primary objective now is to provide an oblivious algorithm for solving the maximum flow problem in a flow network formed by a bipartite graph (which in the fingerprint matching application corresponds to two fingerprints X and Y). Note that in our application it is not necessary to compute the matching itself and instead the size of the matching is sufficient to determine if two fingerprints X and Y are related. This means that it is sufficient to determine the rank of the matrix formed as described above to solve the fingerprint matching problem.

In the search for an approach suitable for solving the maximum flow problem in a data-oblivious way, we chose to concentrate on solutions that work with adjacency matrix representation of the graph. Note that because our graph is bipartite, we only need to consider an approach that works for a bipartite graph and not necessarily for a general graph. Our starting point was the work of Mucha and Sankowski [32] that presents a randomized algorithm for finding maximum matching in an n-node graph in $O(n^\omega)$ time, where ω is the exponent of the best known matrix multiplication algorithm and currently $\omega < 2.38$. The solution of [32] assumes that a perfect matching of size $n/2$ is present, which it will compute. This is not the case for our application, and to use this solution on a graph without perfect matching, we resort to techniques of Ibarra and Moran [21] (which are applicable to bipartite graphs only). The most crucial result listed in [32] that we need is due to Lovasz [28] and can be stated as follows: Let $G = (V, U, E)$ be a bipartite graph with nodes $V \cup U$ and edges

---

[2] In the event that the value of T comes from one of the participants and needs to be protected, the solution can be easily modified to compute with private T.

Algorithm 1. $A = \text{RandAdjMat}(A' = \{A'_{ij}\}_{1 \le i \le n_X, 1 \le j \le n_Y})$	Algorithm 2. $B = \text{GE}(A = \{A_{ij}\}_{1 \le i \le n_X, 1 \le j \le n_Y})$
1: **for** $i = 0, \ldots, n_X$ **do**	1: **for** $i = 1, \ldots, n_X$ **do**
2: **for** $j = 0, \ldots, n_Y$ **do**	2: **for** $j = i+1, \ldots, n_X$ **do**
3: $r_{ij} \overset{R}{\leftarrow} [1, R]$;	3: **for** $k = i, \ldots, n_Y$ **do**
4: $A_{ij} = A'_{ij} \cdot r_{ij}$;	4: $A_{jk} = A_{jk} - A_{ik} \cdot A_{ii}^{-1} \cdot A_{ji}$
5: **end for**	5: **end for**
6: **end for**	6: **end for**
7: **return** A;	7: **end for**

E, where $|V| = |U| = n/2$, $V = \{v_1, \ldots, v_{n/2}\}$ and $U = \{u_1, \ldots, u_{n/2}\}$. Let an adjacency matrix $A = A(G)$ be formed by setting an element A_{ij} of A at row i and column j to a random value from the set $[1, R]$ for some R if $(v_i, u_j) \in E$ and to 0 otherwise. In other words, a matrix cell is set to a random value of a predefined bitlength if the corresponding nodes are adjacent and to 0 otherwise. Then the rank of A is at most the size of the maximum matching, where the equality holds with probability at least $1 - \frac{n}{2R}$. This means that if R is set to 2^κ, where κ is a desired correctness parameter, the rank will be equal to the size of the maximum matching with all but at most a negligible probability in κ. For example, if we set $\kappa = 20$, computing the rank of the randomized adjacency matrix will give the solution to the size of the maximum matching with probability $1 - \text{negl}(20)$.

Because the algorithm above assumes a randomized adjacency matrix as the input, the pre-processing step will consist of creating such a matrix. If a regular adjacency matrix is given, it can be randomized using a simple approach shown in Algorithm 1. In other cases, the matrix needs to be computed, and we defer the description of how it can be done in the context of fingerprint matching to Sect. 7. In Algorithm 1, notation $z \overset{R}{\leftarrow} S$ denotes that the value of z is chosen uniformly at random from set S.

The next step is to compute the rank of A. A standard way to achieve this is to apply Gaussian elimination (LU decomposition) to A. The simplest algorithm for doing so runs in $O(n^3)$ time for an $n \times n$ matrix and asymptotically lower solutions (of the same complexity as that of matrix multiplication) are possible. Before we proceed with further discussion, we include a (non-secure) solution of complexity $O(n^3)$ based on Gaussian elimination. When it is applied to a bipartite graph with n_X and n_Y nodes in the first and second partition, respectively, its complexity is $O((n_X)^2 n_Y)$ assuming that $n_X \le n_Y$ (and $O((n_Y)^2 n_X)$ otherwise). To fully explore our options, in the full version of this work [11] we also consider an alternative approach for matrix rank computation based on Gram-Schmidt orthogonalization process.

The Gaussian elimination algorithm that takes a randomized adjacency matrix A and converts it to a row echelon form is given in Algorithm 2.

It assumes that $n_X \leq n_Y$; otherwise, the matrix dimensions are swapped by using the transpose of A. Following [21], after forming matrix A, we carry out all operations in a field (of size R) in this and other algorithms. That is, we treat A as consisting of random field elements and all consecutive operations are in a field (which is the reason for using multiplicative inverse in place of division). We present the simplest version of the Gaussian elimination algorithm that works only for invertible matrices (with $n_X = n_Y$) and which results in a matrix with only non-zero entries on the diagonal formed by elements A_{ii} and zero elements below the diagonal. In a more general case, some of the matrix rows or columns may either be initially zero or become zero during the computation, and the matrix does not have to be square. In those cases, during the ith iteration, the algorithm may swap row $i+1$ with another row at a higher index so that row $i+1$ contains a non-zero element at the leftmost position (or lowest column index) among all rows with indices $i + 1$ and higher. A column may also be "skipped" during the computation if all of its entries at row i and below are zero, i.e., the leftmost non-zero element at row i is at position $> i$. In that case, the computation will be of the form $A_{jk} = A_{jk} - A_{ik} \cdot A_{it}^{-1} \cdot A_{jt}$ for $t > i$. We note that in the application of fingerprint matching the adjacency matrix is likely to contain a large number of zero elements and we need to use the general algorithm that works for arbitrary matrices. Then the rank of the matrix is computed as the number of non-zero rows (or columns) once the matrix has been converted to a row echelon form.

Lastly, we note that in the traditional setting, when some rows and/or columns are initially zero, they can be eliminated from the matrix before the algorithm is executed because they cannot contribute to the matrix rank. This reduces complexity of the algorithm for sparse matrices, but is not applicable to secure computation because the size of the reduced matrix is likely to reveal information about the size of the matching.

Returning to our prior discussion of rank computation, recall that its asymptotic complexity can be lower than $O(n^3)$ for $n \times n$ matrices and equal to the complexity of matrix multiplication. Upon examining matrix multiplication algorithms of sub-cubic time, we came to the conclusion that only Strassen's algorithm [40] has practical importance to matrices those size is not huge. Its complexity is $O(n^{\log_2 7}) \approx O(n^{2.807})$ for $n \times n$ matrices or $O(n_X^{\log_2 3.5} n_Y)$ for matrices of size $n_X \times n_Y$ with $n_X \leq n_Y$. While this algorithm has reduced numerical stability, it is not an issue when the computation is carried out in a finite field (i.e., on integers without rounding errors).

The original Strassen's algorithm [40] is applicable only to invertible matrices. Solodovnikov [38] later showed how the algorithm can be extended to finding the rank of an arbitrary matrix, which can be used as a starting point for a secure solution. The algorithm is rather complex involving several matrix transformations and produces matrices the size of which determines the rank. While it is possible to make the algorithm oblivious (the most important change will be to force matrices to always be of the same size by padding them with dummy rows or columns), we choose not to expand on this further due to the limited applicability of the algorithm to fingerprint matching. In particular, Strassen's matrix multiplication outperforms the standard $O(n^3)$ matrix multiplication on matrices with sizes ≥ 100 for each dimension, but the number of minutiae in a fingerprint (which define the matrix size) is normally much lower.

6   Oblivious Rank Computation Algorithms

Developing data-oblivious algorithms for computing the rank of a non-invertible matrix of size $n_X \times n_Y$ constitutes the core of this work. In this section, we describe the intuition behind our solution for rank determination followed by its detailed description.

To ensure data-oblivious execution, we must require that the sequence of executed instruction does not depend on the data. This, in particular, means that execution associated with conditional statements is to be modified. In all algorithms we develop, we always execute both branches of conditional statements and the values which may be modified inside conditional statements will be set based on the result of evaluating the condition. In more detail, statements of the type "if (*cond*) then $a = v_1$ else $a = v_2$" will be transformed into evaluating the condition *cond* first and then setting

$$a = cond \cdot v_1 + (1 - cond) \cdot v_2 = (cond \wedge v_1) \vee (\overline{cond} \wedge v_2) \qquad (2)$$

Here, $\vee$ and $\wedge$ denote bitwise OR and AND, respectively. When only one branch is present, the branch gets executed, but the affected values are either updated or kept unchanged depending on the result of the condition evaluation. For example, statements of the type "if (*cond*) then $a = v_1$" can be rewritten as "$a = a + cond \cdot (v_1 - a)$".

When working on Gaussian elimination suitable for secure computation, a major issue we are to overcome is to make the execution oblivious in presence of zero rows and columns. That is, regardless of having zero columns (that need to be skipped) or zero rows (that need to be swapped), we want the algorithm to always execute the same instructions and always access the same matrix cells. For that reason, at each iteration of the solution, we choose to push all zero columns to the right and all zero rows to the bottom. This will allow us to work with row i and column i during the ith iteration of the algorithm (assuming that some non-zero row and column still remain at iteration i). Furthermore, once all non-zero rows and columns have been processed, we cannot reveal this fact and have to continue the computation without affecting its correctness.

To realize swapping of zero rows and columns in an oblivious way, we utilize data-oblivious compaction. Compaction of a sequence of values allows one to move all non-zero elements to the beginning and thus any zero element will appear only after all non-zero elements. Our goal of pushing zero columns and rows to the end can also be achieved by using oblivious sorting, but we choose compaction for performance reasons. Thus, as the first step of each iteration i, we compute whether any given (partial) row and column at position i and higher contains at least a single non-zero element. Note that we only need to consider matrix elements with both row and column indices i and higher and this is why only a part of each row and column is checked. For example, for row $j \geq i$ only cells at position $i \leq k \leq n_Y$ can be non-zero and are checked. Similarly, for column $j \geq i$ only cells at rows $i \leq k \leq n_X$ are relevant and checked. After this step, all zero rows and columns are pushed to the end using oblivious compaction.

At this point we know that the current row and column with index i have at least one non-zero element, but the algorithm requires that the leading coefficient of the (partial) current row i is non-zero. To satisfy this, we add all rows with indices $i + 1$ and higher to the current row i. This has no effect on correctness of the computation (and is a common operation in Gaussian elimination), but ensures that the element $A_{ii} \neq 0$. This is because when (partial) column i has at least one non-zero element, the probability that the sum of its elements (which are random values from $[1, R]$) results in 0 is $1/R$. Thus, with overwhelming probability (in R's bitlength) $A_{ii} \neq 0$ when (partial) column i has at least one non-zero element and correctness of the computation is preserved.

The only part of the algorithm that remains to be modified for oblivious execution is ensuring that the computation can proceed in exactly the same way once all non-zero rows and columns have been processed. That is, for some iteration i of the algorithm all remaining (partial) rows and columns will be zero. To ensure that the algorithm can execute exactly the same steps without revealing this fact and without affecting correctness, the only place we have to modify is computation of the inverse of A_{ii}. When $A_{ii} = 0$, A_{ii} does not have a multiplicative inverse, and we set $A_{ii} = 1$ in that case. Then because $1^{-1} = 1$, multiplying any value by 1^{-1} (as on line 4 of Algorithm 2) will have no effect. To ensure that A_{ii} is unchanged when $A_{ii} \neq 0$, we set A_{ii} to $A_{ii} + c$, where c is the bit corresponding to the result of comparing A_{ii} to 0.

The overall oblivious algorithm for computing matrix rank based on Gaussian elimination is given in Algorithm 3. Lines 2–5 and 7–10 compute row and column flags, respectively, that indicate whether the (partial) rows/columns consist of only zero elements. These flags are used in row-wise and column-wise compaction on lines 6 and 11, respectively. Lines 12–16 update row i to ensure that its leading element is non-zero if non-zero rows still remain. Line 17 adjusts the element A_{ii} for the purpose of computing its inverse as described above. Next, lines 18–23 compute the ith iteration of Gaussian elimination. After executing lines 1–24, matrix A is in a row echelon form and all that remains is to compute its rank by adding the number of non-zero elements on the diagonal A_{ii}. This is performed on lines 25–28, after which the rank is returned.

To realize oblivious compaction, we build on tight order-preserving compaction from [20], which was subsequently used for SMC in [6]. The algorithm proceeds in $\log_2 n$ rounds on input of a sequence of n values. At round i (for $0 \leq i \leq \log n - 1$), an element at position j is either obliviously moved 2^i elements left or is not moved. The former happens when the ith least significant bit in the number $count_j$ of zero elements that precede the jth element is 1. We refer the reader for additional details to [6,20] and provide our realization of it

---

Algorithm 3. rank = OblGERank($\{A_{ij}\}_{1 \leq i \leq n_X, 1 \leq j \leq n_Y}$)

1: **for** $i = 1, \ldots, n_X - 1$ **do**
2:   **for** $j = i, \ldots, n_X$ **do**
3:     Set rowflag$_j = \bigvee_{k=i}^{n_Y} A_{jk}$;
4:     Set $r_j = ($rowflag$_j \overset{?}{\neq} 0)$;
5:   **end for**
6:   Use compaction to "sort" partial rows $i, \ldots, n_X$ using keys r_j, where row j is $(A_{ji}, \ldots, A_{jn_Y})$, so that all rows with $r_j = 0$ are moved to the bottom of A.
7:   **for** $j = i, \ldots, n_Y$ **do**
8:     Set colflag$_j = \bigvee_{k=i}^{n_X} A_{kj}$;
9:     Set $c_j = ($colflag$_j \overset{?}{\neq} 0)$;
10:   **end for**
11:   Use compaction to "sort" partial columns $i, \ldots, n_Y$ using keys c_j, where column j is $(A_{ij}, \ldots, A_{n_X j})$, so that all columns with $c_j = 0$ are moved in the right in A.
12:   **for** $j = i + 1, \ldots, n_X$ **do**
13:     **for** $k = i, \ldots, n_Y$ **do**
14:       Set $A_{ik} = A_{ik} + A_{jk}$;
15:     **end for**
16:   **end for**
17:   Set $A_{ii} = A_{ii} + (A_{ii} \overset{?}{=} 0)$;
18:   Compute A_{ii}^{-1};
19:   **for** $j = i + 1, \ldots, n_X$ **do**
20:     **for** $k = i, \ldots, n_Y$ **do**
21:       Set $A_{jk} = A_{jk} - A_{ik} \cdot A_{ii}^{-1} \cdot A_{ji}$;
22:     **end for**
23:   **end for**
24: **end for**
25: Set ranksum = 0;
26: **for** $i = 1, \ldots, n_X$ **do**
27:   Set ranksum = ranksum $+ (A_{ii} \overset{?}{\neq} 0)$;
28: **end for**
29: Return ranksum;

Algorithm 4. $\langle y_1, \ldots, y_n \rangle = $ Comp($\langle x_1, \ldots, x_n \rangle$)

1: $count_1 = 1 - x_1$;
2: **for** $i = 2, \ldots, n$ **do**
3:   $count_i = count_{i-1} + 1 - x_i$;
4: **end for**
5: Let $b_{i,j}$ denote the ith least significant bit of $count_j$ for $j = 1, \ldots, n$ and $i = 0, \ldots, \lceil \log n \rceil - 1$
6: **for** $i = 0, \ldots, \lceil \log n \rceil - 1$ **do**
7:   **for** $j = 1, \ldots, n$ **do**
8:     **if** $j \geq 2^i$ **then**
9:       $x_j = (1 - b_{i,j})x_j$;
10:     **end if**
11:     **if** $j + 2^i \leq n$ **then**
12:       $x_j = x_j + b_{i,j+2^i} \cdot x_{j+2^i}$;
13:     **end if**
14:   **end for**
15: **end for**
16: Return $\langle x_1, \ldots, x_n \rangle$;

---

with new optimizations in Algorithm 4. It is written for the special case when the input consists of bits and moves all non-zero elements to the beginning of the input sequence. When this algorithm is used in Algorithm 3, it will take 1-bit r_j's or c_j's according to which the values need to be moved, but instead of moving individual elements, the entire (partial) rows or columns are moved.

In the most general case, the element x_j at position j is either kept unchanged or replaced with element x_{j+2^i} during the ith iteration of the algorithm. This corresponds to the computation $x_j = (1 - b_{i,j})x_j + b_{i,j+2^i} \cdot x_{j+2^i}$, where $b_{i,j}$ is the ith least significant bit of $count_j$. At most one of x_j and x_{j+2^i} is guaranteed to be non-zero at any given time. When, however, $j + 2^i$ exceeds the total number of elements, x_j is either kept or erased, i.e., $x_j = (1 - b_{i,j})x_j$. In addition, for the first $2^i - 1$ elements of the sequence, $b_{i,j}$ is always 0, which means that we

Algorithm 5. $A = \mathsf{AdjMat}(X = \langle x_i, y_i, \alpha_i \rangle_{1 \leq i \leq m_X}, Y = \langle x'_i, y'_i, \alpha'_i \rangle_{1 \leq i \leq m_Y})$

1: **for** $i = 0, \ldots, m_X$ **do**
2:     **for** $j = 0, \ldots, m_Y$ **do**
3:         **if** $(\sqrt{(x'_j - x_i)^2 + (y'_j - y_i)^2} < d_0) \wedge (\min(|\alpha'_j - \alpha_i|, 360° - |\alpha'_j - \alpha_i|) < \alpha_0)$
        then
4:             $A_{ij} \xleftarrow{R} [1, R]$;
5:         **else**
6:             $A_{ij} = 0$;
7:         **end if**
8:     **end for**
9: **end for**
10: **return** A;

do not need to multiply x_j by $(1 - b_{i,j})$ and instead set $x_j = x_j + b_{i,j+2^i} \cdot x_{j+2^i}$. This logic (for one general and two special cases) is presented on lines 8–13 of Algorithm 4 in an optimized form.

The complexity of the oblivious compaction algorithm is $O(n \log n)$ for an n-element input. In our case, each invocation of compaction is executed on $m_X - i + 1$ rows (resp., $m_Y - i + 1$ columns) each of size $m_Y - i + 1$ (resp., $m_X - i + 1$). This gives us that the total cost of compaction at all iterations of the algorithm is $O(m_X^2 m_Y \log m_X)$ for rows and $O(m_X^2 m_Y \log m_Y)$ columns. This dominates the algorithm's complexity, as the remaining work is $O(m_X^2 m_Y)$. However, according to our experimental results in Sect. 8, the cost of compaction is small compared to the remaining computation.

In [11] we also present an alternative algorithm based on Gram-Schmidt process.

7   Oblivious Fingeprint Macthing Algorithms

Now we proceed with showing how the above rank computation algorithm can be used to realize oblivious fingerprint matching. To accomplish this, we first need to obliviously build a randomized adjacency matrix from the information contained in two fingerprints. We also need to modify the rank computation algorithms to implement its over-the-threshold version, in which instead of reporting the rank, the output consists of a single bit indicating whether the rank is above the desired threshold.

The regular (non-oblivious) way of computing the adjacency matrix according to Eq. 1 is presented in Algorithm 5. It simply consists of comparing each minutia from X to each minutia in Y and setting the corresponding matrix cell to a random element if the minutiae are a possible match and to 0 otherwise. To make the algorithm oblivious, we have to restructure the computation associated with the conditional statement. Our oblivious algorithm for computation of the adjacency matrix is given as Algorithm 6. For performance reasons, we eliminate

Algorithm 6. $A = \mathsf{OblAdjMat}(X = \langle x_i, y_i, \alpha_i \rangle_{1 \leq i \leq m_X}, Y = \langle x'_i, y'_i, \alpha'_i \rangle_{1 \leq i \leq m_Y})$

1: **for** $i = 0, \ldots, m_X$ **do**
2:    **for** $j = 0, \ldots, m_Y$ **do**
3:      $c_1 = ((x'_j - x_i)^2 + (y'_j - y_i)^2 \overset{?}{<} (d_0)^2);$
4:      $c_2 = (\alpha_i \overset{?}{\geq} \alpha'_j);$
5:      $a_1 = \alpha_i - \alpha'_j;$
6:      $a_2 = \alpha'_j - \alpha_i;$
7:      $a_3 = c_2 \cdot a_1 + (1 - c_2)a_2;$
8:      $c_3 = (a_3 \overset{?}{<} \alpha_0);$
9:      $c_4 = ((360 - a_3) \overset{?}{<} \alpha_0);$
10:     $c = c_1 \wedge (c_3 \vee c_4);$
11:     $r_{ij} \overset{R}{\leftarrow} [1, R];$
12:     $A_{ij} = c \cdot r_{ij};$
13:    **end for**
14: **end for**
15: **return** $A;$

square root computation when computing the Euclidean distance (squared distances are used). Also, in the algorithm a_3 corresponds to $|\alpha_i - \alpha'_j|$ and $(c_3 \vee c_4)$ to $\min(|\alpha'_j - \alpha_i|, 360° - |\alpha'_j - \alpha_i|) \overset{?}{<} \alpha_0$.

To obtain an over-the-treshold version of the rank computation algorithm, we note that the necessary changes are rather simple. In particular, to produce of an over-the-threhold version of Algorithm 3, all we need is to return the result of comparison ($\mathsf{ranksum} \overset{?}{\geq} T$) on line 29 instead of ranksum itself.

Given our oblivious algorithm, it is now not difficult to realize it in the secure computation framework. Because of space considerations, we refer the reader to Appendix B and [11] for our secure protocols in both two-party and multi-party settings.

8 Implementation and Performance

To evaluate performance of our techniques, we implement our oblivious fingerprint matching algorithm in a secure computation framework. Our implementation is based on two-party garbled circuit evaluation and utilizes a tool called JustGarble [5] for efficient circuit garbling and garbled circuit evaluation.

We build Boolean circuits for Algorithm 6 followed by the over-the-threshold version of Algorithm 3 (as described in Sect. 7), with optimizations tailored to specifics of modern garbling techniques. In particular, recent garbled circuit-based techniques allow for XOR gates to be implemented without any use of cryptographic operations, which allows them to become virtually free [26]. This means that a circuit that minimizes the use of non-XOR gates will have performance advantages over other circuits of comparable size with a smaller percentage of XOR gates. One specific optimization that we were able to apply is minimizing the number of non-XOR gates in evaluation of conditional statements. In detail, recall that conditional statements are re-written as given in Eq. 2. The second formula, expressed in terms of Boolean operations, is more suitable for use in Boolean circuits, but we also notice that the bitwise OR operation can be replaced with bitwise XOR operation. This is due to the fact that at most one clause (i.e., $c \wedge v_1$ or $\bar{c} \wedge v_2$) can be non-zero at any time and thus

Table 1. Performance of secure two-party fingerprint matching using JustGarble.

Correctness	Metric	Biometric size (in minutiae)				
parameter		10	15	20	25	30
10	T_G	81.80	84.05	85.29	85.99	87.14
	T_E	50.49	53.18	53.91	54.85	54.74
	Gates	1,843,602	5,238,622	11,543,713	21,741,388	36,796,263
15	T_G	81.30	83.18	84.33	85.25	85.05
	T_E	52.12	53.37	54.16	54.57	54.12
	Gates	4,307,707	11,496,802	24,619,823	45,690,373	76,695,248
20	T_G	80.66	82.35	83.15	82.77	82.85
	T_E	53.02	53.92	54.25	53.80	53.56
	Gates	8,392,862	21,156,282	43,964,983	80,226,158	133,311,283

XOR would accomplish the same functionality as OR or addition. This applies to computation in all of Algorithms 3, 4, and 6. Also note that in compaction algorithm extracting individual bits of counts requires no computation because of bitwise representation of all values.

We measure performance of the algorithms for different numbers of minutiae in fingerprints being compared and different values of the correctness parameter. Note that using synthetic data affects neither performance nor accuracy of the secure algorithm. We varied the number of minutiae in both fingerprints from 10 to 30 and also varied the size of the field $\mathbb{F}_R$ with R's bitlength ranging from 10 to 20. Recall that according to [28], the probability that the rank of a randomized adjacency matrix is not equal to the size of the maximum matching is at most n/R for n-minitia fingerprints. This means that in our experiments the probability that the result is incorrect is approximately between $\leq n/10^3$ and $\leq n/10^6$. In the implementation, we assume that coordinates x_i, y_i of each minutia are represented in a 2-dimensional space of size 250×250 (i.e., $x_i, y_i \in [0, 249]$) and thus the bitlength of each coordinate is 8. Then angle α_i is provided in degrees from range $[0, 359]$ and thus each α_i is represented using 9 bits. In our experiments, circuits with 30 million gates and larger were divided into sub-circuits as the current implementation of JustGarble requires that the entire circuit resides in memory for garbling/evaluation. All experiments were run on a 3.2 GHz machine with Red Hat Linux and 4 GB of memory and are given in Table 1. Each experiment was run 100 times, and the double median (i.e., the median of 10 medians) is reported.

In Table 1, T_G denotes the time it takes to garble the circuit measured in the average number of CPU cycles per gate (as in [5]). Similarly, T_E indicates evaluation time, also measured in the number of CPU cycles per gate. We also provide the total number of gates for each circuit. Note that the number of cycles per gate can vary in different circuits, which is often because circuits contain different percentages of XOR gates (which require substantially less work to create and evaluate than other gates). From Table 1, we can see a slight increase in the per-gate runtimes as the number of minutiae in fingerprints increases and a slight decrease in the runtimes as the correctness parameter decreases. This can be attributed to the varying composition of the circuits from XOR and non-XOR gates. For example, when the correctness parameter increases, a larger portion of the circuit corresponds to field operations that have a higher percentage of XOR gates than other operations. We also observed that paritioning a circuit into small circuits and evaluating the sub-circuits circuits results in slightly faster overall per-gate time compared to the original time, which is due to improved cache performance.

We note that the overall execution consists of circuit garbling, oblivious transfer (OT) for one of the parties' inputs, and garbled circuit evaluation. Circuit garbling and transfer of the garlbed circuit can typically be performed in advance, assuming that the sizes of inputs are known. Similarly, the most expensive portion of OT (which uses public-key operations) can be performed in advance. This means that the online phase will consist of garbled circuit evaluation and communication of inputs associated with the remaining portion of OT. Using an OT extension [22], the number of public-key operations associated with any number of input bits is reduced to a constant corresponding to a security parameter (on the order of 96–128). Furthermore, all public-key operations can be performed in the offline phase and the online phase involves only communicating a number of bits linear in the number of inputs of the circuit evaluator and performing a similar number of hash function operations. Recall that in our application the number of inputs for each party is the number of bits in fingerprint representation (i.e., $25m_X$ or $25m_Y$), which is very small compared to the size of the computation. This means that the cost of OT will not have a noticeable impact on the overall runtime of our solution.

To provide additional information about runtime of our secure fingerprint identification protocols, we translate the numbers from Table 1 into execution times in Fig. 1 in Appendix C. We obtain runtimes on the order of a second or less, which is an acceptable delay for fingerprint authentication. Additional results can be found in [11].

Before we conclude this section, we comment on the performance of our solution compared to that of other secure fingerprint matching protocols. As mentioned earlier, the only secure fingerprint matching protocols that use minutia representations we are aware of are from [10, 36]. They are based on pairing a minutia with the closest possible match minutia and all possible match minutiae, respectively, which does not achieve the same accuracy as in our solution and requires substantially less work. Implementation results are only given in [10] and the runtimes are similar to what we obtain in our solution. (And while no implementation results were reported in [36], we anticipate that performance of that solution will be substantially slower than the solution from [10].) The computation in [10] was structured as comparing fingerprint X to a number of fingerprints Y in a database D. This incurs a one-time cost (per X) and a recurring cost per record Y in D. This means that if we compare X to a single fingerpring Y, the one-time cost will still be present. For fingerprints consisting of 20 minutiae, [10] reports about 5 sec of offline work per Y (total for both parties) and about 4 more seconds for one-time offline work. The online work is approximately 0.85 second per Y. We note that our solution requires even lower overall work for the same fingerprint sizes, but the online work may be higher for large values of the correctness parameter. If we increase the number of minutia points in a fingerprint, the runtime of our solution is expected to increase more rapidly than the runtime of the solution from [10] because of higher complexity of the algorithm we use.

9   Conclusions

This work is motivated by privacy-preserving fingerprint matching in the secure computation framework, using standard minutia-based representation of fingerprints. We show that the maximum (optimal) number of minutiae that match between two fingerprints can be determined by modeling the problem as a flow network in bipartite graphs. Towards this end, we investigate the problem of maximum matching size in a bipartite graph and reduce it to the problem of finding the rank of an adjacency matrix, which has the same complexity as that of matrix multiplication. We build a data-oblivious algorithm for rank computation based on Gaussian elimination, the complexity of which is cubic in the number vertices in the graph (or the number of minutiae in fingerprints). While it is possible to make algorithms of lower asymptotic complexity (such as Strassen's matrix multiplication and its extension to rank computation for non-singular matrices) data-oblivious, we choose to concentrate on simpler algorithms because of smaller constants behind the big-O notation. More advanced techniques of lower asymptotic complexity are also of limited applicability to the problem of fingerprint matching because simpler solutions with higher complexity outperform them on rather small input sizes (the number of minutiae) used in fingerprint matching. Our data-oblivious algorithms for matrix rank, maximum flow size in bipartite graphs and fingerprint matching consequently lead to secure protocols for respective problems using available secure two-party and multi-party techniques. Our implementation builds and evaluates secure two-party protocol for fingerprint matching put forward in this work. Despite having more complex computation to achieve improved accuracy, we show through experiments that performance of our techniques is suitable for this application and is comparable to the performance of other secure fingerprint matching techniques that perform simpler minutia matching.

Acknowledgments. This work was supported in part by grants CNS-1223699 and CNS-1319090 from the National Science Foundation and FA9550-13-1-0066 from the Air Force Office of Scientific Research. Any opinions, findings, and conclusions or recommendations expressed in this publication are those of the authors and do not necessarily reflect the views of the funding agencies.

A   Security Definitions

Security in the semi-honest setting is defined using simulation argument: the protocol is secure if the view of protocol execution for each party is computationally or information-theoretically indistinguishable from the view simulated using that party's input and output only. This implies that the protocol execution does not reveal any additional information to the participants. The definition below formalizes this:

Definition 1. *Let parties $P_1, \ldots, P_n$ engage in a protocol Π that computes function $f(\mathsf{in}_1, \ldots, \mathsf{in}_n) = (\mathsf{out}_1, \ldots, \mathsf{out}_n)$, where in_i and out_i denote the input and output of P_i, respectively. Let $\mathrm{VIEW}_\Pi(P_i)$ denote the view of P_i during the execution of Π. That is, P_i's view is formed by its input, internal random coin tosses r_i, and messages $m_1, \ldots, m_k$ passed between the parties during protocol execution: $\mathrm{VIEW}_\Pi(P_i) = (\mathsf{in}_i, r_i, m_1, \ldots, m_k)$. Let $I = \{P_{i_1}, P_{i_2}, \ldots, P_{i_t}\}$ denote a subset of the parties for $t < n$ and $\mathrm{VIEW}_\Pi(I)$ denote the combined view of the parties in I during the execution of Π (i.e., the union of the views of the parties in I). We say that protocol Π is t-private in presence of semi-honest adversaries if for each coalition I of size at most t there exists a probabilistic polynomial time simulator S_I such that $\{S_I(\mathsf{in}_I, f(\mathsf{in}_1, \ldots, \mathsf{in}_n))\} \equiv \{\mathrm{VIEW}_\Pi(I), \mathsf{out}_I\}$, where $\mathsf{in}_I = \bigcup_{P_i \in I} \{\mathsf{in}_i\}$, $\mathsf{out}_I = \bigcup_{P_i \in I} \{\mathsf{out}_i\}$, and $\equiv$ denotes computational or information-theoretic indistinguishability.*

The second standard, and stronger, malicious security model assumes the participants can behave arbitrarily including deviating from the computation and aborting the execution. Security in this setting is shown using a different security definition, which we omit here due to space considerations and instead refer the reader, e.g., to [18].

B   Secure Protocols

The data-oblivious algorithms that we developed lead to secure protocols for computing maximum bipartite matching size, matrix rank, and fingerprint matching in secure multi-party computation framework. That is, because the execution is now data-oblivious, we can combine each algorithm with available secure arithmetic techniques to provably protect private data throughout the computation. We list two possibilities.

Our first solution is to employ two-party garbled circuit evaluation (originally proposed in [46]). This technique represents the function to be evaluated as a Boolean circuit and one participant, circuit generator, encodes the circuit using two random labels for each (binary) wire. The second participant, circuit evaluator, evaluates the garbled circuit on private inputs in a way that it sees the labels used during function evaluation, but their meaning (i.e., 0 or 1) is not known. After the evaluator computes the output labels, it sends them to the circuit generator, who determines their meaning (it is also possible for the evaluator to learn the output or for both parties to learn the same or individual outputs). To choose labels corresponding to the private inputs, the parties engage in Oblivious Transfer (OT), as a result of which the evaluator obtains labels corresponding to its inputs and the other party learns nothing. The labels for the circuit generator's inputs are sent directly to the evaluator (who does not know their meaning). There are many available OT realizations and their extensions such as, e.g., [33] and [22]. Using garbled circuit evaluation, we can state the following result:

Theorem 1. *Assuming the existence of secure garbled circuit evaluation techniques and OT, our algorithms result in 1-private protocols for maximum bipartite matching size, matrix rank, and fingerprint matching with two participants P_1 and P_2.*

We refer the reader to [11] for the proofs of Theorems 1 and 2.

The second technique we suggest is threshold linear secret sharing in the multi-party setting (such as Shamir's secret sharing [37]). It allows $n > 2$ parties to securely evaluate a function on shares of private data. Before the computation starts, all private data are split into shares and the shares are distributed among the computational parties who carry out the computation on protected data. After the computation, the shares of the result are communicated to the participants who are entitled to learning the result and reconstruct the output from the shares. Note that the participants who provide the data do not have to coincide with computational parties, but instead the sets of input providers, output recipients, and computational parties can be arbitrary with respect to each other. This makes the framework suitable for a variety of settings including secure computation outsourcing by one or more clients to a number of servers.

With linear secret sharing techniques, any linear combination of secret shared data is computed locally by each participant, but multiplication requires their interaction and constitutes a basic (interactive) building block. With (n, t)-threshold linear secret sharing techniques, each private value is split into n shares (and distributed to n participants) such that t or fewer shares information-theoretically reveal no information about the shared value, while $t + 1$ shares allow the value to be reconstructed. For semi-honest participants, it is typically the case that $t < n/2$. Any function can be expressed in this framework, and optimized designs of commonly used operations are available.

Theorem 2. *Assuming the existence of secure (n, t)-threshold linear secret sharing scheme, our algorithms result in t-private protocols for maximum bipartite matching size, matrix rank, and fingerprint matching with n participants and $t < n/2$.*

For both two-party techniques based on garbled circuit evaluation and multi-party techniques based on linear secret sharing, there are general mechanisms for converting solutions secure in the semi-honest model to solutions secure in the stronger malicious model (see, e.g., [27] for garbled circuits and [4] for secret sharing among many others). This means that if we apply such techniques to our computation, we automatically obtain protocols secure in the malicious model. We omit the details here.

C   Additional Performance Results

In Fig. 1, we report circuit evaluation times for experiments with 15 and 20 minutiae. The runtimes were computed from the circuit sizes, per-gate evaluation times, and the machine's clock rate as described in Sect. 8.

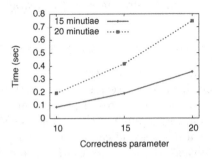

Fig. 1. Performance of garbled circuit evaluation for fingerprint matching.

References

1. Aliasgari, M., Blanton, M.: Secure computation of Hidden Markov Models. In: International Conference on Security and Cryptography (SECRYPT) (2013)
2. Aly, A., Cuvelier, E., Mawet, S., Pereira, O., Van Vyve, M.: Securely solving simple combinatorial graph problems. In: Financial Cryptography, pp. 239–257 (2013)
3. Barni, M., Bianchi, T., Catalano, D., Di Raimondo, M., Labati, R., Failla, P., Fiore, D., Lazzeretti, R., Piuri, V., Scotti, F., Piva, A.: Privacy-preserving fingercode authentication. In: ACM Workshop on Multimedia and Security (MM&Sec), pp. 231–240 (2010)
4. Beerliová-Trubíniová, Z., Hirt, M.: Perfectly-secure MPC with linear communication complexity. In: Canetti, R. (ed.) TCC 2008. LNCS, vol. 4948, pp. 213–230. Springer, Heidelberg (2008)
5. Bellare, M., Hoang, V., Keelveedhi, S., Rogaway, P.: Efficient garbling from a fixed-key blockcipher. In: IEEE Symposium on Security and Privacy, pp. 478–492 (2013)
6. Blanton, M., Aguiar, E.: Private and oblivious set and multiset operations. Cryptology ePrint Archive Report 2011/464 (2011)
7. Blanton, M., Aliasgari, M.: Secure outsourcing of DNA searching via finite automata. In: DBSec, pp. 49–64 (2010)
8. Blanton, M., Aliasgari, M.: Secure outsourced computation of iris matching. J. Comput. Secur. **20**(2–3), 259–305 (2012)

9. Blanton, M., Gasti, P.: Secure and efficient protocols for iris and fingerprint identification. In: Atluri, V., Diaz, C. (eds.) ESORICS 2011. LNCS, vol. 6879, pp. 190–209. Springer, Heidelberg (2011)

10. Blanton, M., Gasti, P.: Secure and efficient iris and fingerprint identification. In: Ngo, D., Teoh, A., Hu, J. (eds.) Biometric Security (2015)

11. Blanton, M., Saraph, S.: Secure and oblivious maximum bipartite matching size algorithm with applications to secure fingerprint identification. Cryptology ePrint Archive Report 2014/596 (2014)

12. Blanton, M., Steele, A., Aliasgari, M.: Data-oblivious graph algorithms for secure computation and outsourcing. In: ASIACCS, pp. 207–218 (2013)

13. Bogdanov, D., Laur, S., Willemson, J.: Sharemind: a framework for fast privacy-preserving computations. In: Jajodia, S., Lopez, J. (eds.) ESORICS 2008. LNCS, vol. 5283, pp. 192–206. Springer, Heidelberg (2008)

14. Damgård, I., Geisler, M., Krøigård, M.: Asynchronous multiparty computation: Theory and implementation. In: Public Key Cryptography (PKC), pp. 160–179 (2009)

15. Erkin, Z., Franz, M., Guajardo, J., Katzenbeisser, S., Lagendijk, I., Toft, T.: Privacy-preserving face recognition. In: Goldberg, I., Atallah, M.J. (eds.) PETS 2009. LNCS, vol. 5672, pp. 235–253. Springer, Heidelberg (2009)

16. Fan, K.-C., Liu, C.-W., Wang, Y.-K.: A fuzzy bipartite weighted graph matching approach to fingerprint verification. IEEE Trans. Syst. Man Cybern. 5, 4363–4368 (1998)

17. Ford, L., Fulkerson, D.: Flows in Networks. Princeton University Press (1962)

18. Goldreich, O.: Foundations of Cryptography: Volume 2, Basic Applications. Cambridge University Press, Cambridge (2004)

19. Goldreich, O., Ostrovsky, R.: Software protection and simulation on oblivious RAMs. J. ACM (JACM) 43(3), 431–473 (1996)

20. Goodrich, M.: Data-oblivious external-memory algorithms for the compaction, selection, and sorting of outsourced data. In: SPAA, pp. 379–388 (2011)

21. Ibarra, O., Moran, S.: Deterministic and probabilistic algorithms for maximum bipartite matching via fast matrix multiplication. Inf. Process. Lett. 13(1), 12–15 (1981)

22. Ishai, Y., Kilian, J., Nissim, K., Petrank, E.: Extending oblivious transfers efficiently. In: Boneh, D. (ed.) CRYPTO 2003. LNCS, vol. 2729, pp. 145–161. Springer, Heidelberg (2003)

23. Jain, A., Prabhakar, S., Hong, L., Pankanti, S.: Filterbank-based fingerprint matching. IEEE Trans. Image Process. 9(5), 846–859 (2000)

24. Jea, T.-Y., Govindaraju, V.: A minutia-based partial fingerprint recognition system. Pattern Recogn. 38(10), 1672–1684 (2005)

25. Keller, M., Scholl, P.: Efficient, oblivious data structures for MPC. Cryptology ePrint Archive Report 2014/137 (2014)

26. Kolesnikov, V., Schneider, T.: Improved garbled circuit: free XOR gates and applications. In: Aceto, L., Damgård, I., Goldberg, L.A., Halldórsson, M.M., Ingólfsdóttir, A., Walukiewicz, I. (eds.) ICALP 2008, Part II. LNCS, vol. 5126, pp. 486–498. Springer, Heidelberg (2008)

27. Kreuter, B., shelat, A., Shen, C.: Billion-gate secure computation with malicious adversaries. In: USENIX Security Symposium (2012)

28. Lovasz, L.: On determinants, matchings and random algorithms. Fundam. Comput. Theor. 79, 565–574 (1979)

29. Lu, S., Ostrovsky, R.: Distributed oblivious RAM for secure two-party computation. In: Sahai, A. (ed.) TCC 2013. LNCS, vol. 7785, pp. 377–396. Springer, Heidelberg (2013)

30. Malkhi, D., Nisan, N., Pinkas, B., Sella, Y.: Fairplay - a secure two-party computation system. In: USENIX Security Symposium, pp. 287–302 (2004)

31. Maltoni, D., Maio, D., Jain, A., Prabhakar, S.: Handbook of Fingerprint Recognition, 2nd edn. Springer, London (2009)

32. Mucha, M., Sankowski, P.: Maximum matchings via Gaussian elimination. In: IEEE Symposium on Foundations of Computer Science, pp. 248–255 (2004)

33. Naor, M., Pinkas, B.: Efficient oblivious transfer protocols. In: SODA (2001)

34. Pathak, M., Portelo, J., Raj, B., Trancoso, I.: Privacy-preserving speaker authentication. In: Gollmann, D., Freiling, F.C. (eds.) ISC 2012. LNCS, vol. 7483, pp. 1–22. Springer, Heidelberg (2012)

35. Sadeghi, A.-R., Schneider, T., Wehrenberg, I.: Efficient privacy-preserving face recognition. In: Lee, D., Hong, S. (eds.) ICISC 2009. LNCS, vol. 5984, pp. 229–244. Springer, Heidelberg (2010)

36. Shahandashti, S.F., Safavi-Naini, R., Ogunbona, P.: Private fingerprint matching. In: Susilo, W., Mu, Y., Seberry, J. (eds.) ACISP 2012. LNCS, vol. 7372, pp. 426–433. Springer, Heidelberg (2012)

37. Shamir, A.: How to share a secret. Commun. ACM **22**(11), 612–613 (1979)

38. Solodovnikov, V.: Extension of Strassen's estimate to the soultion of arbitrary systems of linear equations. USSR Comput. Maths. Math. Phys. **19**, 21–33 (1978)

39. Stefanov, E., van Dijk, M., Shi, E., Fletcher, C., Ren, L., Yu, X., Devadas, S.: Path ORAM: An extremely simple oblivious RAM protocol. In: CCS, pp. 299–310 (2013)

40. Strassen, V.: Gaussian elimination is not optimal. Numer. Math. **13**, 354–356 (1969)

41. The Corbett Report. India fingerprints, iris scanning over one billion people. http://www.corbettreport.com/india-fingerprinting-iris-scanning-over-one-billion-people/

42. Troncoso-Pastoriza, J., Katzenbeisser, S., Celik, M.: Privacy preserving error resilient DNA searching through oblivious automata. In: CCS, pp. 519–528 (2007)

43. UAE Iris Collection. http://www.cl.cam.ac.uk/~jgd1000/UAEdeployment.pdf

44. U.S. Dhs Office of Biometric Identity Management. http://www.dhs.gov/obim

45. Wang, C., Gavrilova, M., Luo, Y., Rokne, J.: An efficient algorithm for fingerprint matching. In: International Conference on Pattern Recognition (ICPR), pp. 1034–1037 (2006)

46. Yao, A.: How to generate and exchange secrets. In: FOCS, pp. 162–167 (1986)

47. Zhang, Y., Steele, A., Blanton, M.: PICCO: a general-purpose compiler for private distributed computation. In: CCS, pp. 813–826 (2013)

Practical Invalid Curve Attacks on TLS-ECDH

Tibor Jager[✉], Jörg Schwenk[✉], and Juraj Somorovsky[✉]

Horst Görtz Institute for IT Security, Ruhr University Bochum,
Bochum, Germany
tibor.jager@rub.de

Abstract. Elliptic Curve Cryptography (ECC) is based on cyclic groups, where group elements are represented as points in a finite plane. All ECC cryptosystems implicitly assume that only valid group elements will be processed by the different cryptographic algorithms. It is well-known that a check for group membership of given points in the plane should be performed before processing.

However, in several widely used cryptographic libraries we analyzed, this check was missing, in particular in the popular ECC implementations of Oracle and Bouncy Castle. We analyze the effect of this missing check on Oracle's default Java TLS implementation (JSSE with a SunEC provider) and TLS servers using the Bouncy Castle library. It turns out that the effect on the security of TLS-ECDH is devastating. We describe an attack that allows to extract the long-term private key from a TLS server that uses such a vulnerable library. This allows an attacker to impersonate the legitimate server to any communication partner, after performing the attack only once.

1 Introduction

Elliptic Curve Cryptography (ECC) is one of the cornerstones of modern cryptography, due to its security and performance features. It is implemented in nearly every cryptographic application, ranging from Bluetooth device level encryption to securing cloud applications via TLS. Mathematically speaking, an elliptic curve is a set of points in a plane (in cryptography: a finite plane), together with a single (associative) operation, namely *point addition*. The set of points are those that satisfy an equation of the form

$$y^2 = x^3 + ax + b \tag{1}$$

and point addition can be defined as a geometric operation in the plane. Each set of elements together with an operation forms an algebraic *group*, if the set is closed under the given operation, if the operation is associative, and if a neutral element exists. Elliptic curves satisfy all these axioms, and thus can be used in any cryptosystem that operates on a mathematical group. For cryptographic applications it is also required that certain assumptions hold in the group G, e.g., the hardness of the discrete logarithm problem, or the CDH and DDH assumptions. An elliptic curve $E_{a,b}$ therefore has to be chosen carefully to guarantee that these assumptions hold.

© Springer International Publishing Switzerland 2015
G. Pernul et al. (Eds.): ESORICS 2015, Part I, LNCS 9326, pp. 407–425, 2015.
DOI: 10.1007/978-3-319-24174-6_21

Now a finite plane also contains points *outside* the elliptic curve $E_{a,b}$, and thus these points are not group elements of G. However they resemble group elements: They have two coordinates, and the functions defining the group operation can be applied to them. They just don't satisfy Eq. (1) with the given parameters a and b. If we use these points with the functions defining our EC cryptosystem, we may get strange results, since the group laws may not apply to them, or they may lie in a diffrent group where the cryptographic assumptions are not valid.

So strictly speaking, any cryptographic application using a cyclic group G should check that any operand that is supposed to be a group element of G is indeed contained in G. Indeed, it is well-known that this check is *in general* necessary to provide security [2,3,6,15]. *But is this check always implemented in the cryptographic libraries that are used in practical applications?*

It is also not clear for which *specific* applications this is inherently necessary. Even though it is considered good practice to *always* perform a test of group membership, we show that sometimes developers of even popular implementations of elliptic curve cryptography *omit* the check. *Which impact does a missing check of group membership have on the* specific *application TLS?*

To answer these questions, we studied the eight most important cryptographic libraries, which are used in TLS-ECDH (and *many* other applications). We found that a check for group membership was missing in three of these libraries, and this omitted check allows to compromise the security of a TLS implementation completely in two libraries (Oracle SunEC, Bouncy Castle), provided that a TLS-ECDH cipher suite is used.

TLS-(EC)DH. Transport Layer Security (TLS) is a security standard originally designed to protect HTTP traffic, but which is today used as a de facto security standard for many applications, e.g. EAP-(T)TLS, IMAPS and secure websockets. TLS consists of two main parts: The *Record Layer encryption*, which protects transported data using a MAC-then-PAD-then-ENCRYPT approach, and the *Handshake Protocol*, which negotiates cryptogra pgorihms and keys to be used by the Record Layer. Three different types of key agreement can be used in the Handshake protocol:

- TLS-RSA: The client chooses a random `PreMasterSecret` *pms*, encrypts it with the RSA public key of the server (contained in the server certificate), and sends this cryptogram to the server.
- TLS-DH: Here the server certificate contains a static Diffie-Hellman share g^s, and the client chooses a fresh DH share g^x. The `PreMasterSecret` is computed as $pms := (g^s)^x = (g^x)^s$.
- TLS-DHE: Here the server also chooses a fresh DH share g^y, and signs this value (plus some additional values). This signature can be verified using the server certificate. The `PreMasterSecret` is computed as $pms := (g^y)^x = (g^x)^y$.

Since only a mathematical group structure is required in the Diffie-Hellman key exchange, we can also use elliptic curves in the last two key agreement

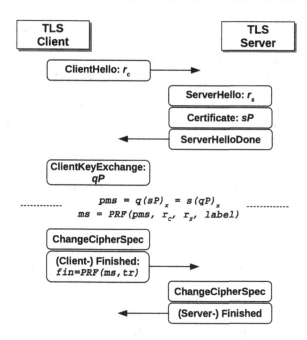

Fig. 1. Structure of the SSL/TLS Handshake protocol for TLS_ECDH cipher suites.

schemes. These variants are denoted as TLS-ECDH and TLS-ECDHE, respectively. The attacks described in this paper are applicable to TLS-ECDH. The structure of this handshake is described in Fig. 1. Our goal is to compute the private server key s. We may learn the public server key sP from the server certificate sent in the Certificate message, but since the Discrete Logarithm assumption (DLP)[1] holds in the elliptic curve group, we cannot compute s from this value.

Attacks on TLS. TLS can be attacked at three points: At the TLS handshake, at the Record Layer, and by using a specific TLS extension. The impact of each attack may range from low to high criticality.

Except where weak export cipher suites were used, the TLS Record Layer seemed secure. This situation changed with the BEAST attack published in 2011 [19]. Although the impact of this attack was low, it showed the practical vulnerability of the MAC-then-PAD-then-ENCRYPT scheme used. Critical attacks followed soon: Lucky 13 [1] and POODLE [17]. However, with these attacks only parts of the plaintext exchanged could be decrypted, and thus the criticality lay in the fact that e.g. HTTP session cookies could be decrypted.

---

[1] Group operations can be written as additive or multiplicative operations. Elliptic curves traditionally use additive notation, so for EC this assumption could be relabeled "discrete factor assumption". However, DLP is the standard term used for this assumption.

The first critical attack on the TLS handshake, which is hard to mitigate and thus resurfaces from time to time, is the famous adaptive chosen ciphertext attack by Daniel Bleichenbacher [5]. With this attack, a single TLS session could be completely broken by computing the `PreMasterSecret` from an intercepted `ClientKeyExchange` message, and from server error messages or timing measurements. Another example of an attack on the TLS handshake is the attack by Brumley et al., who analyzed a bug in EC computation of OpenSSL [6]. The bug allowed the authors to apply practical attacks against TLS servers using NIST secp256r1 and secp384r1 curves, and to extract EC private keys.

Even more critical was the Heartbleed vulnerability,[2] which was not based on a cryptographic attack, but on an implementation error of the OpenSSL Heartbeat extension: An attacker could read the server's private key directly from the memory of the OpenSSL process.

In this paper we describe a cryptographic attack on the TLS handshake which also recovers the private key of the server. Our attack is however less critical than Heartbleed, most importantly because the widely-used OpenSSL library is not affected, and TLS-DH cipher suites are less frequently used in practice than TLS-DHE or TLS-RSA cipher suites.

Our Attack. As a starting point, we used the invalid curve attack sketched by Biehl et al. in [3] and explained in more detail by Antipa *et al.* [2]. The basic idea is to define several different elliptic curves in the same plane as the original curve, by varying the parameter b. The groups defined by these curves may have arbitrary order within a certain range, and this order may be divisible by small primes $2, 3, 5, 7, 11, \ldots$.

For example, if we find a parameter b' where the order of the corresponding group is divisible by 7, then we can find a point P' on this curve that generates a subgroup of order 7. If we send this point P' to the TLS server, then there are only 7 different values for sP'. Thus if we could learn sP', we could compute s mod 7. If we do this for enough different small primes, we can apply the Chinese Remainder theorem to compute the private server key s.

This attack however only works if the result of the EC computation is directly available to the adversary, which is not the case for TLS-ECDH: The resulting value sP' is only used internally by the server as the `PreMasterSecret` *pms*. *Thus we never directly see this value, but we can guess this value and check it against the server.*

Therefore we used the strategy of Brumley et al. [6], and adapted the attack on TLS-ECDH in the following way:

1. We start like in the attacks of [2,3] by generating several different curves with subgroups of small prime order.
2. For each of these small prime orders p_i, we send a generator G_i of the corresponding subgroup in the `ClientKeyExchange` message to the server.

---

[2] http://heartbleed.com/.

3. Additionally, we guess the value sG_j, which can only be one of the p values generated by G_i. Using this guessed value as the `PreMasterSecret` pms, we compute the `MasterSecret` ms and the `ClientFinished` message.
4. If we guessed correctly, the server will accept the `ClientFinished` message, and respond with the `ServerFinished` message. In that case, we have learned $s^2 \bmod p_i$.

Results. We studied eight TLS-ECDH implementations. TLS servers based on Oracle's default Java TLS implementation using the SunEC provider, and the Bouncy Castle library were vulnerable to the presented attack. The WolfSSL library did not validate EC points, but it was not vulnerable. We provide an explanation for this behavior in Appendix A. The results are summarized in Table 1.

Table 1. Overview on the tested libraries

Lib	Bouncy Castle Java 1.50	MatrixSSL 1.3.10	mbed TLS 1.3.10	OpenSSL 1.0.2a	LibreSSL 2.1.6	SunEC Security Provider 1.8	SunPKCS11-NSS Security Provider 1.7	WolfSSL 3.4.6
point check?	no	yes	yes	yes	yes	no	yes	no
vuln.?	yes	no	no	no	no	yes	no	no

We were able to perform the attack against a TLS server with a SunEC provider with about 3300 server queries, and a server based on the Bouncy Castle library with about 17,000 server queries. Both test servers used the secp256r1 NIST curve. The significantly larger values for SunEC resulted from an unidentified computation error in the ECC library:[3] Certain computations resulted in False Positives, and the probability for False Positives was proportional to the inverse of the size of the chosen small group. Thus we had to choose larger primes for our attack, and consequently the average number of guesses increased.

Contribution. The contributions of this paper are the following:

- We adapt attacks of [2,3] to TLS-ECDH, and present a representative study on TLS libraries using TLS-ECDH cipher suites.
- We show that three out of eight analyzed libraries do not include curve point validations, and that two of them are vulnerable to invalid curve attacks. This allowed us to reveal TLS long-term private keys with a few thousands of server requests.
- We present a modified algorithm that allowed us to attack a TLS server using the SunEC security provider even in the presence of invalid EC computations, with high probability.

---

[3] We were not able to investigate this in more detail, because the source code is not publicly available.

– We give additional practical arguments why group membership checks are of prime importance in cryptographic applications.

2   Invalid Curve Attacks on ECC

2.1   A Brief Recap of Elliptic Curve Cryptography

In this section we give a brief introduction to elliptic curve cryptography, mainly in order to introduce our notation. We refer to [7,13] for a more verbose treatment of elliptic curves.

Let $\mathbb{F}$ be a finite field (e.g., $\mathbb{F} = \mathbb{Z}_p$ for prime p) with characteristic not equal to 2 or 3. An elliptic curve in Weierstrass form over $\mathbb{F}$ is described by *curve parameters* $\pi := (\mathbb{F}, a, b)$, where $a, b \in \mathbb{F}$. Let

$$E_\pi := \{(x, y) \in \mathbb{F}^2 : y^2 = x^3 + ax + b\} \cup \{O_\infty\}$$

denote the set of solutions (x, y) to the Weierstrass equation $y^2 = x^3 + ax + b$ over $\mathbb{F}$ defined by π, along with a special symbol O_∞ which is called the *point at infinity*. Let $+_\pi : E_\pi \times E_\pi \to E_\pi$ denote the map that takes as input two points $P, Q \in \mathbb{F}^2$ and outputs the point $R \in \mathbb{F}^2$ computed as

$$R = P +_\pi Q := \begin{cases} \text{ADD}_\pi(P, Q) & \text{if } P \neq Q, \\ \text{DBL}_\pi(P) & \text{if } P = Q. \end{cases}$$

Here, ADD_π and DBL_π denote the algorithms depicted in Fig. 2.

$\text{ADD}(P, Q):$

$(x_P, y_P) := P; (x_Q, y_Q) := Q$
If $P = O_\infty$ **then Return** Q
If $Q = O_\infty$ **then Return** P
$\lambda := (y_P - y_Q)/(x_P - x_Q)$
$x_R := \lambda^2 - x_P - x_Q$
$y_R := y_P + \lambda(x_R - x_P)$
Return (x_R, y_R)

$\text{DBL}(P):$

$(x_P, y_P) := P$
If $P = O_\infty$ **then Return** P
$\lambda := (3x_p^2 - a)/(2y_P)$
$x_R := \lambda^2 - 2x_P$
$y_R := y_P + \lambda(x_R - x_P)$
Return (x_R, y_R)

Fig. 2. Algorithms DBL and ADD for point doubling and addition. Note that both algorithms are independent of the curve parameter b.

Remark 1. Note that algorithm ADD_π depends only on P, Q, and the field $\mathbb{F}$, but not on the curve parameters a and b. Similarly, DBL_π depends only on P, the field $\mathbb{F}$ and curve parameter a, but not on curve parameter b. Thus, *the computation of the group operation $+_\pi$ is independent of curve parameter b*. This is a crucial property for the attack described below.

The set of points E_π along with the group law $+_\pi$ forms an algebraic group $\mathbb{G}_\pi = (E_\pi, +_\pi)$. We will write $P + Q$ shorthand for $P +_\pi Q$ when the reference to parameters π is clear. For $n \in \mathbb{N}$ we write nP for the n-fold sum $P + \cdots + P$.

In the sequel we will furthermore write $[P]_x$ to denote the x-coordinate of a point P. If P is the point at infinity, we set $[P]_x := \emptyset$, where $\emptyset$ is an arbitrary constant.

2.2 Invalid Curve Attacks on Elliptic Curves in TLS

The idea of small subgroup attacks is due to Lim and Lee [14], who described such attacks for groups of integers modulo a prime. The special case of small subgroup attacks, that are based on submitting invalid elliptic curve points (more precisely, points that lie on a *different* curve) were, to our best knowledge, first described in [3]. The attack used in this paper is based on the attack sketched in [3], and explained in detail in [2]. It consists of two phases, an offline pre-computation phase which must only be performed once for each elliptic curve parameters $\pi := (\mathbb{F}, a, b)$, and an online attack phase.

Offline precomputations. First, the attacker performs the following computations, which need to be performed only once for each particular choice of elliptic curve parameters $\pi := (\mathbb{F}, a, b)$ defining an elliptic curve group of order q.

1. Let $p_1, \ldots, p_n$ be the first n primes, such that $\prod_{i=1}^n p_i > q^2$. The attacker first computes integers $b_1, \ldots, b_n \in \mathbb{Z}_p$ such that $(\mathbb{F}, a, b_i)$ defines an elliptic curve of order q_i such that p_i divides q_i. To this end, the attacker sets $b_1 = \cdots = b_n = 0$, and repeats the following algorithm until $b_i \neq 0$ for all i.
   (a) Choose $b^* \xleftarrow{\$} \mathbb{Z}_p$ at random.
   (b) Count the number w of points on the curve $E_{(\mathbb{F}, a, b^*)}$, by running the Schoof-Elkies-Atkin algorithm [7].
   (c) For each $i \in \{1, \ldots, n\}$, check if $p_i \mid w$. If this holds, set $b_i := b^*$.

   Note that the elliptic curve group defined by $(\mathbb{F}, a, b_i)$ has a small subgroup of order p_i, where all p_i are very small. Note also that it is sufficient to have $n \le 2 \cdot \log_2 q$. By the prime number theorem, we may furthermore expect that the largest prime p_n has size about $p_n \approx n \cdot \ln n$. Thus, all primes $p_1, \ldots, p_n$ are very small, in the order of $O(\log q \cdot \log \log q)$. Assuming heuristically that the number of points w on the curve defined by $(\mathbb{F}, a, b^*)$ is distributed nearly uniformly over the interval $[q - 2\sqrt{q} + 1, q + 2\sqrt{q} + 1]$ (the interval given by the Hasse-Weil bounds [7]) for uniformly random $b^* \in \mathbb{Z}_p$, finding all b_i-values is expected to take about p_n iterations of the above algorithm.
   For example, if $q < 2^{193}$ is a 192-bit prime, then $n = 60$ and $p_n = 283$ is sufficient. For a 256-bit prime $q < 2^{257}$ we may have $n = 76$ and $p_n = 383$.
2. Next, the attacker determines points $G_1, \ldots, G_n$ such that G_i generates the subgroup of order p_i of the curve defined by $(\mathbb{F}, a, b_i)$.

For example, performing the above computations on a virtual machine running Ubuntu 12.04 LTS Server x64 with eight 2.3 GHz CPUs and 4 GB RAM takes about 90 min for the NIST P-192 curve, and about 5 h for the NIST P-256 curve, when both computations are started in parallel.

Online attack. In the online attack phase, the attacker interacts with a "target server". This server may, for example, be a TLS server implementing TLS-DH cipher suites. In order to describe the attack independently of a particular server (which would require to go into the details of the service provided by this server and its implementation), we describe the attack with "oracles" that capture the required behavior of a server in an abstract manner. We show later how to instantiate these oracles in practice.

In the sequel let $\mathcal{O}$ be an oracle that performs computations on a curve described by parameters $\pi := (\mathbb{F}, a, b)$. The oracle internally keeps a random secret $s \in \mathbb{Z}_q$. On input $G \in \mathbb{G}$, the oracle computes sG by applying the double-and-add algorithm, using the DBL and ADD procedures from Fig. 2. Finally, the oracle returns $[sG]_x$, the x-coordinate of point sG.[4]

Given the results $(b_i, G_i, p_i)_{1 \leq i \leq n}$ from the precomputation phase and oracle $\mathcal{O}$, the actual attack proceeds as follows.

1. First, $\mathcal{A}$ queries the oracle $\mathcal{O}$ n times, on inputs $G_1, \ldots, G_n$. Given G_i, the oracle computes and returns $[sG_i]_x$. Note that G_i does not lie on the curve defined by the "real" parameters $\pi := (\mathbb{F}, a, b)$, but on the curve defined by adversarially-chosen parameters $(\mathbb{F}, a, b_i)$. However, since the DBL and ADD procedures implemented by $\mathcal{O}$ are independent of b, the oracle will perform this computation correctly.

2. Next, $\mathcal{A}$ computes the points $t \cdot G_i$ for all $t \in \{0, 1, \ldots, (p_i + 1)/2\}$.[5] Then it defines s_i to the unique value t, such that $[sG_i]_x = [tG_i]_x$. Note that either $s_i \equiv s \mod p_i$, or $-s_i \equiv s \mod p_i$. Note also that $s_i^2 \equiv (-s_i)^2 \mod p_i$, thus, s_i^2 is a uniquely determined value.

   Since the group operations implemented by $\mathcal{O}$ are independent of elliptic curve parameter b, and we assume that the oracle does not check whether the given point G_i lies on the correct curve $E_{(\mathbb{F}, a, b)}$, the oracle *implicitly* performs all computations on a different curve $E_{(\mathbb{F}, a, b_i)}$ having a small subgroup of order p_i. This allows $\mathcal{A}$ to determine the unique value $s_i^2 \mod p_i$ for all $i \in \{1, \ldots, n\}$.

3. Finally, $\mathcal{A}$ computes the secret s by determining the unique integer $s \in \mathbb{Z}$ such that $s^2 < q^2$ and $s^2 \equiv s_i^2 \mod p_i$ for all $i \in \{1, \ldots, n\}$, by applying the Chinese Remainder Theorem (CRT) and the fact that the primes p_i have been chosen such that $\prod_{i=1}^n p_i > q^2$.

   The nice trick of computing with $s_i^2 \mod p_i$ is from [3]. It overcomes the issue that we learn either $s_i \mod p_i$ or $-s_i \mod p_i$, but without being able to test immediately which one is correct, by performing all CRT computations with the unique values $s_i^2 \mod p_i$ and finally computing the square root of the result s^2 over $\mathbb{Z}$.

---

[4] Note that keys in elliptic curve cryptography are often derived only from the x-coordinate of a point, which motivates this abstraction.

[5] In principle, this step can also be precomputed. However, we will later have to consider a slightly different setting (and thus a different oracle) where this precomputation is not possible, therefore we explain it here.

Remark 2. We will later describe an oracle $\mathcal{O}$ which takes as input G_i, and immediately returns $s_i^2 \bmod p_i$ (instead of $[sG_i]_x$ as above). This essentially makes Step 2 of the online attack phase obsolete (in particular the computation of the values tG_i), and show how to realize this oracle in practice. Obviously, the above attack works identically with this oracle, by simply omitting Step 2. Describing the above attack with this particular oracle would, however, conceal the idea behind the invalid curve attack.

Remark 3. This attack can easily be prevented by replacing $\mathcal{O}$ with an oracle which checks whether a given point G lies on the "right" curve, that is, the defined by $\pi = (\mathbb{F}, a, b)$ before performing any computation. This is easy, by testing whether $y^2 \equiv x^3 + ax + b \bmod p$. Note also that the test of group membership is relatively inexpensive, as it requires to compute only a small number of multiplications modulo p, which does not increase the complexity of computing sP significantly. Nevertheless, we will show the practical relevance of this attack.

3   Transport Layer Security

In the TCP/IP reference model, the TLS protocol is located between the transport layer and the application layer. Its main purpose is to protect insecure application protocols like HTTP or IMAP. It is also used as a building block in other protocols, like EAP-TLS authentication for WiFi networks.

The first (inofficial) version was developed in 1994 by Netscape, named *Secure Sockets Layer*. In 1999, SSL version 3.1 was officially standardized by the IETF Working Group and renamed to *Transport Layer Security* [8], version 1.0. Since then, two updates of the TLS specification were released, versions 1.1 [9] and 1.2 [10]. Version 1.3 is currently under development [11].

Cipher suites. TLS is rather a protocol framework than a fixed protocol that allows communicating parties to choose from a large number of different algorithms for the various cryptographic tasks performed in the protocol (key agreement, authentication, encryption, integrity protection). A *cipher suite* is a concrete selection of algorithms for all required cryptographic tasks. For example, a connection established with the cipher suite `TLS_RSA_WITH_AES_128_CBC_SHA` uses RSA-PKCS#1 v1.5 public-key encryption [12] to establish a key, and symmetric AES-CBC encryption with 128-bit key and SHA-1-based HMACs. Cipher suite `TLS_DHE_WITH_AES_128_CBC_SHA` uses the same symmetric algorithms, but establishes the key from a Diffie-Hellman key exchange with ephemeral exponents[6] and RSA-PKCS#1 v1.5 signatures [12] for authentication.

The TLS RFCs [8–10] and their extensions [4] specify a large number of different cipher suites. They can be divided into three large groups, depending on the key agreement algorithm used: In `TLS_RSA` cipher suites, the client

---

[6] That is, both communicating partners choose random exponents for each execution of the Diffie-Hellman protocol within TLS. Alternatively, there exist `TLS_DH` cipher suites, where the server uses a static exponent.

chooses a random `PremasterSecret`, encrypts it with the public RSA key of the server, and sends this cryptogram within the `ClientKeyExchange` message to the server. In TLS_DH and TLS_DHE, the Diffie-Hellman key exchange is used to establish the `PremasterSecret`. The difference between these two families is that in TLS_DH, the server DH share is static and contained in the server certificate, whereas in TLS_DHE, only a signature verification key is contained in the server certificate, and an ephemeral server DH share is contained in an additional `ServerKeyExchange` message. Both Diffie-Hellman variants can also be used with elliptic curves, in which case the substring "EC" is added to the cipher suite name. *In this paper, we only consider cipher suites from the* TLS_ECDH *family.*

3.1 The TLS-ECDH Handshake

At the beginning of each TLS session the *TLS Handshake* protocol is executed, to negotiate a cipher suite and cryptographic keys. In the following, we give a brief overview of the TLS_ECDH Handshake for all versions up to the latest version 1.2, in as much detail as required to explain our attack. Note that the sequence of messages exchanged in the handshake depends on the selected cipher suite.

Handshake overview. Let us first give an overview of the messages sent in the TLS Handshake. See also Fig. 1. A TLS handshake is initiated by a TLS client with a `ClientHello` message. This message contains information about the TLS version, a list of references to TLS cipher suites proposed by the client, and a client nonce r_C.

The server now responds with the messages `ServerHello`, `Certificate`, and `ServerHelloDone`. The `ServerHello` message contains a reference to a cipher suite, selected by the server from the list proposed by the client, the selected TLS version, and a server nonce r_S. The `Certificate` message contains an X.509 certificate with the server's public key; in case of TLS_ECDH the public key must be a point sP on the elliptic curve. The `ServerHelloDone` message indicates the end of this step.

The client responds with a `ClientKeyExchange`, which contains the ephemeral DH share of the client, i.e. a point qP on the curve, where q was chosen randomly, and P is the base point.

Finally, both parties send the `ChangeCipherSpec` and `Finished` messages. The former notifies the receiving peer that subsequent TLS messages will be protected (i.e. encrypted and MACed) using the newly negotiated cipher suite. The `Finished` message contains a MAC over all exchanged messages, and is necessary to protect against certain attacks (see [16]).

After the handshake has finished, the peers can start to exchange payload data, which are protected by the negotiated cryptographic algorithms and keys.

TLS_ECDH *cipher suites.* In TLS_ECDH, the `ClientKeyExchange` message contains the client's contribution qP to a EC-based Diffie-Hellman key exchange. Combined with the value sP from the server certificate, the `PremasterSecret` is computed as $pms := [q(sP)]_x = [s(qP)]_x$. Note that only the x-coordinate of the resulting point is used as a `PremasterSecret`.

Using the TLS-PRF function, which is essentially a pseudorandom function based on an iterated HMAC, in a first step the `MasterSecret` ms is derived from pms:

$$ms := \mathsf{TLS\text{-}PRF}(pms; r_C, r_S, label_{ms}).$$

In a second step, the cryptographic keys and the `Finished` messages are derived using the `MasterSecret` as the key of the TLS-PRF:

$$keys := \mathsf{TLS\text{-}PRF}(ms; r_C, r_S, label_{keys}),$$
$$Fin := \mathsf{TLS\text{-}PRF}(ms; transcript)$$

Note that there is no explicit server authentication. The server authenticates implicitly, by being able to compute the `Finished` message correctly. This message depends on the `PremasterSecret`, thus the server must have been able to compute pms.

On client authentication via TLS. Note that we have described only server-authentication. It is in principle also possible to authenticate clients cryptographically in the TLS handshake, however, this would require *client certificates*. If an application requires client-authentication, then it is common to implement this by running an additional protocol over the established TLS channel, e.g. by transmitting a password. TLS is most commonly used with *server-only* authentication, therefore we focus on this setting.

4 Invalid Curve Attack on TLS-ECDH

In Sect. 2.2 we described an invalid curve attack on elliptic curve cryptosystem. In this section we will show how to obtain the required oracle responding with $s_i^2 \bmod p_i$, given a point G_i on a curve $(\mathbb{F}, a, b_i)$ with a small subgroup of order p_i from a TLS server. We assume that this TLS server supports TLS-ECDH cipher suites. Moreover, the server does not validate whether a point sent by the client belongs to a specified curve or not, and implements the group law in a way which is "compatible" with both the real parameters $(\mathbb{F}, a, b)$ and the adversarially-chosen parameters $(\mathbb{F}, a, b_i)$. As explained above, the latter holds in particular if the server implements the standard double-and-add algorithm for multiplication of elliptic curve points with scalars.

The main difficulty in constructing such an oracle from a TLS server is that the server does not directly respond with a result of a multiplication sG. Instead, it uses this result internally to derive cryptographic keys, and expects a suitable TLS `ClientFinished` message. Thus, we will construct an oracle $\mathcal{O}$ which will establish several TLS connections to verify a guessed value sG_i, by sending `ClientFinished` messages. More precisely, given a point G_i and its order p_i prepared by the attacker $\mathcal{A}$, the oracle $\mathcal{O}$ proceeds as follows (see also Fig. 3):

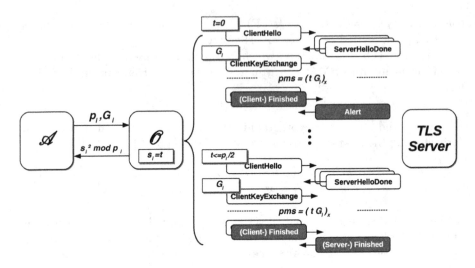

Fig. 3. Constructing an oracle $\mathcal{O}$ from a vulnerable TLS server supporting TLS-ECDH cipher suites.

1. $\mathcal{O}$ sets $t = 0$.
2. $\mathcal{O}$ starts a TLS handshake with a `ClientHello` message containing TLS-ECDH cipher suites (e.g., `TLS_ECDH_ECDSA_WITH_AES_128_CBC_SHA`). It receives TLS messages from the server and sends to the server a `ClientKeyExchange` message containing point G_i.
3. $\mathcal{O}$ guesses the *PremasterSecret* and sets it to $pms = [tG_i]_x$. Based on the *PremasterSecret*, $\mathcal{O}$ computes the *MasterSecret* and derives all keys needed for encryption and HMAC computations. $\mathcal{O}$ uses the derived keys to authenticate and encrypt the `ClientFinished` message.
4. If the TLS server accepts the `ClientFinished` message and responds with a `ServerFinished` message, the guessed *PremasterSecret* was correct and it holds that $s \equiv \pm t \mod p_i$. $\mathcal{O}$ sets $s_i := t$ and responds with $s_i^2 \mod p_i$. Otherwise, if the server responds with a TLS alert message and terminates the connection, the guessed *PremasterSecret* was incorrect. $\mathcal{O}$ increments t and proceeds with Step 2.

Note that $\mathcal{O}$ needs at most $p_i/2$ TLS handshake executions to get $s_i^2 \mod p_i$, and $p_i/4$ executions on average.

This oracle allows the attacker $\mathcal{A}$ to execute the full attack and recover server's private key. $\mathcal{A}$ first queries $\mathcal{O}$ n times, on inputs (G_i, p_i), where $i \in \{1, 2 \ldots, n\}$. It receives equations $s^2 \equiv s_i^2 \mod p_i$. Afterwards, $\mathcal{A}$ computes s^2 using the CRT and finally obtains the server's secret s.

5   Practical Evaluation

In this section we describe the invalid curve attacks on real implementations. To test the TLS implementations and libraries, we implemented a TLS client capable of sending invalid EC points in the `ClientKeyExchange` message, and complete a valid TLS handshake with a given `PremasterSecret`. In case an analyzed implementation was vulnerable to the attack, we used our TLS client to perform the complete attack. Otherwise, we analyzed why the attack was impossible. We conducted all the tests on a localhost, with a machine running on Xubuntu 14.10, with an Intel i7 processor (2.6 GHz).

5.1   Analyzed TLS Libraries

In order to use cryptographic libraries in Java dynamically, a system of cryptographic service providers was introduced. A cryptographic service provider "refers to a package or set of packages that supply a concrete implementation of a subset of cryptography features."[7] Java offers developers cryptographic providers, which are shipped directly with the Java installation (e.g., a SunEC provider for EC computation). The developers can however bind further providers like a Bouncy Castle provider to extend the default behavior of the installed providers.

For testing purposes, we set up a simple TLS server based on the *Java Secure Socket Extension (JSSE)*[8]. JSSE is used, for instance, in JBoss Application Server,[9] Apache Tomcat,[10] or Apache Camel framework.[11] We dynamically exchanged different cryptographic security providers to test their behavior while processing invalid EC points: Bouncy Castle, SunEC 1.8, and SunPKCS11-NSS 1.7. Further C/C++ libraries were tested with TLS test servers provided by these libraries.

- *Bouncy Castle Java 1.50.* Bouncy Castle[12] is a Java-based cryptography library, which can be bound to an implementation as a cryptographic provider. This library was heavily used for EC computations in Java 6, since Java 6 did not support EC by default. It can however also be used with further Java versions. In our work, we first tested Bouncy Castle 1.50 and then reevaluated our results with the 1.52 version.
- *MatrixSSL 3.7.1.* MatrixSSL is a C implementation designed specifically for small and embedded devices.[13]

---

[7] http://docs.oracle.com/javase/7/docs/technotes/guides/security/crypto/ CryptoSpec.html#Provider.
[8] http://docs.oracle.com/javase/6/docs/technotes/guides/security/jsse/ JSSERefGuide.html.
[9] http://jbossas.jboss.org/.
[10] https://tomcat.apache.org/.
[11] http://camel.apache.org/.
[12] https://www.bouncycastle.org/java.html.
[13] http://www.matrixssl.org/.

- *mbed TLS 1.3.10.* mbed TLS (formerly known as PolarSSL) is a lightweight C++ implementation also designed for small devices.[14]
- *OpenSSL 1.0.2a and LibreSSL 2.1.6.* OpenSSL is a cryptographic library with a TLS functionality.[15] LibreSSL is a fork of OpenSSL, created in 2014.[16] Our analysis revealed that the relevant EC implementation parts contain the same code, thus we treat them together as one library.
- *SunEC Security Provider 1.8.* SunEC is an Oracle Java security provider, which supports EC computations.[17] It is by default included in Oracle JDK 7 and 8, and in OpenJDK 8. In our tests, we used the SunEC provider distributed with Oracle JDK 1.8.0_40.
- *SunPKCS11-NSS Security Provider 1.7.* SunPKCS11-NSS is a Java security provider created as a wrapper over Mozilla's NSS library.[18] It is used as a default provider in OpenJDK 7 to support elliptic curves.
- *WolfSSL 3.4.6.* WolfSSL (formerly known as CyaSSL) is an embedded TLS library for small devices, written in C.

5.2 Attacks on Bouncy Castle

Analysis with our TLS client showed that a TLS server based on the Bouncy Castle library does not verify whether a given point lies on the right curve. For the point multiplication, the standard double-and-add algorithm is used. This allowed us to apply the attack described in Sect. 4 in a straightforward way.

Our evaluation with a secp256r1 elliptic curve revealed that the attacker needs about 3300 real server queries to get the private server key. In our localhost setup the online attack phase took about 155 s, see Table 2.

Table 2. Number of queries and time needed to execute the attack against a TLS server using the Bouncy Castle library in version 1.50. Note that a real attack over the Internet would last about ten to hundred times longer, depending on the server response times.

Elliptic curve	# of oracle queries	# of server queries	Duration [sec]
secp256r1	74	3300	155

We informed Bouncy Castle developers about this problem in their official developer mailing list.[19] It was patched one month after our disclosure, with the Bouncy Castle version 1.51. We are not sure whether our disclosure influenced the patch, since we got no official response.

---

[14] https://mbed.org/technology/mbed-tls/.
[15] https://www.openssl.org/.
[16] http://www.libressl.org/.
[17] http://docs.oracle.com/javase/8/docs/technotes/guides/security/SunProviders.html#SunEC.
[18] https://developer.mozilla.org/en-US/docs/Mozilla/Projects/NSS.
[19] http://bouncy-castle.1462172.n4.nabble.com/EC-Implementation-problems-td4657043.html.

5.3   Attacks on SunEC Security Provider

Our analysis of a TLS server using the SunEC security provider indicated that the SunEC provider is also vulnerable to the attacks described above. The server based on this provider processed invalid EC points and we were able to execute valid TLS handshakes. However, a full attack execution was not successful. Further analysis revealed that the SunEC provider introduced failures in the EC point multiplication, which resulted in wrong responses of the oracle constructed using the TLS server. Since the SunEC provider is implemented as a closed source, we needed to provide a black box analysis of the EC multiplication implementation.

Several tests with the EC computation showed that the probability of an invalid point multiplication depends on the order of the elliptic curve. More precisely, point multiplications on an elliptic curve group with order $p_i < 100$ returned a valid result with a probability of less than 60 %. Multiplications on elliptic curves with an order $p_i \approx 300$ returned a valid result with a probability of more than 90 %. Elliptic curves of an order $p_i \approx 1000$ computed correctly with a probability of about 98 %. See some exemplary results in Fig. 4, which depicts the SunEC computation correctness probability as a dependency of the elliptic curve order. The results were generated by applying 100 computations on 256 bit elliptic curves with random scalars.

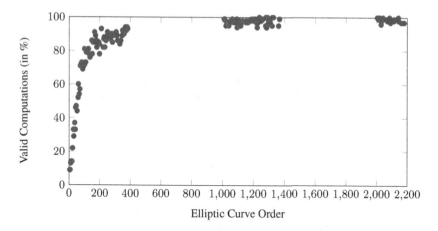

Fig. 4. Exemplary results showing dependency between the elliptic curve order and the percentage of valid EC computations executed by the SunEC provider: When working with custom elliptic curves with a small order ($p_i < 100$), only about one half of the computations were correct. This forced us to use elliptic curves with higher orders.

This is not a unique behavior of an EC implementation. A similar documented behavior of an invalid EC multiplication was observed in 2007 [18], when OpenSSL incorrectly multiplied specific points on a secp384r1 NIST curve. The reason was an incorrect handling of carry bits by the OpenSSL library. In our tests, we were however not able to analyze the reason for the incorrect computation by the SunEC provider due to the fact that the source code is not publicly available.

The SunEC provider behavior forced us to use elliptic curves with an order $p_i > 1000$, where the probability of a valid point multiplication was about $\rho \approx 98\%$. This resulted in a success probability $\rho_s := \rho^n \approx 36\%$ for computing a valid server secret s, where $n = 50$ is the number of oracle queries to attack a server using the secp256r1 curve. In order to increase the chance of computing a valid secret, we adapted the algorithm as follows:

1. The attacker $\mathcal{A}$ sends to the oracle $(n + n')$ queries, where $\prod_{i=1}^{n} p_i > q^2$ and n' are additional attack queries.
2. $\mathcal{A}$ computes $\binom{n+n'}{n}$ possible values for the secret s.
3. $\mathcal{A}$ tests, which of the possible secrets is correct, such that the base point multiplied by the secret returns server public key sP.

Note that both the second and the third steps are offline steps, which can be executed after querying the server.

This adapted algorithm resulted in an overall success probability of

$$\rho_s := \sum_{i=0}^{n'} \binom{n+i}{n} \cdot \rho^{(n+n'-i)} \cdot (1-\rho)^i.$$

We could for example compute a valid server secret s with a probability $\rho_s \approx 75\%$ with $n' = 3$ additional attack queries.

Table 3. Number of queries and time needed to execute the attack against a TLS server using the SunEC security provider. Note that a real attack over the Internet would last about ten to hundred times longer, depending on the server response times.

Elliptic curve	# of oracle queries	# of server queries	Duration [sec]
secp192r1	40	14732	346
secp256r1	52	16897	412

In Table 3 we summarize our attack results. As can be seen, using elliptic curves of a higher order resulted in lesser oracle queries, but in higher number of total server queries (in comparison to the attacks on Bouncy Castle presented in Table 2). We could execute the attacks in less than 7 min, in our localhost setup.

We informed Oracle security team about this vulnerability. Oracle is going to provide a patch in the Oracle Critical Patch Update in July 2015.

6   Attack Impact and Countermeasures

Checking whether a given point lies on the correct curve is a simple and effective countermeasure against the attacks described in this paper, its computational complexity is negligible in comparison to a full scalar multiplication of an elliptic curve point. The library providing elliptic curve point multiplication should therefore always validate whether the incoming point lies on the elliptic curve. Unfortunately, this seems not generally known to implementers of elliptic curve cryptography. Our attacks showed practical examples where this validation was omitted, and highlights that it is dangerous even in applications where the attack of [2] is not immediately applicable. The mentioned vulnerable implementations are already fixed or currently being fixed.

The described attack can be compared with the Heartbleed bug in the sense that the attack leaks the server's long-term private key to an attacker, and thus enables the attacker to impersonate the server in the future. However, we stress that TLS-ECDH cipher suite are less frequently used in practice than TLS-ECDHE or TLS-RSA ciphersuites, thus, the practical impact of these attacks is not as dramatic as the Heartbleed bug. Nevertheless, it is highly recommended to revoke and replace certificates used for static ECDH cipher suites in case the TLS server uses one of the vulnerable libraries or runs on a vulnerable Oracle JDK version, and supports TLS-ECDH cipher suites. This includes for example a JBoss Application Server, Apache Tomcat, or Apache Camel framework.

The attack on TLS is an important and particularly interesting special case. However, we stress that the omitted point validation in the considered libraries may also enable attacks on other protocols and applications beyond TLS. Thus, it is furthermore advisable to replace vulnerable elliptic curve libraries in any application using elliptic curve cryptography with secure ones, and to revoke and replace certificates for static ECDH cipher suites used in these applications.

A   Further Analysis

In Table 4, we provide further analysis of secure TLS libraries and their EC computation processing. Our analysis furthermore includes the Bouncy Castle 1.52 library version, which contains a fix to the attack presented in this paper. We investigate whether the libraries use the standard double-and-add algorithm or a specific window method, where the point validation takes place (before or after point multiplication, or directly after point decoding), and what is the response of the TLS server.

As can be seen, most of the libraries use a window multiplication method and an explicit point validation function. An exception is the WolfSSL library, which does not verify whether the incoming EC point lies on the curve. We were able to send an arbitrary point in the `ClientKeyExchange` message and let the server compute a `PremasterSecret` using this point. However, the invalid curve attacks were not applicable, because the library uses a specific window multiplication method and this method depends on the curve parameter b of $\pi := (\mathbb{F}, a, b)$. We still recommend the developers to fix this issue and implement explicit point validation.

In case of the SunPKCS11-NSS security provider, we were not able to analyze the source code and find out which multiplication method was used or whether

Table 4. Analysis of secure TLS libraries and their processing of elliptic curve multiplication.

Bouncy Castle 1.52

Multiplication	Window method	Package org.bouncycastle.math.ec AbstractECMultiplier.multiply custom.sec.SecP256R1FieldElement.multiply
Point Validation	After multiplication	math.ec.ECAlgorithms.validatePoint
Handshake Termination	Fatal Alert, Internal Error	

MatrixSSL 3.7.1

Multiplication	Window method	crypto/pubkey/ecc.c: function eccMulmod
Point Validation	Point decoding	crypto/pubkey/ecc.c: function eccTestPoint
Handshake Termination	Fatal Alert, Decode Error	

mbed TLS 1.3.10

Multiplication	Window method	library/ecp.c: function ecp_mul_comb
Point Validation	Before multiplication	library/ecp.c: function ecp_check_pubkey_sw
Handshake Termination	Connection termination, no Alert message	

OpenSSL 1.0.2a (and LibreSSL 2.1.6)

Multiplication	Window method	crypto/ec/ec_mult.c: function ec_wNAF_mul
Point Validation	Point decoding	crypto/ec/ecp_oct.c: function EC_POINT_is_on_curve, invoked by ec_GFp_simple_oct2point
Handshake Termination	Connection termination, no Alert message	

SunPKCS11-NSS Security Provider 1.7

Multiplication	–	–
Point Validation	–	–
Handshake Termination	Fatal Alert, Internal Error Caused by: ....InvalidKeySpecException: Could not create EC public key at ....P11ECKeyFactory.engineGeneratePublic(P11ECKeyFactory.java:169)	

WolfSSL 3.4.6

Multiplication	Window method	wolfcrypt/src/ecc.c: function ecc_mulmod
Point Validation	No validation	–
Handshake Termination	Connection termination, no Alert message	

the point validation takes place. Our table thus just includes a visible stack trace provided by the tested TLS server.

References

1. AlFardan, N.J., Paterson, K.G.: Lucky thirteen: breaking the TLS and DTLS record protocols. In: 2013 IEEE Symposium on Security and Privacy, pp. 526–540, Berkeley, California, USA, 19–22 May 2013. IEEE Computer Society Press (2013)
2. Antipa, A., Brown, D., Menezes, A., Struik, R., Vanstone, S.: Validation of elliptic curve public keys. In: Desmedt, Y.G. (ed.) PKC 2003. LNCS, vol. 2567, pp. 211–223. Springer, Heidelberg (2002)

3. Biehl, I., Meyer, B., Müller, V.: Differential fault attacks on elliptic curve cryptosystems. In: Bellare, M. (ed.) CRYPTO 2000. LNCS, vol. 1880, pp. 131–146. Springer, Heidelberg (2000)
4. Blake-Wilson, S., Bolyard, N., Gupta, V., Hawk, C., Moeller, B.: Elliptic Curve Cryptography (ECC) Cipher Suites for Transport Layer Security (TLS). RFC 4492 (Informational), May 2006. Updated by RFCs 5246, 7027
5. Bleichenbacher, D.: Chosen ciphertext attacks against protocols based on the rsa encryption standard PKCS #1. In: Krawczyk, H. (ed.) CRYPTO 1998. LNCS, vol. 1462, pp. 1–12. Springer, Heidelberg (1998)
6. Brumley, B.B., Barbosa, M., Page, D., Vercauteren, F.: Practical realisation and elimination of an ECC-related software bug attack. In: Dunkelman, O. (ed.) CT-RSA 2012. LNCS, vol. 7178, pp. 171–186. Springer, Heidelberg (2012)
7. Cohen, H., Frey, G., Avanzi, R., Doche, C., Lange, T., Nguyen, K., Vercauteren, F. (eds.): Handbook of Elliptic and Hyperelliptic Curve Cryptography. Discrete Mathematics and its Applications (Boca Raton). Chapman and Hall/CRC Press, Boca Raton (2006)
8. Dierks, T., Allen, C.: The TLS Protocol Version 1.0. RFC 2246 (Proposed Standard), January 1999. Obsoleted by RFC 4346, updated by RFCs 3546, 5746, 6176
9. Dierks, T., Rescorla, E.: The Transport Layer Security (TLS) Protocol Version 1.1. RFC 4346 (Proposed Standard), April 2006. Obsoleted by RFC 5246, updated by RFCs 4366, 4680, 4681, 5746, 6176
10. Dierks, T., Rescorla, E.: The Transport Layer Security (TLS) Protocol Version 1.2. RFC 5246 (Proposed Standard), August 2008. Updated by RFCs 5746, 5878, 6176
11. Dierks, T., Rescorla, E.: The Transport Layer Security (TLS) Protocol Version 1.3. draft-ietf-tls-tls13-04, January 2015
12. Kaliski, B.: PKCS #1: RSA Encryption Version 1.5. RFC 2313 (Informational), March 1998. Obsoleted by RFC 2437
13. Katz, J., Lindell, Y.: Introduction to Modern Cryptography. Chapman and Hall/CRC Press, Boca Raton (2007)
14. Lim, C.H., Lee, P.J.: A key recovery attack on discrete log-based schemes using a prime order subgroup. In: Kaliski Jr., B.S. (ed.) CRYPTO 1997. LNCS, vol. 1294, pp. 249–263. Springer, Heidelberg (1997)
15. McGrew, D., Igoe, K., Salter, M.: Fundamental Elliptic Curve Cryptography Algorithms. RFC 6090 (Informational), February 2011
16. Meyer, C., Schwenk, J.: SoK: lessons learned from SSL/TLS attacks. In: Kim, Y., Lee, H., Perrig, A. (eds.) WISA 2013. LNCS, vol. 8267, pp. 172–189. Springer, Heidelberg (2014)
17. Möller, B., Duong, T., Kotowicz, K.: This POODLE Bites: Exploiting the SSL 3.0 Fallback, September 2014. Technical report
18. Reimann, H.: Bn_nist_mod_384 gives wrong answers. openssl-dev mailing list #1593 (2007). http://marc.info/?t=119271238800004
19. Rizzo, J., Duong, T.: Here Come The $\oplus$ Ninjas, Ekoparty, May 2011

Crypto Applications and Attacks

Challenging the Trustworthiness of PGP: Is the Web-of-Trust Tear-Proof?

Alessandro Barenghi, Alessandro Di Federico, Gerardo Pelosi[✉],
and Stefano Sanfilippo

Department of Electronics, Information and Bioengineering – DEIB,
Politecnico di Milano, Milano, Italy
{alessandro.barenghi,alessandro.difederico,
gerardo.pelosi,stefano.sanfilippo}@polimi.it

Abstract. The OpenPGP protocol provides a long time adopted and widespread tool for secure and authenticated asynchronous communications, as well as supplies data integrity and authenticity validation for software distribution. In this work, we analyze the Web-of-Trust on which the OpenPGP public key authentication mechanism is based, and evaluate a threat model where its functionality can be jeopardized. Since the threat model is based on the viability of compromising an OpenPGP keypair, we performed an analysis of the state of health of the global OpenPGP key repository. Despite the detected amount of weak keypairs is rather low, our results show how, under reasonable assumptions, approximately 70 % of the Web-of-Trust *strong set* is potentially affected by the described threat. Finally, we propose viable mitigation strategies to cope with the highlighted threat.

Keywords: Web-of-Trust · WoT · OpenPGP · GPG · PGP

1 Introduction

The continuous increase in the size of computing systems, and the amount of data processed and exchanged by them calls for a widespread and trustworthy infrastructure for secure communications, encompassing both synchronous data transport and asynchronous messaging. Secure and endpoint-authenticated transport is nowadays provided by the Transport Layer Security (TLS) protocol [6], which is regarded as the most widespread solution when it comes to interactive communications between a server and a client. By contrast, the main workhorse in providing both confidentiality of the contents and sender authenticity, when it comes to secure e-mails, is the Open Pretty Good Privacy (OpenPGP) protocol [3]. The use of OpenPGP has been recently encouraged as a practical countermeasure to dragnet surveillance actions involving e-mail inspection. In particular the Free Software Foundation has promoted a campaign [29] to foster its use even among non technically-savvy users. Finally, the OpenPGP protocol is widely used to ensure data authentication and integrity of

© Springer International Publishing Switzerland 2015
G. Pernul et al. (Eds.): ESORICS 2015, Part I, LNCS 9326, pp. 429–446, 2015.
DOI: 10.1007/978-3-319-24174-6_22

binary packages of both all the Debian and RedHat derived GNU/Linux distributions, and a significant number of other popular ones such as Arch, Slackware and Gentoo. Therefore, the authenticity of the software binaries installed on the overwhelming majority of GNU/Linux systems is provided by OpenPGP signatures.

Since 2010, the official implementation of the OpenPGP protocol is available as a commercial technology by Symantec Corp., even if its source code is publicly available for peer review [28]. In addition to its employment as a solution to provide confidentiality and sender-authentication for e-mails, Symantec's products also employ the same protocol for securing files and documents. The OpenPGP protocol, first defined in the RFC2440 [4] and then amended and extended in the RFC4880 [3] by the Internet Engineering Task Force (IETF), has its best known implementations both in proprietary solutions (e.g., the *Google Chrome* browser extension called `end-to-end` [26], which has also been forked and adopted by *Yahoo! Mail* [32]) and in the free alternative GNU Privacy Guard (GPG) software suite [13].

The security services offered by OpenPGP all hinge on the requirement to perform sound public key authentication. The adopted approach relies on a distributed, asynchronous trust model as an alternative to both the hierarchical Public Key Infrastructure (PKI) [5,7], and the distributed and synchronous approach of *Perspectives* [31]. The mainstay of the OpenPGP protocol is its Web-of-Trust (WoT), which provides a way to establish the binding of a public key to an identity through having a number of peers a specific user trusts acting as certification authorities for it. This is realized through having all the OpenPGP users sign the public key-identity pairs belonging to anyone they could directly verify the identity of (e.g., via meeting in person). This practice, under the "small world assumption", grows a tightly knit network of trust-relationships, which allows anyone to authenticate public key-identity pairs.

Contribution. In this work we provide a survey of the state of health of the key material employed by OpenPGP, and globally distributed via a public network of keyservers. Subsequently, we describe a practical threat model, aiming at invalidating the public key authentication mechanism provided by OpenPGP, on the basis of a broken keypair either directly or indirectly authenticated by a trustworthy user. We evaluate the effective applicability of the proposed threat model, as a result of the weak keypairs we detected, reporting the portion of the most trusted subset of the OpenPGP WoT for which the authentication mechanism can be fooled. Finally, we suggest viable countermeasures to mitigate the effect of the described threat, and evaluate their actuation cost.

Organization of the paper. Section 2 provides a detailed overview of the inner workings of the OpenPGP protocol, and a survey of the current state of the WoT, Sect. 3 proposes our threat scenario, Sect. 4 reports the state of health of the global key storage, and Sect. 5 evaluates the applicability of the described threat, and proposes mitigation measures.

2   OpenPGP Infrastructure

A user in OpenPGP is associated with one or more *user-IDs*, each of which is composed by a text string usually including his real name and e-mail address. Each user generates a bundle of public key/private key pairs. Among the public key/private key pairs, one is denoted as a *primary key* pair, while each one of the others is denoted as a *subkey* pair. Conventionally, the primary key pair is employed only for signing purposes, while subkey pairs are employed to either encrypt or sign messages. The message encryption function employs a hybrid scheme using a combination of symmetric key cryptography for speed, and public key cryptography for ease of secure symmetric-key exchange between the sender and the receiver of the data transfer. In particular, OpenPGP employs a symmetric key cipher, with a randomly generated ephemeral key, to encrypt the message to be transferred. The ephemeral key is sent encrypted with the recipient's public key along with the encrypted message.

Users issue *certificates* to each other to authenticate the binding between user-IDs and public keys (primary or subkey). This is obtained signing with their primary private keys a subset of certificate data including the user-ID and one public key. A certificate contains one primary public key, and at least a self-signature binding it to the user-ID. In addition, it may contain several signatures verifiable via public keys of other users. The global distribution of OpenPGP certificates is realized via a network of public key directories, known as *keyservers*, which provide a synchronized billboard accessible via either a dedicated interface over HTTP, known as the HKP protocol [25]. We note that the available implementations of the OpenPGP keyserver do not support TLS, although it is possible to add it employing a reverse proxy. The synchronization across keyservers is maintained with a set-reconciliation algorithm [17], which guarantees that the uploading of a certificate on one of the servers will be mirrored by all the others. The servers are not required to perform any integrity or sanity checks.

2.1   Key Management

Each user keeps his own local key storage, known as *keyring*, containing a number of certificates, plus his own private keys (which are never disclosed). The keyring is complemented with two local maps, stored in the so-called *trust-db*. The first map associates each public key in the keyring to its *trust level*, i.e., the amount of trust the owner of the trust-db has in the actions of the public key owner. The second one binds each public key in the keyring to its *validity level*, i.e., the extent to which the keyring owner deems the key authentic.

Trust level assignment. The admissible trust values, according to the default trust model of GPG are: *(i)* `ultimate`, which is reserved for the keyring owner's public keys; *(ii)* `full`, *(iii)* `marginal`, *(iv)* `untrusted`, *(v)* `undefined`, and *(vi)* `unknown`. Trust levels from *(i)* to *(iv)* can only be explicitly assigned by the user through a direct interaction with the OpenPGP client. This is typically done after the user has ascertained the identity and trustworthiness of the public key owner either meeting her in person, or by any other means he sees fit. The unknown trust level is automatically assigned by the OpenPGP client to a new public key whenever it is imported into the keyring. Whenever a public key contained in the keyring is employed to verify a signature on a different public key, the client checks whether its trust level is set to unknown, and, if possible, asks the user to provide one. In case it is not possible to obtain an explicit trust level from the user, the client sets the trust level to undefined.

Validity level computation. The admissible validity values for a public key are: *(i)* full, *(ii)* marginal, *(iii)* untrusted, and *(iv)* unknown. The validity level of a public key is computed by the OpenPGP client employing the certificates contained in the keyring, and both the trust and validity values in the trust-db. The public key is deemed authentic if its validity level is full. Whenever a new public key is imported into the user keyring, its validity is automatically set to the unknown level. The computation of the validity level of a public key takes place every time it needs to be employed, and its validity level in the trust-db is unknown. All public keys having an ultimate trust level have their validity level set to full. Public keys carrying a signature verified with a public key having an ultimate trust level are considered to have full validity. Thus any piece of key material carrying a signature verifiable by the public key of the keyring owner is considered fully valid. Subsequently, all the public keys carrying a signature verified by a fully valid, fully trusted public key are assigned a full validity level. If the signature on a public key is verified by a fully valid, but marginally trusted public key its validity level is set to marginal. Whenever three such signatures are verified on the same public key, its validity level is promoted to full. Signatures which can be verified by public keys with an untrusted trust level are not taken into account in the computation. If a signature on a public key is verified by a public key having an undefined trust level, the signed public key validity is set to undefined. The aforementioned validity level computation rules allow the client to assign a value to the validity of a signed public key taking into account the one which verifies the signature. This process effectively creates chains of validity dependence among public keys, where each signed one depends on the one verifying the signature to be validated.

Revocations management. The revocation of both public keys and signatures made to certify the binding between an identity and a public key are performed creating a *revocation signature*. Three types of revocation signatures are possible: (i) a primary key revocation, (ii) a subkey revocation, and (iii) a signature revocation, which voids the authenticity of a signature, regardless of whether it is correctly verified by the corresponding public key or not. The OpenPGP revocation management allows to mark a signature as *non revocable*: in this case, all the revocation signatures on it are ignored. Finally, it is possible to indicate an expiration date for both public keys and signatures.

2.2 The OpenPGP Web-of-Trust

Each OpenPGP user is endowed with a keyring and a trust-db, which represent the means by which he will authenticate the public keys contained in the former. The most common way to analyze the effectiveness of the authentication mechanism is to examine the certifier-certified relation among the different public keys of the keyring. This certifier-certified relation is commonly represented in terms of a directed graph [30] with public keys as nodes and signatures as directed edges exiting from the certifying node and entering into the certified one. Such a representation implies that the public key contained in the source node can be used to verify a signature on the destination node. The direction of the arcs is a convention chosen for the sake of clarity: we note that the authors of [30] employ arcs in the opposite direction. This graph is known as the Web-of-Trust (WoT) of a keyring, although it is indeed the certifier-certified relationship being represented, instead of the user specified trust.

Table 1. Contents of the OpenPGP keyservers as of March 2015, reporting a ≈41 % increase of the number of certificates w.r.t. the figures reported in 2011 by [30]

	Total	Revoked	Expired
Primary public keys (certificates)	3, 867, 397	181, 833	13, 754
Public subkeys	3, 597, 910	27, 670	2
Signatures	13, 866, 817	78, 976	1, 828, 630

Willing to obtain information on the state of all the publicly available certificates, we analyzed the contents of the distributed keyserver network as if it were a single large keyring, and its corresponding WoT. We obtained a snapshot of the whole keyserver contents as of March 2015, of which we report a synoptic overview in Table 1. Note that it is possible for an OpenPGP user to generate a keypair and never upload the corresponding certificate on the keyservers. The number of subkeys is smaller than the number of primary keys: this is caused by the old certificate formats of OpenPGP (Ver. 3 and earlier) not mandating the generation of separate subkeys to relieve the primary keypair from encryption uses. We also note that the amount of revoked keys is comparatively small (≈4.7 %), and the number of expired ones is almost negligible (0.35 %). In particular, we ascertained that 99.6 % of the primary public keys do not have an expiration date set, which may be ascribed to the optional nature of the expiration date field [3]. We report the presence of 3, 828, 825 unique user-IDs, thus pointing strongly at a one-to-one correspondence between user-IDs and primary public keys for most of the OpenPGP users, although the standard [3] allows for multiple user-IDs. The mean number of identity-public key binding signatures per certificate, including the mandatory self-signature, is 2.08, pointing to the whole WoT as a rather sparse graph. The current global keyring contains 33, 136 non revocable signatures.

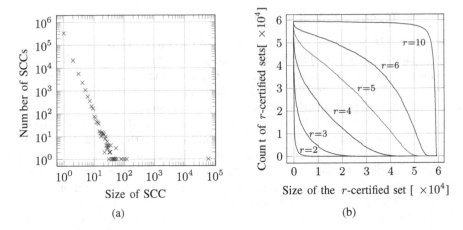

Fig. 1. Structural features of the WoT and the strong set as of March 2015. (a) reports the number of distinct SCCs of the WoT and their size. (b) depicts the distribution of the r-certified sets sizes over the strong set (GPG default: $r = 5$, in blue) (Color figure online)

The concept of Strongly Connected Components (SCCs) of a directed graph is a key tool to analyze the usefulness of the WoT [30]. A SCC is a maximally connected subgraph where there is at least one path between every node pair. Computing the number of SCCs and their size yields the data reported in Fig. 1(a), taking into account only non-revoked and non-expired public keys and signatures. Examining the sizes of the SCCs, it can be noticed that around 300 k nodes are indeed isolated (top left point in figure), and all but one SCCs have a size smaller than or equal to 117. The largest SCC of the WoT (bottom right point in figure), is composed by 59,466 primary public keys, and is commonly known as the *strong set*. The strong set is significantly less sparse than the rest of the WoT: its nodes have an average of 27.39 signatures on them. However, we note that the distribution of signatures on each certificate of the strong set (incoming arcs in nodes) is rather skewed: in particular, only $\approx$18 % of the strong set users have more than 27 signatures. The nodes in the strong set are the ones able to better exploit the structure of the WoT to perform public key authentication since, in principle, there is a path between any two of them. However, a bound on the allowed certifier-certified chains length exists, limiting their length to 5 in both in the original PGP and in the GPG trust model; thus, not all the strong set paths are useful. In fact, the maximum length among all such paths, known as the graph diameter, is 27, and only 38.7 % of the distances between pairs of strong set nodes are smaller or equal to 5. To the end of analyzing the effectiveness of the OpenPGP WoT as a public key certifier, we define the concept of r-certified set as follows.

Definition 1 (r-certified set). *Let n be a node of the WoT, and r be an integer $r \geq 1$. The set of nodes reachable from n via a valid certifier-certified chain of length shorter or equal to r is defined as the r-certified set of n.*

Since each OpenPGP user acts as both user and certification authority, the size of the r-certified set of a given node n is a measure of: (i) the extent of the strong set which is actually useful for n to perform public key authentication when acting as a user, and (ii) the usefulness of n as a certification authority.

Figure 1(b) reports the evaluation of the count of r-certified sets for the nodes in the strong set, and $r \in \{2, 3, 4, 5, 6, 10\}$. Considering the case of the PGP and GPG default value $r = 5$, highlighted in blue, it can be seen how only a little more than 10 k nodes have a r-certified set exceeding 40 k in size (represented by the values on the bottom right corner), out of $\approx$60 k, while around 15 k nodes have an r-certified set not exceeding 10 k in size (values on the top left corner). Lowering the maximum certifier-certified chain length r yields an effective decrease of the usefulness of the strong set, up to the point where, with $r = 2$, no nodes have a r-certified set larger than 10 k elements. By contrast, increasing the chain length boosts the certifying capability of the nodes, at the expense of the need for a longer trust chain to be effectively exploited. For instance, for $r = 10$ the overwhelming majority of the nodes have an r-certified set exceeding 50 k elements out of $\approx$60 k, at the expense of the requirement to trust a rather long certifier-certified chain.

3 Threats to the WoT Authentication Capabilities

In this section we provide a description of the scenario and the threat model to OpenPGP public key authentication capabilities.

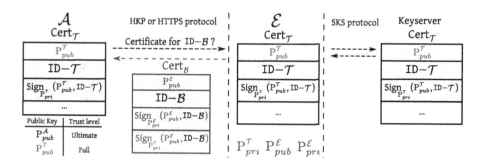

Fig. 2. Compromising a fully trusted key scenario. $\mathcal{A}$ queries the keyserver network for $\mathcal{B}$'s certificate, receiving instead one forged by $\mathcal{E}$. Blue portions of the picture are forged by the adversary $\mathcal{E}$, red portions are compromised by $\mathcal{E}$, black portions are genuine (Color figure online)

Assume a user, $\mathcal{A}$, wants to retrieve an OpenPGP certificate containing the public key of whom she wants to communicate with, $\mathcal{B}$. $\mathcal{A}$ will query a keyserver to retrieve $\mathcal{B}$'s certificate. A malicious keyserver, or an adversary able to act as an active man-in-the-middle, say $\mathcal{E}$, is willing to supply a forged OpenPGP certificate to $\mathcal{A}$, as depicted in Fig. 2. If $\mathcal{B}$'s certificate is considered authentic by $\mathcal{A}$ after running the signature validation procedure, both the confidentiality, and the authenticity of the messages between $\mathcal{A}$ and $\mathcal{B}$ are compromised.

Compromising a fully trusted key. Assume $\mathcal{A}$ is trusting a public key $P_{pub}^{\mathcal{T}}$, with full trust level. If the adversary $\mathcal{E}$ is able to compromise $\mathcal{T}$'s keypair, i.e., she is able to obtain $\mathcal{T}$'s private key, she will be able to forge a certificate containing an arbitrary public key $P_{pub}^{\mathcal{E}}$, generated by herself. She will use this to forge a certificate binding $\mathcal{B}$'s identity ID$-\mathcal{B}$ to her public key $P_{pub}^{\mathcal{E}}$, and perform a self signature on $(P_{pub}^{\mathcal{E}}, \text{ID}-\mathcal{B})$ with $P_{pri}^{\mathcal{E}}$. Subsequently, $\mathcal{E}$ will compute a signature on $(P_{pub}^{\mathcal{E}}, \text{ID}-\mathcal{B})$ with $\mathcal{T}$'s private key $P_{pri}^{\mathcal{T}}$, and append it to the forged certificate $\text{Cert}_\mathcal{B}$ (depicted in blue in Fig. 2).

Upon receiving the forged certificate, $\mathcal{A}$ will verify both signatures and, trusting the actions of $\mathcal{T}$ fully, she will consider $P_{pub}^{\mathcal{E}}$ fully valid, according to the key authentication mechanism described in Sect. 2.

A noteworthy point is the fact that $\mathcal{E}$ generates the forged certificate for $\mathcal{B}$ from scratch. In case a certificate for $\mathcal{B}$ is already present on the keyservers, $\mathcal{E}$ simply refrains from synchronizing the forged one, effectively presenting to $\mathcal{A}$ a different view on the state of the distributed key storage with respect to the other keyservers. This strategy is viable as the SKS synchronization protocol between keyservers allows each member to choose which certificates should be included in the synchronization, without any enforcement on the inclusion of all of them. In case a certificate for $\mathcal{B}$ is not present, $\mathcal{E}$ can refrain from performing an active man-in-the-middle attack, and simply upload the forged certificate on the global directory, leaving the delivery to $\mathcal{A}$ up to the keyserver network.

Compromising a key verified by a fully trusted one. Consider the alternate scenario where $\mathcal{A}$ is trusting $\mathcal{I}$ fully, and has $\mathcal{I}$'s certificate in her own keyring, as depicted in Fig. 3(a). $\mathcal{E}$ has compromised $\mathcal{T}$'s keypair and has generated a keypair $P_{pri}^{\mathcal{E}}, P_{pub}^{\mathcal{E}}$ which she desires to substitute to the legitimate one for $\mathcal{B}$. $\mathcal{A}$ gets to know that $\mathcal{T}$ is on a certifier-certified chain leading to $\mathcal{B}$ (for instance using an online tool [23]), and fetches $\text{Cert}_\mathcal{T}$ from the keyserver with the intent of verifying the signature made with $P_{pri}^{\mathcal{T}}$ present in $\text{Cert}_\mathcal{B}$. The resulting state of $\mathcal{A}$'s keyring is depicted in Fig. 3(a), and the trust level of $P_{pub}^{\mathcal{T}}$ is set to unknown. Subsequently, $\mathcal{A}$ attempts to compute the validity of $P_{pub}^{\mathcal{E}}$ contained in $\text{Cert}_\mathcal{B}$. To this end $\mathcal{A}$ requires a definite validity level for $P_{pub}^{\mathcal{T}}$, which is computed to be full, through verifying both $\mathcal{I}$'s and $\mathcal{T}$'s signatures on $\text{Cert}_\mathcal{T}$ and knowing that $P_{pub}^{\mathcal{I}}$ is fully trusted. $\mathcal{A}$'s client will ask $\mathcal{A}$ to set a trust value for $P_{pub}^{\mathcal{T}}$ in order to proceed with the validation of $P_{pub}^{\mathcal{E}}$. Assume $\mathcal{A}$ sets the trust level of $P_{pub}^{\mathcal{T}}$, to full on the basis that $\mathcal{I}$ and $\mathcal{T}$ cross-signed their certificates, thus providing reasonable evidence for the presence of a mutual trust relationship among them. This assumption is reasonable especially whenever both $\mathcal{T}$ and $\mathcal{I}$ are members of the strong set, and thus highly regarded in terms of reliability in the use of OpenPGP. We note that, in case $\mathcal{A}$ decides against setting the trust level to `full`, she will be forfeiting the usefulness of this WoT path as a mean for authenticating $\mathcal{B}$'s public key, effectively decreasing the WoT usefulness as a public key authenticator from $\mathcal{A}$'s point of view. Once the trust level for $P^{\mathcal{T}}_{pub}$ is set to `full`, $\mathcal{A}$ will set the validity level of $P^{\mathcal{E}}_{pub}$ to `full` as it is correctly signed by $P^{\mathcal{T}}_{pub}$, thus effectively believing $\mathcal{E}$'s forgery.

By induction on the length of the certifier-certified chains of the aforementioned scenario, $\mathcal{E}$ will be able to forge an arbitrary certificate whenever $\mathcal{A}$ **fully** trusts a key containing in its $(r-1)$-certified set the compromised key $\mathcal{T}$ (recall that $r \geq 1$). Figure 3(b) reports an example of WoT, including the forged $P^{\mathcal{E}}_{pub}$, and the compromised $P^{\mathcal{T}}_{pub}$, drawn, together with their signatures, in blue and red respectively. The portion of the graph (both keys and signatures) drawn in black is genuine and non compromised. The red-filled nodes are the ones having in the $(r-1)$-certified set the compromised public key $P^{\mathcal{T}}_{pub}$ considering the GPG default value $r = 5$. If $\mathcal{A}$ trusts any one of the red-filled nodes, and extends the trust to the ones which have mutual signatures with respect to it, $\mathcal{E}$ will be able to forge a certificate for an arbitrary identity and get it validated by $\mathcal{A}$. In this respect, we note that, if $\mathcal{A}$ requires mutual signatures between a trusted node and one with an **unknown** trust level to extend her trust, it is possible for $\mathcal{E}$ to forge $\mathcal{T}$'s signature on $P^{\mathcal{I}}_{pub}$ (the red arc from $P^{\mathcal{T}}_{pub}$ to $P^{\mathcal{I}}_{pub}$ in Fig. 3(b), should it be missing. We can thus state our attacker model as follows.

Definition 2 (Threat model). *Consider the OpenPGP public key authentication scheme based on the PGP/GPG trust model with a certifier-certified chain bound $r = 5$ and the WoT signature verification infrastructure. Assume an adver-*

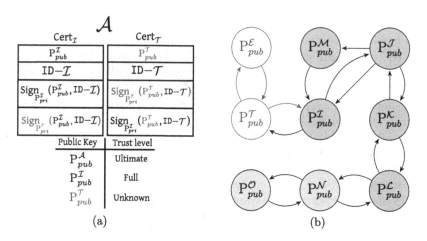

(a)   (b)

Fig. 3. Compromising a key verified by a fully trusted one scenario. Subfigure (a) represents the state of $\mathcal{A}$'s keyring and trust-db after fetching the certificate for the compromised key Cert$_{\mathcal{T}}$. Subfigure (b) depicts a sample WoT, highlighting the extent to which the attack is successful (red filled nodes), and the immune portion (green filled ones). Items drawn in blue are forged by $\mathcal{E}$, the ones in red are compromised by $\mathcal{E}$, the black ones are genuine (Color figure online)

sary $\mathcal{E}$ able to compromise the keypair of a user $\mathcal{T}$, $\left(P_{pri}^{\mathcal{T}}, P_{pub}^{\mathcal{T}}\right)$. $\mathcal{E}$ is also able to either act as a keyserver or perform active man-in-the-middle between a targeted user $\mathcal{A}$ and $\mathcal{A}$'s keyserver of choice. Whenever $\mathcal{A}$ tries to fetch the certificate of another user $\mathcal{B}$, the adversary $\mathcal{E}$ is able to forge a valid Cert$_\mathcal{B}$, provided: (i) the public key of the compromised keypair, $P_{pub}^{\mathcal{T}}$, is within $r - 1$ certifier-certified steps from a public key deemed fully trusted and fully valid by $\mathcal{A}$ and (ii) $\mathcal{A}$ extends her trust to the intermediate certifier public keys.

Consequentially, compromising a well connected public key in the WoT will yield a potentially larger attack surface against the target user $\mathcal{A}$. In particular, compromising nodes in the strong set has the maximum potential for certificate forgery, both due to the strongly connected nature of the strong set (each of its nodes has an average of 27.39 signatures in contrast with the 2.08 average of the global WoT as mentioned in Sect. 2.2), and to the potential willingness of $\mathcal{A}$ to trust them as certifiers. Note that the capability of $\mathcal{E}$ of performing signatures on behalf of $\mathcal{T}$ allows her to connect $P_{pub}^{\mathcal{T}}$ to the strong set as long as $\mathcal{T}$'s certificate contains a signature from a strong set member. This observation allows to extend the effectiveness of the described threat model to keys which are not members of the strong set, as we will highlight in Sect. 5.

The practical impact of the described attacker model is thus dependent on the robustness of the generated keypairs, and the location of their public keys within the OpenPGP WoT. In the following we will examine the factors allowing $\mathcal{E}$ to compromise a keypair present in the current OpenPGP global keyring, thus meeting the former requirement.

4   State of Health of the OpenPGP Global Keyring

In the following, we report, for each one of the asymmetric key cryptosystems employed to perform signatures in OpenPGP, the possible issues on the key material which may lead to compromise a keypair. A similar analysis, tackling keypairs employed in the SSL/TLS and SSH protocols was performed in [11]. The asymmetric key ciphers available for signature purposes in OpenPGP are RSA [24], DSA [19], ElGamal [8] and ECDSA [9]. ECDSA signatures have been recently introduced in OpenPGP and currently account for a negligible portion (<0.01%) of the total keypairs, and were thus ignored in our analysis. Table 2 reports, for each examined issue, the number of affected keypairs, and the number of signatures performed by strong set members on their certificate.

Note that the expiration of a compromised key does not prevent an adversary from performing the certificate forgery. In fact the expiration date of a key can be updated by performing a new self-signature which is feasible by the adversary, as he owns the corresponding private key. Moreover, in the man-in-the-middle scenario, we note that the adversary is also able to drop revocation signatures, thus practically voiding their effect. However, willing to take into account the scenario where the adversary uploads a forged certificate for a non-existent recipient, and does not need to perform an active man-in-the-middle attack, we will assume that revoked keys are unusable.

Table 2. Report on the state of health of the global OpenPGP keyring, highlighting which issues are present, how many keypairs are affected, and how many of them were signed by strong set members

Cryptosystem	Keypair issue	Public keys		
		Affected	Not revoked	Signed by strong set
RSA	$\lceil \log_2 N \rceil < 600$	8,260	89.48 %	1.79 %
	$600 \leq \lceil \log_2 N \rceil \leq 800$	11,205	91.79 %	2.03 %
	Prime modulus	1	100.00 %	100.00 %
	Common primes	4	100.00 %	0.00 %
DSA	None	–	–	–
ElGamal	Use as a signing key	1,383	89.73 %	2.60 %
Any	MD5 Hash function	155,760	89.79 %	3.78 %

4.1 RSA Cryptosystem

The RSA algorithm is a very popular choice in the OpenPGP ecosystem both for signing and encryption purposes. In particular, it gained popularity in 2009, when the first version of GnuPG using it as default algorithm for the key generation process was released (i.e., Ver. 1.4.10). An RSA public key is constituted of a pair of integers (e, N) where N is obtained as the product of two large, randomly chosen primes p and q, having substantially the same bit-size. The RSA private key d is computed as $d = e^{-1} \bmod \varphi(N)$, where Euler's Totient function $\varphi(\cdot)$ can be evaluated only by the keypair owner who knows the factorization of the modulus N, since $\varphi(N) = (p-1)(q-1)$. The values of p, q and $\varphi(N)$ should be kept as secret as the value d. The security margin of the RSA cryptosystem hinges on the difficulty of factoring N, provided nothing else is known on the form of the two factors: p and q [14]. In the following, we present the aspect on which we focused our attention during the analysis of the RSA public keys contained in the WoT.

Outdated key sizes. The OpenPGP system has a long history, which means that a good share of the key-pairs were generated in an era when security margins were significantly lower, and were never revoked. Nowadays RSA keys using a modulo N smaller than 768 bits are considered weak, as it was proven the practical feasibility of factoring one in [12], while factoring 512-bit RSA moduli was proven to be feasible in about 10 h of computation time on Amazon EC2 for a cost around 100 USD [10]. Moreover, as shown in [2], the cost of factoring multiple RSA moduli with the same size increases less than linearly with their number. As a consequence, we consider all the 8,260 RSA moduli smaller than 600 bits to be compromised, and the 11,205 ones using a modulus between 600 and 800 bits-long as nearly compromised. As reported in Table 2 only $\approx$10 % of the keys were revoked, and none of them are part of the strong set. However, there are more than 1,000 signatures from the strong set vouching for their authenticity, thus meeting the requirement of Sect. 3 for 1.79 % keys smaller than 600 bits, and 2.03 % of the ones between 600 and 800 bits.

Prime modulus. If the modulus N is prime, $\varphi(N)$ can be trivially computed as $\varphi(N) = N - 1$, thus allowing an adversary to compute the private exponent d. We found a single instance of this issue, running a primality test on all the moduli of the RSA public keys available. This compromised key does not belong to the strong set, but was signed by one of its members.

Common primes. Given two moduli $n = p \cdot q$ and $n' = p' \cdot q'$, if they share a factor (e.g., $p = p'$), then it is possible to efficiently factor both. In fact, computing the greatest common divisor (using Euclid's algorithm), it is possible to obtain the common factor $p = p'$, and, via trivial division operations, the q and q' too. Looking for common primes is a technique which has been proven successful in discovering flaws in the TLS certificate pool [11]. The causes for the repeated use of the same primes were either a low entropy availability on the generating system, in particular on embedded devices or during the boot process, or simply faulty PRNG implementations. The results of our survey point to substantially different results: only two pairs of public key shared a common prime, thus providing good evidence of the soundness of the prime generators employed in OpenPGP implementations. We note that none of the public keys sharing primes were in the strong set, nor they were signed by one of its members, and thus are not exploitable in the described threat model. We also report the presence of 253 RSA moduli which are not the product of two large primes. They share a large amount of small factors and the self signatures on the corresponding public keys are not valid, nor there are other valid signatures on them.

4.2   Digital Signature Algorithm

The examination of keypairs generated to perform signatures with the DSA algorithm were found to be sound, and passed all the tests mandated by the [19] standard (prime generation methodology, check on the order of the generator). The only keys found not to be passing the tests were belonging to corrupted certificates where neither the public key was respecting the constraints of [19], nor the signatures made by others on it were verified correctly.

4.3   ElGamal Cryptosystem

The ElGamal cryptosystem is formed by two primitives, signature and encryption, based on the Discrete Logarithm Problem [1,8] over a multiplicative cyclic subgroup of order q of $\mathbb{Z}_p^*$, the set of equivalence classes of signed integers modulo p, with both p, q primes and $p \geq 2^{1024}, q \geq 2^{160}$. The ElGamal signature algorithm produces an output longer than DSA, and, for this reason, it has been historically discouraged. Thus, ElGamal keys are assigned two separate algorithm identifiers depending on whether they are only employed to perform encryptions, or if they are also used for signatures. In 2004, Nguyen et al. [20]

discovered a significant flaw in how ElGamal signatures were implemented in GPG. The ElGamal signature requires the generation of an unpredictable random integer l of the same bit-size of p. The issue with the GPG implementation of the ElGamal signature is that l is generated as an unpredictable random integer q bits long, with $q \ll p$, for efficiency reasons. This allows to recover the ElGamal private key exploiting the material of a single signature. Since all the ElGamal primary keys must have signed their own certificate, we consider them to be all compromised. It is interesting to note how the WoT still contains $1,241$ unrevoked keys ElGamal public keys allowed to perform signatures, and bearing signatures from members of the strong set.

4.4 MD5 Based Signatures

In digital signatures, the choice of the cryptographic hash to be employed to reduce the signed content size to a fixed length is crucial. The MD5 hash algorithm has been proven vulnerable to a specific collision attack, where it is possible for an attacker to choose the prefix of the colliding messages. In particular, Stevens et al. [27] exploited the aforementioned issue to construct a rogue X.509 certificate, splicing out a valid signature, and forging a set of certificate contents colliding with the signed hash. This was possible especially as the X.509 standard allows an arbitrary comment field to be placed as the suffix of the material to be hashed [5]. The same attack can be performed also on a OpenPGP certificate signature, since the RFC4880 [3] allows to add arbitrary subpackets at the end of the data to be signed. Despite, RFC4880 explicitly discourages the use of MD5, signatures made with it are still quite widespread. In fact, our analysis shows that ≈ 115 k unrevoked keys performed at least a MD5 signature, and 3.78 % of them were signed by a strong set member as reported in Table 2.

5   Vulnerability Evaluation

In this section we provide concrete evidence of the extent of applicability of the attack scenario described in Sect. 3 against the public OpenPGP keyring. To this end, all the certificates in the public keyring were parsed and stored in a database, from which the relevant data was extracted and further processed.

In order to avoid GPG-specific parsing behaviors, we adopted a parsing library [15] independently built on RFC4880 OpenPGP format specifications. The library was modified to extract the RSA and DSA/ElGamal signature material for subsequent analysis steps and to make the parsing process more robust towards recoverable errors caused by corrupted entries in packets.

We point out that parsing the dumps available for keyserver bootstrapping, split in chunks of 10 k–50 k certificates, results in a few non recoverable errors, due to corrupted packet metadata, which in turn cause the parser to go out-of-sync with the underlying format. The issue was made worse by the lack of synchronization points, as an OpenPGP certificate bundle has no recognizable trailer to skip to. In fact, when such an error is encountered, the parsing process cannot proceed further and the rest of the chunk is discarded. Such an issue was encountered in [30], and prevented the parsing of around 50 k certificates. However, we observed that the main implementation of the SKS server [16] reported no errors in importing the certificate dumps, while the GnuPG client fails in parsing them in the same way our parser does. Combining the observations above, we decided to bootstrap our own instance of the SKS keyserver with the provided dump and re-export the dataset as a separate file for each certificate bundle. By doing so, we were able to limit the impact of unrecoverable parsing errors to the single certificate in which they were located. All the certificates in the public keyring dump were correctly parsed.

We imported the information contained in the global keyring into a `MySQL` 5.5.41 database with `MyISAM` backend. The parsing stage lasted approximately 3 h and resulted in 10 GB of database files being stored on disk. The underlying schema was modeled on the content of the OpenPGP packets composing a certificate bundle, with a table for each packet type. With said database in place, the various datasets used for the analysis presented in this paper were gathered as SQL queries and prepared for further processing steps. In particular, each analysis step was coded as a `Python` script with specified dependencies onto the results of previous steps. The whole set of analysis was then orchestrated by a `makefile`, making the whole process fully automatic and therefore easily reproducible. The WoT was exported as a graph, with arcs being trust signatures and keys as nodes, and all connectivity and reach-ability measures and the related graph processing were carried on using `graph-tool` [22], a comprehensive `Python` toolkit for graph analysis. The `fastgcd` tool [11] was used to find common RSA primes in an efficient way. With the aforementioned infrastructure in place, and after performing the analyses which produced the results shown in Table 2 and described in Sect. 4, we proceeded to compute the portion of the WoT affected by the threat model described in Sect. 3.

Figure 4 reports the amount of public keys which allow an adversary to forge an arbitrary certificate, should one of them be trusted by an end-user, and should the end-user trust the certifier-certified chain up to the compromised key. Full grey bars take into account only public keys belonging to the *strong set*, while thatched bars represent keys not in the *strong set*. In particular, Fig. 4(a) reports the amount of certifiers which pose a risk in being trusted, considering as compromised all the short and mis-generated RSA, Elgamal keypairs: in both cases compromising the keypair (i.e., computing the private key) is feasible with limited resources, and further signatures made with the compromised keypairs will be accepted by any client as valid. We note that such a key compromise is performed fully offline, and thus is most likely not alerting the legitimate keypair owner. Figure 4(b) complements the previous information reporting the extent of the risk whenever spliced MD5-based signatures can be reused, and RSA keypairs with a modulus size between 600 and 800 bits are compromised. These two cases will either require a significant amount of computational effort to compromise the keypair, or yield signatures which may be discarded by modern

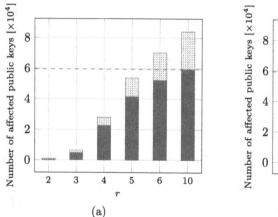
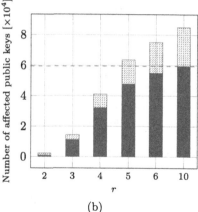

(a)   (b)

Fig. 4. Number of public keys affected by the attack described in Sect. 3 as a function of r. Subfigure (a) reports the amount of public keys which allow an adversary to forge a certificate considering short (≤ 600 bits) RSA moduli, mis-generated RSA keypairs and ElGamal keypairs employed for signature purposes. Subfigure (b) provides the same results for RSA keys with insufficient sized moduli (between 600 and 800 bit in length) and keys which performed at least an MD5 based signature. The red dashed line marks the size of the strong set

clients (GPG stopped taking into account MD5-based signatures starting from June 2014, with GnuPG 2.0.23).

Considering the default bound on the length of certifier-certified trust chains, $r = 5$, the reported results show that around 70 % of the keys in the *strong set* of the WoT are affected by the described threat scenario if all the keypairs breakable with limited resources are effectively broken. This significant amount of keys is cut down to 37 % of the strong set, if the user is willing to cap the length of the maximum chain on the WoT to $r = 4$ (or, equivalently, not to extend her trust), and is further cut down to 8 % in case $r = 3$. However, we note that such a restriction also reduces the effectiveness of the strong set as an authenticator (see Fig. 1(b)), and thus comes at a usability expense. In particular, this link between the effectiveness of the threat and the size of the longest certifier chain r would allow a threat coverage of above 87 % in case the default chain length were one step longer, i.e., $r = 6$. Moreover, in the extreme case where it is desired for the overwhelming majority of the users to be able to use the entire strong set as a certifier, setting $r = 10$ (as shown in Fig. 1(b) and described in Sect. 2), substantially the whole strong set (99.6 % of the keys) are affected by the described threat. The effects of either compromising moderately sized RSA moduli, or splicing MD5 signatures yields similar effects to the aforementioned ones, as reported in Fig. 4(b), although providing a slightly higher coverage of the strong set (83 % of the keys for $r = 5$).

Mitigation strategies. We now propose three viable mitigation strategies for the described threat scenario. A first approach to counteract the actions of the adversary, while preserving usefulness of WoT, is to employ redundant chains of authentication to validate a public key. However, this approach requires two, or more, disjoint paths on the WoT to be present in order to effectively thwart the certificate forgery. To evaluate the practical feasibility of such an approach, we computed how many public keys in the strong set are the unique way to reach a portion of it (i.e., removing one of such keys would split a portion of the strong set out). There are 8,804 such nodes (14.8 % of the strong set), thus pointing to a lack of practical viability of such an approach, especially for certification chains of lengths up to 5. An alternate approach is to prevent the attacker from successfully impersonating a keyserver, fetching the certificates from multiple ones. In this case, even if a single malicious keyserver tries to present a "split world"-view to a targeted user, fetching certificates from multiple servers and comparing them will allow to detect the malicious intent. This approach is rather feasible in practical terms, although it may be a concern in rare cases where the user is trusting only a single keyserver to be safe.

Finally, we point out that the nature of the OpenPGP protocol makes the phase out of an outdated hash algorithm trickier than in a common hierarchical PKI infrastructure. In fact, cases such as the current one with MD5, need to be tackled through dropping altogether the support for it. However, such a solution may potentially endanger the soundness of the WoT in case many signatures are removed from it, as it could happen dropping the support for SHA-1 based signatures (which currently constitute 88.9 % of the entire WoT arcs). To the end of preventing a significant alteration in the WoT structure, it is advisable to exploit the nature of OpenPGP certificates, which allow for more than one signature coming from the same issuer to be appended. To allow a graceful phase out of SHA-1, or any other hash which should be phased out, it is thus sufficient to modify the OpenPGP clients so that signatures on the same key material signed with SHA-1 are made, exploiting a better algorithm (e.g., the OpenPGP message standard supports SHA-2-256). As it is already happening in the public web PKI [18, 21], this operation should be performed while it is not yet possible to find meaningful collisions on SHA-1. This allows a graceful, and transparent deployment of a stronger hash algorithm, allowing safe disposal of SHA-1 signatures, should the need come anywhen in the future.

6   Conclusion

In this paper we proposed a threat scenario to the authentication capability of the OpenPGP WoT, relying on the possibility for an adversary to perform a man in the middle attack, trying to forge a requested certificate. Under the described threat scenario, the adversary needs to compromise a keypair and get the target user to be trusting the compromised keypair certifiers to be able to forge a certificate for an arbitrary identity. Willing to provide an evaluation of the impact of the threat, we performed a survey of the current state of health of the OpenPGP WoT, both in structural terms, and concerning the security of the individual keypairs. The results show how, in a context where public key authentication can be performed indirectly exploiting verification made by trusted users, even a limited amount of broken or outdated keys can have a dramatic impact on the security of the whole system. Another relevant aspect that emerged from our analysis is the impact of the recent decision to reject MD5-based signatures by some OpenPGP clients, namely GnuPG. A unilateral decision to disable MD5 for public key authentication effectively removed more than 432 k signatures for the WoT, without any preemptive measures being taken to compensate for the loss. For this reasons we suggest a strategy to perform a graceful phase-out of SHA-1, which is currently used in the vast majority of OpenPGP signatures, through a signature refreshment strategy amenable to automation, performed by the clients, using a more modern algorithm.

References

1. Barenghi, A., Beretta, M., Di Federico, A., Pelosi, G.: Snake: an end-to-end encrypted online social network. In: Bourgeois, J., Magoulès, F. (eds.) 2014 IEEE International Conference on High Performance Computing and Communications, 6th IEEE International Symposium on Cyberspace Safety and Security, 11th IEEE International Conference on Embedded Software and Systems, HPCC/CSS/ICESS 2014, Paris, France, 20–22 August 2014. IEEE (2014)
2. Bernstein, D.J., Lange, T.: Batch NFS. In: Joux, A., Youssef, A. (eds.) SAC 2014. LNCS, vol. 8781, pp. 38–58. Springer, Heidelberg (2014)
3. Callas, J., Donnerhacke, L., Finney, H., Shaw, D., Thayer, R.: OpenPGP Message Format. RFC 4880, updated by RFC 5581 (2007)
4. Callas, J., Donnerhacke, L., Finney, H., Thayer, R.: OpenPGP Message Format. Internet RFC 2440 (1998)
5. Chokhani, S., Ford, W.: Internet X.509 Public Key Infrastructure Certificate Policy and Certification Practices Framework. RFC 2527, obsoleted by RFC 3647 (1999)
6. Dierks, T., Rescorla, E.: The Transport Layer Security (TLS) Protocol Version 1.2. RFC 5246, updated by RFCs 5746, 5878, 6176 (2008)
7. Diffie, W., van Oorschot, P.C., Wiener, M.J.: Authentication and authenticated key exchanges. Des. Codes Crypt. 2(2), 107–125 (1992)
8. El Gamal, T.: A public key cryptosystem and a signature scheme based on discrete logarithms. IEEE Trans. Inf. Theory 31(4), 469–472 (1985)
9. Hall, T.A., Keller, S.S.: The FIPS 186-4 Elliptic Curve Digital Signature Algorithm Validation System. NIST (2014). http://csrc.nist.gov/groups/STM/cavp/documents/dss2/ecdsa2vs.pdf
10. Heininger, N.: Factoring as a Service. CRYPTO 2013 Rump session (2013). https://www.cis.upenn.edu/nadiah/projects/faas/
11. Heninger, N., Durumeric, Z., Wustrow, E., Halderman, J.A.: Mining your Ps and Qs: detection of widespread weak keys in network devices. In: Kohno, T. (ed.) Proceedings of the 21th USENIX Security Symposium, Bellevue, WA, USA, 8–10 August 2012, pp. 205–220. USENIX Association (2012)
12. Kleinjung, T., Aoki, K., Franke, J., Lenstra, A.K., Thomé, E., Bos, J.W., Gaudry, P., Kruppa, A., Montgomery, P.L., Osvik, D.A., te Riele, H., Timofeev, A., Zimmermann, P.: Factorization of a 768-bit RSA modulus. In: Rabin, T. (ed.) CRYPTO 2010. LNCS, vol. 6223, pp. 333–350. Springer, Heidelberg (2010)

13. Koch, W.: The GNU Privacy Guard (2015). https://www.gnupg.org
14. Lenstra, A.K.: Integer factoring. Des. Codes Crypt. **19**(2/3), 101–128 (2000)
15. McGee, D.: PGP Packet Parser Library (2015). https://github.com/toofishes/python-pgpdump
16. Minsky, Y., Clizbe, J., Fiskerstrand, K.: Synchronizing Key Server (SKS) Software Package (2015). https://bitbucket.org/skskeyserver/sks-keyserver/wiki/Home
17. Minsky, Y., Trachtenberg, A., Zippel, R.: Set reconciliation with nearly optimal communication complexity. IEEE Trans. Inf. Theory **49**(9), 2213–2218 (2003)
18. Mozilla Security Engineering Team: Phasing Out Certificates with SHA-1 based Signature Algorithms (2014). https://blog.mozilla.org/security/2014/09/23/phasing-out-certificates-with-sha-1-based-signature-algorithms/
19. National Institute of Standards and Technology: Digital Signature Standard (DSS). Federal Information Processing Standards Publication (FIPS) 186-4. U.S. Department of Commerce (2013). http://dx.doi.org/10.6028/NIST.FIPS.186-4
20. Nguyên, P.Q.: Can we trust cryptographic software? Cryptographic flaws in GNU privacy guard v1.2.3. In: Cachin, C., Camenisch, J.L. (eds.) EUROCRYPT 2004. LNCS, vol. 3027, pp. 555–570. Springer, Heidelberg (2004)
21. Palmer, C., Sleevi, R.: Gradually Sunsetting SHA-1 (2014). http://blog.chromium.org/2014/09/gradually-sunsetting-sha-1.html
22. Peixoto, T.P.: The Graph-tool Python Library (2014). http://figshare.com/articles/graph_tool/1164194
23. Penning, H.P.: PGP Pathfinder and Key Statistics (2015). http://pgp.cs.uu.nl/
24. Rivest, R.L., Shamir, A., Adleman, L.M.: A method for obtaining digital signatures and public-key cryptosystems. Commun. ACM **21**(2), 120–126 (1978)
25. Shaw, D.: OpenPGP HTTP Keyserver Protocol (HKP). Expired Internet-Draft (2013). http://tools.ietf.org/html/draft-shaw-openpgp-hkp-00
26. Somogyi, S.: End-to-End Chrome Browser Extension (2015). https://github.com/google/end-to-end/wiki
27. Stevens, M., Sotirov, A., Appelbaum, J., Lenstra, A., Molnar, D., Osvik, D.A., de Weger, B.: Short chosen-prefix collisions for MD5 and the creation of a rogue CA certificate. In: Halevi, S. (ed.) CRYPTO 2009. LNCS, vol. 5677, pp. 55–69. Springer, Heidelberg (2009)
28. Symantec Corp.: Symantec Encryption (PGP) Docs. Article Tech202483 (2015)
29. The Free Software Foundation: Email Self-Defense Campaign (2015). https://emailselfdefense.fsf.org/
30. Ulrich, A., Holz, R., Hauck, P., Carle, G.: Investigating the OpenPGP web of trust. In: Atluri, V., Diaz, C. (eds.) ESORICS 2011. LNCS, vol. 6879, pp. 489–507. Springer, Heidelberg (2011)
31. Wendlandt, D., Andersen, D.G., Perrig, A.: Perspectives: improving SSH-style host authentication with multi-path probing. In: Isaacs, R., Zhou, Y. (eds.) 2008 USENIX Annual Technical Conference, Boston, MA, USA, 22–27 June 2008, pp. 321–334. USENIX Association (2008)
32. Zhu, Y., et al.: End-to-End for Yahoo! Mail (2015). https://github.com/yahoo/end-to-end

Transforming Out Timing Leaks, More or Less

Heiko Mantel and Artem Starostin[✉]

Computer Science Department, TU Darmstadt, Darmstadt, Germany
{mantel,Starostin}@mais.informatik.tu-darmstadt.de

Abstract. We experimentally evaluate program transformations for removing timing side-channel vulnerabilities wrt. security and overhead. Our study of four well-known transformations confirms that their performance overhead differs substantially. A novelty of our work is the empirical investigation of channel bandwidths, which clarifies that the transformations also differ wrt. how much security they add to a program. Interestingly, we observe such differences even between transformations that have been proven to establish timing-sensitive noninterference. Beyond clarification, our findings provide guidance for choosing a suitable transformation for removing timing side-channel vulnerabilities. Such guidance is needed because there is a trade-off between security and overhead, which makes choosing a suitable transformation non-trivial.

1 Introduction

Side channels are unintended communication channels that transmit information during the execution of programs. Running time [4,15,34], power consumption [35], EM radiation [26,49], cache behavior [48], and other characteristics can cause side channels. Side channels might reveal information about secrets processed by a program, and this makes them a serious security concern. Timing side channels are particularly critical since they can be exploited remotely [4,15].

The idea of program transformations, in general, dates back to the seventies [33] and since then has attracted a lot of attention for improving programs, e.g., [5,12,16]. More specifically, a spectrum of program transformations has been proposed for removing timing side-channel vulnerabilities [2,13,38,47]. The objective of such transformations is to improve the security of programs. That a program is secure wrt. timing side channels can be formalized by a timing-sensitive noninterference-like property (see, e.g., [2]). That a transformation is sound wrt. its objective can then be shown by proving that each transformed program satisfies the property based on a timing-sensitive program semantics [2].

The objective of our research project was to improve the understanding of program transformations for eliminating timing side-channel vulnerabilities. We wanted to better understand how much security is added by such transformations at which costs, in practice. Hence, we chose an experimental approach. In our study we focused on four well-known source-to-source transformations: cross-copying [2], conditional assignment [47], transactional branching [13], and unification [38]. Each of these transformations is transparent in the sense that it

© Springer International Publishing Switzerland 2015
G. Pernul et al. (Eds.): ESORICS 2015, Part I, LNCS 9326, pp. 447–467, 2015.
DOI: 10.1007/978-3-319-24174-6_23

does not change a sequential program's input/output behavior. Hence, the only negative consequence of these transformations is the overhead that they induce.

Our experimental results clarify that all four program transformations reduce the capacity of timing side channels. These capacity reductions are substantial, but they differ between the transformations. Regarding negative consequences, our experimental results show that all four program transformations cause some performance overhead. The worst-case overhead substantially differs between the transformations, ranging from 18 to 372 % in our experiments.

Previously, the effectiveness of program transformations for removing timing side-channel vulnerabilities was evaluated mostly analytically. In [2,13,38], it is proven that cross-copying, transactional branching, and unification, respectively, establish timing-sensitive noninterference. In [47], it is proven that conditional assignment establishes the program counter security (PC-Security). The only prior experimental study of the effectiveness of transformations is the investigation of cross-copying in [3]. The overhead of program transformations also was evaluated mostly analytically, based on the code-size blow-up wrt. the definitions of transformations. The only prior experimental study of the overhead induced by transformations is the investigation of conditional assignment in [47].

In contrast to most prior work, we perform our evaluation empirically. We measure the running time of baseline and transformed programs in a series of experiments. From these experimental results, we estimate the performance overhead induced by a transformation by computing the percentage increase of a program's mean running time caused by the transformation. We estimate the effectiveness of a transformation by computing the percentage reduction of the timing side-channel capacity in a program achieved by the transformation. We run all our experiments on a contemporary laptop using realistic Java programs.

Our observation, which might be surprising, is that there are substantial differences in the capacity reduction even between transformations that have been proven before to establish fairly similar definitions of timing-sensitive noninterference. This suggests that analytical investigations of the security established by such program transformations are not yet satisfactory wrt. practice.

In summary, the two main novel contributions of this article are

- the quantification of the positive and negative consequences of different program transformations based on experiments, and
- the clarification of the trade-off between performance overhead and security in this context.

In addition, we provide guidance for selecting a suitable transformation by exploiting our results of the performance and security evaluations in combination.

The article is structured as follows. In Sect. 2, we define the class of timing side channels relevant for this article. In Sect. 3, we recall the aforementioned transformations and explain our implementations of them. In Sect. 4, we introduce our benchmark programs and our experimental setup. In Sects. 5 and 6 we present the performance and security evaluation, respectively. In Sect. 7 we analyze the performance-security trade-off. After a discussion of related work in Sect. 8, we conclude in Sect. 9.

2 Timing Side Channels

An illustrative example [34] of a timing side channel can be found in the square-and-multiply modular exponentiation. Such exponentiation is used, e.g., during private-key operations in RSA [50] for computing $R = y^k \bmod n$, where n is public, y can be eavesdropped by the attacker, and k is the secret key. A vulnerable Java implementation containing a timing side channel is given in Fig. 1.

```
public int modExp(int y, int k) {
   int r = 1;
   for (int i = 0; i < 32; i++) {
      if (k % 2 == 1)
         r = (r * y) % n;
      y = (y * y) % n;
      k >>= 1;
   }
   return r % n;
}
```

Fig. 1. Square-and-multiply modular exponentiation.

The secret key is stored in integer parameter k. It is processed bitwise starting from the least significant bit. Each bit of k is tested. If the current bit is set, extra multiplication and modulo operations are performed (highlighted lines in Fig. 1). Since these extra operations are performed only for the set bits of the secret key, the running time of this implementation varies depending on the number of the set bits. More concretely, the running time encodes the Hamming weight of the secret key. Therefore, the Hamming weight of the secret key is leaked through the timing behavior in one run.

This example illustrates how a conditional statement may result in a timing side channel. If the Boolean condition of a conditional statement contains secret information, then the resulting timing side channel leaks secret information. We will refer to conditional statements that may result in timing side channels leaking secret information as *critical conditionals*.

Previously proposed program transformations for removing timing side channels [2,13,38,47] aim at eliminating timing side channels that result from critical conditionals, like the one in the above example program. This is the class of timing side channels on which we focus in this article.

3 Program Transformations

We consider four transformations: cross-copying [2], conditional assignment [47], transactional branching [13] and unification [38]. Their original definitions from the respective articles assume special statements like skip, dummy assignments, etc. Such statements are not available in real-world programming languages by default. In order to analyze program transformations in practice one first needs to implement the missing special statements. These implementations are not obvious because for each special statement there is a spectrum of design decisions.

The four transformations were defined for different programming languages. For instance, transactional branching was defined for an object-oriented programming language in [13], while unification was defined for a simple language with conditionals and loops in [38]. For our comparison, we use a language that provides all features that are in the intersection of the languages in [2,13,38,47]. This resulting language is a high-level programming language that restricts bodies of critical conditionals to contain only assignments to variables or fields of primitive data types or arrays, and other conditional statements.

3.1 Cross-Copying

Cross-copying [2] pads the branches of critical conditionals in order to equalize the timing behavior of both branches. Technically, cross-copying appends a sequence of dummy statements that shall mimic the timing behavior of one branch to the respective other branch, hence the name "cross-copying". The inserted dummy statements perform the same computations as the statements that shall be mimicked, but dummy statements do not update program variables that are relevant for the program's behavior.

Realization in [2]. Padding is realized with the help of a special statement SKIPASN x e. It shall take the same time to execute as the assignment x := e, but that does not change the value of x. SKIPASN-versions of all assignments in one branch of a critical conditional are appended to the other branch, and vice versa. For instance, the critical conditional from Fig. 1 is transformed to

if (k % 2 == 1) { r = (r * y) % n; } **else** { SKIPASN r ((r * y) % n); }

Our Implementation in Java. We implement SKIPASN by assignments to dummy variables. For each statement SKIPASN x e that needs to be inserted, we introduce a dummy field xSkip assuming xSkip is not present in the original program. We implement then SKIPASN x e by xSkip = e. Such implementation is transparent because assignments to dummy fields do not affect the values in the original computation while introducing the desired delays in the running time.

3.2 Conditional Assignment

Conditional assignment [47] removes critical conditionals, so that both branches are consecutively executed. Boolean conditions of the removed conditionals are encoded directly in the assignments from both branches of the original code. The encoding is done with the help of bit masks and bitwise logical operators.

Realization in [47]. Function MASK(b) is used for encoding a boolean condition b of a critical conditional. It satisfies MASK(false) $= 0$ and MASK(true) $= 2^l - 1$, where l is the length in bits of the variables assigned under the critical conditional. Suppose that in a program, x is assigned e_t if b evaluates to true, and e_f if b evaluates to false. Then, in the transformed program, x is assigned $(m$ & $e_t) | (\tilde{\ }m$ & $e_f)$, where $m =$ MASK(b) and &, |, and ˜ are bitwise conjunction, disjunction, and negation. For instance, the critical conditional from Fig. 1 is transformed to

r = (MASK(k % 2 == 1) & ((r * y) % n)) | (˜MASK(k % 2 == 1) & r);

Our Implementation in Java. In [47], it is shown that MASK can be implemented in C without conditional statements by defining MASK(b) as $-b$. Such implementation is not suitable for Java because type casting from booleans to integers is not allowed in Java. We came up with a different solution: MASK(a == b) is implemented for 32-bit integers as `~(((a-b)>>31) | ((b-a)>>31))`, where `>>` is the sign-extending right shift. Such implementation is correct because Java uses two's complement integer numbers, and the check whether two integers a and b are equal is equivalent to checking $\neg(((a - b) < 0) \vee ((b - a) < 0))$.

3.3 Transactional Branching

Transactional branching [13] leverages a transaction mechanism for cross-copying. Each branch of a critical conditional is wrapped in a transaction and sequentially composed with the respective other branch. The transaction of the original branch is committed, while the transaction of the cross-copied branch is aborted.

Realization in [13]. Three transaction primitives are used. BEGINT starts a new transaction. ABORTT aborts a transaction dismissing all changes made since BEGINT. COMMITT commits a transaction making all changes since BEGINT effective. The original branch is wrapped by the pair BEGINT-COMMITT. The cross-copied branch is wrapped by the pair BEGINT-ABORTT. For instance, the critical conditional from Fig. 1 is transformed to

> **if** (k % 2 == 1) { BEGINT; ABORTT; BEGINT; r = (r ∗ y) % n; COMMITT; }
> **else** { BEGINT; r = (r ∗ y) % n; ABORTT; BEGINT; COMMITT; }

Our Implementation in Java. We implement transaction primitives by methods that operate on copies of variables that are not yet committed. For each assignment x := e under a critical conditional we introduce a field xCopy assuming that xCopy is not present in the original program. We implement then BEGINT as xCopy = x, ABORTT as x = xCopy, and leave the body of COMMITT empty. Such implementation is correct because it straightforwardly realizes the required functionality of the transaction primitives.

3.4 Unification

Unification [38] is similar to cross-copying in the sense that dummy statements are added to the branches of critical conditionals in order to equalize the timing behavior of both branches. In contrast to cross-copying, these dummy statements might be inserted into the branches instead of being appended only at the end of branches. A unification algorithm is used to determine where dummy statements need to be inserted into each branch, hence the name "unification". Unification can be viewed as an optimization of cross-copying that inserts never more, but often fewer dummy statements into a program.

Realization in [38]. In [38], unification assumes a program semantics in which execution of every statement consumes one time unit, but its adaptation to a more fine-grained timing-sensitive program semantics is straightforward. Padding is realized in [38] using the special statement SKIP. It has no effect on the values of variables, but its execution consumes one time unit. For instance, the critical conditional from Fig. 1 is transformed to

if (k % 2 == 1) { r = (r * y) % n; } **else** { SKIP; }

Note that the advantage of unification over cross-copying does not become apparent in this example, because the critical conditional in the original program lacks an else-branch.

Our Implementation in Java. In our implementation of unification, we use the same dummy statements as in our implementation of cross-copying. Such implementation is transparent because assignments to dummy fields do not affect the values in the original computation while introducing the desired delays.

4   Our Benchmark Programs and Experimental Setup

An existing suite of benchmark Java programs that contain timing side-channel vulnerabilities would be an ideal candidate for an empirical evaluation of program transformations for removing such vulnerabilities. To the best of our knowledge, there is unfortunately no such suite. That is why, we identify meaningful candidates for benchmark programs ourselves. We choose four programs: (i) square-and-multiply modular exponentiation from RSA [50], (ii) computation of a share's value [2], (iii) Kruskal's algorithm for calculating the minimum spanning tree (MST) of a graph [40], and (iv) modular multiplication from the IDEA cipher [41]. These four programs should not be seen as a complete benchmark that is sufficient to investigate transformations in full detail. However, since these programs come from different domains and have different degree of sophistication, they offer themselves as meaningful candidates for our experiments.

4.1   Our Benchmark Programs

Modular Exponentiation. Program modExp is the square-and-multiply modular exponentiation discussed in Sect. 2. The security concern is that the Hamming weight of the secret key k is leaked via a timing side channel.

Share's Value. Program shareValue computes the total market value of a specified share form the user's portfolio. In [2], similar program was used to illustrate timing side channels. The portfolio is represented by two arrays, ids and qty, that store identifiers of shares and the number of corresponding shares possessed by the user, respectively. Which shares are possessed by the user is a secret. Method **public int** shareValue(**int** [] ids , **int** [] qty) computes the total market value of a specified share from the portfolio. The security concern is that the fact whether the user possess the specified share is leaked via a timing side channel.

Kruskal's Algorithm. Program kruskal implements Kruskal's algorithm [40] for calculating the minimum spanning tree of a graph. Kruskal's algorithm is used among others for compression of database queries and responses to them [29]. In case a secret is stored in a database, both queries and responses may contain secret information. Method **public int []** kruskal (**int []** g) computes the MST for graph g represented by its adjacency array. The security concern is that the number of graph's vertices is leaked via a timing side channel.

Modular Multiplication. Program mulMod16 is a modular multiplication from the IDEA cipher's [41] implementaion in cryptographic library FlexiProvider [1]. The encryption and decryption of this IDEA's implementation use mulMod16{ several times for computing with the secret key. Method **private int** mulMod16(**int** a, **int** b) implements multiplication modulo $2^{16} + 1$ for operands a and b. The security concern is that 16 bits of the secret key leak via a timing side channel. Corresponding timing side-channel attacks have been reported [32,43].

4.2   Our Experimental Setup

We run all experiments on a typical laptop, a Lenovo ThinkPad T510 with Intel Core i7 CPU @2.67 GHz×4 and 4 Gb RAM under Ubuntu 12.04 LTS with Open-JDK 64-Bit Server VM. We measure the running time of programs in nanoseconds using System.nanoTime(). We want to stay close to the program semantics in which the transformations have been originally defined. In particular, we want to avoid aggressive compiler optimizations that might revert transformations. Because of that we disable the JIT compilation. This might be seen as a simplification of a practical environment, however the main goal of this research project is to empirically evaluate theoretical concepts of different program transformations and to clarify the relationship between them. It is not the goal of this research project to fully solve the problem of timing side channels in practice.

5   A Performance Evaluation

Our goal is to quantify the performance overhead induced by program transformations in practice. Estimating performance of Java programs in a statistically sound fashion requires a careful experimental design and analysis of the obtained data. We guide our decisions for such a design and analysis by the principles of statistically rigorous Java performance evaluation by Georges et al. [28].

5.1   Experimental Design

We estimate the running time of Java programs by random sampling. We draw each sample of the running time from a different invocation of the Java VM. This is necessary because the running time samples drawn from the same invocation will not be independent. We measure the running time of a program directly after the invocation of the Java VM, i.e., we do not perform any warm-up computations. It has been recognized [28] that because of the JIT compilation the performance of Java programs may improve after certain amount of warm-up computation is made. We however excluded the JIT compilation from our setup.

To estimate the running time of a program, we first generate a vector of random inputs. We run the program on each input in a freshly invoked Java VM. We measure the running time of the program within each Java VM invocation in nanoseconds using System.nanoTime(). The measured time value constitutes a sample of the running time. From all collected samples, we reject outliers that lie further than three median absolute deviations from the median.

5.2 Experiments and Experimental Results

We apply each of the 4 transformations to each of the 4 benchmark programs. By that we obtain 17 unique programs: 4 baseline and 13 transformed ones. We obtain 13 unique transformed programs instead of 16 because the resulting programs for cross-copying and unification coincide for modExp, shareValue, and kruskal. Next, we perform the timing measurements for these 17 programs.

The inputs to modExp are pairs of random integers. The inputs to shareValue are pairs of arrays of random integers. Each array has 10 elements. The inputs to kruskal are random graphs. Each graph has 7 vertices and 7 edges. That is, each input is an array of 15 integers: The first element stores the number of vertices, and the next 14 elements store 7 edges as the pairs of source and target vertices. The inputs to mulMod16 are pairs of random integers.

We collect 1000 samples of the running time for each baseline and transformed programs. From these samples we compute 95 % confidence intervals [11] for the estimated mean running time. The results are presented in Fig. 2.

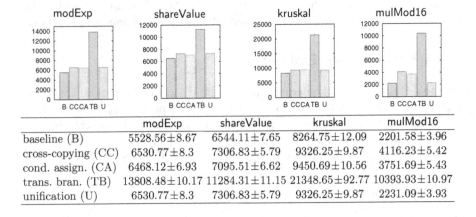

	modExp	shareValue	kruskal	mulMod16
baseline (B)	5528.56±8.67	6544.11±7.65	8264.75±12.09	2201.58±3.96
cross-copying (CC)	6530.77±8.3	7306.83±5.79	9326.25±9.87	4116.23±5.42
cond. assign. (CA)	6468.12±6.93	7095.51±6.62	9450.69±10.56	3751.69±5.43
trans. bran. (TB)	13808.48±10.17	11284.31±11.15	21348.65±92.77	10393.93±10.97
unification (U)	6530.77±8.3	7306.83±5.79	9326.25±9.87	2231.09±3.93

Fig. 2. Estimated mean running time, in ns, 95 % confidence intervals.

5.3   Our Findings in the Performance Evaluation

In order to clarify how much overhead is introduced by transformations, we use the estimated mean running time to compute the percentage increase of the running time due to each transformation. The result of this is given in Fig. 3.

We observe that program transformations generally introduce some performance overhead. The observed overhead substantially differs between the transformations. Altogether, the observed overhead varies from 1 to 372 %. The worst-case overhead of transformations among different benchmark programs varies from 18 to 372 %. The experimental results suggest that transactional branching introduces the largest overhead that varies from 72 to 372 %. We observe moderate difference between the overhead introduced by cross-copying and conditional assignment. For mulMod16 we observe substantial difference between unification and all other transformations. In this case, unification introduces only a marginal overhead of about 1 %.

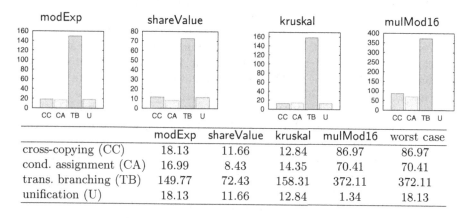

	modExp	shareValue	kruskal	mulMod16	worst case
cross-copying (CC)	18.13	11.66	12.84	86.97	86.97
cond. assignment (CA)	16.99	8.43	14.35	70.41	70.41
trans. branching (TB)	149.77	72.43	158.31	372.11	372.11
unification (U)	18.13	11.66	12.84	1.34	18.13

Fig. 3. Performance overhead based on the estimated mean running time, in %.

Comparison with Findings in [47]. The only prior experimental study of the overhead induced by transformations is the investigation of conditional assignment by Molnar et al. in [47]. The experiments were done on three programs implemented in C. The experimental results in [47] indicate a much larger overhead for conditional assignment than the one observed in our experiments. The worst case overhead observed in [47] is about 480 %. Interestingly, in [47] a modular exponentiation from RSA and a modular multiplication from IDEA are also used as benchmark programs. For these programs, the overhead observed in [47] is about 150 and 200 %, respectively. We, however, observe an overhead of only 17 and 70 % for our versions of these programs, respectively. Note that the versions of these programs in [47] and in our work originate from different cryptographic libraries and are implemented in C and Java, respectively.

6   A Security Evaluation

Our goal is to quantify the effectiveness of program transformations in practice. In the spirit of Millen [46], we model a timing side channel as a discrete information-theoretic channel [21] with input X and output Y. The input alphabet of the channel models the space of secret inputs to a program and the output alphabet models possible timing observations. We measure the correlation between the secret inputs and possible timing observations with the Shannon's channel capacity [51], denoted $C(X;Y)$. We statistically estimate [17] the channel capacity $C(X;Y)$ from empirically collected timing observations. To quantify the positive effects of a transformation we compute the percentage reduction of the timing side-channel capacity achieved by the transformation.

6.1   Experimental Design

For each benchmark program we design the following experiment to which we will refer as the *distinguishing experiment*. We generate two distinct secret input values for a program. Our security concern is that the fact whether the program has received the first or the second secret input value is leaked via a timing side channel. For each of the two secret input values we repeatedly run the program. For each run we freshly invoke the Java VM. We measure the running time of the program within each Java VM invocation in nanoseconds using System.nanoTime(). The resulting value of the time measurement constitute a sample of the running time. From all collected samples, we reject outliers that lie further than three median absolute deviations from the median. We augment each sample with a Boolean variable that stores whether the sample resulted from the first or the second secret input value. We pass the list of such augmented samples into the procedure for statistical measurement of information leakage [17]. This procedure estimates the capacity $C(X;Y)$ of the timing side channel using iterative Blahut-Arimoto algorithm [8,14].

6.2   Experiments

Similarly to our performance evaluation, we run our security evaluation experiments on 4 baseline and 13 transformed programs. We run a distinguishing experiment for each of these 17 programs.

Two distinct secret inputs for each of the programs are generated as follows.

In modExp, the timing side channel of our interest results from a critical conditional with the Boolean condition over parameter k. Hence, we supply two different secret inputs to k: fixed integers with the Hamming weight of 5 and of 25, respectively. The other parameter of modExp receives a fixed integer.

In shareValue, the timing side channel of our interest results from a critical conditional with the Boolean condition over parameter ids. Hence, we supply two different secret inputs to ids: an array of 10 fixed integers that does not contain the value representing the user's specified share, and an array of 10 fixed integers that contains at one element a value representing the user's specified share. The other parameter of shareValue receives an array of 10 fixed integers.

In kruskal, the timing side channel of our interest results from a critical conditional with the Boolean condition depending on parameter g. Hence, we supply two different secret inputs to g: an array encoding a fixed graph with 5 vertices and 7 edges, and an array encoding a fixed graph with 7 vertices and 7 edges.

In mulMod16, the timing side channel of our interest results from a critical conditional with the Boolean condition over parameter a. Hence, we supply two different secret inputs to a: a fixed integer whose 16 least significant bits are all zeros, and a fixed integer whose 16 least significant bits contain ones and zeros. The other parameter of mulMod16 receives a fixed integer.

We collect 10000 samples of the running time for each of the two secret inputs for each baseline and each transformed version of benchmark programs.

6.3 Experimental Results

Already just by visualizing the collected samples of the running time one can get a first impression about timing side channels in each program and about the effects of program transformations on these timing side channels.

Figure 4a depicts a portion of the collected running time samples for the baseline version of modExp. Blue (filled) boxes correspond to the first 800 running time samples that resulted from executing modExp on the secret input with the Hamming weight of 5. Red (unfilled) boxes correspond to the first 800 running time samples that resulted from executing modExp on the secret input with the Hamming weight of 25. Figure 4b depicts the frequency with which different running time samples occurred in the experiment. Again, blue (filled) and red (unfilled) bars correspond to the samples that resulted from executing modExp on the secret inputs with the Hamming weights of 5 and 25, respectively. On both Figs. 4a and b we can clearly observe differences in the running time values that correspond to two different secret input values. This gives us a hint that modExp indeed contains a timing side channel.

Similarly, Fig. 4c depicts a portion of the collected running time samples for modExp transformed with cross-copying. Figure 4d depicts the frequency with which different running time samples occurred in the experiment. Blue and red (filled and unfilled, respectively) correspond to the running time samples that resulted from executing the transformed program on the secret inputs with the Hamming weights of 5 and 25, respectively. In contrast to Figs. 4a and b, we cannot observe much difference in the running time values that correspond to two different secret input values. This gives us a hint that cross-copying was effective in removing the timing side channel in modExp.

From the collected samples we estimate the capacity of the timing side channels using a procedure for statistical measurement of information leakage [17]. The resulting estimated capacity is depicted in Fig. 5. Since in our distinguishing experiments the size of the secret is 1 bit, the maximal possible capacity of the timing side channel in each program is also 1 bit.

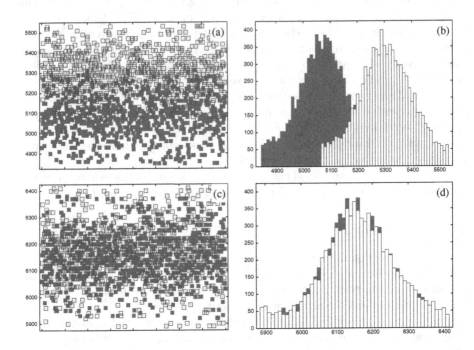

Fig. 4. Running time values and frequencies of their occurrence in the distinguishing experiment for modExp in the baseline and cross-copied versions.

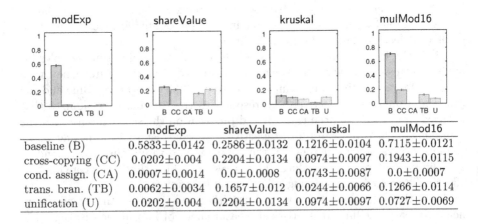

	modExp	shareValue	kruskal	mulMod16
baseline (B)	0.5833±0.0142	0.2586±0.0132	0.1216±0.0104	0.7115±0.0121
cross-copying (CC)	0.0202±0.004	0.2204±0.0134	0.0974±0.0097	0.1943±0.0115
cond. assign. (CA)	0.0007±0.0014	0.0±0.0008	0.0743±0.0087	0.0±0.0007
trans. bran. (TB)	0.0062±0.0034	0.1657±0.012	0.0244±0.0066	0.1266±0.0114
unification (U)	0.0202±0.004	0.2204±0.0134	0.0974±0.0097	0.0727±0.0069

Fig. 5. Estimated capacity of timing side channels, in bits, 95 % confidence intervals.

6.4   Our Findings in the Security Evaluation

The results of our experiments show that executing each benchmark program opens timing side channels that have various capacities. The experimental results also show that all program transformations in all experiments reduce the capacity of timing side channels, i.e., all considered transformations have positive effects wrt. side-channel mitigation. In order to clarify how large these positive effects of transformations are, we use the estimated capacity of timing side channels to compute the percentage reduction of the side channel's capacity due to each transformation. The result of this is given in Fig. 6.

We observe that program transformations generally reduce the capacity of timing side channels, and that the observed reduction substantially differs between the transformations. Altogether, the observed reduction varies from about 15 to 100 %. We also observe that the reduction of the capacity of timing side channels varies between cross-copying, transactional branching, and unification. These transformations have been previously proven in [2,13,38] to establish respective definitions of timing-sensitive noninterference.

The transformation "conditional assignment" has been proven in [47] to establish PC-Security. We observe that, in shareValue and mulMod16, conditional assignment completely removes timing side channels, and, in modExp, it achieves a 99.88 % reduction of the estimated timing side-channel capacity. For these three programs, conditional assignment removes timing side channels more effectively than the other transformations. One might wonder: Why is conditional assignment so much worse for kruskal, achieving a reduction of only 38.9 % and being outperformed by transactional branching? We investigated this question and suspect that the remaining timing side-channel capacity in kruskal is caused by the recursive function find (see Fig. 9 in the appendix).

Our experimental results clarify that, in practice, there are differences in the effectiveness of program transformations for removing timing side-channel vulnerabilities. The differences are substantial, and therefore our results indicate that there is still much to be understood about such transformations. Under which conditions should a program developer prefer one transformation over another? Can a program developer maximize the positive effects of a transformation by his programming style, and, if yes, how? Such questions will require answers until we fully understand how to use program transformations for writing programs that are free from timing-side channel vulnerabilities.

Comparison with Findings in [3]. The only prior experimental study of the effectiveness of transformations is the investigation of a Java bytecode implementation of cross-copying by Agat in [3]. This investigation had a qualitative nature and did not consider bandwidths of timing side channels. The experiments were done on synthetic benchmark programs. In contrast to our findings, no significant timing differences for the transformed programs have been observed. There might be several reasons for that: The transformation was implemented in Java bytecode, and different experiments, programs, and a setup were used.

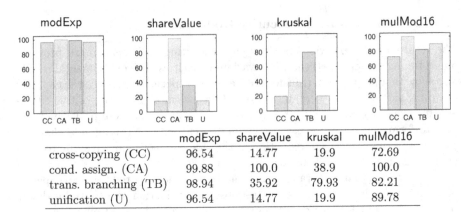

Fig. 6. Reduction of the estimated capacity of timing side channels, in %.

	modExp	shareValue	kruskal	mulMod16
cross-copying (CC)	96.54	14.77	19.9	72.69
cond. assign. (CA)	99.88	100.0	38.9	100.0
trans. branching (TB)	98.94	35.92	79.93	82.21
unification (U)	96.54	14.77	19.9	89.78

7   Navigating in the Performance-Security Trade-Off

Usually security comes at a price. Our evaluation of the overhead introduced by four program transformations for removing timing side-channel vulnerabilities shows that these transformations are no exception. But what is the relationship between the security and its price?

In this section we attempt to explore this relationship for the considered program transformations. In Fig. 7 we plot together the results of our performance and security evaluations. The ordinate denotes the values of the performance overhead from Fig. 3. The abscissa denotes the values of the side-channel capacity reduction from Fig. 6. Red crosses, yellow triangles, blue circles, and green boxes correspond to cross-copying, conditional assignment, transactional branching, and unification, respectively. There are four markers of each marker type. Each marker corresponds to an experiment with one benchmark program.

We are interested in analyzing which transformations satisfy a performance-security requirement of the form "We are willing to pay α percent in performance overhead for 1 % of side-channel capacity reduction" for different values of α. Let p denote the performance overhead in percent, and let s denote the side-channel capacity reduction in percent. Equation $p = \alpha s$ represents the above performance-security requirement. In Fig. 7 we plot beams that satisfy the equation $p = \alpha s$ for different values of α. Whenever all four markers of the same marker type lie below the beam for particular α, the transformation that corresponds to this marker type satisfies the performance-security requirement for this α. We vary α from 0 to 5 with the step 0.25.

Our experimental results suggest: (1) Conditional assignment satisfies $p = 0.75s$. (2) Unification satisfies $p = s$. (3) Cross-copying satisfies $p = 1.25s$. (4) Transactional branching satisfies $p = 4.75s$. (In three cases, it satisfies $p = 2.25s$.)

We conclude that conditional assignment satisfies our performance-security requirement of interest for the smallest value of α among all transformations. Furthermore, the above list allows us to identify the ordering between the trans-

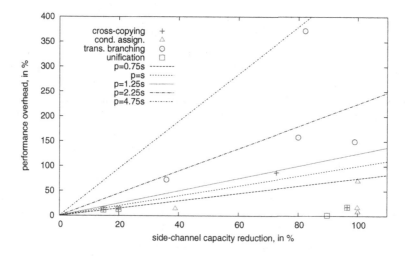

Fig. 7. Analyzing performance-security requirements for transformations.

formations wrt. how expensive is the security offered by them. This list can serve as an initial guidance for reducing the search space of candidate program transformations that one may want to deploy in practice.

One weakness of the considered requirement is that it suggests that a transformation not impacting performance, but only very slightly decreasing the side-channel capacity might be considered superior to any other transformation. This weakness can be overcome by requiring in addition all transformations to achieve a minimum threshold in reduction of the side-channel capacity. Naturally, further performance-security requirements may also be of one's interest. In this section, we illustrate how one can use our experimental results for analyzing how good different program transformations satisfy such requirements.

8   Related Work

There is a large body of work on the analysis of side channels from the attacker's perspective, e.g., [4,15,19,26,32,34,35,48,49]. Timing side channels have been for the first time exploited by Kocher to attack an implementation of RSA [34].

A successful attack against an implementation proves that the implementation is vulnerable. On the contrary, timing-sensitive noninterference-like properties have been used to express that an implementation is secure wrt. timing side channels [2,13,23,30,38]. Noninterference-like properties express very strong security, which usually implies that an attacker cannot gain any information about given secrets. In practice, however, some leakage might be unavoidable.

Quantitative theories of information-flow security allow one to limit how much information is actually leaked [52]. In the eighties, Millen [46] proposed to use the Shannon's channel capacity [51] for quantifying the capacity of covert channels. Later, attention was attracted by the development of new leakage measures that more closely express the danger of real attacks, most notably min-entropy [52] and g-leakage [7]. Generalizing the Shannon's capacity, a theory of channel capacity applicable to g-leakage has also been recently proposed [6].

For quantitative analysis of side channels, in general, Köpf and Basin [36] present an information-theoretic model of side-channel attacks that allows quantification of the information revealed to an attacker. Macé et al. [44] propose an approach for information-theoretic evaluation of side-channel resistant logic styles. Standaert et al. [53] present a framework for analysis of side-channel attacks that enables comparisons of different implementations wrt. side channels.

For quantitative analysis of timing side channels, Köpf and Backes [10] propose an approach for quantifying resistance to unknown-message side-channel attacks and use this approach to assess the resistance of cryptographic implementations against timing attacks. Köpf and Smith [39] derive leakage bounds for blinded cryptography under timing attacks. Doychev et al. [24] present a tool for automatic derivation of upper bounds on the cache side-channel leakage in x86 binaries, including cache-related side channels that are based on timing.

Yet, there seems to be a deficit of reports on *empirical* quantitative evaluation of timing side channels. We are aware only of the work by Cock et al. [19] who present an empirical evaluation of timing side channels on the seL4 microkernel. The results of our own research project contribute to this line of research.

Related to side channels, the problem of covert channels [42] has also attracted a lot of attention. For covert channels that are based on timing, there are reports on their informal [55], analytical [45], and empirical [19,27] analysis.

Besides program transformations [2,13,38,47], there is a spectrum of other techniques for controlling timing side channels. Hu [31] proposes to reduce timing channels by adding noise to the observable timing signal. Kocher [34] proposes blinding that unpredictably changes the correlation between the secret input of a cryptographic operation and its observable running time. Chevallier-Mames et al. [18] propose side-channel atomicity, a method to convert a cryptographic algorithm into an algorithm protected against simple side-channel attacks. Köpf and Dürmuth [37] improve blinding to allow a choice between the strength of the security guarantee and the resulting performance overhead. Svenningsson and Sands [54] present a method for controlled declassification of the side-channel leakage. Coppens et al. [20] propose to remove timing side channels by a transformation in a compiler backend. Askarov et al. [9] introduce black-box mitigators for controlling timing side channels in a system by delaying the system's outputs. Zhang et al. [56] leverage this approach for a programming language. Crane et al. [22] propose automated software diversity to mitigate cache side channels.

While performance costs of side-channel mitigation are generally addressed in the literature, e.g., in [20,23,37,47,56], a trade-off between the performance and security in this context is explored to a lesser extent. Köpf and Dürmuth [37] study such a trade-off for their countermeasure. Di Pierro et al. [23] investigate such a trade-off for a probabilistic variant of cross-copying, but only analytically. Doychev and Köpf [25] propose a game-theoretic approach for finding cost-effective configurations for countermeasures against side channels.

9   Conclusion

We presented the first systematic empirical evaluation of source-to-source transformations for removing timing side-channel vulnerabilities wrt. security and
overhead. Our experimental results suggest that there are substantial differences
between the transformations both in the introduced performance overhead and
in the achieved reduction of timing side-channel capacities. In prior work, such
transformations were analyzed mostly theoretically. However, it was speculated
that some of the transformations are of unclear practical significance due to
their potential inefficiency [54] or ineffectiveness [38]. In this research project,
we obtain objective numbers that allow one to clarify such concerns wrt. one's
own criteria of efficiency and effectiveness. Beyond this clarification, our findings
provide guidance for choosing a suitable program transformation. Such choice is
non-trivial because of the trade-off between security and performance.

Our work deepens the understanding about the effectiveness and efficiency
of program transformations for removing timing side-channel vulnerabilities in
practice, but this is only a first step in the empirical evaluation of such transformations. As future work, we will experimentally investigate effects of JIT
compilation on program transformations. We also plan to consider alternative
implementations of transformations as well as alternative measures of leakage.

Acknowledgements. We thank Boris Köpf, David Sands, and the anonymous reviewers for valuable comments. We thank Patrick Metzler for help in the early phase of this
work. This work has been partially funded by the DFG as part of project E2 within
the CRC 1119 CROSSING and by CASED (www.cased.de).

A   Source Code of Benchmarks

(see Figs. 8, 9, and 10)

```
public int shareValue(int[] ids, int[] qty) {
    shareVal = 0;
    int i = 0;
    while (i < ids.length) {
        int id = ids[i];
        int val = lookupVal(id) * qty[i];
        if (id == SPECIAL_SHARE)
            shareVal = shareVal + val;
        i++;
    }
    return shareVal;
}
```

Fig. 8. Benchmark program shareValue, the critical conditional is highlighted.

```java
public int[] kruskal(int[] g) {
  int[] mst = new int[g.length];
  par = new int[g.length];
  for (int i = 0; i < par.length; ++i) {
    mst[i] = -1;
    par[i] = i;
  }
  int idx = 0;
  for (int i = 1; i < g.length; i += 2) {
    int src = find(g[i]);
    int tgt = find(g[i + 1]);
    if (src != tgt) {
      mst[++idx] = src;
      mst[++idx] = tgt;
      par[src] = tgt;
    }
  }
  mst[0] = idx / 2 + 1;
  return mst;
}

private int find(int x) {
  if (par[x] != x)
    return find(par[x]);
  return x;
}
```

Fig. 9. Benchmark program kruskal, the critical conditional is highlighted.

```java
private int mulMod16(int a, int b) {
  int p;
  a &= mulMask;
  b &= mulMask;
  if (a == 0) {
    a = mulModulus - b;
  } else if (b == 0) {
    a = mulModulus - a;
  } else {
    p = a * b;
    b = p & mulMask;
    a = p >>> 16;
    a = b - a + (b < a ? 1 : 0);
  }
  return a & mulMask;
}
```

Fig. 10. Benchmark program mulMod16, the critical conditional is highlighted.

References

1. FlexiProvider (Version 1.7p7) (2013). http://www.flexiprovider.de
2. Agat, J.: Transforming out Timing Leaks. In: POPL 2000, pp. 40–53. ACM (2000)
3. Agat, J.: Type Based Techniques for Covert Channel Elimination and Register Allocation. PhD thesis, Chalmers University of Technology (2000)
4. AlFardan, N.J., Paterson, K.G.: Lucky Thirteen: Breaking the TLS and DTLS Record Protocols. In: S&P 2013, pp. 526–540. IEEE (2013)
5. Alglave, J., Kroening, D., Nimal, V., Tautschnig, M.: Software verification for weak memory via program transformation. In: Felleisen, M., Gardner, P. (eds.) ESOP 2013. LNCS, vol. 7792, pp. 512–532. Springer, Heidelberg (2013)
6. Alvim, M.-S., Chatzikokolakis, K., McIver, A., Morgan, C., Palamidessi, C., Smith, G.: Additive and Multiplicative Notions of Leakage, and Their Capacities. In: CSF 2014, pp. 308–322. IEEE (2014)
7. Alvim, M.S., Chatzikokolakis, K., Palamidessi, C., Smith, G.: Measuring Information Leakage using Generalized Gain Functions. In: CSF 2012, pp. 265–279. IEEE (2012)
8. Arimoto, S.: An algorithm for computing the capacity of arbitrary discrete memoryless channels. IEEE Trans. Inf. Theory 18(1), 14–20 (1972)
9. Askarov, A., Zhang, D., Myers, A.C., Predictive Black-Box Mitigation of Timing Channels. In: CCS 2010, pp. 297–307. ACM (2010)
10. Backes, M., Köpf, B.: Formally bounding the side-channel leakage in unknown-message attacks. In: Jajodia, S., Lopez, J. (eds.) ESORICS 2008. LNCS, vol. 5283, pp. 517–532. Springer, Heidelberg (2008)
11. Baron, M.: Probability and Statistics for Computer Scientists. CRC Press (2006)
12. Barthe, G., Crespo, J.M., Devriese, D., Piessens, F., Rivas, E.: Secure multi-execution through static program transformation. In: Giese, H., Rosu, G. (eds.) FORTE 2012 and FMOODS 2012. LNCS, vol. 7273, pp. 186–202. Springer, Heidelberg (2012)
13. Barthe, G., Rezk, T., Warnier, M.: Preventing Timing Leaks Through Transactional Branching Instructions. In: QAPL 2005, pp. 33–55. Elsevier (2006)
14. Blahut, R.E.: Computation of channel capacity and rate-distortion functions. IEEE Trans. Inf. Theory 18(4), 460–473 (1972)
15. Brumley, B.B., Tuveri, N.: Remote timing attacks are still practical. In: Atluri, V., Diaz, C. (eds.) ESORICS 2011. LNCS, vol. 6879, pp. 355–371. Springer, Heidelberg (2011)
16. Burstall, R.M., Darlington, J.: A transformation system for developing recursive programs. J. ACM 24(1), 44–67 (1977)
17. Chatzikokolakis, K., Chothia, T., Guha, A.: Statistical measurement of information leakage. In: Esparza, J., Majumdar, R. (eds.) TACAS 2010. LNCS, vol. 6015, pp. 390–404. Springer, Heidelberg (2010)
18. Chevallier-Mames, B., Ciet, M., Joye, M.: Low-cost solutions for preventing simple side-channel analysis: side-channel atomicity. IEEE Trans. Comput. 53(6), 760–768 (2004)
19. Cock, D., Ge, Q., Murray, T.C., Heiser, G.: The last mile: an empirical study of timing channels on seL4. In: CCS 2014, pp. 570–581. ACM (2014)
20. Coppens, B., Verbauwhede, I., De Bosschere, K., De Sutter, B.: Practical mitigations for timing-based side-channel attacks on modern x86 processors. In: S&P 2009, pp. 45–60. IEEE (2009)
21. Cover, T.M., Thomas, J.A.: Elements of Information Theory, 2nd ed. Wiley (2006)

22. Crane, S., Homescu, A., Brunthaler, S., Larsen, P., Franz, M.: Thwarting cache side-channel attacks through dynamic software diversity. In: NDSS 2015. The Internet Society (2015)
23. Di Pierro, A., Hankin, C., Wiklicky, H.: Probabilistic timing covert channels: to close or not to close? Int. J. Inf. Sec. **10**(2), 83–106 (2011)
24. Doychev, G., Feld, D., Köpf, B., Mauborgne, L., Reineke, J.: CacheAudit: a tool for the static analysis of cache side channels. In: USENIX Security 2013, pp. 431–446. USENIX (2013)
25. Doychev, G., Köpf, B.: Rational protection against timing attacks. In: CSF 2015. IEEE (2015)
26. Gandolfi, K., Mourtel, C., Olivier, F.: Electromagnetic analysis: concrete results. In: Koç, Ç.K., Naccache, D., Paar, C. (eds.) CHES 2001. LNCS, vol. 2162, pp. 251–261. Springer, Heidelberg (2001)
27. Gay, R., Mantel, H., Sudbrock, H.: An empirical bandwidth analysis of interrupt-related covert channels. In: QASA 2013 (2013)
28. Georges, A., Buytaert, D., Eeckhout, L.: Statistically rigorous Java performance evaluation. In: OOPSLA 2007, pp. 57–76. ACM (2007)
29. Guttoski, P.B., Sunyé, M.S., Silva, F.: Kruskal's algorithm for query tree optimization. In: IDEAS 2007, pp. 296–302. IEEE (2007)
30. Hedin, D., Sands, D.: Timing aware information flow security for a JavaCard-like Bytecode. El. Notes Th. Comp. Science **141**(1), 163–182 (2005)
31. Hu, W.-M.: Reducing timing channels with fuzzy time. In: S&P 1991, pp. 8–20. IEEE (1991)
32. Kelsey, J., Schneier, B., Wagner, D., Hall, C.: Side channel cryptanalysis of product ciphers. In: Quisquater, J.-J., Deswarte, Y., Meadows, C., Gollmann, D. (eds.) ESORICS 1998. LNCS, vol. 1485, pp. 97–110. Springer, Heidelberg (1998)
33. Knuth, D.: Structured programming with go to statements. ACM Comput. Surv. **6**(4), 261–301 (1974)
34. Kocher, P.C.: Timing attacks on implementations of Diffie-Hellman, RSA, DSS, and other systems. In: Koblitz, N. (ed.) CRYPTO 1996. LNCS, vol. 1109, pp. 104–113. Springer, Heidelberg (1996)
35. Kocher, P.C., Jaffe, J., Jun, B.: Differential power analysis. In: Wiener, M. (ed.) CRYPTO 1999. LNCS, vol. 1666, pp. 388–397. Springer, Heidelberg (1999)
36. Köpf, B., Basin, D.A.: An information-theoretic model for adaptive side-channel attacks. In: CCS 2007, pp. 286–296. ACM (2007)
37. Köpf, B., Dürmuth, M.: A provably secure and efficient countermeasure against timing attacks. In: CSF 2009, pp. 324–335. IEEE (2009)
38. Köpf, B., Mantel, H.: Transformational typing and unification for automatically correcting insecure programs. Int. J. Inf. Sec. **6**(2–3), 107–131 (2007)
39. Köpf, B., Smith, G.: Vulnerability bounds and leakage resilience of blinded cryptograph under timing attacks. In: CSF 2010, pp. 44–56. IEEE (2010)
40. Kruskal, J.B.: On the shortest spanning subtree of a graph and the traveling salesman problem. Proc. American Math. Soc. **7**(1), 48–50 (1956)
41. Lai, X.: On the design and security of block ciphers. PhD thesis, ETH Zürich (1992)
42. Lampson, B.W.: A note on the confinement problem. Commun. ACM **16**(10), 613–615 (1973)
43. Lux, A., Starostin, A.: A tool for static detection of timing channels in Java. J. Crypt. Eng. **1**(4), 303–313 (2011)

44. Macé, F., Standaert, F.-X., Quisquater, J.-J.: Information theoretic evaluation of side-channel resistant logic styles. In: Paillier, P., Verbauwhede, I. (eds.) CHES 2007. LNCS, vol. 4727, pp. 427–442. Springer, Heidelberg (2007)
45. Mantel, H., Sudbrock, H.: Comparing countermeasures against interrupt-related covert channels in an information-theoretic framework. In: CSF 2007, pp. 326–340. IEEE (2007)
46. Millen, J.K.: Covert channel capacity. In: S&P 1987, pp. 60–66. IEEE (1987)
47. Molnar, D., Piotrowski, M., Schultz, D., Wagner, D.: The program counter security model: automatic detection and removal of control-flow side channel attacks. In: Won, D.H., Kim, S. (eds.) ICISC 2005. LNCS, vol. 3935, pp. 156–168. Springer, Heidelberg (2006)
48. Osvik, D.A., Shamir, A., Tromer, E.: Cache attacks and countermeasures: the case of AES. In: Pointcheval, D. (ed.) CT-RSA 2006. LNCS, vol. 3860, pp. 1–20. Springer, Heidelberg (2006)
49. Quisquater, J.-J., Samyde, D.: ElectroMagnetic Analysis (EMA): measures and counter-measures for smart cards. In: Attali, S., Jensen, T. (eds.) E-smart 2001. LNCS, vol. 2140, pp. 200–210. Springer, Heidelberg (2001)
50. Rivest, R.L., Shamir, A., Adleman, L.M.: A method for obtaining digital signatures and public-key cryptosystems. Commun. ACM 21(2), 120–126 (1978)
51. Shannon, C.E.: A mathematical theory of communication. Bell Syst. Tech. J. 27(379–423), 623–656 (1948)
52. Smith, G.: On the foundations of quantitative information flow. In: de Alfaro, L. (ed.) FOSSACS 2009. LNCS, vol. 5504, pp. 288–302. Springer, Heidelberg (2009)
53. Standaert, F.-X., Malkin, T.G., Yung, M.: A unified framework for the analysis of side-channel key recovery attacks. In: Joux, A. (ed.) EUROCRYPT 2009. LNCS, vol. 5479, pp. 443–461. Springer, Heidelberg (2009)
54. Svenningsson, J., Sands, D.: Specification and Verification of Side Channel Declassification. In: Degano, P., Guttman, J.D. (eds.) FAST 2009. LNCS, vol. 5983, pp. 111–125. Springer, Heidelberg (2010)
55. Wray, J.C.: An analysis of covert timing channels. In: S&P 1991, pp. 2–7. IEEE (1991)
56. Zhang, D., Askarov, A., Myers, A.C.: Language-based control and mitigation of timing channels. In: PLDI 2012, pp. 99–110. ACM (2012)

Small Tweaks Do Not Help: Differential Power Analysis of MILENAGE Implementations in 3G/4G USIM Cards

Junrong Liu[1], Yu Yu[1,2,3]($\boxtimes$), François-Xavier Standaert[4], Zheng Guo[1,5],
Dawu Gu[1]($\boxtimes$), Wei Sun[1], Yijie Ge[1], and Xinjun Xie[6]

[1] School of Electronic Information and Electrical Engineering,
Shanghai Jiao Tong University, Shanghai, China
{liujr,yyuu,guozheng,dwgu,ruudvn}@sjtu.edu.cn

[2] State Key Laboratory of Information Security, Institute of Information
Engineering, Chinese Academy of Sciences, Beijing 100093, China

[3] State Key Laboratory of Cryptology, P.O. Box 5159, Beijing 100878, China

[4] ICTEAM/ELEN/Crypto Group, Université catholique de Louvain,
Louvain-la-Neuve, Belgium
fstandae@uclouvain.be

[5] Shanghai Viewsource Information Science and Technology Co., Ltd,
Shanghai, China

[6] Shanghai Modern General Recognition Technology Corporation, Shanghai, China

Abstract. Side-channel attacks are an increasingly important concern
for the security of cryptographic embedded devices, such as the SIM
cards used in mobile phones. Previous works have exhibited such attacks
against implementations of the 2G GSM algorithms (COMP-128, A5). In
this paper, we show that they remain an important issue for USIM cards
implementing the AES-based MILENAGE algorithm used in 3G/4G
communications. In particular, we analyze instances of cards from a variety of operators and manufacturers, and describe successful Differential
Power Analysis attacks that recover encryption keys and other secrets
(needed to clone the USIM cards) within a few minutes. Further, we
discuss the impact of the operator-defined secret parameters in MILE-
NAGE on the difficulty to perform Differential Power Analysis, and show
that they do not improve implementation security. Our results back up
the observation that physical security issues raise long-term challenges
that should be solved early in the development of cryptographic implementations, with adequate countermeasures.

Keywords: Side-channel attacks · Mobile network security · SIM cards
cloning

1 Introduction

The mathematical and physical security of cryptographic algorithms used in
cellular networks has been a long standing concern. Starting with the reverse

© Springer International Publishing Switzerland 2015
G. Pernul et al. (Eds.): ESORICS 2015, Part I, LNCS 9326, pp. 468–480, 2015.
DOI: 10.1007/978-3-319-24174-6_24

engineering of the COMP-128 algorithm (i.e. the A3/A8 algorithms used to authenticate GSM subscribers and generate session keys), Briceno, Goldberg and Wagner first showed that its compression function was fatally flawed due to a lack of diffusion. The resulting "narrow pipe attack" takes roughly 131,000 challenge-response pairs to recover a GSM SIM card master key [10]. Furthermore, several cryptanalytic results have been published about the A5 algorithm – i.e. the stream cipher used to encrypt the GSM communications based on a session key (see, e.g. [6–9,15]). Besides, different implementations of COMP-128 deployed in actual SIM cards have also been proved susceptible to Differential Power Analysis (DPA). For example, it was shown in [18] that a specialized (so-called partitioning) side-channel attack could lead to the cloning of 8-bit GSM SIM cards after monitoring its power consumption for only a couple of minutes. More recently, Zhou et al. reached a similar conclusion for implementations in 16-bit CPUs [20]. The latter reference also discussed the negative impact of closed-source algorithms (such as COMP-128) on physical security, as it limits the amount of research on dedicated countermeasures against physical attacks for these algorithms. As a result of this state-of-the-art, the move towards UMTS/LTE and the 3G/4G communication technology, whose security is based on standardized algorithms, was a very welcome improvement.

In this paper, we pay attention to the implementation of the MILENAGE algorithm in 3G/4G USIM cards, for which the recommended underlying primitive is the Advanced Encryption Standard (AES) Rijndael. MILENAGE is typically used for authentication and key agreement in UMTS/LTE networks. As for previous works on side-channel analysis against SIM cards, this focus is motivated by the fact that breaking this part of the system is most damaging, since it allows eavesdropping, card cloning, and therefore bypassing the one-time-password authentication mechanism with mobile phones. In this context, we evaluated the security of eight commercial USIM cards, coming from a variety of operators and manufacturers, in order to tackle two main questions.

First, are the AES implementations used by MILENAGE systematically protected by state-of-the-art countermeasures against side-channel attacks? We answer this question negatively, as the different cards against which we performed experiments did not exhibit any particular mechanisms to prevent such attacks, leading to the same conclusions as [20] regarding the need to consider physical security issues early in the development of cryptographic products.

Second and more importantly, we analyzed the impact of small tweaks in MILENAGE – such as the use of secret (operator-defined) constants – regarding the difficulty of performing the attacks. As a main contribution, we show that these secrets have very limited impact on the attacks complexity. In particular, they do not bring the security improvements that would be expected from unknown-plaintexts, and allow successful divide-and-conquer key recoveries after a few minutes of power consumption measurements, as standard unprotected implementations of the AES in similar devices. The latter result is of more general interest, since it applies to any implementation of MILENAGE.

Cautionary Note. The experiments presented in this paper were performed more than one year before submission to ESORICS 2015. We contacted the operators with feedbacks and suggestions (on countermeasures against side-channel analysis) before publication of the results. Upgrades towards more physically secure implementations are under development (or maybe already deployed). We do not claim that the USIM cards we measured and analyzed are reflective of the majority of deployed USIM cards and the paper does not contain any specific detail allowing to reveal the operators and manufacturers that were considered.

2   Background

2.1   The UMTS/LTE Infrastructure

The Universal Mobile Telecommunications System (UMTS) and Long-Term Evolution (LTE) are respectively third generation (3G) and fourth generation (4G) mobile cellular systems for networks based on the Global System for Mobile Communication (GSM) standard. The technologies have been developed and maintained by the 3rd Generation Partnership Project (3GPP), and they have been widely adopted in many countries in Asia, Europe and the USA (see [3,4] for a list of mobile operators who adopt the 3G/4G technologies). For convenience, we only provide a simplified overview of the infrastructure by considering only two parties (omitting intermediate nodes such as Visitor Location Registers), namely, the Universal Subscriber Identity Module (USIM), which is typically a smart card embedded in a subscriber's telephony device, and an Authentication Center (AuC), which is a security function running on the operator's server. The cryptographic protocol engaged between two parties is symmetric, so that USIM and AuC need to share necessary information such as a unique identifier IMSI (International Mobile Subscriber Identity), a symmetric master key K, and operator-defined secrets OPc (operand code), $r1, \ldots, r5, c1, \ldots, c5$.

3G/4G AUTHENTICATION AND KEY AGREEMENT. Unlike GSM whose authentication was one-way and based on flawed algorithms, UMTS and LTE enforce a mutual authentication and key agreement (AKA) protocol, which in turn builds upon an AES-based algorithm called MILENAGE. As shown in Fig. 1, the 3G authentication starts with a user id request and a response from USIM with its unique IMSI. Upon the authentication request, the AuC samples a random RAND, assigns a sequence number SQN, and computes the MILENAGE algorithm (a suite of AES-based functions $f1, \ldots, f5$) with the symmetric key K and the AMF (Authenticated and key Management Field) constant to produce as output the masked (i.e. XORed with anonymity key AK) sequence number $SQN \oplus AK$, tag MAC, expected response XRES, cipher key CK and integrity key IK. The USIM then receives RAND and $AUTN = (SQN \oplus AK, AMF, MAC)$, and computes with MILENAGE symmetrically to recover SQN, and to obtain XMAC (the expected MAC), response RES, CK and IK. The USIM rejects if the SQN is out of the expected range or the MAC is not the same as XMAC,

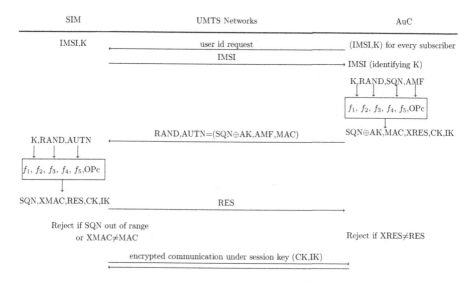

Fig. 1. Simplified AKA protocol between a USIM card and an AuC in 3G networks.

and the AuC rejects if the response is not as expected (RES $\neq$ XRES). The 4G protocol slightly differs from the 3G one described in the figure (see, e.g. [5, Fig. 1] for the details). However, none of its changes are relevant to our attacks. Note that while mostly based on public algorithms, MILENAGE still includes a slight amount of secrets in its specifications, e.g., the (fixed) parameter OPc is usually kept secret by mobile operators. Once an adversary recovers all the secrets stored in the USIM, he can clone it by loading the same configuration into a blank card. As mentioned in introduction, the next sections will investigate the impact of these secret parameters for physical security.

2.2   The MILENAGE Algorithm

The MILENAGE algorithm [13] is a suite of mathematical functions, $f1, \ldots, f5$, that are based on the AES-128. For the purposes of this paper, it suffices to consider the computation of this algorithm on the USIM side of the AKA protocol, as depicted in Fig. 2. In particular, we will focus on $f5$. It is used to compute $AK = f5_k(RAND)$ and thus allows to recover $SQN = (SQN \oplus AK) \oplus AK$, which is in turn used to compute $XMAC = f1_k(SQN, RAND, AMF)$. Note that if XMAC does not equal to MAC, the USIM authentication will terminate and signal an error message, which means the rest of the functions (i.e. $f2, f3$ and $f4$) will not be computed. Therefore, $f5$ is a target of choice for our power analysis investigations. Yet, we mention that other functions $f1, f2, f3$ and $f4$ are similarly defined, and we refer to [16] for details on their specifications.

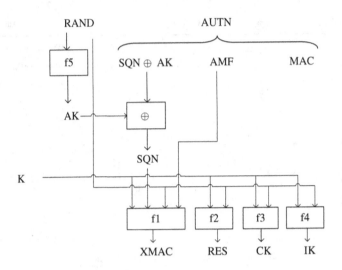

Fig. 2. Illustration of the computation of MILENAGE on a USIM.

$$RAND \xrightarrow{\oplus}_{OPc} E_k \xrightarrow{\oplus}_{OPc} \boxed{\begin{array}{c} \text{rotate} \\ \text{by } r2 \end{array}} \xrightarrow{\oplus}_{c2} E_k \xrightarrow{\oplus}_{OPc} AK$$

Fig. 3. Illustration of $f5$.

As depicted Fig. 3, $f5$ takes RAND, OPc and K as 16-byte inputs, and computes:

$$M_1 = E_k(RAND \oplus OPc), \quad M_2 = Rotate_{r2}(M_1 \oplus OPc),$$
$$M_3 = E_k(M_2 \oplus c2), \qquad AK = M_3 \oplus OPc, \tag{1}$$

where $\oplus$ denotes bitwise XOR, $Rotate_{r2}$ denotes rotate-by-$r2$-bits, and E_k is the AES-128 [12].

OPERATOR-DEFINED PARAMETERS. OPc is a secret value chosen by the operator and fixed once for all its USIMs. Other parameters such as $r1, \ldots, r5$ and $c1, \ldots, c5$ have default values suggested by 3GPP specification [1], but they are also configurable (to secret values) by operators.

2.3   Side-channel Attacks

Side-channel attacks generally exploit the existence of data-dependent and physically observable phenomenons caused by the execution of computing tasks in microelectronic devices. Typical examples of such information leakages include the power consumption and the electromagnetic radiation of integrated circuits. We will focus on the first one in the rest of this paper. The literature usually divides such attacks in two classes. First, Simple Power Analysis (SPA) attempts to interpret the power consumption of a device and deduce information about its performed operations. This can be done by visual inspection of the power consumption measurements in function of the time. SPA in itself does not always lead to key recovery, e.g. with block ciphers, distinguishing the encryption rounds does not reveal any sensitive information. Yet, it can be a preliminary step in order to reduce the computational requirements of more advanced attacks. Second, Differential Power Analysis (DPA) intends to take advantage of data-dependencies in the power consumption patterns. In its standard form [14], DPA is based on a divide-and-conquer strategy, in which the different parts of a secret key (usually denoted as "subkeys") are recovered separately. The attack is best illustrated with an example. Say one targets the first round of a block cipher, where the plaintext is XORed with a subkey and sent through a substitution box S. DPA is made of three steps:

1. For different plaintexts x_i and subkey candidates k^*, the adversary predicts intermediate values in the implementation, e.g. the S-box outputs $v_i^{k^*} = \mathsf{S}(x_i \oplus k^*)$.
2. For each of these predicted values, the adversary models the leakages. For example, if the target block cipher is implemented in a CMOS-based micro-controller, the model can be the Hamming weight (HW) of the predicted values[1]: $m_i^{k^*} = \mathsf{HW}(v_i^{k^*})$.
3. For each subkey candidate k^*, the adversary compares the modeled leakages with actual measurements, produced with the same plaintexts x_i and a secret subkey k. In the univariate DPA attacks (that we will apply), each $m_i^{k^*}$ is compared independently with many single points in the traces, and the subkey candidate that performs best is selected by the adversary.

Different statistical tools have been proposed to perform this comparison. In our experiments, we will consider a usual DPA distinguisher, namely Pearson's correlation coefficient [11]. In this case, and denoting a leakage sample produced with plaintext x_i and subkey k as l_i^k, the adversary selects the subkey candidate as:

$$\tilde{k} = \underset{k^*}{\arg\max} \ \frac{\sum_i (m_i^{k^*} - \overline{m}^{k^*}) \cdot (l_i^k - \overline{l}^k)}{\sqrt{\sum_i (m_i^{k^*} - \overline{m}^{k^*})^2 \cdot \sum_i (l_i^k - \overline{l}^k)^2}}, \qquad (2)$$

where $\overline{m}^{k^*}$ and $\overline{l}^k$ are the sample means of the models and leakages. By repeating this procedure for every subkey (and enumarting if needed [19]), the complete master key is finally recovered.

---

[1] This assumption relates to the observation that in CMOS circuits, a significant part of the power consumption is dynamic, i.e. caused by the switching activity. A first-order approximation of this switching activity is given by the Hamming weight of the intermediate values produced when performing the cryptographic computations.

Fig. 4. The actual measurement setup for our experiments.

3 DPA Against MILENAGE Implementations in USIM Cards

3.1 Measurement Setup and Target USIM Cards

As depicted in Fig. 4, we used a self-made card reader (with a resistor inserted for power acquisition) and ran some open source software [2] on a PC to control the test cards and execute the MILENAGE algorithm. At the same time, we used a LeCroyScope oscilloscope to acquire the power traces, and connected it with a Card-to-Terminal adapter providing an external DC power (+5V). Finally, we used MP300 SC2 to intercept the authentication messages between USIM and AuC, which provides useful information for our experiments (e.g. whether authentication succeeds or not). Our target USIM cards are listed in Table 1. They all include secret OPc. As for the other configurable parameters ($r1$, $c1$, ..., $r1$, $c5$), some of the USIM cards use standard (public) suggested values, and the rest use secret ones.

To initiate the authentication, the PC (which plays the role of AuC) typically communicates with the USIM in the language of application protocol data unit (APDU) as following:

```
00 A4 08 04 02 2F 00  select file with 2(0x02)-byte argument 2F 00
00 C0 00 00 1C        get response of 29(0x1C) bytes
00 B2 01 04 26        read records
00 A4 04 04 10 A0 00 00 00 87 10 02 FF 86 11 04 89 FF FF FF FF
                      select file with 16(0x10)-byte argument A0**FF
00 C0 00 00 35        get response of 53(0x35) bytes
00 A4 00 04 02 6F 07  select file with 2(0x02)-byte argument 6F 07
00 C0 00 00 19        get response of 25(0x19) bytes
```

Table 1. List of target USIM cards with anonymized operators, manufacturers and countries of origin. (C1-1 stands for continent 1, country 1). The data and time complexity are measured respectively by the number of power traces and the total amount of time needed for the attack (including power acquisition, data processing and DPA).

USIM	Operator	Manufacturer	Technology	Secrets	# of traces	Time
#1	C1-1	C1-I	3G UMTS	K, OPc	200	10 min
#2	C1-1	C2-II	3G UMTS	K, OPc	200	10 min
#3	C1-1	C1-III	3G UMTS	K, OPc	200	10 min
#4	C1-2	C3-I	3G UMTS	K, OPc, $r_1, \ldots, r_5, c_1, \ldots, c_5$	1000	60 min
#5	C2-1	C2-I	3G UMTS	K, OPc, $r_1, \ldots, r_5, c_1, \ldots, c_5$	1000	70 min
#6	C1-3	C1-IV	4G LTE	K, OPc, $r_1, \ldots, r_5, c_1, \ldots, c_5$	1000	60 min
#7	C1-3	C1-II	4G LTE	K, OPc, $r_1, \ldots, r_5, c_1, \ldots, c_5$	1000	60 min
#8	C2-2	C2-II	4G LTE	K, OPc, $r_1, \ldots, r_5, c_1, \ldots, c_5$	1000	80 min

```
00 B0 00 00 09       read binary
00 88 00 81 22 10 AA AA AA AA AA AA AA AA AA AA AA AA AA AA AA AA
---------------10 BB BB BB BB BB BB BB BB BB BB BB BB BB BB BB BB
run authentication on 16(0x10)-byte RAND=(AA**AA),AUTN=(BB**BB)
```

where the '−'s are padded for alignment only. Roughly speaking, one needs to apply a sequence of "select file" APDUs from the master file (through the directory tree) to reach the application that invokes MILENAGE. The last APDU runs MILENAGE on two 16-byte arguments "AA...AA" and "BB...BB" (highlighted in blue), which can be replaced with any values for RAND and AUTN. Note finally that the structure of the APDU is defined by ISO/IEC 7816-4, but the "command data" fields (highlighted in red) of some APDUs may vary for different manufacturers. In the latter cases, we used some brute force search in order to remove the uncertainties.

3.2 Attack Strategy

In order to recover OPc and K from the USIM, we interact with the card and execute the AKA protocol based on full knowledge of the inputs being processed (i.e. RAND and AUTN), which allows us to collect power consumption traces for the implementation of MILENAGE. We then perform DPA using the Hamming weight model with the following steps.

1. *Recovering $K \oplus OPc$.* As illustrated in Fig. 5, the (known) RAND is XORed with (secret) OPc before going through E_k (i.e. the AES-128 encryption [12]). In this step, we therefore focus on the first round of E_k, where the 16-byte plaintext RAND $\oplus$ OPc is parsed as a 4×4 byte state matrix. This 16-byte plaintext is first bitwise XORed with 16-byte secret key in *AddRoundKey*. Then, each updated state byte is replaced by another one using the S-box (16 invertible lookup tables) in *SubBytes*. As a result, a simple DPA attack can be performed by considering the output of *SubBytes* as target intermediate

value, viewing RAND (instead of RAND $\oplus$ OPc) as plaintext, and OPc $\oplus$ K (rather than K) as the first round key.

2. *Recovering K (and OPc).* Given that K $\oplus$ OPc is already known, we just need to recover either K or OPc. A straightforward way to do this is to target at the XOR operation between RAND and OPc[2], but DPA usually works better after a non-linear operation (as explained in [17]). Therefore, a much better approach is to attack the second block cipher round. That is, upon successful key recovery in the first round, we obtain the output of the first round (i.e. x_2 in Fig. 5), which enables us to perform another DPA on the second round to recover the 2nd round key RK_2, from which we compute the corresponding encryption key K.

3. *Recovering the other secret parameters.* One of our target USIMs contained secret values for $r1, \ldots, r5$ and $c1, \ldots, c5$, which can also be recovered with a divide-and-conquer side-channel attack, as we now explain for $c2$ and $r2$ (the same techniques applies to the other secret parameters). Based on the previous attacks, we now know the 128-bit intermediate result prior to the $Rotate_{r2}$ operation (illustrated in Fig. 3), say $v_0 v_1 \ldots v_{127}$. $Rotate_{r2}$ is simply a right cyclic shift of this known value by r_2 bits. In order to recover r_2, we first write it as a multiple of some i plus remainder j, i.e. $r2 = 8i + j$. Then we consider the sequence:

$$\underbrace{(v_j v_{j+1} \ldots v_{j+7})}_{\text{byte 0}} \ldots \underbrace{(v_{j+120} \ldots v_{127} v_0 \ldots v_{j-1})}_{\text{byte 15}} \tag{3}$$

which represents $v_0 v_1 \ldots v_{127}$ rotated by j bits. Assuming that the power trace is correlated with the Hamming weight of every individual byte of this rotated value, we can simply make guesses about j (which has only 8 possibilities) and test these guesses with a correlation analysis between the Hamming weight of any byte in (3) and the power trace. Once we recovered j, we then take into account the fact that the sequence was shifted by $8i + j$ bits, which means that the correlations for the 16 bytes above should appear in the order of byte numbers $15 - i + 1, \ldots, 15, 0, \ldots, 15 - i$. Therefore, we can again identify the value of i by doing a correlation analyses (with Hamming weight model) for every byte, and finding out the order in which significant correlations appear for those bytes. Eventually, a simple attack as previously described can be used against the second E_k in Fig. 3 to recover $c2$.

3.3   Experimental Results

For conciseness, we show power traces and coefficients plots for one of the USIM cards we investigated (with secret parameters). Results were essentially similar for the other USIM cards. In all cases, successful attacks were obtained based on several hundred power traces that were acquired in a few minutes, and pre-processed with a low-pass filter. We began with SPA to identify the relevant

---

[2] Which succeeded as well, but less efficiently than the following proposal.

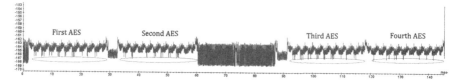

Fig. 5. AES S-box lookups for the first two rounds.

Fig. 6. An overview of a power trace.

parts of the power traces, sent the USIM card authentication commands with randomized inputs for this purpose, and as expected received a *"user authentication reject"* error due to the mismatch of XMAC and MAC (or SQN out of range). For illustration, Fig. 6 gives a view of an entire power trace collected, where we identify 4 similar parts, and each part has 10 rounds. We observe that the last round is less obvious to spot than the other ones, which can be justified by the fact that AES-128 computes no *MixColumns* in its last round. Note that in this case, the power consumption we measured only corresponds to that of f_1 (to compute XMAC for verification) and f_5 (to obtain AK and thus recover SQN) since f_2, f_3 and f_4 are not computed on an authentication failure. We could therefore safely assume that the first two parts represent the two AES executions of $f5$, and the last two parts of the trace correspond to the two AES executions of $f1$.

We aligned the traces corresponding to the randomized inputs with a standard pattern matching method. That is, we choose a unique pattern close to the part of the traces of our interest (e.g. the header part of Fig. 6), used cross-correlation tools to identify this pattern in all the traces in an automated manner, and then aligned the traces based on those cross-correlations. This simple technique was sufficient in our experiments, due to the relatively low noise level of our traces.

Thanks to the iterative nature of the AES, we could then divide the traces into segments that correspond to their respective rounds. Furthermore, for each round we identified the parts of the *AddRoundKey* and *MixColumns* operations, by comparing the differences between that round and the 10-th round. Figure 7 is a zoomed-in view of the trace segment nearby the first round, where the four operations *AddRoundKey*, *SubBytes*, *ShiftRows*, and *MixColumns* are identified. We could also verify with correlation analysis that the part of trace prior to *AddRoundKey* corresponds to the operation of RAND $\oplus$ OPc. The fact that all operations appeared to be carried out sequentially gave us strong hints that the MILENAGE algorithm was implemented in software. This suggested that trying an attack with a Hamming weight leakage model might be a good option.

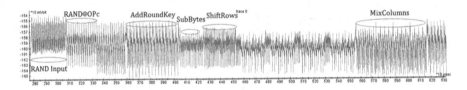

Fig. 7. A zoomed-in view of part of a power trace.

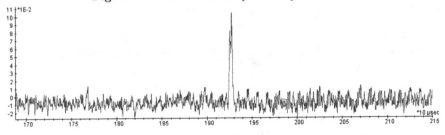

Fig. 8. DPA result on SubBytes to recover $K \oplus OPc$.

We finally discuss the key recovery following the strategies described in Sect. 3.2.

1. *Recovering $K \oplus OPc$.* We focused on the *SubBytes* part of Fig. 7 and performed our DPA attack exactly as described in the previous section. The result of the correlation analysis for the first byte is shown in Fig. 8. Note that the peak was clearly sufficient to recover all key bytes without ambiguity. Furthermore, the time at which they appeared were in line with our previous assumptions regarding when the S-box computations take place.
2. *Recovering K (and OPc).* As previously detailed, a straightforward DPA against the second AES round allowed us to recover the second subkey, from which K (and OPc) can be derived. Correlation plots (and hence, attack efficiencies) were similar as for recovering $K \oplus OPc$.
3. *Recovering the Other Secret Parameters.* As mentioned in Sect. 3.2, we can write $r2 = 8i + j$ and find out the value of j by correlating the Hamming weight of any single byte from (3) (with different hypothetical values about j) with the power trace. As depicted in Fig. 9, we indeed obtained high correlations upon correct guesses about j. We then correlated all bytes in (3) (based on the correct value of j) to the power trace, and we expected to see that correlations occur in sequential order for bytes $15 - i + 1, \ldots, 15, 0, \ldots, 15 - i$. For instance, the value of i in Fig. 9 should be 8. Eventually, we performed an additional DPA against the second E_k in Fig. 3 to recover $c2 \oplus K$ (and thus $c2$), which yielded not particular challenge. The process for recovering other parameters $r1, c1, r3, c3, \ldots, r5$ and $c5$ is identical.
4. *Correctness Verification.* We used MP300 SC2 to acquire the actual messages (RAND and AUTN) communicated between the USIM card and the AuC.

Based on the K and OPc values we recovered thanks to side-channel analysis, XMAC can be calculated accordingly. We could therefore verify that our calculated XMAC equals to the MAC contained in AUTN, and thus confirm that the key recovery of K and OPc was successful in all cases.

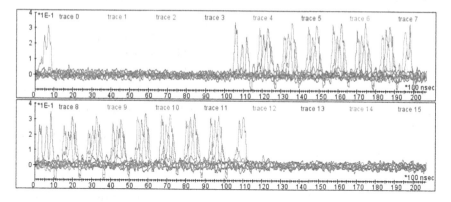

Fig. 9. Correlation traces between the Hamming weight of the bytes in (3) and the power trace, where traces 0, 1, ..., 15 correspond to bytes 0, 1, ..., 15, and are drawn in different colors.

4   Conclusions

Technically, the results in this work are essentially based on known techniques (i.e., differential power analysis attacks). Yet, they are useful to illustrate that the move to AES-based encryption algorithms in 3G/4G USIM cards did not systematically take advantage of state-of-the-art countermeasures against side-channel attacks. Indeed, the USIM cards we analyzed essentially relied on plain (unprotected) software implementations of the AES. Besides, it is interesting to observe that the (minor) obfuscation of the MILENAGE specification with operator-defined secrets has essentially no impact on side-channel security. Needless to say, it would be interesting to exploit the broad literature on secure AES implementations to improve this situation.

Acknowledgments. This research work was supported in parts by the National Basic Research Program of China (Grant 2013CB338004) and the European Commission through the ERC project 280141 (CRASH). Yu Yu was supported by the National Natural Science Foundation of China Grant (Nos. 61472249, 61103221). F.-X. Standaert is a research associate of the Belgian Fund for Scientific Research (FNRS-F.R.S.). Zheng Guo was supported by the National Natural Science Foundation of China Grant (Nos. 61402286, 61202371). Dawu Gu was supported by the National Natural Science Foundation of China Grant (No. 61472250), the Doctoral Fund of Ministry of Education of China (No. 20120073110094), the Innovation Program by Shanghai Municipal Science and Technology Commission (No. 14511100300), and Special Fund Task for Enterprise Innovation Cooperation from Shanghai Municipal Commission of Economy and Informatization (No. CXY-2013-35).

References

1. 3GPP specification: 35.206 (Specification of the MILENAGE algorithm set). http://www.3gpp.org/DynaReport/35206.htm
2. Cryptography for mobile network - C implementation and Python bindings. https://github.com/mitshell/CryptoMobile
3. List of LTE networks. http://en.wikipedia.org/wiki/List_of_LTE_networks
4. List of UMTS networks. http://en.wikipedia.org/wiki/List_of_UMTS_networks
5. Security Technology for SAE/LTE. https://www.nttdocomo.co.jp/english/binary/pdf/corporate/technology/rd/technical_journal/bn/vol11_3/vol11_3_027en.pdf. Accessed 6 January 2015
6. Barkan, E., Biham, E., Keller, N.: Instant ciphertext-only cryptanalysis of GSM encrypted communication. In: Boneh, D. (ed.) CRYPTO 2003. LNCS, vol. 2729, pp. 600–616. Springer, Heidelberg (2003)
7. Biham, E., Dunkelman, O.: Cryptanalysis of the A5/1 GSM stream cipher. In: Roy, B., Okamoto, E. (eds.) INDOCRYPT 2000. LNCS, vol. 1977, pp. 43–51. Springer, Heidelberg (2000)
8. Biryukov, A., Shamir, A., Wagner, D.: Real time cryptanalysis of A5/1 on a PC. In: Schneier, B. (ed.) FSE 2000. LNCS, vol. 1978, pp. 1–18. Springer, Heidelberg (2001)
9. Bogdanov, A., Eisenbarth, T., Rupp, A.: A hardware-assisted realtime attack on A5/2 without precomputations. In: Paillier, P., Verbauwhede, I. (eds.) CHES 2007. LNCS, vol. 4727, pp. 394–412. Springer, Heidelberg (2007)
10. Briceno, M., Goldberg, I., Wagner, D.: GSM Cloning (1998). http://www.isaac.cs.berkeley.edu/isaac/gsm-faq.html. Accessed 6 January 2015
11. Brier, E., Clavier, C., Olivier, F.: Correlation power analysis with a leakage model. In: Joye, M., Quisquater, J.-J. (eds.) CHES 2004. LNCS, vol. 3156, pp. 16–29. Springer, Heidelberg (2004)
12. Daemen, J., Rijmen, V.: The Design of Rijndael: AES - The Advanced Encryption Standard. Springer, Heidelberg (2002)
13. Gindraux, S.: From 2G to 3G: a guide to mobile security. In: 3rd International Conference on 3G Mobile Communication Technologies, pp. 308–311 (2002)
14. Mangard, S., Oswald, E., Standaert, F.: One for all - all for one: unifying standard differential power analysis attacks. IET Inform. Secur. 5(2), 100–110 (2011)
15. Maximov, A., Johansson, T., Babbage, S.: An improved correlation attack on A5/1. In: Handschuh, H., Hasan, M.A. (eds.) SAC 2004. LNCS, vol. 3357, pp. 1–18. Springer, Heidelberg (2004)
16. Niemi, V., Nyberg, K.: UMTS Security. Wiley Online Library (2003)
17. Prouff, E.: DPA attacks and S-boxes. In: Gilbert, H., Handschuh, H. (eds.) FSE 2005. LNCS, vol. 3557, pp. 424–441. Springer, Heidelberg (2005)
18. Rao, J.R., Rohatgi, P., Scherzer, H., Tinguely, S.: Partitioning attacks: or how to rapidly clone some GSM cards. In: 2002 IEEE Symposium on Security and Privacy, Berkeley, California, USA, pp. 31–41 (2002)
19. Veyrat-Charvillon, N., Gérard, B., Renauld, M., Standaert, F.-X.: An optimal key enumeration algorithm and its application to side-channel attacks. In: Knudsen, L.R., Wu, H. (eds.) SAC 2012. LNCS, vol. 7707, pp. 390–406. Springer, Heidelberg (2013)
20. Zhou, Y., Yu, Y., Standaert, F.-X., Quisquater, J.-J.: On the need of physical security for small embedded devices: a case study with COMP128-1 implementations in SIM cards. In: Sadeghi, A.-R. (ed.) FC 2013. LNCS, vol. 7859, pp. 230–238. Springer, Heidelberg (2013)

Risk Analysis

Should Cyber-Insurance Providers Invest in Software Security?

Aron Laszka[1]([✉]) and Jens Grossklags[2]

[1] Vanderbilt University, Nashville, TN, USA
laszka.aron@gmail.com
[2] Pennsylvania State University, University Park, PA, USA

Abstract. Insurance is based on the diversifiability of individual risks: if an insurance provider maintains a large portfolio of customers, the probability of an event involving a large portion of the customers is negligible. However, in the case of cyber-insurance, not all risks are diversifiable due to software monocultures. If a vulnerability is discovered in a widely used software product, it can be used to compromise a multitude of targets until it is eventually patched, leading to a catastrophic event for the insurance provider. To lower their exposure to non-diversifiable risks, insurance providers may try to influence the security of widely used software products in their customer population, for example, through vulnerability reward programs.

We explore the proposal that insurance providers should take a proactive role in improving software security, and provide evidence that this approach is viable for a monopolistic provider. We develop a model which captures the supply and demand sides of insurance, provide computational complexity results on the provider's investment decisions, and propose different heuristic investment strategies. We demonstrate that investments can reduce non-diversifiable risks and can lead to a more profitable cyber-insurance market. Finally, we detail the relative merits of the different heuristic strategies with numerical results.

Keywords: Economics of security · Cyber-insurance · Software security · Vulnerability discovery

1 Introduction

Most software suffers from vulnerabilities. Partly, the reason is technical and related to the inherent complexity of software development projects. In addition, economic factors play a significant role. For example, software companies may find it undesirable to invest heavily in the security of their products because customers may not immediately reward such actions (in particular, when they impact the time-to-market, or create backwards-compatibility issues). However, the quality of software critically impacts the security of most parts of an organization's information system. Moreover, popular software products influence the security of *many* organizations. Even though systems may be independently

© Springer International Publishing Switzerland 2015
G. Pernul et al. (Eds.): ESORICS 2015, Part I, LNCS 9326, pp. 483–502, 2015.
DOI: 10.1007/978-3-319-24174-6_25

owned and administrated, they may often exhibit similar software configurations leading to so-called monoculture risks [3,12].

It is a matter of considerable debate on how to address these monoculture risks. For example, organizations may desire some security warranties for the software they deploy, however these are not offered as part of software licenses for commercial software which may even contain substantial warranty disclaimers. In response, a number of public policy changes have been proposed. For example, assigning loss liability for security breaches related to insecure software products to software vendors has been argued to be beneficial [27] and can be welfare-enhancing [2]. But such proposals have not found sufficient policy support.

Some organizations have partially taken matters into their own hands by improving the security of software which is critical for their own operations. For example, Samsung and Google have invested a significant amount of resources into making key software products, such as the Linux kernel, more secure by finding and patching vulnerabilities [8]. In addition, several large companies are now running software and web vulnerability rewards programs to limit the risks related to their own businesses. However, these isolated efforts cannot fully address the security risks related to the diverse landscape of widely used software products, such as popular web-based content-management systems etc.

As an alternative, companies of various sizes may wish to purchase *cyber-insurance* to transfer risks related to the consequences of potentially insecure software. This raises the question whether cyber-insurers would find the prospect of offering such contracts attractive.

From an insurance provider's perspective, the total risk related to each insured company can be decomposed into two parts: *diversifiable risk* and *non-diversifiable risk* (also known as systematic risk or market risk). Diversifiable risk arises from vulnerabilities that pertain to a particular company. For example, the possibility of insider attacks, hardware failures, weak passwords, configuration errors, and human mistakes all contribute to the diversifiable risk of a company (e.g., [22]). In contrast, monoculture risks associated with widely used software products in its client base are a key contributor to non-diversifiable risk of a cyber-insurer.

The existence of diversifiable risk is typically desirable from the perspective of an insurance provider: it provides incentives for companies to purchase insurance, and insurers can account for those risks by maintaining a large and diverse portfolio. In contrast, non-diversifiable risk can cause significant fluctuations in the arrival of cyber-insurance claims, which requires an insurer to set aside a substantial safety capital and may provide a price-barrier impeding the growth of the cyber-insurance market [6].

Insurance providers often incentivize companies to reduce risk with security investments by offering premium reductions. However, typical security investments such as the purchase of security products (including firewalls, IDS, and IPS) and the hiring of auditors who can point out and fix company-specific vulnerabilities do not address non-diversifiable risks. Further, most companies lack both the resources and expertise to make valuable contributions to improving the security of widely used software products. Consequently, these incentives lower the level of diversifiable risk without having a significant impact on the level of non-diversifiable risk. An insurer would prefer the reverse outcome to increase revenue and to limit its exposure to significant risks.

In this paper, we tackle two interrelated issues. First, we propose a model about the insurability of monoculture risks. Second, we propose to lower these risks by investigating a scenario which provides direct incentives to increase the security of widely used software products.

More specifically, we explore the proposal that cyber-insurers should take a *proactive approach* to improve the security of widely used software products in its customer population and to reduce its aggregate non-diversifiable risk. Specifically, we study whether an insurance provider would find it beneficial to adhere to the following two propositions: (1) An insurer should *not* ask companies to individually invest in security *in exchange* for lower premiums, which is the currently dominant practice. (2) An insurer should rather invest the surplus from the resulting higher premiums into making widely used software products more secure. Measures facilitated by the insurer could include: (1) targeted direct investments in software companies (similar to economically targeted investments of public funds which aim to provide positive collateral benefits [15]), (2) vulnerability reward programs which benefit the software used by its customers, and (3) the hiring of external developer teams for popular open-source software.

For the case of a monopolistic cyber-insurer, we provide evidence that this approach is viable. We develop a model which captures the supply and demand sides for insurance when security outcomes are related to the software products chosen by the insured companies, and insurers can invest in the security of the utilized software. We provide theoretical results highlighting the computational complexity of the insurer's decision-making problem, and propose different heuristic strategies to allocate an investment budget to software security. We demonstrate how investments in software security reduce the occurrence of non-diversifiable risk and lower the insurer's required safety capital. We further detail the relative merits of the different heuristic strategies with numerical analysis.

The proposed approach would constitute a paradigm change for insurance. We argue that novel ways to overcome the currently existing impediments are needed to make cyber-insurance viable for non-diversifiable risks. The approach is feasible because insurance companies are strongly incentivized to lower the magnitude of non-diversifiable risks to reduce their probability of ruin, and they have access to privileged information which could guide their investment decisions. Finally, the approach would have significant positive spillover effects on home users and other typically uninsured entities.

The remainder of this paper is organized as follows. In Sect. 2, we summarize relevant previous work from the areas of cyber-insurance and software-security investments. In Sect. 3, we introduce our modeling framework for cyber-insurance. Then, we present our theoretical and numerical results in Sects. 4 and 5, respectively. Finally, in Sect. 6, we provide concluding remarks and outline future work.

2   Related Work

2.1   Cyber-Insurance

A key objective of our work is to improve the insurability of risks from an insurer's perspective. A functioning market for cyber-insurance and a good understanding of the insurability of diversifiable and non-diversifiable risks both matter, because they signal that stakeholders are able to manage modern threats that cause widespread damage across many systems [1,5]. However, the market for cyber-insurance is developing at a frustratingly slow pace due to several complicating factors, which are discussed in the detailed review of the security economics and cyber-insurance literature by Böhme and Schwartz [7].

In particular, from an attacker's perspective, a group of defenders might appear as a very appealing target because of a high correlation in the risk profiles of the defended resources. For example, even though systems may be independently owned and administrated, they may exhibit similar software configurations leading to monoculture risks [3,12]. Böhme and Kataria study the impact of correlation which is readily observable for an insurer and found that the resulting insurance premiums to make the risks insurable would likely endanger a market for cyber-insurance [6]. Similarly, Chen et al. study correlated risks by endogenizing node failure distribution and node correlation distribution [9]. Lelarge and Bolot model interdependent security with insurance, but assume that there is an insurance provider with an exogenously priced premium [23]. Johnson et al. study the viability of insurance in the presence of weakest-link interdependencies [17].

Non-diversifiable risks may also be caused by interdependent security issues, which have been thoroughly studied outside the context of cyber-insurance (e.g., [13,28]). These works have been reviewed by Laszka et al. [20]. Recently, Johnson et al. investigated interdependent security from an insurance provider's perspective [18,19,21]. They found that real-world networked systems can exhibit substantial non-diversifiable risk, and that estimating the magnitude of this risk is a complex problem due to both theoretical and practical challenges.

2.2   Software Security Investments

Potential improvements to software security frequently focus on finding vulnerabilities in deployed code which is also most relevant to our context (since we focus on widely used software). Public vulnerability disclosure programs (VDP), such as the BugTraq mailing list that emerged more than 20 years ago, have been an important source for companies and the public to receive vulnerability reports from white hats. See also recent work on the Wooyun VDP [29]. However, there has always been a debate on whether VDPs are beneficial to society [10]. On the one hand, Rescorla showed that the pool of vulnerabilities in a software product is very deep with respect to the effort and potential impact of vulnerability discovery efforts [26]. On the other hand, Ozment showed that the pool of vulnerabilities in OpenBSD 2.2 is being depleted and vulnerability rediscovery is common. He concludes that vulnerability hunting by white hats is socially beneficial [25].

Conceptual work has discussed different approaches to organize and design vulnerability markets [4]. For example, Ozment proposed a vulnerability auction mechanism that allows a software company to measure its software quality as well as encourage vulnerability discovery at an acceptable cost [24]. In addition, some companies such as Facebook, Google and Mozilla have established vulnerability reward programs (VRP) that pay white hats to hack. A study based on the Google VRP and Mozilla VRP has shown that harvesting vulnerabilities from the white hat community is cost effective, and compares favorably to hiring full-time vulnerability researchers [11].

3 Model

Now, we present our modeling framework for studying security investments for cyber-insurance. First, in Sect. 3.1, we describe our model of software-security investments and how software security determines the probability of a company suffering an incident. Then, in Sect. 3.2, we discuss cumulative risks, that is, the expected value and variability of the aggregate loss over all companies. Next, in Sect. 3.3, we first describe the demand-side of the insurance model, which is based on utility-maximizing risk-averse companies. Finally, in Sect. 3.4, we discuss the supply-side and how the insurance provider's profit is affected by individual and cumulative risks. For a list of symbols used in this paper, see Table 1.

3.1 Software Security and Individual Risks

We assume that there are N software products that the insurance provider might invest into, and we let d_i denote the amount of resources that the provider invests into the ith product. For every software product, there is a non-zero probability that a new vulnerability is discovered and exploited before it is patched. We call this probability the vulnerability level of software i and let $V_i(d_i)$ denote its value. We assume that the vulnerability level V_i decreases exponentially with the value of the provider's investment, that is,

$$V_i(d_i) = BV_i \cdot e^{-\gamma_i d_i} , \tag{1}$$

where BV_i is the level of vulnerability when there is no security investment from the provider, and γ_i is the efficiency of security investments into software product i.

We assume that there are M companies that want to purchase insurance from the provider. Each company j may use any subset S_j of all the N software products in our model. We assume that each software product $i \in S_j$ has a vulnerability with V_i probability independently of the other software products, and a company suffers an incident if any of its software products has a vulnerability. Furthermore, a company may also suffer an incident due to an individual

Table 1. List of Symbols

Symbol	Description
	Constants
BV_i	base vulnerability level of software i
γ_i	efficiency of investing into software i
IR_j	individual risk of company j
W_j	base wealth of company j
L_j	loss of company j in case of an incident
I	interest rate for the insurer
ε	insurer's probability of ruin
	Variables and Functions
V_i	vulnerability level of software i
R_j	risk level of company j
d_i	insurer's investment into securing software i
D	insurer's sum investment into securing software products (i.e., $D = \sum_i d_i$)
S	insurer's safety capital

vulnerability, such as a configuration error, which occurs with IR_j probability. Formally, the probability of company j suffering an incident, denoted by R_j, is

$$R_j = 1 - (1 - IR_j) \prod_{i \in S_j} (1 - V_i) \,. \tag{2}$$

3.2 Cumulative Risk

In the previous subsection, we described a stochastic risk model that captures security vulnerabilities and individual incidents. Now, consider an aggregate outcome of this model:

1. each software product i had a vulnerability with probability $V_i(d_i)$ (independently of the other software products);
2. every company j that uses a vulnerable software had an incident;
3. each remaining company j had an incident with probability IR_j (independently of the other companies).

We are interested in the total amount of losses over all companies due to incidents. Let L_j denote the loss suffered by company j when an incident happens, and let TL denote the sum of the loss values L_j over all the companies j that suffered incidents (either due to vulnerable software or due to individual vulnerabilities).

First, notice that we can compute the expected total amount of losses $\mathrm{E}[TL]$ easily as

$$\mathrm{E}[TL] = \sum_j L_j R_j \,, \tag{3}$$

where each R_j can be computed efficiently (i.e., in polynomial time) using Eq. (2).

On the other hand, measures of variability (e.g., variance) and quantiles cannot be computed simply from the companies' risk levels R_j, due to the correlations between the incident events caused by the software products. For example, consider two companies with $R_1 = R_2 = 0.5$ and $L_1 = L_2 = 1$. Then, from these values only, we cannot determine the probability of both companies suffering an incident (i.e., the probability $\Pr[TL = 2]$): It is possible that the two companies use completely different sets of software, which means that there are no correlations between the incidents and $\Pr[TL = 2] = 0.25$. However, it is also possible that both companies use exactly the same set of software and $IR_1 = IR_2 = 0$, which means that there is perfect correlation and $\Pr[TL = 2] = 0.5$. In Sect. 4.1, we will show that computing certain properties of TL, which are crucial to providing insurance, is in fact computationally hard.

3.3 Demand-Side Model

For a functioning cyber-insurance market, we need both demand and supply: companies that are willing to purchase insurance and insurers that are willing to provide it.

Now, we introduce our demand-side model, which is based on utility-maximizing risk-averse companies. As it is usual in the literature (see, e.g., [6]), we assume that companies have Constant Relative Risk Aversion (CRRA) utility functions. Furthermore, we also assume that the constant of the relative risk aversion is equal to 1, which means that for a given amount of wealth w, a company's utility is $\ln(w)$. Finally, we let the initial wealth of company j (i.e., the amount of wealth when no incident occurs) be denoted by W_j. Then, the expected utility of company j is

$$R_j \ln(W_j - L_j) + (1 - R_j) \ln(W_j) . \tag{4}$$

In the above equation, the first term corresponds to the case when the company suffers an incident and loses L_j, which happens with probability R_j, and the second term corresponds to the case when the company does not suffer an incident, which happens with probability $1 - R_j$.

Since companies are risk averse, they are interested in trading off expected wealth for decreased risks. In the case of purchasing insurance, this means that the company pays a fixed premium p_j to the provider, but in case of an incident, the provider will pay the amount of loss L_i suffered by the company. Hence, when company j purchases insurance for premium p_j, its expected utility is simply

$$\ln(W_j - p_j) . \tag{5}$$

As companies are assumed to be utility maximizing, it is optimal for company j to purchase insurance if and only if its utility with insurance is greater than or equal to its expected utility without insurance. Building on Eqs. 5 and 4, we can express the condition for purchasing insurance as

$$\ln(W_j - p_j) \geq R_j \ln(W_j - L_j) + (1 - R_j) \ln(W_j) \tag{6}$$
$$W_j - p_j \geq e^{R_j \ln(W_j - L_j) + (1 - R_j) \ln(W_j)} \tag{7}$$
$$p_j \leq W_j - e^{R_j \ln(W_j - L_j) + (1 - R_j) \ln(W_j)} . \tag{8}$$

In our model, we assume that all companies purchase insurance from the provider, who chooses the maximum premiums such that purchasing insurance is the optimal choice for the companies.

3.4   Supply-Side Model

Next, we discuss the final piece in our model, the supply-side of insurance. We assume a monopolist insurance provider who maximizes its expected profit, where profit is defined as the difference between income and expenditure. Besides maximizing its profit, the insurance provider is also risk-averse in the sense that it keeps the probability of ruin below a certain threshold by setting aside a safety capital, which we will discuss shortly.

First, the insurance provider's income is the sum of all the premiums paid by the companies, that is,

$$\text{Income} = \sum_j p_j . \tag{9}$$

Since the provider is assumed to be a monopolist, it can ask for the maximal premium (see Eq. 8); hence, we can compute the income as

$$\text{Income} = \sum_j W_j - e^{R_j \ln(W_j - L_j) + (1 - R_j) \ln(W_j)} . \tag{10}$$

We assume that insurance premiums are flexible in the sense that the premium values p_j are affected by the provider's investments d_i: higher investment values d_i lead to lower vulnerability values V_i, which in turn lead to lower risk levels R_j and lower premiums p_j. The flexibility of premiums poses challenges to the provider, which we will discuss in Sect. 5.3.

Second, the insurance provider's expected expenditure is

$$\text{Expenditure} = \text{E}[TL] + \sum_i d_i + A + I \cdot S , \tag{11}$$

where

- $\text{E}[TL]$ is the expected total amount of claims (i.e., the sum of the losses suffered by the companies),
- $\sum_i d_i$ is the total amount of investments into software security,
- A is the sum of all administrative costs,
- I is the interest rate,
- and S is the safety capital required to keep the probability of ruin below a given probability ε.

The safety capital is set aside by the provider to ensure that it remains solvent. To see why this capital is required, consider the total amount of losses TL: On average, the insurance provider has to pay the expected value $E[TL]$ of these losses (hence the first term in the right-hand side of Eq. (11)). However, in many outcomes, the realization of the total amount of losses TL exceeds $E[TL]$; hence, the provider has to set aside S to be able to pay all the claims. More formally, the safety capital is the amount necessary to ensure that

$$\Pr[TL > E[TL] + S] \leq \varepsilon . \tag{12}$$

Since this capital has to be set aside, the provider bears the opportunity cost $I \cdot S$.

4 Theoretical Results and Heuristic Investment Strategies

In this section, we study the computational problems faced by the insurance provider. First, in Sect. 4.1, we show that determining whether a given safety capital is sufficient is computationally hard. Then, in Sect. 4.2, we prove that simulations can approximate the amount of necessary safety capital and, hence, the provider's profit. Finally, in Sect. 4.3, we propose efficient heuristic investment strategies.

4.1 Complexity of Computing the Optimal Safety Capital

Assume for the following analysis that the security-investment values d_i are given and fixed for every software product i, and the insurance provider's decision space is limited to choosing the amount of safety capital S. Recall from Eq. (11) that higher amounts of safety capital lead to higher expenditures for the provider. Consequently, a rational and profit-maximizing provider will try choose the minimum amount of safety capital that will keep its probability of ruin below a threshold ε. We show that this problem is computationally challenging by proving that its decision version, that is, determining whether a given amount of safety capital keeps the probability of ruin below ε, is an NP-hard problem.

Theorem 1. *Given a safety capital S and a threshold probability of ruin ε, determining whether the probability of the total amount of losses TL exceeding $S + E[TL]$ is greater than or equal to ε is NP-hard.*

The proof of the theorem can be found in Appendix A.1.

4.2 Approximating the Loss Distribution

From Theorem 1, we have that it is computationally hard to find the minimal amount of safety capital that keeps the provider's probability of ruin below a given threshold ε. Consequently, computing the provider's profit for given security-investment values $(d_1, \ldots, d_N)$ is also computationally hard, since the provider's expenditure is determined by the amount of safety capital.

However, we can approximate the minimal amount of safety capital using simulations as follows. First, generate K outcomes of the risk model as described in Sect. 3.2, and let $tl_1, tl_2, \ldots, tl_K$ be the realizations of TL. Second, let the approximate safety capital $\hat{S}$ be the $\lceil (1-\varepsilon)K \rceil$-th smallest realization (note that if multiple realizations have the same value, they have to be counted separately). The following theorem shows that the probability of ruin for the approximate safety capital $\hat{S}$ converges quickly to the actual probability of ruin.

Theorem 2. *Let* $TL_1, TL_2, \ldots, TL_K$ *be* K *independent random variables having the same distribution as* TL, *and let* $\hat{S}$ *be the* $\lceil (1-\varepsilon)K \rceil$-*th smallest of these random variables. Then,*

$$\Pr[TL > \hat{S}] \leq \varepsilon + \frac{1}{K} \ . \tag{13}$$

The proof of the theorem can be found in Appendix A.2.

4.3   Investment Strategies

Since computing the provider's profit is challenging, so is finding the investments $(d_1, \ldots, d_N)$ that maximize the profit. In this subsection, we propose heuristic investment strategies, which we will evaluate numerically in Sect. 5.

First, suppose that we are given an aggregate investment amount D, and our goal is to find the optimal investments $(d_1, \ldots, d_N)$ satisfying $\sum_i d_i = D$, that is, we have to divide the aggregate amount D among the N software products. Here, we propose four heuristic strategies for dividing D: uniform, most-used, proportional, and greedy. Then, we can find good investments $(d_1, \ldots, d_N)$ using these heuristics by searching for the best value of D, which is a simple scalar optimization problem.

Uniform. The *uniform* strategy invests the same amount into all software products. Formally, for every software product i,

$$d_i = \frac{D}{N} \ . \tag{14}$$

The rationale behind this heuristic is that the provider needs to mitigate all common vulnerabilities in order to decrease non-diversifiable risks.

Most-Used. The *most-used* strategy invests only into the most popular software product. Let P_i denote the number of companies that use software product i, that is, $P_i = |\{j : i \in S_j\}|$. Then, for every software product i,

$$d_i = \begin{cases} D & \text{if } P_i = \max_l P_l \\ 0 & \text{otherwise.} \end{cases} \tag{15}$$

The rationale behind this heuristic is that the provider needs to invest into the most-used software only, since vulnerabilities in less popular software cannot cause a large number of incidents.

Proportional. The *proportional* strategy invests into each software product an amount that is proportional to the number of companies using that software. Formally, for every software product i,

$$d_i = \frac{P_i}{\sum_l P_l} . \tag{16}$$

This heuristic is a middle ground between the first two heuristics, combining their advantages.

Greedy. The *greedy* strategy divides the aggregate investment amount D according to the following greedy algorithm. First, let the investment into each software be zero. Then, the investments are increased iteratively: in every iteration, compute for each software product i how much would the profit increase if we invested an additional δ into software i, and invest into the software product for which the profit increase is maximal. Formally, the greedy strategy divides the aggregate investment amount D as follows:

$\forall i : d_i \leftarrow 0$
while $\sum_i d_i < D$ **do**
    for $i = 1, \ldots, N$ **do**
        $\text{Profit}_i \leftarrow \text{Profit}(d_1, \ldots, d_{i-1}, d_i + \delta, d_{i+1}, \ldots, d_N)$
    end for
    $i^* \leftarrow \text{argmax}_i \text{Profit}_i$
    $d_{i^*} \leftarrow d_{i^*} + \delta$
end while

5   Numerical Results

In this section, we present numerical results on our insurance modeling framework. With these results, we strive to answer two important questions:

– Can the insurance provider increase its expected profit by investing into software security?
– Which heuristic investment strategy leads to the highest expected profit?

First, in Sect. 5.1, we describe how we instantiate our model. Then, in Sect. 5.2, we present the resulting loss distributions both in the case of no software-security investments and in the case of substantial investments. Finally, in Sect. 5.3, we compare the various investment strategies in terms of expected profit to answer the above questions.

5.1 Setup

We instantiated the model with exemplary values to illustrate the relative effect of the investment strategies. First, we generated a set of 15 software products such that, for each software i,

- base vulnerability BV_i was randomly drawn from $[0.09, 0.11]$,
- investment efficiency γ_i was randomly drawn from $[0.9, 1.1]$.

Second, we generated a set of 1500 companies such that, for each company j,

- individual risk IR_j was randomly drawn from $[0.4, 0.6]$,
- base wealth W_j was randomly drawn from $[10, 20]$,
- loss in case of an incident L_j was randomly drawn from $[0.25 \cdot W_j, 0.75 \cdot W_j]$.

For each company, we choose 3 software products to be used by the company using a popularity-based preferential-attachment model as follows. For the first few companies, the set of software products used by the company was chosen uniformly at random. For the remaining companies, the probability of choosing each software was proportional to the number of companies already using the software. This process models the widely-observed phenomena in which businesses and people tend to choose more popular software products with higher probability, leading to a long-tailed usage distribution [14,16].

Finally, we let the insurance provider's probability of ruin ε be 0.1 %, the interest rate I be 5 %, and the administrative costs A be 0 (i.e., negligible). Note that the value of administrative costs does not affect our analysis, since it is a constant term in the provider's profit, which does not depend on the investment strategy.

5.2 Distribution of the Total Amount of Losses

Figure 1a shows the distribution of the total amount of losses (or, equivalently, the total amount of claims) without any security investments from the provider. We can see that the distribution has a very heavy tail with multiple local maxima, each of which corresponds to vulnerabilities being discovered in one or more widely used software products. Due to this heavy tail, the provider has to set aside a substantial safety capital to avoid ruin: even though the expected amount of claims to be paid is only E[TL] = 7032 (marked by dotted blue line on the plot), the amount exceeds 10510 with probability 0.1 %, that is, Pr[$TL > 10\,510$] = 0.1 % (marked by dashed red line on the plot). Consequently, in order to keep the probability of ruin below 0.1 %, the provider has to set aside a safety capital of $10\,510 - 7\,032 = 3\,478$.

Figure 1b shows the distribution of the total amount of losses with uniform security investments $d_i = 7.5$ into every software product i. As expected, we can see that the investments decrease both the expected value of the total amount of losses (i.e., total amount of claims) and the necessary safety capital. The expected amount of claims to be paid is E[TL] = 5536 (marked by dotted blue line on the plot), while the 0.999 % quantile is 6051, that is, Pr[$TL > 6\,051$] = 0.1 % (marked by dashed red line on the plot). Hence, the amount of safety capital that the provider needs to set aside is only $6\,051 - 5\,536 = 515$.

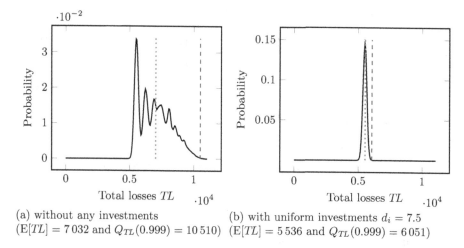

Fig. 1. Probability distribution of the total amount of losses with and without investments. The dotted blue lines mark the expected values, while the dashed red lines mark the 99.9 % quantiles $Q_{TL}(0.999)$ of the distributions (Color figure online).

5.3 Security Investment Strategies

Now, we compare the various investment strategies that we have introduced in Sect. 4.3. For each investment strategy, we compute the insurance provider's income (see Eq. (10)), expenditure (see Eq. (11)), and profit for aggregate investment amounts $D = \sum_i d_i$ ranging from 0 to 200. In each case, we divide the aggregate investment amount D among the software products according to the investment strategy (e.g., with uniform strategy, we let $d_i = \frac{D}{N}$), and approximate the resulting expenditure value using 500 000 simulations of the risk-model outcome.

Recall from Sect. 3.4 that insurance premiums are flexible, that is, the premium values take into account the reductions in risk levels due to the provider's security investments. Consequently, as we increase the value of security investments, we will see a decrease not only in the provider's expenditure, but also in its income due to the decreasing premium values. If we assumed fixed premiums, that is, if the premium values were determined by the base vulnerability levels, then the provider's profit would be strictly higher. Hence, by assuming flexible premiums, we study the conservative scenario, where investments are less beneficial for the insurer (or where the benefits of the security investments are shared between the insurer and the insured companies).

First, Fig. 2a shows the provider's income, expenditure, and profit for the uniform investment strategy. We observe that, as expected, the provider's expenditure drops sharply at first as we increase the investments, due to the rapid decrease in the non-diversifiable risks caused by software vulnerabilities and, hence, in the necessary safety capital. However, once the aggregate investment amount reaches around 110, further investments cannot significantly decrease

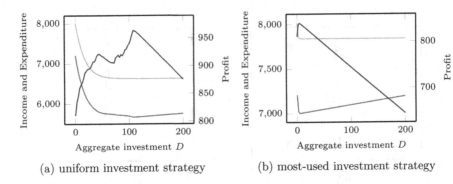

(a) uniform investment strategy   (b) most-used investment strategy

Fig. 2. Income (green), expenditure (red), and profit (blue) of the uniform and the most-used investment strategies for various aggregate security investments. Please note that the scale of the vertical axis for the most-used strategy differs from that for the other strategies (Color figure online).

the necessary safety capital; hence, the expenditure starts increasing due to the increasing cost of investments. The provider's income also drops sharply at first as we increase the investments, due to the rapid decrease in risk levels and, hence, in premium values. Even though the income decreases monotonically for all investment values, once the aggregate investment reaches around 70, the decrease becomes negligible.

On the other hand, the insurance provider's profit is a highly irregular function of the aggregate investment amount, with many local maxima. These irregularities are caused by the combined effects of decreases in expenditure and income, which make finding the optimal investment amount non-trivial. In this example, the maximum profit for the uniform investment strategy is 962, and the maximizing aggregate investment is 107.5. Note that this is substantially better than the case of zero investments, where the profit is only 810.

Second, Fig. 2b shows the provider's income, expenditure, and profit for the most-used investment strategy. Similarly to what we observed for the uniform strategy, we see that the provider's expenditure and income drop sharply at first as we increase the investment, while the profit increases rapidly. However, the profit quickly reaches its maximum value 840 at the investment value 5; and after this point, it decreases monotonically. The explanation for this is the following: securing the most used software eliminates the non-diversifiable risk caused by it, which has a substantial impact due to the large number of companies that are affected; however, once this software product is secure, any further investments will only increase the insurance provider's investment costs without eliminating the non-diversifiable risks caused by the other software. Compared to the other investment strategies, the most used strategy is clearly inferior.

Third, Fig. 3a shows the provider's income, expenditure, and profit for the proportional investment strategy. Again, we see that the income and expenditure take a sharp drop at first, after which the income decreases slowly but monotonically, while the expenditure starts increasing after reaching its minimum at the

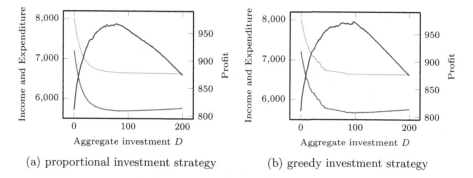

(a) proportional investment strategy   (b) greedy investment strategy

Fig. 3. Income (green), expenditure (red), and profit (blue) of the proportional and the greedy investment strategies for various aggregate security investments (Color figure online).

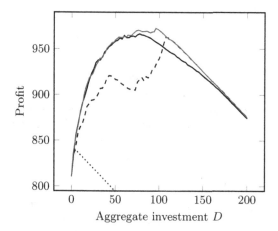

Fig. 4. Profits of the proportional (solid line), uniform (dashed line), most-used (dotted line), and greedy (red line) investment strategies for various investment values. Please note that the profit of the most-used strategy is outside of the plotted vertical range for investment values 50 and above (Color figure online).

aggregate investment 90. However, the profit is a surprisingly smooth function of the investment: it is approximately concave with only a few local maxima, none of which deviate from the general trend substantially.[1] For this strategy, the maximum profit is 967 and the maximizing investment value is 77.5, which means that this strategy is slightly better than the uniform strategy, but the difference is not significant.

Fourth, Fig. 3b shows the provider's income, expenditure, and profit for the greedy investment strategy with increment size $\delta = 2$. We see that the income, expenditure, and profit functions are all very similar to the ones plotted for

---

[1] Note that these deviations do not diminish as we increase the number of iterations.

the proportional strategy. However, both the maximal profit value 972 and the maximizing investment value 96 are greater than those of the proportional strategy, which shows that this strategy is superior. Furthermore, compared to not investing in security, the maximum profit of the greedy strategy is 20 % higher.

Finally, Fig. 4 compares the proportional (solid line), uniform (dashed line), most-used (dotted line) and greedy (red line) investment strategies for various aggregate investment amounts. This comparison shows how the greedy strategy outperforms the other strategies: For lower investment amounts, where the proportional strategy is optimal (among the considered strategies), the profit of the greedy strategy is almost indistinguishable from that of the proportional strategy. After the proportional strategy reaches its maximum at 77.5, the greedy strategy keeps increasing, until it reaches its maximum at 96. Then, the profit of the greedy strategy decreases until it reaches the maximum of the uniform strategy at 96, after which the profits of the uniform and greedy strategies are almost indistinguishable.

6   Conclusion

In this paper, we have introduced a model for cyber-insurance which incorporates software-security investments. Based on this model, we have shown that the insurance provider's decision-making involves computationally hard problems, and we have proposed different heuristics for security investments. Using numerical results, we have demonstrated that security investments can substantially decrease non-diversifiable risks and increase the profitability of cyber-insurance. Our results show that the viability of the cyber-insurance market, which has been growing very slowly, could be increased through software-security investments. Even though this approach requires a paradigm shift for insurance providers, we believe that they are strongly incentivized to take such a more proactive role.

Our proposal would have significant positive spillover effects on home users and other typically uninsured entities. In future work, we aim to quantify this effect and to also explore the viability of the approach in competitive insurance markets when multiple insurers have to make decisions about which software products to improve.

Acknowledgments. We thank the reviewers for their comments. We gratefully acknowledge the support by the National Science Foundation under Award CNS-1238959, and by the Penn State Institute for CyberScience.

A   Proofs

A.1   Proof of Theorem 1

Proof. We prove NP-hardness by showing that a well-known NP-hard problem, the Set Cover Problem, can be reduced to the above decision problem in polynomial time. Given an instance of the Set Cover Problem, that is, a base set U, a set of subsets $\mathcal{F}$, and limit k on the number of subsets, we construct an instance of our problem as follows:

- For every element of the base set U, there exists a corresponding company.
- For every set in $\mathcal{F}$, there exists a corresponding software product.
- Let the vulnerability level V_i of every software be $\frac{1}{|\mathcal{F}|!}$.
- Let the individual risk IR_j and loss L_j of every company be 0 and 1, respectively.
- Let company j use software i if and only if the corresponding element j is a member of the corresponding set i.
- Let the safety capital S be $|U| - 1 - \mathrm{E}[TL]$.
- Finally, let the probability ε be $\frac{1}{|\mathcal{F}|!^k}$.

Firstly, observe that the above reduction can be performed out in polynomial time.

Next, observe that, in the above instance of our problem, the safety capital S is insufficient to cover all claims if and only if $TL = \sum_j L_j = |U|$, that is, if and only if all companies suffer an incident. Since the individual risk IR_j of every company is 0, this can happen iff, for every company i, there is a vulnerable software product j that is used by i. In other words, it can happen iff the sets in $\mathcal{F}$ corresponding to the compromised software form a cover of the base set U. Hence, it remains to show that the probability of the compromised software forming a set cover is greater than or equal to ε if and only if there exists a set cover of size at most k.

First, suppose that there exists a set cover $\mathcal{C}$ such that $|\mathcal{C}| \leq k$. Then, the probability of all the software products corresponding to the sets in $\mathcal{C}$ being vulnerable is $\frac{1}{|\mathcal{F}|!^k}$. Since $\mathcal{C}$ is a set cover, for every company j, there exists a software product i such that j uses i. Thus, with probability at least $\frac{1}{|\mathcal{F}|!^k}$, every company will suffer an incident and the total amount claims TL will exceed $S + \mathrm{E}[TL]$.

Second, suppose that, for every set cover $\mathcal{C}$, $|\mathcal{C}| > k$. Then, the probability of every company suffering an incident is

$$\Pr[TL > S + \mathrm{E}[TL]] = \Pr\left[\begin{array}{l}\text{some collection } C \text{ of software} \\ \text{forming a cover of } U \text{ is vulnerable}\end{array}\right] \qquad (17)$$

$$= \Pr\left[\begin{array}{l}\text{some collection } C \text{ of software} \\ \text{such that } |C| > k \text{ is vulnerable}\end{array}\right] \qquad (18)$$

$$= \sum_{l=k+1}^{|\mathcal{F}|} \binom{|\mathcal{F}|}{l} \left(\frac{1}{|\mathcal{F}|!}\right)^l \qquad (19)$$

$$< |\mathcal{F}|! \left(\frac{1}{|\mathcal{F}|!}\right)^{k+1} \qquad (20)$$

$$= \left(\frac{1}{|\mathcal{F}|!}\right)^k = \varepsilon . \qquad (21)$$

Since the inequality is strict, we have that the probability of ruin is less than ε if there is no set cover size at most k, which concludes our proof. □

A.2   Proof of Theorem 2

Proof. Let $A_1, A_2, \ldots, A_K, A_{K+1}$ be $K+1$ independent random variables having the same distributions as TL. Then, since all the random variables in $A_1, \ldots, A_{K+1}$ are independent, it follows readily from the definition of $\hat{S}$ that $\Pr[TL > \hat{S}]$ is equal to the probability of a randomly chosen variable in $A_1, \ldots, A_{K+1}$ being greater than $\lceil (1-\varepsilon)K \rceil$ of the other variables in $A_1, \ldots, A_{K+1}$.

Now, we introduce an upper bound for the latter probability as follows. Suppose that we order the realizations $a_1, \ldots, a_{K+1}$ of the random variables $A_1, \ldots, A_{K+1}$ according to their values, with equal realizations being ordered in an arbitrary way. Then, the probability of a randomly chosen variable A_i being greater than $\lceil (1-\varepsilon)K \rceil$ other variables is less than or equal to the probability of choosing a random variable whose realization is not among of the first $\lceil (1-\varepsilon)K \rceil$ realizations, that is, choosing a random variable whose realization is among the last $K + 1 - \lceil (1-\varepsilon)K \rceil$ realizations. Note that the two probabilities are not necessarily equal because multiple realizations may have the same value. Since we choose a variable from $A_1, \ldots, A_{K+1}$ at random, the probability of picking one whose realization is among the last $K + 1 - \lceil (1-\varepsilon)K \rceil$ realizations is

$$\frac{K+1-\lceil (1-\varepsilon)K \rceil}{K+1} \tag{22}$$

$$= \frac{K+1-(K-\lfloor \varepsilon K \rfloor)}{K+1} \tag{23}$$

$$= \frac{1+\lfloor \varepsilon K \rfloor}{K+1} \tag{24}$$

$$\leq \frac{1+\varepsilon K}{K} \tag{25}$$

$$= \varepsilon + \frac{1}{K} . \tag{26}$$

Consequently, $\Pr[TL > \hat{S}]$ has to be less than or equal to $\varepsilon + \frac{1}{K}$. □

References

1. Anderson, R.J.: Liability and computer security: nine principles. In: Gollmann, D. (ed.) ESORICS 1994. LNCS, vol. 875, pp. 231–245. Springer, Heidelberg (1994)
2. August, T., Tunca, T.: Who should be responsible for software security? A comparative analysis of liability policies in network environments. Manag. Sci. **57**(5), 934–959 (2011)
3. Birman, K., Schneider, F.: The monoculture risk put into context. IEEE Secur. Priv. **7**(1), 14–17 (2009)
4. Böhme, R.: A comparison of market approaches to software vulnerability disclosure. In: Müller, G. (ed.) ETRICS 2006. LNCS, vol. 3995, pp. 298–311. Springer, Heidelberg (2006)
5. Böhme, R.: Towards insurable network architectures. IT - Inf. Technol. **52**(5), 290–293 (2010)

6. Böhme, R., Kataria, G.: Models and measures for correlation in cyber-insurance. In: Proceedings of the 5th Workshop on the Economics of Information Security (WEIS) (2006)
7. Böhme, R., Schwartz, G.: Modeling cyber-insurance: Towards a unifying framework. In: Proceedings of the 9th Workshop on the Economics of Information Security (WEIS) (2010)
8. Brodkin, J.: Google and Samsung soar into list of top 10 Linux contributors (2013). http://arstechnica.com/information-technology/2013/09/google-and-samsung-soar-into-list-of-top-10-linux-contributors/
9. Chen, P., Kataria, G., Krishnan, R.: Correlated failures, diversification, and information security risk management. MIS Q. **35**(2), 397–422 (2011)
10. Egelman, S., Herley, C., van Oorschot, P.: Markets for zero-day exploits: ethics and implications. In: Proceedings of the 2013 New Security Paradigms Workshop (NSPW), Banff, Canada, pp. 41–46 (2013)
11. Finifter, M., Akhawe, D., Wagner, D.: An empirical study of vulnerability rewards programs. In: Proceedings of the 22nd USENIX Security Symposium, Washington, DC, August 2013
12. Geer, D., Pfleeger, C., Schneier, B., Quarterman, J., Metzger, P., Bace, R., Gutmann, P.: Cyberinsecurity: The cost of monopoly. How the dominance of Microsoft's products poses a risk to society (2003)
13. Grossklags, J., Christin, N., Chuang, J.: Secure or insure?: a game-theoretic analysis of information security games. In: Proceedings of the 17th International World Wide Web Conference, pp. 209–218 (2008)
14. Hanson, W., Putler, D.: Hits and misses: Herd behavior and online product popularity. Mark. Lett. **7**(4), 297–305 (1996)
15. Hoffer, D.: A survey of economically targeted investments: opportunities for public pension funds (2004). http://www.vermonttreasurer.gov/sites/treasurer/files/pdf/misc/econTargetInvestReport20040216.pdf
16. Huang, J., Chen, Y.: Herding in online product choice. Psychol. Mark. **23**(5), 413–428 (2006)
17. Johnson, B., Böhme, R., Grossklags, J.: Security games with market insurance. In: Baras, J.S., Katz, J., Altman, E. (eds.) GameSec 2011. LNCS, vol. 7037, pp. 117–130. Springer, Heidelberg (2011)
18. Johnson, B., Laszka, A., Grossklags, J.: The complexity of estimating systematic risk in networks. In: Proceedings of the 27th IEEE Computer Security Foundations Symposium (CSF), pp. 325–336 (2014)
19. Johnson, B., Laszka, A., Grossklags, J.: How many down? toward understanding systematic risk in networks. In: Proceedings of the 9th ACM Symposium on Information, Computer and Communications Security (ASIACCS), pp. 495–500 (2014)
20. Laszka, A., Felegyhazi, M., Buttyan, L.: A survey of interdependent information security games. ACM Comput. Surv. **47**(2), 23:1–23:38 (2014)
21. Laszka, A., Johnson, B., Grossklags, J., Felegyhazi, M.: Estimating systematic risk in real-world networks. In: Christin, N., Safavi-Naini, R. (eds.) FC 2014. LNCS, vol. 8437, pp. 412–430. Springer, Heidelberg (2014)
22. Laszka, A., Johnson, B., Schöttle, P., Grossklags, J., Böhme, R.: Managing the weakest link. In: Crampton, J., Jajodia, S., Mayes, K. (eds.) ESORICS 2013. LNCS, vol. 8134, pp. 273–290. Springer, Heidelberg (2013)
23. Lelarge, M., Bolot, J.: Economic incentives to increase security in the internet: the case for insurance. In: Proceedings of the 33rd IEEE International Conference on Computer Communications (INFOCOM), pp. 1494–1502 (2009)

24. Ozment, A.: Bug auctions: vulnerability markets reconsidered. In: Proceedings of the 3rd Workshop on the Economics of Information Security (WEIS), Minneapolis, MN, May 2004

25. Ozment, A.: The likelihood of vulnerability rediscovery and the social utility of vulnerability hunting. In: Proceedings of the 4th Workshop on the Economics of Information Security (WEIS), Cambridge, MA, June 2005

26. Rescorla, E.: Is finding security holes a good idea? IEEE Secur. Priv. **3**(1), 14–19 (2005)

27. Schneier, B.: Schneier on security: liability changes everything (2003). https://www.schneier.com/essays/archives/2003/11/liability_changes_ev.html

28. Varian, H.: System reliability and free riding. In: Camp, J., Lewis, S. (eds.) Economics of Information Security, pp. 1–15. Kluwer Academic Publishers, Dordrecht (2004)

29. Zhao, M., Grossklags, J., Chen, K.: An exploratory study of white hat behaviors in a web vulnerability disclosure program. In: Proceedings of the 2014 ACM Workshop on Security Information Workers (SIW), pp. 51–58 (2014)

Lightweight and Flexible Trust Assessment Modules for the Internet of Things

Jan Tobias Mühlberg$^{(\boxtimes)}$, Job Noorman, and Frank Piessens

iMinds-DistriNet, KU Leuven, Celestijnenlaan 200A, 3001 Leuven, Belgium
jantobias.muehlberg@cs.kuleuven.be

Abstract. In this paper we describe a novel approach to securely obtain measurements with respect to the integrity of software running on a low-cost and low-power computing node autonomously or on request. We propose to use these measurements as an indication of the trustworthiness of that node. Our approach is based on recent developments in Program Counter Based Access Control. Specifically, we employ Sancus, a light-weight hardware-only Trusted Computing Base and Protected Module Architecture, to integrate trust assessment modules into an untrusted embedded OS without using a hypervisor. Sancus ensures by means of hardware extensions that code and data of a protected module cannot be tampered with, and that the module's data remains confidential. Sancus further provides cryptographic primitives that are employed by our approach to enable the trust management system to verify that the obtained trust metrics are authentic and fresh. Thereby, our trust assessment modules can inspect the OS or application code and securely report reliable trust metrics to an external trust management system. We evaluate a prototypic implementation of our approach that integrates Sancus-protected trust assessment modules with the Contiki OS running on a Sancus-enabled TI MSP430 microcontroller.

Keywords: Internet of Things · Wireless sensor networks · Trust assessment · Trust management · Protected software modules

1 Introduction

In the past decades, security research and security practice has focused on desktop and server environments. While threats to these systems grew with increased interconnectivity and deployment in safety-critical environments, elaborate security mechanisms were added. Of course these mechanisms impose certain costs in terms of a performance decrease on the host system. However, with the availability of more potent hardware, these costs quickly became acceptable to a degree where virus scanners, firewalls and intrusion detection systems can operate in the background of every modern off-the-shelf PC.

Ongoing developments in our ever-changing computing environment have lead to a situation where every physical object can have a virtual counterpart on the Internet. These virtual representations of things provide and consume

© Springer International Publishing Switzerland 2015
G. Pernul et al. (Eds.): ESORICS 2015, Part I, LNCS 9326, pp. 503–520, 2015.
DOI: 10.1007/978-3-319-24174-6_26

services and can be assigned to collaborate towards achieving a common goal. While this Internet of Things (IoT) brings us unpreceded convenience through novel possibilities to acquire and process data from our environment, the situation with respect to the safe and secure deployment and use of such extremely interconnected devices is quite different from the server-and-desktop world [26].

Devices in the IoT may be equipped with inexpensive low-performance microcontrollers that provide just enough computing power to periodically perform their intended tasks, i.e. obtain sensor readings and communicate with other nodes. Many nodes are required to operate autonomously for extended periods of time, solely relying on battery power as they are deployed in environments where maintenance is difficult or even impossible. Yet, all these devices are interconnected and thereby exposed to physical as well as virtual attacks. Even if we do not consider malicious attempts to disrupt a node's function, the autonomous mode of operation, exposure to harsh environmental conditions and the resource scarceness of small microcontrollers, make these systems prone to malfunction and the effects of software aging [7] – while other systems may critically depend on the reliability and timeliness of information obtained from these devices.

The problem of trustworthiness and trust management of low-power low-performance computing nodes has been discussed in previous research, in particular in the context of Wireless Sensor Network (WSNs) [12,16,19]. Importantly, most techniques proposed in this field focus on observing the communication behaviour and on validating the plausibility of sensor readings obtained from network nodes so as to assess the trustworthiness of these nodes. This approach to trust management is suitable to detect the systematic failure or misbehaviour of single nodes. However, failures or misbehaviour of a node may not be detected immediately: the quality of readings from a sensor may degrade gradually, software failures may lead to non-deterministic behaviour or a node may be captured by an attacker, exposing benign and malicious behaviour alternately. In all these cases the malfunctioning node may produce a number of measurements that are accepted as trustworthy by the network before the network will begin to distrust the node. We believe that this shortcoming can be mitigated by employing light-weight security mechanisms that guarantee the integrity and secrecy of programs and data directly on WSN or IoT nodes. An approach to do so with only marginal interference with legacy code is presented in this paper.

Our Contribution. We describe a novel approach to securely obtain measurements with respect to the integrity of the software that runs on a minimalist computing node autonomously or on demand. We use these measurements as an indication of the trustworthiness of that node. Our approach is based on Sancus [23], a light-weight hardware-only Trusted Computing Base (TCB) and Protected Module Architecture (PMA) [28]. Sancus allows us to integrate trust assessment modules into a largely unmodified and untrusted embedded Operating System (OS) without using techniques such as virtualisation and hypervisors, which would incur unacceptable performance overheads for many embedded applications.

Sancus targets low-cost embedded systems which have no virtual memory. Recent research on Program Counter Based Access Control (PCBAC) [30] shows that, in this context, the value of the program counter can be used unambiguously to identify a specific software module. Whenever the program counter is within the address range associated with the module's code, the module is said to be executing. Memory isolation can then be implemented by configuring access rights to memory locations based on the current value of the program counter.

Sancus also provides attestation by means of built-in cryptographic primitives to provide assurance of the integrity and isolation of a given Protected Module (PM) to a third party. By using this feature, our trust assessment modules can be deployed dynamically, limiting memory consumption and restricting attacker adaptation. The module may then inspect the OS or application code and securely report trust metrics to an external trust management system.

Beyond trust assessment, our approach can be used to remotely test and debug code on a node and to facilitate the deployment of formally verified code in an untrusted context [1]. We describe and evaluate a prototypic implementation of our approach that integrates Sancus-protected trust assessment modules with the Contiki [9] OS, running on a Sancus-enabled TI MSP430 microcontroller, a single-address-space architecture with no memory management unit. The source code of the evaluation scenario is available at http://distrinet.cs.kuleuven.be/software/sancus/esorics15/.

2 Background

This section provides background information on the IoT and the Contiki OS, which enables extremely light-weight hardware such as TI MSP430 microcontrollers to be active components in the IoT. We emphasise on safety and security limitations of this setup and outline key features of the Sancus PMA as a way to cope with these limitations.

2.1 Contiki and the IoT

Contiki [9] is one of the most used OSs in the IoT. It is open source and designed for portability and to have a small memory footprint. Contiki readily runs on a range of different hardware platforms, including a number of small 8-bit and 16-bit microcontrollers, including the TI MSP430. On these machines, a Contiki system that supports full IPv6 networking can be deployed in less that 10 KiB of RAM and 30 KiB of ROM. While the IoT certainly requires the use of light-weight software on similarly light-weight, low-cost and low-power hardware, the use of this kind of configurations comes at the expense of safety and security. That is, microcontrollers such as the TI MSP430 do not feature the hierarchical protection domains, virtual memory and process isolation that are known as key mechanisms to implement safe and secure operation in the server and desktop world. Moreover, implementing computationally expensive cryptography and complex secure networking protocols is often contradictory with the constraints on power consumption and computation power on tiny autonomous devices. As a result, one would expect WSNs or the IoT in general to become a safety hazard and a key target for attacks in the near future [26]. Recent attacks on Internet connected light bulbs [6] already give an outline of this future.

In particular the lack of protection domains on extremely light-weight hardware makes it very difficult to implement extensible systems securely since software components cannot easily be isolated from each other. In the remainder of this section we present the features of Sancus, a hardware-only TCB and PMAs that aims to mitigate this difficulty.

2.2 PMAs and Sancus

Sancus [23] guarantees strong isolation of software modules, which are generally referred to as Protected Modules or PM, through low-cost hardware extensions. Moreover, Sancus provides the means for remote parties to attest the state of, or communicate with, the isolated software modules.

Isolation. Like many PMAs [28], Sancus uses Program Counter Based Access Control (PCBAC) [30] to isolate PMs. Software modules are represented by a *public text section* containing the module's executable code and a *private data section* containing data that should be kept private to the module. The core of the PCBAC model is that the private data section of a module can only be accessed from code in its public text section. In other words, if and only if the program counter points to within a module's code section, memory access to this module's data section is allowed.

To prevent instruction sequences in the code section from being misused by external code to extract private data, entry into a module's code section should be controlled. For this purpose, PMAs allow modules to designate certain addresses within their code section as *entry points*. Code that does not belong to a module's code section is only allowed to jump to one of its entry points. In Sancus, every module has a single entry point at the start of its code section. Table 1 gives an overview of the access control rules enforced by Sancus.

Attestation. Sancus allows external parties to verify the correct isolation of a module as well as to securely communicate with it. For this, Sancus extends the underlying MSP430 processor with a cryptographic core that includes symmetric

Table 1. Memory access control rules enforced by Sancus using the traditional Unix notation. Each entry indicates how code executing in the "from" section may access the "to" section. The "unprotected" section refers to code that does not belong to a PM.

From/to	Entry	Text	Data	Unprotected
Entry	r-x	r-x	rw-	rwx
Text	r-x	r-x	rw-	rwx
Unprotected/ Other SM	r-x	r--	---	rwx

authenticated encryption and key derivation primitives. Sancus also defines a key hierarchy to ease the establishment of a shared symmetric key.

The root of this hierarchy is a *node master key*, K_N. This node-unique key is known only to the owner of the node and is not accessible by software. Each software provider that wants to deploy modules on a node gets assigned a unique ID, SP, by the node's owner. This ID is then used to derive a *software provider key*, $K_{N,SP}$, from K_N and the software provider is provided with this key along with its ID. The last level in the key hierarchy is the *software module key*, $K_{N,SP,SM}$. This key is derived from $K_{N,SP}$ using the *module identity SM*. The identity of a module is defined as the concatenation of the contents of its text section and the load addresses of its text and data sections.

When a module is isolated, the hardware will first derive $K_{N,SP}$ and then use that key to derive $K_{N,SP,SM}$. Sancus enforces that this key is only accessible by the newly isolated module. This construction ensures that (1) the key $K_{N,SP,SM}$ can *only* be used by a module with identity SM deployed by software provider SP on node N; and (2) isolation has been enabled for this module.

Since the software provider has access to $K_{N,SP}$, it can also calculate $K_{N,SP,SM}$. The latter key can then be used as the basis for attestation and secure communication. Indeed, because of the properties listed above, if the software provider receives a message created with $K_{N,SP,SM}$, it will have strong guarantees that this message was created by a module with identity SM isolated on node N.

3 Trust Assessment Modules

Our approach to trust assessment is designed to integrate seamlessly with the deployment of low-cost and low-power hardware in WSNs and in the IoT. In particular, we make use of a Sancus-enabled CPU to run a protected trust assessment module and to facilitate secure and authenticated communication with a remote operator of this module. This operator can be, for example, a human operator with a particular interest in inspecting a specific device, or a trust management system that keeps track of the integrity and trustworthiness of a larger network of devices. Our trust assessment module executes as a PM, in isolation from a base of largely unmodified and generally untrusted OS and application code. Yet, our approach partially relies on services provided by this untrusted code, e.g. networking, scheduling and memory management, in a way such that failure is detected by the trust assessment module or by the remote operator. Trust assessment modules are capable of inspecting and modifying the state of the untrusted OS and applications autonomously or on request, giving the operator a trustworthy means of assessing the integrity of the software on a node and to take actions accordingly.

In this section we describe the process of deploying and communicating with Sancus-protected trust assessment modules and discuss inspection targets and trust metrics. We further outline weaknesses and attack scenarios to our approach. While the examples in this section are given with respect to the Contiki OS and its internals, we believe that our approach can be easily adapted to support other OSs in the domain of the IoT, such as TinyOS [18] or FreeRTOS [5].

3.1 Module Deployment

This section describes how the operator of a trust assessment module can deploy such a module on a Sancus-enabled computing node. We focus on getting assurance of correct deployment and on establishing a secure and authenticated communication channel with the module. The principal deployment process is originally described in [23], where details on the underlying cryptographic machinery are given. Figure 1 illustrates the process and highlights the TCB. In summary, each Sancus-enabled computing *node N* possesses a unique *node master key*, K_N, which is managed by the hardware, not directly accessible by the software running on the node, and shared only with the Infrastructure Provider (IP). It is the responsibility of the IP to manage the hardware and deployment of the nodes, and to derive a *software provider key*, $K_{N,SP}$, for each party that is to install PMs on the node N. We refer to these parties as Software Provider (SPs); they are identified by a unique public ID SP. $K_{N,SP}$ is computed using a key derivation function that takes K_N and SP as input. The computing node includes a hardware implementation of this derivation function so as to independently compute $K_{N,SP}$. Thus, $K_{N,SP}$ is shared between the IP, an SP and a specific node N.

The SP, in our scenario equivalent with the operator or Trust Management System, may now deploy a trust assessment module on N. This module can be sent as a binary program over an untrusted network and be loaded by an untrusted loader on the node. Each software module has a unique identity SM, which comprises of the module's text section (code) and the effective start and end-addresses of the

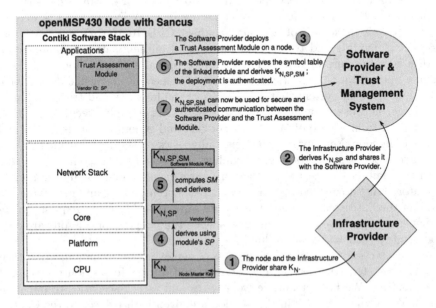

Fig. 1. Deployment of a trust assessment module on a Sancus node. The TCB, from the perspective of the operator, is shaded in orange.

loaded module's text- and protected data sections. As the module is loaded, the Sancus-enabled hardware computes a secret *software module key* $K_{N,SP,SM}$, which is derived from $K_{N,SP}$ and SM, and stored in hardware. Software cannot access $K_{N,SP,SM}$ directly but may use it to encrypt or decrypt data. The SP may derive $K_{N,SP,SM}$ if he is provided with a symbol table of the linked module, containing the start and end-addresses of the module's text- and protected data sections and the effective addresses of library code used by the module. This layout information is not confidential and may be transferred by the module loader back to the SP without integrity protection.[1] As can be seen, the proceeding outlined above establishes a shared secret between the SP and the correctly deployed PM SM on node N. All further data exchanged between these two parties can be encrypted with $K_{N,SP,SM}$, providing a secure and authenticated channel. Nonces may be used to guarantee freshness of messages.

The trust assessment module SM is now ready to execute on the computing node and may access all data and code on that node, with the exception of data belonging to other PMs. Consequentially, the module may inspect arbitrary address ranges and report its findings to the operator as an indication of the trustworthiness of the node. In the following section we discuss a number of these trust indicators in detail.

3.2 Trust Indicators

Our approach to trust assessment readily supports measuring a number of trust indicators as listed and explained in detail below. Importantly, our system is not limited to these indicators and we believe that additional or alternative indicators may be more suitable for specific application scenarios. Research, in particular in the context of software aging and software rejuvenation [7] names many such indicators that may be securely measured using our approach.

Code Integrity. A particularly useful measurement is code integrity. Sancus-enabled hardware features a keyed cryptographic hash function to compute a Message Authentication Code (MAC) of a section of memory using the module's secret key. This MAC may then either be reported to the remote operator or be compared with a MAC stored in the secret section of the trust assessment module in autonomous operation. Code integrity checks with a MAC are used by the trust assessment module to establish whether a particular section of code has been modified, which is then securely communicated to the operator. Unexpected code modifications may be caused by an attack against the device or by a malfunction. Candidates for integrity checks are core functions of the OS such as the scheduler, the memory management system or the network stack, or application code. MACing all code sections is technically feasible but may impose unacceptable computational overheads.

---

[1] It is possible for an attacker to modify the module or layout information during loading. However, this will be detected as soon as SM communicates with SP. Successful communication attests that SM has not been compromised during deployment to N and that the hardware protection has been correctly activated.

OS Data Structures. Trust assessment modules are further capable of inspecting and reporting the content of internal data structures of the OS. Interesting candidates for this are the process table or the interrupt vector table. Similar to code integrity checks, unexpected changes of these data structures are a strong indication of a malfunction or a successful attack against a device.

Available Resources. A group of indicators that is heavily used in the domain of software aging is the availability of resources such as memory and swap space: as software runs for extended periods of time, small memory leaks can accumulate and degrade performance, eventually leading to failure. In the context of Contiki and the MSP430 we use the general availability of program memory and data memory and the size of the largest available chunks of these as trust indicators. The chunk size is an important characteristic as our architecture does not feature a Memory Management Unit that could mitigate the fragmenting effect of repeated allocation and deallocation. Importantly, reliably measuring the availability of program and data memory requires implementing part of the allocator, typically a OS component, as part of the trust assessment TCB.

Application Data Structures. Similar to monitoring OS data structures, we have experimented with using application data as trust indicators. For example, on WSN nodes that run a webserver, activity can be measured by monitoring the length of the request queue. Also static content that is used to compile dynamic websites can be inspected to detect modification due to a bug or a malicious attempt. Generally all these measures are highly specific with respect to critical use cases of a node.

Event Occurrence and Timing. A key feature of our trust assessment infrastructure is to monitor and attest intentional activity on a node. More specifically, by integrating part of the OS's scheduler into the TCB, our approach can attest when critical code on a node has been executed. This allows an operator to infer which parts of a node are behaving within expected parameters.

Combined Indicators. In particular in the context of autonomous operation of a trust assessment module, combining trust indicators is desired so as to automatically adapt to changing deployment scenarios. In particular, we have experimented with modules that combine the inspection of OS data structures, i.e. the process table, and periodically performing integrity checks on the functions associated with each process. This can be interleaved with measuring the frequency of process invocation and execution times, giving the operator a detailed picture of the behaviour of a computing node and allowing for specific autonomous responses to faults.

3.3   Fault Recovery

As a trust assessment module or the operator detect anomalies on a node, the module is even capable of responding to the situation. Responses may range from a simple reset of the node over a more thorough investigation of the fault up to actively manipulating the system state and restoring damaged code and data.

4 Evaluation

We have implemented the approach described in the previous section as a number of flexibly configurable trust assessment modules that can be loaded into a Contiki OS at runtime. In this section we evaluate our implementation with respect to overheads in terms of module sizes and runtime. We further discuss security gains, attack scenarios and their mitigation.

4.1 Scenario and Implementation

Our prototypic implementation is based on a developmental version of Contiki 3.x running on a Sancus-enabled openMSP430 [15,23]. We evaluate an application scenario in which the trust assessment module regularly reports on the application processes running on a node, periodically checks the integrity of a number of code sections of these processes and integrates with Contiki's scheduler to detect and log process invocations. We have further added a public entry point to the trust assessment module that allows an application to register invariant address ranges, which are then included in periodic integrity checks. This section gives an overview of entry points and the internal behaviour of our trust assessment module and the demo scenario.

As outlined in Table 2, our example module provides a number of entry points to be called from unprotected code. Most importantly, the TAMainFunc is invoked by the scheduler. In a first run, it will initialise internal data structures of the module and then populate these data structures with initial measurements from the unprotected OS. This involves shadowing part of the scheduler's process list and MACing the process functions and the interrupt vector table. Subsequent

Table 2. *Entry Points* of our trust assessment module.

Function Name	Description
TAMainFunc	Main entry point controlling initialisation and periodic behaviour
TARegisterInvar	Can be used by application code and internally to register an address range for regular integrity checks
TASecureCallProcess	Used by the OS scheduler to invoke application functions; the trust assessment module extends the call with counting the number of invocations and measuring time
TAInvarsStatus	Returns an encrypted status report on the integrity checked address ranges
TAProcessStatus	Returns an encrypted status report on the processes currently running on a node

Table 3. Size and execution time of different trust assessment components on an MSP430 running at 20 MHz: 1 cycle corresponds to 50 ns. Function sizes include protected helper functions.

Function	Size in Bytes	Runtime in Cycles	Description
TACoreEnable	58	236,440	Enables module protection and initiates key generation
TAMainFunc	430	578	Main function, initialisation
		73,678	... validation run (5 processes, 9 integrity checks)
TARegisterInvar	402	1,242	Stores meta-data and MACs of 32 B
		10,762	... 199 B
		19,930	... 399 B
TACheckInvars	498	69,659	Checks integrity of 9 address ranges (1833 B)
TAAddProcess	568	≤ 18,374	Shadows and entry from the process list and determines length of process function
TACheckProcesses	288	2,371	Checks shadowed process data against process list (5 processes)
TASecureCallProcess	392	266	Process invocation with no logging
		≤ 731	... logs time and number of invocations
TAInvarsStatus	202	10,254	Encrypts meta-data on integrity-checked code and data (160 B + 16 B nonce)
TAProcessStatus	202	17,488	Encrypts meta-data on running processes (320 B + 16 B nonce)
total	3,742	n/a	Code (.text) and data (part of .bss)

invocations result in the current state of the unprotected OS being compared with the internal state of the module. In addition, TASecureCallProcess is used by the scheduler to start process functions. As this function is part of the trust assessment module, it can securely log which process is invoked and keep track of meta data. Of course, all data, including MACs and meta data on process invocations is stored in the trust assessment module's private data section. The functions TAInvarsStatus and TAProcessStatus return a snapshot of this data, encrypted with the module's $K_{N,SP,SM}$ and using a nonce to guarantee freshness. Thus, the module's state can be reported to the operator for further assessment.

To test the effectiveness of our trust assessment module, our scenario integrates a number of trivial application processes and a "malicious" process that aims to perform alterations to OS data and application code. Specifically, our *attacker* is invoked by an event timer. With every invocation it performs one of the following random actions: do nothing, modify a function pointer in the process list, remove an entry from the process list, overwrite a process function, or modify an entry in the interrupt vector. Event timing and the Contiki's scheduler typically result in alternating invocation of the attacker and the trust assessment module. Expectedly, all changes performed by the attacker are detected with the next invocation of the trust assessment module.

4.2   Overheads

Our evaluation shows at what expenses the alterations made by the attacker are detected. In Table 3 we list measurements of the size of our trust assessment components and these components' execution time. All code of the demo scenario is compiled either with MSP430-GCC 4.6.3[2] if no Sancus features are involved, or with the LLVM-based Sancus toolchain[3]. The trust assessment module is executed on an MSP430 configured with 41 KiB of program memory[4] and 16 KiB of data memory, running at 20 MHz. In Table 3 we report execution times in terms of CPU cycles. With the given clock speed, 1 cycle corresponds to 50 ns and 10,000 cycles correspond to 0.5 ms. For our evaluation, the MSP430 CPU is programmed on a Xilinx Spartan-6 FPGA. This renders a precise assessment of overheads in terms of power consumption infeasible. For a discussion of the power consumption of the Sancus extensions we refer the reader to [23].

As can be seen from Table 3, our approach does imply non-negligible overheads. Whether these overheads are acceptable depends largely on the constraints on reactivity and energy consumption versus safety and security requirements in a specific deployment scenario. Our trust assessment module is designed to keep the cost of periodic validation tasks small, typically below 70,000 cycles (3.5 ms), at the expense of incurring higher initial overheads. Overall, most overheads are caused by the use of Sancus-provided cryptographic operations. The performance and security provided by these operations is evaluated in [23].

As mentioned in Sect. 3.2 certain trust indicators, such as logging process invocations, required us to modify the Contiki core. These modifications are always very small, i.e., replacing a call to a Contiki internal function with a PM-equivalent. Yet, the resulting overhead is considerably high due to switching protection domains – 26 cycles for an unprotected call and return versus 160 cycles for calling a protected entry point function. Due to passing arguments, return values, and logging the function invocation with a time stamp, process invocations through TASecureCallProcess incurs an overhead of 731 cycles.

With respect to runtime performance it is important to mention that Sancus does not support interruption of protected code execution. Thus, protected modules run with interrupts disabled, which may lead to important interrupts not being served by the OS and certain properties of the unprotected code potentially being broken. Examples for this could be real-time deadlines not being met due to extensive integrity checks. This issue can be mitigated by splitting up periodic validation tasks, e.g., do not perform all integrity checks but only one per scheduled invocation of the trust assessment module. Similar approaches have been used to perform expensive validation tasks in desktop and server environments [14]. Ongoing research aims to resolve this issue by making Sancus PMs fully interruptible and re-entrant. Mechanisms for securely handling interrupts in the context of PMAs have been discussed in [8,17]. The non-interruptibility of Sancus PMs also makes it necessary to use trampoline functions that re-enable and again disable interrupts when transferring control to an application

---

[2] http://www.ti.com/tool/msp430-gcc-opensource/.
[3] http://distrinet.cs.kuleuven.be/software/sancus/.
[4] ROM is often used as program memory in embedded devices. On platforms that support module deployment at runtime, as we do, program memory is writable.

process in `TASecureCallProcess`, incurring relatively high overheads for scheduled process invocations.

We do neither evaluate nor provide an integration with a trust management system. In particular, we do not evaluate the infrastructure that has to be in place to load a software module at runtime, and to communicate with a PM on the OS level. This infrastructure performs fairly generic tasks, yet its implementation is highly dependent on the deployment scenario. Contiki and many other embedded OSs provide module loaders and a network stack that is fully sufficient to implement the required functionality. Yet, the performance of these components depend on the storage and communication hardware connected to the MSP430 and is, thus, beyond the scope of this paper.

4.3   Security Evaluation

Bootstrapping Autonomous Operation. An obvious issue of the scenario presented and evaluated here is with respect to the suggested autonomous mode of operation: the trust assessment module automatically discovers running processes and then periodically checks the discovered data structures and code sections for unexpected changes. Of course, an attacker may tamper with these sections at or before boot time, effectively preventing detection in regular checks. In our scenario it would be the responsibility of the operator to request and evaluate the output of `TAInvarsStatus` and `TAProcessStatus` to detect such modifications. Alternatively, a trust assessment module may also be provided with a list of expected processes and MACs by the operator at runtime, using encrypted communication.

Communication Failure. While the code and the internal state of the PM cannot be tampered with, it is of course possible that malfunctions or an successful attack against the node prevent the trust assessment module from successfully communication with the operator or from executing altogether. Yet, this is detected by the operator who then may conduct actions appropriate for the deployment scenario.

Preventing Invocation of the Trust Assessment Module. In the evaluated application scenario, the trust assessment module is invoked by the scheduler and its entry point is stored in the unprotected process list. This gives the attacker process the opportunity to tamper with the pointer to the entry point, allowing it to disable execution of the trust assessment module. Alternatively, an attacker or a malfunction may disable interrupts while preventing control flow from returning to the scheduler. In our evaluation scenario these attack would not be detected by the trust assessment module directly but rather by the operator who would not be able to communicate with the module.

For autonomous operation, this attack can be easily mitigated by configuring the trust assessment module to be invoked as an interrupt service routine for a non-maskable timed interrupt. We can simulate this behaviour by using the watchdog as a source of timed interrupts, which we have implemented as an optional configuration option in our evaluation scenario. To ensure that the module will complete its tasks, this approach requires the worst-case execution time of the trust assessment module to be smaller than the interrupt rate. It is possible to guarantee that the watchdog configuration is not modified by an attacker by making the control register and the respective entry in the interrupt vector table part of the secret section of a PM. In combination with extensive integrity checks, this approach also hinders stealthy attacks where malicious code would attempt to restore a valid system state before the trust assessment module is executing. Yet, using a non-maskable interrupt to invoke the trust assessment infrastructure requires some consideration: It must be possible to determine the worst-case execution time of the trust assessment module and it must be acceptable to interrupt application code for that time as the PM itself is non-interruptible. Using a scheduler to invoke the trust assessment module allows for more permissible policies that prevent starvation of applications.

Attacker Adaptation. As mentioned in the previous paragraph, a stealthy attacker that is well adapted to a specific trust assessment module may be able to hide code or data in address ranges that are not inspected by the module. The attacker may also restore inspected memory content to the state that is expected by the trust assessment module right before inspection takes place. Our approach to trust assessment counters these attacks by allowing the operator to deploy trust assessment modules at runtime, confronting the attacker with an unknown situation. Alternatively, a generic module may inspect targets by request from the operator rather than controlled by a deterministic built-in policy.

Process Accounting. Our trust assessment module features logging and reporting a time stamp of the latest invocation and the total number of invocations of scheduled processes. Of course, these numbers are only exact as long as processes are called through the scheduler, which passes the call through our trust assessment module. As processes may be invoked without using the scheduler, the numbers reported by our module represent a lower bound on the actual number of invocations. If more precise measures are needed for a particular process, this process should be implemented as a PM and perform its own accounting.

Extending the TCB. Of course, the safety and security of a node could be improved greatly by implementing larger parts of the OS, e.g. the scheduler, or applications as PMs. PMAs imply a number of complications that are a direct consequence of the strong isolation guarantees provided: resource sharing between components is generally prohibited, yet it is often desired for efficiently implementing communication between components. In Sancus, for example, one would have to explicitly copy the protected state of a module so as to share it with another module or unprotected code. While technically feasible, we believe that it is not trivial to re-implement a more complex code base as a set of neatly separated PMs. Alternatively one could think of compiling an entire embedded OS together with its applications as a single PM. This would ensure integrity but does not provide for isolation between components and severely restricts runtime extensibility and the use of dynamic memory. Thus, the trust assessment modules provided here present a pragmatic approach to measure and improve safety and security of an IoT node while not interfering with the existing code on that node. This results in low development overheads and runtime overheads that should be acceptable for many deployment scenarios.

5   Related Work

This section discusses some related work in the domains of WSNs, trust assessment on high-end systems, and PMAs. Where applicable, we compare the work with our contributions. Note that this section is not meant as an exhaustive exposition on trust assessment – a domain that can be interpreted rather broadly – but as an overview of the work that we consider closely related to ours.

5.1   Trust Management in Wireless Sensor Network

Many schemes for trust management in WSNs have been devised by researcher over the years [12,16,19]. Most of these schemes deal with the problem of distributing trust management over a network of sensor nodes. Individual nodes usually obtain trust values about neighboring nodes by observing their externally visible behavior. These trust values are then propagated through the network allowing nodes to make decisions based on the trustworthiness of other nodes.

Although our approach does not deal directly with distributed networks, it can be used to enhance trust metrics used by existing trust management systems. Indeed, our trust assessment modules can provide nodes with a detailed view on the internal state of their neighbors; allowing them to make better informed decisions about their trustworthiness. Moreover, since the produced trust metrics are attested, the bar is significantly raised for existing attacks on trust management systems where malicious nodes try to impersonate good nodes.

5.2   Trust Assessment on Desktop and Server Systems

Techniques similar to our trust assessment modules have been described for the domain of desktop and server systems. Copilot [24] and Gibraltar [4] employ specialised PCI hardware to access OS kernel memory with negligible runtime overhead. Both systems detect and report modifications to kernel code and data.

A number of approaches use virtualisation extensions of modern general purpose CPU. Here, a hypervisor is employed to inspect a guest operating system. SecVisor [27] protects legacy OSs by ensuring that only validated code can be executed in kernel mode. Similarly, NICKLE [25], shadows physical memory in a hypervisor to store authenticated guest code. At runtime, kernel mode instructions are then only loaded from shadow memory and an attempt to execute code that is not shadowed is reported as an attack. Hello rootKitty [14] inspects guest memory from a hypervisor to detect and restore maliciously modified kernel data structures. Due to frequent transitions between execution hypervisor and guest code, and expensive address translation between those domains, these inspection systems typically incur significant performance overheads. HyperForce [13] mitigates this problem by securely injecting the inspection code into the guest and forcing guest control flow to execute this code.

Our approach to trust assessment using PMs on a Sancus-enabled TI MSP430 provides isolation guarantees that are equivalent to executing the trust assessment code in a hypervisor. Yet, our PM executes in the same address space as the OSs and application, which makes expensive domain switches and address mapping unnecessary. In addition, Sancus provides attestation features in hardware that the above systems do not employ. On modern desktop architectures, these features can be implemented using the Trusted Platform Module.

Sancus enables the implementation of effective security mechanisms on extremely light-weight and low-power hardware. In terms of inspection abilities and isolation guarantees, these mechanisms are similar to the state-of-the-art in the desktop and server domain. Our approach to trust assessment modules illustrates that, using Sancus, comprehensive inspection mechanisms can be implemented efficiently, incurring runtime overheads that should be acceptable in many deployment scenarios with stringent safety and security requirements.

5.3 Alternatives to Sancus

The trust assessment infrastructure proposed in this paper is built upon Sancus [23], a PMA [28]. A number of PMAs have been proposed and can be used to implement our approach, as long as memory isolation and attestation features are provided, which we discuss below.

A PMA is typically employed as a core component of a TCB. The key feature of all PMA is to provide *memory isolation* for software components. That is, to enable the execution of a security sensitive component, a PM, so that access to the component's runtime state is limited to the TCB, the component itself, and if supported, to other modules specifically chosen by the protected component. In addition, execution of the module's code is guaranteed to happen in a controlled way so as to prevent code misuse attacks [2]: a module may specify a public Application Programming Interface (API) to be used by other modules. A range of PMAs for general purpose CPU has been presented in the last years, including Intel SGX [21], ARM TrustZone [3], TrustVisor [20] and Fides [29].

Recent research [10,17] has brought PMA techniques to small embedded microprocessors at an acceptable cost. PMAs such as SMART [10], TrustLite [17] as well as Sancus [23] utilise the PCBAC [30] approach to provide isolation an thereby guarantee the integrity of software modules executing on low-power embedded processors.

A second crucial feature of many trusted computing platforms is the ability to provide assurance of the integrity and isolation of a given PM to a third party. This party can be, e.g. another module on the same hosts or a software component on a remote host. We refer to the process of providing this assurance as *attestation*, which is typically implemented by means of cryptographic primitives that operate on the PM's identity. Attestation can be reused to establish a shared secret for secure communication between the PM and a third party. To the best of our knowledge, only Intel SGX, SMART and Sancus readily implement attestation.

6 Conclusions

In this paper we present an approach to trust assessment for extremely light-weight and low-power computing nodes as they are often used in the Internet of Things (IoT). Instead of relying on the externally observable behaviour of a node, we deploy flexible trust assessment modules directly on the node. These modules are executing in isolation from an unprotected OS and application code. Yet, the modules are capable of inspecting the unprotected domain and report measurements that are indicative for the trustworthiness of a node to a trust management system. We employ Sancus [23] to guarantee isolation, to facilitate remote attestation of the correct deployment of a trust assessment module, and to secure communication between a module and a trust management system. Sancus is a Protected Module Architecture as well as a minimal hardware-only Trusted Computing Base. In terms of inspection abilities and isolation guarantees, Sancus-protected trust assessment modules are similar to using virtualisation technology or specialised security hardware in the desktop and server domain.

We have implemented our approach to trust assessment modules on a Sancus-enabled TI MSP430 microcontroller. Our results demonstrate that, using Sancus, comprehensive inspection mechanisms can be implemented efficiently, incurring runtime overheads that should be acceptable in many deployment scenarios with stringent requirements with respect to safety and security. Indeed, we believe that our approach enables many state-of-the-art inspection mechanisms and countermeasures against attacks to be adapted for IoT nodes and in the domain of Wireless Sensor Networks, which are in dire need of modern security mechanisms [26]. These mechanisms include integrity checks and data structure inspection as discussed in this paper. Yet, more complex mechanisms such as automatic invariant detection and validation [14], stack inspection [11] or protection against heap overflows [22] are in scope for our approach.

In the future we aim to improve performance and scalability of the inspection and reporting process by making Sancus modules fully interruptible and re-entrant. We are further interested in investigating alternative trust indicators and fault recovery mechanisms, and integrate our trust assessment modules with a trust management system. Finally we will investigate the deployment of formally verified code in an untrusted context [1] for Sancus, which can lead to proving the absence of runtime errors for Sancus-protected security critical code that runs on an IoT node.

Acknowledgements. This research is partially funded by the Intel Labs University Research Office, the Research Fund KU Leuven, and by the FWO-Vlaanderen. Job Noorman holds a PhD grant from the Agency for Innovation by Science and Technology in Flanders (IWT).

References

1. Agten, P., Jacobs, B., Piessens, F.: Sound modular verification of c code executing in an unverified context. In: Proceedings of the 42nd Annual ACM SIGPLAN-SIGACT Symposium on Principles of Programming Languages, POPL 2015, pp. 581–594. ACM (2015)
2. Agten, P., Strackx, R., Jacobs, B., Piessens, F.: Secure compilation to modern processors. In: 2012 IEEE 25th Computer Security Foundations Symposium (CSF 2012), pp. 171–185. IEEE, August 2012
3. Alves, T., Felton, D.: Trustzone: integrated hardware and software security. ARM white paper **3**(4), 18–24 (2004)
4. Baliga, A., Ganapathy, V., Iftode, L.: Detecting kernel-level rootkits using data structure invariants. IEEE Trans. Dependable Secure Comput. **8**(5), 670–684 (2011)
5. Barry, R.: FreeRTOS: A portable, open source, mini real time kernel (2010). http://www.freertos.org/
6. Chapman, A.: Hacking into internet connected light bulbs (2014). http://www.contextis.com/resources/blog/hacking-internet-connected-light-bulbs/
7. Cotroneo, D., Natella, R., Pietrantuono, R., Russo, S.: A survey of software aging and rejuvenation studies. J. Emerg. Technol. Comput. Syst. **10**(1), 8:1–8:34 (2014)
8. de Clercq, R., Piessens, F., Schellekens, D., Verbauwhede, I.: Secure interrupts on low-end microcontrollers. In: 2014 IEEE 25th International Conference on Application-Specific Systems, Architectures and Processors (ASAP), pp. 147–152. IEEE (2014)
9. Dunkels, A., Gronvall, B., Voigt, T.: Contiki - a lightweight and flexible operating system for tiny networked sensors. In: 29th Annual IEEE International Conference on Local Computer Networks, pp. 455–462 (2004). http://www.contiki-os.org/
10. Eldefrawy, K., Francillon, A., Perito, D., Tsudik, G.: SMART: secure and minimal architecture for (establishing a dynamic) root of trust. In: 19th Annual Network and Distributed System Security Symposium, NDSS 2012, San Diego, USA (2012)
11. Feng, H., Kolesnikov, O., Fogla, P., Lee, W., Gong, W.: Anomaly detection using call stack information. In: 2003 Symposium on Security and Privacy, pp. 62–75. USENIX Association (2003)
12. Fernandez-Gago, M., Roman, R., Lopez, J. : A survey on the applicability of trust management systems for wireless sensor networks. In: Third International Workshop on Security, Privacy and Trust in Pervasive and Ubiquitous Computing, SECPerU 2007, pp. 25–30 (2007)
13. Gadaleta, F., Nikiforakis, N., Mühlberg, J.T., Joosen, W.: HyperForce: hypervisor-enforced execution of security-critical code. In: Gritzalis, D., Furnell, S., Theoharidou, M. (eds.) SEC 2012. IFIP AICT, vol. 376, pp. 126–137. Springer, Heidelberg (2012)
14. Gadaleta, F., Nikiforakis, N., Younan, Y., Joosen, W.: Hello rootKitty: a lightweight invariance-enforcing framework. In: Lai, X., Zhou, J., Li, H. (eds.) ISC 2011. LNCS, vol. 7001, pp. 213–228. Springer, Heidelberg (2011)
15. Girard, O.: openMSP430 (2009). http://opencores.org
16. Granjal, J., Monteiro, E., Silva, J.S.: Security in the integration of low-power wireless sensor networks with the internet: a survey. Ad Hoc Netw. **24**(Part A), 264–287 (2015)
17. Koeberl, P., Schulz, S., Sadeghi, A.-R., Varadharajan, V.: Trustlite: a security architecture for tiny embedded devices. In: Proceedings of the Ninth European Conference on Computer Systems, EuroSys 2014, pp. 10:1–10:14. ACM (2014)

18. Levis, P., Madden, S., Polastre, J., Szewczyk, R., Whitehouse, K., Woo, A., Gay, D., Hill, J., Welsh, M., Brewer, E., Culler, D.: Tinyos: an operating system for sensor networks. In: Weber, W., Rabaey, J.M., Aarts, E. (eds.) Ambient Intelligence, pp. 115–148. Springer, Heidelberg (2005)
19. Lopez, J., Roman, R., Agudo, I., Fernandez-Gago, C.: Trust management systems for wireless sensor networks: best practices. Comput. Commun. **33**(9), 1086–1093 (2010)
20. McCune, J.M., Li, Y., Qu, N., Zhou, Z., Datta, A., Gligor, V., Perrig, A.: Trustvisor: efficient tcb reduction and attestation. In: Proceedings of the 2010 IEEE Symposium on Security and Privacy, SP 2010, pp. 143–158. IEEE (2010)
21. McKeen, F., Alexandrovich, I., Berenzon, A., Rozas, C.V., Shafi, H., Shanbhogue, V., Savagaonkar, U.R.: Innovative instructions and software model for isolated execution. In: Proceedings of the 2nd International Workshop on Hardware and Architectural Support for Security and Privacy, HASP 2013, pp. 10:1–10:1. ACM (2013)
22. Nikiforakis, N., Piessens, F., Joosen, W.: HeapSentry: kernel-assisted protection against heap overflows. In: Rieck, K., Stewin, P., Seifert, J.-P. (eds.) DIMVA 2013. LNCS, vol. 7967, pp. 177–196. Springer, Heidelberg (2013)
23. Noorman, J., Agten, P., Daniels, W., Strackx, R., Van Herrewege, A., Huygens, C., Preneel, B., Verbauwhede, I., Piessens, F.: Sancus: low-cost trustworthy extensible networked devices with a zero-software trusted computing base. In: Proceedings of the 22nd USENIX Conference on Security, SEC 2013, pp. 479–494. USENIX Association (2013)
24. Petroni Jr., N.L., Fraser, T., Molina, J., Arbaugh, W.A.: Copilot-a coprocessor-based kernel runtime integrity monitor. In: USENIX Security Symposium, pp. 179–194. USENIX Association (2004)
25. Riley, R., Jiang, X., Xu, D.: Guest-transparent prevention of kernel rootkits with VMM-based memory shadowing. In: Lippmann, R., Kirda, E., Trachtenberg, A. (eds.) RAID 2008. LNCS, vol. 5230, pp. 1–20. Springer, Heidelberg (2008)
26. Roman, R., Najera, P., Lopez, J.: Securing the internet of things. Computer **44**(9), 51–58 (2011)
27. Seshadri, A., Luk, M., Qu, N., Perrig, A.: SecVisor: a tiny hypervisor to provide lifetime kernel code integrity for commodity OSes. In: Proceedings of Twenty-First ACM SIGOPS Symposium on Operating Systems Principles, pp. 335–350. ACM (2007)
28. Strackx, R., Noorman, J., Verbauwhede, I., Preneel, B., Piessens, F.: Protected software module architectures. In: Reimer, H., Pohlmann, N., Schneider, W. (eds.) ISSE 2013 Securing Electronic Business Processes, pp. 241–251. Springer, Heidelberg (2013)
29. Strackx, R., Piessens, F.: Fides: selectively hardening software application components against kernel-level or process-level malware. In: Proceedings of the 2012 ACM Conference on Computer and Communications Security, CCS 2012, pp. 2–13. ACM (2012)
30. Strackx, R., Piessens, F., Preneel, B.: Efficient isolation of trusted subsystems in embedded systems. In: Jajodia, S., Zhou, J. (eds.) SecureComm 2010. LNICST, vol. 50, pp. 344–361. Springer, Heidelberg (2010)

Confidence Analysis for Nuclear Arms Control: SMT Abstractions of Bayesian Belief Networks

Paul Beaumont[1], Neil Evans[2(✉)], Michael Huth[1], and Tom Plant[2]

[1] Department of Computing, Imperial College London, London SW7 2AZ, UK
{paul.beaumont09,m.huth}@imperial.ac.uk
[2] AWE Aldermaston, Reading, Berkshire RG7 4PR, UK
{Neil.Evans,Tom.Plant}@awe.co.uk

Abstract. How to reduce, in principle, arms in a verifiable manner that is trusted by two or more parties is a hard but important problem. Nations and organisations that wish to engage in such arms control verification activities need to be able to design procedures and control mechanisms that capture their trust assumptions and let them compute pertinent degrees of belief. Crucially, they also will need methods for reliably assessing their *confidence* in such computed degrees of belief in situations with little or no contextual data. We model an arms control verification scenario with what we call *constrained* Bayesian Belief Networks (cBBN). A cBBN represents a set of Bayesian Belief Networks by symbolically expressing uncertainty about probabilities and scenario-specific constraints that are not represented by a BBN. We show that this abstraction of BBNs can mitigate well against the lack of prior data. Specifically, we describe how cBBNs have faithful representations within a Satisfiability Modulo Theory (SMT) solver, and that these representations open up new ways of automatically assessing the confidence that we may have in the degrees of belief represented by cBBNs. Furthermore, we show how to perform symbolic sensitivity analyses of cBBNs, and how to compute global optima of under-specified probabilities of particular interest to decision making. SMT solving also enables us to assess the relative confidence we have in two cBBNs of the same scenario, where these models may share some information but express some aspects of the scenario at different levels of abstraction.

1 Introduction

AWE's Arms Control Verification Research programme supports and advises UK Government, through the UK Ministry of Defence (MOD), on verification measures that might be put into operation in the context of future arms control agreements. Specifically, the UK may one day be involved in a bilateral or multilateral agreement regarding the monitoring or reduction of arms. Any such agreement would very likely contain provisions for verifying that parties to this agreement are indeed compliant with their obligations expressed within said agreement. These provisions may be in the form of inspections, deployment

G. Pernul et al. (Eds.): ESORICS 2015, Part I, LNCS 9326, pp. 521–540, 2015.
DOI: 10.1007/978-3-319-24174-6_27

of monitoring equipment, use of satellite imagery, agreement of formal notice periods for certain activities and so forth.

An understanding of the reliability of such provisions and their interaction will be paramount: an agreement is more likely to be signed, and honoured, if all parties can be confident that the agreement's provisions allow them to verify compliance of other parties with the agreement. These provisions will be informed by strategic and conflicting interests of the parties. We propose to further such understanding by using mathematical analysis in this problem space, based on mathematical representations of arms control verification scenarios. In such scenarios, we are primarily interested in three types of quantities:

- **Trust**: a bias in the processing of imperfect information about another party
- **Degree of Belief**: the amount we believe a proposition is true
- **Confidence**: a measure of the uncertainty we should have in our degree of belief in a proposition.

Assuming that verification measures have been deployed, a mathematical representation of an arms control verification scenario should then allow a party to have high confidence in its degrees of belief (even if these degrees of belief are low), regardless of what trust it places in other parties. Such trust may, e.g., be based on past dealings between the parties or may be affected by the conduct exhibited within the verification activities themselves.

Mathematical representations should therefore give us measures of **Trust**, **Degree of Belief**, and **Confidence** so that we can investigate the trade-offs between these measures, assess their relative merits, or perform optimisation – e.g. to determine extremal cases of interest. Other desired capabilities of such mathematical representations are:

(1) ability of non-technical users (e.g. diplomats) to understand these representations and their results
(2) ability to represent both subjective (e.g. expert opinion) and objective data
(3) ability to determine which representational aspects or results are due to different subjective modelling decisions
(4) ability to represent and analyse dynamic, time-dependent scenarios
(5) ability to perform optimisation for measures of interest and their trade-offs
(6) ability to certify or formally prove that analysis outputs are correct.

In this paper, we explore the suitability of one such mathematical representation, Bayesian Belief Networks (BBNs) – see e.g. [10] – against the aforementioned desired capabilities in understanding the measures of **Confidence, Degrees of Belief**, and **Trust**.

We assume that little or no prior data is available for modelling arms control verification scenarios. This prevents us from using methods for estimating probabilities within BBNs. Moreover, control mechanisms may be subject to non-probabilistic, logical rules so we want to enrich BBNs with logical constraints. Thus we propose to use symbolic representations of both the uncertainty of probabilities within a BBN and of logical constraints of such a symbolic BBN. These constrained BBNs (cBBN) generalise BBNs in that the latter have no such uncertainty and no logical constraints. cBBNs also generalize Credal networks (see e.g. [9]), where the latter abstract probabilities of BBNs with convex intervals – a particular form of uncertainty – but cannot capture logical constraints.

To get the ability to assess confidence in degrees of belief of cBBNs, we develop techniques for determining whether one or more cBBNs are satisfiable at the same time, where satisfiability witnesses are BBNs that meet all constraints expressed in the cBBNs. We also show how to compute optimal such witnesses for measures of interest such as the probability of a cBBN node that informs decision making or such as the worst-case sensitivity of a node in a cBBN. Technically, we achieve this by specifying cBBNs in the Satisfiability Modulo Theories (SMT) solver Z3 [20], and by formulating confidence queries directly in SMT.

The contributions of this paper are therefore in proposing a new approach and methods for representing and analysing Bayesian Belief Networks, with a concrete application in national security in mind. We also demonstrate that our new methods genuinely enrich the modelling capabilities that exist to date in this application domain, notably (2), (3), and (5) above. We also began a case study [3] demonstrating that our approach can accommodate the temporal capability in (4) but we cannot report on this within the scope of this paper.

We note that our approach, an SMT-based analysis of constrained BBNs, can not only express logical rules of arms control verification, it can also use such logical rules to ensure a consistent relationship between different levels of abstraction in the comparison of two or more cBBNs that model the same arms verification control scenario. Our SMT-based approach is also consistent with realising the capabilities listed in (1) and (6) above, and scoping out the potential for this is subject to future work. The reader is hoped to appreciate that this paper emphasises the exposition of our new methods and their utility for this case study, at the expense of providing less detail on the more routine tool building activities that support and animate these methods.

We emphasise that our methods are of general interest to those who model any security aspects with BBNs but have little contextual data that informs their models or to those that may need to constrain these BBNs logically.

Outline of Paper: In Sect. 2 we present our arms control verification scenario and model it with a simple Bayesian Belief Network. The scenario is designed to be comprehensible to a non-expert of the application domain. Section 3 contains a gentle introduction to Satisfiability Modulo Theory solving and explains how constrained Bayesian Belief Networks can be represented as input for an SMT solver. Our methods for assessing the confidence in constrained Bayesian Belief Networks are developed in Sect. 4. The context of our work and related work are discussed in Sect. 5 and the paper concludes and discusses future work in Sect. 6.

2   An Arms Control Verification Scenario

Consider two fictitious nation states (referred to as "nations" below to avoid confusion with "states" of a BBN), N1 and N2, the latter of which is tasked with identifying whether boxes A and B belonging to the former and installed in a controlled inspection facility contain nuclear weapons. Nation N2 is also given declarations from nation N1 as to what is supposed to be in these boxes. The purpose of this inspection within an arms control agreement may be that the contents of the boxes are on their way for decommissioning, destroying, storage, civilian reuse, etc. Our mathematical model of the scenario does not reflect what may happen to the material post-inspection, but more detailed models may well reflect this. It should be noted that the models of this case study are created by nation N2 in order to assess this scenario.

Nation N1 declares that one box does indeed include nuclear weapons, and that the other does not. To illustrate that we can also add some gamification (unrealistic in a real scenario), let us assume that nation N1 won't reveal in which box the nuclear weapon might be, and that the inspecting party is allowed to inspect only one of these two boxes. The inspecting party, say nation N2 or some third party, is given a radiation detector with a specific, known sensitivity and known false-error reporting rate. The detector shows a green or red light based on whether nuclear materials in a particular ratio of a particular isotope are present or not. No other information bar this colour outcome is provided, which establishes an information barrier that can hide, e.g., important weapon design secrets of nation N1 – a requirement for agreeing to such inspections [18].

The design of the detector has been agreed upon by both nations N1 and N2. Nation N2 believes that it may be possible for nation N1 to spoof a radioactive signal (or indeed block a radioactive signal through under-saturation or over-saturation of gamma signals), to fool the detector, or indeed, to have just placed radioactive material in the boxes, but no weapon (in which case, nation N2 even needs to consider its degree of belief of nation N1 being able to build a nuclear weapon). There is also a possibility that the nuclear material may have been enriched to a physical state that is outside the detectable ratio range of the detector, but nation N2 thinks this is unlikely.

There are of course multiple ways of modelling this scenario. One advantage of our approach developed below is that it is able to compare different such models analytically and automatically. In this case study, we consider a simple and a more detailed model – both of which have some nodes in common (demonstrating that we can accommodate such overlap). The simple BBN model is depicted in Fig. 1. In a BBN, nodes represent (probabilistic) events. Such events may be conditional on other events (their parent nodes in a dependency graph). In our simple model, we have the following set of nodes:

- Box: which box will be inspected, that choice will determine whether nation N2 expects nuclear weapons to be present or not
- Spoof: determining nation N2's belief in a spoofed signal
- Detectable Ratio: probability that the fissile material of the object in the box has an isotopic ratio that the system is designed to give a green light for

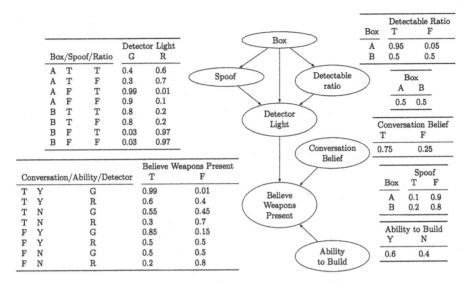

Fig. 1. Simple Bayesian Belief Network modelling our nuclear arms verification scenario

- Detector Light: accounts for false positive and false negative rates of the detector itself, and determines the green/red light state on the detector
- Conversation Belief: models whether or not external discussions with nation N1 would lead nation N2 to believe declarations of nation N1
- Ability to Build: captures nation N2's uncertainty over the technical abilities of nation N1, irrespective of the detector result
- Believe Weapons Present: the overall belief of nation N2 in a nuclear weapon being present in the inspected box.

The BBN $\mathcal{B}$ in Fig. 1 shows the dependency graph of the simple model. For example, the belief in the presence of nuclear weapons depends (through incoming edges) on the events Detector Light, Ability to Build, and Conversation Belief. Each node in the BBN $\mathcal{B}$ has a probability table from which one can compute its probability. For node Box we see that the inspection of a box is determined by flipping a fair coin. For node Believe Weapons Present, this probability table lists the probability distributions conditionally on the three aforementioned parent events. The probabilities used in this scenario are fictitious but convey plausible perceived levels of trust and degrees of belief.

Figure 2 shows how to compute probabilities for all nodes via the Law of Total Probability, by "summing out" conditional probabilities so that probabilities at a node are expressed in terms of probabilities of its parent nodes only.

3   Expressing Constrained BBNs in an SMT Solver

Satisfiability modulo theories [1,20] is an approach to automated deduction supported with robust and powerful tools that combine the state-of-the-art of deduc-

$$\sum_i \sum_j \sum_k \mathbb{P}(\text{BWP} = T \mid \text{AB} = i, \text{CB} = j, \text{DL} = k) \cdot \mathbb{P}(\text{AB} = i) \cdot \mathbb{P}(\text{CB} = j) \cdot \mathbb{P}(\text{DL} = k)$$
$$\sum_i \sum_j \sum_k \mathbb{P}(\text{BWP} = T \cap \text{AB} = i \cap \text{CB} = j \cap \text{DL} = k)$$

Fig. 2. Two ways of computing node marginal $\mathbb{P}(\text{BWP} = T)$ for Believe Weapons Present (BWP): via summing (first line) over all possible combinations of the conditional probability, multiplied by the parent marginals Ability to Build (AB), Conversation Belief (CB), Detector Light (DL); or via the joint probability distributions (second line)

tive theorem proving with that of SAT solving for propositional logic. We choose Z3 as SMT solver within our tool, although it would be relatively easy to replace it with another solver such as CVC3 [2].

The SMT solver Z3 has a declarative input language for defining constants, functions, and assertions about them [20]. Figure 3 shows Z3 input code to illustrate that language and its key analysis directives. On the left, constants of Z3 type Bool and Real are declared. Then an assertion defines that the Boolean constant q means that x is greater than $y + 1$, and the next assertion insists that q be true. The directives check-sat and get-model instruct Z3 to find a witness of the satisfiability of the conjunction of all visible assertions, and to report such a witness (called a model, but we will refer to Z3 models as "witnesses" to avoid any ambiguous use of the word "model" in the paper). On the right of Fig. 3, we see what Z3 reports for the input on the left: sat states that there is a witness; other possible replies are unsat (there cannot be a witness), and unknown (Z3 does not know whether or not a witness exists).

```
(declare-const q Bool)          sat
(declare-const x Real)            (model
(declare-const y Real)              (define-fun q () Bool true )
(assert (= q (> x (+ y 1))))        (define-fun y () Real (-2.0) )
(assert q)                          (define-fun x () Real 0.0)
(check-sat)                       )
(get-model)
```

Fig. 3. Left: sample Z3 input code with a directive to find and to generate a witness. Right: raw Z3 output for the left input code (edited to save space), saying that the conjunction of all assertions is satisfiable, and supporting this claim with a witness.

We encode a BBN in SMT using an automated code generator we have written; it converts a specification of a BBN given in a form similar to that seen in Fig. 1 automatically into SMT code. All state variables of a BBN node are declared in SMT by an appropriate enumeration type. In our simple BBN $\mathcal{B}$, these are mostly Boolean variables or tuples of such Boolean variables. But in general, such variables may take on other values such as integers.

The probability of a node is expressed in SMT as an arithmetic constraint that captures the definition of that probability as a function of the probability of its parent nodes and its own probability table. Although this is merely restating the familiar definitions for BBNs (see e.g. [10] and Fig. 2), we carefully circumscribe any use of divisions (occurring through the use of Bayes' Theorem) as equivalent equations of multiplicative terms. This syntactic change avoids the use of division, whose presence complicates automated reasoning and often makes an SMT solver report analysis result **unknown**.

We add constraints that ensure that all probabilities for all nodes add up to 1. Doing this will likely detect any accidental transcription errors in the specifications of probability tables and, more importantly, will ensure that the semantics of a cBBN (where some or all probabilities are under-specified) is still that of a set of concrete BBN that "refine" it by resolving such under-specifications to concrete probability distributions – in the spirit of abstract interpretation [8].

Having this SMT encoding in place, it is now easy to extend it to a cBBN. For example, suppose that we want to relax the probability for when the detector reports a green light in the BBN of Fig. 1 in the state in which box A is inspected, nation N2 believes that the signal is being spoofed, and nation N2 believes that a detectable ratio of radioactive material is being used. In that state, we want to change the probability distribution from 0.4 and 0.6 to α and $1-\alpha$, respectively, where α is constrained to be in a convex interval, say the interval $[0.3, 0.4]$. The choice of such intervals may be informed by external sources such as expert opinions, and the interval may have further non-convex restrictions via logical constraints of the cBBN.

We can represent this in our SMT encoding by declaring a real variable α, and using it and its complement $1-\alpha$ in place of 0.4 and 0.6 in the assertions of our SMT encoding that contain references to these probabilities (e.g. definitions of overall probabilities at nodes). Additionally, we add the assertion that α be in $[0.3, 0.4]$ by adding (`assert` (`and` ($<=$ 0.3 α) ($<=$ α 0.4))) to the SMT code for this model. In this manner, we can generalise the BBN $\mathcal{B}$ in Fig. 1 to a cBBN, referred to as $\mathcal{C}$ subsequently, in SMT. We note that we can relax more than one such probability in a similar manner and Z3 seems to cope well with multiple such relaxations.

Let us now turn to discussing how we can ask questions about cBBNs in SMT. The simplest possible question is to ask whether the SMT encoding of a cBBN is satisfiable, and failure of satisfiability would point out crude encoding or modelling errors. But we may use the power of an SMT solver to ask more interesting questions. For example, we may ask whether the probability of a node in a cBBN is always below a certain threshold (a form of *vacuity checking* [15]). Our tool allows us to declare such an analysis and to generate Z3 input code that, when run, will try to answer this whilst reflecting all probabilistic constraints represented in the network (its BBN aspect) and all arithmetic or logical constraints (the relaxations of concrete probabilities and logical rules that make a BBN into a cBBN). In the next section, we discuss richer questions that would not be solvable with BBN tools, and how we use SMT to answer them.

So far we have only discussed encodings of cBBNs that reflect no means of updating evidence. BBNs can model hard evidence, which changes the probabilities in a BBN upon observation of an event as seen for example in Fig. 4.

These changes propagate through the BBN and algorithms exist that compute this propagation of belief update (see e.g. [10]); our tool uses the Junction Tree Algorithm [17] to that end.

$$\mathbb{P}(\text{Box} = A \mid \text{SO} = T) = \frac{\mathbb{P}(\text{SO} = T \mid \text{Box} = A) \cdot \mathbb{P}(\text{Box} = A)}{\sum_i \mathbb{P}(\text{SO} = T \mid \text{Box} = i) \cdot \mathbb{P}(\text{Box} = i)}$$

Fig. 4. Updated marginal for node Box (Box) via Bayes' Rule once Spoof On (SO) is observed as true

Our tool can accommodate the processing of hard evidence in cBBNs as follows. Since probabilistic uncertainty is expressed via symbolic parameters, we use a Python script of the Junction Tree algorithm supplied within an open-source BBN package from eBay at github.com/eBay/bayesian−belief−networks to compute the updated probabilities symbolically. Then we remove the assertions in the SMT code that express the marginal probabilities and replace them (where applicable) with the symbolic assertions computed by this algorithm to reflect the marginals after their update based on this hard evidence. Note that this process is independent of any logical, non-probabilistic constraints of the cBBN and won't modify the SMT code of such constraints.

This update mechanism is external to the SMT solver and needs to post-process the SMT code of the cBBN before the modified SMT code can be further analysed, but now with the hard evidence properly reflected. Furthermore, it is important to realise that the propagation of hard evidence is different from analysing "soft" evidence. In our model we also pull out events of interest by just adding a constraint to our SMT code saying that a state variable at a node has a particular value – *without* propagating this as one would do for hard evidence.

4   Assessing Confidence in cBBNs

Our SMT encodings of constrained BBNs allow new forms of analysis, one of them being a comparison of different such models. To demonstrate this, we present the dependency graph of a more detailed model $\mathcal{B}'$ in Fig. 5.

The BBN $\mathcal{B}'$ shares some nodes with the BBN $\mathcal{B}$, and has the same probability tables for these nodes. But $\mathcal{B}'$ refines some nodes of $\mathcal{B}$ to take a more nuanced view of the ability to spoof and the assessment of whether a detectable ratio of nuclear material is present. The new nodes are:

– Intention to Mislead: the belief of nation N2 about nation N1's said intent
– Deliberately Saturates: probability of nation N1 to saturate the information barrier, dependent on nation N1's intention to mislead
– Manufactured Gamma: probability of manufactured gamma being used, also dependent on nation N1's intention to mislead

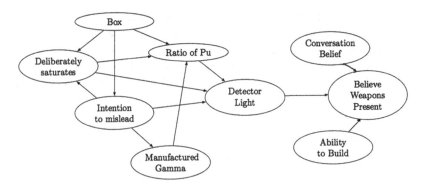

Fig. 5. More detailed BNN $\mathcal{B}'$ of scenario (probabilities of new nodes are in Fig. 11 in the appendix)

- Ratio of Plutonium: models said ratio, depends on events Box, Manufactured Gamma, and Deliberately Saturates, and informs event Detector Light.

We write $\mathcal{C}'$ for the constrained BBN that relaxes $\mathcal{B}'$ with the same uncertainty α as $\mathcal{C}$ relaxes $\mathcal{B}$, and pose the following questions:

Q1 For the constrained BBN $\mathcal{C}$, what is the maximal/minimal probability of nation N2 believing that a weapon is present given that nation N2 is uncertain about the prior probability of the detector light turning green?

Q2 How different can the probabilities of nation N2 believing that a weapon is present be between cBBNs $\mathcal{C}$ and $\mathcal{C}'$, i.e. when nation N2 is uncertain about the prior probability of the detector light going green?

Q3 Can the constrained BBNs $\mathcal{C}$ and $\mathcal{C}'$ return different results when we ask whether the probability of nation N2 believing that a weapon is present can be above a threshold, which we are uncertain about?

Q4 For what threshold ranges can such different results for Q3 occur?

Almost all of these questions require us to compute optimal values of a potentially non-linear objective function. We realise this in our tool by implementing unbounded binary search through the Python API for the SMT solver Z3. The pseudo code for this computation is depicted in Fig. 12 in the appendix for the case of global maxima. This method computes optimal values within a desired accuracy $\delta > 0$, and also truncates the mantissa of witness real numbers to a size commensurate to the value of δ. We do this as larger mantissas tend to increase the complexity of reasoning in the SMT solver within the unbounded binary search.

4.1 Optimising a Probability over Uncertainty

Let us reconsider the cBBN $\mathcal{C}$ obtained from the BBN $\mathcal{B}$ so that the probability distribution for Detector Light is α and $1 - \alpha$ and where α is constrained to be in the interval $[0.3, 0.4]$. We then maximise the variable of the SMT encoding of $\mathcal{C}$ that represents the overall probability of event Believe Weapons Present.

COP_Believeweaponspresent represents the largest joint probability contributing to the marginal and C_4_S1 is the marginal probability for event Believe Weapons Present. The witness returned by the SMT solver for this query is shown in Fig. 6.

```
[Believeweaponspresent = 1,
COP_Believeweaponspresent = 72836577/320000000,
C_4_S1 = 100021751/160000000,
x = 2/5,
Abilitytobuild = 1, Conversationbelief = 1, ...]
```

Fig. 6. Excerpt of the witness of the SMT solver (hand-edited to save space) for our SMT-based encoding of cBBN $\mathcal{C}$, where variable x denotes the value of α from $[0.3, 0.4]$ for which event Believe Weapons Present has maximal probability C_4_S1 given that our event of interest is Believeweaponpresent $= T$

The real values of a witness are rational numbers since SMT solvers use exact arithmetic – another aspect that helps to establish **Confidence** in computed degrees of belief. The maximal value of C_4_S1 is $100021751/160000000$ which equals 0.6251, and this maximal value is attained when the α (modelled as x in the SMT code) has value $2/5 = 0.4$. Witness values relevant to this optimisation query are those of x and C_4_S1; but the witness reported in Fig. 6 also offers some states of the event for which the maximal joint probability (with the node's parents), COP_Believeweaponspresent, is attained.

We find that the global minimum of C_4_S1 is 0.6233, occurring when x is 0.3.

4.2   Optimisation for Hard Evidence

We can also optimise probabilities in cBBNs for hard evidence. The Junction Tree Algorithm (JTA) implemented in the aforementioned open-source code of eBay can also be executed for symbolic input such as for the variable x in the SMT representation of $\mathcal{C}$. We then take this symbolic output of the JTA and post-process it so that divisions are expressed in terms of multiplications (where possible). Figure 7 illustrates what kind of assertions this adds to the SMT model of $\mathcal{C}$, where x is the variable that captures the uncertainty in $\mathcal{C}$.

```
s.add((C_4_S1*0.15) == (0.0158175*x+0.09513975))
s.add((C_4_S2*(0.095*x+0.88845)) == (0.02014*x+0.1883514))
```

Fig. 7. Some marginal probabilities revised by hard evidence via the symbolic Junction Tree Algorithm, post-processed to replace divisions with equivalent multiplications

Then we update the relevant portions of the SMT representation with this symbolic input to reflect the hard evidence. Thereafter, we can compute maxima in the same manner as described above.

To illustrate, let us now think of `Believeweaponspresent` = T as our parameter of interest and let us consider `Spoof` = T as hard evidence. Then we transform $\mathcal{C}$ and its SMT representation as just outlined, and compute the maximum for C_4_S1 over this transformed SMT code, and find that this is 135289/200000 which equals 0.6764. We can similarly compute the minimum of C_4_S1 and find that this equals 6659/10000 = 0.6659.

Note that if nation N2 definitely observes the crude node `Spoof On`, its confidence increases that a weapon is present. We can see this here since the maximal probability increases from 0.6251, when x is 0.4, to 0.6764, when x is also 0.4, but `Spoof` = T. If nation N2 knew that always `Box` = A (instead of also allowing for `Box` = B in our gamified scenario), then observing spoofing would lead to a drop in confidence as it would hint that there is no weapon. The results above though are in keeping with the probabilities assigned in the node tables for the gamified scenario which crudely models that a spoofed signal can be used to both hide and mimic a weapon.

4.3   Confidence in Comparison of cBBNs

Consider two cBBNs that have a common node whose probability will support decision making. We want to compute the maximal difference that these respective probabilities could have, in order to assess with confidence by how much they could differ in principle. We illustrate how this can be done in SMT by considering again the CBBN $\mathcal{C}$ for the simple model, and the BBN $\mathcal{B}'$ for the detailed model (noting that BNNs are also cBBNs). The event of interest in both models is `Believe Weapons Present`. We want to compute the maximal difference of the joint probability of this event (with its parent nodes) in both models, expressed in our SMT model as

```
(declare-const DIFF Real)
(assert (= DIFF (abs
  (- COP_Believeweaponspresent_mod1 COP_Believeweaponspresent_mod2)))))
```

where the suffixes `mod1` and `mod2` separate the name spaces for these two cBBNs within the same SMT model. Since these cBBNs contain also common aspects, we use the logical constraints of the SMT language to specify the "semantic glue" between these common aspects. Doing so prevents the computation of values for DIFF that would arise from inconsistent instances of these two cBBNs. Figure 8 illustrates how this is done for the two models considered here. In many cases, we just state that variables have the same meaning.

In other cases, we need to provide glue between different levels of abstraction. For example, that state `SpoofOn` = F and only that state of the simple model is mapped to a certain level of ratio of element Pu in the detailed model. Specifically, in the scenario only a ratio of `About 10:1` is deemed acceptable (see the last table in Fig. 11 of the appendix for how ratio levels are modelled in $\mathcal{B}'$);

```
(assert (= Box_mod1 Box_mod2))
(assert (= DetectorLight_mod1 DetectorLight_mod2))
(assert (= Believeweaponspresent_mod1 Believeweaponspresent_mod2))
(assert (ite (= SpoofOn_mod1 2) (= RatioOfPu_mod2 3) (not (= RatioOfPu_mod2
3)))))
```

Fig. 8. Excerpts of SMT code that semantically connects common aspects of $\mathcal{C}$ and $\mathcal{B}'$:
e.g. its $if-then-else$ assertion logically relates Spoof On of $\mathcal{C}$ to Ratio of Pu of $\mathcal{B}'$

all other levels would indicate a spoof. The figure shows such an assertion with
ite (if-then-else) where integers encode states of these variables, e.g., 3 encodes
ratio About10 : 1.

Now we can compute the maximum of DIFF, which equals 0.0921. The witness
for this tells us that the simple model has probability 0.0843 and the detailed
one probability 0.176 which realise this difference. In fact, we could in principle
extract two BBNs from that witness to study how these probabilities come about.

4.4   Two-Dimensional Difference Analysis

We may also compute such maximal differences for a probability of interest as a
function of how uncertainty in two models gets resolved. Let x be the probability
for Conversation Belief being true in the simple model, whereas y denotes the
corresponding probability in the detailed model. We can now maximise DIFF
above again, but for each data point (x, y) in $[0, 1] \times [0, 1]$ at some granularity.
The result of this analysis is seen in Fig. 9.

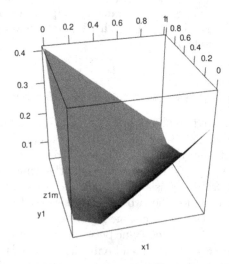

Fig. 9. 3-D plot showing the maximum of variable DIFF where x and y axes represent
the probability of ConversationBelief = T in the simple, respectively, detailed model

If both models have the same priors, meaning when $x = y$, we would expect both models to agree most. And we do see a trough of DIFF at the $x = y$ axis even though it is somewhat shifted and distorted by the different ways in which these models represent event Detector Light, for example.

4.5 Computing Agreement Intervals

We are interested in the probability of event Believe Weapons Present in both cBBNs $\mathcal{C}$ and $\mathcal{B}'$. Let us write pr and pr' for this probability in these models, respectively. Consider a threshold th such that truth of $th < pr$, respectively, $th < pr'$, would support a decision, e.g., for nation N2 to declare that the inspection has been successful. We want to understand for which values th these two cBBNs would agree on that decision. Using their common SMT representation discussed above, we can ask whether

$$((th < pr) \wedge (pr' \le th)) \vee ((th < pr') \wedge (pr \le th))$$

is satisfiable in that SMT model. If not, then the two models would support the same decision for threshold value th. Using our global maximum method, where th is now the variable to optimise, we can compute ranges of th for which both models agree in their support of the decision of successful inspections. One such interval of agreement that we can compute for these models is $[0.307, 1.0]$, implying that thresholds at or above 0.307 render the same decisions.

4.6 Sensitivity Analyses

We refer to [16] for a discussion of pertinent sensitivity analysis of Bayesian Belief Networks called *Bound, Score*, and *Vertex Proximity* (respectively), and their use in an application of digital forensics.

We conducted such sensitivity analyses for our models as well (not shown here). Such methods don't rely on SMT and complement the approach advocated in this paper. But we claim that there is benefit in leveraging our SMT-based approach to compute symbolic sensitivity results. Figure 10 shows such results for sensitivity analysis *Score* [16], for the cBBN $\mathcal{C}$. These symbolic assertions can then be further analysed within an SMT model, e.g., to compute maximal values of these expressions to learn worst-case sensitivities.

5   Wider Context of Work and Related Work

We first put the research reported in this paper into a wider context of the problem space. Article VI of the Treaty on the Non-Proliferation of Nuclear Weapons (NPT) states that each of the parties to the Treaty

"... undertakes to pursue negotiations in good faith on effective measures relating to cessation of the nuclear arms race at an early date and to nuclear disarmament, and on a treaty on general and complete disarmament under strict and effective international control."

Name	Sensitivity Score
Box	-148.0*(0.0004275*x - 0.00336683986467894)*(0.0158175*x + 0.633562925005377)
Spoof On	-44.4444444444444*(0.0158175*x - 0.0548602500019255)*(0.0158175*x + 0.633562925005377)
Detectable ratio	-1.90249702734839*(0.0158175*x - 0.238873075001069)*(0.0158175*x + 0.633562925005377)
Detector Light	1.0*(0.01007*x + 0.113679700000125)*(0.0158175*x + 0.633562925005377)/(0.0475*x + 0.536225)**2
Conversation belief	-1.0*(0.01189875*x - 0.255675637493819)*(0.0158175*x + 0.633562925005377)/(1.73472347597681e-18*x + 0.75)**2
Ability to build	-2.77777777777778*(0.01083*x - 0.132740700000797)*(0.0158175*x + 0.633562925005377)
Average	(-0.702999999999999*x + 2.43823333341891)*(0.0158175*x + 0.633562925005377)/6 + (-0.06327*x + 0.498292299972483)*(0.0158175*x + 0.633562925005377)/6 + (-0.0300927467300832*x + 0.454455315103103)*(0.0158175*x + 0.633562925005377)/6 + (-0.0300833333333334*x + 0.368724166668881)*(0.0158175*x + 0.633562925005377)/6 + (-0.01189875*x + 0.255675637493819)*(0.0158175*x + 0.633562925005377)/(6*(1.73472347597681e-18*x + 0.75)**2) + (0.01007*x + 0.113679700000125)*(0.0158175*x + 0.633562925005377)/(6*(0.0475*x + 0.536225)**2)

Fig. 10. Sensitivity of cBBN $\mathcal{C}$ with respect to event Believe Weapons Present, as a function of the sole parameter x that is under-specified in $\mathcal{C}$. The last row computes symbolic averages of all node sensitivities

The UK and Norway have explored, since 2007, how effective verification procedures could be established that could play a vital part in meeting the obligations set out in Article VI [14,18]. This collaboration made clear that security and safety requirements are essential for the creation of verification technologies and processes, and that more effort is needed at devising such technologies and processes such that all parties can gain and maintain confidence in them. In the past 15 years, the US and UK engaged in a technical cooperation that explored and evaluated methodologies and technologies for the verification of arms control treaties [24]. This work showed that it is feasible to monitor and verify nuclear warheads, components and processes; but it also identified the need for further research. Our work reported here can be seen as making a contribution to methods that would allow parties to build and sustain confidence in particular arms control verification mechanisms.

We now discuss related work outside this problem space. Robust optimisation is an approach to optimisation in which one seeks a measure of robustness against deterministic uncertainty in parameters of the optimisation problem [4]. Robust optimisation has already been applied in computer security, e.g. to model human adversaries in complex security resource allocation problems [21]. Mixed Integer Linear Programming (MILP) and its non-linear variant MINLP can express constraints stated in propositional logic, but – unlike SMT – seem unable to express relational or functional structure within atomic propositions. Robust optimisation has been applied to MINLP problems of scheduling under bounded uncertainty [13]. This is related to our work in [3] where we use SMT to robustly compute optimal schedules for nuclear arms inspection regimes over measures of interest to participating parties.

Z3opt is an SMT solver based on Z3 that incorporates optimisation within the SMT solver itself, including the ability to compute Pareto fronts [19]. Our work in [3] scales better if we use Z3opt instead of Z3 plus our own optimisation seen in Fig. 12 in the appendix. However, we were not able to use Z3opt successfully for the work reported in this paper, which may be due to the fact that we here work with non-linear objective functions.

Next, we discuss additional work on sensitivity analysis of BBNs. One such analysis studies the sensitivity of queries in BBNs to changes of a sole parameter, including an understanding of which changes would realise a given query constraint [7]. It seems possible to extend such work to multiple parameters at moderate computational overheads [6]. In [23] it is noted that naive Bayesian classifiers perform quite well even in the presence of inaccuracies, and that standard sensitivity functions suffice to describe scenario sensitivities [23].

In [11], methods from constructive real analysis are used to decide whether a formula is satisfiable if the values occurring in it can be perturbed by at most a specified, uniform value $\delta > 0$. This approach can support a good range of non-linear functions, including some transcendental ones, and can be applied to solutions of Lipschitz-continuous ordinary differential equations. This should therefore also enable a form of robust optimisation.

Our introduction is similar to the motivation given in [22], which poses a problem to the European Study Group with Industry (ESGI 107), held in Manchester in March 2015 [22]. Although our introduction shares this exposition of the problem, our paper advocates the use of BBNs, and cBBNs as their suitable abstractions, as one method of probing scenarios in application domain.

We view our approach as complementing other approaches in that problem domain – be they based on game theory, economic considerations of trust cultures, policy and reputation based formalisms, dynamical systems and so forth. For example, we considered predicates asking whether the probability of a cBBN node can be above some threshold; and such predicates may inform rules within policy-based languages that evaluate trust – of which the language Peal and its tool PEALT is a more recent example [12].

6   Conclusions

We have proposed the use of BBNs in the modelling and assessment of nuclear arms verification scenarios, because such networks have several desirable features, e.g., their ability to represent both subjective and objective data that can interact in the model. BBNs formulated for this problem domain contain **Trust**, e.g., in the form of biases expressed as probabilities; and they capture **Degrees of Belief** by computing probabilities of events. However, in this problem domain it is paramount to assess the **Confidence** that we have in such degrees of belief. Yet in this problem space **Confidence** is hard to come by, given that little or no prior data are available to inform probabilities within model BBNs.

In this paper, we addressed this modelling problem by abstracting BBNs to constrained BBNs, which are subject to logical constraints and whose probabilities may contain symbolic uncertainties. We then addressed the corresponding analysis problem by representing these cBBNs in Satisfiability Modulo Theories, so that SMT solvers can answer queries about one or more of such cBBNs.

We demonstrated these new capabilities by developing constrained BBNs that model a particular arms control verification scenario, and by then analysing scenario-specific queries over those constrained BBNs but expressed in SMT. The types of queries that we analysed included the optimisation of the overall probability of an event in a constrained BBN, optimisation for hard evidence and its resulting model update, optimisation to determine worst-case differences between two cBBNs that model the same scenario, the computation of threshold ranges for which two constrained BBNs would inform decisions in the same manner, and worst-case sensitivities of critical nodes in a constrained BBN.

Our approach has several advantages: the query language is open-ended, queries merely have to be expressible in SMT; satisfiability witnesses for queries found by an SMT solver subsume the description of concrete BBNs that can subsequently be fed into BBN tools for external validation and feedback to non-expert users; and we may add logical constraints freely, for example to provide consistency between levels of abstractions of two or more constrained BBNs.

In future work, we want to design a domain-specific language in which we can specify constrained BBNs as well as a host of analysis methods, including those represented in this paper. And we want to write code generators that transform such specifications into SMT code. Finally, it would be of great interest to certify unsatisfiability results (e.g. that a computed maximum probability really is a global maximum). In that context, it is worth noting that Z3 can provide proofs of unsatisfiability, and there has been work on independently certifying such proofs in interactive theorem provers [5].

Acknowledgements. The authors from Imperial College London would like to thank AWE for sponsoring a PhD studentship under which the research reported in this paper was carried out.

Open Access of Research Data and Code: The Python code for the queries and models of this paper, and raw SMT analysis results are publicly available at https://bitbucket.org/pjbeaumont/beaumontevanshuthplantesorics2015/

A   Ancillary Material

In order to make this paper more self-contained, we provide in this appendix two figures that show probability tables of our more detailed Bayesian Belief Network and details of our optimisation algorithms, respectively.

Box A	B
0.5	0.5

Ability to Build Y	N
0.6	0.4

Conversation Belief T	F
0.75	0.25

		Manufactured Gamma	
Saturates/Intention		T	F
T	T	0.99	0.01
T	F	0.01	0.99
F	T	0.3	0.7
F	F	0.0	1.0

	Intention to mislead	
Box	T	F
A	0.2	0.8
B	0.1	0.9

		Deliberately saturates	
Box/Intention		T	F
A	T	0.8	0.2
A	F	0.02	0.98
B	T	0.7	0.3
B	F	0.01	0.99

	Detector Light	
Ratio of Pu	G	R
Significantly less	0.05	0.95
Less	0.2	0.8
Around 10:1	0.01	0.99
More	0.2	0.8
Significantly more	0.95	0.05

		Believe Weapons Present	
Ability/Conversation/Detector		T	F
Y T	G	0.99	0.01
Y T	R	0.6	0.4
Y F	G	0.55	0.45
Y F	R	0.3	0.7
N T	G	0.85	0.15
N T	R	0.5	0.5
N F	G	0.5	0.5
N F	R	0.2	0.8

Saturates	Gamma	Box	Significantly less	Less	Around 10:1	More	Significantly more
T	T	G	0.4	0.09	0.02	0.09	0.4
T	T	R	0.4	0.1	0.0	0.1	0.4
T	F	G	0.5	0.4	0.1	0.0	0.0
T	F	R	0.2	0.2	0.2	0.2	0.2
F	T	G	0.0	0.1	0.25	0.25	0.4
F	T	R	0.0	0.0	0.1	0.3	0.6
F	F	G	0.0	0.15	0.7	0.15	0.0
F	F	R	0.2	0.2	0.2	0.2	0.2

Fig. 11. Probability tables for model $\mathcal{B}'$ of the arms verification control scenario. The last two tables specify node Believe Weapons Present and node Ratio of Pu, respectively

```
def maxopt(X, delta):

# unbounded search begins
    r = s.check()
    if r == unsat:
        return unsat
    else:
        t = s.model()

    while r == sat:
        s.push()
        s.add(X > 2*t[X])
        r = s.check()
        if r == sat:
            t = s.model()
        s.pop()
# unbounded search ended

# bisection method begins
    v = t[X]
    v = float(v.as_decimal(10)[:-1])
    max = 2*v
    min = v
    while (max-min) > delta:
        s.push()
        s.add(((max-min)/2)+min <= X)
        r = s.check()
        if r == sat:
            min = ((max-min)/2)+min
        else:
            max = ((max-min)/2)+min
        s.pop()
    y = (max_min)/2
# bisection method ended
return y
```

Fig. 12. Pseudo-code that returns the global maximum of real variable X within an accuracy of $\delta > 0$, where X is declared in the SMT input and is the subject of this optimisation. Variable s is an instance of the SMT solver, and expression s.model() refers to a witness found by that solver on its current input. The use of **float** above controls the mantissas of max and min to be commensurate with the desired accuracy δ to mitigate the complexity of reasoning. Directives **push** and **pop** control the visibility of assertions for incremental satisfiability checks

References

1. Barrett, C., de Moura, L., Ranise, S., Stump, A., Tinelli, C.: The SMT-LIB initiative and the rise of SMT (HVC 2010 award talk). In: Raz, O. (ed.) HVC 2010. LNCS, vol. 6504, p. 3. Springer, Heidelberg (2010)
2. Barrett, C.W., Tinelli, C.: CVC3. In: Damm, W., Hermanns, H. (eds.) CAV 2007. LNCS, vol. 4590, pp. 298–302. Springer, Heidelberg (2007)
3. Beaumont, P., Evans, N., Huth, M., Plant, T.: Modelling and analysis of constrained iterative systems: a case study in nuclear arms control. Submitted to AVoCS 2015, June 2015
4. Ben-Tal, A., El Ghaoui, L., Nemirovski, A.: Robust Optimization. Princeton Series in Applied Mathematics. Princeton University Press, 9-16, Princeton (2009)
5. Böhme, S., Weber, T.: Fast LCF-Style proof reconstruction for Z3. In: Kaufmann, M., Paulson, L.C. (eds.) ITP 2010. LNCS, vol. 6172, pp. 179–194. Springer, Heidelberg (2010)
6. Chan, H., Darwiche, A.: Sensitivity analysis in bayesian networks: From single to multiple parameters. CoRR abs/1207.4124 (2012)
7. Chan, H., Darwiche, A.: When do numbers really matter? CoRR abs/1408.1692 (2014)
8. Cousot, P., Cousot, R.: Abstract interpretation: past, present and future. In: Joint Meeting of the Twenty-Third EACSL Annual Conference on Computer Science Logic (CSL) and the Twenty-Ninth Annual ACM/IEEE Symposium on Logic in Computer Science (LICS), CSL-LICS 2014, Vienna, Austria, July 14–18, 2014, p. 2 (2014)
9. Cozman, F.G.: Credal networks. Artif. Intell. **120**(2), 199–233 (2000)
10. Fenton, N., Neil, M.: Risk Assessment and Decision Analysis with Bayesian Networks. CRC Press, Boca Raton (2013)
11. Gao, S., Avigad, J., Clarke, E.M.: Delta-complete decision procedures for satisfiability over the reals. CoRR abs/1204.3513 (2012)
12. Huth, M., Kuo, J.H.-P.: PEALT: an automated reasoning tool for numerical aggregation of trust evidence. In: Ábrahám, E., Havelund, K. (eds.) TACAS 2014 (ETAPS). LNCS, vol. 8413, pp. 109–123. Springer, Heidelberg (2014)
13. Lin, X., Janak, S.L., Floudas, Ch.A.: A new robust optimization approach for scheduling under uncertainty: I. Bounded uncertainty. Comput. Chem. Eng. **28**(6–7), 1069–1085 (2004)
14. Kingdom of Norway and the United Kingdom of Great Britain and Northern Ireland: The United Kingdom - Norway Initiative: Further Research into the Verification of Nuclear Warhead Dismantlement. In: 2015 Review Conference on the Parties to the Treaty on the Non-Proleferation of Nuclear Weapons, NPT/CONF 2015, WP.31, New York, USA, 27 April–22 May 2015
15. Kupferman, O., Vardi, M.Y.: Vacuity detection in temporal model checking. STTT **4**(2), 224–233 (2003)
16. Kwan, M.Y.K., Overill, R.E., Chow, K., Tse, H., Law, F.Y.W., Lai, P.K.Y.: Sensitivity analysis of bayesian networks used in forensic investigations. In: Peterson, G., Shenoi, S. (eds.) Advances in Digital Forensics VII. IFP AICT, vol. 361, pp. 231–243. Springer, Heidelberg (2011)
17. Lauritzen, S.L., Spiegelhalter, D.J.: Local computations with probabilities on graphical structures and their application to expert systems. J. Roy. Stat. Soc. Ser. B (Methodol.) **50**(2), 157–224 (1988)

18. Ministry of Defence of the United Kingdom: the UK/Norway initiative: report on the UKNI nuclear weapons states workshop, March 2010

19. Bjørner, N., Phan, A.-D., Fleckenstein, L.: νZ - An optimizing SMT solver. In: Baier, C., Tinelli, C. (eds.) TACAS 2015. LNCS, vol. 9035, pp. 194–199. Springer, Heidelberg (2015)

20. de Moura, L., Bjørner, N.S.: Z3: an efficient SMT solver. In: Ramakrishnan, C.R., Rehof, J. (eds.) TACAS 2008. LNCS, vol. 4963, pp. 337–340. Springer, Heidelberg (2008)

21. Pita, J., John, R., Maheswaran, R.T., Tambe, M., Yang, R., Kraus, S.: A robust approach to addressing human adversaries in security games. In: Proceedings of AAMAS 2012, pp. 1297–1298 (2012)

22. Plant, T., Stapleton, M.: Decision support for nuclear arms control. Problem Statement for ESGI 107, Manchester, UK, 23–27 March 2015

23. Renooij, S., van der Gaag, L.C.: Evidence and scenario sensitivities in naive Bayesian classifiers. Int. J. Approx. Reasoning 49(2), 398–416 (2008)

24. US NISA, US NAPC, UK Ministry of Defence and AWE: Joint U.S. - U.K. Report on Technical Cooperation for Arms Control (2015)

Author Index

Printed in the United States
by Baker & Taylor Publisher Services